# www.wadsworth.com

*www.wadsworth.com* is the World Wide Web site for
Thomson Wadsworth and is your direct source to dozens
of online resources.

At *www.wadsworth.com* you can find out about supple-
ments, demonstration software, and student resources.
You can also send email to many of our authors and pre-
view new publications and exciting new technologies.

www.wadsworth.com
Changing the way the world learns®

# THE UNITED NATIONS

# THE UNITED NATIONS

## *International Organization and World Politics*

### FOURTH EDITION

LAWRENCE ZIRING
*Western Michigan University*

ROBERT RIGGS
*Brigham Young University*

JACK PLANO

THOMSON
WADSWORTH

*Australia · Canada · Mexico · Singapore · Spain
United Kingdom · United States*

THOMSON
WADSWORTH

Publisher: Clark Baxter
Executive Editor: David Tatom
Assistant Editor: Rebecca Green
Editorial Assistant: Reena Thomas
Technology Project Manager:
  Michelle Verdeman
Marketing Manager: Janise Fry
Marketing Assistant: Mary Ho
Advertising Project Manager:
  Kelley McAllister

Project Manager, Editorial Production:
  Jennifer Klos
Print Buyer: Barbara Britton
Permissions Editor: Kiely Sexton
Production Service: G & S Book Services
Copy Editor: Jessie Dolch
Cover Designer: Brian Salisbury
Cover Image: AP/Wide World Photos
Compositor: G & S Book Services
Printer: Malloy Incorporated

Thomson Wadsworth
10 Davis Drive
Belmont, CA 94002-3098
USA

Asia
Thomson Learning
5 Shenton Way #01-01
UIC Building
Singapore 068808

Australia/New Zealand
Thomson Learning
102 Dodds Street
Southbank, Victoria 3006
Australia

Canada
Nelson
1120 Birchmount Road
Toronto, Ontario M1K 5G4
Canada

Europe/Middle East/Africa
Thomson Learning
High Holborn House
50/51 Bedford Row
London WC1R 4LR
United Kingdom

Latin America
Thomson Learning
Seneca, 53
Colonia Polanco
11560 Mexico D.F.
Mexico

Spain/Portugal
Paraninfo
Calle Magallanes, 25
28015 Madrid, Spain

For more information about our products, contact us at:
**Thomson Learning
Academic Resource Center
1-800-423-0563**

For permission to use material from this text or product, submit a request online at **http://www.thomsonrights.com.**

Any additional questions about permissions can be submitted by email to **thomsonrights@thomson.com.**

Library of Congress Control Number:
2004101398

ISBN 0-534-63186-X

*This book is dedicated to*
*Raye, Leona, and Sarah*
*for their inspiration and love*

# CONTENTS

PREFACE     xi

1.  THE UNITED NATIONS IN HISTORICAL PERSPECTIVE     1
    *Prologue*     1
    *In the Beginning*     8
    *The State System and International Organization*     9
    *The Emergence of International Institutions*     11
    *The League Experiment*     13
    *Organizing the United Nations*     23

2.  LEGAL FRAMEWORK, INSTITUTIONAL STRUCTURES, AND
    FINANCIAL REALITIES     31
    *The Constitutional Structure*     31
    *Instruments of Political Decision Making*     38
    *Financing the United Nations*     65

3.  THE UN POLITICAL PROCESS     74
    *Participants in the UN Decision Process*     74
    *UN Decision Making*     85
    *The Consequences of UN Action*     125

4.  POLITICS AND THE UN SECRETARIAT     133
    *The International Civil Service*     136
    *The UN Secretariat*     138
    *The UN Secretariat in the Political Process*     145
    *Revitalizing the United Nations*     160

5.  SECURITY THROUGH COLLECTIVE ACTION     167
    *Balance of Power and Collective Security*     168
    *The United Nations and Collective Security*     174
    *The Peacekeeping Alternative*     213

6.  THE SETTLEMENT OF INTERNATIONAL DISPUTES     264
    *Procedures for Settling International Disputes*     264
    *UN Practice*     267
    *Case Studies in UN Conflict Resolution*     282
    *Settling International Disputes and Humanitarian Law*     313
    *Global Security and the United Nations*     316
    *Conclusions on Dispute Settlement*     318

7.  DISARMAMENT AND ARMS CONTROL     324
    *Disarmament in Historical Perspective*     325
    *The UN and Arms Negotiations in the Nuclear Era*     332
    *Disarmament and Arms Control—A Balance Sheet*     338

*Obstacles to Disarmament*     357
*Approaches to the Disarmament Problem*     366
*Conclusion*     370

8.   THE REVOLUTION OF SELF-DETERMINATION     373
*Mandates Under the League*     374
*The Effect of World War II*     378
*UN Trusteeship*     379
*The United Nations and Total Decolonization*     383
*The UN Role: An Appraisal*     390
*Self-Determination in the Twenty-first Century*     392

9.   SOCIAL AND TECHNICAL COOPERATION     397
*Functional Cooperation in Theory and Practice*     397
*Human Rights Rule-Making*     404
*Rules in Other Functional Settings*     424
*Information and Promotion*     440
*Internationally Administered Programs*     448
*Conclusion*     464

10.   PROMOTING ECONOMIC DEVELOPMENT     470
*Problems of Development*     470
*A Blueprint for Economic Development*     477
*Promoting International Action*     486
*UN Programs*     488
*The Role of the International Monetary Fund*     500
*UN Development Financing Programs:*
   *The World Bank Group*     503
*Conclusion on Economic Development*     509

11.   THE UNITED NATIONS IN THE TWENTY-FIRST CENTURY     515
*Rethinking the United Nations in the Age of Terrorism*     518
*The United Nations and the Definition of Terrorism*     522
*Terrorism in the Twenty-First Century*     524
*The Realities of the Global Condition*     527
*Toward World Order*     529

APPENDIX   THE CHARTER OF THE UNITED NATIONS     535

NAME INDEX     557

SUBJECT INDEX     561

# PREFACE

Four years have passed since the third edition of *The United Nations* saw the light of day. Much has happened in the interim, and this fourth edition has been thoroughly revised to examine the critical challenges facing the world organization—many challenges that were not forecast with the previous volume. Although terrorism was a known phenomenon and had much earlier become a transnational problem, the horrific events of September 11, 2001, deeply affected a world unprepared for their magnitude and portent. Central headquarters of the United Nations stood city blocks from the site of the World Trade Center, "ground zero" for the single most violent attack on the United States in its history. Physically as well as psychologically the United Nations could not be separated from the catastrophe perpetrated by suicidal operatives representing not a national state but a worldwide network of religious zealots. Founded on the theme of political secularism, the United Nations addressed the universality of humankind and the gathering of all the world's nations into a common facility espousing cooperation and accommodation on a broad plane of social and economic endeavor. In targeting the United States, the terrorists of September 11 knew full well the central role played by the one remaining superpower in the maintenance of global equilibrium. They also understood Washington's major influence in the globalization movement, including American power in shaping ideas and performance inside and outside the United Nations. With the strike against the United States, therefore, the world became witness to the maturation of a mortal threat that not only focused attention on the United States as besieged *hegemon,* but also on international organization and its future capacity to meld humanity into a viable union dedicated to peace and mutual understanding.

The fourth edition of *The United Nations* describes the efforts made by the world body to sustain its normal routine amid conditions that demand innovation and conceptual reform. The difficulty in pursuing the latter, however, is no easier today than in years past. While the United Nations remains rooted in its original structure, the individual nation-states that constitute it have not marked time. Most important is the organization's central organ, the Security Council, with its five permanent members—the United States, the United Kingdom, France, Russia, and China. Charged with overall responsibility for collective security actions, the Security Council has again been divided by the terrorist assault on the United States. Unlike the era of the Cold War, however, the division is not drawn along ideological lines as much as it is over the right of a state or states to ignore the imprimatur of the high body. Concern is with the right of a state or states to resort to preemptive and unilateral action in clear violation of the intent and wording of the UN Charter. The question raised by the events of September 11 centers on the UN principle of ultimate state sovereignty and the exclusive preserve of the state to enjoy jurisdiction over its domestic scene. The United Nations reminds states of their obligations to one another, to honor national integrity and to respect individual expression. But how, in an age of proliferating weapons of mass destruction and the ability of homicidal non-states to acquire and use them, can the United Nations protect the attributes of state independence?

Actions of the United States that were aimed at neutralizing the suspected perpetrators of the September 11 tragedy resulted in conflicts between what is legally proper and what is instrumentally necessary, between the rules of the state system and the demands of national self-preservation. Whereas the United Nations represented the former, the United States could not be constrained in its attempt to manage the latter. Self-defense has been an honored feature of the UN Charter from its inception, but self-defense was never interpreted as operating outside the realm of UN responsibilities. NATO's immediate reaction after September 11 to declare an attack on one an attack on all appeared to cover for the legalities of the UN Charter in the U.S. war in Afghanistan, but the unilateral action by Washington against Baghdad was another matter. For the United Nations the fanatical regime of the Taliban in Afghanistan stood in vivid contrast to the tyrannical regime in Iraq. Making war on Afghanistan could be equated with making war against transnational terror. But making war on Iraq could not be equally justified. The one could be framed within the constitutional requirements of the UN system; the other was judged by no less than the UN Secretary-General to be a blow against the international order that the world organization had been created to preserve. The minions of worldwide terror made a quantum leap on September 11. The United States argued that it could do no more than meet the challenge, even if in doing so it was forced to compromise international practices tediously erected over the decades. While the United Nations confronted the reality of its most significant member augmenting the very essence of international security, it nonetheless was compelled to acknowledge the passage of a threshold. On one side the trail appeared to lead to still a different kind of interdependence, while on the other it seemed to reaffirm the individuality of the nation-state.

*Plus ça change, plus c'est la même chose*—the more things change, the more they remain the same. The fourth edition of *The United Nations* contains all that is relevant to the UN system from its inception to these opening years of the new millennium. Readers familiar with the previous editions will find much that they valued retained and, where necessary, expanded upon. The format is essentially as it was when Robert Riggs and Jack Plano wrote the first edition of the book, but with this edition every word, every line, every paragraph has been reviewed and, where necessary, rewritten. Particular attention has been given to the march of time and the new elements that have become integral parts of the UN discourse. New to this edition is the changing interface between the United Nations as peacekeeper and the United Nations as peacemaker. While the thread of terrorism weaves its way through the text, every effort has been made to discuss the world organization's continuing role in assisting nations and peoples in distress from underdevelopment, from population overload, from pandemic disease, and from political instability.

# NEW TO THIS EDITION

Here is a partial list of what has been included in this new volume: Where required, all tables, charts, and figures have been updated and others added. The role played by the Secretary-General has been revisited and expanded. Contemporary conflict engaging the permanent powers of the Security Council is analyzed. Despite the capacity of states to ignore or bypass the United Nations, the organization preserves an inherent validity, especially in an era of greater state vulnerability. Collective security therefore is reexamined and receives new emphasis. Continuing regional and civil conflicts are described, and the actions of the United Nations are detailed. All new peacekeeping missions are accounted for, with a notable emphasis on background as well as detailed operations. Expanded reviews of the Israeli-Palestinian conflict, the North Korean nuclear threat, and conditions in Iraq through and after the U.S. invasion have been given particular prominence. Discussion has been reserved for the opening of the International Criminal Court and the sustained controversy over the international effort to punish former and serving state officials for offenses committed in office.

On the development side, the Millennium Congress is examined for its work and ongoing projects. Attention is given to environmental issues, notably the dilemma of global warming and its effect. Similarly, demographic matters ranging from the question of population increases outpacing development to the spread and impact of infectious disease, especially HIV/AIDS, are explored. The roles played by international organizations such as the World Bank and the International Monetary Fund are all revisited and updated, with the pros and cons of programs and strategies in the arena of globalization covered.

Most significant in this volume, however, is the omnipresence of terrorism and its effect on the everyday operations of the United Nations. The volume centers on the capacity of the United Nations to face the terrorist challenge. It analyzes the call to the member states to transcend cultural limitations and to combine their efforts for what is generally deemed to be a scourge not only on the United Nations but indeed on all humanity.

## A FINAL NOTE

To paraphrase a comment from the third edition of *The United Nations*, the United Nations today remains as vital as the day it was conceived—perhaps even more so; the world needs the United Nations as never before. In a world where established national and international institutions are questioned for their legitimacy, the United Nations stands above all others. Only the United Nations has the aura needed to both honor the sovereignty of states and encourage the deeper integration of world community. In a twenty-first-century world divided more by social and cultural distinctions and less by political geography, attention is drawn less to the frontiers separating one state actor from another and more to the revolution in science and technology that brings people into immediate proximity. Changes in communications have made the planet one as never before, while the flowering of the global economy addresses conditions that hold out the promise of a better life for more people. In the decades to come the United Nations is destined to become the vanguard of the revolution in information technology. To that extent it will be the world organization, not the nation-states, that bridges the gap not only between the "haves" and "have-nots" but between the different civilizations. This fourth edition heralds a United Nations at the crossroads of history.

While drafting this fourth edition of *The United Nations,* one of the original authors, Jack C. Plano, a life force behind the volume, passed away. Jack was a scholar of superior talent and a man devoted to the idea of the United Nations. A veteran of World War II, Jack saw in the United Nations what other idealists of his generation envisaged, the one great hope that war and conflict could be purged from the earth. Also the realist, however, Jack understood the relevance of the United Nations in a world of disparate and often desperate states and people. A true patriot, he saw the need to sustain the alliance that won World War II and to impart to ever-new generations the understanding that peace is a product of joint endeavor and shared responsibility. As *The United Nations* is Jack Plano's legacy, so too it will always be his gift to those who make the future.

As with the third edition, I had full responsibility for drafting the fourth edition of *The United Nations*. I would be remiss if I did not note that this fourth edition was more challenging than the third. Indeed, I also must cite the assistance I received from Jane Okwako, who helped me with the research; and my wife, Raye, not only for her encouragement and patience, but for her technical skills in helping to assemble the manuscript. I also want to acknowledge the services provided by Gretchen Otto, production coordinator at G&S Book Services, and my team at Thomson Wadsworth: Reena Thomas, editorial assistant; Jennifer Klos, production project manager; Janise Fry, marketing manager; Kiely Sexton, permissions editor; and David Tatom, executive editor, who mentored this fourth edition. In the end, however, as always, I take full responsibility for any errors of omission or commission in the preparation of this work.

## ADDITIONAL RESOURCES

For the Covenant of the League of Nations, the Universal Declaration of Human Rights, and peacekeeping maps, visit the Book Companion Site at http://politicalscience .wadsworth.ziring.4e.

# I

# The United Nations in Historical Perspective

## PROLOGUE

International organization does not come naturally to a world of nation-states. Nations draw pride from their independence, and their sovereign status suggests an unerring concern for individuality and aloofness. The exclusive aspects of the territorial states reinforce go-it-alone posturing, and it is not without hesitation, and often much reluctance, that they seek community in organizations that transcend their unique character and peculiar stated purposes. Indeed, states behave as though they would rather not be burdened by arrangements that seem to dilute their private interests. Coalescence therefore is a feature of state behavior only because states must live in a world of many nation-states, each of which shares the same desire to be free of the restrictions that transcendent organizations require. It is only despite their otherwise limited inclinations that states join with other states and thus accept the limitations on their sovereignty that collective membership demands. States, after all, are seldom, if ever, self-sustaining, and barring costly autarkic ambitions, they cannot avoid external commitments.

In the greater realm of the nation-states, each actor is something less than the omnipotent entity it aspires to be; in the end, therefore, nation-states will join with others in order to compensate for their shortcomings, to make up for their obvious and not-so-obvious weaknesses. International organization promises something that individual states cannot achieve in isolation, and security, development, and prosperity are hardly realizable goals in the absence of cooperative arrangements. In no arrangement is this more obvious than in the system of the United Nations.

Emerging from the ashes of World War II, the United Nations projected a world order that in principle elevated international organization above that of sovereign states. The United Nations was conceived as the answer to a world torn by license and anarchy and ravaged by the excesses of aggressive, self-centered national states. Limitation on sovereignty was a notable outcome of a world no longer divided into colonial and colonized peoples. Retreating empires left behind national actors, none of whom were capable of making it alone, and all enthusiastically sought association in the organization of nations that became the United Nations. The United Nations was not only called humankind's best hope for an enduring peace, it also promised a cooperative grouping of nations whose concerns centered on social and economic advances.

The new states of the immediate postwar generation saw in the United Nations a guarantee against the aggressiveness of big powers as well as the promise of a helpful hand to those struggling to find their way in an uncharted wilderness. And although the role of the United States loomed large over the organization, the character of the colossus of the Western Hemisphere projected a charitable, benevolent, and amiable presence. Unlike earlier super actors, the United States was prompted by a substantial portion of the international community to assume global responsibility, and an overwhelming number of states applauded and welcomed its leadership and guidance. Moreover, the country that conceived a League of Nations after World War I (only to reject its own innovation), now in the changed conditions wrought by World War II, could not fail to make the United Nations central to its foreign policy.

American idealism was never so heavily tested. The nation that had contributed so much to the defeat of fascism and militarism stood alone at the apex of world power. The only major state emerging from World War II without serious damage, the United States in fact was more prosperous after the war than when it had entered it. Thus it was the United States that addressed the need to restructure the world's economic and banking institutions; and it was also only the United States that appeared capable of reviving a world that literally lay in ruins. With its forces in occupation in Japan and in a divided Germany, and with its network of military bases and installations in virtually every region of the world, the United States assumed the dual role of policing the defeated nations and restoring the world's socioeconomic equilibrium. Seeking not to suggest a policy of *Pax Americana,* however, the United States endeavored to legitimize its external policies and programs through the institutions of the UN system. By so doing, Washington hoped to give special credence to an experiment in international living that, while not entirely without precedent, was nevertheless as innovative as it was self-limiting.

U.S. membership in the United Nations involved the sublimation of national proclivities. It also meant the organization would guide the powerful as well as the weaker actors along a path requiring their accommodation to policies and programs not necessarily of their particular choosing. Such national transcendence, however, was deemed a small price after the tragedy of World War II. In an atmosphere of relief and self-examination, during a period of heightened idealism, the joint enterprise that was the United Nations was deemed a noble undertaking, one that promised a future far more positive and manifestly more beneficial than anything preceding it.

But the expectations of the architects of the UN system in that heady moment of creation were not to be realized. The era that came to be known as the *Cold War* began as the dust of World War II was just beginning to settle. The bipolar conditions that positioned the United States on the one side of a geopolitical frontier and the Soviet Union on the other imposed an enormous burden on the new international organization. Moreover, the fact that both countries were chiefly responsible for the success or failure of the UN system, in fact had assumed primary responsibility for the operations of the organization, distorted UN purposes. As a consequence, the United Nations was handicapped from the outset, and its weakness was written large in its lack of capacity to meld and transcend national experiences. Even UN expansion to include the newly independent states did more to heighten national rather than international organization. The peculiar characters of the different nation-states were exaggerated, hardly muted, by membership in the United Nations.

In the initial years following its formation, therefore, the United Nations became an extension of U.S. foreign policy, and Washington did not hesitate to exploit the bona fide character of the organization in its contest with Moscow. The collapse of the European empires, however, forced the release of their colonies, and the latter's emergence as sovereign nation-states soon altered the U.S. monopoly. At the same time, the Soviets freely employed their veto power against efforts that would use the United Nations to thwart Soviet ambitions. Thus, many member states were conditioned to view the United Nations as an instrument for the advancement of their exclusive policies. With the principal powers showing the way, virtually all the states endeavored to squeeze some justification from the organization for their otherwise parochial behavior. But none of the member states were more obvious in their exploitation of the organization than the major powers. Almost from its inception, the United Nations was transformed into an arena of major power jousting, and the lesser states were not long in using the world body for their own largely exclusive pursuits.

While still in its infancy, the United Nations was embroiled by a war on the Korean peninsula, but the nature of its involvement merely demonstrated the weakness of the central enforcement section of the UN Charter. The desperate transference of peacemaking and peacekeeping functions from the Security Council to the General Assembly exposed structural weaknesses in the organization that were to carry forward through all the decades of the Cold War and beyond. The United Nations proved less the instrument for controlling the aggressive use of national power and more a vehicle for the projection of unrealized national and bloc objectives. More a forum for debate during the Cold War, the United Nations found that many of the issues with which it was seized proved insoluble, and as a consequence, their cumulative weight only imposed still heavier burdens on the organization.

The United Nations received little if any credit for the termination of the Cold War, but it is not without noting that the last major incident before its ending was the UN-sanctioned coalition that drove Iraq from Kuwait. The revival of the UN Security Council during the Persian Gulf crisis of 1990–91 appeared to breathe new life into the organization. The bridging of U.S.–Soviet differences during that episode hinted at a new beginning for the international organization, but this new accommodation came just as the Soviet Union was about to self-destruct. The breakup of the communist superpower left a new

Russian Federation as the Soviet Union's heir. Moreover, Russia's largely amicable approach to the United States appeared to indicate a heavier reliance on the institutions of the United Nations. The People's Republic of China also appeared inclined to play a more cooperative role in the world body, and indeed, the appearance of permanent power unity tended to herald a reduction in the leverage achieved by the lesser states during the period of East-West hostility.

Given what appeared to be a major power preference for multilateral assertiveness immediately after the Cold War, the United Nations once more was viewed as the primary instrument for the maintenance of international equilibrium. It was not surprising therefore that the pacification of numerous small state incidents became the responsibility of the organization. During the 1990s, UN peacekeeping forces were assembled and ordered to manage state problems at unprecedented levels. Nevertheless, the enthusiasm with which the United Nations assumed these tasks, often at the behest of one or more of the permanent powers, could not conceal deep divisions among the many member states. Called upon to make substantial contributions to expanded UN activities, the permanent powers were notably hesitant, or in different situations, unwilling to honor their expressed commitments. Indeed, with the end of the Cold War, the U.S. Congress refused to honor U.S. financial obligations to the United Nations, and considerable mainstream public sentiment in the United States began to verbalize opposition to UN policies and activities.

The Clinton administration was in no position to dampen these sentiments, and by its actions it appeared to shift its emphasis from the United Nations. Confronted with major tests, whether in the Balkans with the breakup of Yugoslavia, in the Middle East with the sustained Israeli-Palestinian conflict, in the Indian subcontinent with the nuclear face-off between India and Pakistan, or in North Korea with that nation's determination to establish itself as a nuclear power, Clinton's policies tended to stress unilateral actions. With the Cold War ended, only the United States could be described as a world superpower. Nor was Washington eager to be burdened by UN institutions and procedures in its assumption of responsibility for the maintenance of world peace. The failure of UN member states to implement Chapter VII of the UN Charter in the immediate aftermath of World War II, most notably the formation of a supranational UN military command structure, was critical. The end of the Cold War, in the view of U.S. decision makers, was hardly propitious for the subordination of U.S. armed forces to UN authority.

Moreover, much of the European community appeared to follow similar thinking. The enlargement of the North Atlantic Treaty Organization (NATO) to include the former East European countries of the defunct Soviet-inspired Warsaw Pact was pressed by France and Germany as well as the United States. National security remained a high priority of the individual states, and although the UN Security Council continued to authorize the deployment of UN peacekeepers to numerous trouble spots, national governments maintained effective control over their foreign policies and armed forces. Indeed, the primacy of national self-interest reinforced American attitudes, both governmental and public, that the UN security system was hardly more than a secondary consideration in the maintenance of global stability. Moreover, American dissatisfaction with United Nations peacekeeping operations was transformed into a major issue during the U.S. presidential campaign in 2000. None of the major candidates believed it politically sound to emphasize a major role for the United Nations in matters of immediate concern to the United States. In fact, the candidate most critical of UN performance, George W. Bush, would emerge as Clinton's successor.

The assumption of the U.S. presidency by Bush in January 2001 brought into the White House policymakers with little interest in UN practices. With the ground already prepared by the election campaign for an even more publicly declared unilateral policy on international questions, the new Bush administration lost no time in declaring its opposition to UN-associated issues ranging from global warming and the environment to family planning to the International Criminal Court. But more significantly in the security area where the United States had already demonstrated a preference for military actions outside the United Nations, particularly in Bosnia and Kosovo, Washington rejected placing U.S. armed forces under UN leadership. The Bush administration reinforced this posture, and even in the matter of U.S. arrears in its financial obligations to the United Nations, only scant attention was given to the payment of the U.S. debt. In this climate, a solid segment of central Bush administration supporters were heard calling for a drastic reduction in U.S. activities in the United Nations. More extreme elements called for the abandonment of the organization altogether. Washington seemed more determined than ever to follow a unilateralist course, especially where majority UN opinion was judged to run counter to American interests.

The events of September 11, 2001, reinforced American negative thinking on matters related to the United Nations. Terrorists hijacked four American airliners and flew two of them into the towers of the World Trade Center in New York City, while a third was crashed into the Pentagon in Washington, D.C. The fourth plane missed its target when passengers aboard the ill-fated craft forced it to crash in a Pennsylvania field. The Pentagon was severely damaged, and the World Trade Center towers fell to the ground not blocks from UN headquarters. The death toll from the combined attacks approximated three thousand, the heaviest loss of life perpetrated by a foreign hand on U.S. soil. Until that moment the most secure country in the world, the United States was suddenly counted among the most vulnerable. By citing that the enemies of the United States had declared war on his country, President Bush responded with his own declaration. Noting the relative invisibility of the enemy, he insisted that the United States not only was at war with terrorists everywhere, but with those states and governments that sponsored, harbored, and, whether deliberately or not, aided and abetted terrorist actions.

There was no appeal to the United Nations from Washington, although the organization was quick to add terrorism to its list of concerns. The international organization, however, had been constructed with states as the essential actors. And while terrorism was not a new phenomenon, the action of September 11 had opened another chapter in the uses of violence. In an age of advances in science and technology, it was immediately apparent that a determined foe did not have to represent or be directly connected to an established government. Resolute individuals with access to weapons of mass destruction, many dedicated to expending their lives in the act of terror, were judged a mortal threat to any nation, most significantly to the most complex and open society on the planet. Insulating the United States from this threat was hardly something the United Nations had been organized to accomplish. Nor was the United Nations in a position to buttress U.S. defenses, or even to signal willingness to abide by U.S. counteractions. The war on terrorism was described as protracted, without a foreseeable end. Although sympathies could be expressed for the loss of life on American soil, the United States alone was responsible for protecting its citizenry and vital assets at home and abroad.

On one side, therefore, the events of September 11 reinforced the determination of the Bush administration that it alone was responsible for the defense of the United States. On the other, however, the declared UN role as the primary organ for the maintenance of international security was made even more questionable. Cooperation among nations in the war on terrorism was an acknowledged imperative, but arranging such support was less a capability of the United Nations and more a matter of interstate affiliation and cooperation. The war on terrorism did not require the United Nations to give it legitimacy or sanction. Nor was a traumatized Washington establishment prepared to seek the good graces of the United Nations in striking targets determined to be a mortal threat to the United States. Thus, President Bush ordered U.S. forces to strike at what was deemed to be the operational base for the September 11 attack. Declaring that the Al-Qaeda organization of Osama bin Laden had planned and executed the assault from Afghanistan, the United States, without UN approval, demanded that the Taliban government of Afghanistan surrender bin Laden and his compatriots. When the Afghan government refused to comply, the United States unleashed an intense and wide-scale attack on Al-Qaeda bases in the country and in short order introduced land forces that not only targeted the terrorist camps but the Afghan government as well. President Bush declared that the Afghan campaign was only a beginning in the war on terrorism, and U.S. forces were deployed to other countries around the globe.

The destruction and removal of the Afghan Taliban government was a direct outcome of September 11, but it did not end the war. With assistance provided by neighboring countries, notably Pakistan, the United States sustained a presence in Afghanistan where it maintained pressure on dispersed but well-hidden Al-Qaeda and Taliban operatives. Moreover, with the United Nations more a bystander to unfolding events, the United States turned its attention to Iraq and the government of Saddam Hussein. Insisting that Iraq possessed weapons of mass destruction and that Hussein's government was in league with terrorists, Washington renewed the call for the destruction of Iraq's unconventional weapons, and if necessary, for regime change in Baghdad. This time, compelled by events to seek UN authorization for an assault on an Iraq that was universally acknowledged to be in noncompliance with previous UN resolutions on disarmament, President Bush reluctantly agreed to address the UN General Assembly. Urging the Security Council to demand that Baghdad reveal its weapons of mass destruction or face the combined force of the United Nations, the UN body unanimously adopted an American-drafted resolution. Saddam Hussein, it was said, was given one last chance to avoid still another, more decisive, Persian Gulf War. While U.S. forces were mobilized in the region to pressure the Iraqi regime, the UN Security Council, nevertheless, ran into difficulty in authorizing action against another sovereign state. Saddam had agreed to permit UN inspectors back into the country to verify that Iraq no longer possessed, nor was then in the process of producing, weapons of mass destruction. Security Council members therefore were divided over whether Baghdad was in full and complete compliance with this most recent resolution. In the end, only Great Britain stood with the United States. The other permanent powers, especially France and Russia, threatened the use of their veto power to prevent the United States from committing the United Nations to an unprovoked war against Iraq. Citing what it deemed to be a paralyzed UN Security Council, and insisting that Iraq posed an imminent threat to world security, Washington decided to forgo further UN authorization and take immediate action against the Hussein government, with what the Bush administration called an "alliance of the willing."

The war on Iraq, perpetrated by the United States, was an act of preemption, and because it was without immediate provocation, it challenged the United Nations as never before. The United States nevertheless claimed that forty-nine countries supported the action aimed at removing the Iraqi government. Washington also argued that UN Security Council Resolution 678 of 1990 authorized military action in such circumstances. Moreover, according to the Americans, Resolution 687, which set the terms for the cessation of hostilities that ended the 1991 Gulf War, and Resolution 1441 of 2002 declaring that Iraq was in continued material breach of its obligation to disarm, arguably provided the necessary international legitimacy for the use of force. Although few nations were on record supporting the U.S. position, the virtually unilateral U.S. action to proceed with the war elevated as never before the question, "Whither the United Nations?". The United States was central to the functioning of the United Nations, but the divisions caused by the American-driven war in Iraq in 2003 had caused the permanent powers to grow estranged from one another. Moreover, the war and its aftermath raised anew the issue of the international organization's future, or at least its restructuring in light of events never envisaged in the days following the end of World War II.

Although conversant with the basic features of the Cold War, the United Nations of the twenty-first century was unprepared for the conditions that now demanded its attention. Restructuring had been contemplated and sometimes debated, but action had been slow in developing. Moreover, the need for collective action appeared to be in conflict with the forces of nationalism that now again heavily determined state policy. The penchant of nation-states, especially in an age of terror, to respond to events instinctively and without time for consultation, that is, to pursue exclusive interests, contradicted the inclusive, more deliberative and collective purpose of the United Nations. With the twentieth century already history, the world of nations had yet to demonstrate that the twenty-first century promised a heavier commitment to deeper integration through international organization.

## IN THE BEGINNING

Scholars have traced the origins and have cited features of international organization in the numerous ancient leagues and assemblies that were aimed at warding off threats posed by more formidable powers. The quest for security encouraged cooperation among the lesser states confronting the imperial power of China and Rome, but international organization was perhaps more relevant in the amphicytonic councils of the Greek city-states. Bound by a common culture and devoted to shared ceremonial temples, the different Hellenistic tribes pledged themselves to observe established rules, particularly in matters related to warfare. From the amphictyonic councils emerged the confederations of the Phocian, Akarnian, and Boetian leagues, which in turn gave rise to the Lycian and Achaean leagues that promised even richer accommodations. By the fourteenth century more functional arrangements were developed that centered on trade and commerce, particularly among the commercial towns around the North and Baltic Seas. The formation of the Hanseatic League represented some fifty evolving cities, and for two hundred years their combined power not only monopolized trade and commerce, but also demonstrated considerable strategic prowess. The fading of Hanse power culminated with the emergence of a territorial, though absolutist, dynastic state system that was formally acknowledged with the Peace of Westphalia in 1648. Although international organization was not made a feature of the Westphalian settlement, the assembly of great and lesser European powers heralded the opening of a new era in international relations, and indeed, Europe ushered in the epoch of the nation-states. No longer guided by mythology or priest, let alone by emperor or pope, the evolution of a secular state system necessitated cooperation no less than it projected individual sovereignty. Clearly, a traceable thread runs through the history that links these early and rudimentary efforts at state accommodation to the contemporary world of the United Nations.

Despite monumental and continuing failures to eliminate violence and war, peoples and governments continue to reach beyond existing political boundaries to build on the orderly, brotherly, and cooperative side of human nature rather than give free rein to the suspicious, destructive, dark side. The founding of the United Nations is in this tradition. While falling short of its high ideals and purposes, the UN system nevertheless represents that human outreach toward peace and cooperation. In the rest of this chapter we place the United Nations in historical perspective by looking at the modern state system that gave rise to it, by describing the emergence of earlier international institutions, and by reviewing events leading to the establishment of the United Nations at the end of World War II. In Chapter 2 we will discuss the structure and operation of the United Nations.

# THE STATE SYSTEM
# AND INTERNATIONAL ORGANIZATION

As the many separate political units created during the European feudal era were fused into larger communities, the national state, on which the contemporary UN system rests, emerged as the dominant political unit. Through conquest and annexation the number of small political entities was progressively reduced, and a Europe of nation-states began to take shape. The legal inception of the modern state system is commonly dated from the 1648 Treaty of Westphalia, which ended the Thirty Years' War and recognized the territorial state as the cornerstone of the system.

The new European State System was characterized not only by rivalry and disunity but also by forces moving peoples and nations toward closer contact and agreed rules of conduct. Political and economic rivalries were the chief source of competition, and periodic wars were a constant reminder that resolving them peaceably would not be easy. Nevertheless, increased contacts among the new states also brought an awakening in the realm of economic activity, and this created a need for state cooperation. In response to this need, rules were established for the adjustment of differences that inevitably arise through commercial intercourse. This resulted in a progressive elaboration of the system of international law that had begun to develop before Westphalia and in the growing use of consular interchange for the promotion and adjustment of commercial contacts. As trade competition among the new nations increased, it began to spill over into a race to acquire overseas colonies. This, in turn, produced a need for further international rules by which nations could recognize one another's titles to new lands, settle boundary disputes, and undertake joint action against piracy. Nations began to deal more directly with such problems by entering into agreements and treaties with one another. Hence rivalries and antagonisms, while continuing to grow, tended to produce countervailing forces leading to increased cooperation.

The closing decades of the eighteenth century witnessed the emergence of two powerful new ideas destined to have a profound effect on the nature of the state system. These were the two concepts of laissez-faire and democratic nationalism, each of which dramatically recognized the new role to be played by the individual in human affairs. In the economic realm, the mercantilist doctrine of state-controlled economic activity for the enhancement of state power gave way to a new concept of economic liberalism that placed greater emphasis on individual choice and initiative, rather than on government regulation, as the focus of activity. This philosophy of laissez-faire was buttressed by a new technology that provided the means for producing goods with machines. The ensuing Industrial Revolution not only changed the methods of economic production but also spectacularly increased the interdependence of states.

The forces of science and invention responsible for developing the new machine technology also helped shrink the world through new and better devices for communication and transportation. Steamships, railroads, telegrams, and telephones made closer contacts possible, accelerated trade expansion, and produced a new awareness in the minds of Western peoples. Their common societal relationship in a larger community of nations assumed particular prominence. Thus, in a progressive and dramatic way, heretofore patterns of individual and national self-sufficiency began to erode, and expression began to focus on new and rapidly developing systems of interdependence, which, in turn, produced the rudiments of a new philosophy of internationalism among Western nations.

At the same time, political developments triggered forces of individualism that were destined to have far-reaching effects on the state system. The salient events were the American and French revolutions, which were centered on democratic expression and individual rights. By producing, on a national scale, working political systems built upon principles of popular sovereignty and the importance of the individual, the political revolutions on both sides of the Atlantic Ocean ushered in the era of democratic nationalism. Democracy, as a political doctrine, presumes individuals to be rational creatures who will submit to a higher authority only of their own choosing and as a means of achieving order and prosperity in society. Translated to the international level, democratic individualism also supported a rational search for cooperative alternatives and acceptable rules of uniform state conduct. It was not historical accident that modern international law and institutions were created largely at the initiative of nations enjoying the greatest measure of individual freedom.

## THE PROCESS OF INTERNATIONAL ORGANIZATION

With the onset of the machine age and the appearance of democracy in the Western world, the stage was set for the emergence of modern international organization. Democracy fosters the growth of international organization because both involve, in essence, commitment to a *consensual process.* Just as democracy in a national political setting implies a process of public decision making by consent of the governed, international organization implies a process of international action achieved through the consent of sovereign states.

The process of building international organizations is thoroughly pragmatic; most, if not all, international institutions have been created to achieve procedural and practical objectives. The process assumes the multistate system as fact and seeks only to provide an effective means to reconcile interstate rivalry, or contradictions that emerge from state interaction. As Dag Hammarskjöld, the second Secretary-General of the United Nations, observed,

> The United Nations is not in any respect a superstate, able to act outside the framework of decisions by its member governments. It is an instrument for

negotiation among, and to some extent for, governments. It is also an instrument for concerting action by governments in support of the Charter. Thus the United Nations can serve, but not substitute itself for, the efforts of its member governments.[1]

In the absence of supranational government, only voluntary agreement among the states was considered successful in mitigating international rivalry. International organization provides the institutionalized means for eliciting such agreement. It provides the principles, the machinery, and the encouragement, but it also is the catalytic agent needed to bring about tangible results that enhance cooperation. When international cooperation is forthcoming, positive goals are made possible. When cooperation is lacking, however, international organizations represent mere "debating societies." An international organization like the United Nations therefore is only as useful as its members want it to be.

## THE EMERGENCE OF INTERNATIONAL INSTITUTIONS

International institutions dating from the early nineteenth century represent a creative response to the need for a joint approach to common problems in areas such as commerce, communication, and transportation. Early examples of modern international organization were the river commissions in Europe. The Central Rhine Commission was created in 1804 by an agreement between France and Germany; it provided for extensive regulation of river activity, the maintenance of navigation facilities, and the hearing and adjudication of complaints for alleged violations of the Commission's rules. The European Danube Commission was created in 1856 to regulate international movement on the Danube River. Both river commissions still function today in much the same way as they did when originally established.

The development of international organization was carried a step further with the creation of international public administrative unions in the latter half of the nineteenth century. In many cases the public unions were developed as a result of demands placed on national governments by the members of private international associations. Such demands resulted in the establishment of the International Telegraphic Union in 1865 and the Universal Postal Union in 1874. The success of these two unions paved the way for the creation of numerous international public agencies in such diverse areas as narcotic drugs, agriculture, health, weights and measures, railroads, patents and copyrights, and tariffs. The rapid growth of technical international agencies was a reaction to the new world of science and technology that was compressing space and overcoming political boundaries. States were willing to collaborate because it was essential to business and commerce and useful in protecting the lives, health, and other interests of their citizens.

As cooperation among states increased during the nineteenth century, a pattern of organization and procedures developed. Each new international agency established institutional machinery that was unique in some respects, yet each possessed certain basic characteristics in common with its contemporaries. The following pattern was typical:

1. Membership in organizations was usually limited to sovereign states. With the exception of organizations that were regional in scope, such organizations typically held membership open to all states without political conditions.
2. Each functional organization was created through the instrument of a multilateral treaty. The treaty served as a constitution, specifying the obligations of members, creating the institutional structure, and proclaiming the objectives of the organization.
3. A conference or congress was usually established as the basic policy-making organ. The conference included all members of the organization and met infrequently, typically once in a five-year period.
4. Decision making in the organization was based on the principle of egalitarianism, with each member having an equal vote, and decisions made on the basis of unanimous consent. In time, this gave way to majoritarianism, especially in voting on procedural questions.
5. A council or other decision-making organ of an executive nature was often created to implement policies. It usually had a limited membership, and its primary responsibility was to administer the broad policy decisions laid down by the conference.
6. A secretariat was established to carry out the policies of the conference and council and to conduct routine functions of the organization. The secretariat was made the responsibility of a secretary-general or director-general, usually a professional civil servant with an international reputation.
7. Some organizations, such as the river commissions, exercised judicial or quasi-judicial powers. Some created special international courts to decide controversies arising out of their administrative operations.
8. Many organizations were endowed with a legal personality enabling them to own property, to sue and be sued in defined areas, and, in some cases, to enjoy a measure of diplomatic immunity.
9. Financial support was provided by contributions from member governments, using a formula for contributions based on principles such as "ability to pay," "satisfaction to be gained," "equality," or any combination of such principles.
10. The competence of the organization was usually limited to a functional or specialized problem area, as set forth in its constitution. Organizations of general competence in political, economic, and social areas were not established until the twentieth century.
11. Decision making was carried on in two ways: by drafting international treaties and submitting them to member governments for their official acceptance, and by adopting resolutions recommending action by member governments. A few organizations possessed administrative and minor policy-making powers.

An important by-product of political cooperation on technical matters was the growth of the belief that political cooperation might be equally productive in securing agreement among states in the more weighty matters of war and peace. Such thinking helped prepare the ground for the calling of two conferences at The Hague, Netherlands, in 1899 and 1907, the earliest general international conferences concerned with building a world system based on law and order. The 1899 Hague Peace Conference was attended by delegates from only twenty-six nations and was largely European in complexion; the second conference, however, moved toward universality, with representatives from forty-four states, including most of the countries of Latin America. The principle of the sovereign equality of states was accepted at the conferences, with the result that the system emerging from the conferences helped break the monopoly of the great powers in handling matters of war and peace and economic and colonial rivalry. The Hague system also established precedents that contributed to the later development of an international parliament. Headquarters at The Hague provided international machinery to facilitate the peaceful settlement of international disputes. The Hague system in effect proclaimed a new era of cooperation and indicated that a global political organization to keep the peace and promote interstate cooperation was now a possibility. But expectations and realities were not the same. The Hague system did not deter the empires from their more aggressive impulses, and World War I appeared to make a mockery of the idealism that underpinned it. Nevertheless, the Great War that was World War I had altered the game of states. The magnitude of the calamity demonstrated that incredible forces had produced a fusion of popular nationalism and modern technology that needed to be controlled. Therefore, instead of acknowledging failure, the diplomats of the period found new urgency in structuring an international system that, they hoped, could prevent a recurrence of the tragic experience. Indeed, World War I revealed that something more formidable than a Hague system was needed to deal with the issues that compelled modern states to ferociously and recklessly assault one another.

## THE LEAGUE EXPERIMENT

Americans were living in an age of innocence when the United States declared war against the Central Powers in 1917. Both sides were then close to exhaustion, their idealism and egoistic nationalism largely dissipated by nearly three years of savage trench warfare. In the early years of the war, the carnage in Europe produced U.S. consensus that involvement should be avoided at all costs. But as the war dragged on, that consensus was eroded by a growing belief that the New World somehow had to save the Old World from extinction. If Europeans of all nationalities could live in peace under the U.S. system of democracy, why not apply these same principles to the international community?

The United States entered World War I fired with a holy mission to "make the world safe for democracy." U.S. idealism was summed up in President Woodrow Wilson's peace program, submitted to Congress on January 8, 1918, in which he enunciated Fourteen Points aimed at rekindling Allied idealism and determination while weakening the enemy's resolve by promising a just peace and a new world of security and democracy. In his fourteenth point Wilson declared that "a general association of nations must be formed under published covenants for the purpose of affording mutual guarantees of political independence and territorial integrity to great and small powers alike."

The chief architect of the League of Nations, unquestionably, was Woodrow Wilson. Without his support the idea of a League would probably not have gone beyond the point of intellectual germination. While many Allied politicians thought more cynically of how the victory won at a terrible cost could be exploited for national gain and political advantage, Wilson sought to materialize his dreams of a just world based on law and democracy. Because his program appealed to millions of Europeans emerging from the trauma of war, Allied leaders were forced by public opinion to pay more than lip service to his ideas. Wilson's vision of a just peace was focused on the building of a League of Nations, and Allied politicians accepted his demands that the League be created as an integral part of the Treaty of Versailles. Wilson believed that the League Covenant would support and reinforce provisions of the Treaty, especially Article 10 of the Covenant, which was aimed at preserving the territorial integrity of signatory states from aggression. But while Wilson's dream of a new, formally structured international organization was realized with the formation of the League of Nations, the U.S. Senate refused to ratify the Treaty of Versailles, thus rejecting American membership in the world body. Decrying what it called an assault on U.S. sovereignty, the Senate opened the way for those nations that had joined the organization to violate its principles, again in the name of state sovereignty. In sum: the League of Nations, although structurally more elegant than the earlier Hague system, was no less at the mercy of the individual states and their exclusive interests.

## STRUCTURE AND FUNCTIONS OF THE LEAGUE

The League Covenant provided for the establishment of three permanent organs—the Assembly, the Council, and the Secretariat. Two semiautonomous bodies were created outside the Covenant framework—the Permanent Court of International Justice (PCIJ) and the International Labor Organization (ILO). The objectives of the PCIJ and the ILO were similar to those of the League, however, and their budgets were part of the League budget. The Council and Assembly also elected the judges of the World Court. Of greater importance than structures were the obligations that members assumed toward the organization and toward one another. Each state undertook to "respect and preserve as against external aggression the territorial integrity and existing political independence of all Members of the League" (Article 10). Members agreed to submit all of their disputes to arbitration, adjudication, or Council inquiry and in no case to resort to war until three months after a settlement was offered. If any state resorted to war in violation of the Covenant, members would apply diplomatic and economic sanctions and consider the violation an act of war against the world community. Members further agreed to work together to control national armaments and to cooperate in solving social, economic, colonial, humanitarian, and other common problems.

## LEAGUE INNOVATIONS

In its basic design and role, the League was both old and new. It was old in the sense that the system was founded on the sovereignty of the member states, and no new obligation could be imposed on a member without that member's consent. As with earlier attempts to establish some degree of international order, the powers of the League were limited to recommendations. The Covenant, in keeping with the traditional guidelines of international law, did not seek to outlaw war but only to regulate a state's resort to this ultimate action. A special security role was accorded to the great powers, a role that they had always played (along with war making) in the international political system. The League's decisions were made on the basis of mutual agreements that embodied each state's particular interests, a decision-making system as ancient as the state system itself. Progress in technical, social, economic, and humanitarian areas was, as in the past, a consequence of common treaty actions and based on national statutory concerns. All in all, there was much in the new League of Nations system that was merely a continuation of the old traditions, customs, institutions, and decision-making procedures of the pre-League world. But there was also much that was new, some quietly evolutionary in nature, others dramatically revolutionary in scope.

The League, for example, attempted to establish a permanent international organization of a general political nature with machinery functioning on a continuing basis. State security was made a community responsibility in which the collective force of the state system would be used to constrain an international lawbreaker. Although the League could hardly be compared to a domestic political system with its superior authority, independent police force, and automatic action against lawbreakers, it was, nonetheless, a step toward internationalizing the responsibility of enforcing peace and security. Military action against an aggressor always had been a right of state; but under the League Covenant it was made a collective duty. What was intended and what was simple reality, however, was seldom if ever realized. In point of fact the individual right of states to choose their individual course of action, to judge their own circumstances, and to act militarily remained elevated over that of the League's internationalized "collective state duties." In its approach to the problem of war, the Covenant made no general statement that war was illegal. The traditional right of states to engage in war was circumscribed in the Covenant by provisions that made it illegal to make war outside the organization, that mandated delay in taking individual action, and that prescribed community sanctions against the war maker. But the sovereign status of the individual state remained paramount, and League limitations on state behavior proved unenforceable.

Acknowledging this weakness in the League machinery, in 1928, the major nations, this time with the United States playing a primary role, entered into a treaty that renounced war as an instrument of national policy. The Kellogg-Briand Pact, however, did little more than create false assurances. Peaceful relations between the signatories to the Pact could not be guaranteed by words and solemn promises alone.

## The League in Action

The two major functions of the League, as stated in the Preamble to the Covenant, were "to achieve international peace and security" and "to promote international cooperation." These functions were expected to be complementary. A secure world would encourage state cooperation in many areas, and a common attack on economic, social, and technical problems would help eliminate state rivalry by developing a genuine sense of community. Of the two functions, however, the security function was regarded as the more pressing.

There was little agreement on how the League should pursue its security objectives. In French eyes the primary responsibility of the League was to enforce the provisions of the peace treaties and guard against a resurgence of German military power. Britain, in contrast, viewed the League as an agency for fostering the peaceful settlement of disputes and protecting the vital interests of the Empire. Each member, in fact, tended to explain the League's peace-preserving role largely in terms of its own national interest, so that when the League was confronted with threats to the peace, it often spoke in a cacophony rather than with a single voice.

## The Manchurian Case

The League's great test in coping with war initiated by a great power came in 1931 when Japan, claiming Chinese destruction of its railway properties, attacked Manchuria and occupied its capital city of Mukden. China, charging aggression by Japan, appealed to the League under Article 11 of the Covenant. Attempts by the Council to secure a cease-fire and a Japanese withdrawal were vetoed by Japan, which requested an on-the-spot inquiry into the facts of the dispute before League action followed.

As the war in Manchuria intensified, the Council appointed a Commission of Inquiry under Lord Lytton's direction and ordered it to go to the region to ascertain the facts. By the time the Commission arrived in the Far East, in April 1932, however, the Japanese had seized all of Manchuria and had transformed it into a fictional independent state, renaming it Manchukuo and providing it with a puppet government loyal to Tokyo. League indecision infuriated China, which denounced the Council's procrastination and utter failure to act. China asked that the matter be transferred to the League's Assembly, but all it could do was issue a condemnation of Japanese aggression and adopt the U.S.-initiated

Stimson Doctrine of nonrecognition of new states or governments that were created illegally by the use of force. The Lytton Commission authored a lengthy report that condemned Japan's aggressive actions in Manchuria. It subsequently was adopted unanimously by the Assembly. But it was too late and too little to affect the outcome. Japan's conquest of Manchuria was an accomplished fact. In the end, the Assembly's action condemning Japan of blatant aggression only led to Tokyo's formal withdrawal from membership in the League of Nations.

The Manchurian case emphasized that situations involving overt aggression could not be successfully handled by using League procedures for peaceful settlement. Japan proved, and the lesson was not lost on potential European aggressors, that the cumbersome machinery and procedures of the League demonstrated the ineffectiveness of collective action. Overall, however, the League failed this first test because leadership from the great powers was lacking on the Council and because the United States, the major power most concerned with Japanese aggressive tendencies, was not a League member. The United States managed to send an observer to Geneva, but the representative sat quietly as the debate raged around him. Washington condemned Japan's actions on moral grounds but nonetheless continued doing business with the East Asian country. Thus the League of Nations failed its first major test and quickly gained the reputation as a weak and indecisive body.

## THE ETHIOPIAN CASE

A second critical test for the League was not long in coming. In the winter of 1934, League-member Italy attacked League-member Ethiopia in violation of their mutual Covenant obligations to respect each other's political and territorial integrity and to adjust their differences peacefully. Italy, following the Japanese example, launched a diplomatic offensive in Geneva, claiming that Ethiopian forces had struck the first blow. Ethiopia, not recognizing the Italian master plan to build an African empire, sought to negotiate and to use the power of the League facilities for conciliation rather than collective action. Under cover of negotiations, Mussolini mobilized Italian reserves for war, granting minor concessions each time it appeared that the Council would intervene. Outside the main arena of the League, a diplomatic web of intrigue developed as Britain and France, concerned more with the rising power of Nazi Germany, sought to keep Italy as a buffer to Germany. Permitting Mussolini to seize a piece of African territory seemed to the diplomats in London and Paris a small price to pay for the containment of German power. Incredibly, the United States remained aloof and President Franklin Roosevelt refused Ethiopian Emperor Haile Selassie's request that he call on the parties to observe their commitment under the Kellogg-Briand Pact of 1928 not to use war as an instrument of national policy.

By the autumn of 1935 Italy had completed its mobilization, and on October 2, disregarding many League resolutions and Covenant provisions, it launched a full-scale attack on Ethiopia. Ethiopia at once invoked Article 16 of the Covenant, holding that Italy's resort to war was undertaken in defiance of the Covenant and that League members must conclude that an act of war had been committed against the League itself. The Ethiopian delegate at Geneva argued that all members must honor their Covenant obligations by applying immediate economic sanctions against Italy, and he called on the Council to recommend military sanctions as well. Under an interpretation of the Covenant agreed on in 1921, however, neither the Council nor the Assembly was empowered to determine that aggression had been committed. Each member state was entitled to decide for itself. The levying of economic and other sanctions was likewise controlled by each state, emphasizing the veto power held by each member under the League system. Of the fifty-four League members polled, fifty indicated that Italy was the aggressor, thus obligating them to apply economic sanctions at once and to undertake military sanctions if these were recommended by the Council.

Historically, it was the first time economic sanctions were levied against an international lawbreaker. Fifty League members had participated. Numerous questions, however, arose concerning what kinds of materials should be embargoed, whether imports from Italy should be banned, what would happen to private long-term contracts, and whether an effort should be made to prevent nonmember states from violating the embargoes. A League consensus developed that economic sanctions should include an embargo on arms and a number of essential minerals (but not coal and oil). A ban on loans and other kinds of funding, a restriction against all imports from Italy and its possessions, and mutual support among League members to minimize their economic injury from the embargoes were all considered. By November 1935 the economic sanctions were in effect, and within a period of several months the sanctions began to affect Italy's economy. Within two months after the levying of sanctions in November 1935, Italian exports declined 43 percent over the same month of the previous year, and imports dropped 47 percent. In three months imports fell to 56 percent of the previous year, and imports of strategic items such as iron ore, tin, and raw rubber had almost ceased. Thus, within a short period of time economic sanctions proved generally effective in reducing Italy's economic activity.

Despite economic sanctions, however, the Italian armies swept into the Ethiopian capital of Addis Ababa. On May 5, 1936, Mussolini boasted that victory had been achieved. Eight months after sanctions had been imposed, the Assembly voted to withdraw all sanctions against Italy. Why had the economic sanctions failed? Why were they terminated after Italy had completed its conquest, thus condoning the aggression? Why had the Council not recommended military sanctions? These and similar questions were aired in Assembly debates following the withdrawal of sanctions. The answers to them, incomplete as they may be, help explain the problem of carrying out a policy of collective security. Basic to the League's dilemma was the British and French objective of building a coalition to balance the power of Hitler's Germany. The struggle in the 1930s to contain Nazi Germany's power took precedence over the League's attempt to realize collective security, and London and Paris were eager to have Mussolini on their side.

Moreover, other nations besides Britain and France contributed to the weak-sanctions syndrome. The United States condemned Italian aggression but avoided any cooperation with the sanctions decision other than placing both belligerents off-limits for arms shipments under the American Neutrality Acts. U.S. trade, especially shipments of oil, increased sizably, however, with most of the increase going to the Italian African colonies. Many Latin American countries, straining under gluts of primary commodity surpluses, agreed in principle to sanctions, but they too failed to apply them in practice. Four League members refused to apply any kind of sanctions, one refused to reduce imports from Italy, while seven never applied the arms embargo. For these countries, the need to stimulate national economies that had stagnated during the world economic depression proved to be a more powerful motivator of national actions than idealistic considerations or League member obligations.

In the end, the gains of appeasement were illusory. While the worldwide economic depression spread and intensified, Italy joined Germany and the Axis Powers (which included Japan), and together their actions precipitated World War II. With major war beginning in Europe and East Asia, the United States insisted on neutrality and did nothing as the League of Nations was allowed to slip into oblivion. League sanctions were something of a first for an international organization, but there was nothing to celebrate as history's most costly war began to unfold. The Ethiopian case only demonstrated that it took more to deter aggression than covenants, organizations, institutions, and procedures. The failure of not only sanctions but also collective security was illustrated in Hitler's attack on Poland in September 1939, commencing the formal start of World War II.

## AN APPRAISAL: THE LEAGUE'S BALANCE SHEET

A review of the League record might be summarized as a study in utility and futility. Conclusions about the degree of success or failure attained by the League must obviously depend on the standard of measurement used. If the League of Nations is to be measured by what the Covenant framers intended, or what millions of people hoped for, or what the principles of the Covenant actually called for, the League fell far short. If, on the other hand, the League is measured by the performances of past international organizations, or what skeptics and critics predicted for it, or what the nature of the rivalry-ridden state system would permit, the League probably rated high. Any evaluation, however, faces the danger of falling into the old pro-League–anti-League controversy that characterized the great American debate on the subject and kept it on a largely emotional level for the lifetime of the organization.

## A CAPSULE HISTORY OF THE LEAGUE

Obviously, an appraisal of the League must recognize that its effectiveness varied in response to changes in the international environment. The peace, stability, and relative prosperity of its first decade permitted the League to make a promising start in several directions. Numerous international disputes were settled peacefully, the complex problem of disarmament was tackled, and the Kellogg-Briand Pact of 1928 attempted to close a gap in the League Covenant by outlawing war as an instrument of national policy. Cooperation in welfare areas was explored, and foundations were laid for extensive programs that emerged during the subsequent decade.

The period from 1930 to 1935 was one of challenge and uncertainty for the League. The economic depression that started with the U.S. stock market crash in 1929 and spread across the world in a chain reaction reduced the League's carefully cultivated channels of cooperation to a shambles. Economic nationalism and ideological rivalries spawned in the depression's wake split the status quo world into hostile camps. Japanese, Italian, and German fascism posed successive political and military challenges with which the organization and its members were unwilling or unable to cope. A new wave of nationalism erased many of the gains of internationalism during the 1920s as League members became increasingly obsessed with their own limited conceptions of national security as well as with domestic problems. Government after government fought desperately to rescue its people from the brink of economic ruin, social disintegration, and political revolution. As Germany rearmed, disarmament talks collapsed and the world witnessed the start of a new arms race. Economic and monetary conferences failed, and the world depression deepened. The world of the 1930–35 era was not of the League's making, but it was the one in which the League had to function.

The world stage was now set for the League's inevitable demise. Nine members withdrew between 1935 and 1939, some for political reasons, others claiming funding problems. A desperate reform movement initiated by the Assembly in 1936 sought to stem the tide of despair and refurbish the League's tarnished image. The organization's security provisions were revised, and the League Covenant was altered to avoid all references to the peace treaties of World War I. The Axis Powers, however, were bent on aggression and were not interested in returning to the League, nor were other former member states, which continued to pursue independent courses of action. With the failure of the reform movement, the League became inoperative in the security area. The one exception was the vote expelling the Soviet Union from membership because of its attack on Finland in 1939. By contrast, a majority of the members professed neutrality in the crises growing out of German annexations in Central Europe. When general war came to Europe in September 1939, the League became quiescent, a posture it retained through the six years of World War II. A shell of the League organization lived on at its Geneva headquarters through the war period. Shunned by the architects of still another world organization, the discredited League of Nations was not allowed to influence the construction of a body that was being heralded as the best hope of humankind.

## AN AUTOPSY

Just as friends of the League in its early years tended to exaggerate its novelty and its potential, critics have in retrospect emphasized its failures and under-valued its contributions. All evaluations, however, eventually return to the central question: Why did the League fail to keep peace? Since the maintenance of peace and security was the primary objective of the League, it is only natural that the historical verdict on the League has been delivered mainly in that area and in condemnatory terms.

In fixing blame, some observers have sought to explain the League's demise as a failure of its member states to support the principles of the Covenant. Such a rationalization fails to recognize that in the area of international organization members *are* the organization, that the League had no real existence independent of its component parts. No organization made up of sovereign and independent entities can possibly be stronger than the will and support for common action that exists within the group. Thus, to blame the members rather than the League is a circular argument. One could as well make the point that the pre–World War I balance of power worked well in keeping the peace but eventually failed because the states involved did not play their proper roles within the system.

Procedural problems growing out of the League's machinery have also been blamed for its failure. It is quite true that the requirement of unanimity in both Council and Assembly on most substantive questions enabled aggressor nations to veto some countermeasures. Also, because the Kellogg-Briand Pact could not effectively outlaw war, and the League Covenant permitted members to use the provisions regulating resort to war to block serious collective responses to aggression, the use of state violence was still deemed a sovereign act of state. Covenant provisions dealing with disarmament were so loosely worded that no particular responsibility existed for members to reduce their arms. The sanctions system was weakened in the League's early years by a Covenant interpretation permitting each member to decide for itself the question of invoking an economic embargo. Many other technical problems also contributed to the League's failure, but it would be inaccurate to assign organizational weaknesses a major role in the debacle since most of the weaknesses could be, and many were, overcome by interpretation and by the use of alternative pathways.

Probably the most popular explanation for the League's failure was U.S. defection. Unquestionably, the refusal of the United States to participate in a world organization sponsored by its own president created a psychological and power vacuum that the League never fully overcame. In the security area U.S. policymakers offered only moral condemnation of aggression, while permitting U.S. businesses to continue extensive trade with the aggressors. The popular myth—if U.S. military forces had combined with those of League members, the

League would have been successful against aggressors—overlooks the fact that U.S. power during the 1920s and 1930s was only a potentiality awaiting the full mobilization of World War II. Contributions from the small, garrison-bound U.S. Army could hardly have changed the outcome of any major military action during the League period. Americans also were psychologically unprepared for major war. Indeed, it was not until Japan's surprise attack on the U.S. naval base at Pearl Harbor in December 1941 that Americans were galvanized to stem the tide of aggression. The U.S. defection from the League therefore weakened the organization, but it was not the central reason for its ultimate collapse.

Some critics of the League have sought to explain its failure as resulting from its close association with the "unjust" peace treaties of World War I. The League, it is argued, was placed in the impossible position of defending the status quo, that is, of reinforcing the victors against the vanquished who wished to undo the peace treaties. The League acknowledged the importance of the argument when it appointed a committee in the late 1930s to propose reforms that would free it from this incubus and, it was hoped, regain the support of nations—especially Germany—that had been the most alienated. Yet the League would still have had to operate within a world based on the peace settlements even if it had in no way been associated with them. Moreover, to the League's credit, the status quo was not tenaciously defended. Justice and equity often took precedence over the status quo, as in the case of the German Saar territory, whose people, in a League-supervised plebiscite, voted for reunion with Germany.

Finally, some groups of critics have seen in the League's failure an example of the fundamental inability of a collective security system to keep the peace. One such group rejected the League as an impractical and idealistic concept that was foredoomed to failure because it ignored the power realities of the world. Only by fostering a balance of power through military preparedness and alliances could peace be preserved, so ran the argument of these critics, and the League diverted the status quo great powers from such a course, making disaster inevitable. Another group also criticized the League's utopianism, but its alternative was a world government with substantial powers acting directly on individuals. Since peace can be adequately preserved within nations by a federal government, this group argued, the world scene likewise demanded a world authority with a near monopoly of power. Compelling as arguments favoring world federalism may be in theory, the world of sovereign states was hardly ready then, nor is it now, to undergo such a radical metamorphosis. Moreover, if the will to resist the aggressors had been broadly based and deeply rooted, if conditions approaching a consensus had existed, the cooperation of member states could probably have done the job as expeditiously as a world federal system. Conversely, the absence of consensus under either system would have had equally deleterious results.

In conclusion, no single theory explains the League's failure. One might even conclude that bad luck had something to do with it. A combination of many factors, often appearing at inopportune times, made success in the security area an elusive quarry. Unquestionably, the economic nationalism engendered by world depression created an environment uncongenial to international cooperation. And once the world had been irretrievably split between revisionist and status quo powers, the malfunctioning of the League's collective security apparatus became a matter of course.

# ORGANIZING THE UNITED NATIONS

The failure of the major nations to promote collective security after World War I meant that the League of Nations would be helpless in meeting the challenges of the aggressive states determined to recast the world in their own image. The rise and popularity of fascism in Italy, Japan, and Germany coincided with the emergence of Marxist Bolshevism in the Soviet Union. The League, a manifestation of the imperial conditions existing before the Great War, was not prepared to confront these new and more bombastic expressions of exclusive nationalism on one side and ideological internationalism on the other. Moreover, having failed to repel aggression in Manchuria and Ethiopia, the League demonstrated it was hardly an obstacle to the ambition of a violence-prone and vengeful Hitlerian Germany. But as much as World War II was attributed to the failure of the League, and it ceased playing a role in that long and costly war, the central idea of collective security remained. Furthermore, the alliance that was eventually forged to defeat the Axis Powers and demand their unconditional surrender had assumed an identity as the United Nations. It was for the purpose of sustaining that alliance once the war was over that the UN organization was created. Energized again by the United States, and this time with a guarantee that the Americans would play a central role in UN operations as well as in its establishment, the League of Nations was allowed to fade into history.

## THE ROAD TO SAN FRANCISCO

The UN Charter, which emerged from the UN Conference on International Organization in San Francisco, was a product of extensive wartime planning. The seed for a new postwar world organization was planted in the Atlantic Charter of August 14, 1941, by U.S. President Franklin Roosevelt and British Prime Minister Winston Churchill. The date is important because it was four months before the Japanese attack on Pearl Harbor and the United States was not yet a belligerent in World War II. Churchill wanted explicit endorsement of a postwar international political organization included in the joint statement of aspirations. Roosevelt, however, recognized that U.S. public opinion was still basically isolationist and might not be favorably disposed to such a clear-cut internationalist objective. The Atlantic Charter therefore called for "fullest collaboration between all nations in the economic field" and hinted of the future "establishment of a wider and permanent system of general security." Even in this watered-down form the Charter carried the clear implication that progress toward a world organization having security and economic responsibilities was a joint objective of the two leading democracies. On January 1, 1942, with the United States now in the war, twenty-six nations subscribed to a Declaration by the United Nations that cited the principles of the Atlantic Charter. This declaration established the UN military alliance, to which twenty-one other nations subsequently adhered, each agreeing to employ its full resources against the Axis, to cooperate with one another, and not to make a separate peace.

The vague references to international organization in these early war documents were made explicit in the Moscow Declaration on General Security signed in October 1943 by the foreign ministers of the Big Four (Cordell Hull of the United States, Anthony Eden of Great Britain, Vyacheslav Molotov of the Soviet Union, and Foo Ping-sheung of Nationalist China). The Moscow Declaration pledged continuance of wartime cooperation "for the organization and maintenance of peace and security" and explicitly recognized "the necessity of establishing at the earliest practicable date a general international organization." It was also the first clear commitment by the Soviet Union to support the establishment of a world organization.

## THE DUMBARTON OAKS CONFERENCE

With the three major powers diligently working on drafts of a constitution for a general international organization, the U.S. State Department suggested to the Soviet and British governments that they meet to work out a single set of proposals. After negotiations the three governments agreed that they would participate in the drafting of a proposed charter. It also was decided that China should participate, although not directly with the Soviet Union because the latter desired to preserve its position of neutrality in the Far Eastern war (the Soviet Union had yet to declare war on Japan). The four governments met at Dumbarton Oaks, an estate in Washington, D.C., in two separate phases. Conversations were held among the U.S., Soviet, and British delegations from August 21 to September 28, 1944, and among the U.S., British, and Chinese delegations from September 29 to October 7, 1944. At the conclusion of the conference, the areas of joint agreement were published as the Dumbarton Oaks Proposals.

A surprisingly large area of agreement emerged from the conference in an atmosphere that was cordial and cooperative. Although the Allies were taking the offensive on all fronts by the summer of 1944, victory was not yet assured and all four governments still felt the close attachment of nations seriously threatened by common enemies.

The four governments intended the Dumbarton Oaks Proposals to constitute a basis for discussions at the forthcoming general conference on international organization. The following summarizes some of the major areas covered by the Proposals:

*Purposes:* To maintain international peace and security, encourage friendly relations among nations, and achieve international cooperation.

*Nature:* To be based on the sovereign equality of its members, in the tradition of early international organizations and the League of Nations.

*Membership:* To be open to all peace-loving states, on the assumption that all states will eventually become "peace-loving," hence eligible for membership. New members to be admitted through action by the Security Council and the General Assembly.

*Organs:* To have five major organs: a Security Council including all great powers as permanent members, a General Assembly comprising all members, a Secretariat, a Court, and an Economic and Social Council, plus such subsidiary agencies as might be found necessary.

*Competence:* To have primary responsibility, through the Security Council, for maintaining peace and security, with all decisions in this crucial area reached only by unanimous agreement of the permanent members.

## THE YALTA CONFERENCE

Several important topics were not settled during the Dumbarton Oaks conversations. No decision was reached on whether a new court should be established to replace the existing Permanent Court of International Justice. The question of how the new world organization would deal with the mandates system and the general problem of colonialism was avoided. More important than the omissions were the disagreements that were to prove too fundamental to settle at any but the highest levels. These disagreements were eventually resolved at the final wartime conference of the Big Three—Roosevelt, Churchill, and Stalin—meeting at Yalta in the Russian Crimea February 4–11, 1945. At Dumbarton Oaks the Soviets had demanded a comprehensive and unlimited veto power in the Security Council; at Yalta Stalin accepted a compromise that the great power veto would not apply to decisions on procedural matters and could not be invoked by a party to a dispute. At Dumbarton Oaks the Soviets had sought the admission of each of the fifteen Soviet republics as original members; at Yalta this demand was reduced to additional seats for two Soviet republics, Ukraine and Byelorussia, which was acceptable to Roosevelt and Churchill. The term *peace-loving,* adopted at Dumbarton Oaks as a criterion of fitness for membership, was defined at Yalta to provide original membership for any state that had declared war on the common enemy by March 1, 1945, a definition that was somewhat anomalous but operational. Agreement was reached on the question of territories then governed under mandates from the League of Nations: A trusteeship system would be established, and the territories placed under it would include existing League mandates, colonial holdings from the enemy states, and other areas voluntarily placed under trusteeship. A trusteeship council would be established to oversee the trust system. Finally, at Yalta the Big Three (the United States, the USSR, and Great Britain) agreed that the five great powers would sponsor a UN Conference on International Organization to meet on April 25, 1945. San Francisco was selected as the site of the conference.

The Yalta Conference helped resolve outstanding issues among the Big

Three, but the publication of the Dumbarton Oaks Proposals raised questions among the small powers. The views of some of the small states were carefully set forth, somewhat to the annoyance of the U.S. delegation, at the Inter-American Conference on Problems of Peace and War held at Mexico City in February and March 1945. These states called for universality of membership, a more powerful General Assembly, more emphasis on a world court, a special agency to promote intellectual and moral cooperation, adequate representation for Latin America on the Security Council, and the settlement of regional disputes by regional organizations. The Inter-American system was to be organized to act in harmony with the new organization. Clearly, the small powers were not going to accept passively domination by the great powers in the framing of the new Charter or in the power structure of the organization itself.

To some extent, the Dumbarton Oaks Proposals also collided with the views of informed public opinion in the United States. The wartime propaganda for a new international organization had fostered a wave of idealism bordering on utopianism among segments of the public. The Proposals, conversely, were based on the bedrock of diplomatic realism, as were the compromises reached at Yalta. Consequently, many idealists regarded the Proposals as a step backward from the League of Nations Covenant. They pointed out that the principle of national sovereignty was proclaimed more strongly than it had been in 1919, that great power domination was more solidly entrenched, and that references to law and justice were vaguer. Idealists who had been thinking in terms of a world federal union were brought harshly back to reality.

The great powers, however, could not wait for the building of a full public consensus; to prolong the process of constructing the framework of the new organization might run the risk of destroying existing areas of agreement as the war drew to a close. Suggestions for revisions and improvements could be explored at San Francisco. In the words of Franklin D. Roosevelt, addressing the Congress on his return from Yalta, "This time we shall not make the mistake of waiting until the end of the war to set up the machinery of peace."

## THE UN CONFERENCE ON INTERNATIONAL ORGANIZATION

The UN Conference on International Organization (UNCIO) opened in San Francisco on April 25, 1945, with forty-six nations represented. Four additional delegations representing Argentina, Denmark, Byelorussia, and Ukraine were subsequently admitted to participate in drafting the Charter. The fifty nations represented, plus Poland, became the original members of the United Nations. The latter did not participate in the San Francisco Conference because the United States and Britain refused to recognize the Soviet-sponsored Provisional Government, but Poland was permitted to sign the completed Charter as an original member. The controversy over Poland's participation hinted strongly of the coming ideological struggle within the new organization.

The process of writing the UN Charter resembled that of a democratic constituent body drafting a constitution. The Big Three provided the leadership and initiative in most of the decision making. The U.S. delegation was particularly conspicuous in its role as godfather of the new organization. Although diplomatic practice demands that the foreign minister of the host country be chosen as the presiding officer of an international conference, in the interest of unity among the great powers the conference chose the foreign ministers of the four sponsoring governments (including China) as cochairmen. France was invited to become a sponsoring government but had declined.

The Conference agenda was based on the Dumbarton Oaks Proposals as modified by the Yalta Conference. The Conference rules provided for freedom of discussion, voting equality, and substantive decision making by a two-thirds vote of those present and voting. These ground rules theoretically gave the small states an opportunity to undo the work of the great powers, but in fact no substantial change in the position of the great powers was effected. The threat of empty great power chairs at the UN table was inducement enough for the majority to defer to the few. The middle and small powers did sometimes obtain concessions on matters of secondary importance that, in total, added up to an important modification of the Proposals. Bloc politics were also used at the Conference, with the twenty Latin American states and five Arab states particularly active and effective. The Commonwealth states, however, did not join Britain in a voting bloc, preferring to provide leadership to the attempts to modify the position of the great powers.

The UN Charter was signed on June 26, 1945, by the delegates of fifty-one nations. On the same date the delegates also established a Preparatory Commission consisting of representatives of all member states. The Preparatory Commission met in London during November to make arrangements for the first meetings of the new organization's major organs and for the transfer of certain activities from the League of Nations.

## PUBLIC SUPPORT AND RATIFICATION

After signing the UN Charter, the fifty-one signatory states undertook its ratification through their respective constitutional processes. The process of ratification varies from nation to nation, although it generally involves some measure of approval by the national legislative body. Such approval may be automatic in authoritarian nations, and it may even be perfunctory in democratic nations, but in some nations, such as the United States, it may be the crucial test for a treaty. Although the great majority of treaties submitted to the U.S. Senate over the years have received its consent, some of the most important ones, such as the Covenant of the League of Nations and the Statute of the first World Court, have been rejected. Many others have been effectively denied by remaining buried in the Senate Foreign Relations Committee.

On July 28, 1945, the U.S. Senate approved the Charter of the United Nations by a vote of eighty-nine to two. The lopsided vote surprised no one. Never before in U.S. history had a treaty been studied and debated so extensively both before and after its drafting. Never had the Senate participated so directly in

the major steps of the treaty process or had bipartisanship operated so successfully in removing a major treaty from politics. Never before, or since, had the
State Department been so successful in stimulating organized group support for
a major policy objective. In a very real sense the U.S. decision to participate in
the United Nations was in accord with the democratic principle expounded in
the Preamble of the Charter: "We the peoples of the United Nations . . . have
resolved to combine our efforts . . . and do hereby establish an international organization to be known as the United Nations."

On August 8, 1945, President Truman ratified the Charter of the United
Nations and the Statute of the International Court of Justice, which was annexed to it. The United Nations came into being on October 24, 1945, which
has since been established as United Nations Day. At that time, the Soviet Union
deposited its ratification, and Secretary of State James F. Byrnes, acting for the
United States, signed the Protocol of Deposit of Ratifications, affirming that a
majority of the fifty-one original signers (twenty-nine nations), including all five
great powers, had deposited ratifications with the United States. All fifty-one
signers of the Charter had ratified the Charter by December 27, 1945. On January 10, 1946, with the opening of the First General Assembly, the United Nations began its work.

# NOTE

1. *New York Times Magazine,* September 15, 1957, p. 21.

# SELECTED READINGS

Acheson, Dean. *Present at the Creation: My Years in the State Department.* New York: Norton, 1969.

Armstrong, James D. *From Versailles to Maastricht: International Organization in the Twentieth Century.* New York: St. Martin's Press, 1996.

Ball, George W. *The Discipline of Power: Essentials of a Modern World Structure.* Boston: Little, Brown and Company, 1968.

Bennett, A. Leroy. *Historical Dictionary of the United Nations.* Lanham, MD: Scarecrow Press, 1995.

Boulding, Elise. *Building a Global Civic Culture: Education for an Interdependent World.* New York: Teachers College Press, 1988.

Bretton, Henry L. *International Relations in the Nuclear Age.* Albany: State University of New York Press, 1986.

Burton, M. E. *The Assembly of the League of Nations.* Chicago: University of Chicago Press, 1943.

Churchill, Winston. *The Gathering Storm.* Boston: Houghton Mifflin, 1948.

Claude, Inis L., Jr. *Swords into Plowshares: The Problems and Progress of International Organization.* 2nd rev. ed. New York: Random House, 1962.

Diehl, Paul F., ed. *The Politics of International Organizations.* Chicago: Dorsey Press, 1989.

Eagleton, Clyde. *International Government.* New York: Ronald Press, 1948.

Goodrich, L. M. "From League of Nations to United Nations." *International Organization* (February 1947): pp. 3–21.

Gorbachev, Mikhail. *Perestroika—New Thinking for Our Country and the World.* New York: Harper & Row, 1987.

Hilderbrand, Robert C. *Dumbarton Oaks: The Origins of the United Nations and the Search for Postwar Security.* Chapel Hill: University of North Carolina Press, 1990.

Hoopes, Townsend, and Douglas Brinkley. *FDR and the Creation of the UN.* New Haven, CT: Yale University Press, 1997.

Hull, Cordell. *The Memoirs of Cordell Hull.* 2 vols. New York: Macmillan, 1948.

Iriye, Akira. *Cultural Internationalism and World Order.* Baltimore: Johns Hopkins University Press, 1997.

Kegley, Charles W., Jr., and Eugene R. Wittkopf. *World Politics: Trend and Transformation.* New York: St. Martin's Press, 1985.

Kennan, George F. *Memoirs, 1925–1950.* Boston: Little, Brown and Company, 1967.

Mangone, Gerard J. *A Short History of International Organization.* New York: McGraw-Hill, 1954.

Perlmutter, Amos. *Making the World Safe for Democracy: A Century of Wilsonianism and Its Totalitarian Challengers.* Chapel Hill: University of North Carolina Press, 1997.

Potter, Pitman B. *An Introduction to the Study of International Organization.* New York: Appleton-Century-Crofts, 1948.

Reinsch, Paul S. *Public International Unions.* Boston: Ginn, 1911.

*Report to the President on the Results of the San Francisco Conference.* Department of State Publication 2349, Conference Series 71. Washington, DC: U.S. Government Printing Office, 1945.

Reuter, Paul. *International Institutions.* New York: Rinehart, 1958.

Russell, Ruth B., and Jeanette E. Muther. *A History of the United Nations Charter: The Role of the United States, 1940–45.* Washington, DC: Brookings Institution, 1958.

Smith, S. S. *The Manchurian Crisis: A Tragedy in International Relations.* New York: Columbia University Press, 1948.

Walters, F. P. *A History of the League of Nations.* London: Oxford University Press, 1952.

Zolo, Danilo. *Cosmopolis: Prospects for World Government.* Cambridge: Polity Press, 1997.

## 2

# LEGAL FRAMEWORK, INSTITUTIONAL STRUCTURES, AND FINANCIAL REALITIES

## THE CONSTITUTIONAL STRUCTURE

Written as a multilateral treaty and ratified by the drafting member states, the UN Charter became the de facto constitution for the establishment of the UN organization. Like most constitution makers, the framers had sought to create a document that would facilitate the development of an administrative substructure, allocate responsibilities, grant and circumscribe powers, and demarcate jurisdictions—in short, do the jobs that are typical of a national constitution. Also common to every constitution is the enunciation, usually in hortatory language, of the principles and objectives underlying the organization, and the framers of the UN Charter answered that test as well. The real test of any constitution, however, comes in the transition from principle to practice. Meeting this test is an ongoing process. Words constantly take on new meanings as different people interpret them and as changing situations and fresh problems call for solutions not in keeping with older interpretations. This is the process of constitution building; it exists because constitution makers can never fully anticipate the changes that will occur. Although the Charter is a lengthy and verbose document, its framers created a document that was flexible and adaptable to changing conditions and changing times, and the almost sixty-year history of the United Nations indicates that they achieved their overall goals.

### CONSTITUTIONAL EVOLUTION

Constitutional development for an international organization like the United Nations may closely parallel that of a national constitutional system. A comparison can be a useful enterprise if the analogy is not carried too far. Over the years the U.S. Constitution, for example, has developed largely through the process of executive, legislative, and judicial interpretation. Similarly, the Charter of the United Nations has evolved through interpretation by its members and by its major organs, particularly the General Assembly, the Security Council, the Secretariat, and the International Court of Justice. Custom and usage, where mandates are lacking or ambiguous, have been important forces in shaping both national constitutional systems and the UN system. In both instances, when the constitutional text has been too limiting, ways have been found to bypass or ignore the strict letter of the law. Formal amendments have been adopted only infrequently in U.S. constitutional history and for the United Nations as well; there have been only three formal UN Charter amendments in nearly a half century. Two amendments to the Charter were proposed by the Eighteenth General Assembly in 1963, one enlarging the Security Council from eleven to fifteen, while changing its voting majority from seven to nine. The other increased the size of the Economic and Social Council from eighteen to twenty-seven. Both amendments were accepted by the member states through their individual legal processes. They took effect in 1965. A third amendment, which took effect in 1973, enlarged the Economic and Social Council to fifty-four members. For a proposed amendment to take effect it must be approved by a two-thirds vote of the General Assembly and ratified by two-thirds of the member states, including all permanent members of the Security Council (China, the United Kingdom, France, Russia, and the United States). Each permanent member thus retains the power of veto over all *formal* changes to the Charter, with the exception of changes that are a consequence of interpretation.

Constitutional development in the United Nations is largely a political process. As a multilateral treaty, the Charter was a product of extensive international negotiations, with the precise meaning and application of many words and phrases in the Charter masked by the need for agreement at the time of negotiations. Since 1945, problems in translations, the vagaries of power politics, rival national interests, the admission of new members, ideological differences, the role of nongovernmental organizations, the uses of violence by non-states, and the lack of a higher judge have all contributed to the continuing problems of interpretation and development.

Like the U.S. Constitution, the Charter does not provide for a constitutional umpire. Who, then, shall decide what the Charter means when questions of jurisdiction, powers, competence, and procedures arise? Should the International Court of Justice as the principal judicial organ appoint itself "guardian of the UN constitutional system" and undertake a role similar to that assumed by the U.S. Supreme Court in the historic case of *Marbury* v. *Madison*? Should the final arbiter be the General Assembly, where all members are represented? The Charter bestows on the General Assembly the power to "discuss any questions or any matters within the scope of the present Charter or relating to the powers and functions of any organs provided for in the present Charter." Should each major organ determine the nature and extent of its own jurisdiction and procedures? Should unanimity prevail, as it did traditionally with multilateral treaties, with constitutional issues resolved through agreement of all signatory governments? Or should each member interpret the Charter for itself?

The question of establishing a constitutional umpire was never resolved at San Francisco, nor was it considered directly. The result has been that all of the preceding methods, and many others, have been used to deal with constitutional issues in the UN system. Decisions on constitutional questions have included interpretations made by presiding officers. Different organs of the United Nations have ruled by majority and extramajority votes. Decisions of the Secretary-

General and other members of the Secretariat, as well as advisory opinions of the Court, have in some instances defined the limits of the organization. Decisions of member governments, made outside the UN framework but based on interpretations of Charter provisions, also have framed the use of the Charter in circumstances not otherwise stated in the document. Thus, most interpretations of the Charter leading to development of the UN system have been made *politically* by political organs or individuals, more in the name of diplomacy than in the context of law.

## CHARTER PRINCIPLES

The analogy between national constitutions and the constitutional system of the United Nations can also be extended to the realm of principles. Underlying the U.S. governmental system, for example, are basic principles that provide the philosophical underpinning and moral strength for its constitutional structure. Most of these principles are also found, explicitly or implicitly, in the UN system, supplemented by others that are more germane to an international body. Those that can be observed or implied from the operations of the United Nations include democracy, self-determination, parliamentary preeminence, majority governance, the rule of law and justice, horizontal federalism (regionalism), and the separation of powers. In addition, principles described in Article 2 of the UN Charter are accepted by states upon their ratification of the Charter. These principles include the following: (1) the sovereign equality of all members of the United Nations; (2) the good-faith acceptance of Charter obligations; (3) the peaceful settlement of international disputes; (4) the non-use of force, or the threat of force, for aggressive purposes; (5) the support for UN enforcement action; and (6) the nonintervention by the United Nations in matters that are essentially within a state's domestic jurisdiction. Together these principles constitute basic rules of international conduct that all member states are ostensibly committed to observe. These rules are a projection into the international arena of purposes and principles already having national validity. In this sense the Charter moves in the direction of an organized international community independent of the organs set up for international decision making. Even in the most democratic of states, these ideals are never perfectly realized, and certainly a great gulf exists between theory and practice in the United Nations. Nevertheless, the Charter principles can provide guidelines for action, and they are frequently invoked in General Assembly debates. Although these and other principles will be discussed throughout this book as they relate to the operations of the United Nations, two of them—domestic jurisdiction and regionalism—will be examined now in their constitutional context.

### Domestic Jurisdiction

In federal states such as Canada, Mexico, Germany, and the United States, a written constitution provides for a division of powers between a central government and the governments of provincial or "state" subdivisions. In a somewhat related manner, Article 2 of the UN Charter recognizes a dual authority when it proclaims that nothing in the Charter should be interpreted to "authorize the United Nations to intervene in matters that are essentially within the domestic jurisdiction of any state." The application of enforcement measures to maintain peace and security under Chapter VII is deliberately excluded from the limiting clause. The domestic jurisdiction clause resembles the Tenth Amendment of the U.S. Constitution in that it makes explicit a division of powers and responsibilities between two levels of political organization and provides a limitation on the higher level to safeguard the lower from unwarranted intrusions. In effect, this Charter principle suggests that only *international* problems and issues are proper subjects for UN inquiry and action and that *national* questions remain within the complete jurisdiction of member states (unless, of course, the state consents to UN involvement). The Charter leaves open to controversy, however, the questions of who shall determine what is national and what is international, how that determination should be made, and what is meant by "intervene."

Controversy within the organization has also centered on the nature and intent of the domestic jurisdiction clause, with differences over whether it provides a *legal* limitation or merely proclaims a *political* principle. In practice, the latter has generally been accepted, with decisions made by UN organs in keeping with the political realities of the situation. Problems within the Republic of South Africa, for example, were debated extensively. UN resolutions condemning South African apartheid policies (the strict and deliberate separation of the races) were adopted by the General Assembly over the repeated invocations by South Africa that its domestic jurisdiction was being violated. Most UN members took the position that South African apartheid practices constituted a threat to international peace and security and were therefore subject to UN jurisdiction. Persistence in the condemnation of apartheid practices by the United Nations eventually paid off when the practice was abandoned in 1991, and in 1994, Nelson Mandela, a black African leader, was elected South African president. Some states—France and Portugal, for example—invoked the domestic jurisdiction clause for many years in refusing to submit reports to the United Nations on conditions in their colonies, holding that their overseas possessions were part of their "metropolitan territory" and therefore matters of purely local concern. These problems were eliminated when the colonies gained their independence. Serbia too claimed violation of its domestic jurisdiction in the 1990s, notably over the issue of Kosovo. Belgrade complained bitterly about the violation of its sovereignty and domestic jurisdiction over the territory, but none of these complaints registered with NATO that had intruded itself in Kosovo or the United Nations that was made responsible for humanitarian programs there.

Over the years, domestic jurisdiction has become increasingly ineffective as a deterrent to UN action. UN majorities have grown more and more inclined to express UN competence so broadly that virtually nothing is left to domestic jurisdiction. The arms inspection requirements, no-fly zones, and sanctions imposed on Iraq after the 1991 Persian Gulf War and again in 1994 and 1997–98 constituted a particularly intrusive invasion of Iraqi jurisdiction. Iraqi efforts to force an end to the UN-directed inspections caused the UN Secretary-General to personally seek reassurance from Iraq's head of state that his country's full compliance with UN resolutions governing inspections would be honored. Seeking to prevent a U.S. air attack in 1998, Baghdad accepted the terms offered by the Secretary-General. Nonetheless, by October, and after repeated violations of UN resolutions, and especially interference with the work of the UN Special Commission (UNSCOM) inspectors, what to do with Iraq burdened Security Council deliberations. Although military action was initially forestalled, in December 1998 the United States and Great Britain, acting alone, but assuring other members that they were complying with previous UN resolutions, launched raids against Iraqi military targets. The contest engaging Iraq and the United Nations entered still another phase in 1999, and no end to the crisis was forecast as long as Saddam Hussein remained at the head of the Baghdad government. With UN sanctions still in place, the United States, with cooperation from Great Britain, got the Security Council to approve still another resolution against Iraq in 2002. The Iraqi government was called upon still another time to disclose its weapons of mass destruction, and a team of UN inspectors, known as UNMOVIC (the UN Monitoring, Verification, and Inspection Commission), again was sent to the country. The United States, however, had grown impatient with Iraqi authorities, and despite assurances from UNMOVIC that no weapons of mass destruction could be identified and that the inspectors required more time to pursue their mission, Washington insisted on direct action. Although the Security Council was divided on the matter of still another resolution authorizing the use of force, the United States, with assistance from Great Britain but in opposition to the other permanent powers of Russia, China, and France, invaded Iraq. In the early spring of 2003, the U.S.-led force unleashed a violent assault on the Iraqi regime and in rapid order brought the rule of Saddam Hussein to an abrupt end. Avoiding discourse on the matter of domestic jurisdiction, the United States announced it had assumed the role of an occupation force, and Washington indicated a minor, ancillary role for the United Nations in the reconstruction and rehabilitation of Iraq.

UN involvement in internal conflict with the consent of the parties, as in Cambodia and El Salvador, has further blurred the line between domestic and international concerns. Demands for UN intervention to protect human rights, as in Croatia and Bosnia, in the Serbian province of Kosovo, or in East Timor, would also subordinate sovereignty to broader values of world order. UN resolutions, however, are generally ineffective when addressed to matters believed by nonconsenting states, notably among the greater powers, to be within their domestic jurisdiction except in cases where the organization is willing and able to enforce its mandates. Whether or not observed by UN majorities, the domestic jurisdiction clause, certainly in theory and precept, mirrors a world of sovereign states not yet ready to yield power to the United Nations over their internal affairs.

*Regionalism*

Interstate cooperation, a halfway house in the U.S. constitutional system between the central government and the state units, has its international counterpart in the form of regionalism. The U.S. Constitution refers to this middle-level organization as "interstate relations"; in its politically activist form it is known as "horizontal federalism," connoting an extensive system of teamwork among states to solve common problems through uniform laws, joint actions, and common agencies.

International regionalism is recognition by participating governments that not all problems are either national or global in scope. Some international problems may be limited to a geographic region; their solutions may require action by only a limited number of states, or psychological, technical, or administrative problems may limit the ability of international agencies to function beyond the region. International regionalism exists, therefore, because groups of states have found it to be the most appropriate means of solving some common problems.

The framers of the UN Charter, although theoretically committed to a universal system, recognized the political investment in regional organizations and accepted the feasibility of decentralizing some international operations concerned with security, political action, and economic and social welfare. The framers compromised on the issue by providing that regional organizations would serve as adjuncts of the UN system subject to a measure of control and direction by it. All such arrangements and activities must also be consistent with the purposes and principles of the Charter, although no apparent means exist for enforcing this rule. Under these provisions a host of regional political, security, economic, social, and technical organizations have been established over the past sixty years in all areas of the globe.

Collective self-defense, expressly authorized by Article 51 of the Charter, has served from time to time as a basis for the construction of numerous regional alliances. The Charter further provides that regional organizations should contribute to security by making "every effort to achieve pacific settlement of local disputes . . . before referring them to the Security Council" (Article 52). The framers assumed that some disputes might be better resolved without inviting the whole world in, and this in turn would reduce the load on the United Nations. In practice, both assumptions have to some extent been borne out, although a number of disputes have been referred to the United Nations as well as a regional organization. Moreover, with the volume of UN work at unprecedented levels at the end of the Cold War, and with the funds and capabilities needed to address world issues inadequate to meet the many challenges, in 1998 the UN Secretary-General called for greater acceptance of a "co-deployment principle." Co-deployment meant that regional organizations capable of addressing an area problem would be encouraged to play a primary role in establishing and enforcing order. Thus, regional organizations, or regional alliances (for example, the Commonwealth of Independent States [CIS], Organization for African Unity [OAU], Economic Community of West African States [ECOWAS], and NATO), have assumed enforcement responsibilities generally found under Chapter VII of the Charter, while UN peacekeeping has become more an activity of Chapter VI or peaceful resolution of disputes. Although no clear criteria have emerged, either in theory or in practice, there are indications that a formula may yet be arrived at that would determine which level is most appropriate in dealing with threats or breaches of the peace. Co-deployment, however, in no way alters the Charter's stated purpose that the Security Council could decide to consider a dispute already handled in a regional forum.

Still another role for regional organizations involves political, economic, and social cooperation. In this regard, the concept of regionalism has sometimes been applied to limited-membership organizations such as the Organization for Economic Cooperation and Development (OECD). Although OECD is primarily Europe based, it nevertheless includes members from other geographic regions. Thus Japan, the United States, and Canada are members of the organization. Collaboration rather than competition has characterized the relationship between the United Nations and such groups as the OECD, the Organization of American States (OAS), the Association of Southeast Asian Nations (ASEAN), and the European Union (EU). Economic regionalism, in particular, has expanded as states have tried to solve their problems associated with trade, balance of payments, economic development, and technical assistance through arrangements with neighboring or interdependent states.

Regionalism is offered as either an alternative or a complement to the quest for universal organization. Debates involving the respective advantages of regionalism over universal systems have usually focused on the following points.

## ARGUMENTS FOR REGIONALISM

1. Regionalism permits a sharper focus on local problems.
2. Regionalism involves fewer actors and offers greater propensities for consensus because of common traditions; similar political, economic, and social systems; and the regional nature of the problem to be solved.
3. Regionalism tends to produce greater support from the peoples of the participating states because of a closer identity on common interests.
4. Regionalism permits a more appropriate handling of administrative, technical, and functional problems because the organization's machinery is better matched with the nature and scope of its operations.
5. Regionalism is a necessary precursor to effective global cooperation because it lays the groundwork for a broader consensus.

## ARGUMENTS FOR UNIVERSALISM

1. A universal system is a more appropriate means for preserving peace than regionalism because peace is indivisible; a war anywhere in the world threatens to engulf all.

2. The universal system encourages the more effective pooling of resources for attacking economic and social problems; a pooling of African regional resources, for example, would result only in a sharing of African poverty.
3. The universal approach encourages a consensus of humankind based on global principles.
4. Universal approaches to problems such as disease, hunger, illiteracy, and poverty acknowledge their commonality in all areas of the world and that joint action in dealing with them is the most effective use of available resources.
5. The universal idea as embodied in the United Nations already exercises broader powers over a greater variety of subjects. Its deepening experience in the long term promises advantages that can only be imagined in a world of many different nation-states.

Although the arguments on both sides have intrinsic merit, such debates tend to be detached from reality because the operational dichotomy between regionalism and universalism is largely a false one. Both types of international organization exist today; both serve useful purposes, and their functions are usually—if not always—complementary. For example, in electing members of the various organs of the United Nations, including the Secretary-General, regional factors are generally considered relevant in reaching electoral decisions. Regionalism is perhaps best understood for the advances achieved in transcending national frontiers and in gaining greater cooperation between and among sovereign entities. In a way regionalism can be seen as both a way station and a learning experience as the different components of the state system begin to see real value in an ever-expanding community of integrated states.

# INSTRUMENTS OF POLITICAL DECISION MAKING

UN operations revolve around the functions of six principal organs: the General Assembly, the Security Council, the Economic and Social Council, the Trusteeship Council, the Secretariat, and the International Court of Justice. The organization and processes of each of these major organs will be discussed in this chapter.

In addition to the six principal organs, eighteen specialized agencies and other autonomous organizations within the overall framework of the United Nations operate in technical, economic, and social areas (see Figure 2-1). Added to the specialized agencies and related bodies are a number of major programs and organizations that have been created by the United Nations to deal with particular problem areas. These UN bodies have their own directors and governing boards but are not legally autonomous because they are subject to the direction of the General Assembly. The major ones are listed in Figure 2-1. Of these programs and organizations, the UN Relief and Works Agency for Palestine refugees in the Near East reports directly to the General Assembly, whereas the rest report to the General Assembly through the Economic and Social Council. Peacekeeping missions, which are created and disbanded as necessary, report to the Security Council. Finally, the UN system includes regional commissions, functional commissions, and a variety of committees that report to the Economic and Social Council and, indirectly, to the General Assembly.

The vast array of agencies and programs subject to supervision by the major organs of the United Nations, or at least reporting to them, addresses the global nature of the UN *system,* as distinct from the political decision-making apparatus headquarters in New York. The latter is merely the tip of a huge organizational and bureaucratic iceberg with its operations carried on in one way or another in almost every country in the world. Isolated, indeed, is the country or society that has not been touched by one of the many UN programs. Hundreds of millions of the earth's inhabitants have received assistance from UN programs, and all human beings stand to gain from UN activities directed toward such objectives as mediating conflict, controlling pollution, and improving health. The actions and programs and the problems and issues that are the concern of UN and UN-related agencies will be covered in later chapters.

## THE GENERAL ASSEMBLY

Central to the sprawling UN organization, resembling somewhat the British prototype Parliament at Westminster in its unifying role, the General Assembly functions as the main focus for most UN activities. "Global Parliament," "Town Meeting of the World," "Sun of the UN Solar System"—these and other catchphrases are used to sum up, perhaps somewhat inaccurately, the General Assembly's widely diffused activities and diverse roles. Unlike the Security Council, which pays homage to the elitism of great power politics, the Assembly effuses the democratic ethos of *egalitarianism, parliamentary* or *representative government,* and *majority decision making.*

### Equality of Members

The Assembly's *egalitarian* nature should be obvious to even the casual UN visitor: The Assembly is the only one of the six principal UN organs in which all member states are equally represented, with a maximum of ten delegates and one vote for each member (see Table 2-1). Efforts by some of the great powers to push for a change, that is, to a voting system that represents their larger stake, and hence weighted votes, have never been taken seriously by the small and middle powers. The traditional equality of all states, large and small, under international law and as participants in international conferences provides the legitimacy for retaining equal voting. The political defensiveness of the new states, some of which formed their Assembly delegations at the same time that they established their initial governments, safeguards the principle. This equality permeates the work of the Assembly, including that carried on by its seven main committees, on each of which all members are represented. The seven main committees of the Assembly are the First (Political and Security); Special

| INTERNATIONAL COURT OF JUSTICE | SECURITY COUNCIL | GENERAL ASSEMBLY |
|---|---|---|

Military Staff Committee
Standing Committee and ad hoc bodies
International Criminal Tribunal for the Former Yugoslavia
International Criminal Tribunal for Rwanda
UN Monitoring Verification and Inspection Commission
  (Iraq)
Peacekeeping Operations and Missions

Main committees
Other sessional committees
Standing committee
and ad hoc bodies
Other subsidiary organs

## PROGRAMMES AND FUNDS

**UNCTAD**
United Nations Conference
on Trade and Development

  **ITC**
  International Trade Centre
  (UNCTAD, WTO)

**UNDCP**
United Nations Drug
Control Programme

**UNEP**
United Nations
Environment Programme

**UNDP**
United Nations
Development Programme

  **UNIFEM**
  United Nations Development
  Fund for Women

  **UNV**
  United Nations Volunteers

**UNFPA**
United Nations
Population Fund

**UNHCR**
Office of the United Nations
High Commissioner for Refugees

**UNICEF**
United Nations Children's Fund

**WFP**
World Food Programme

**UNRWA\*\***
United Nations Relief and
Works Agency for Palestine
Refugees in the Near East

## OTHER UN ENTITIES

**OHCHR**
Office of the United
Nations High
Commissioner for
Human Rights

**UNCHS**
United Nations Centre
for Human Settlements
(Habitat)

**UNOPS**
United Nations Office
for Project Services

**UNU**
United Nations
University

## RESEARCH AND TRAINING INSTITUTE

**INSTRAW**
International Research and
Training Institute for the
Advancement of Women

**UNICRI**
United Nations Interregional Crime
and Justice Research Institute

**UNITAR**
United Nations Institute for
Training and Research

**UNIRISD**
United Nations Research Institute
for Social Development

**UNIDIR\*\***
United Nations Institute for
Disarmament Research

SOURCE: UN Department of Public Information (February 2003), DPI 2299.

\* Autonomous organizations working with the United Nations and each other through the coordinating machinery of the Economic and Social Council.

\*\* Reports only to the General Assembly.

| ECONOMIC AND SOCIAL COUNCIL | TRUSTEESHIP COUNCIL | SECRETARIAT |
|---|---|---|

## FUNCTIONAL COMMISSIONS

Commission for Social Development
Commission on Human Rights
Commission on Narcotics Drugs
Commission on Crime Prevention and Criminal Justice
Commission on Science and Technology for Development
Commission on Sustainable Development
Commission on the Status of Women
Commission on Population and Development
Statistical Commission

## REGIONAL COMMISSIONS

Economic Commission for Africa
Economic Commission for Europe
Economic Commission for Latin America and the Caribbean
Economic and Social Commission for Asia and the Pacific
Economic and Social Commission for Western Asia

---

Sessional and Standing Committee
Expert ad hoc and related bodies

## RELATED ORGANIZATIONS

**IAEA**
International Atomic Energy Agency

**WTO**
World Trade Organization

## SPECIALIZED AGENCIES*

**ILO**
International Labour Organization

**FAO**
Food and Agriculture Organization of the United Nations

**UNESCO**
United Nations Educational, Scientific and Cultural Organization

**WHO**
World Health Organization

**WORLD BANK GROUP**

**IBRD**
International Bank for Reconstruction and Development

**IDA**
International Development Association

**IFC**
International Finance Corporation

**MIGA**
Multilateral Investment Guarantee Agency

**ICSID**
International Centre for the Settlement of Investment Disputes

**IMF**
International Monetary Fund

**ICAO**
International Civil Aviation Organization

**IMO**
International Maritime Organization

**ITU**
International Telecommunication Union

**UPU**
Universal Postal Union

**WMO**
World Metereological Organization

**WIPO**
World Intellectual Property Organization

**IFAD**
International Fund for Agricultural Development

**UNIDO**
United Nations Industrial Development Organization

**OSG**
Office of the Secretary General

**OIOS**
Office of Internal Oversight Services

**OLA**
Office of Legal Affairs

**DPA**
Department of Political Affairs

**DDA**
Department for Disarmament Affairs

**DPKO**
Department of Peacekeeping Operations

**OCHA**
Office for the Coordination of Humanitarian Affairs

**DESA**
Department of Economic and Social Affairs

**DGAACS**
Department of General Assembly Affairs and Conference Services

**DPI**
Department of Public Information

**DM**
Department of Management

**OPI**
Office of the Iraq Programme

**UNSECOORD**
Office of the United Nations Security Coordinations

**ODCCP**
Office for Drug Control and Crime Preservation

**UNOG**
United Nations Office at Geneva

**UNOV**
United Nations Office at Vienna

**UNON**
United Nations Office at Nairobi

Political (originally an ad hoc committee, this committee has remained numberless although it is now a permanent committee); Second (Economic and Financial); Third (Social, Humanitarian, and Cultural); Fourth (Trusteeship; the work of the Trusteeship Committee was suspended with the independence of the last Trust territory in the 1990s); Fifth (Administrative and Budgetary); and Sixth (Legal). Consideration of agenda items usually begins in one of the main committees, which meet and carry on business as committees of the whole. Most matters receive their most thorough airing and consideration at this stage, since the press of time permits the Assembly in plenary session to explore extensively only the most politically explosive issues. Increasingly, as in legislative bodies like the U.S. Congress, a committee's report has been accepted in plenary session with only perfunctory debate. This trend has had the effect of creating eight assemblies with a full complement of members in each, a development that has helped keep the business of the Assembly moving forward but also has added to the general confusion of Assembly decision making. The General Assembly also utilizes various procedural committees and subsidiary bodies in carrying out its decision-making functions (see Table 2-1).

*Parliamentary Role*

The parliamentary nature of the UN General Assembly becomes evident in observing its modus operandi. It may be, as an astute British observer has noted, that the Assembly's operations are "a far cry from anything at Westminster." The British system's focus on a legislative program, its emphasis on responsibility and party discipline, and its organized majority and opposition are missing or hardly discernible in the UN General Assembly. Yet the agenda is adopted, debate proceeds, votes are taken, and decisions are made. Our British observer described the process in this picturesque language: "Like a herd of grazing cattle, that moves as it chews, head down, the Assembly gets through its day (or more often its morning) without any particular drive, yet not without a certain vaguely diffused sense of purpose." [1]

In a search for analogies, the Assembly's parliamentary qualities may be found to resemble the continental European parliaments, with their multiparty coalitions, ideological rivalries, and shifting centers of power, more closely than the orderly, compact British model. Or a watchful observer might note some similarities between the Assembly's operations and those of the U.S. Congress. Both are, more often than not, caught up in clashes of parochial interests and must attempt to harmonize regional, class, credal, and racial differences. Both must grapple with procedural rules that often complicate rather than expedite the process of decision making. The U.S. federal system produces an attachment to states' rights in somewhat the same manner that the sovereign states of the world with their attachments to national interests produce a loose, untidy, somewhat anarchic General Assembly. Yet a parliament's main role is concerned with freedom of debate, in which issues can be discussed, decisions made, budgets approved, taxes determined, and administrative operations supervised.

TABLE 2-1    **Membership of Principal UN Organs in 2003**

GENERAL ASSEMBLY

All UN Members

SECURITY COUNCIL

Permanent members: China, France, Russian Federation, United Kingdom, United States

Nonpermanent members (two-year term expires 31 December of the year indicated):

| | | |
|---|---|---|
| Angola (2004) | Chile (2004) | Philippines (2005) |
| Algeria (2005) | Germany (2004) | Romania (2005) |
| Benin (2005) | Pakistan (2004) | Spain (2004) |
| Brazil (2005) | | |

ECONOMIC AND SOCIAL COUNCIL

Fifty-four members (three-year term expires 31 December of the year indicated):

*African states:*

| | | |
|---|---|---|
| Benin (2005) | Libyan Arab | Senegal (2005) |
| Burundi (2004) | Jamahiriya (2004) | Tunisia (2006) |
| Congo (2005) | Mozambique (2005) | Tanzania (2006) |
| Ghana (2004) | Namibia (2006) | Zimbabwe (2004) |
| Kenya (2005) | Nigeria (2006) | |

*Asian states:*

| | | |
|---|---|---|
| Bangladesh (2006) | Indonesia (2006) | Qatar (2004) |
| Bhutan (2004) | Japan (2005) | Republic of Korea (2006) |
| China (2004) | Malaysia (2005) | Saudi Arabia (2005) |
| India (2004) | Mauritius (2006) | United Arab Emirates (2006) |

*Eastern European states:*

| | | |
|---|---|---|
| Armenia (2006) | Hungary (2004) | Russian Federation (2004) |
| Azerbaijan (2005) | Poland (2006) | Ukraine (2004) |

*Latin American and Caribbean states:*

| | | |
|---|---|---|
| Belize (2006) | Ecuador (2005) | Jamaica (2005) |
| Chile (2004) | El Salvador (2004) | Nicaragua (2005) |
| Colombia (2006) | Guatemala (2004) | Panama (2006) |
| Cuba (2005) | | |

*Western European and other states:*

| | | |
|---|---|---|
| Australia (2004) | Germany (2005) | Sweden (2004) |
| Belgium (2006) | Greece (2005) | Turkey (2005) |
| Canada (2006) | Ireland (2005) | United Kingdom (2004) |
| Finland (2004) | Italy (2006) | United States (2006) |
| France (2005) | | |

TRUSTEESHIP COUNCIL

The Trusteeship Council suspended operation on November 1, 1994, with the independence of Palau, the last remaining United Nations Trust Territory, on October 1, 1994. By resolution adopted on May 25, 1994, the Council amended its rules of procedure to drop the obligation to meet annually and agreed to meet as occasion required—by its decision or the decision of its president, or at the request of a majority of its members or the General Assembly or the Security Council.

*(continued)*

TABLE 2-1   *(continued)*

---

INTERNATIONAL COURT OF JUSTICE

---

Fifteen judges, elected individually (nine-year term ends 5 February of the year indicated):

Awn Shawkat Al-Khasawneh of Jordan (2009)

Thomas Buergenthal of the United States (2006)

Nabi Elaraby of Egypt (2006)

Gilbert Guillaume of France (2009)

Rosalyn Higgins of the United Kingdom (2009)

Shi Jiuyong of China (2012)

Pieter H. Kooijmans of the Netherlands (2006)

Abdul G. Koroma of Sierra Leone (2012)

Hisashi Owada of Japan (2012)

Gonzalo Parra-Aranguren of Venezuela (2009)

Raymond Ranjeva of Madagascar (2009)

Jose Francisco Rezek of Brazil (2006)

Bruno Simma of Germany (2012)

Peter Tomka of Slovakia (2012)

Vladlen S. Vereshchetin of the Russian Federation (2006)

---

SOURCE: Adapted from United Nations Department of Public Information, 2003.

---

The General Assembly resembles all national parliaments in these functions. Although it does not possess a direct lawmaking authority, its competence to discuss and debate extends to *any* problem of the world or of the organization itself that a majority of members regard as proper for Assembly consideration. The only exceptions to this broad power are the domestic jurisdiction clause (Article 2) and the limitation on the Assembly concerning matters under consideration by the Security Council (Article 12).

## Majority Rule

The Assembly's *majority* approach to decision making is an improvement over that of the Assembly of the League of Nations, which required unanimity for most actions. Article 18 of the UN Charter provides that decisions on "important questions" be made by a two-thirds majority of members present and voting. All other questions require only a simple majority. "Important questions" include those mentioned in Article 18 (peace and security recommendations; elections to the three UN councils; admission, suspension, and expulsion of members; trusteeship and budgetary questions; and those questions that the Assembly decides by a majority vote are to be considered "important").

Consensus, not overpowering majority votes, is the objective of Assembly politics. Consensus demands compromise, and compromises in the Assembly are sought through negotiations, pressures, demands, debates, promises, and other techniques of parliamentary diplomacy that, in art and form, closely resemble the "politics" that keeps the wheels turning in a national legislative body. Groups of delegates meet, plan strategy, and negotiate with other groups before decisions are made. On economic and related issues, when the issue comes to a vote, decision making is dominated by the Group of 77 (G-77), which consists of more than 130 Third World countries that caucus to determine a common approach to issues that arise before the General Assembly. In recent years, however, the Assembly has decided more issues by consensus than by voting.

## Formal Organization

Regular sessions of the General Assembly are held each year, beginning usually on the third Tuesday in September. At the beginning of each session, the Assembly establishes a target date for adjournment, usually mid-December. A three-week period of "general debate" opens each Assembly session, with most delegations taking the opportunity to express their views on the full range of issues on the global agenda. Heads of state or government often participate. A Special Session may be convoked after the Assembly adjourns its regular annual session and can be requested by a member state, the Security Council, or the General Assembly. A majority of the Special Sessions have been convened by the General Assembly. They require majority support from the member states. When the need for Assembly action beyond the regular December adjournment date is anticipated in advance, the Assembly will recess its session and reconvene as later needed. Table 2-2 describes the Special Sessions convened from 1947 to 2003.

In addition to General Assembly Special Sessions, the General Assembly can also meet in Emergency Special Sessions. Dealing with more contentious issues of critical importance, Emergency Sessions are convoked under the 1950 Uniting for Peace Resolution. Such sessions can be convened within twenty-four hours. Between 1956 and 2003 ten Emergency Sessions were held. Table 2-3 lists the General Assembly Emergency Special Sessions.

The initial task facing a new Assembly each year is to elect a President and seventeen Vice Presidents who serve for one year. It has become traditional to select as President a leading international diplomat from an important small- or middle-power state, usually from the Third World. The vice presidencies are allocated to the five great powers and to geographic areas of the world to ensure their representative character and a fair apportionment of prestige. In 1963 the number of Vice Presidents was increased from thirteen to seventeen. A formula was adopted to provide for the election of seven Vice Presidents from Asia and Africa, one from Eastern Europe, three from Latin America, two from Western Europe and "other states" (Canada, Australia, and New Zealand), and one from each of the five permanent members of the Security Council. The total of eighteen is because the region from which the President is elected receives one less than the formula indicates. The President, the Vice Presidents, and the chairs of the seven standing committees constitute the General Committee, which functions as a steering committee for each session (see Table 2-4).

Although his formal powers are limited, the President may accomplish much through personal persuasive capacities and political adeptness. As the Assembly's presiding authority, the President must possess a special temperament, including, it has been said, the capacity to show interest when otherwise bored. He or she must possess "a memory for faces, a capacity to slough off private and national partialities, a sense of humor coupled with a concern for the dignity of his office, a ready grasp of procedural technicalities, a proper sense of

TABLE 2-2    General Assembly Special Sessions

| SPECIAL SESSION | DATE OF SESSION | REQUESTED OR CONVENED BY |
|---|---|---|
| 1  Palestine | 28 April–15 May 1947 | Great Britain |
| 2  Palestine | 16 April–14 May 1948 | Security Council |
| 3  Tunisia | 21–25 August 1961 | 38 member states |
| 4  UN Finances | 14 May–27 June 1963 | General Assembly |
| 5  South West Africa (Namibia) | 21 April–13 June 1967 | General Assembly |
| 6  Raw Materials and Development | 9 April–2 May 1974 | Algeria |
| 7  Development and International Economic Cooperation | 1–16 September 1975 | General Assembly |
| 8  Financing the UN Interim Force in Lebanon | 20–21 April 1978 | General Assembly |
| 9  Namibia | 24 April–3 May 1978 | General Assembly |
| 10 Disarmament | 23 May–1 July 1978 | General Assembly |
| 11 New International Economic Order | 25 August–15 September 1980 | General Assembly |
| 12 Disarmament | 7 June–10 July 1982 | General Assembly |
| 13 Africa | 27 May–1 June 1986 | General Assembly |
| 14 Namibia | 17–20 September 1986 | General Assembly |
| 15 Disarmament | 7 June–10 July 1988 | General Assembly |
| 16 Apartheid | 12–14 December 1989 | General Assembly |
| 17 Drug Abuse | 20–23 February 1990 | General Assembly |
| 18 International Economic Cooperation | 23–27 April 1990 | General Assembly |
| 19 Earth Summit+5 | 23–27 June 1997 | General Assembly |
| 20 World Drug Problem | 8–10 June 1998 | General Assembly |
| 21 Population and Development | 30 June–2 July 1999 | General Assembly |
| 22 Small Island Developing States | 27–28 September 1999 | General Assembly |
| 23 Women 2000: Gender Equality, Development and Peace for the Twenty-first Century | 5–9 June 2000 | General Assembly |
| 24 Social Development | 26–30 June 2000 | General Assembly |
| 25 Implementation of the Outcome of the United Nations Conference on Human Settlements (Habitat II) | June 2001 | General Assembly |
| 26 Problem of Human Immunodeficiency Virus/Acquired Immuno-deficiency Syndrome (HIV/AIDS) in All Its Aspects | 25–27 June 2001 | General Assembly |
| 27 World Summit for Children | 8–10 May 2002 | General Assembly |

SOURCE: United Nations Department of Public Information, 2003.

TABLE 2-3    General Assembly Emergency Special Sessions

| EMERGENCY SPECIAL SESSION | TOPIC | DATE OF SESSION | CONVENED BY |
|---|---|---|---|
| 1 | Middle East | 1–10 November 1956 | Security Council |
| 2 | Hungary | 4–10 November 1956 | Security Council |
| 3 | Middle East | 8–21 August 1958 | Security Council |
| 4 | Congo Question | 17–19 September 1960 | Security Council |
| 5 | Middle East | 17 June–18 September 1967 | USSR |
| 6 | Afghanistan | 10–14 January 1980 | Security Council |
| 7 | Palestine | 22–29 July 1980 | |
| | | 20–28 April 1982 | Senegal (Chairman, |
| | | 25–26 June 1982 | Palestine Rights |
| | | 16–19 August 1982 | Committee) |
| | | 24 September 1982 | |
| 8 | Namibia | 3–14 September 1981 | Zimbabwe |
| 9 | Occupied Arab Territories | 29 January–5 February 1982 | Security Council |
| 10 | Occupied East Jerusalem and the rest of the occupied Palestinian territory | 24–25 April 1997 | Qatar |
| | | 15 July 1997 | |
| | | 13 November 1997 | |
| | | 17 March 1998 | |
| | | 5, 8–9 February 1999 | |
| | | 18–20 October 2000 | |
| | | 20 December 2001 | |
| | | 7 May 2002 | |
| | | 5 August 2002 | |
| | | 19 September 2003 | |
| | | 20–21 October 2003 | |
| | | 3 December 2003 | |

SOURCE: UN Department of Public Information, 2003.

pace, and a quick feeling for the sense of the meeting." [2] Seated beside the President at all Assembly sessions is the Executive Assistant to the Secretary-General, who, as Secretary of the General Assembly, functions as parliamentarian and adviser to the President. Although the President's formal powers to control or shape the direction of debate and action are weak and tend to resemble those of the President of the U.S. Senate or the Speaker in the House of Commons, the disarray of the Assembly demands a strong yet tactful guidance. The international reputations of the Presidents have helped each of them to weather many verbal storms and to develop the UN presidency into a respectable source of Assembly power.

## Assembly Functions

Against a backdrop of politics and diplomacy, the General Assembly carries out its various roles and diverse activities, some assigned by the Charter and others assumed by the Assembly.

TABLE 2-4   UN Presidents of the General Assembly since the First Session

| SESSION | YEAR | NAME | COUNTRY |
|---|---|---|---|
| 1 | 1946 | Mr. Paul-Henri Spaak | Belgium |
| 1st special | 1947 | Mr. Oswaldo Aranha | Brazil |
| 2 | 1947 | Mr. Oswaldo Aranha | Brazil |
| 2nd special | 1948 | Mr. Jose Arce | Argentina |
| 3 | 1948 | Mr. H. V. Evatt | Australia |
| 4 | 1949 | Mr. Carlos P. Romulo | Philippines |
| 5 | 1950 | Mr. Nasrollah Entezam | Iran |
| 6 | 1951 | Mr. Luis Padilla Nervo | Mexico |
| 7 | 1952 | Mr. Lester B. Pearson | Canada |
| 8 | 1953 | Mrs. Vijaya Lakshmi Pandit | India |
| 9 | 1954 | Mr. Eelco N. van Kleffens | Netherlands |
| 10 | 1955 | Mr. José Maza | Chile |
| 1st emergency special | 1956 | Mr. Rudecindo Ortega | Chile |
| 2nd emergency special | 1956 | Mr. Rudecindo Ortega | Chile |
| 11 | 1956 | Prince Wan Waithayakon | Thailand |
| 12 | 1957 | Sir Leslie Munro | New Zealand |
| 3rd emergency special | 1958 | Sir Leslie Munro | New Zealand |
| 13 | 1958 | Mr. Charles Malik | Lebanon |
| 14 | 1959 | Mr. Victor Andrés Belaúnde | Peru |
| 4th emergency special | 1960 | Mr. Victor Andrés Belaúnde | Peru |
| 15 | 1960 | Mr. Frederick H. Boland | Ireland |
| 3rd special | 1961 | Mr. Frederick H. Boland | Ireland |
| 16 | 1961 | Mr. Mongi Slim | Tunisia |
| 17 | 1962 | Sir Muhammad Zafrulla Khan | Pakistan |
| 4th special | 1963 | Sir Muhammad Zafrulla Khan | Pakistan |
| 18 | 1963 | Mr. Carlos Sosa Rodríguez | Venezuela |
| 19 | 1964 | Mr. Alex Quaison-Sackey | Ghana |
| 20 | 1965 | Mr. Amintore Fanfani | Italy |
| 21 | 1966 | Mr. Abdul Rahman Pazhwak | Afghanistan |
| 5th special | 1967 | Mr. Abdul Rahman Pazhwak | Afghanistan |
| 5th emergency special | 1967 | Mr. Abdul Rahman Pazhwak | Afghanistan |
| 22 | 1967 | Mr. Corneliu Manescu | Romania |
| 23 | 1968 | Mr. Emilio Arenales Catalán | Guatemala |

| Session | Year | President | Country |
| --- | --- | --- | --- |
| 24 | 1969 | Miss Angie E. Brooks | Liberia |
| 25 | 1970 | Mr. Edvard Hambro | Norway |
| 26 | 1971 | Mr. Adam Malik | Indonesia |
| 27 | 1972 | Mr. Stanislaw Trepczynski | Poland |
| 28 | 1973 | Mr. Leopoldo Benítes | Ecuador |
| 6th special | 1974 | Mr. Leopoldo Benítes | Ecuador |
| 29 | 1974 | Mr. Abdelaziz Bouteflika | Algeria |
| 7th special | 1975 | Mr. Abdelaziz Bouteflika | Algeria |
| 30 | 1975 | Mr. Gaston Thorn | Luxembourg |
| 31 | 1976 | Mr. H. S. Amerasinghe | Sri Lanka |
| 32 | 1977 | Mr. Lazar Mojsov | Yugoslavia |
| 8th special | 1978 | Mr. Lazar Mojsov | Yugoslavia |
| 9th special | 1978 | Mr. Lazar Mojsov | Yugoslavia |
| 10th special | 1978 | Mr. Lazar Mojsov | Yugoslavia |
| 33 | 1978 | Mr. Indalecio Liévano | Colombia |
| 34 | 1979 | Mr. Salim A. Salim | United Republic of Tanzania |
| 6th emergency special | 1980 | Mr. Salim A. Salim | United Republic of Tanzania |
| 7th emergency special | 1980 | Mr. Salim A. Salim | United Republic of Tanzania |
| 11th special | 1980 | Mr. Salim A. Salim | United Republic of Tanzania |
| 35 | 1980 | Mr. Rüdiger von Wechmar | Federal Republic of Germany |
| 8th emergency special | 1981 | Mr. Rüdiger von Wechmar | Federal Republic of Germany |
| 36 | 1981 | Mr. Ismat T. Kittani | Iraq |
| 7th emergency special (resumed) | 1982 | Mr. Ismat T. Kittani | Iraq |
| 9th emergency special | 1982 | Mr. Ismat T. Kittani | Iraq |
| 12th special | 1982 | Mr. Ismat T. Kittani | Iraq |
| 37 | 1982 | Mr. Imre Hollai | Hungary |
| 38 | 1983 | Mr. Jorge E. Illueca | Panama |
| 39 | 1984 | Mr. Paul J. F. Lusaka | Zambia |
| 40 | 1985 | Mr. Jaime de Piniés | Spain |
| 13th special | 1986 | Mr. Jaime de Piniés | Spain |
| 41 | 1986 | Mr. Humayun Rasheed Choudhury | Bangladesh |
| 14th special | 1986 | Mr. Humayun Rasheed Choudhury | Bangladesh |
| 42 | 1987 | Mr. Peter Florin | German Democratic Republic |

*(continued)*

TABLE 2-4 *(continued)*

| Session | Year | Name | Country |
|---|---|---|---|
| 15th special | 1988 | Mr. Peter Florin | German Democratic Republic |
| 43 | 1988 | Mr. Dante M. Caputo | Argentina |
| 44 | 1989 | Mr. Joseph Nanven Garba | Nigeria |
| 16th special | 1989 | Mr. Joseph Nanven Garba | Nigeria |
| 17th special | 1990 | Mr. Joseph Nanven Garba | Nigeria |
| 18th special | 1990 | Mr. Joseph Nanven Garba | Nigeria |
| 45 | 1990 | Mr. Guido de Marco | Malta |
| 46 | 1991 | Mr. Samir S. Shihabi | Saudi Arabia |
| 47 | 1992 | Mr. Stoyan Ganev | Bulgaria |
| 48 | 1993 | Mr. Samuel R. Insanally | Guyana |
| 49 | 1994 | Mr. Amara Essy | Côte d'Ivoire |
| 50 | 1995 | Prof. Diogo Freitas do Amaral | Portugal |
| 51 | 1996 | Mr. Razali Ismail | Malaysia |
| 10th emergency special (resumed) | 1997 | Mr. Razali Ismail | Malaysia |
| 19th special | 1997 | Mr. Razali Ismail | Malaysia |
| 52 | 1997 | Mr. Hennadiy Udovenko | Ukraine |
| 20th special | 1998 | Mr. Hennadiy Udovenko | Ukraine |
| 53 | 1998 | Mr. Didier Opertti | Uruguay |
| 10th emergency special (resumed) | 1999 | Mr. Didier Opertti | Uruguay |
| 21st special | 1999 | Mr. Didier Opertti | Uruguay |
| 54 | 1999 | Mr. Theo-Ben Gurirab | Namibia |
| 22nd special | 1999 | Mr. Theo-Ben Gurirab | Namibia |
| 23rd special | 2000 | Mr. Theo-Ben Gurirab | Namibia |
| 24th special | 2000 | Mr. Theo-Ben Gurirab | Namibia |
| 55 | 2000 | Mr. Harri Holkeri | Finland |
| 10th emergency special (resumed) | 2000 | Mr. Harri Holkeri | Finland |
| 25th special | 2001 | Mr. Harri Holkeri | Finland |
| 26th special | 2001 | Mr. Harri Holkeri | Finland |
| 56 | 2001 | Mr. Han Seung-soo | Korea |
| 10th emergency special (resumed) | 2001 | Mr. Han Seung-soo | Korea |
| 10th emergency special (resumed twice) | 2002 | Mr. Han Seung-soo | Korea |
| 57 | 2002 | Mr. Jan Kavan | Czech Republic |
| 58 | 2003 | Mr. Julian Robert Hunte | Saint Lucia |

SOURCE: The United Nations Department of Public Information, 2003.

One frequently indulged activity is exhortation by means of resolutions aimed at member states, nonmembers, great powers, the Security Council, other major organs, and even the General Assembly itself. Sometimes referred to as "manifestos against sin," these resolutions permit the Assembly to carry out what its supporters regard as the role of guardian of Charter principles and the conscience of humankind and what its detractors write off as sheer hypocrisy. Through such resolutions the Assembly has, among other things, called on the permanent members of the Security Council to use the veto with restraint, the great powers to cease their war propaganda, all states to accept the maxim of peaceful coexistence, and disputants to settle their controversies peacefully.

The Assembly's quasi-legislative function, carried on through the adoption of resolutions, declarations, and conventions, goes beyond exhortation in seeking to develop and codify international law. In this role the Assembly most closely approximates the lawmaking activities of a national legislature. Assembly resolutions governing internal matters, such as procedural rules, control of funds and property, and staff regulations, have the force of law. Resolutions directed toward state conduct outside the organization are not ipso facto binding, but the rules thus enunciated may have legal force if they are regarded as statements of customary international law or authoritative interpretations of the UN Charter. The Assembly may also engage in lawmaking through the drafting of multilateral treaties. Conventions adopted by the Assembly, such as the Genocide Convention (outlawing acts aimed at the destruction of a national, ethnic, racial, or religious group) or the Law of the Sea Treaty, become operative law among the consenting parties after they have been ratified by the required number of states. The Assembly's International Law Commission is regularly engaged in the codification of rules of international law to be presented to members in treaty form. The numerous Assembly-approved treaties now in force illustrate the quasi-legislative function. When members are motivated to act, the Assembly can truly function like a world parliament.

In its investigative role the Assembly complements its quasi-legislative functions. This role can be illustrated by frequent resolutions asking the Secretariat, or a special committee, to study a problem and report to the next General Assembly. As in a national legislature, facts are often helpful before the Assembly acts. In the settlement of disputes, investigation is an essential prelude to a determination of the issues involved and the working out of a just solution.

Although the Security Council has primary responsibility for international peace and security, the Assembly also has a role. That role was more important in earlier decades when the Security Council was often deadlocked by the veto. Commonly, the Assembly has pursued peaceful settlement through discussion and recommendation, tendering good offices, mediation, conciliation, commissions of inquiry, and appointment of individual mediators. Since 1950 the Uniting for Peace Resolution has authorized the Assembly to make recommendations for economic or military sanctions when the Security Council is unable to deal with a breach of the peace or act of aggression. Assembly creation of the UN Emergency Force (UNEF) in the Middle East (1956), when the Security

Council was unable to fulfill its responsibility, illustrates this backup role in a threatening situation.

The Assembly's budgetary function resembles that of a national legislature's traditional "power of the purse." All UN programs and all activities of subsidiary UN bodies come under a measure of surveillance and control since all must be supported with adequate funds. Budget decisions have on occasion become the tail that has wagged the dog of substantive actions in the United Nations, as happened during the money crisis of the 1960s, when lack of funds forced the discontinuance of the UN operation in the Congo. In the 1980s and 1990s, the huge backlog of unpaid dues owed by the United States, along with smaller amounts owed by many other members, put serious constraints on UN activities. In 1996, Secretary-General Boutros Boutros-Ghali called on the General Assembly to deal with what he described as "a grave set of problems," in part a product of the heavier and more complex workload of the United Nations and in part caused by the failure of members to pay their assessments. His successor, Kofi Annan, has labored with similar problems, but despite severe austerity measures that resulted in a drastic reduction in UN staff, the financial status of the organization has not improved. Attention remains riveted on the U.S. Congress, which must be won over if the United States is expected to satisfy its financial obligations to the world body.

Closely related to the Assembly's budgetary function is its supervisory role. It is to the Assembly that the Security Council, the Economic and Social Council, and the Trusteeship Council (when still operative) submit annual and special reports on their respective operations. Although the Security Council is not a subsidiary organ, the Charter empowers the Assembly to make recommendations to it and to call peace-threatening situations to its attention. The Economic and Social Council and the Trusteeship Council, although designated as "principal organs," are actually subsidiary and operate "under the authority of the General Assembly" (Articles 60 and 85). Decisions on economic issues, social questions, and, heretofore, trusteeship matters are made by the Assembly on recommendations from the councils. The Secretariat also is concerned with serving the Assembly and in turn is controlled by it. Decisions on organization, personnel, and the Secretariat budget are made by the Assembly. Annual reports on selected activities and on the work of each organ and agency of the United Nations enable the Assembly to receive, to criticize, and hence to supervise the entire UN operation.

The Assembly exercises a twofold elective function. One phase involves the admission of new members into the United Nations; the other relates to the selection of the elective members of other organs. The election to membership takes place following a recommendation by the Security Council, a prerequisite affirmed by the International Court of Justice in an advisory opinion in 1950. Prospective UN members file an application with the Secretary-General for transmission to the Security Council. Before 1955 membership decisions were often delayed in the Security Council, sometimes for years, but once the Council has made its recommendations, Assembly action to admit is swift. The Assembly's second elective function helps shape the outlook and decision-making capabilities of other major UN organs. Some elections are conducted jointly with the Security Council, as in selecting the judges of the International Court and appointing the Secretary-General. Others occur through Assembly action alone, as in the election of the ten nonpermanent members of the Security Council and all members of the Economic and Social Council. Annual elections to fill vacancies in various organs are preceded by extensive group consultation, which ordinarily, but not always, has prevented sharp wrangling in the Assembly over the more prestigious seats, especially those in the Security Council.

Finally, as previously noted, the Assembly exercises a constituent function in proposing formal amendments to the Charter that take effect when ratified by two-thirds of the member states, and including all the permanent members of the Security Council. Amendments to enlarge the Security Council and Economic and Social Council are the only ones that have been added to the Charter.

## Assembly Decision Making

Changes in global political and economic systems have also meant important changes in General Assembly decision making. In 1990, the forty-fifth year of Assembly operation, for example, President Guido de Marco of Malta described it as "the first Assembly session in the post-cold-war era." The forty-fifth Assembly, he noted, was "marked by a rising tide of consensus decisions . . . with fewer meetings, fewer debates, fewer votes." This "calm," however, proved short-lived as crises erupted in several regions of the world, particularly in the former Yugoslavia, where Bosnia-Herzegovina was the scene of a European war not experienced since the end of World War II. So too the African continent exploded in a series of civil wars that demanded the attention of the United Nations, and of which Rwanda proved to be the most tragic. Involvement in Somalia and Haiti was also of major importance. But it was the Persian Gulf War, precipitated by the Iraqi invasion and conquest of Kuwait, that necessitated an aggressive UN response as well as a sustained policing operation that kept the lights burning at UN headquarters.

Nonetheless, the passing of the Cold War appeared to bring promise as well as new problems. The democratization of Eastern Europe was begun, although tempered by the realization that integrating these countries into the world of free political expression and an open market economy would be painful. Perhaps even more affected by revolutionary changes in the global economy were the Third World countries that found the competition for international assistance far more problematic in a world liberated from the command economies of the communist bloc. But for the first time in the history of the United Nations, the East European states no longer voted as a bloc, and the merger of East and West Germany meant that the German state would be represented by one united voice. The post–Cold War period also saw the further integration of

Europe as the European Community became the European Union and in 1998 the EU agreed to establish its European Monetary Union. At the turn of the twenty-first century a majority of EU members agreed to adopt a uniform currency, the euro, shedding their historic and emotional ties to their individual currencies. With the world passing through a period of dynamic change, and with enhanced cooperation an apparent reality, the General Assembly was nevertheless far from the proverbial quiet refuge, nor could it ignore the forces and conditions that made for greater instability. Examples of the latter were found in the General Assembly Emergency Special Sessions on Jerusalem and the West Bank territory from 1997 to 2002. Concern over the nuclear arms race and the heightened tensions over Kashmir between India and Pakistan in 2002, as well as the convening of the Open Ended Panel of the General Assembly on Afghanistan in November 2002, reflected the unsettled political conditions, despite the passing of the Cold War.

But nothing was more compelling than the events of September 11, 2001. The horrific assault on the United States by members of the Al-Qaeda terrorist organization became a defining moment for the United Nations as a whole. The United Nations Counter-Terrorism Committee (CTC) was charged with erecting global standards for dealing with terrorist cells in every part of the globe. Toward that objective, the CTC was made responsible for enlisting the services of regional and subregional organizations. Among these were the Association of Southeast Asian Nations, the League of Arab States, the EU, the Organization of American States, the Organization of the Islamic Conference, NATO, and Interpol. The purpose of the CTC was to commit the United Nations to the struggle against non-state doers of violence and declared enemies of the international system. Members, however, were quick to point out that the United Nations was not an operational agency and that the essential security work remained the responsibility of states.

While acknowledging the unstable security environment created by the forces of worldwide terrorism, the extended UN system and the General Assembly in particular devotes a good portion of its attention and resources to the promotion of the development of human skills and potentials. The system's annual disbursements, including loans and grants, amounted to more than $12 billion in 2000. Examples of these activities were found in the UN Development Program (UNDP), which worked in close cooperation with more than 170 member states and other UN agencies. UNDP designs and implements projects centered on agriculture, industry, education, and the environment. The Earth Summit, the UN Conference on Environment and Development that was called by the General Assembly, has resulted in treaties on biodiversity and climate change. The "Agenda 21" blueprint promotes sustainable development, a commitment reaffirmed at the General Assembly's Special Session (Earth Summit+5) in June 1997, and again, at the World Summit for Children in May 2002. The General Assembly's role in maintaining peace and security, in promoting democracy and human rights, in preventing nuclear proliferation, in strengthening international law, in promoting human rights and social development, and in combating disease have made it a central organ in the management of an increasingly complex world.

### Proposals to Streamline the Assembly Procedures

Despite a relatively greater harmony in recent sessions, Assembly delegations still agree as they have for years that the Assembly must somehow find the means for streamlining its procedures in order to expedite the work of the organization. The growth in membership has added a degree of urgency to this need. The Assembly has too often become mired in the procedural quicksand of its own making, and little agreement exists on the means necessary for achieving greater effectiveness. Suggestions and recommendations over the years have included the following:

1. Reduce the time wasted during each session. Better scheduling of speakers and regulating those not prepared to speak at their appointed time to the bottom of the list have been suggested. Joint statements by a number of delegations with the same viewpoint and written statements instead of oral statements have been encouraged.
2. Expedite the "general debate" that opens each Assembly session. Avoid repetition of speeches by heads and members of the same governments.
3. Speed up committee work and organize it better. Committees should start their work early in each session and should coordinate their activities through the steering committee. The creation of more subcommittees might help free the main committees from the detailed work of drafting resolutions.
4. Accelerate the debate and voting processes in the Assembly and its main committees.

Many proposals to speed the deliberative process have been considered, such as placing time limits on general debate. Ultimately, the orderliness and dispatch with which a body like the General Assembly conducts its procedural work depend on the expertise of the committee chairs and members and on the willingness of heads of delegations to exercise self-restraint in the interest of reducing tedium.

## THE SECURITY COUNCIL

In both the planning and writing of the UN Charter, the primacy of the Security Council was generally accepted. Nothing seemed more certain to the framers than the logic of its role: The primary responsibility of the United Nations is to keep the peace; keeping the peace is mainly a function of the great powers; ergo, the Security Council is the logical focus for this responsibility. For more than forty years, however, the Security Council did not fully measure up to the framers' hopes. Then, beginning in the late 1980s, a new spirit of cooperation among the great powers permitted unified action to deal with crises in Afghanistan, Iran and Iraq, Cambodia, and other troubled areas. When Iraq invaded Kuwait in 1990, the Council was able to act with unanimity in condemning Iraq's aggression against Kuwait and authorizing collective military action to expel the aggressor. (For further analysis of the Persian Gulf crisis see Chapter 5.)

## Council Composition

The Security Council has fifteen members. Five countries—China, France, the United Kingdom, the Soviet Union, and the United States—were designated by the Charter as *permanent* members. With the demise of the Soviet Union, its permanent seat was filled by Russia. This sparked discussion of possibly adding other states, such as Japan, Germany, or India, as permanent members, but no serious attempt at Charter amendment followed. Ten (originally six) *nonpermanent* or *elected* members are chosen by the General Assembly for staggered two-year terms, five elected each year (see Table 2-1). On retirement from the Council, elected members are not immediately eligible for reelection. This provision was inserted because under the League the elective seats on the Council were controlled by the middle powers in most elections to the near exclusion of the small powers. Although all members of the United Nations, other than the five permanent members, are eligible for election to the Security Council, the Charter stipulates that in the selection of nonpermanent members, due regard would be paid to "the contributions of Members of the United Nations to the maintenance of international peace and security." This is because of pressures exerted by the middle powers at San Francisco. Concern also was to be given to the matter of equitable geographical distribution (Article 23). These two considerations obviously can be contradictory, since states with strategic locations or reserves of economic or human resources are not evenly distributed about the globe.

During the early years of the United Nations, the Western powers held a majority on the Council. By virtue of a "gentlemen's agreement" in 1946, two elective Council seats were assigned to Latin America and one each to Western Europe, Eastern Europe, the Middle East, and the British Commonwealth, an arrangement that normally assured the West a majority on the Council.

In the late 1950s, pressed by demands for Asian and African representation, the United States succeeded in shifting the seat allocated for Eastern Europe to Asia. This shift proved to be only a temporary tranquilizer, however, as African, Eastern European, and Asian states clamored for greater representation for their areas. An amendment to the Charter, proposed in 1963 and adopted and ratified in 1965 by a requisite number of states, emerged out of these pressures for greater representation. It provided for enlarging the Council from eleven to fifteen members by increasing the elective members from six to ten, and it changed the majority needed for a decision from seven to nine. By Assembly resolution, the ten nonpermanent seats are now allotted as follows: five seats to Asia and Africa, one to Eastern Europe, two to Latin America, and two to Western European and other states. The keen competition in Assembly elections and the demands for "area representation" demonstrate that a seat at the Council table is one of the most coveted honors and crucial power positions available to members of the United Nations.

### Council Functions

The Security Council's two main functions under the Charter are to settle disputes peacefully (Chapter VI) and to meet threats to peace with the concerted action of the organization (Chapter VII). Whenever possible the Council has handled situations under Chapter VI of the Charter as simple disputes rather than considering collective action under Chapter VII, even when both sides to the dispute have been engaged in extensive military actions. The Korean War (1950–53) and the Persian Gulf hostilities (1990–91) were two exceptions to this general rule of trying to avoid a UN military action.

Division on the Security Council over the renewed use of force against Iraq in 2003 was in major part caused by a majority of Security Council members, including three of the permanent members, opting for the more diplomatic procedures of Chapter VI. Nevertheless, a minority, led by the United States, argued for military enforcement measures provided by Chapter VII. This controversy went unresolved when the United States, insisting it had sufficient legal justification for launching a war against Iraq, led a coalition into battle without final Security Council approval. The problems arising from this episode will be examined in more detail subsequently.

Generally, techniques the Council employs in the application of either Chapter VI or Chapter VII vary from case to case. Much depends in each situation on the political considerations involved, the degree of unity on the Council, the extent of the danger to peace, and the relationship of the dispute and the disputants to Council members, particularly the permanent members. Typical techniques the Council uses to deal with peace and security matters include deliberation, investigation, recommendation, exhortation, mediation, conciliation, interposition of a peacekeeping presence, and, in extreme cases, economic or military sanctions. These are discussed at greater length in Chapters 5 and 6. In Article 26 of the Charter, the Council is assigned the additional security responsibility of developing plans "for the establishment of a system for the regulation of armaments" (see Chapter 7).

Other Council functions are elective or supervisory in nature and were designed by the framers to permit the great powers to maintain some control over organizational matters. These functions are shared with the General Assembly. They include the election of a Secretary-General, the admission of new members, the election of the judges of the International Court of Justice, the deprivation and restoration of members' rights and privileges, and the expulsion of members. In addition, the Council supervised a trusteeship system that was left in suspension after the last trust territory, Palau, was declared independent in October 1994.

*Council Procedures*

Each Council member, permanent and elected, appoints a representative and an alternate to the Council. Unlike other UN organs, the Security Council is in permanent session and meets whenever a need exists. Under its rules of procedure, intervals between meetings should not exceed fourteen days. The President of the Council may convene it at any time on his or her own initiative when requested to do so by a member of the Council or, under circumstances prescribed in the Charter, when requested to do so by the General Assembly or the Secretary-General.

Under the Security Council's rules of procedure, its presidency rotates each month among its members. This provision, while safeguarding the Council from continuing domination or abuse by a presiding officer who is out of sympathy with its objectives, gives the organ a discontinuity that has not always been consistent with its high responsibilities. The brief two-year terms of the ten nonpermanent members add to the impromptu quality of the Council. Moreover, debates in the Council lack spontaneity and continuity because important statements must often be studied thoroughly before they are answered and because comments are often reserved until home governments can be contacted for instructions.

Although debates are carried on in the Security Council under rules of procedure established by the Council, the Charter provides that any UN member may be invited to participate in any discussion if its interests are affected by the question under debate. Also, any state, whether a UN member or not, must be invited to participate in the discussion if it is a party to a dispute being considered by the Council. In neither case does the invited state have a vote.

When debate on a measure has been completed, a vote is taken, with each member of the Council having one vote. Decisions are of two types: *procedural* and *substantive*. The Charter provides that all decisions on procedural questions be made by an approving vote of any nine members; thus permanent and elected members have equal voting power on procedural questions. On all other, or substantive, matters, the Charter declares that decisions shall be made "by an affirmative vote of nine members including the concurring votes of the permanent members," except that when a member of the Council is a party to a dispute, it must abstain from voting. Although the words of the Charter clearly denote that substantive decisions require a "yes" vote of all five permanent members, in a practice based on numerous precedents, a permanent member's abstention from voting is not regarded as constituting a veto of the pending measure. To "kill" or veto a matter of substance that is supported by at least nine members of the Council, a permanent member must cast a negative vote.

The Charter does not specify how the Security Council, in the event of disagreement, decides whether a question is procedural or nonprocedural. At San Francisco the great powers agreed that the issue would be treated as a nonprocedural question and therefore subject to the veto. This meant that a permanent member could gain the right to veto any matter simply by voting against the preliminary motion to declare it procedural. In practice, this so-called double veto has not been attempted often enough to be a serious problem.

## THE ECONOMIC AND SOCIAL COUNCIL

Although afforded the status of principal organ by the Charter, the Economic and Social Council (ECOSOC) functions under the authority of the General Assembly. In many respects its activities resemble those of the main Assembly committees, and it has occasionally been accused of duplicating or competing with the work of the Second (Economic and Financial) and Third (Social) Committees of the Assembly.

Originally established with eighteen members, ECOSOC was enlarged to twenty-seven in 1965 and to fifty-four in 1973. Both enlargements were implemented through Charter amendments and were the product of growing demands by the Third World bloc for a greater voice in determining economic and social policy. Members are elected by a two-thirds vote in the Assembly for staggered three-year terms. Although all UN members are equally eligible for election, in practice members representing First World countries of industrial importance have been consistently elected over the years. This practice contributed to the expansion of ECOSOC in 1965 and again in 1973 to meet the demands of the developing countries for a larger voice in economic and social policy-making. A president is elected each year from one of the small or middle powers represented on ECOSOC. Sessions are held twice annually, the first in New York in the spring and the second in Geneva in the summer. Decisions are made by a simple majority of those present and voting.

### ECOSOC Functions

ECOSOC's mandate is very broad, and it has the power only to recommend. In all things it must defer to the General Assembly, which means that ECOSOC can scarcely be the final word on anything of importance. It can hold meetings, do research, produce studies and reports, draft multilateral conventions for submission to the Assembly, and make recommendations. It is authorized to coordinate the activities of the UN specialized agencies but is given no power to make this mandate effective. Despite a persisting gap between aspirations and reality, ECOSOC has carried on some useful if usually unspectacular work.

Recent ECOSOC agendas have included such diverse topics as housing, narcotic drug control, water resources, desertification, world population, trade, the UN Children's Fund (UNICEF), industrial development, literacy, refugees, the environment, science and technology, the status of women, the needs of children, and the problems of the disabled. Always on the agenda are two subjects of perennial concern and overriding importance: human rights and economic development. In these and other areas, ECOSOC has from time to time generated proposals that have affected state practice.

All development programs begin with exhaustive studies. Through studies and reports ECOSOC has done much to overcome the dearth of statistical and other kinds of data on economic and social conditions in the world. In performing this function ECOSOC operates as a research agency and clearinghouse, attempting to coordinate the work of numerous committees, commissions, study groups, and private or nongovernmental organizations. The information thus gathered is vital to helping the United Nations and states across the globe come to grips with world problems, and no other agency in history has had such a broad research mandate.

Often, studies and preliminary recommendations originate in ECOSOC's functional commissions or regional economic commissions. The functional commissions established by ECOSOC are Human Rights (with its subcommission on the Prevention of Discrimination and Protection of Minorities), Narcotic Drugs, Population, Statistical, Status of Women, and a Social Commission. Regional economic (or economic and social) commissions have been set up for Africa (ECA), Asia and the Pacific (ESCAP), Western Asia (ESCWA), Europe (ECE), and Latin America and the Caribbean (ECLAC).

## Decision-Making Role

Based on its deliberations and extensive studies, ECOSOC appraises situations and, by Charter directive, may make recommendations "with respect to any such matters to the General Assembly, to the Members of the United Nations, and to the Specialized Agencies concerned" (Article 62). Sometimes, ECOSOC resolutions embody a statement of general principles and require only a favorable vote in the General Assembly for implementation, such as the proclamation of the Universal Declaration of Human Rights of 1948. They may also take the form of conventions requiring approval by the Assembly and subsequent ratification of the agreement by a stipulated number of member states.

Drafting conventions provides a quasi-legislative role for ECOSOC because the Council is often involved in the early phases of consensus building for many UN-sponsored treaties. This resembles the national lawmaking function in that the resulting convention binds consenting states, often limits governments in their relationship to their own citizens, and makes an addition to international law. While ECOSOC cannot make law, it plays a role in helping UN members develop law. This is a much more tedious process than the mere proclaiming of principles, and some nations that voted for the Universal Declaration of Human Rights in 1948 have failed to ratify the international covenants that would make these rights enforceable.

One such covenant, the Convention on the Political Rights of Women, serves as an example of what can be accomplished in the form of international legislation when states reach agreement. Consensus, in that case, was not easily developed. Women's groups from many countries, banding together as an international pressure group, demanded and obtained from ECOSOC a Commission on the Status of Women. They followed this up by promoting the idea of feminine political equality in the Commission, ECOSOC, General Assembly, and national acceptance stages. The Convention guarantees women the right to vote and to hold public office equally with men in all adhering states.

## Coordination Responsibilities

ECOSOC is supposed to exercise a coordination function relating to the specialized agencies of the United Nations and several autonomous organizations. The Charter charges ECOSOC with bringing the specialized agencies into a relationship with the United Nations through agreements negotiated by ECOSOC and approved by the General Assembly. The specialized agencies range in nature from the highly technical and functionally determined (such as the International Civil Aviation Organization and the International Telecommunication Union) to those that are involved in highly controversial political matters (such as the UN Educational, Scientific, and Cultural Organization [UNESCO] and the International Monetary Fund). Each of the specialized agencies began its existence as an intergovernmental organization with its own treaty or constitution. At the initiative of the agency, negotiations are conducted between it and ECOSOC, with the resulting agreement subject to approval by the General Assembly. Eighteen agencies have gone this route (see Figure 2-1) and thus are classified as specialized agencies of the United Nations. In addition to the specialized agencies, five other intergovernmental agencies function in a somewhat similar capacity as largely autonomous agencies within the UN system. These are the International Atomic Energy Agency (IAEA) and the General Agreement on Tariffs and Trade (GATT), which was superseded by the World Trade Organization. A World Tourism Organization, the Preparation Committee for the Nuclear Test Ban Treaty Organization, and the Organization for the Prohibition of Chemical Weapons were subsequently declared related organizations.

Integrating the activities of diverse intergovernmental agencies that are largely autonomous in their powers, have their own organizational machinery, adopt their own budgets, select their own secretariats, and, in some cases, antedate the UN organization is no simple task. The permissive authorization given to ECOSOC in the Charter has, as a result, not proved adequate to the challenge of securing effective "coordination," although various agreements have been concluded.

The growing assertion of power by the Assembly and its main committees in the 1980s and 1990s has produced a closer working relationship between them and the specialized agencies than between the agencies and ECOSOC, but this relationship tends to involve general oversight rather than coordination. More effective coordination on a voluntary consultative basis is effected through the Administrative Committee on Coordination, a committee of high officials from the UN Secretariat and the secretariats of the specialized agencies, functioning as an international administrative cabinet. Much of the important work of the UN family is carried on by the eighteen specialized agencies and by other UN-related bodies that report to ECOSOC or directly to the General Assembly. Most of them will be discussed in their proper context in later chapters.

## THE TRUSTEESHIP COUNCIL

Although the Charter designates the Trusteeship Council as a principal organ of the United Nations, like ECOSOC, it was subordinate to the General Assembly. Its function, to supervise nonstrategic trust territories for the Assembly and strategic trusts for the Security Council, involved only recommendation powers.

Membership on the Trusteeship Council was accorded by the Charter to three types of members: (1) states that administer trust territories, (2) permanent members of the Security Council that did not administer trust territories, and (3) enough additional elected members. Elected members were eliminated when the remaining trusts were all located in the strategic category. And with the last strategic trust territory, Palau, gaining independence in 1994, this category of membership also was eliminated. The Council's work has therefore been concluded. Its remaining permanent members have suspended meetings, and it only remains for a Charter amendment to be approved declaring the Trusteeship Council abolished.

### Trusteeship Functions

In carrying out its responsibilities the Trusteeship Council exercised power in performing a variety of functions. Two of these functions were similar to those of ECOSOC: The Council deliberated on matters within its jurisdiction through studies and debates, and it made recommendations for action based on its evaluations. Its recommendations, however, related to problems of particular trust territories or their administration and, unlike those of ECOSOC, did not usually take the form of proclamations or treaties.

The Council's supervisory role involved overseeing the governance of trust territories by administering states. An elaborate questionnaire drawn up by the Council served as a basic supervisory tool. The Council also received petitions, sometimes several hundred in a year, from individuals and groups in the trust territories seeking redress of real or imagined grievances. Reports and petitions were supplemented by periodic on-the-spot investigations by visiting missions of the Trusteeship Council composed of two people chosen by administering powers and two by nonadministering states. The missions evaluated economic and social conditions, examined progress toward self-government, sought answers to certain questions raised by the Council and the General Assembly, and consulted a wide cross section of the population, including labor leaders, tribal chiefs, local administrative leaders, and private individuals.

The information thus gathered was subjected to rigorous scrutiny in the Council, forcing each trust-holding state to defend its actions or lack of them. Out of these confrontations emerged the Council's annual report to the Assembly, permitting, this time by the Assembly, another inquiry, another debate, and another evaluation of how well administering states lived up to their mandated responsibilities. Little wonder that most trust states impatiently pushed their trust territories toward independence and self-government!

The work of the Trusteeship Council will be further examined in Chapter 8.

## THE INTERNATIONAL COURT OF JUSTICE

Although the International Court of Justice (ICJ) functions largely outside the UN framework as a semi-independent entity headquartered at The Hague in the Netherlands, the Charter recognizes it as one of the six principal organs of the United Nations. The ICJ, or World Court, is the successor to the Permanent Court of International Justice (PCIJ), which functioned as the world's chief judicial organ from 1922 to 1946. The Charter, in Article 92, recognizes this successor status in noting that the annexed Statute for the ICJ "is based upon the Statute of the Permanent Court of International Justice."

Although some of the organization and powers of the ICJ are set forth in the Charter (Articles 92 to 96), most are contained in the ICJ Statute, a multilateral treaty that serves as its basic constitution. All members of the United Nations are automatically parties to the ICJ Statute, but a state that is not a member of the United Nations can join the Court on conditions determined by the General Assembly following a recommendation by the Security Council. Switzerland, for example, refused to join the United Nations because of its centuries-old position of neutrality, but it accepted membership in the World Court almost from its inception. Moreover, Switzerland broke with its long-standing tradition of neutrality and joined the United Nations as a full member in September 2002.

Fifteen judges serve on the ICJ. Judges are elected by Security Council and General Assembly procedures, voting separately. Five judges are elected every three years for nine-year terms. Each judge is eligible for reelection. Article 9 of the Statute of the ICJ provides that judges should be selected on the basis of their individual merit and together should represent the main forms of civilization and the principal legal systems of the world. No two judges may be of the same nationality. Although the judges strive for objectivity, their voting behavior on the Court can often be predicted. With opinions based on the nature of the cases and the issues involved, their records as national judges, their publications in the areas of expertise in international law, their ideological persuasions, and other factors affect their judicial decision making.

The Court's competence to hear and decide cases extends to all controversies submitted to it by contending parties. If there is no judge on the Court of the nationality of one or several of the parties to a case, the party or parties so deprived may under Court rules appoint a judge to participate in that case with full voting rights. While such action is unknown in national courts, the World Court provisions mirror the sovereign independence of the parties in such cases. Some states have accepted the compulsory jurisdiction of the Court under what has been described as the Optional Clause of the Statute (Article 36). Because of a myriad of reservations and amendments, however, the general rule is that only those states that are willing to have their controversies adjudicated by the Court will be parties to cases before it. Cases are decided by a majority vote, with a quorum of nine needed for voting, unless by agreement the case is submitted to a smaller panel of judges. Decisions and awards cannot be appealed. In case of a tie, the President of the Court is entitled to a "casting" (tie-breaking) vote.

The Court's jurisdiction also extends to the rendering of advisory opinions on legal questions submitted to it by the principal organs of the United Nations and the UN special agencies.

To reach a decision, the Court interprets and applies treaties, international customs, the general principles of law, and decisions of international tribunals. Decisions of national courts and the teachings of respected international jurists can be used as subsidiary means for determining rules of international law. If the parties agree, the Court can render a decision *ex aequo et bono* (based on the Court's conception of justice and fairness rather than on law).

The ICJ is a symbol of the widespread yearning to replace the use of force with the rule of law. Within its scope of operation it has performed well, but its reach is necessarily limited by the willingness of all affected parties to place a dispute before it. For this reason it has had little part in resolving the major issues of peace and war and resource distribution that persistently plague the international system. The modest successes and inherent limitations of the Court in dispute settlement will be explored in depth in Chapter 7.

## THE SECRETARIAT

The UN Secretariat under Article 7 of the Charter is included as one of the six "principal organs" of the United Nations. The Secretariat consists of international civil servants who perform administrative, budgetary, secretarial, linguistic, staff, and housekeeping functions for the other principal organs and carry out the programs of the organization. Members of the Secretariat are recruited individually and do not serve as representatives of their governments, as do those who serve as delegates to the General Assembly and the three councils. They are full-time employees of the United Nations who bring diverse skills to the organization. They are supposed to serve the entire membership of the United Nations in a politically neutral manner, although reality sometimes falls short of the ideal.

Heading the Secretariat is a Secretary-General who in Article 97 is designated "the chief administrative officer of the Organization." Appointment of the Secretary-General for a five-year term is the culmination of a political process that includes recommendation by the Security Council, with the veto power applicable, and appointment by a two-thirds vote of the General Assembly.

The responsibilities of the Secretary-General, with the assistance of staff, include the following: preparing the agenda for major UN organs, providing essential services and sometimes expert advice at meetings, drawing up the biennial budget of the organization, expending funds, supervising day-to-day operations, taking the initiative in suggesting new programs, offering political leadership when requested to do so, serving as a diplomatic agent to iron out problems among member delegations, and serving as the ceremonial head of the United Nations in formal affairs. The Secretary-General is the only person in the United Nations who can speak for or represent the entire organization. The Secretariat's role in the administration and politics of the United Nations will be further elaborated in Chapter 4.

# FINANCING THE UNITED NATIONS

The effectiveness of a multilateral organization such as the United Nations and the dedication of its members can often be evaluated by an analysis of its budget. The short history of international organizations reveals that many states have been penurious to an extreme and often grudging in providing the needed funds. This propensity of members to invest only relatively meager resources in the work of international organizations may mirror the limited character of their commitment, the poverty of their societies, or their disagreement with some of the activities carried on by these organizations. Demands by countries for substantial payoffs from such organizations are often balanced by inclinations to contribute little more than lip service to their operations.

## ASSESSMENT PROBLEMS

When the United Nations began its work in 1946, the need to find an equitable but adequate funding formula was given high priority. The task of preparing a scale of budgetary assessments was assigned to a special Committee on Contributions under guidelines laid down by the General Assembly. The Committee has since continued to provide periodic review and to recommend necessary revision of the assessment scale. Members of the Committee are supposed to be experienced in money matters and drawn from states providing a broad geographic representation. In determining assessments, the Committee was originally charged by the General Assembly to utilize the criterion of ability to pay as determined by each state's total national income, per capita income, economic dislocation caused by the war, and foreign exchange earnings. These factors, with the exception of dislocation caused by war, remain the main criteria for arriving at assessments today, although "floor" and "ceiling" limitations have been added. The United States pays the largest assessment of the regular budget. Many of the small, poor states of the Third World are assessed the minimum payment of 0.01 percent. Assessments are paid as "contributions," but they are considered binding once the General Assembly has adopted the organization's annual budget. Unlike the technical programs of the League of Nations, whose funds were included within the League's general budget, each of the specialized agencies of the United Nations has its own budgetary considerations, with Assembly oversight limited to consultation and recommendations. The UN budget system also differs from that of the League because the General Assembly operates by a two-thirds majority formula. This is different from the League of Nations where unanimity was required.

In 1946 assessments acknowledged the dominant economic position of the United States in a world suffering from the aftermath of war. The U.S. assessment amounted to almost 40 percent, with the remaining 60 percent paid by the other fifty member states. Objections were raised by U.S. leaders who argued that the United States did not have that great a capacity to pay and did not wish to weaken the organization by a heavy dependence on a single source of revenue. U.S. opposition took the form of a demand that a ceiling be established prohibiting contributions of more than one-third of the UN budget by any one state. This position was accepted for a ten-year period and until the economic revival of older members as well as the admission of new members offered another formula. In years past, the contributions of the United States to the UN system have sometimes approached 50 percent despite an annual budget assessment of 25 percent. The United States also provided support, through voluntary contributions, to special UN programs. These heavy U.S. contributions, however, are less impressive if measured strictly in terms of ability to pay, since a number of members contribute a greater percentage of their gross national product than does the United States. Moreover, in recent years U.S. voluntary contributions to UN programs have declined to about 25 percent.

The poorer states of the world prefer that budget assessments be based strictly on each state's national income and ability to pay. The use of national per capita income as a factor in the assessment scale has encountered objections from states with high national incomes and small populations. In deference to this protest, the Assembly established a rule that no state should be assessed more per capita than the largest contributor. Canada is the only state that has had its assessment reduced under this rule.

In previous years much of the debate over budgetary questions involved Cold War animus as well as controversies over money and other issues between countries north and south of the equator, the latter often referred to as the North-South dialogue. The Soviet Union's share of the regular budget was 6.34 percent in 1946, but after a vigorous campaign pushed by the United States, the Soviet share was increased to 12.95 percent, a figure that included the separate assessments for the Byelorussian and Ukrainian republics. The breakup of the Soviet Union and the near collapse of the surviving Russian Federation's economy caused a reduction in its assessments from 9.41 to 2.87 percent between 1992 and 1998. Japan, with the world's second largest economy, was the recipient of the second largest assessment, amounting to 17.98 percent in 1998, with Germany following at 9.63 percent, France at 6.49, Italy at 5.39, and the United Kingdom at 5.07 percent. The 1998–99 two-year budget was set at $2.532 billion, $51 million below the 1996–97 budget, and there was considerable complaint from the member states that the reduction as well as the overall budget had been set at a level imposed by the United States. The U.S. Congress had in fact insisted that the United Nations could not exceed its earlier budget. On the basis of capacity to pay, however, the poorest thirty members of the United Nations saw their assessments reduced from 0.01 to 0.001 percent in 1998. But perhaps the most heated debate resulted from a demand by the United States that its 25 percent share be reduced to 20 percent. The reaction from the other member states, especially from members of the European Union, to the U.S. demand was that the request could only be considered after Washington paid all its arrears. When the United States refused to comply, its assessment was left at 25 percent. Earlier, the U.S. ambassador had argued in the Fifth Committee that the U.S. assessment must be reduced to 22 percent by 1998 and 20 percent by the year 2000 in order to prevent serious damage to the U.S. relationship with the United Nations. In May 2001 the United States agreed to pay $582 million of its debt, but in doing so the Congress insisted that this sum represented a payment in keeping with Washington's reduced share of UN dues and peacekeeping costs. In other words, the United Nations was to receive the money in exchange for cutting the U.S. share of the operating budget from 25 to 22 percent, and the peacekeeping budget from 31 to 25 percent. The United Nations, apparently yielding to the U.S. demand for a reduction in their funding quota, nevertheless insisted that the U.S. share of peacekeeping could not be reduced below 26.5 percent.

Under the 1998–99 assessment scales, however, ten members were made responsible for 80 percent of the UN budget, with the United States, Japan, and Germany accounting for more than half. And because assessments were made on a capacity-to-pay arrangement, that is, the country's share of the world economy, it meant that three countries with less than 10 percent of the world's population controlled more than half the world's wealth, an issue that did not go unnoted by the more-numerous, less-endowed states.

## Budget Procedures and Politics

Overall UN operations are divided into four major budget categories: (1) the regular budget, (2) the specialized agencies, (3) voluntary programs related mainly to economic development, and (4) peacekeeping operations.

The regular budget pays the day-to-day costs of the organization, including buildings and equipment, conferences, travel, salaries and retirement pay, and other administrative costs arising from the operations of the major UN organs. Each specialized agency has its own budget, which is presented to the General Assembly for formal approval but is in fact arrived at independently. Economic aid and technical assistance through the UN Development Program (UNDP) is one of the larger voluntary programs. Some programs, such as the expenses of the office of the UN High Commissioner for Refugees (UNHCR), operate largely on voluntary contributions but are partly supported by the regular budget.

The UN two-year program budget requires the administrative staff to plan organizational goals, to establish the programs needed to achieve the goals, and to provide budgetary support for the programs. The budget process is the responsibility of members of the Secretariat under the direction of the Secretary-General. The Secretary-General proposes; the majority of member states dispose. This means that nations of the Third World, which pay the least, have the voting power to determine how much should be spent, and for what. The eight richest countries pay more than 75 percent of the total budget but can be outvoted by the huge Third World majority, which pays only a small portion of the remaining 25 percent (see Figure 2-2). No effective budget ceiling has ever been established, and new programs and rising costs for old programs that have been approved regularly over the years have added to the total cost of UN operations.

FIGURE 2-2    **Relationship of Assessments to Voting Strength in the General Assembly, January 1998**

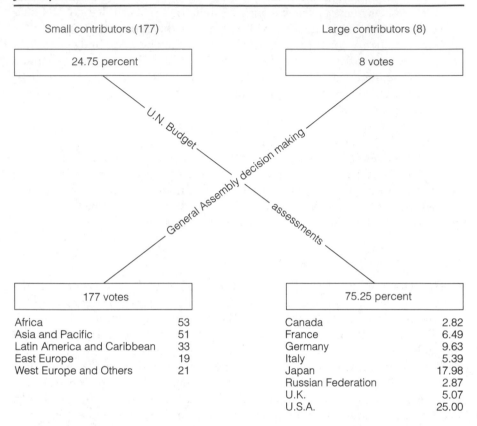

Small contributors (177)

| 24.75 percent |

Large contributors (8)

| 8 votes |

U.N. Budget

General Assembly decision making

assessments

| 177 votes |

| 75.25 percent |

| Africa | 53 |
| Asia and Pacific | 51 |
| Latin America and Caribbean | 33 |
| East Europe | 19 |
| West Europe and Others | 21 |

| Canada | 2.82 |
| France | 6.49 |
| Germany | 9.63 |
| Italy | 5.39 |
| Japan | 17.98 |
| Russian Federation | 2.87 |
| U.K. | 5.07 |
| U.S.A. | 25.00 |

In 1982 the United States, Great Britain, and the Soviet Union tried to halt budgetary escalation by jointly demanding that the Secretary-General set a ceiling on the 1982–83 budget and accept stringent limits on future budgets. Although the Secretary-General agreed to try budgetary restraint, he also faced pressures from Third World members to expand various programs. Neither side was happy when the budget for 1984–85 was fixed at $1.606 billion, an increase of $133 million, or 9 percent, over the previous biennium. The tide turned against the Third World nations after the Cold War, however. The United States, chastened by lack of support in the General Assembly on numerous policy issues, exacted revenge. Given earlier failures to impress the majority members by withholding payment of its assessed fees, the United States insisted on a greater assumption of responsibility by all the member states in paying the UN's bills. With the United States in a singular role and the dominant actor in strategic as well as economic and money matters, this contest between the one surviving superpower and the vast majority of member states was protracted.

Quite apart from budget ceiling controversies, UN budgetary planning has been complicated by failure of numerous states to pay their assessed contributions. In past years some twenty-five member governments have at various times withheld portions of their assessments for political reasons. A number refused to pay their share for peacekeeping operations because they opposed the use of UN peacekeeping forces in particular situations. As of mid-July 1997, member states owed the United Nations a total of $2.3 billion—$1.6 billion for peacekeeping, $681 million for the regular UN budget, and $8.7 million for international tribunals. The U.S. debt stood at $1.4 billion, or over half of the total. This included $498 million for the regular budget and $920 million for peacekeeping. After tallying the entire UN membership in 1998, only 78 of 185 states had paid their obligations in full.

Theoretically, continued nonpayment of compulsory assessments could lead to loss of voting rights in the General Assembly. Article 19 of the Charter provides that a member shall lose its vote when its budgetary arrearage equals or exceeds its total assessment for the preceding two years. That sanction lost most of its teeth in 1964 and 1965, however, when the United States tried—and failed—to persuade the Assembly to impose the penalty on the Soviet Union for failure to pay peacekeeping assessments. The Assembly went through the entire 1964 session without taking a formal vote. The United States, somewhat in disgust, reserved to itself the right to reject compulsory assessments in the future if compelling reasons arose. As a result, Article 19 has never been used to deprive a state of a vote.

Since the mid-1980s the United States has been the greatest offender in withholding assessed contributions. Moreover, dissatisfaction with the United Nations has been more obvious within the U.S. Congress than in the U.S. President's office. In 1985 the Congress adopted the Kassebaum Amendment, which required the United States to reduce its regular budget payments from 25 percent to 20 percent, beginning with the 1987 UN fiscal year. Under the amendment, this cut was to be continued until the United Nations adopted a system of reforms on budgetary matters by which the major funding contributors would no longer be subjected to budgetary decisions arrived at arbitrarily by the Third World majority. Additional reductions in the U.S. contribution were made necessary by subsequent congressional action.

The UN's financial crisis worsened with the end of the Cold War when it was assumed that the world body would accept major responsibility for a variety and multiplicity of political, economic, and social upheavals. Indeed, the United Nations found itself expanding its peacekeeping and peacemaking operations, but not without considerable encouragement from its member states. As a consequence, the organization was soon financially overextended and so heavily burdened that it became necessary to request even heavier funding commitments from the major member states, especially the United States. By 1996, the Secretary-General was forced to call a Special Session of the General Assembly to discuss the organization's financial crisis and propose remedies. Faced with UN insolvency and unpaid bills estimated at $3.3 billion, the Secretary-General declared it would be necessary to scale back the number of peacekeeping missions as well as cut a wide range of social and economic programs. Assessments for peacekeeping operations, however, were the main problem. They fell from $3 billion in 1995 to $1.3 billion in 1997, and by 1998 the United Nations owed some seventy-one countries more than $800 million for troops and equipment. The UN's two-year budget for 1998 and 1999 represented a zero-growth plan that required the Secretary-General to carry on the work of the organization with $372 million less than he had for 1996 and 1997. Thus, the UN staff was reduced from twelve thousand in the mid-1980s to nine thousand at the end of the 1990s, and although the United States approved such cuts, the U.S. Congress still insisted on exacting a price for meeting the country's financial obligations.

The new millennium witnessed important new directions in UN expenditures, and the intense pressure imposed on the organization by the United States met with some improvement in the world organization's cash flow. In 2003 a report issued by the UN Secretary-General for Management described a turnaround in UN financial fortunes. The year 2002 had been a surprisingly good one for the world body. The United Nations had $1.4 billion cash in hand, the highest liquidity in seven years. Unpaid assessments, while still substantial, had nevertheless declined compared with 2001 when delinquent states owed the organization $2.11 billion; 2002 arrears totaled $1.68 billion. Total collected receipts in 2002 totaled more than $4 billion despite smaller payments than forecast from the United States (owing 62 percent of the UN debt), Brazil (owing 12 percent), and Argentina (owing 10 percent). UN frugality and prudent financial management, however, not the beneficence of member states, was the chief reason given for the surplus. Still important, therefore, was the increase in unpaid assessments in 2002. A total of 117 member states paid their regular budget contributions in 2002, whereas 141 had done so in 2000. In effect, a number of responsible states were contributing more than their standard assessment to the organization.

The peacekeeping budget showed a decline in arrears, but it still remained high at $1.34 billion. Again, the U.S. share of this failure to meet the UN's peacekeeping obligations was the highest, representing 40 percent of the total, or $536 million. The next fourteen major delinquent contributors amounted to $494 million or 37 percent of the total. In the matter of support for International Tribunals, there was even greater reluctance on the part of member states to meet their obligations. A total of 133 states had unpaid assessments, with five states—the United States, Russia, Brazil, Argentina, and the Republic of Korea—owing the largest portion. Each of the five states owed between $3 million and $12 million, or 84 percent of the uncollected total budget of $217 million for 2003. On the other side of the issue were those states that had paid all their assessments, in all categories. They included Angola, Australia, Botswana, Cameroon, Canada, the Czech Republic, Denmark, Finland, France, Ireland, Kuwait, Latvia, Lithuania, Madagascar, Monaco, Norway, Seychelles, Sierra Leone, Singapore, South Africa, Sweden, Tuvalu, and the United Kingdom.

## FUTURE FINANCING PROBLEMS

Paying for UN operations remains a problem, and given the continuing prospect of nonpayment, late payment, and selective withholding, even prudent management may prove futile in meeting the organization's responsibilities. One answer, at least in theory, would be to seek sources of income for the United Nations independent of its members. Although many such sources would require Charter amendment or basic changes in the UN structure, the principle of revenue production independent of members' contributions is already in practice. Each year the organization nets several million dollars from its headquarters' businesses involving stamp sales, a gift shop, investment income, and guided tours. Although this amounts to only a small percentage of the annual regular budget, other proposals to secure independent sources of revenue could be regarded as extensions of this principle.

Suggestions for new sources run the gamut from those that would provide minor amounts of supplemental income to those that might fund most or all UN activities. As might be expected, sources that offer the greatest potential for substantial income are also the least feasible politically. Many members, of course, do not regard financial independence for the United Nations as a virtue because it would reduce their control over the organization and its activities. Potential sources for UN income might include the following:

1. Private contributions in the form of individual gifts, inheritances, and foundation grants encouraged through a joint policy of making such contributions deductible from national taxes.
2. Charges levied by UN agencies for services performed; for example, the World Meteorological Organization could charge a service fee for its weather data and the International Telecommunication Union could issue international radio licenses for substantial fees.
3. Tolls charged for various kinds of transportation and communications, facilitated in today's world by UN programs.
4. Fees for international travel imposed through levies on passports and visas or through surcharges on national customs duties.
5. Income earned through implementation of the 1982 Law of the Sea Treaty by which a UN international investment corporation could exploit the mineral and other forms of wealth in international waters or the subterranean seabed.
6. Charters sold to private companies or governmental agencies authorizing them to exploit the resources of the seabed, as well as Antarctica, with royalty rights reserved by the United Nations.
7. Fishing, whaling, and sealing rights in international waters, assigned to countries or private companies upon the payment of "conservation" fees to the United Nations.
8. Rights to the use of outer space, or the operation of outer space programs by the United Nations, aimed at producing revenues through

communications satellites, meteorological systems, and the future development of resources on the moon and the planets.

9. Taxes levied on member states, collectible by their governments, and based on ability to pay judged by national income.

10. Taxes levied directly on individuals through the cooperation of member states, based on income and with a mild graduation of rates.

11. Issuance of an international trading currency backed by national reserves that could serve the dual function of funding UN programs and providing a supplementary international monetary unit to encourage greater trade.

Recent Secretaries-General have addressed the serious short-term cash problems created by late payment of assessments, including charging interest on late payments, increasing the working capital fund, establishing a temporary Peacekeeping Reserve Fund, and authorizing the Secretary-General to borrow commercially to meet temporary cash needs. Other suggested plans include a levy on arms sales, a tax on international air travel, UN authority to borrow from the World Bank and the International Monetary Fund, and a general tax exemption for private contributions to the United Nations.

# NOTES

1. H. G. Nicholas, *The United Nations as a Political Institution,* 5th ed. (London: Oxford University Press, 1975), p. 104.
2. Ibid., p. 92.

# SELECTED READINGS

Ali, Sheikh R. *The International Organizations and World Order Dictionary.* Santa Barbara, CA: ABC-CLIO, 1992.

Beigbeder, Yves. *The Internal Management of United Nations Organizations: The Long Quest for Reform.* New York: St. Martin's Press, 1997.

Boutros-Ghali, Boutros. *An Agenda for Peace.* New York: United Nations, 1992.

Feld, Werner J., and Robert S. Jordan. *International Organizations: A Comparative Approach.* 2nd ed. New York: Praeger, 1988.

Galey, Margaret E. "Reforming the Regime for Financing the United Nations." *Howard Law Journal* 31, no. 4 (1988): 543–74.

Gati, Toby Trister, ed. *The US, the UN, and the Management of Global Change.* New York: New York University Press, 1983.

Goodrich, Leland M., Edvard Hambro, and A. P. Simons. *Charter of the United Nations, Commentary and Documents.* 3rd rev. ed. New York: Columbia University Press, 1967.

Gordenker, Leon. *Thinking About the United Nations System.* Hanover, NH: The Academic Council on the United Nations, 1990.

Jacobson, Harold K. *Networks of Interdependence.* 2nd ed. New York: Knopf, 1984.

Kaufmann, Johan. *Conference Diplomacy: An Introductory Analysis.* 2nd rev. ed. Dordrecht: Martinus Nijhoff, 1988.

Nicholas, H. G. *The United Nations as a Political Institution.* 5th ed. London: Oxford University Press, 1975.

Riggs, Robert E. *Politics in the United Nations.* Urbana: University of Illinois Press, 1958. Reprinted by Greenwood Press, 1984.

Russell, Ruth B. *A History of the United Nations Charter: The Role of the United States, 1940–1945.* Washington, DC: Brookings Institution, 1958.

Schachter, Oscar, ed. *United Nations Legal Order.* Cambridge: Cambridge University Press, 1995.

Stoessinger, John G., and Associates. *Financing the United Nations System.* Washington, DC: Brookings Institution, 1964.

Van Dervort, Thomas R. *International Law and Organization.* Thousand Oaks, CA: Sage, 1997.

Yoder, Amos. *The Evolution of the United Nations System.* New York: Crane Russak, 1989.

# 3

# THE UN POLITICAL PROCESS

The United Nations provides a setting for the practice of international politics. The principal participants are representatives of governments, secretariat employees, representatives of other international organizations, and spokespeople for nongovernmental interests. The UN political process is the sum of their efforts in the making and implementing of international decisions. This chapter will examine the several types of UN participants, how their interaction is affected by the UN institutional setting, and the events that stem from their activity.

## PARTICIPANTS IN THE UN DECISION PROCESS

### MEMBER STATES

The chief participants in any intergovernmental organization are the representatives of member states. When the process calls for a vote, these representatives are ordinarily the only ones entitled to vote. They also control most of the resources essential for implementing decisions. What the organization does is thus heavily dependent on its members, their interests, and their capabilities.

Today, membership in the United Nations is virtually universal. This was not so in the beginning. The organization took its name from the wartime United Nations, a coalition formed during World War II to defeat the Berlin-Rome-Tokyo Axis. Charter membership provisions were designed to permit at least the temporary exclusion of former enemy states until they could meet the test of membership among the "peace-loving" states. Thus the original membership consisted of states that had demonstrated their status as "peace-loving" by having declared war on the Axis Powers before March 1, 1945. Membership, under Article 4, paragraph 1, of the Charter subsequently was to be

> open to all other peace-loving states which accept the obligations contained in the present Charter and, in the judgment of the Organization, are able and willing to carry out these obligations.

The question of a state's identity as peace-loving was not taken lightly, since favorable action required a decision of the Security Council, including the acquiescence of the five permanent members as well as a two-thirds voting majority in the General Assembly.

During the United Nation's first decade, admission was granted grudgingly—only nine new members were added to the original fifty-one members. The few admissions to the United Nations had more to do with the developing Cold War and far less to do with World War II or the would-be candidate's love of peace. As East-West lines hardened, the U.S.-led majority denied the necessary seven Security Council votes to applicants from the Soviet bloc, while the Soviet Union used the veto to block the admission of most other applicants. Indeed, the Soviet Union hoped to break the logjam by its use of the veto, using it as leverage to secure the admission of its own protégés.

The break in the stalemate came in 1953 with the relaxation of Cold War tensions that followed the Korean Armistice and the death of Joseph Stalin. In this new atmosphere the United States and the Soviet Union in 1955 agreed on a package deal for the admission of sixteen new members, including several communist applicants. Since then, UN membership has been available virtually for the asking. Table 3-1 shows the present UN member states by years of admission.

The principal exceptions to the new open-door policy were the partitioned states of Germany, Vietnam, and Korea, a persisting legacy of the Cold War and the domestic conditions of the divided countries. Political détente led to the admission of both German states in 1973, and a single Vietnam was admitted in 1977 in the aftermath of the Vietnam War that brought its unification. Problems associated with the partition of Korea in the immediate aftermath of World War II, and hardened by the Korean War of 1950–53, kept the two Koreas outside the organization until 1991. The end of the Cold War in 1991, however, softened Korean attitudes on both sides of their thirty-eighth parallel boundary. With the permanent powers leading the way, both North and South Korea were admitted to membership in the United Nations as two separate and independent sovereign Korean governments.

An exception of a different kind was Switzerland, the former seat of the League of Nations and the present site of UN European headquarters. Switzerland voluntarily remained aloof from the United Nations out of its conviction that membership was incompatible with Swiss neutrality. When the issue of UN membership was put to a national referendum in March 1986, Swiss voters rejected it by a margin of three to one. When the matter was put before the Swiss nation some years later, Switzerland, acknowledging a changed world, voted in the affirmative for membership. In September 2002 it became the 190th member of the United Nations. Some days later Timor-Leste became the 191st member. The Holy See and the Palestine Authority presently maintain Permanent Observer status at the United Nations but they do not have voting privileges.

Membership issues regarding China also reflect political issues that wait for resolution. An original member of the United Nations, China also became a partitioned state in 1949 when the forces representing the People's Republic won the civil war on the mainland and the deposed Nationalist government was forced to seek refuge on the island of Taiwan. With each rival force still claiming to represent "one China," the issue of who spoke for "China" was left

TABLE 3-1   Growth in United Nations Membership, 1945–2003

| YEAR | NUMBER | MEMBER STATES |
|---|---|---|
| 1945 | Original 51 | Argentina, Australia, Belgium, Bolivia, Brazil, Belarus, Canada, Chile, China, Colombia, Costa Rica, Cuba, Czechoslovakia, Denmark, Dominican Republic, Ecuador, Egypt, El Salvador, Ethiopia, France, Greece, Guatemala, Haiti, Honduras, India, Iran, Iraq, Lebanon, Liberia, Luxembourg, Mexico, Netherlands, New Zealand, Nicaragua, Norway, Panama, Paraguay, Peru, Philippines, Poland, Russian Federation, Saudi Arabia, South Africa, Syrian Arab Republic, Turkey, Ukraine, United Kingdom of Great Britain and Northern Ireland, United States of America, Uruguay, Venezuela, Yugoslavia* |
| 1946 | 55 | Afghanistan, Iceland, Sweden, Thailand |
| 1947 | 57 | Pakistan, Yemen |
| 1948 | 58 | Burma (Myanmar) |
| 1949 | 59 | Israel |
| 1950 | 60 | Indonesia |
| 1955 | 76 | Albania, Austria, Bulgaria, Cambodia, Finland, Hungary, Ireland, Italy, Jordan, Lao People's Democratic Republic, Libyan Arab Jamahiriya, Nepal, Portugal, Romania, Spain, Sri Lanka |
| 1956 | 80 | Japan, Morocco, Sudan, Tunisia |
| 1957 | 82 | Ghana, Malaysia |
| 1958 | 82** | Guinea |
| 1960 | 99 | Benin, Burkina Faso, Cameroon, Central African Republic, Chad, Congo, Côte d'Ivoire, Cyprus, Democratic Republic of the Congo, Gabon, Madagascar, Mali, Niger, Nigeria, Senegal, Somalia, Togo |
| 1961 | 104 | Mauritania, Mongolia, Sierra Leone, United Republic of Tanzania |
| 1962 | 110 | Algeria, Burundi, Jamaica, Rwanda, Trinidad and Tobago, Uganda |
| 1963 | 112 | Kenya, Kuwait |
| 1964 | 115 | Malawi, Malta, Zambia |
| 1965 | 117 | Gambia, Maldives, Singapore |
| 1966 | 122 | Barbados, Botswana, Guyana, Lesotho |
| 1967 | 123 | Democratic Yemen |
| 1968 | 126 | Equatorial Guinea, Mauritius, Swaziland |
| 1970 | 127 | Fiji |
| 1971 | 132 | Bahrain, Bhutan, Oman, Qatar, United Arab Emirates |
| 1973 | 135 | Bahamas, Federal Republic of Germany, German Democratic Republic |
| 1974 | 138 | Bangladesh, Grenada, Guinea-Bissau |
| 1975 | 144 | Cape Verde, Comoros, Mozambique, Papua New Guinea, Sao Tome and Principe, Suriname |
| 1976 | 147 | Angola, Samoa, Seychelles |
| 1977 | 149 | Djibouti, Viet Nam |
| 1978 | 151 | Dominica, Solomon Islands |

Table 3-1    *(continued)*

| Year | Number | Member States |
|---|---|---|
| 1979 | 152 | Saint Lucia |
| 1980 | 154 | Saint Vincent and the Grenadines, Zimbabwe |
| 1981 | 157 | Antigua and Barbuda, Belize, Vanuatu |
| 1983 | 158 | Saint Kitts and Nevis |
| 1984 | 159 | Brunei Darussalam |
| 1990 | 159*** | Liechtenstein, Namibia |
| 1991 | 166 | Democratic People's Republic of Korea, Estonia, Federated States of Micronesia, Latvia, Lithuania, Marshall Islands, Republic of Korea |
| 1992 | 179 | Armenia, Azerbaijan, Bosnia and Herzegovina,* Croatia,* Georgia, Kazakhstan, Kyrgyzstan, Moldova, San Marino, Slovenia,* Tajikistan, Turkmenistan, Uzbekistan |
| 1993 | 184 | Andorra, Czech Republic, Eritrea, Monaco, Slovak Republic, The former Yugoslav Republic of Macedonia* |
| 1994 | 185 | Palau |
| 1999 | 188 | Kiribati, Nauru, Tonga |
| 2000 | 189 | Tuvalu, Serbia and Montenegro* |
| 2002 | 191 | Switzerland, Timor-Leste |

Source: "Basic facts about the UN," at http://www.un.org/overview/growth.htm.

*The Socialist Federal Republic of Yugoslavia was an original Member of the United Nations, the Charter having been signed on its behalf on 26 June 1945 and ratified 19 October 1945, until its dissolution following the establishment and subsequent admission as new members of Bosnia and Herzegovina, the Republic of Croatia, the Republic of Slovenia, The former Yugoslav Republic of Macedonia, and the Federal Republic of Yugoslavia.

The Republic of Bosnia and Herzegovina was admitted as a Member of the United Nations by General Assembly resolution A/RES/46/237 of 22 May 1992.

The Republic of Croatia was admitted as a Member of the United Nations by General Assembly resolution A/RES/46/238 of 22 May 1992.

The Republic of Slovenia was admitted as a Member of the United Nations by General Assembly resolution A/RES/46/236 of 22 May 1992.

By resolution A/RES/47/225 of 8 April 1993, the General Assembly decided to admit as a Member of the United Nations the State being provisionally referred to for all purposes within the United Nations as "The former Yugoslav Republic of Macedonia" pending settlement of the difference that had arisen over its name.

The Federal Republic of Yugoslavia was admitted as a Member of the United Nations by General Assembly resolution A/RES/55/12 of 1 November 2000.

Following the adoption and the promulgation of the Constitutional Charter of Serbia and Montenegro by the Assembly of the Federal Republic of Yugoslavia on 4 February 2003, the name of the State of the Federal Republic of Yugoslavia was changed to Serbia and Montenegro.

**The total remains the same because from 21 January 1958 Syria and Egypt continued as a single member (United Arab Republic).

***The Federal Republic of Germany and the German Democratic Republic were admitted to membership in the United Nations on 18 September 1973. Through the accession of the German Democratic Republic to the Federal Republic of Germany, effective from 3 October 1990, the two German States have united to form one sovereign State. Thus, the total remains the same.

essentially to the parties, but the world had to come to grips with there being two de facto Chinas. Because neither of the two Chinas would admit to there being two Chinas, however, the United Nations was compelled to treat the matter as one of representation rather than of admission to membership. Each year from 1950 to 1971, the General Assembly was forced to decide whether China was to be represented by delegates from the mainland or from the island of Taiwan. A string of Nationalist voting victories, made possible by vigorous support from the United States, was broken in November 1971, however, when the United States stepped aside and permitted the UN General Assembly to recognize the People's Republic of China as the legitimate holder of the China seat. Other UN organs quickly followed the lead of the Assembly, and the Nationalist representatives from Taiwan were required to leave the UN scene. Although the People's Republic of China Beijing government has continued to insist it is the government of all of China, including Taiwan, that island nation remains beyond its grasp. Considering this a delicate diplomatic and political issue, the United Nations has avoided opening Taiwan to separate membership in the world body, nor has Taiwan called for membership, although since the turn of the twenty-first century there is considerably more discussion within Taiwan about its separate status and independence. Beijing would hear none of this, however, and the situation remains outside the purview of the United Nations.

The few exceptions aside, essentially all states have valued the status of UN membership. The United Nations now welcomes all comers with adequate political credentials. For a time some members agonized over the mini-state problem—the admission of new states with equal voting rights in the General Assembly but without the population or resources to contribute much to UN programs (or, indeed, to exercise much activity in international affairs). But the admission of Antigua and Barbuda, the Seychelles, Dominica, the Marshall Islands, Micronesia, Liechtenstein, Monaco, and San Marino—all with populations of less than one hundred thousand—as well as more than thirty other states with populations less than one million indicates that no state is too small to qualify for membership.

The policy of unrestricted admission has made membership in the United Nations virtually universal and in the process has changed the character of the organization. With the growth in membership coming primarily from newly created states in Africa, Asia, and the Caribbean (see Table 3-2), Western (and in particular the U.S.) dominance of the United Nations gave way to the numerical dominance of the Third World. The new states have differed from the Western industrialized world in their needs and priorities, and they have not hesitated to refocus UN priorities according to their own visions. The changes, of course, have been more profound in the General Assembly, where all members have a voice and a vote, than in the Security Council with its great power veto.

In summary, the addition of new members has changed the United Nations by enlarging the cast of characters who make decisions. Developments within member countries, particularly changes in national leadership and national policies, also have affected UN politics and policies by placing new actors on the

TABLE 3-2    UN Membership and Geographic Region, 1945–2002

| Date | Western Europe[1] | Eastern Europe | Asia and Pacific[2] | Africa | Latin America & Caribbean | Others[3] | Total |
|------|-------------------|----------------|---------------------|--------|---------------------------|-----------|-------|
| 1945 | 9  | 6  | 8  | 4  | 20 | 4 | 151 |
| 1950 | 11 | 6  | 15 | 4  | 20 | 4 | 160 |
| 1955 | 17 | 10 | 20 | 5  | 20 | 4 | 176 |
| 1960 | 17 | 10 | 23 | 26 | 20 | 4 | 100 |
| 1965 | 18 | 10 | 27 | 37 | 22 | 4 | 118 |
| 1970 | 18 | 10 | 29 | 42 | 24 | 4 | 127 |
| 1975 | 19 | 11 | 36 | 47 | 27 | 4 | 144 |
| 1980 | 19 | 11 | 39 | 51 | 30 | 4 | 154 |
| 1985 | 19 | 11 | 41 | 51 | 33 | 4 | 159 |
| 1993 | 21 | 19 | 51 | 52 | 33 | 4 | 180 |
| 1998 | 23 | 20 | 52 | 53 | 33 | 4 | 185 |
| 1999 | 23 | 20 | 54 | 53 | 33 | 4 | 187 |
| 2000 | 24 | 21 | 55 | 53 | 33 | 4 | 190 |
| 2002 | 24 | 21 | 56 | 53 | 33 | 4 | 191 |

[1]Includes Turkey.

[2]Includes Israel as well as the former Soviet Republics that are geographically located in Asia.

[3]Includes Australia, Canada, New Zealand, and the United States.

stage and by giving them important lines to speak. A major example in the 1980s was the change in Soviet policy under the leadership of Mikhail Gorbachev. Moscow shifted from its narrow ideological course to make international cooperation through the United Nations an important Soviet priority. Indeed, the larger consequence of this shift was the end of the Cold War. The breakup of the Soviet Union that followed also led to each of the Soviet Union's fifteen republics becoming independent states and, in quick order, members of the United Nations.

## PRIVATE INTEREST GROUPS

While states are the central actors, the twentieth century saw a very important meshing of activity by private interest groups ("nongovernmental organizations" or NGOs in UN parlance) with the processes of intergovernmental bodies ("international governmental organizations" or IGOs). Business and commercial private organizations are often called BINGOs (business international nongovernmental organizations) or TNCs (transnational corporations) or MNCs (multinational corporations). International organizations having both governmental and nongovernmental members are sometimes categorized as IQUANGOs (international quasi-nongovernmental organizations). Although much of the contact is informal in nature, like the lobbying activity of domestic special interest groups in democratic states, a great deal of interest group consultation now takes place in all international organizations.

The International Labor Organization has gone the farthest in this direction, allowing participation with full voting rights to representatives of private interests. The ILO permits each member state to send four delegates to its general conference—two representing the government, one representing employer interests, and one chosen in consultation with national labor organizations. This combination of public and private interest representation dates from the formation of the ILO in 1919 and is still unique, but consultation without right of participation in debate and voting has become common in other intergovernmental bodies as well.

The UN Economic and Social Council, under Article 71 of the Charter, is authorized to "make suitable arrangements for consultation with nongovernmental organizations." ECOSOC acknowledges the right of these organizations to express their views and accepts that they often possess special experience or technical understanding vital to its work. More than fifteen hundred nongovernmental organizations had consultative status with ECOSOC in the closing years of the twentieth century, and these were divided into three categories: Category I, organizations having consultative interests that coincide with those of the Council; Category II, organizations having special competence in particular areas; and Category III, including so-called roster organizations, which are judged worthy of making occasional contributions to ECOSOC or its subsidiary organs, or other UN bodies. NGOs with consultative status may send observers to public meetings of ECOSOC and its subsidiary organizations and may also submit written statements relevant to ECOSOC's work. They are also permitted to consult with the UN Secretariat on matters of mutual concern.

The General Assembly has no formal consultative arrangements separate from the ECOSOC system, but representatives of NGOs try to make their presence felt in corridors, lounges, and meeting halls while the Assembly is in session. In 1978, during the tenth Special Session devoted to disarmament, the Assembly broke precedent by allowing representatives from a number of private organizations to address the assembled delegates.

Observer status was granted to the Palestine Liberation Organization (PLO) as the representative of the Palestinian people and to the South West Africa People's Organization (SWAPO) before Namibian independence. The African National Congress (ANC) was also an observer in debates on questions related to South Africa.

The importance of UN recognition is illustrated in the subsequent achievements of these different movements. The PLO was transformed into the Palestine Authority when Israel granted it political and administrative responsibility over most of the urban areas in the West Bank in mid-1990s. In July 1998, the UN General Assembly voted to upgrade the status of the Palestinian Authority to that of a virtual state. The Assembly voted 124 in favor and only 4 against, with 10 abstentions, to give the Palestinian Observer Group the new status of a nonvoting member in the General Assembly. With the new designation, Palestinian representatives could raise issues, cosponsor draft resolutions, and have a right to reply. The Palestinian representative, however, could not vote or put forward candidates for UN committees. In justifying the resolution, it was noted that the Palestinians already enjoyed membership in the Arab League, the Group of 77, and other regional organizations. The resolution also noted that the Palestinian Authority had been established only on part of what was described as occupied Palestinian territory. By its actions, therefore, the United Nations sought to increase the pressure on Israel to withdraw from the remaining Palestinian-defined territory. Only the United States, Israel, Micronesia, and the Marshall Islands voted against the resolution, which was seen as paving the way for full Palestinian membership in the world body. In fact, many of the member states already assumed that the Palestinian Authority was a credible member of the United Nations. Actual Palestinian membership, however, had to wait on still more favorable circumstances.

In the case of SWAPO, its observer status was transformed into full membership when Namibia achieved statehood in 1990. The ANC also discarded its observer status when it gained control of the South African government following its victory at the polls in 1994.

Most intergovernmental organizations have formal or informal arrangements for consultation with private groups. The volume of contacts frequently depends on the perceived capacity of the organization to affect group interests. The European Union, for example, is lobbied heavily because it has extensive power to regulate, reward, and punish the conduct of private groups and individuals. On a lesser scale, UNESCO is also an important focus of private group activity. Private groups and individuals are involved directly in many of its programs for education, science, and cultural interchange; and UNESCO can reward some of them with fellowships and scholarships, contracts for writing and publication, and subsidies to support private international societies fostering such interchange. UNESCO maintains additional private contacts through the national UNESCO commissions that have been formed in many member countries.

Private groups have been particularly active in environmental areas. Such groups have influence in many countries, and they have extended their efforts to the international arena as the global scope of environmental issues has come to be recognized. The UN Environment Programme (UNEP) has been effective in building links with national and international groups through which it cultivates support for programs to preserve the environment. Private groups also play an important and growing role in IGO activities relating to human rights and development assistance.

A notable increase in private group activity has been stimulated by the practice of holding special world conferences under UN auspices. As early as 1963, and again in 1970, the World Food Congresses sponsored by the Food and Agriculture Organization (FAO) were designed primarily for NGOs as a means of publicizing and enlisting support for FAO objectives. Since the 1972 Stockholm Conference on the Human Environment, the more common pattern has been to hold intergovernmental conferences on special subjects with informal participation and sometimes "parallel" conference activities by NGO representatives. Among the conferences that attracted interest and vigorous NGO participation were the Conference on Environment and Development held in Rio de Janeiro (1992), a conference on women's issues assembled in Beijing

(1995), the UN Framework Convention on Climate Change convened in Kyoto (1997), and the Rome conference concerned with the Establishment of an International Criminal Court (1998). Also of note in recent years were the General Assembly Special Sessions on the world drug problem (1998), on population and development (1999), on women (2000), on HIV/AIDS (2001), and on children (2002).[1]

Participation at world conferences includes the usual forms of lobbying at meetings and, often, working with Secretariat administrators or national governments in preparation for the conference program. Increasingly, it has included appeals to the media and their mass public audiences. NGOs lobby media representatives at international conferences, hoping to shape the reporting. Many NGO representatives themselves hold press accreditation from local newspapers or broadcasting stations and send out their own news reports. Such NGO activity has carried over to General Assembly Special Sessions on economic development and on disarmament.

Generalizing about the role of private interest groups is not always helpful. There is wide variation from one intergovernmental organization to another, and it is all too easy to equate such activity with gaining leverage. UN representatives often tend to view NGOs as vehicles for building public support for IGO programs rather than as coparticipants in UN decision making. Speeches delivered by NGO representatives (where permitted) or papers submitted to ECOSOC or some other UN body are easily ignored, and most have little effect beyond the satisfaction felt by the NGO representatives in expressing their points of view. The same, of course, can be said of most speeches delivered by governmental delegates.

In other contexts, NGO activity may be important. Where NGO cooperation is essential or helpful in carrying out IGO programs—for example, refugee relief, cultural exchange, or programs for economic and social development—their emphasis on the details of a situation may be considerable. NGOs with national constituencies may also affect policy decisions through their connections with national governments. Groups that have political clout with governments are likely to have the ear of international secretariats as well, especially if the interests of the group and the secretariat converge. When Secretariat administrators recognize the need for NGO involvement, group input can be substantial in developing position papers and documentation for UN conferences. Environmental groups, for example, have been politically effective in the United States, Western Europe, and some other countries and as a result have been able to work closely with the staff of international agencies in environmental areas to promote common goals. Advice and support of environmental groups was extensively utilized by the international staff assigned to prepare for the 1992 UN Conference on Environment and Development (UNCED).

As in the national arena, lobbying by private groups is a matter of resources. Thus vigorous lobbying can be expected in a setting such as the European Union, where supranational agencies have a capacity to promote—or injure—private interests in a direct and substantial way. Many of the affected groups, including large national and multinational corporations, have resources to conduct extensive lobbying with community organs and member governments and do not hesitate to use those resources when important interests are at stake.

Sometimes, special circumstances enhance the role of a particular group. In preliminary negotiating sessions preceding the June 1992 UNCED meetings, the United States took a strong stand against including in the global warming treaty any reference to achieving environmental goals by reducing economic consumption in the Northern Hemisphere. In retaliation, the developing countries proposed to remove from the treaty all reference to slowing population growth. This opened the way for vigorous and effective lobbying by the Vatican, a political force in many countries, against inclusion of provisions that might be inconsistent with the Catholic Church's position on birth control.

Even groups with limited lobbying resources can sometimes have an effect through high-quality research or a good idea proposed at the right time. Once a resolution or recommendation has been adopted, NGOs may serve as gadflies to the international body politic, monitoring compliance by governments and the subsequent follow-up by the Secretariat. This is particularly evident in the area of human rights where private humanitarian groups have been very active in revealing evidence collected on human rights violations and making them public. With the growth of extensive national and transnational group networks having international interests, NGO participation in international organizations must be regarded as an important part of the political process.

How important NGOs have become was dramatized in 1997–98 when Secretary-General Kofi Annan proposed sweeping reforms aimed at preparing the United Nations for its role in the twenty-first century. Although a description of these reforms is reserved for the following chapter, it is important to cite Annan's strategy to more heavily enlist the services of the NGOs and to make them "welcome partners" in UN efforts dealing with humanitarian causes. UN coordination efforts in 1997–98 assumed new credence after directives were issued from the Secretary-General to the Office of the UN High Commissioner for Refugees, UNICEF, and the World Food Program. These directives called on these agencies to work "in close concert" with the NGOs in all regions around the world. Most notable was the concern shown for the famine-stricken areas of the People's Democratic Republic of Korea and the drought-affected region of the Great Lakes region of Africa that had brought untold suffering to hundreds of thousands of people. The directives also focused attention on Iraq in the aftermath of the 1990–91 Gulf War, where UN sanctions had imposed a special burden on the country's young people.

## THE INTERNATIONAL ADMINISTRATOR AS POLITICAL PARTICIPANT

The political functions of international secretariats will be discussed in a subsequent chapter, but a description of participants in the political process would be incomplete without a brief reference to the international civil servant. The executive head of an international secretariat is often in a position to have an influence on policy. In organizations with large budgets for operational programs, this executive is likely to be the most effective individual participant and may initiate proposals as well as join actively in formal and informal discussion of matters to be decided by members of the organization. Success will of course vary with the type of organization, the nature of the issue, and the individual attributes of the incumbent. All UN Secretaries-General have felt a responsibility to bring the weight of their authority to bear on issues confronting the United Nations, some with more success than others.

Secretariat leverage on the political process is not restricted to the activities of the chief administrator. Others farther down the hierarchy participate as well. Experience and expertise may qualify secretariat civil servants for the role of counselor or informal adviser to delegates whose respect and friendship they have earned, or sometimes for an intermediary's role when compromise is required. Many seasoned secretariat members, steeped in the practice of an agency, provide an indispensable institutional memory that many member states rely on. Formal reports or opinions prepared by secretariats provide part of the informational base for some decisions. Decisions relating to the operation of agency programs often depend on information from the people who administer the programs. Nor can one overlook the substantial policy implications of budget preparation, a task regularly performed by secretariats, albeit with careful supervision by representatives of member states.

## INTERNATIONAL ORGANIZATIONS AS PARTICIPANTS

The participation of international organizations in the decisions of other international organizations, including organizations outside the UN system, is now a pervasive feature of international relations. Representatives of the European Union speak for the community in international tariff negotiations, and the World Trade Organization maintains contact with EU authorities in Brussels. Members of the European Union frequently address economic matters in UN forums through a common spokesperson. In the UN Development Program, the participating intergovernmental organizations jockey vigorously to leverage the allocation of available funds. Coordination in technical assistance matters is indispensable and often facilitated by interagency committees. Representatives of UN specialized agencies regularly participate in the work of ECOSOC, and regional organizations frequently collaborate with UN bodies in dealing with common problems. The General Assembly has adopted resolutions granting formal consultative status to a number of regional organizations, including the Commonwealth of Nations, the European Union, the Islamic Conference, the League of Arab States, the Organization of African Unity, the Organization of American States, and the Caribbean Community. The International Committee of the Red Cross, a hybrid IGO/NGO, also participates as an Assembly observer. Such arrangements illustrate an often forgotten political fact—that international organizations are more than mere channels for national diplomatic activity. An international organization with permanent institutions is itself a political entity capable of participating in the political processes of the international system.

# UN DECISION MAKING

National interest and power may ultimately determine who gets what in the international arena, but perceptions of interest and use of power are influenced by the institutions through which power is exercised. The most important questions that can be asked about international organization relate to the ways in which participation changes national perceptions of interest and affects the exercise of national power. Absolute answers have not been found—and perhaps never will be—but the questions should be asked. The following sections present information that may be helpful in framing tentative answers.

## NATIONAL ORGANIZATION FOR UN PARTICIPATION

Membership in the United Nations requires countries to adopt positions on a multitude of issues ranging in diversity from war in the Middle East to stabilization of world prices for copper and cotton to refugee relief in Africa. Many countries feel compelled to formulate policy on particular issues that never would have concerned them except for their participation in the United Nations. There is, of course, a wide variation in the thoroughness of preparation for UN discussions. States with substantial resources and broad foreign policy interests are likely to prepare detailed instructions for their UN representatives. Delegates from tiny states with limited interests and meager resources may have little guidance beyond the country's general foreign policy orientation, level of development, bloc associations, and the known predilections of its leaders.

The United States illustrates a very extensive adaptation to UN participation. Within the State Department, a Bureau of International Organization Affairs (IO) is concerned exclusively with coordinating U.S. policy in the United Nations and other multilateral agencies. The IO does not do it alone, however. Every major unit of the State Department is involved in preparation for UN meetings because the agendas run the full range of U.S. foreign policy interests. Indeed, every major department of government has interests in the activities of one or more international groups. People from every department participate in international conferences. Interagency clearances are utilized to make sure that all relevant governmental interests are represented and, it is hoped, to bring consistency to U.S. representation at different international meetings. Perfect consistency is usually an unattained ideal because of the varying agency perspectives (health, labor, commerce, defense, etc.) and the different personnel representing the United States in different international organizations. Other countries have the same problems of coordinating their own policies, often to a greater degree.

If an issue is to come before the United Nations, the IO has responsibility for clarifying the possible policy alternatives and preparing position papers to guide U.S. representatives in the United Nations. This, again, is not a self-contained operation. It is usually accomplished through a small working group—a temporary interoffice committee that includes representation from geographic and other interested bureaus—that does the groundwork and makes the initial policy recommendations. Position preparation may also require coordination with other executive departments through an interdepartmental coordination committee. This is a far cry from the behavior of a microstate, which may send no instructions at all to its UN representatives, but it shows the extent to which a major state must adapt its governmental machinery to the needs of UN participation.

## Missions and Delegations

Nearly all UN members maintain permanent missions to the United Nations in New York. Most also have permanent representation at the UN European office in Geneva. The mission chief, or permanent representative, usually holds the diplomatic rank of ambassador. Mission size varies with the interests and resources of the state. The smaller missions may have only one or two people of diplomatic rank plus a couple of clerical employees, whereas the United States maintains a permanent staff of about 150. In times past the size of the Soviet mission approached 300 (including personnel assigned to the ostensibly separate missions for Ukraine and Byelorussia), but the Russian mission now maintains a staff comparable to that of the United States.

The permanent mission represents a country's interests in the United Nations much as an embassy represents its interests in a foreign capital. The functions of the permanent mission differ in many respects from those of the traditional diplomatic mission, however, because the United Nations is a multilateral organization rather than a government. Members of the permanent mission perform the traditional diplomatic functions of representation, negotiation, information gathering, and reporting. But at the United Nations this is done multilaterally with more than 190 states rather than bilaterally with one. Although bilateral and multilateral contacts occur among diplomats assigned to any national capital, such contacts are incidental to the primary mission of representation to the host government and are not the fundamental object. The UN diplomat, on the other hand, deals constantly with many national viewpoints and policies and often operates through procedures more congenial to national parliaments than to chanceries and foreign departments. The UN diplomat also deals with a broader spectrum of issues, frequently of a technical nature. This, as Seymour Maxwell Finger observes, "promotes a greater degree of autonomy for the mission, as few governments can keep track of so many details and the government is more dependent on the mission for relevant information."[2]

Permanent representation at the United Nations is essential for the fifteen members of the Security Council, which, under Article 28 of the Charter, must "be so organized as to be able to function continuously." Most other countries also believe it useful for a variety of reasons. The Assembly is in session for at least three months of every year. The fifty-four states elected to ECOSOC generally hold one five- to six-week-long substantive session each year, alternating between New York and Geneva, and one organizational meeting in New York City. The substantive session includes a high-level special meeting, attended by ministers and other high officials, who discuss major economic and social issues. The year-round work of ECOSOC is carried out in its subsidiary bodies—commissions and committees—which meet at regular intervals and report back to the main ECOSOC body. Numerous other UN committees, commissions, and subsidiary bodies hold meetings in New York as well. (See Table 3-3 for a sample of the diversity of UN meetings.) For states that have no current meeting in session, there is a continuing need to prepare for forthcoming meetings, engage in preliminary negotiations, maintain working relations with the UN Secretariat, monitor the operation of UN activities, and stay in contact with other UN missions.

Diplomatic discussions in New York are by no means limited to matters on a UN agenda. The existence of so many diplomatic missions in one location makes the United Nations the world's busiest center for bilateral diplomacy. Most UN members are small states that cannot afford to maintain embassies in very many other countries. If they are geographically distant from one another, the volume of contacts among their government and citizens does not justify the expense. Yet they may have some common interests, and the United Nations provides a setting where they can discuss issues and maintain diplomatic contact, whether or not the matter is a subject of immediate UN concern.

The United Nations is not the only alternative to exchanging ambassadors. Other possibilities range from unilateral representation (receiving but not sending an ambassador) to multiple accreditation (accrediting an ambassador in one country to others in the area) to third-country representation (communicating with a second country through the embassy of a third) to joint representation (two governments accrediting a single envoy). Permanent representation at the United Nations is helpful, but in normal circumstances it is not absolutely essential, especially where the smaller states are concerned. UN representation in fact does not replace direct representation in countries that are vital to the functioning of small states. The United Nations nevertheless provides states with the opportunity to dramatically assert their sovereignty, and, not to be overlooked, it also provides lesser as well as larger powers with two representatives in the United States. In sum, the United Nations is a useful channel of communication. Moreover, contacts made at the United Nations may be particularly helpful for states confronted with hostile challenges or threats, for whom the normal channels of communication may not be fully adequate.

A "delegation" in UN parlance consists of personnel accredited to represent a country at a particular UN meeting or series of meetings. For the General Assembly, each state is entitled by the Charter to five representatives and

TABLE 3-3    Past UN Conferences and General Assembly Special Sessions, 1994–2002

| Date | Event |
| --- | --- |
| 1994 | Global Conference on Sustainable Development of Small Island Developing States (Barbados, 25 April–6 May)<br>International Conference on Population and Development [ICPD] (Cairo, September)<br>World Conference on Natural Disaster Reduction<br>World Summit on Trade Efficiency |
| 1995 | Fourth World Conference on Women (Beijing, China, September)<br>World Summit for Social Development (Copenhagen, Denmark, 6–12 March)<br>Conference on Straddling & Highly Migratory Fish Stocks |
| 1996 | Second United Nations Conference on Human Settlements [Habitat II] (Istanbul, Turkey, 3–14 June) |
| 1997 | Earth Summit+5 (23–27 June) |
| 1998 | World Conference of Ministers Responsible for Youth (Lisbon, Portugal, 8–12 August)<br>UN Conference on the Establishment of an International Criminal Court (Rome, Italy, 15 June–17 July)<br>General Assembly Twentieth special session—World Drug Problem (New York, 8–10 June) |
| 1999 | Small Island Developing States (Special Session of the General Assembly, 27–28 September)<br>52nd Annual DPI/NGO Conference—Challenges of a Globalized World: Finding New Directions (New York, 15–17 September)<br>Third United Nations Conference on the Exploration and Peaceful Uses of Outer Space [UNISPACE III] (Vienna, 19–30 July)<br>Webcast of the High-level segment of the substantive session of the Economic and Social Council (Geneva, 5–7 July)<br>International Conference on Population and Development [ICPD+5] (Special Session of the General Assembly, New York, 30 June–2 July)<br>Fighting Landmines: First Meeting of States Parties (Maputo, Mozambique, 3–7 May) |
| 2000 | United Nations Convention against Transnational Organized Crime (Palermo, Italy, 12–15 December)<br>Millennium Summit: "The role of the United Nations in the 21st century" (New York, 6–8 September)<br>53rd Annual DPI/NGO Conference (New York, 28–30 August)<br>World Summit for Social Development and Beyond: Achieving Social Development for All in a Globalized World (Session of the General Assembly—Geneva, Switzerland, 26–30 June)<br>Review the implementation of the Nairobi Forward-looking Strategies for the Advancement of Women and of the Declaration and Platform for Action—Beijing +5 Review (Special Session of the General Assembly, 5–9 June)<br>Crime and Justice: Meeting the Challenges of the Twenty-first Century (Vienna, Austria, 10–17 April)<br>UNCTAD X—Tenth Session of the Conference on Trade and Development (Bangkok, 12–19 February) |
| 2001 | Conference on facilitating the entry into force of the Comprehensive Nuclear-Test-Ban treaty (New York, 11–13 November) |

TABLE 3-3    *(continued)*

| Date | Event |
|------|-------|
| | World Conference against racism, racial discrimination, xenophobia and related intolerance (Durban, South Africa, 31 August–7 September) |
| | United Nations Conference on the Illicit Trade in Small Arms and Light Weapons in All Its Aspects (New York, 9–20 July) |
| | Problem of human immunodeficiency virus/acquired immunodeficiency syndrome (HIV/AIDS) in all its aspects (Special Session of the General Assembly, New York, 25–27 June) |
| | Implementation of the outcome of the United Nations Conference on Human Settlements [Habitat II] (Special Session of the General Assembly, New York, 6–8 June) |
| | Third United Nations Conference on the Least Developed Countries (Brussels, 14–20 May) |
| 2002 | The World Summit on Sustainable Development (Johannesburg, South Africa, 26 August–4 September) |
| | World Food Summit: five years later (Rome, Italy, 10–13 June) |
| | General Assembly Special Session on Children (New York, 8–10 May) |
| | Second World Assembly on Ageing (Madrid, Spain, 8–12 April) |
| | International Conference on Financing for Development (Monterrey, 18–22 March) |
| | United Nations Conferences and Observances (Reference Paper 41) |

SOURCE: UN Web site (http://www.un.org/events/conferences.htm).

five alternates, with no constitutional limitation on the clerical or advisory staff, which usually consists of permanent mission personnel as well as people from foreign offices, diplomatic posts, or other governmental agencies. It is customary for the permanent representative to be the chief delegate, but he or she is often outranked on the delegation by the foreign minister. Occasionally, a permanent representative's head of state or head of government, who may attend part of a session, will supercede him or her. Some states send a full delegation of professional diplomats while others include people from other ministries of government. Many, including the United States, send one or more members of the national legislature and prominent people from private life.

UN delegates are akin to both legislators and diplomats. This duality is recognized by use of the term *parliamentary diplomacy* to designate what goes on at meetings of the United Nations and other international organizations. Procedures for agenda setting, debate, and decisions by vote are not unlike those in a national legislature. So also are the informal activities of discussion, persuasion, and compromise in drafting resolutions embodying areas of common interest that are designed to command a voting majority.

But delegates are still diplomats. They come as representatives of their governments to negotiate agreements rather than as representatives of their constituency to enact laws. Except for procedural and organizational matters, General Assembly resolutions are not legally binding on states. As governmental agents, delegates must act not only in the interest of their countries but also in conformity with their governments' instructions. There are, of course, vast differences in the quality of instructions from one delegation to another. Some delegations are given lengthy and detailed instructions that severely limit their freedom to maneuver. Some governments instruct their delegations in terms of the positions of other governments, that is, vote like . . . or if . . . votes "no," abstain. Some governments provide no instructions at all, leaving matters to the discretion of the delegation. Instructions are likely to be more detailed on questions of great importance to a government, such as a war in which that government is involved.

Even the most meticulous instructions do not rule out all freedom of action. Like all diplomats, UN delegates can alter the content of their instructions by the information and advice they send to their foreign offices. Their degree of influence, however, depends on their political standing at home, as well as on the force of their arguments. If a government has a strong interest in the United Nations as an institution, it may be more willing to listen to members of the delegation or the permanent mission. If, on the other hand, a particular issue touches important interests of a country, the UN representatives' margin for maneuver and their ability to shape policy may be reduced.

The UN setting demands leeway for delegates because no government can fully anticipate every twist and turn of UN parliamentary diplomacy. All delegations have a large measure of discretion as to tactics and at least some discretion to make minor adjustments of substance. If changed instructions are desired, the delegation's judgment will be given weight because of its position on the UN firing line. The bottom line, nevertheless, is the government's control over its diplomats. Notwithstanding the freedom of action and policy entailed by the parliamentary setting, delegations to international meetings have a responsiveness to their governments that is unmatched by any ordinary relationship of a national legislator to a voting constituency or, in democratic societies at least, to a political party.

## The Institutional Setting of UN Decision Making

National interest and national power supply the dynamics of the political process in international organization, but the outcome is also affected by the institutional setting. One obvious institutional constraint is the subject matter competence of the organization. Limited-purpose organizations such as the UN specialized agencies are limited by their Charters to a particular subject area, such as the promotion of world health, funding of development, or regulation of maritime transport. Regional organizations, by reason of membership as well as constitutional prescription, focus on matters of particular concern to states of the region. The United Nations, by its nature as a general international organization, is much less restrictive in scope. Its legal purview extends to virtually everything under the sun except matters "essentially within the domestic jurisdiction" of a state. Never very limiting, the domestic jurisdiction restriction has grown smaller as human rights, the environment, and other formerly domestic concerns have become subjects of extensive international action. In practice, UN members discuss any subject they wish because the issue of jurisdiction has always been reduced to who has the votes to put an item on the agenda or keep it off.

Two other institutional features must be considered in greater detail because they so profoundly affect the perception of national interests and the exercise of national power within the United Nations. One is the body of rules and practices that govern voting and formal decision making in the organization. The other consists of the formal and informal communication structures that characterize the UN's political process. Each will be examined in the pages that follow.

### Voting in the International Arena

If decision-making procedures within an international organization accurately mirror the actual distribution of national power, the effect of procedure on the exercise of power is minimal. But this rarely occurs because power is not easily measured, power patterns change over time, less-powerful states are generally unwilling to accept rules that show their impotence, and larger states have learned to live with rules that emphasize sovereign equality above national power. In practice, the three most common decision rules of modern international organizations are decision by vote, one vote per state, and majority rule. When these three rules are combined in an organization of wide membership, an imbalance between internal and external power relationships is unavoidable.

Voting has become so common on the international scene that one can easily forget its recent origins. Modern international organizations emerged only in the nineteenth century, and voting as a means of international decision making is a product of that development. The international conferences of an earlier period were primarily negotiating bodies without "action" responsibilities. Their function was to negotiate agreements to be embodied in treaty form for approval by the respective national governments. Voting implies a process of deciding—and the right of decision belonged to governments individually, not to representatives of states gathered at international meetings. Moreover, the principles of national sovereignty and sovereign equality demanded nothing less than complete dispersal of decision-making authority among national units.

With the development of international organizations having permanent secretariats, organizational budgets, and special subject matter expertise, a new dimension was added to interstate relations. The organizations themselves became entities with legal personalities distinct from those of their member states. Budgeted funds, though raised primarily through national contributions, were disbursed by the organization, and secretariats did the bidding of the collectivity—not of the individual members. A growing number of decisions of international organizations became operative immediately, without referral to the treaty approval process. Voting, a time-honored practice in domestic processes, was readily transferred to the new setting.

The shift of real, if limited, decision-making power to international organizations placed unavoidable strain on national sovereignty and equality. In a strictly juridical context states may be equal in their legal rights and duties with respect to the world community. In any other context, including that of international organizations, the notion of state equality verges on pure fantasy because states neither have equality of interest in the substance of organizational decisions nor equal capacity to implement them. Sovereign equality suggests that each state should have an equal voice in the decisions of the organization, but this can only result in a divorce of power to decide responsibility for implementing a decision.

The principle of sovereignty gives rise to the further implication that no state can be bound without its consent. Carried to a logical conclusion, this could mean that decisions should be taken only by a unanimous vote. The problem is practical rather than legal. If a state joins the United Nations, it consents to the decision rules of the organization. Thus it is not bound without its consent. In practice, however, states are very reluctant to assume particular obligations to which they object even if they have given general assent to the voting procedures. But such hesitation or reluctance strikes at the capacity of the organization to produce meaningful decisions, and the United Nations often is compelled to seek something less than unanimity on controversial issues. If unanimity is insisted upon, decisions may never be made on subjects of vital interest to the international community. It is also true that decisions taken without full support of the member states may result in the dilution of the action so that nothing of substance is agreed upon. Some decisions, of course, cannot be carried out very effectively without the concurrence of the states most directly connected. Economic aid programs will falter without the support of the wealthier contributors. Resolutions will not achieve their aims without acceptance by the targeted governments. But many decisions, certainly those involving joint action among states disposed to cooperate, can be made and acted on without the concurrence of other states having little practical interest in or responsibility for the matter.

International organizations often display varying kinds of compromise between principle and practicality. Equality of voting rights is the general rule, although its effect has been blunted in several ways, and a few organizations have rejected it in favor of a distribution of voting rights more accurately revealing differences in national interests and the distribution of power. This is true of some organizations whose primary function is the handling of money—the International Bank, the International Monetary Fund, the International Finance Corporation, and the International Development Association—where voting power is governed by amount of contribution. Commodity councils, such as the wheat and sugar councils, allot votes according to the volume of imports and exports of the commodity. Still another form of unequal or weighted voting is found in the Central Commission for the Navigation of the Rhine, where voting rights, for certain purposes, are roughly proportional to river frontage. These illustrations suggest that weighted voting is most feasible where the weighting principle can be tied to a single measurable criterion directly related to the primary function of the organization.

When weighted voting is not acceptable, organizations often recognize differences among states by the creation of special executive or deliberative bodies of limited membership on which representation can be granted according to some rough approximation of interest and power. Thus the five largest states in the World War II UN coalition were made permanent members of the Security Council. Ten of the twenty-eight seats on the International Labor Organization governing body are given to states of high "industrial importance." States of "chief importance in air transport" are given preference in the election of the International Civil Aviation Organization Council, and eligibility for selection to the Council of the International Maritime Organization is determined by a state's interest in shipping and maritime trade. As further recognition of their special status, the five permanent members of the Security Council were given representation on the UN Trusteeship Council, ECOSOC, and most other UN bodies on which they desire membership. A national of each permanent member is usually chosen to sit on the fifteen-member International Court of Justice.

If sovereign equality has been somewhat eroded by schemes of weighted voting and unequal representation on limited-membership bodies, the rule of unanimity has suffered a more far-reaching eclipse. Unanimity still governs some organizations of limited membership, including the NATO Council, the Arab League Council, and the Council of the Organization for Economic Cooperation and Development, but most international organizations now can act by a simple or qualified majority. Even in the UN Security Council, which retains the principle of unanimity for permanent members, decisions require only nine of fifteen votes.

Majority voting, with its inherent derogation from sovereign prerogatives, is the price paid for some degree of organizational success. The spread of majority voting in international organizations does not necessarily mean the triumph of "majority rule" in international affairs, however. To pass a resolution by majority vote is one thing; to take action that is practically effective and legally binding on all members is quite another. A careful examination of the law and practice of international organizations reveals that majorities have much more authority to recommend than to command and that their authority to command is largely limited to matters eliciting a high degree of consensus or not seriously impinging on the vital interests of states. The Universal Postal Union, for example, can alter certain postal regulations by a two-thirds majority vote. This is possible because of the substantial consensus on Union objectives. Most international organizations can adopt binding rules governing the operations of their secretariats, for example, the filling of electoral posts, the expenditure of budgeted funds, and other housekeeping activities. Although such "lawmaking" power is important, it does not ordinarily affect the vital interests of states.[3]

Except for power over internal operations, one looks almost without success for authority to make binding decisions in any of the policy-making organs of the United Nations. The General Assembly, the Economic and Social Council, and the virtually defunct Trusteeship Council are clearly limited to nonbinding recommendations. Under Chapter VII of the Charter, members are obligated to assist with military, economic, and diplomatic sanctions imposed by the Security Council in dealing with a "threat to the peace, breach of the peace, or act of aggression." However, the Security Council's authority to make binding decisions for the use of military force has thus far remained dormant for lack of special agreements, under Article 43, on the composition of forces to be available on call for UN use. And, until the 1990s, a majority in favor of compulsory nonmilitary sanctions has been a rarity. For most purposes the Security Council, like the General Assembly, has been limited to exhortation rather than command.

## Voting in the General Assembly

Decision procedures in the General Assembly combine the elements of sovereign equality and majority voting with persistent reluctance to let majorities legislate. Each member state is allotted one vote, regardless of size or capacity to contribute to the purposes of the organization. Decisions on "important questions" require a two-thirds majority of members present and voting. Certain types of "important questions" are specified in the Charter. As listed in Article 18, such questions include

> recommendations with respect to the maintenance of international peace and security, the election of the non-permanent members of the Security Council, the election of members of the Economic and Social Council, the election of members of the Trusteeship Council . . . , the admission of new Members to the United Nations, the suspension of the rights and privileges of membership, the expulsion of Members, questions relating to the operation of the trusteeship system, and budgetary questions.

Other matters are decided by a simple majority vote, including the decision to designate other questions or categories of questions as "important" enough to require a two-thirds majority. In calculating the existence of a required majority, the General Assembly has adopted the practice of excluding abstentions as well as absences from the count of states present and voting. With a large number of abstentions, even an important measure can be adopted by considerably less than a majority of the total membership. Decisions in the Economic and Social Council, the now-suspended Trusteeship Council, and subordinate UN committees and commissions are made by simple majority of the members present and voting, but their decisions are all subject to review by the General Assembly, with its two-thirds requirement for important questions. Just a few categories of decisions require a majority based on total membership. These include an absolute majority for election to the International Court of Justice, under Article 10 of the ICJ Statute, and a two-thirds majority for the proposal of Charter amendments, as provided in Article 109 of the UN Charter.

In the decades since the framing of the UN Charter, dissatisfaction with Assembly voting rules has frequently been voiced. Equality of voting rights has been the most persistent source of concern. The expansion of the United Nations to include many small states created since 1945 has multiplied the voting disparity of small states over large. Third World states now have the voting strength to obtain a two-thirds majority on any issue of importance to them. Mathematically, a two-thirds vote could even be mustered by states collectively representing less than 15 percent of the world's population. This extreme case does not occur, however, because the prevailing Third World majority usually includes such populous countries as China, India, and Indonesia.

Even in the days of U.S. ascendance, the Assembly was prone to adopt resolutions that were totally unacceptable to states in the minority whose cooperation was essential to achieving the purposes of the resolutions. Today, with voting dominance of mostly small and poor developing countries, the gap between the power to decide and the power to implement decisions has further increased. The readiness of small states to use their collective voting power to sway UN outcomes is understandable. It is a form of political leverage. It can sometimes be used to win meaningful compromises from industrialized states. It can in any event be used to win parliamentary victories. But major power disenchantment with equality of voting rights is also understandable. And the effectiveness of the organization is diminished when groups of states, through frustration over the course of events or with the slow pace of negotiations or enthusiasm for a parliamentary cause, resort to an empty display of voting power that cuts short the hard search for genuine agreement. The long-running General Assembly Tenth Emergency Session on Palestine may be a case in point. The Security Council, hampered by a U.S. veto, failed to approve a resolution condemning Israel for its construction of a wall separating Israel from the occupied West Bank territory. The General Assembly Emergency Session immediately assumed control of the issue, and on October 21, 2003, it approved a resolution condemning Israel and demanding it to cease action and remove the wall. The vote was 144 to 4, with 12 abstentions. Member states opposing the resolution were the United States, Israel, the Federated States of Micronesia, and the Marshall Islands. Various forms of weighted voting have been broached as a remedy to this problem, but no one has yet devised a plan acceptable to a majority of states, not to mention the two-thirds majority required for Charter amendment. Small states, certainly, are unlikely to voluntarily relinquish the advantage they enjoy under the present system. The remedy, if any, must lie in national self-restraint, but given the volatility of issues such as the Israeli-Palestinian conflict, such is not anticipated.

Even though formal amendment of UN voting arrangements has not been possible, the members have come to recognize the need for alternatives to deciding by majority vote. The result has been extensive use of a "consensus" approach to decision making. Instead of taking a vote on a proposed resolution, a procedural decision, or some other matter, the presiding member simply announces his or her understanding that the measure commands general support and is hence to be considered adopted by consensus. This expedites the decision procedure when there is genuine consensus on an agreed text. It is also useful when general agreement has been reached on action to be taken, but drafting a concise text might prove taxing. Approving the chair's more or less vague summation averts possibly extensive wrangling over details. Sometimes the consensus procedure is used when substantial disagreement exists but the meeting is willing to adopt a particular text without a vote. This permits a decision without forcing a defeated minority to make its opposition or abstention part of the permanent public record, although some members may still choose to express their objections or reservations to the adopted text. In some sessions of the Assembly, decisions by consensus have outnumbered decisions by majority vote. For example, of 387 resolutions and decisions adopted by the 1990 General Assembly, 297 (77 percent) were decided without a vote, that is, by consensus.[4]

### Voting in the Security Council

At the 1945 San Francisco Conference the great powers insisted that their special responsibility for maintaining international peace and security should be recognized in the voting procedures of the Security Council. Thus China, France, the United Kingdom, the United States, and the Soviet Union were made permanent members of the Security Council, and each was given a veto over "nonprocedural" matters. The issue involved far more than mere concern for the status of the great powers. Without the concurrence of all the major powers, the United Nations could conceivably engage in an enforcement action that it could not complete for lack of cooperation from an essential collaborator. Worse yet, a decision to use force in the name of the United Nations over the objection of a state controlling large military forces could be the means of turning localized violence into world war. The veto was intended to avoid such situations and, above all, to preclude initiation of enforcement action directly against one of the major powers. In the words of one of the architects of the Charter, "This would be the equivalent of a world war, and a decision to embark upon such a war would necessarily have to be made by each of the other nations for itself and not by any international organization."[5]

In practice, the United Nations has not had the important military enforcement role envisioned by the framers, but the veto has still served a useful purpose in preventing the organization from overreaching itself by treading too heavily on the toes of the great powers. All of the permanent members continue to value its protection. From 1946 to 1969, the Soviet Union cast 105 vetoes and the United States none. Between 1976 and September 2003, however, the United States cast 66 vetoes to only 8 by the Soviet Union/Russia. Since the founding of the United Nations to 2003, the United States had cast a grand total of 78 vetoes to 121 for the Soviet Union/Russia. Of the 252 vetoes cast by all the permanent members from 1945 to 2003, China registered 3, France 18, and Great Britain 32 (see Table 3-4).

TABLE 3-4 Vetoes in the Security Council, 1946–2003

| PERIOD | CHINA | FRANCE | BRITAIN | UNITED STATES | USSR/ RUSSIA | TOTAL |
|---|---|---|---|---|---|---|
| 1946–55 | — | 2 | — | — | 80 | 82 |
| 1956–72 | 1 | 2 | 10 | 2 | 32 | 47 |
| 1973–85 | — | 11 | 14 | 44 | 7 | 76 |
| 1986–91 | — | 3 | 8 | 23 | — | 34 |
| 1992–2003 | 2 | — | — | 9 | 2 | 13 |
| Total | 3 | 18 | 32 | 78 | 121 | 252* |

SOURCE: Table prepared by Celine Nahory, Giji Gya and Misaki Watanabe (http://www.global policy.org/security/membership/veto/vetosubj.htm) from data in Sydney D. Bailey and Sam Daws, *The Procedures of the UN Security Council,* 3rd edition (Oxford: Clarendon Press, 1998). Updated by author.

*Only a minority of vetoes was cast in cases concerned with vital security issues. Fifty-nine vetoes were cast to block admission of member states. These vetoes appear in the table. In addition, 43 vetoes have been used to block nominees for Secretary-General. These vetoes were cast in closed sessions and are not included in the table.

A new and disturbing use of the veto was registered when China in 1999 cast a negative vote against the continuation of the UN Preventive Deployment Force (UNPREDEP) in the Former Yugoslav Republic of Macedonia. UNPREDEP, a force meant to quell unrest before it intensified, was the first preventive peacekeeping operation in UN history. Moreover, China's veto of UNPREDEP was used because Macedonia had diplomatically and formally recognized the Republic of China (Taiwan) in return for its economic assistance. The closing of the UNPREDEP mission, however, did not mean the withdrawal of all the peacekeeping forces.

*Bypassing the Veto: The Kosovo Case*

NATO forces that had been linked with the UN mission in Macedonia had in fact been increased and were formed into an extraction force, to be used if required, to assist in the removal of UN, OSCE (Organization for Security and Cooperation in Europe), and other observer monitors in Kosovo, across the Macedonian border. In fact, the monitors were ordered out of Kosovo after Serbia rejected a NATO plan for settling the strife in the Serbian province. Thus when NATO began its air campaign against Serbia, the NATO extraction force was given still another mission. NATO's presence provided assurance that the territorial integrity of neighboring states would be protected from Serbian forces in embattled Kosovo. Moreover, the allied bombing of Serbia had accelerated Belgrade's ethnic cleansing, and Serbian military and paramilitary forces had moved aggressively against the Kosovo Liberation Army and the entire population of Albanian Kosovars. The result was a flood of refugees, forcibly removed from their land and forced to take refuge in neighboring areas of Macedonia, Albania, and Montenegro. NATO's intrusion, however, stemmed the flow of this refugee tide. NATO indeed proved a formidable force in opposing Serbia, and its success in Kosovo amply demonstrated the utility of the codeployment principle when the United Nations was itself unable to take forceful action because of the use of the veto.

Serbia's humiliation in Bosnia and ultimately in Kosovo in time prompted the ouster of the government of Slobodan Milošević and the eventual arrest of Milošević and many of his political followers, who were transferred by the new Belgrade government to the International Criminal Court in The Hague. Milošević's trial for war crimes began in 2002, and a verdict was not expected before 2005. Serbia's shift to a more democratic form of governance under new leadership nevertheless left NATO forces in Kosovo, with the United Nations confined to a humanitarian role. A major consideration in using NATO forces against Milošević's Serbia was the paralysis in the UN Security Council. Moreover, Russia had voiced support for Belgrade and adamantly opposed interference in Kosovo, which Moscow argued affected Serbia's territorial integrity and exclusive jurisdiction. Debate in the Security Council delayed the taking of a firm stand against Serbia. It no doubt also would have produced a veto on any resolution authorizing the use of force against Belgrade. The decision by Washington and its European allies, therefore, was to bypass the United Nations and deploy NATO troops in Kosovo. In the end, the China veto of a UN peacekeeping operation did not change the direction of the war in the Balkans, but it did highlight the continuing weakness of the Security Council to manage difficult situations.

## The United States and Contemporary Use of the Veto

The use of the veto in subsequent years focused on the actions of the United States. In March 2001 the United States vetoed a Security Council resolution centered on the establishment of a UN observer force in the Middle East, ostensibly to protect Palestinian civilians from Israeli military operations in the West Bank and Gaza territories. Then in December 2001 the United States vetoed a resolution that called for an Israeli withdrawal from territory supposedly under the Palestinian Authority. Condemning what was described as acts of terror against civilians, the resolution singled out the Israelis and left unspoken Palestinian attacks on Israeli civilians. In 2002 the United States cast another veto involving UN peacekeeping in Bosnia. The resolution also questioned peacekeeper immunity from the jurisdiction of the International Criminal Court. In December 2002, the United States vetoed another resolution that would have subjected Israel to condemnation when its military forces destroyed a World Food Program warehouse, killing several UN employees. In September 2003 the United States cast a veto when a Syrian resolution condemning Israel for its threat on the life of Yasir Arafat received general approval (there were also three abstentions). In October 2003 the United States used the veto again in thwarting a resolution condemning Israel for its construction of a barrier that cut across Palestinian-designated territory. In both instances in 2003 the United States argued that the resolutions were one-sided against Israel. The same argument was used in March 2004 when the United States vetoed a Security Council resolution condemning Israel for killing the founder of the Palestinian HAMAS.

In sum, the use of the veto has remained a desired instrument of the permanent powers, increasingly by the United States, which often has found itself isolated and consistently outvoted in the Security Council. Much of U.S. isolation in recent times has been attributed to Washington's go-it-alone policy in making war on Iraq after the terrorist attacks of September 11, 2001, despite the fact that France, China, and Russia declared they would veto any resolution authorizing the use of force there. With division among the permanent powers deep and unbridgeable over this issue, the Bush administration took it upon itself to lead a "coalition of the willing" against Iraq that included Great Britain and Australia, and to a lesser extent Poland. The effect of the Iraqi episode on the Security Council and the UN in general will be explored in subsequent chapters.

Vetoes have been a source of irritation to states on the opposite sides of an issue, but up to 1999, and especially after 2003, they did not seriously hamper the United Nations in performing its security functions. Fifty-one of the Soviet vetoes, all before 1960, were used to deny approval of UN membership applications that had been pressed to a vote over Soviet objection. All of the vetoed applicants were subsequently admitted, most of them in 1955. Other vetoes have been almost frivolous or inconsequential in their practical effects. In 1949 the Soviet Union vetoed a resolution of congratulations to the Netherlands and Indonesia upon successful conclusion of their negotiations for Indonesian independence. In 1963 the Security Council was not permitted to utter condemnation of the murder of two Israelis in an incident along the Syrian border. Still other vetoes have been circumvented through action by the General Assembly. This was notably true of the Korean War, the 1956 Suez crisis, and the 1960 UN Congo operation. It also has been true of numerous resolutions of condemnation or censure that were initially vetoed in the Security Council but subsequently adopted by the General Assembly with perhaps only some change in wording. Assembly resolutions condemning Soviet intervention in Hungary and Afghanistan; U.S. intervention in Nicaragua, Grenada, and Panama; and many Israeli actions in the Middle East are examples of the practice. Generally speaking, only a few of the vetoes cast since the inception of the United Nations have been concerned with vital international security issues. Between 1946 and 1997, fifty-nine vetoes were cast to block admission of member states. Forty-three vetoes were used to prevent nominations for Secretary-General, although these latter vetoes were cast in closed sessions of the Security Council and are not included in Table 3-4. China's veto of the continuing deployment of UNPREDEP in the Former Yugoslav Republic of Macedonia, however, involved a vital security matter, especially given instability in neighboring Kosovo. If Security Council peacekeeping missions are rejected as a consequence of purely domestic issues that have no bearing on the mission itself, the United Nation's future capacity to buttress world security could be considerably reduced. China's 1999 veto of UNPREDEP may not have been a major factor in the war over Kosovo, but the use of the veto by a permanent power for reasons having nothing to do with a peacekeeping mission hinted at new problems for UN peacekeeping.

Some vetoes, of course, have achieved their purpose of preventing UN action opposed by one or more of the permanent members. British and U.S. vetoes successfully fended off mandatory UN sanctions against South Africa, except for an arms embargo. China's veto in 1981 denied a third term as Secretary-General to Kurt Waldheim, and a U.S. veto barred the election of Tanzanian Salim A. Salim. A 1961 Soviet veto of a Security Council resolution calling for a cease-fire and the withdrawal of Indian forces from the Portuguese enclave of Goa was never overruled by the General Assembly. Moreover, Soviet vetoes of cease-fire resolutions in December 1971 left India uninhibited in its military action against Pakistan, which secured the independence of East Pakistan (now Bangladesh). Likewise, the British veto of a call for cessation of hostilities in the Falkland Islands permitted the war there with Argentina to be resolved on British terms before the Assembly, meeting later in the fall of 1982, could intervene.

Thus the veto has given some protection to the interests of the permanent members but has not prevented UN action in situations where effective UN action was possible. When action has been feasible and desired by member states, the General Assembly has usually found a way to act. If a UN resolution will not alter any state's behavior for the better, a veto of that resolution can scarcely be considered a disservice to the organization or to the cause of peace. The veto simply prevents the Security Council from undermining its own authority by issuing orders that cannot be carried out. The Security Council was saved from an even more ignominious fate when Great Britain withdrew its resolution of 2003 that would have authorized the United Nations to act aggressively in Iraq. Since France and Russia, and possibly China, were determined to veto the resolution, and, moreover, since the resolution would not have received a requisite nine votes, Britain realized that leaving the resolution on the table might well have fractured an already weakened Security Council.

Viewed from another perspective, the veto may be crucial to UN viability as a world organization. During the years of Western dominance in the General Assembly, the Soviet Union might have left the United Nations altogether if it had been forced to accept the will of the Western coalition in the Security Council. Through hard diplomatic times the Soviet Union stayed, perhaps in part because the veto provided an institutional power base that could not be shaken by numerical majorities. From the 1960s onward the Soviet Union was no longer politically isolated in either the Assembly or the Security Council. But the United States, often confronted with hostile Third World majorities in the Assembly, welcomed the protection of the veto in the Security Council and for example blocked resolutions dealing with Israel (May 1990) and the U.S. invasion of Panama (January 1990).

The veto also has had the salutary effect of promoting the search for consensus. The same forces that encourage consensus in the Assembly are at work in the Security Council, but the veto provides an additional incentive. If the Council is to act at all, it must have the concurrence—or at least the abstention—of each permanent member. The need for great power consensus was the fundamental assumption underlying the UN security system, and the veto was the institutional embodiment of that assumption. For several decades the availability of the veto to the permanent powers demonstrated both the correctness of the assumption and the utility of the veto as an incentive for reaching consensus. Nevertheless, the Security Council's division over Iraq in 2003 highlighted U.S. insistence on forceful action against Iraq, and France and Russia's threat to use the veto to prevent the United Nations from legitimizing a U.S. decision to make war on Baghdad. On one side was Washington's claim of the right to make preemptive war under certain circumstances, and on the other was Paris and Moscow's argument that attacking without provocation did not come within the realm of UN procedures or actions. In the new circumstances after September 11, the question of the veto as a consensus-building mechanism required still another evaluation. Questions have also been raised that not only focus new attention on the veto, but also on the need to restructure the international organization to meet the exigencies and uncertainties of a world not foreseen when the UN Charter was drafted in 1945.

## The United Nations as a Communications Network

Voting procedures set important constraints on decision making. The exchange of information among the participants that precedes voting is even more important in determining the kinds of decisions that will be reached.

The United Nations generates a constant stream of information that must be evaluated by foreign departments. The United Nations also directs a flow of information directly between governments. The approach of a General Assembly session, for example, is always the signal for increased intergovernmental consultations both through regular diplomatic channels and in New York. Members with a special interest in an issue use presession discussion to obtain the widest measure of support for their positions. On issues in which they have no special interest, they consult to obtain the information necessary to appraise their own policies intelligently in the light of positions held by others. Whatever the scope of presession consultations, the beginning of an Assembly session brings a new phase in the communication process. National governments now become sources of information that move into and through the UN system. The United Nations provides both formal and informal channels for such movement. Formal debate in committee and plenary session has symbolic importance but usually does little to facilitate agreement on disputed questions. A public address may dramatize or occasionally clarify positions, but a committee of 191 members is too large for useful document drafting or for working out detailed compromise. Furthermore, reconciliation of differences requires give-and-take in a more private setting. This can occur among smaller groups of states in vacant rooms of the UN building or perhaps in the offices of the delegations. Social gatherings also have their part in the communication process. Although casual meetings in a UN bar or lounge, luncheon engagements, cocktail parties, or formal receptions are unlikely settings for resolution drafting, they can provide occasions for important exchanges of views and information.

## UN "Groups"

The private, ad hoc interchange between delegates drawn temporarily together by their common interest in an issue is a persistent and inevitable part of the UN process. But other forms of interchange occur on a more routine basis. The least formal may include the regular luncheon engagements of two friendly delegates sharing a range of common interests. At a higher level of activity and important to the discussion process are organized groups having more or less regular meeting times, established routines for the conduct of conversations, and secretarial assistance drawn from one or more of the delegation staffs.

Groups have formed at the United Nations for the obvious purpose of achieving common objectives through concerted action. Consultation within regional groups received its initial impetus from electoral contests in the General Assembly. By seeking agreement beforehand, groups of members might hope to obtain an "equitable share" of Assembly influence, as well as through elective positions on the Security Council, ECOSOC, and other UN bodies with rotating membership. This ultimately can lead to agreed arrangements for allotting positions among geographic regions and permitting regional groups to nominate candidates to serve in the allotted positions. For electoral purposes nearly every UN member is assigned to one of five regional groups: the African group, the Asian group, the Latin American group, the Eastern European group, or the Western European and Others group, which includes Australia, Canada, and New Zealand (see Table 3-5). Israel does not meet with a regional group, not by choice but because of the politics of the United Nations that operates often in opposition to the Jewish entity. The United States is not a member of any group but consults with Western Europe on electoral matters.

The formal geographic groups exist primarily for elections and exchange of relevant information, but other groups, sometimes called caucusing groups, are concerned with policy matters. Such groups mirror common interests and often enjoy organizational ties developed outside the United Nations. The Commonwealth of Independent States, the Organization of Security and Cooperation in Europe, the League of Arab States, the Organization of African Unity, the Organization of American States, the Association of Southeast Asian Nations, the European Union, the Organization for Economic Cooperation and Development, the Nordic Group, the Contact Group, the Group of 77, the G-7 (with Russia, G-8), the Islamic Conference, and others, meet periodically or as their interests dictate. All are known to exchange views and canvass prospects for common action.

Occasionally, an issue may call for consultation among members of NATO or the Commonwealth. Not infrequently, a group appoints a common spokesperson to represent its views in debate on a particular issue. No group matched the voting unity of the East European states during the years of Soviet domina-

TABLE 3-5    UN Membership Regional Groups, 2003

### AFRICAN STATES

| | | | |
|---|---|---|---|
| Algeria | Equatorial Guinea | Madagascar | Seychelles |
| Angola | Eritrea | Malawi | Sierra Leone |
| Benin | Ethiopia | Mali | Somalia |
| Botswana | Gabon | Mauritania | South Africa |
| Burkina Faso | Gambia | Mauritius | Sudan |
| Burundi Cameroon | Ghana | Morocco | Swaziland |
| Cape Verde | Guinea | Mozambique | Togo |
| Central African | Guinea-Bissau | Namibia | Tunisia |
| Republic | Ivory Coast | Niger | Uganda |
| Chad | Kenya | Nigeria | United Republic of |
| Comoros | Lesotho | Rwanda | Tanzania |
| Congo | Liberia | São Tomé and | Zaire |
| Djibouti | Libyan Arab | Principe | Zambia |
| Egypt | Jamahiriya | Senegal | Zimbabwe |

### ASIAN STATES

| | | | |
|---|---|---|---|
| Afghanistan | India | Marshall Islands | Singapore |
| Bahrain | Indonesia | Mongolia | Solomon Islands |
| Bangladesh | Iraq | Myanmar | Sri Lanka |
| Bhutan | Iran | Nauru | Syrian Arab |
| Brunei Darussalam | Japan | Nepal | Republic |
| Cambodia | Jordan | Oman | Thailand |
| China | Kiribati | Pakistan | Timor-Leste |
| Cyprus | Kuwait | Palau | Turkey* |
| Democratic Peo- | Lao People's | Papua New Guinea | Tuvalu |
| ple's Republic | Democratic | Philippines | United Arab |
| of Korea | Republic | Qatar | Emirates |
| Federated States of | Lebanon | Republic of Korea | Vanuatu |
| Micronesia | Malaysia | Samoa | Vietnam |
| Fiji | Maldives | Saudi Arabia | Yemen |

### EASTERN EUROPEAN STATES

| | | | |
|---|---|---|---|
| Albania | Czech Republic | Poland | Turkmenistan |
| Armenia | Estonia | Republic of | Ukraine |
| Azerbaijan | Georgia | Moldova | Uzbekistan |
| Belarus | Hungary | Romania | Yugoslavia |
| Bosnia and | Kazakhstan | Russian Federation | The former |
| Herzegovina | Kyrgyzstan | Slovak Republic | Yugoslav |
| Bulgaria | Latvia | Slovenia | Republic of |
| Croatia | Lithuania | Tajikistan | Macedonia |

(continued)

tion there, but coordination of policy initiatives and UN voting has been a frequent product of group consultation, with considerable effect on voting outcomes. The overlapping membership of various groups is shown in Figure 3-1.

During the past two decades two interrelated groups have held a special preeminence among groups in UN politics. One is the Group of 77 (G-77), representing the interests of the Third World countries, which are the vast major-

TABLE 3-5    *(continued)*

### LATIN AMERICAN STATES

| | | | |
|---|---|---|---|
| Antigua and | Costa Rica | Haiti | Saint Lucia |
| Barbuda | Cuba | Honduras | Saint Vincent and |
| Argentina | Dominica | Jamaica | the Grenadines |
| Bahamas | Dominican | Mexico | Suriname |
| Barbados | Republic | Nicaragua | Trinidad and |
| Belize | Ecuador | Panama | Tobago |
| Bolivia | El Salvador | Paraguay | Uruguay |
| Brazil | Grenada | Peru | Venezuela |
| Chile | Guatemala | Saint Kitts and | |
| Colombia | Guyana | Nevis | |

### WESTERN EUROPEAN AND OTHER STATES

| | | | |
|---|---|---|---|
| Andorra | France | Luxembourg | San Marino |
| Australia | Germany | Malta | Spain |
| Austria | Greece | Monaco | Sweden |
| Belgium | Iceland | Netherlands | Switzerland |
| Canada | Ireland | New Zealand | Turkey* |
| Denmark | Italy | Norway | United Kingdom |
| Finland | Liechtenstein | Portugal | |

NOTE: The United States and Israel are not members of regional groups.

*Turkey, which is in the Western European Group for election purposes, is also a member of the Asian group.

ity of UN members. The other is the Non-Aligned Movement (NAM). Although "Third World" does not suggest an institution or an organized lobby, NAM and, more notably, the G-77 do speak for the less-developed states that achieved independence after World War II. The term "Third World" is a term believed to have been first used in France during the 1950s, more or less to describe those nations emerging from the tutelage of colonialism. Because the majority of these nations are found south of the equator, they are also described as the "South," as in the "North-South" dialogue. The G-77 was actually formed at the 1964 inaugural meeting in Geneva of the UN Conference on Trade and Development (UNCTAD), which was attended by seventy-seven Third World nations. During that conference the developing countries agreed to form an organization through which they could better represent their economic and trade problems at future UNCTAD sessions, as well as within the UN General Assembly and the entire UN system. The membership of the Group of 77 expanded to include almost double that number in subsequent years, but the original description, that is, G-77, has nonetheless been retained.

Organizationally, the G-77 has no secretariat but is formally divided into Africa, Asia, and Latin America groupings and creates committees and working groups as the need arises. The group has been the driving force in the United Nations for promoting developing countries' interests in trade, aid, investment, technical cooperation, and related matters. Developed countries have come to

FIGURE 3-1   Regional and Other UN Groups: Overlapping Membership, 2003

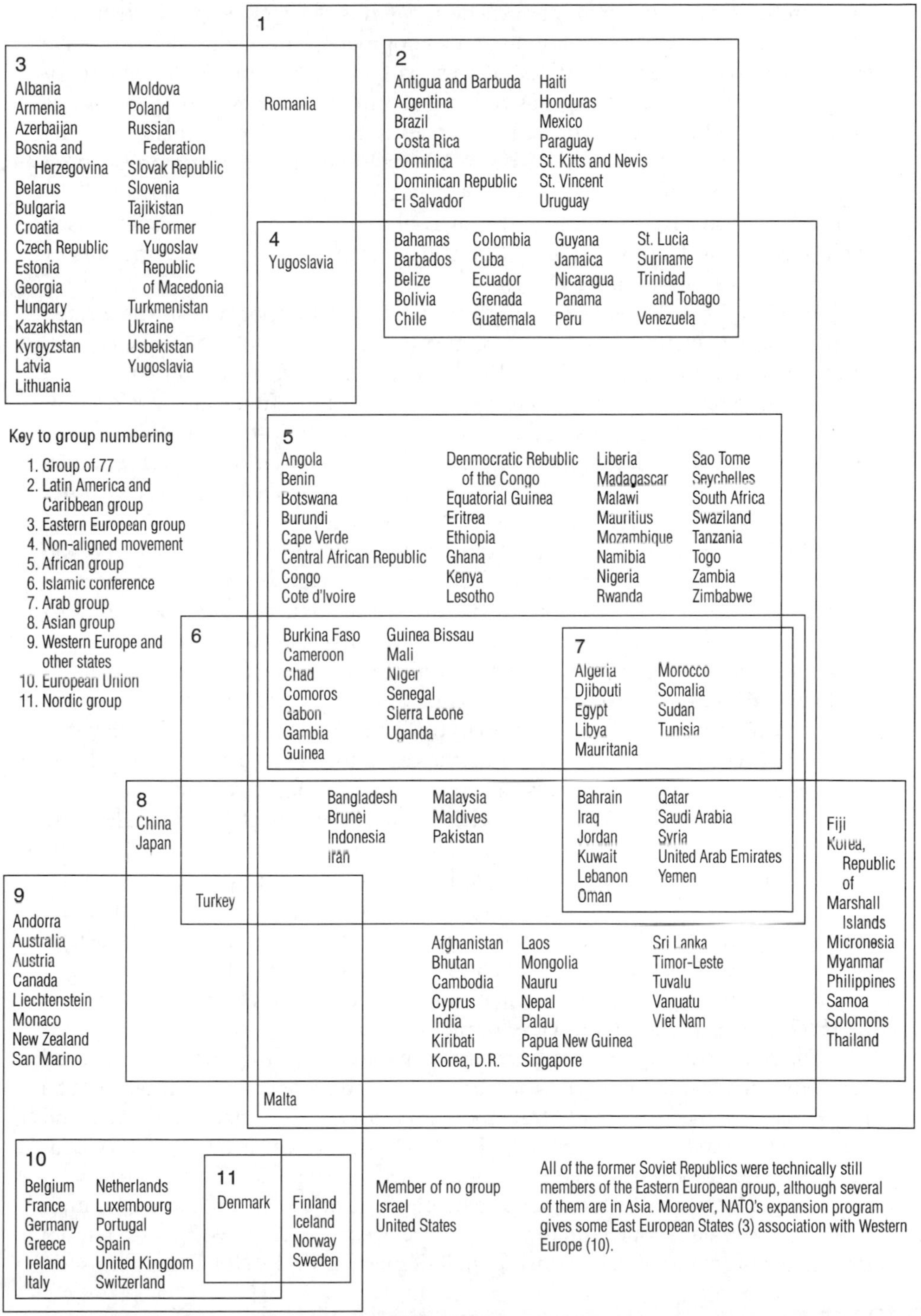

**1**

**3**

| | |
|---|---|
| Albania | Moldova |
| Armenia | Poland |
| Azerbaijan | Russian |
| Bosnia and | Federation |
|   Herzegovina | Slovak Republic |
| Belarus | Slovenia |
| Bulgaria | Tajikistan |
| Croatia | The Former |
| Czech Republic | Yugoslav |
| Estonia | Republic |
| Georgia | of Macedonia |
| Hungary | Turkmenistan |
| Kazakhstan | Ukraine |
| Kyrgyzstan | Usbekistan |
| Latvia | Yugoslavia |
| Lithuania | |

Romania

**2**

| | |
|---|---|
| Antigua and Barbuda | Haiti |
| Argentina | Honduras |
| Brazil | Mexico |
| Costa Rica | Paraguay |
| Dominica | St. Kitts and Nevis |
| Dominican Republic | St. Vincent |
| El Salvador | Uruguay |

**4**

Yugoslavia

| | | | |
|---|---|---|---|
| Bahamas | Colombia | Guyana | St. Lucia |
| Barbados | Cuba | Jamaica | Suriname |
| Belize | Ecuador | Nicaragua | Trinidad |
| Bolivia | Grenada | Panama | and Tobago |
| Chile | Guatemala | Peru | Venezuela |

**Key to group numbering**

1. Group of 77
2. Latin America and
   Caribbean group
3. Eastern European group
4. Non-aligned movement
5. African group
6. Islamic conference
7. Arab group
8. Asian group
9. Western Europe and
   other states
10. European Union
11. Nordic group

**5**

| | | | |
|---|---|---|---|
| Angola | Denmocratic Rebulic | Liberia | Sao Tome |
| Benin |   of the Congo | Madagascar | Seychelles |
| Botswana | Equatorial Guinea | Malawi | South Africa |
| Burundi | Eritrea | Mauritius | Swaziland |
| Cape Verde | Ethiopia | Mozambique | Tanzania |
| Central African Republic | Ghana | Namibia | Togo |
| Congo | Kenya | Nigeria | Zambia |
| Cote d'Ivoire | Lesotho | Rwanda | Zimbabwe |

**6**

| | |
|---|---|
| Burkina Faso | Guinea Bissau |
| Cameroon | Mali |
| Chad | Niger |
| Comoros | Senegal |
| Gabon | Sierra Leone |
| Gambia | Uganda |
| Guinea | |

**7**

| | |
|---|---|
| Algeria | Morocco |
| Djibouti | Somalia |
| Egypt | Sudan |
| Libya | Tunisia |
| Mauritania | |

**8**

China
Japan

Turkey

| | |
|---|---|
| Bangladesh | Malaysia |
| Brunei | Maldives |
| Indonesia | Pakistan |
| Iran | |

| | |
|---|---|
| Bahrain | Qatar |
| Iraq | Saudi Arabia |
| Jordan | Syria |
| Kuwait | United Arab Emirates |
| Lebanon | Yemen |
| Oman | |

Fiji
Korea,
   Republic
of
Marshall
   Islands
Micronesia
Myanmar
Philippines
Samoa
Solomons
Thailand

**9**

Andorra
Australia
Austria
Canada
Liechtenstein
Monaco
New Zealand
San Marino

| | | |
|---|---|---|
| Afghanistan | Laos | Sri Lanka |
| Bhutan | Mongolia | Timor-Leste |
| Cambodia | Nauru | Tuvalu |
| Cyprus | Nepal | Vanuatu |
| India | Palau | Viet Nam |
| Kiribati | Papua New Guinea | |
| Korea, D.R. | Singapore | |

Malta

**10**

| | |
|---|---|
| Belgium | Netherlands |
| France | Luxembourg |
| Germany | Portugal |
| Greece | Spain |
| Ireland | United Kingdom |
| Italy | Switzerland |

**11**

Denmark

Finland
Iceland
Norway
Sweden

Member of no group
Israel
United States

All of the former Soviet Republics were technically still
members of the Eastern European group, although several
of them are in Asia. Moreover, NATO's expansion program
gives some East European States (3) association with Western
Europe (10).

expect position papers or other statements from the G-77 at most UN meetings, and draft resolutions are frequently submitted on behalf of the whole group by the state holding the current chair. The G-77 has maintained a fair degree of cohesiveness on issues of economic development, although divisions have emerged in recent years. Unity is greatest in formulating broad statements of purpose or general concepts that reflect the interests of developing countries vis-à-vis the industrialized states. Differences in levels of development and particular economic interests have often made negotiation of a common position difficult. At the UN Law of the Sea Conference, for example, members of the group were frequently divided on the basis of their differing maritime interests, their locations as landlocked or coastal states, or their positions as importers or exporters of certain minerals.

The G-77 has the voting strength to override all opposition in the United Nations, and sometimes it does. Since meaningful action often depends on voluntary cooperation from industrialized states, however, the group has shown an increasing tendency to negotiate consensus decisions. In the negotiation process the number of members and the unity of the group provide political leverage but are far from determinative. Occasionally, negotiations with the industrialized states break down and end in a display of raw voting power. At other times, a degree of genuine consensus can be reached.

The end of the Cold War reduced the leverage of the group because it could no longer play off East against West. The retreat from socialist economics in Eastern Europe, and the obviously superior performance of the Western market economies, had the further effect of undermining the economic presuppositions of some developing countries that relied heavily on state economic management. Moreover, the states of the former Soviet bloc became competitors for economic aid that might otherwise go to the Third World. None of this changed the basic needs of the Third World or the drive for development. It did, however, make developing countries more receptive to market-oriented solutions suggested by the United States and other Western industrialized countries, and this in turn moved the G-77 into a more conciliatory position on some economic matters. It has also led the G-77 to emphasize the "environmental card"—that is, to make a case that developing states cannot afford the cost of controlling industrial pollution, preserving rain forests, and other environmental measures without more assistance from rich countries. This was an underlying theme at the 1992 Conference on Environment and Development, the Earth Summit+5 in 1997, and Population and Development in 1999.

The NAM was organized separately from the G-77, although the two shared economic goals and reinforced each other on matters of common interest. The NAM had a somewhat smaller membership than the G-77 had, 105 states and the PLO (representing "Palestine"). The NAM dates from a 1961 summit conference in Belgrade, convoked by Yugoslavia's Marshal Tito for the purpose of exploring a common foreign policy independent of the superpowers. Summit meetings were held approximately every three years (except 1967), with annual meetings of foreign ministers during the fall meeting of the UN General Assembly and meetings of lower-level experts as necessary. The NAM had no headquarters or permanent secretariat.

The NAM took positions on a broader range of issues than did the Group of 77. In addition to being concerned with economic development, the NAM was highly active on issues pertaining to the Middle East and southern Africa, as well as other political questions. Its anticolonial, anti-Western bias frequently put the movement at odds with the United States. In its summit pronouncements and UN voting, the NAM was far less likely to make common cause with the United States than with the Soviet Union, which for years maintained a posture of general support and encouragement for the NAM. In 1983 the U.S. permanent representative to the United Nations called the NAM "the most important bloc of all" because of it size and effectiveness. Still a lively organization after the Cold War, the NAM was one of the more vocal organizations rejecting the U.S. decision to invade Iraq in 2003.

Nevertheless, with East and West no longer strategic rivals, with NATO including as members the former Warsaw Pact states of Eastern Europe, and with Russia a member of the U.S.-inspired Partnership for Peace (PFP), G-8, and Contact Group, the notion of nonalignment has become anachronistic. The NAM is under pressure to find its role in the new millennium. As a movement the NAM always had internal divisions, and group discipline was a problem. Exceptions perhaps were found in UN votes on the issue of apartheid in South Africa or the Palestinian question in the Middle East, but on many other matters there were always important defections. Indeed, the termination of apartheid and South Africa's rebirth under black majority leadership, as well as the Palestine Authority's on-again, off-again peace talks with Israel, further divides and confuses the organization's members. So too on economic questions where the G-77 is a more dominant actor, the NAM's purpose reflects considerable ambiguity. And because the NAM never established a permanent secretariat or central headquarters, it may well fade away, its work assumed by other, more formal organizations.

Opinions differ on whether the group system has a salutary effect on UN politics. On the negative side, the group system introduces elements of rigidity into the political process. When a group has agreed on its position, the need for constant reference back to the group may make negotiation of compromise solutions more problematic. An individual member of the group also loses opportunity when pressures to conform to the group position prevent the public expression of any misgivings that the member may have. The dilemma may be excruciating when an individual spokesperson for a group passes off his or her own extremist views as the group position or when the group position in fact represents the views of its more extremist elements. The group system has the further disadvantage of fostering power relationships within the United Nations that are at variance with the actual distribution of national power. Large groups of small states can dominate voting, but they may have little power to carry out the mandates they have issued.

The system nevertheless has a positive side. For the smaller or less-developed countries, which constitute the majority of UN members, regional and extraregional groups play a very useful role in promoting shared interests—most notably in dealing with issues of economics and anticolonialism. For new and smaller members, the groups perform an important socializing function, helping new governments and delegates identify roles in the UN community. For nearly all members, the groups provide additional channels of communication and a forum for harmonization of views. Such discussions are an important means of building consensus at the group level, in some instances eliminating the need for an extensive series of bilateral negotiations. If the formulation of group positions adds rigidity to UN decision making, that rigidity is mitigated by the trend toward consensus decisions in UN meetings generally. As a further advantage, the group system saves time in meetings by permitting speaking assignments to be accomplished by one or a few delegates from a group in place of the many who might otherwise speak.

## UN Decisions: Who Wins?

Action by the General Assembly or the Security Council, as in most other intergovernmental bodies, is symbolized by the adoption of a resolution. The winners, in a parliamentary sense, are those who vote for a resolution that succeeds or against a resolution that fails. When the political process works at its best, an adopted resolution is the expression of a common interest among states having the will and the ability to do whatever its implementation requires. At other times the "win" is purely parliamentary or symbolic.

### Changes in Security Council Dynamics

Most resolutions are the product of extensive negotiation and compromise. The frequent adoption of resolutions by consensus indicates that this process can be successful in identifying the requisite area of common interest (or at least in watering down the resolution so that no one is seriously offended). Often, however, opinion in the Assembly is strongly divided, so that adoption of a resolution is a victory for some and a defeat for others. In such a situation the delegations most directly interested will lobby vigorously to achieve victory or avoid defeat.

An example of massive lobbying was the successful U.S. campaign in December 1991 to secure the repeal of the General Assembly's 1975 resolution equating Zionism with racism. The groundwork was laid months in advance, in the first instance by consulting close allies and subsequently extending the contacts to other states as possible cosponsors of the measure. Advance contact was also made with moderate Arab states that might be persuaded not to oppose repeal. In early December, when the United States concluded that prospective support was enough to justify a repeal attempt, State Department telegrams went out to every U.S. embassy in the world. Each ambassador was instructed to solicit not only the foreign government's support of the repeal but also cosponsorship. In some cases, the United States sought a further commitment to lobby for repeal so that the campaign would appear more than a U.S.-Israeli effort. The initial area of focus was Europe, both East and West, and reluctance had to be overcome in both places. Initially, Moscow did not commit itself out of concern for antagonizing its own Muslim republics in Central Asia, but eventually the Kremlin agreed to support the resolution. Many Latin American states also displayed reluctance, but when Argentina and Mexico agreed to cosponsor the resolution, their compliance was assured. Eventually, a list of eighty-six sponsors was obtained, representing every regional group. The resolution's final form was a product of American persistence, heavily dependent on personal contacts, including letters and telephone calls from President George Bush, Vice President Dan Quayle, and Secretary of State James Baker. In the end, the vote was 111 states supporting repeal, with 25 opposed and 13 abstaining. Fifteen states were absent when the vote was taken. Not a single Arab state voted in support of the repeal, nor did any abstain. Seven Arab states, however, were among those absenting themselves from the Assembly.

What is the content of "pressure" when a country decides to turn it on? For the most part, it is insistence, persistence, and seeking ways to neutralize objections. The lobbying is most effective where there is an important relationship between the parties concerned—ties of friendship, military security, cultural homogeneity, or economic dependence. Regional and group solidarity have become especially important in UN meetings, particularly for the small or less-developed countries whose parliamentary strength lies in unity. On many issues, group pressures are determinative. As between individual governments, pressure may consist not so much in what is said as in how it is said. When reluctant delegates are repeatedly buttonholed in New York and their governments subjected to insistent appeals at home, the pressure is noticed. In this context an appeal for "good relations" carries a hint that relations may be strained by failure to cast an appropriate vote. For a large country merely to communicate a strong opinion to a smaller dependent country may constitute pressure. If no more is said, the smaller country is left to weigh the uncertain consequences of taking a position displeasing to its more powerful patron. Such interchanges constitute a kind of diplomatic pressure and are a common occurrence in connection with UN meetings.

The crasser forms of threat or promise are seldom used because they are too costly to invoke often. Threats arouse resentment, and bribes do not build mutual esteem and respect over the long run. Most Assembly decisions are not important enough to justify the threat to alter levels of foreign aid or to take other forms of retaliatory action. Seldom do the stakes of UN action appear to justify strong bilateral pressures. Undoubtedly, the occasions when such pressures would bring a favorable vote are even fewer. Another form of pressure, exerted primarily as a deterrent to action, is the threat of noncooperation with proposed UN programs. This kind of bargaining power is still important for a country like the United States, whose cooperation may be essential to the effective functioning of particular economic programs.

The discussion of pressure tactics may convey the picture of a great power using its muscle to induce small states to vote the way the larger power wants. Within Eastern Europe this once was true, but East bloc solidarity was not enough to win an Assembly vote. The Soviet Union never had enough reliable friends to constitute anything close to a UN majority, and the days of a dependable U.S.-led majority are also long gone. As Table 3-6 indicates, except for Western Europe, no regional group of states votes with the United States on contested votes even half of the time. In fact, neither Russia nor the United States consistently votes with the majority as often as do most members. A tabulation of majority agreement scores for seventy-nine resolutions adopted by roll-call votes during the 1954, 1959, and 1962 sessions of the Assembly shows that the United States voted in the minority more often than did 93 of the 110 member states. Only four members had a poorer win-loss record than the former Soviet Union. Since the early years of the Cold War, U.S. agreement with the majority on contested roll-call votes has grown much worse, falling below 15 percent in the 1980s, while the Soviet (now Russian) score has improved markedly. The U.S. decline and the corresponding rise in Soviet agreement with the Assembly majority are shown in Table 3-7 and Figure 3-2. The improved Soviet position was not the result of Soviet leadership initiatives or of pressures effectively exerted on smaller states. It mirrored mainly General Assembly dominance of the Third World majority, with which the Soviet Union was able to make common cause.

This state of affairs led a Reagan-appointed U.S. ambassador to the United Nations to observe that the United States had no leverage at all in the General Assembly (see Table 3-7). Continuing frustration with the United Nations, as expressed by some U.S. government leaders as well as by segments of the media and lay public, is traced to the changing patterns of UN membership. The "one state one vote" conception that provided Third World nations with a sense of state equality in the General Assembly early on had the favor of the United States. But in the changed conditions of the twenty-first century it was an expression that had lost its appeal, especially when it provided the smaller nations with virtual veto power. The more-determined U.S. use of the veto in Security Council deliberations in the latter years of the Cold War also was an indication of U.S. frustration that the organization it had done so much to create no longer followed its lead. Moreover, this dissatisfaction with the United Nations carried over and into the post–Cold War era. Public opinion in the United States had become demonstrably divided between those favoring a larger role for the United Nations and those vehemently opposed to it. Washington's failure to meet its funding obligations, and congressional statements adverse to UN-sponsored programs, however, appeared to cause more distress in UN headquarters than in individual member states.

Clearly, the United States does not have a monopoly on pressure tactics or persuasive capacity within the United Nations. And given the leverage enjoyed by Third World nations in the General Assembly, the U.S. Congress will continue to promote NATO over the United Nations in security matters. It is interesting

TABLE 3-6  UN Regional Group Voting Practices Coinciding with United States Votes in General Assembly, 2002

| COUNTRY | IDENTICAL VOTES | OPPOSITE VOTES | ABSTENTIONS | ABSENCES | VOTING COINCIDENCE | |
|---|---|---|---|---|---|---|
| | | | | | INCLUDING CONSENSUS | VOTES ONLY |
| AFRICAN GROUP | | | | | | |
| Swaziland | 26 | 55 | 1 | 8 | 81.5% | 32.1% |
| Rwanda | 13 | 32 | 10 | 35 | 83.0% | 28.9% |
| Mauritius | 22 | 57 | 7 | 4 | 81.1% | 27.8% |
| Cameroon | 18 | 47 | 13 | 12 | 82.5% | 27.7% |
| Nigeria | 22 | 61 | 6 | 1 | 80.6% | 26.5% |
| Burundi | 16 | 46 | 8 | 20 | 81.1% | 25.8% |
| Sierra Leone | 17 | 50 | 11 | 12 | 81.2% | 25.4% |
| Madagascar | 14 | 44 | 21 | 11 | 83.6% | 24.1% |
| UR Tanzania | 18 | 59 | 13 | 0 | 81.0% | 23.4% |
| Senegal | 19 | 63 | 2 | 6 | 79.0% | 23.2% |
| Eritrea | 18 | 60 | 9 | 3 | 79.9% | 23.1% |
| Kenya | 17 | 57 | 16 | 0 | 81.5% | 23.0% |
| Zambia | 17 | 59 | 11 | 3 | 80.6% | 22.4% |
| Uganda | 16 | 56 | 14 | 4 | 81.0% | 22.2% |
| Gambia | 13 | 47 | 8 | 22 | 79.9% | 21.7% |
| Burkina Faso | 16 | 60 | 14 | 0 | 80.5% | 21.1% |
| Togo | 16 | 60 | 13 | 1 | 80.5% | 21.1% |
| South Africa | 16 | 61 | 13 | 0 | 80.4% | 20.8% |
| Djibouti | 16 | 62 | 9 | 3 | 79.7% | 20.5% |
| Lesotho | 15 | 59 | 15 | 1 | 80.7% | 20.3% |
| Egypt | 15 | 60 | 15 | 0 | 80.6% | 20.0% |
| Ethiopia | 13 | 53 | 18 | 6 | 81.5% | 19.7% |
| Malawi | 12 | 49 | 15 | 14 | 81.4% | 19.7% |
| Ghana | 14 | 58 | 18 | 0 | 81.0% | 19.4% |
| Cape Verde | 14 | 59 | 13 | 4 | 80.2% | 19.2% |
| Mozambique | 12 | 51 | 7 | 20 | 78.1% | 19.0% |
| Benin | 6 | 26 | 6 | 52 | 77.6% | 18.8% |
| Congo | 14 | 61 | 6 | 9 | 78.2% | 18.7% |

(continued)

TABLE 3-6  (continued)

| COUNTRY | IDENTICAL VOTES | OPPOSITE VOTES | ABSTENTIONS | ABSENCES | VOTING COINCIDENCE | |
|---|---|---|---|---|---|---|
| | | | | | INCLUDING CONSENSUS | VOTES ONLY |
| AFRICAN GROUP | | | | | | |
| Namibia | 12 | 53 | 13 | 12 | 79.9% | 18.5% |
| Mali | 14 | 62 | 12 | 2 | 79.6% | 18.4% |
| Libya | 14 | 65 | 11 | 0 | 79.2% | 17.7% |
| Angola | 12 | 57 | 10 | 11 | 79.5% | 17.4% |
| Guinea | 12 | 58 | 13 | 7 | 79.7% | 17.1% |
| Sudan | 14 | 68 | 8 | 0 | 78.5% | 17.1% |
| Botswana | 11 | 56 | 13 | 10 | 79.3% | 16.4% |
| Côte d'Ivoire | 11 | 56 | 7 | 16 | 78.4% | 16.4% |
| Sao Tome and Principe | 11 | 57 | 7 | 15 | 78.3% | 16.2% |
| Comoros | 9 | 47 | 11 | 23 | 79.2% | 16.1% |
| Morocco | 10 | 58 | 18 | 4 | 80.2% | 14.7% |
| Seychelles | 7 | 42 | 0 | 41 | 76.3% | 14.3% |
| Tunisia | 10 | 60 | 20 | 0 | 80.1% | 14.3% |
| Zimbabwe | 7 | 42 | 11 | 30 | 78.7% | 14.3% |
| Algeria | 9 | 61 | 18 | 2 | 79.5% | 12.9% |
| Gabon | 5 | 39 | 1 | 45 | 75.1% | 11.4% |
| Mauritania | 7 | 58 | 19 | 6 | 79.5% | 10.8% |
| Chad | 3 | 28 | 10 | 49 | 78.5% | 9.7% |
| Equatorial Guinea | 2 | 21 | 2 | 65 | 73.1% | 8.7% |
| Somalia | 3 | 42 | 7 | 38 | 75.1% | 6.7% |
| Dem. Rep. of the Congo | 2 | 34 | 13 | 41 | 77.8% | 5.6% |
| Guinea–Bissau | 0 | 2 | 5 | 83 | 88.5% | 0.0% |
| Central African Rep. | 0 | 0 | 0 | 90 | * | * |
| Liberia | 0 | 0 | 0 | 90 | * | * |
| Niger | 0 | 0 | 0 | 90 | * | * |
| Average | 11.9 | 48.6 | 10.2 | 19.3 | 80.0% | 19.6% |

| Asian Group | | | | | | |
|---|---|---|---|---|---|---|
| Palau | 39 | 0 | 5 | 46 | 100.0% | 100.0% |
| Marshall Islands | 47 | 1 | 4 | 38 | 99.4% | 97.9% |
| Micronesia | 53 | 6 | 10 | 21 | 97.4% | 89.8% |
| Uzbekistan | 13 | 13 | 19 | 45 | 91.2% | 50.0% |
| Japan | 34 | 36 | 20 | 0 | 88.2% | 48.6% |
| Republic of Korea | 32 | 38 | 19 | 1 | 87.4% | 45.7% |
| Nauru | 26 | 35 | 19 | 10 | 87.2% | 42.6% |
| Cyprus | 34 | 49 | 7 | 0 | 84.5% | 41.0% |
| Tonga | 17 | 26 | 21 | 26 | 87.9% | 39.5% |
| Solomon Islands | 22 | 40 | 21 | 7 | 85.3% | 35.5% |
| Timor-Leste | 12 | 25 | 0 | 53 | 78.9% | 32.4% |
| Papua New Guinea | 19 | 40 | 25 | 6 | 85.5% | 32.2% |
| Fiji | 21 | 46 | 15 | 8 | 83.5% | 31.3% |
| Samoa | 21 | 47 | 8 | 14 | 82.5% | 30.9% |
| Kazakhstan | 18 | 45 | 22 | 5 | 84.3% | 28.6% |
| Mongolia | 20 | 53 | 6 | 11 | 81.1% | 27.4% |
| Maldives | 21 | 56 | 3 | 10 | 80.5% | 27.3% |
| Kuwait | 22 | 61 | 7 | 0 | 80.8% | 26.5% |
| Thailand | 19 | 58 | 13 | 0 | 81.4% | 24.7% |
| Philippines | 19 | 60 | 11 | 0 | 80.8% | 24.1% |
| Singapore | 17 | 54 | 19 | 0 | 82.3% | 23.9% |
| Nepal | 15 | 51 | 13 | 11 | 80.9% | 22.7% |
| Tajikstan | 10 | 34 | 8 | 38 | 81.0% | 22.7% |
| Malaysia | 17 | 59 | 14 | 0 | 81.0% | 22.4% |
| Indonesia | 17 | 60 | 13 | 0 | 80.7% | 22.1% |
| Kyrgyzstan | 9 | 32 | 7 | 42 | 80.8% | 22.0% |

*(continued)*

TABLE 3-6  *(continued)*

| COUNTRY | IDENTICAL VOTES | OPPOSITE VOTES | ABSTENTIONS | ABSENCES | VOTING COINCIDENCE | |
|---|---|---|---|---|---|---|
| | | | | | INCLUDING CONSENSUS | VOTES ONLY |
| **ASIAN GROUP** | | | | | | |
| Afghanistan | 9 | 33 | 0 | 48 | 79.2% | 21.4% |
| Bangladesh | 16 | 59 | 15 | 0 | 80.9% | 21.3% |
| Brunei Sarussalam | 16 | 59 | 15 | 0 | 80.9% | 21.3% |
| India | 14 | 52 | 24 | 0 | 82.7% | 21.2% |
| Qatar | 15 | 60 | 14 | 1 | 80.4% | 20.0% |
| Oman | 15 | 61 | 12 | 2 | 80.0% | 19.7% |
| Iran | 14 | 57 | 8 | 11 | 79.7% | 19.7% |
| Sri Lanka | 14 | 57 | 19 | 0 | 81.3% | 19.7% |
| Cambodia | 14 | 58 | 16 | 2 | 80.6% | 19.4% |
| Pakistan | 13 | 54 | 23 | 0 | 81.9% | 19.4% |
| Vanuatu | 3 | 13 | 20 | 54 | 87.8% | 18.8% |
| Bahrain | 14 | 61 | 9 | 6 | 79.2% | 18.7% |
| China | 13 | 61 | 13 | 3 | 79.8% | 17.6% |
| United Arab Emirates | 13 | 61 | 13 | 3 | 79.6% | 17.6% |
| Yemen | 13 | 61 | 5 | 11 | 78.3% | 17.6% |
| Bhutan | 8 | 42 | 15 | 25 | 80.3% | 16.0% |
| Myanmar (Burma) | 11 | 58 | 21 | 0 | 80.9% | 15.9% |
| Turkmenistan | 3 | 16 | 3 | 68 | 80.7% | 15.8% |
| Saudi Arabia | 10 | 59 | 14 | 7 | 79.2% | 14.5% |
| Jordan | 10 | 64 | 15 | 1 | 79.1% | 13.5% |
| Syria | 10 | 66 | 11 | 3 | 77.8% | 13.2% |
| Lebanon | 9 | 61 | 18 | 2 | 79.5% | 12.9% |
| DPR of Korea | 7 | 57 | 11 | 15 | 77.5% | 10.9% |
| Vietnam | 6 | 61 | 7 | 16 | 76.5% | 9.0% |
| Tuvalu | 1 | 12 | 10 | 67 | 83.5% | 7.7% |

| | | | | | |
|---|---|---|---|---|---|
| Laos | 3 | 53 | 8 | 26 | 75.6% | 5.4% |
| Kiribati | 0 | 6 | 0 | 84 | 74.6% | 0.0% |
| Iraq | 0 | 0 | 0 | 90 | * | * |
| Average | 16.1 | 44.2 | 12.4 | 17.4 | 82.2% | 26.7% |

LATIN AMERICAN AND CARIBBEAN GROUP (LAC)

| | | | | | |
|---|---|---|---|---|---|
| St. Kitts and Nevis | 9 | 14 | 4 | 63 | 83.9% | 39.1% |
| Guatemala | 26 | 47 | 8 | 9 | 83.6% | 35.6% |
| Argentina | 26 | 50 | 14 | 0 | 83.9% | 34.2% |
| Peru | 26 | 53 | 9 | 2 | 82.8% | 32.9% |
| El Salvador | 26 | 54 | 2 | 8 | 81.6% | 32.5% |
| Nicaragua | 25 | 52 | 1 | 12 | 81.3% | 32.5% |
| Barbados | 26 | 57 | 4 | 3 | 81.2% | 31.3% |
| Uruguay | 26 | 57 | 7 | 0 | 82.0% | 31.3% |
| Brazil | 26 | 58 | 6 | 0 | 81.8% | 31.0% |
| Costa Rica | 26 | 58 | 3 | 3 | 81.2% | 31.0% |
| Trinidad and Tobago | 26 | 58 | 3 | 3 | 81.4% | 31.0% |
| Chile | 27 | 61 | 2 | 0 | 81.1% | 30.7% |
| Paraguay | 26 | 60 | 4 | 0 | 81.3% | 30.2% |
| Honduras | 25 | 58 | 5 | 2 | 81.4% | 30.1% |
| St. Vincent/Gren. | 21 | 49 | 11 | 9 | 82.6% | 30.0% |
| Bolivia | 26 | 63 | 1 | 0 | 80.5% | 29.2% |
| Ecuador | 26 | 63 | 1 | 0 | 80.5% | 29.2% |
| Dominica | 13 | 32 | 9 | 36 | 81.7% | 28.9% |

*(continued)*

TABLE 3-6  *(continued)*

| Country | Identical Votes | Opposite Votes | Abstentions | Absences | Voting Coincidence Including Consensus | Voting Coincidence Votes Only |
|---|---|---|---|---|---|---|
| **Latin American and Caribbean Group (LAC)** | | | | | | |
| Dominican Republic | 26 | 64 | 0 | 0 | 80.2% | 28.9% |
| Panama | 25 | 62 | 2 | 1 | 80.4% | 28.7% |
| Colombia | 24 | 60 | 3 | 3 | 80.7% | 28.6% |
| Grenada | 22 | 57 | 7 | 4 | 81.3% | 27.8% |
| Bahamas | 21 | 56 | 11 | 2 | 81.7% | 27.3% |
| Mexico | 23 | 62 | 4 | 1 | 80.4% | 27.1% |
| Antigua and Barbuda | 15 | 42 | 2 | 31 | 79.1% | 26.3% |
| Guyana | 20 | 59 | 11 | 0 | 81.2% | 25.3% |
| Jamaica | 20 | 59 | 10 | 1 | 81.0% | 25.3% |
| Belize | 17 | 58 | 7 | 8 | 79.9% | 22.7% |
| Venezuela | 18 | 63 | 8 | 1 | 79.9% | 22.2% |
| St. Lucia | 13 | 59 | 10 | 8 | 79.4% | 18.1% |
| Haiti | 12 | 58 | 13 | 7 | 79.9% | 17.1% |
| Cuba | 12 | 62 | 8 | 8 | 78.5% | 16.2% |
| Suriname | 5 | 39 | 2 | 44 | 75.8% | 11.4% |
| Average | 21.4 | 54.7 | 5.8 | 8.2 | 81.0% | 28.1% |
| **Western European and Others Group (WEOG)** | | | | | | |
| Israel | 63 | 5 | 22 | 0 | 98.3% | 92.6% |
| United Kingdom | 44 | 33 | 13 | 0 | 89.4% | 57.1% |
| France | 42 | 33 | 15 | 0 | 89.3% | 56.0% |
| Monaco | 37 | 34 | 11 | 8 | 88.0% | 52.1% |
| Australia | 38 | 35 | 17 | 0 | 88.6% | 52.1% |

| | | | | | |
|---|---|---|---|---|---|
| Belgium | 37 | 37 | 15 | 1 | 87.9% | 50.0% |
| Italy | 39 | 39 | 12 | 0 | 87.5% | 50.0% |
| Netherlands | 37 | 37 | 15 | 1 | 87.9% | 50.0% |
| Spain | 38 | 39 | 13 | 0 | 87.5% | 49.4% |
| Canada | 37 | 38 | 15 | 0 | 87.7% | 49.3% |
| Germany | 37 | 38 | 15 | 2 | 87.5% | 49.3% |
| Portugal | 37 | 38 | 13 | 1 | 87.3% | 49.3% |
| Denmark | 37 | 39 | 13 | 0 | 87.3% | 48.7% |
| Iceland | 37 | 39 | 14 | 1 | 87.4% | 48.7% |
| Luxembourg | 37 | 39 | 14 | 0 | 87.4% | 48.7% |
| Norway | 37 | 39 | 14 | 0 | 87.4% | 48.7% |
| Greece | 37 | 40 | 13 | 0 | 87.1% | 48.1% |
| Finland | 36 | 39 | 15 | 0 | 87.4% | 48.0% |
| San Marino | 36 | 40 | 12 | 2 | 86.9% | 47.4% |
| Switzerland | 35 | 39 | 15 | 1 | 87.2% | 47.3% |
| Andorra | 37 | 42 | 11 | 0 | 86.6% | 46.8% |
| Austria | 36 | 41 | 13 | 0 | 86.8% | 46.8% |
| Sweden | 35 | 41 | 14 | 0 | 86.8% | 46.1% |
| Liechtenstein | 35 | 42 | 13 | 0 | 86.5% | 45.5% |
| Ireland | 34 | 42 | 14 | 0 | 86.5% | 44.7% |
| New Zealand | 33 | 42 | 13 | 2 | 86.2% | 44.0% |
| Malta | 36 | 48 | 6 | 0 | 84.9% | 42.9% |
| Turkey | 33 | 44 | 12 | 1 | 85.8% | 42.9% |
| | | | | | | |
| Average | 37.8 | 37.9 | 13.6 | 0.7 | 87.7% | 49.9% |

(continued)

TABLE 3-6 *(continued)*

| COUNTRY | IDENTICAL VOTES | OPPOSITE VOTES | ABSTENTIONS | ABSENCES | VOTING COINCIDENCE | |
|---|---|---|---|---|---|---|
| | | | | | INCLUDING CONSENSUS | VOTES ONLY |
| EASTERN EUROPEAN GROUP (EE) | | | | | | |
| Bosnia/Herzegovina | 35 | 34 | 14 | 7 | 88.1% | 50.7% |
| Poland | 39 | 39 | 12 | 0 | 87.5% | 50.0% |
| Republic of Moldova | 34 | 34 | 15 | 7 | 88.1% | 50.0% |
| Bulgaria | 37 | 38 | 14 | 1 | 87.6% | 49.3% |
| Hungary | 37 | 38 | 15 | 0 | 87.6% | 49.3% |
| Latvia | 35 | 36 | 17 | 2 | 88.0% | 49.3% |
| Romania | 37 | 39 | 13 | 1 | 87.2% | 48.7% |
| Lithuania | 36 | 38 | 16 | 0 | 87.7% | 48.6% |
| Slovenia | 36 | 38 | 16 | 0 | 87.7% | 48.6% |
| Albania | 31 | 33 | 16 | 10 | 87.8% | 48.4% |
| Czech Republic | 37 | 40 | 12 | 1 | 87.0% | 48.1% |
| Slovak Republic | 37 | 40 | 13 | 0 | 87.1% | 48.1% |
| TFYR Macedonia | 36 | 40 | 14 | 0 | 87.1% | 47.4% |
| Yugoslavia | 36 | 40 | 14 | 0 | 87.1% | 47.4% |
| Croatia | 35 | 40 | 15 | 0 | 87.1% | 46.7% |
| Georgia | 32 | 39 | 18 | 1 | 87.1% | 45.1% |
| Ukraine | 31 | 49 | 10 | 0 | 84.4% | 38.8% |
| Russia | 21 | 48 | 20 | 1 | 83.9% | 30.4% |
| Armenia | 22 | 53 | 14 | 1 | 82.7% | 29.3% |
| Azerbaijan | 14 | 51 | 22 | 3 | 82.6% | 21.5% |
| Belarus | 14 | 60 | 14 | 2 | 80.2% | 18.9% |
| Average | 32.0 | 41.3 | 15.0 | 1.8 | 86.4% | 43.7% |

SOURCE: U.S. Department of State, Voting Practices in the United Nations for 2002, Bureau of International Affairs, Report to the Congress submitted pursuant to Pub. L. 101-246, March 31, 2003, pp. 66–70.

TABLE 3-7    United States and Soviet Union Agreement with the Majority, UN General Assembly Roll-Call Votes, Regular Plenary Sessions, 1946–90

| YEARS | UNITED STATES (%) | SOVIET UNION (%) |
|---|---|---|
| 1946–50 | 74.0 | 34.1 |
| 1951–55 | 60.1 | 52.4 |
| 1956–60 | 72.5 | 47.2 |
| 1961–65 | 54.5 | 54.7 |
| 1966–70 | 43.9 | 59.4 |
| 1971–75 | 38.9 | 65.1 |
| 1976–80 | 32.6 | 67.4 |
| 1981–85 | 14.3 | 79.3 |
| 1986–90 | 12.3 | 93.0 |

SOURCE: For years 1946–85: Inter-University Consortium for Political Research, Ann Arbor, Michigan; for 1987–91: United Nations, *Index to Proceedings of the General Assembly,* ST/LIB/SER. B/A. 41–46, Part 1.

to note that in votes in the U.S. Congress in 1998, the enlargement of NATO received almost unanimous support, whereas the same body could not muster the necessary majority to pay the country's back dues to the United Nations.

On one side, the United States represents the only surviving superpower. On the other, however, it is not just the Third World nations that believe the Americans are too eager to display their prowess in strategic and economic matters. The virtual unilateral action by the United States in making war on Iraq in March 2003 was condemned the world over, but nowhere were the street protests more vitriolic and expansive than in Western Europe. U.S. allies were distressed by what they judged to be an overbearing and demanding American posture. American "go-it-alone" policy and "the world be damned" attitude had become a general European reaction to George W. Bush's decision to unleash U.S. superior weapons technology against a small state. Even though the United Nations agreed that Iraq was a threat to its neighbors and peace in the Middle East, little if any justification could be found for the U.S. military action. The European reaction against U.S. hegemony, led by France, began before the war on Iraq, but Washington's demonstration of unbridled power confirmed in the minds of many that American ambitions had to be resisted. The overall European reaction to what was described as American arrogance was mirrored in the UN General Assembly. Moreover, the many nations of the United Nations were forced to compare Washington's enthusiasm for unilateral action with its reluctance to consider permanent power status on the Security Council for countries acknowledged to play significant roles in international affairs. The general conclusion was that the United States did not want to see the United Nations mature into a more formidable opposition.

FIGURE 3-2    Graph of U.S. and Soviet Union Percentage Agreement with the Majority, UN General Assembly Roll-Call Votes, Regular Plenary Sessions, 1946–90

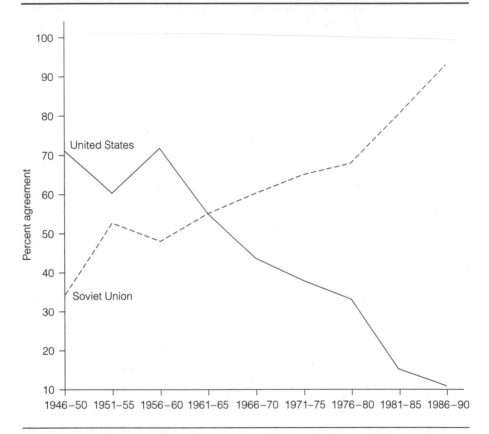

SOURCE: Roll call voting data for 1946–85 obtained from Inter-University Consortium for Political Research, Ann Arbor, Michigan; for 1986–90, from United Nations, *Index to Proceedings of the General Assembly*, ST/LIB/Ser. B/A. 41–46, Part 1 (1987–91).

The voting dynamics in the Security Council are quite different from those in the General Assembly, and here the United States was more likely to vote with the majority (see Table 3-8). If 1994 is taken as a pivotal year in the escalation of UN activity following the end of the Cold War, it also reveals a marked increase in Security Council cooperation. While the number of formal meetings and resolutions adopted were slightly lower than in 1993, there were more than in any other previous year. More important, Security Council consensus was extremely high. After the Cold War the Council had become involved even more deeply in the world community's collective efforts to resolve intranational as well as international differences.

The Security Council authorized new operations in Haiti, Tajikistan, and the Aouzou Strip, a border between Libya and Chad. It also began the closing

TABLE 3-8    UN Security Council Voting Behavior, 1988–2002

| YEAR | MEETINGS | RESOLUTIONS CONSIDERED | RESOLUTIONS ADOPTED | U.S. VETOES | PRESIDENTIAL STATEMENTS |
|------|----------|------------------------|---------------------|-------------|-------------------------|
| 2002 | 238 | 70 | 68 | 2 | 42 |
| 2001 | 192 | 54 | 52 | 2 | 39 |
| 2000 | 167 | 52 | 50 | 0 | 41 |
| 1999 | 124 | 67 | 65 | 0 | 34 |
| 1998 | 116 | 73 | 73 | 0 | 38 |
| 1997 | 117 | 57 | 54 | 2 | 57 |
| 1996 | 114 | 59 | 57 | 1 | 49 |
| 1995 | 130 | 67 | 66 | 1 | 63 |
| 1994 | 160 | 78 | 77 | 0 | 82 |
| 1993 | 171 | 95 | 93 | 0 | 88 |
| 1992 | 129 | 74 | 74 | 0 | 94 |
| 1991 | 53 | 42 | 42 | 0 | 21 |
| 1990 | 69 | 40 | 37 | 2 | 14 |
| 1989 | 69 | 25 | 20 | 5 | 17 |
| 1988 | 55 | 26 | 20 | 6 | 8 |

SOURCE: http://www.state.gov/p/io/conrpt. U.S. Department of State, *Voting Practices in the United Nations for 2002,* Bureau of International Organization Affairs, Report to Congress Submitted Pursuant to Public Law, 101-246, March 31, 2003, p. 15.

NOTE: In addition to the five permanent members—China, France, Russia, the United Kingdom, and the United States—the Security Council in 2002 was composed of Bulgaria, Cameroon, Colombia, Guinea, Ireland, Mauritius, Mexico, Norway, Singapore, and Syria. In 2002, the Security Council considered 70 draft resolutions and adopted 68, including two adopted by acclamation. The United States was the only permanent member of the council to exercise its veto, this year vetoing two draft resolutions. The Council was again heavily engaged in the international community's efforts to resolve conflicts and in giving direction to UN peacekeeping missions. Much of the Council's attention was focused on: Africa (23 resolutions), the Middle East (9 resolutions, including one that was vetoed), Afghanistan (6 resolutions), international terrorism (5 resolutions), Iraq (5 resolutions) and International Courts/Tribunals (4 resolutions). The Council also adopted resolutions on Bosnia and Herzegovina (one was vetoed), Croatia, Cyprus, East Timor (including one recommending that East Timor become a member of the United Nations), Georgia, and Switzerland (recommending that Switzerland become a member of the United Nations).

down of operations in Mozambique, South Africa, Somalia, and El Salvador. It responded to acts of genocide in Rwanda, if belatedly, and it sought peaceful solutions to disputes in the Persian Gulf, Georgia, Liberia, Angola, Burundi, and Cyprus. Measured against the popularity contest in the General Assembly, it was the Security Council that more accurately mirrored the realities of UN voting behavior in the mid-1990s. Of the seventy-seven resolutions adopted by the Security Council in 1994 (only one was rejected), three were approved without a vote and sixty-two won unanimous approval. Of the twelve resolutions adopted without unanimous approval, the United States voted in favor of eleven and abstained in one. Russia was the only permanent member to cast a veto in 1994, its first such action following the collapse of the Soviet Union.

This apparent harmony was sustained through the 1990s and into the new millennium, but the number of Security Council actions also was becoming ever more burdensome. While the UN's peacekeeping role was largely run by the smaller states, it was the major powers, and most notably the United States, that made the operations possible. And in the United States the antipathy always present toward the United Nations began to assume greater significance. The Clinton administration was positively disposed toward UN peacekeeping operations. But Clinton inherited the Somalia peacekeeping task from his predecessor, George Bush, and what the United States initiated, the United Nations was expected to conclude. When the United Nations expanded its mandate, however, to involve establishing a government for Somalia, the intervention in East Africa became protracted. Clinton's detractors in the American political scene found cause to condemn Washington's close association with the United Nations in Somalia, especially when a U.S. force was set upon by warring locals who exacted a heavy toll of American lives. Clinton's critics blamed the White House, but they also condemned the United Nations for what they called its unauthorized "mission creep" activity. Clinton was compelled by events and an unrelenting media to pull U.S. forces out of the country. When the United Nations decided it too would leave, that portion of the American public consistently opposed to the United Nations saw its ranks swelled by an even larger segment of the public that attributed American retreat to the failure of the United Nations to adequately respond to the Somali situation.

The development of the Internet and the changing character of the electronic and print media in the mid-1990s, especially that represented by more conservative American commentators, also was a vital factor in America's more negative perception of the United Nations. Neoconservatives associated with the extreme political right in the United States had been rejuvenated during the years of President Ronald Reagan. Echoed by the U.S. President, they saw little value in an organization that seemed to demand much from the United States but offered little and nothing, in their judgment, in return. As they mobilized their followers, viewers, and listeners with the power of the new technologies, their role in what was being described as an "information revolution" was to elevate the voice of conservative America. In the absence of the Cold War and the Soviet enemy, neoconservatives centered much of their assault on the United Nations. The international organization was viewed as a bastion of anti-Americanism and hence unworthy of U.S. support, and the call went out for the United States to withdraw from it. American highways were suddenly dotted with billboards demanding moving the United Nations out of the United States, and indeed, for the United States to announce its withdrawal from the institution that it was chiefly responsible for creating.

In this atmosphere, George W. Bush succeeded Bill Clinton. Bush's election campaign platform reserved a special place for renewed U.S. unilateralism, if not isolationism, rebuffing UN programs that centered on global warming, on de-mining, and in fact on bringing an end to the practice of laying land mines, as well as the effort by the international community to establish an International Criminal Court. As a candidate for the U.S. presidency, Bush presented himself as the champion of those wishing to see a neutered United Nations. With Bush victorious in the 2000 election, the anti-UN neoconservatives now had every reason to anticipate a radical change in U.S. foreign policy, especially with regard to the U.S. commitment to the world body. True to his campaign promises, President Bush formally rejected the Kyoto treaty on global warming, removed the U.S. signature from the treaty establishing the International Criminal Court, and denied all efforts that would have ended U.S. military mining practices.

But hardly eight months into Bush's term, the United States suffered the egregious assaults of September 11, 2001. Apart from the heavy loss of life, the two great symbols of American power—the seat of capitalism at the World Trade Center and the central command of the U.S. armed forces at the Pentagon—had been successfully targeted by a determined and vicious adversary. September 11 signaled the need for cooperation across the planet, but the Bush administration that declared war on terrorism did not see the United Nations as a major partner in what was described as a protracted enterprise. In October 2001 U.S. forces attacked the Afghanistan-based Al-Qaeda organization that led the assault on the United States, as well as the Taliban government of Afghanistan, identified as Al-Qaeda's primary supporter. The action was not taken for approval to the UN Security Council or General Assembly. The consensus gained in the mid-1990s between Security Council permanent members—moreover, the idea that the Security Council could take chief responsibility for maintaining the peace after the Cold War—had evaporated. Washington hoped to enlist the help of the world in its fight against global terrorism, but from the outset it was clear that Washington, not the United Nations, would determine the strategy and tactics for that war.

## The Structure of General Assembly Coalitions

The United Nations was never meant to cater to the interests and needs of a single power. Representing almost every sovereign actor in the world today, 191 in 2004, the United Nations must reflect the interests of all its members, rich and impoverished, powerful and weak, sophisticated and complex as well as primitive and simple. Issues abound in the organization, and each one has a special place in the affairs of a particular member. To the major powers, the objectives and concerns of a minor actor may carry little weight. But all issues no matter how limited are the stuff of UN activity, and no state wants to see its goals belittled, let alone ignored. Thus, the makeup of winning coalitions in the United Nations differs in detail with the nature of the issue, but UN membership patterns guarantee that any majority in the General Assembly must depend heavily on votes from African, Asian, and Latin American countries. The large powers win, however, when they can achieve common ground with the developing, non-Western majority. On many issues, the larger and wealthier states have important leverage in the negotiation process because their cooperation is essential to carrying out proposed resolutions.

In economic matters the majority understandably favors proposals for redistributing the world's wealth. Assembly majorities have routinely voted anti-Israel and anticolonial. On Middle East issues, the United States and Israel frequently stand alone on the losing side of the vote, with a few U.S. allies abstaining. Before the breakup of the Soviet Union, the UN majority purported to be nonaligned but their speeches and votes indicated more suspicion of the United States than of the Soviet Union.

The cohesiveness of the majority is shown by the extreme rarity of close votes. The African, Asian, and developing countries simply overwhelm the opposition when agreement cannot be negotiated. The division of 93 to 27 with 37 abstaining that occurred during the Forty-Sixth Assembly (1991) on a vote demanding immediate and complete Israeli withdrawal from occupied territories was a close decision by UN standards. More typical examples from the same session were the vote of 104 to 2, with 43 not only abstaining but intent on setting forth principles for a Middle East peace that were unacceptable to Israel (opposed by only Israel and the United States). A resolution that called for the return or restitution of cultural property to countries deemed to possess an original claim drew 23 abstentions but no opposing votes. Winning coalitions thus have a remarkable quality of sameness. Nothing can pass that does not minimally satisfy the Third World. The fact that Western industrialized states, East European states, and individual Third World states slide in and out of the majority is almost incidental to the outcome. With small, poor, developing states winning far more often than large, rich, developed states, the UN General Assembly appears to be a place where, to parody Thucydides' maxim, "the weak do what they can and the strong suffer what they must."

But that is not the whole story. In recent years the United States has prepared an annual report on General Assembly voting practices for the purpose of identifying how frequently other UN members vote with the United States. One feature of the report is a congressionally mandated discussion of "votes on issues which directly affected important United States interests and on which the United States lobbied extensively."[6] Of the twelve decisions in the 1991 Assembly meeting these criteria, the United States prevailed on eight. These included defeat of an Iraqi proposal to again condemn Israel for its 1981 attack on an Iraqi nuclear reactor, and another commending the International Atomic Energy Agency for monitoring Iraqi violations of its nuclear nonproliferation obligations. The other resolutions provided for a registry of conventional arms transfers, urged support of the UN Relief and Works Agency in Palestine, and repealed the 1975 resolution equating Zionism with racism (two recorded votes). The United States also got the United Nations to focus international attention on Iraqi human rights violations in Kuwait and on streamlining UN procedure for providing electoral assistance to countries requesting it. On the other side, the United States unsuccessfully opposed resolutions calling for discontinuance of all nuclear testing. It also voted against the resolution proposing a Middle East peace settlement on terms unfavorable to Israel (two decisions) and another deploring "coercive measures" against developing countries by some developed states (a Cuban initiative aimed at the United States). Although the United States voted with the majority on about 15 percent of all contested issues in the Forty-Sixth Assembly, the U.S. position prevailed on two-thirds of the twelve important votes. The outcome of all this jousting seemed to indicate that the United States could only win in the General Assembly when it was willing to lobby intensively for a position that was not diametrically opposed to interests of Third World states.

The picture of small states routinely outvoting the large ones is further blurred by the growing tendency for the Assembly to make decisions by consensus. In its report on voting in the 1991 Assembly the United States rated fifteen of the consensus resolutions as "important." Adding these to the twelve "important" recorded votes, the United States was with the majority in twenty-three of twenty-seven important decisions, or 85 percent of the time. Furthermore, when decisions by consensus are taken into account, the United States seems to vote with the majority most of the time. In 1984 the proportion of Assembly decisions by consensus was 55 percent; in 1987 it rose to 61 percent; and in 1991 more than 78 percent of all decisions (272 of 348) were by consensus. With 272 consensus decisions and ten recorded votes in which the United States joined the majority, the overall majority agreement score for the United States in 1991 was 81 percent.[7] Nevertheless, it is important to note that this was a lower score than any other UN member with the exception of Israel.

The voting power of the Third World clearly does not make the General Assembly either a useless or a dangerous place for the major powers or a superpower like the United States. Even when a resolution objectionable to one or more states is adopted, it has only the force of a recommendation. A parliamentary victory of one group over another may induce temporary euphoria in the winners, and even have some weight as an expression of world opinion, but no dissenting state is bound to comply. Also not to be overlooked is the UN function of harmonizing differences and promoting action in the common interest. The large and growing number of resolutions adopted without objection demonstrates that differences are usually harmonized, at least at the verbal level, and especially in widely approved UN programs in such disparate areas as peacekeeping, economic development, and refugee relief. Agreement therefore often extends beyond rhetoric. The Assembly undoubtedly could accomplish more if its members behaved better, that is, were more empathetic and cooperative, but the body has utility for all of them. If nothing else, the General Assembly is a good place for listening and learning.

## THE CONSEQUENCES OF UN ACTION

The UN political process normally focuses on the adoption of a resolution. But what are the consequences of this action? Will the resolution be enforced, ignored, or acted on in any way? There is no single answer to these questions because UN resolutions are not all alike and much depends on the circumstances. Partial answers will be supplied as particular UN activities are examined in subsequent chapters. Here we will present a more general framework for identifying and explaining the differing consequences of a variety of UN actions. In developing this analysis, an examination of conditions that give weight to the decisions of national governments will be helpful. These include the sanction of physical force, the authority of law, customary obedience, and the economic and human resources available for carrying out programs.

Physical force is important, primarily as a deterrent to law violation. Without it society would be at the mercy of the deviant lawbreaker, vulnerable to a general breakdown in order and respect for law. Physical coercion works best when its use is the exception rather than the rule. A government that habitually resorts to violence to obtain compliance with its rules is unstable at best. In a well-ordered state people obey the law because it is the law. The law is respected because it is legitimate; that is, the people accept the government's right to make it. The legitimacy of the law is also reinforced by customs of compliance. While the state's coercive power may lurk in the background, the daily homespun of obedience is woven from threads of habit, legitimacy, underlying consensus on the goals of the state, and rational recognition that obedience to law is in the general interest. The viability of a state and its government rests heavily on the capacity to command widespread compliance without the necessity of physical coercion.

The protective and regulatory functions of government require general obedience to law. Governments also perform service functions, and these are dependent not so much on the obedience of the citizenry as on the availability of material resources and of administrative apparatus for application of the resources to the task at hand. All governments have the power to raise money by various forms of compulsory levy, and all have some type of administrative machinery. Given a satisfactory level of obedience to law, the effectiveness of government action is closely correlated with the availability of taxable resources and the expertise of public administration. The states of Western Europe and North America, for example, have effective governments not only because of general obedience to law but also because their resources are adequate and their administrative machinery is relatively well trained. In contrast, some of the smaller, poorer countries lack resources, administrative capacity, and even an adequate level of obedience to law.

To what extent can the United Nations draw on the sources that give force to decisions of national governments? On its face the UN Charter appears to confer on the United Nations a legal monopoly on the right to use physical coercion in international affairs, with the exception of self-defense. In practice, however, states—individually and through alliances—have retained control over the instruments of coercion. The United Nations neither has a monopoly of such force nor makes any grandiose claim to it. At best, the United Nations can serve as a catalytic agent for mobilizing force for UN objectives when enough members are willing to cooperate.

Most UN decisions also lack the force of law. The organization has much authority to recommend but little to command. Recommendations might be effective if they were supported by a strong tradition of customary obedience, but the United Nations has not yet developed such a tradition. Some UN specialized agencies do much better. The regulations of the Universal Postal Union, for example, are observed with a regularity that would do credit to national administrations. All the elements of customary obedience are there—habit legitimacy, broad consensus on goals, and recognition of a common interest in international postal operations. As one moves away, however, from purely technical activities to the more political subjects debated by the General Assembly and other UN organs the degree of customary obedience declines markedly. States have not yet developed habits of indiscriminate compliance with General Assembly recommendations. As a result, compliance rests on a coincidence of national interest in particular UN policies and programs. The action of a UN majority may sometimes create political pressure in favor of compliance, but that is no substitute for the kinds of forces that induce voluntary compliance with national laws.

International organization also stands in a different position from that of national governments in its ability to command vital resources, such as money. Although budgetary assessments are usually paid, international organizations are ultimately dependent on the resources that individual states are willing to supply, not on what majorities are moved to demand. This should not suggest that the sums raised by contribution are inconsequential. The regular UN budget for 1997 was reduced from five years earlier partly because of a failure of the United States to meet its obligations, but also as a consequence of the organization's overextension in dealing with world problems after the end of the Cold War. From a budget of $2.39 billion in 1992–93, the 1997 budget, including UN core functions in New York, Geneva, Nairobi, Vienna, and five regional commissions, was a mere $1.3 billion. This sum represented about 4 percent of New York City's annual budget and nearly $1 billion less than the yearly cost of Tokyo's fire department. As the UN public relations department noted, the UN budget was considerably less than the $3.7 billion of the New York State university system. The sum given for UN peacekeeping operations in 1996 was $1.4 billion, or less than 1 percent of the U.S. military budget and hardly 0.2 percent of worldwide military spending.

Eighty percent of the work of the UN system was still devoted to helping developing countries improve their economies, but also to encouraging them to build democratic institutions and protect human rights. No other organization was so deeply involved in administering to needy children, warding off infectious disease, or assisting refugees and disaster victims, let alone those exposed to the dangers of land mines. Granted organizations such as UNICEF, UNDP, the UN Fund for Population Activities (UNFPA), and the World Food Program (WFP) spend an additional $4.6 billion, but even this represents only the equivalent of 80 cents per human being. In 1994, by contrast, the world's governments spent approximately $778 billion on their armed forces, the equivalent of $134 per human being. In all of this the U.S. share of the 1997 UN budget was $312 million, and the assessment for peacekeeping was another $400 million, down from $1 billion in 1995. Despite deep personnel cuts (approximately 25 percent in 1997), U.S. citizens still held more UN Secretariat positions than did citizens of any other member state, and Americans also served in more top posts at UNICEF, the UNDP, the World Bank, the WFP, and the Universal Postal Union. Nevertheless, the U.S. Congress demanded still more drastic reductions in the UN workforce.

In 1998 the UN regular budget was reduced still further, to $1,190 billion, and the peacekeeping budget from July 1998 to June 1999 was less than $1 billion dollars, that is, lower than the $992 million in the same period for 1997–98. But even these reductions did not cause the organization's delinquents to pay their full share. As of October 31, 1998, the total amount owed the United Nations was approximately $2.3 billion. Of this amount $650,594,871 involved the regular budget, $20,951,563 was for the operations of international tribunals, and $1,630,178,650 was for the peacekeeping program. The nations most delinquent in 1999 were the United States ($1,477,107,967), Ukraine ($223,310,477), Russian Federation ($131,826,307), Japan ($96,558,681), Belarus ($56,251,700), and Brazil ($46,820,811).

With pressure exerted from numerous sources, delinquent payments in 2001 were reduced to $2.11 billion, and $1.68 billion at the end of 2002. The latter figure was the lowest in seven years. Nevertheless, the aggregate level of unpaid contributions, though having decreased from previous years, showed the United States delinquent in meeting its peacekeeping obligations by $536 million in 2002. In fact, the United States was first among three member countries that owed 84 percent of the regular budget debt. It also was first among the five member states that owed 84 percent of the debt on funding international tribunals, and first among the ten states owing 77 percent of peacekeeping assessments in January 2003.

The United Nations must depend on the willingness of members to provide funds. The sale of UN publications and postage stamps does not yet constitute an important source of independent income, and substantial revenues from resources of the common seabed area are yet in the distant future. The remaining condition of effective action, administrative capability, will be discussed in more detail in the following chapter. Here, we may observe that the UN Secretariat has performed reasonably well the administrative tasks imposed on it, whereas decisions dependent on member state compliance have frequently been dead letters.

Given UN capabilities as we have assessed them, the consequences of UN action may be summarized. Where UN resolutions have initiated programs to be administered by the Secretariat and members are willing to contribute the necessary resources, the consequences of UN action have been important. The United Nations has solid accomplishment in areas ranging from research studies to development assistance to peacekeeping operations. On the other hand, where resolutions have depended on compliance by member states, the record is very checkered. In many instances, members comply because they are in sympathy with the resolution. Occasionally, states are moved to compliance, or a show of compliance, by a desire not to appear out of step with a large UN majority. In numerous other instances, UN recommendations are flat-out ignored by governments that perceive no self-interested basis—however broadly or narrowly construed—for compliance. No UN majority could persuade the Soviet Union to withdraw its troops from Afghanistan in 1979 or induce the United States to refrain from invading Iraq in 2003. In the absence of rules having the force of law, compelling habits of obedience, and physical sanctions to support the rules, the United Nations must rely on a convergence of national interests to secure compliance.

There is still another way in which UN resolutions affect international politics. More than three decades ago Inis L. Claude Jr. observed that the United Nations "has come to be regarded, and used, as a dispenser of politically significant approval and disapproval of the claims, policies, and actions of states." [8] He called this phenomenon "collective legitimization." Former UN Ambassador Jeane J. Kirkpatrick, a persistent critic of UN decision making, made a similar point in explaining why UN decisions are important to the conduct of foreign affairs: UN votes clarify "world opinion" on major issues. Since there are no other arenas in which all the countries of the world express their opinions on policy, the decisions of UN bodies are widely taken as the most valid expression of "world opinion." [9]

UN resolutions, by the very fact of their adoption, become intangible resources for their supporters and liabilities for their opponents. UN decisions may not confer the legitimacy of law, but they do confer the legitimacy of majority approval in a body representing virtually every sovereign state. The legitimizing force of a resolution varies according to the size and composition of the voting majority and the forcefulness and clarity of the language used. Objective data cuts sharper than ambiguity. A unanimous Security Council resolution is weightier than one on which several permanent members abstain (and even more so if it is a "decision" under Article 25, which members have agreed to "accept and carry out"). Overwhelming approval in the Assembly is more convincing than a two-vote margin. A series of resolutions that clarify a position will have more impact than an isolated case. Repeated UN declarations of support for decolonization, aid to developing countries, and human rights have helped to make such concepts almost articles of faith (if not of unfailing practice) in the global system. Even states that deny the validity of particular UN pronouncements are sometimes reluctant to violate them, or appear to violate them, in tacit recognition of the importance of collective legitimization.

The United Nations is not a supergovernment. Its resources are limited; its words are seldom law. Its mandates can be enforced against an unwilling state only if members are willing to use the necessary coercion. But its decisions do make a difference. Funds are raised and expended; economic and social programs are launched; peacekeeping missions are maintained; disputes are sometimes settled. Much voluntary cooperation is encouraged. And no state can disregard UN processes without paying some penalty, or losing some advantage in its relations with other states.

# NOTES

1. Some others include UN world conferences on population (1974), food (1974), the International Women's Year (1975), human settlements (1976), world employment (1976), water (1977), desertification (1977), racial discrimination (1978 and 1983), technical cooperation among developing countries (1978), agrarian reform and rural development (1979), science and technology for development (1979), the UN Decade for Women (1980), energy (1981), outer space (1982), Palestine (1983), population (1984), fisheries (1984), status of women (1985), sanctions against South Africa (1986), peaceful uses of nuclear energy (1987), disarmament and development (1987), children (1990), education for all (1990), environment and development (1992), human rights (1993), population and development (1995), and women (1995).
2. Seymour Maxwell Finger, *Your Man at the UN* (New York: New York University Press, 1980), p. 20.
3. See Robert E. Riggs, "The United Nations and the Politics of Law," in *Politics in the United Nations System,* ed. Lawrence S. Finkelstein (Durham, NC: Duke University Press, 1988), pp. 41–74.
4. U.S. Department of State, *Report to Congress on Voting Practices in the United Nations 1990,* submitted pursuant to Public Law 101-167, March 31, 1991, p. 61.
5. Leo Pasvolsky, "The United Nations in Action," in *Edmund J. James Lectures on Government* (Urbana: University of Illinois Press, 1951), pp. 80–81.
6. For example, U.S. Department of State, *Report to Congress on Voting Practices in the United Nations 1991,* submitted pursuant to Public Law 101-167, March 31, 1992, p. 33.
7. The percentage figures for Assembly consensus voting, 1976 through 1991, are found *ibid.,* p. 63. For 1984 the figures are taken from U.S. Department of State, *Report to Congress on Voting Practices in the United Nations,* submitted pursuant to Public Law 99-190 and Public Law 98-164, May 20, 1985, p. 3. The ten recorded votes in which the United States was with the UN majority are found in *Resolutions and Decisions Adopted by the General Assembly during the First Part of Its Forty-Sixth Session,* United Nations Press Release GA/8307, January 21, 1992.
8. Inis L. Claude Jr., *The Changing United Nations* (New York: Random House, 1967), pp. 73, 93.
9. "Testimony of U.S. Permanent Representative to the United Nations Jeane J. Kirkpatrick before the Senate Foreign Operations Subcommittee of the Senate Appropriations Committee, March 25, 1985," reproduced in U.S. Department of State, *Report to Congress on Voting Practices in the United Nations,* submitted pursuant to Public Law 98-151 and Public Law 98-164, May 30, 1985, p. 3.

# SELECTED READINGS

Alker, Hayward R., and Bruce M. Russett. *World Politics in the General Assembly.* New Haven, CT: Yale University Press, 1965.

Ameri, Houshang. *Politics and Process in the Specialized Agencies of the United Nations.* Aldershot, UK: Gower, 1982.

Baehr, Peter R. *The Role of a Delegation in the General Assembly.* Occasional paper no. 9. New York: Carnegie Endowment for International Peace, 1970.

Bailey, Sydney D. *The Procedure of the United Nations Security Council.* 2nd ed. Oxford: Clarendon Press, 1988.

Chiang Pei-Heng. *Non-Governmental Organizations at the United Nations.* New York: Praeger, 1981.

Cox, Robert W., Harold K. Jacobson, et al. *The Anatomy of Influence: Decision Making in International Organization.* New Haven, CT: Yale University Press, 1973.

Finger, Seymour Maxwell. *American Ambassadors at the U.N.: People, Politics, and Bureaucracy in Making Foreign Policy.* New York: Holmes & Meier, 1988.

Hovet, Thomas, Jr. *Bloc Politics in the United Nations.* Cambridge, MA: Harvard University Press, 1960.

Jackson, Richard L. *The Non-Aligned, the UN and the Superpowers.* New York: Praeger, 1983.

Kaufmann, Johan. *Conference Diplomacy: An Introductory Analysis.* 2nd rev. ed. Dordrecht: Martinus Nijhoff, 1988.

———. *United Nations Decision Making.* Alphen aan den Rijn: Sijthoff & Noordhoff, 1980.

McConnell, W. H., and Ron Wheeler, eds. *Swords and Plowshares: The United Nations in Transition.* Toronto: Canadian Scholars Press, 1997.

McWhinney, Edward. *United Nations Law Making.* New York: Holmes & Meier, 1984.

Mortimore, Robert. *The Third World Coalition in International Politics.* Boulder, CO: Westview Press, 1984.

Peterson, M. J. *The General Assembly in World Politics.* Winchester, MA: Allen & Unwin, 1986.

Rajan, M. S., et al., eds. *The Nonaligned and the United Nations.* Dobbs Ferry, NY: Oceana, 1987.

Riches, Cromwell A. *Majority Rule in International Organization.* Baltimore, MD: Johns Hopkins University Press, 1940.

Riggs, Robert E. *Politics in the United Nations: A Study of United States Influence in the General Assembly.* Urbana: University of Illinois Press, 1958. Reprinted by Greenwood Press, 1984.

Rosenau, James N. *The United Nations in a Turbulent World.* International Peace Academy, Occasional Paper Series. Boulder, CO: Lynne Rienner, 1992.

Sauvant, Karl P. *The Group of 77: Evolution, Structure, Organization.* Dobbs Ferry, NY: Oceana, 1981.

Sloan, Blaine. *United Nations General Assembly Resolutions in Our Changing World.* Los Angeles: Transnational, 1991.

Sonnenfeld, Renata. *Resolutions of the United Nations Security Council.* Dordrecht: Martinus Nijhoff, 1989.

Stoessinger, John G. *The United Nations and the Superpowers.* 4th ed. New York: Random House, 1977.

White, Nigel D. *The United Nations System: Toward International Justice.* Boulder, CO: Lynne Rienner, 2002.

Whittaker, David J. *United Nations in Action.* Armonk, NY: M. E. Sharpe, 1995.

Willetts, Peter, ed. *The Conscience of the World: The Influence of Non-Governmental Organizations in the UN System.* Washington, DC: Brookings Institution, 1996.
———. *Pressure Groups in the Global System: The Transnational Relations of Issue-Oriented Nongovernmental Organizations.* London: Frances Pinter, 1982.
Williams, Marc. *Third World Cooperation: The Group of 77 in UNCTAD.* New York: St. Martin's Press, 1991.

# 4

# POLITICS AND THE UN SECRETARIAT

"I am a free man; I feel light as a feather." These words captured the exhilaration and the relief of Javier Pérez de Cuéllar as he left UN headquarters in the early hours of New Year's Day 1992. His tenth and last year as UN Secretary-General had just drawn to a close, only minutes after the completion of lengthy negotiations leading to a cease-fire agreement between El Salvador's contending factions. A compromise candidate for the Secretary-Generalship in 1982, he had become Secretary-General when UN fortunes had sunk to new lows. In 1992, however, he left an organization much closer to the center of world politics, as well as a position with a greatly enlarged role in the promotion of world peace and security. Beginning without great expectations, this bland, determined diplomat-professor from Lima made his exit with a standing ovation from the General Assembly and a nomination for the Nobel Peace Prize.

Pérez de Cuéllar did not have a direct role in ending the Cold War, but he was very much responsible for the new prominence the United Nations enjoyed in 1992. It was in fact the Secretary-General who quickly took advantage of the changed global climate and propelled the organization into the mainstream of world politics. Such a role for the United Nations was not inevitable, and without the Secretary-General and his staff it would have been impossible. Pérez de Cuéllar was the right choice at the right time. More than a decade after his departure it can still be said that Pérez de Cuéllar added a luster and credibility to the office of the Secretary-General, and in so doing elevated the United Nations to heights not seen since its founding.

The importance of an international secretariat to the functioning of international organizations is hard to exaggerate. It is fair to say that modern international organization did not, indeed could not, exist until the invention of the permanent international secretariat. Without a staff to administer its affairs between meetings, an international organization is little more than a series of conferences. With a permanent secretariat, the organization is no longer just an arena where states and other actors play out their roles but is itself an actor on the international scene. A permanent staff creates the capacity to gather and disseminate information, monitors state compliance with rules and recommendations of the organization, and provides services to member states and their people. These functions include a wide range of activities for the Secretariat and its economic, social, and technical agencies. Lending money, giving advice on agricultural questions, confronting disease, reducing illiteracy, improving meteorological services, regulating labor standards, promoting human rights, safeguarding the environment, and providing refugee relief are just some of the UN activities that come within the purview of the UN Secretariat. Within its sphere of operation, the United Nations becomes a continuing presence among the states and in their relations with one another, often affecting their domestic policies.

Secretariat employees perform many tasks that often affect the substance of UN decisions. Internal housekeeping activities, such as personnel management, money issues, UN property care, and the procurement of needed supplies, are important institutionally and are kept politically neutral. Hundreds of language specialists are employed by the Secretariat to interpret speeches at UN meetings, often simultaneously, into each of the organization's six languages—English, French, Russian, Spanish, Chinese, and Arabic—and to prepare documentation in the same six languages. The designation of "official" and "working" languages became a political issue in the early years of the United Nations. Initially, the United Nations had five "official" languages but only two "working" languages—English and French—into which all documents were routinely translated. Arabic was subsequently added to the group of official UN languages. All the official languages later were declared working languages, thus satisfying a large number of members, but also considerably increasing the cost of producing documentation.

The UN Secretariat conducts its own postal service and maintains a large-scale publishing operation to supply the world with reports, meeting records, and other UN publications. But secretariats also do much that is politically important. At meetings of the United Nations and other international agencies, the staff is concerned not only with translation and documentation but also with the substantive problems being discussed. Whether the subject is human rights, social welfare, disarmament, environmental protection, or the peaceful settlement of disputes, staff members are assigned duties of information gathering, research, and reporting. Staff reports are often the basis for discussion and decision in meetings of UN bodies. Specialists in economic development, international law, or particular political problem areas must be prepared to advise the Secretary-General and, on occasion, national delegates. Countries lacking adequate expertise within their delegations sometimes rely heavily on the experts in the Secretariat. In organizations whose principal business is supplying technical assistance and other services to member states, the budget proposal prepared by the Secretariat dominates the organization's agenda.

Even internal matters such as staff recruitment can become intensely political as member states intervene to secure Secretariat positions, especially high-level positions, for their nationals. Budgeting in any international agency is also an intensely political process. Staff members and governmental representatives consult extensively in negotiating a budget that will satisfy their special interests and yet win the necessary majority of votes. Budget controversies are generally the responsibility of government representatives, but secretariats are intimately involved in the political give-and-take.

Beyond advising, reporting, budgeting, and otherwise shaping organizational decisions, the Secretary-General and other high-level Secretariat officers may become intimately involved in the politics of the world as intermediaries in the settlement of international disputes. The services of Pérez de Cuéllar and his deputies were utilized widely in the closing years of his administration to help resolve the war in Afghanistan. The Secretary-General's hand can also be seen in bringing order, if not peace, to Iran and Iraq, El Salvador, Western Sahara, Angola, and other trouble spots. In such situations UN representatives become political actors, on a par with ambassadors and foreign ministers, and have a capacity to effect desired outcomes. The effectiveness of the Secretary-General and his associates is derived from their identity as neutral, international civil servants, rather than rival members of a national constituency. By contrast, however, Boutros Boutros-Ghali, who succeeded Pérez de Cuéllar, had a stormy term as Secretary-General. As the first Secretary-General following the end of the Cold War, Boutros-Ghali found himself and the United Nations more involved in peacekeeping ventures than previously. Moreover, major operations such as in Bosnia and Somalia ended in disaster, and the Secretary-General was singled out for the organization's ineptitude in managing its responsibilities. During this period the U.S. government was split between a comparatively liberal President and a very conservative Congress, and in the melee between the two institutions the United Nations suffered. When the United States rejected Boutros-Ghali's quest for reelection, and the search for a compromise candidate was undertaken, Kofi Annan, a long-term international civil servant at the United Nations, was identified for his neutral, apolitical record; he was ultimately elected to succeed Boutros-Ghali.

Elected in January 1997, Annan is perhaps the best example of a Secretary-General, who is supposed to be all things to all people and nations. One of Annan's major initiatives has been his plan to reform the United Nations and bring "new life" to it. He has focused needed attention on Africa in a number of ways and been instrumental in actions from Libya to East Timor to the Middle East. In April 2000 he presented his Millennium Report, which called upon member states to do more to improve education, reduce the incidence of HIV/AIDS, and safeguard the environment. For all these efforts and more, Annan received the Nobel Peace Prize in 2001. In 2001, Annan was extended to another term as Secretary-General, this time by acclaim. His second term will run until December 31, 2006.

Before considering the political role of the UN Secretariat in detail, this chapter will examine the origin of the international civil service and some of the special problems that it raises for those who serve in it. The discussion will then turn to the UN Secretariat, with emphasis on political problems associated with recruiting personnel and preserving staff independence from national suasion. The last section will elaborate the principal theme of the chapter—the role of secretariats in organizational decision making and their impact on international politics. The discussion will center on the United Nations and its Secretary-General, but a broader perspective will be added by occasional comparison with other international organizations.

# THE INTERNATIONAL CIVIL SERVICE

## ORIGIN

The international civil service dates only from the establishment of the League of Nations and the International Labor Organization at the close of World War I. Before that time the permanent bureaus or secretariats of such technical organizations as the Universal Postal Union were not international in composition. The personnel were typically citizens of the headquarters host state, and often they were nationals on temporary leave from their normal assignments with the home government.

The League Covenant made no express provision for internationalization of the staff. It simply stated, "The Secretariat shall comprise a Secretary-General and such secretaries and staff as may be required." Credit goes to Sir Eric Drummond, the first League Secretary-General, for insisting on a truly international secretariat. The decision to establish a multinational civil service recruited individually rather than as contingents of national representatives has been called, in an authoritative history of the League, "one of the most important events in the history of international politics."[1] The secretariat of the ILO, under the leadership of Albert Thomas, adopted a similar concept of an international civil service.

Codifying the experience of the League and the ILO, the UN Charter expressly provided for a Secretariat that was to be appointed by a Secretary-General as its administrative head, and recruited individually on the basis of merit and personal probity. With their loyalty due to the international organization, the individuals chosen for service with the League embodied the ideals of the international civil service, notably, the "highest standards of *efficiency, competence,* and *integrity*" as well as *independence* from national pressures, and *impartiality* toward all member states. Wide geographic distribution of appointments was recognized as an important subsidiary principle. Other intergovernmental organizations have looked to these standards and have applied them to an ever-growing international public service. At their peak the staff of the League and ILO together numbered scarcely more than a thousand. Although the UN Secretariat employs many more people, when judged by its greater complexity and the number of specialized international agencies that have emerged since the end of World War II, its overall workforce is very modest. Indeed, McDonald's hamburger chain employs three times as many people! The worldwide UN system in 2002, that is, the Secretariat and twenty-eight other organizations (for example, UNICEF, and including its specialized agencies and related intergovernmental organizations) employed something more than sixty thousand people. Tough new standards introduced in 1997 cut the overall Secretariat staff (which includes those based in Geneva, Nairobi, and Vienna) from twelve thousand to nine thousand employees.

## PROBLEMS OF DIVERSITY AND POLITICAL SUPPORT

An international secretariat faces the problems that bureaucracies face everywhere—problems of internal decision making, communication, lines of authority and responsibility, and recruitment and retention of competent personnel. But compared with national civil services, an international secretariat has special problems stemming from its political environment.

One obvious challenge is to integrate within a single administrative machine the diverse attitudes, languages, backgrounds, and abilities of people who are recruited from every region on earth. The central problem here is the absence of a shared political culture. A national civil service operates within a relatively homogeneous value framework. There is broad consensus on the functions of government, the means by which political decisions are reached, and the limits of legitimate governmental authority. With no shared global political culture, the UN Secretariat lacks both the guidelines that would make its own choice of actions easier and the legitimacy that would make its functions acceptable to its clientele. In any governmental system the conduct of administration requires some bargaining and negotiation with the clientele to be served or regulated. In international administration the lack of shared political values greatly widens the range of issues that must be negotiated. Even when norms for particular activities are developed through practice, such as standards for technical assistance programs, the process is complicated by the need for adapting standards to differing national contexts.

The international secretariat also lacks sustaining links with sources of political support that national civil services enjoy. At the apex of the national administrative structure is a President or Prime Minister, who is in most instances a dominant person. In the United States the President draws power from his constitutional prerogatives, his control of the executive branch, his electoral mandate, and his relationship with his political party and other important support groups within the larger society. The administrative departments work under his direction and draw political support from that relationship. Parliamentary systems have the further advantage of a chief executive who speaks for a dominant political party or coalition within the national legislature. In addition, administrative agencies often receive support from groups within the community that receive agency services.

In contrast, the links that join an international secretariat to sources of power within the international system are more fragile and tenuous. The typical Secretary-General or Director-General has very limited political prerogatives, no important ties with a public constituency, no broad electoral mandate, and scarcely anything resembling leadership of a dominant political party or legislative coalition. The executive head can cultivate the support of governments within his or her organization. But governments change, as do their UN representatives, and governments are motivated very little by a sense of loyalty, obligation, or feelings of support for a UN Secretary-General.

Sometimes, international bureaucracies can develop important ties of mutual interest with their counterparts in national ministries of government. Periodic personal contacts at international meetings and regular communication between staff members of national and international agencies concerned with similar problems can lead to mutually supportive behavior. Thus civil servants in national ministries of health may feel a vested interest in the work of the World Health Organization, or national finance ministries may provide support for the work of the International Monetary Fund. Such relationships are more likely to be developed in technical, relatively noncontroversial areas and in economic and social activities rather than in matters affecting national security.

In some international secretariats, for example, UNESCO, the ILO, the United Nations Environment Programme, the International Civil Aviation Organization, the World Bank, or even the United Nations, mutually advantageous relationships with private groups have a way of developing, but in range and intensity of support, they cannot be compared to the agency-clientele relationships that sustain a particular country's national bureaucracy.

## THE UN SECRETARIAT

The UN Secretariat is undergoing major reforms that are proposed to meet the demands of the twenty-first century with far less financial support. The Secretariat of the future is slated to be smaller, better trained, more versatile, and more integrated. The average age of the UN staff at the end of the century was forty-nine, with only 14 percent younger than forty and fewer than 5 percent younger than thirty-five. Within the next decade almost half of the Secretariat staff are expected to retire, and the opportunity will exist to refashion the organization so that it has better geographic and gender representation. Some member states are still not represented, and women hold less than 20 percent of senior-level posts. Indeed, women constituted 35 percent of the total Secretariat staff. UN Secretariat personnel have been cut significantly, almost 20 percent since 1999 levels. The administrative budget also was reduced substantially. Scrutinized especially by the United States, the UN Secretariat of the future will have to be much leaner, more efficient, less concerned with internal personnel matters, and more prepared for external development.

### RECRUITING UN PERSONNEL

The UN Secretariat, like a national bureaucracy, faces the constant problem of recruiting competent employees to fill available positions. For support staff positions, the problems of recruitment are much the same as those other employers face. Such jobs are commonly filled by local recruitment without regard to geographic distribution and mostly with nationals of the host country. About two-thirds of the employees at UN headquarters in New York and Geneva fall into these categories.

For higher-level employees, the search for talent is limited to people with the necessary language skills and the willingness to live in an alien environment. There is also the very serious problem of reconciling competence with the demands of wide geographic distribution. This applies to positions at the professional level and higher, except for language specialists. These professionals are mandated to do all the substantive work of analyzing global and regional developments in the political, security, disarmament, economic, social, human rights, and environmental areas. They also are authorized to direct peacekeeping and other emergency operations and prepare the Secretary-General's reports to the General Assembly, Security Council, Economic and Social Council, and their related organs and agencies. Finally, the professional staff oversees the implementation of works programs and other detailed assignments.

The Secretariat's professional-level civil service numbered 5,733 in 2003, with an emphasis on gender distribution. Women represented 35 percent of staff with appointments of one year or more, an increase of 0.4 percent over 2001–02. In the matter of geographical distribution, women made greater strides, representing 41 percent, or an increase 0.8 percent. Appointment of women to higher levels in the United Nations, however, declined by 7.5 percent in the same period, with women constituting 32.2 percent of these appointments. Women accounted for 57.9 percent of staff recruited through the national competitive and language examinations. In the field service category, out of 55 promotions, however, only two women were promoted. This contrasts with the 546 promotions in the General Service category, of which 63.6 percent were women. Nevertheless, only 14 women moved between departments and offices on promotion, indicating only marginal upward mobility. Although the goal is gender balance, the UN Secretariat still has a considerable way to go. (See Tables 4-1 and 4-2; this subject will also be treated in more detail below.)

According to Article 101 of the UN Charter, the "paramount consideration" in recruitment and conditions of service should be "the necessity of securing the highest standards of efficiency, competence, and integrity." Article 101 further provides that "due regard shall be paid to the importance of recruiting the staff on as wide a geographical basis as possible," but the Charter makes this clearly secondary to the merit principle. In practice, the Secretary-General has given first importance to efficiency, with substantial support from the United States and countries of Western Europe, which have always been heavily represented in the UN Secretariat. Areas less well represented, especially Eastern Europe and the newer states of Asia and Africa, have fought for the principle of equitable geographic distribution as though it were the paramount consideration. They contend that efficiency in the broader sense is not possible unless all national viewpoints are adequately represented in the Secretariat.

TABLE 4-1    Gender Representation in United Nations Secretariat
Professional Staff, 1996

| DEPARTMENT OR OFFICE | MEN | WOMEN | TOTAL | PERCENTAGE WOMEN |
|---|---|---|---|---|
| Administration and Management | 14 | 17 | 31 | 54.8 |
| Human Resources Management | 36 | 41 | 77 | 53.2 |
| Interorganization Body | 3 | 3 | 6 | 50.0 |
| Public Information | 131 | 128 | 259 | 49.4 |
| Policy Coordination & | | | | |
| Sustainable Development | 47 | 44 | 91 | 48.4 |
| Joint Staff Pension Fund | 18 | 15 | 33 | 45.5 |
| UN Environmental Program | 11 | 9 | 20 | 45.0 |
| Program Planning Budget 7 | | | | |
| Accounts | 51 | 40 | 91 | 44.0 |
| UN Center for Human Rights | 33 | 25 | 58 | 43.1 |
| Development Support & | | | | |
| Management Services | 49 | 37 | 86 | 43.0 |
| UN Office in Geneva | 55 | 38 | 93 | 40.9 |
| UN Drug Control Program | 27 | 18 | 45 | 40.0 |
| Political Affairs | 84 | 52 | 130 | 38.2 |
| Legal Affairs | 49 | 30 | 79 | 38.0 |
| International Oversight Services | 31 | 18 | 49 | 36.7 |
| Economic & Social Information | | | | |
| & Analysis | 83 | 42 | 125 | 33.6 |
| Conference Services | 91 | 46 | 137 | 33.6 |
| Peacekeeping Operations | 53 | 26 | 79 | 32.9 |
| Office of the Secretary General | 17 | 8 | 25 | 32.0 |
| Economic & Social Commission | | | | |
| for Western Asia | 50 | 22 | 72 | 30.6 |
| Economic & Social Commission | | | | |
| for Asia & Pacific | 93 | 40 | 133 | 30.1 |
| Economic Commission for Latin | | | | |
| America & Caribbean | 101 | 38 | 139 | 27.3 |
| Humanitarian Affairs | 33 | 12 | 45 | 26.7 |
| UN Office in Vienna | 38 | 13 | 51 | 25.5 |
| Regional Commissions | 3 | 1 | 4 | 25.0 |
| Center for Human Settlements | 34 | 11 | 45 | 24.4 |
| Economic Commission for | | | | |
| Europe | 68 | 20 | 88 | 22.7 |
| UN Commission on Trade and | | | | |
| Development | 157 | 46 | 203 | 22.7 |
| Economic Cooperation | | | | |
| Administration | 128 | 36 | 164 | 22.0 |
| Peacekeeping-Field | | | | |
| Administration & Logistics | 39 | 6 | 45 | 13.3 |
| UN Compensation Commission | 5 | 0 | 5 | 0.0 |
| Total* | 1,632 | 882 | 2,514 | 35.1 |

SOURCE: UN Department of Public Information, Gender Distribution of United Nations Staff, 1996.

*The highest grades of Under-Secretary-General, Assistant Secretary-General, Directors, and top professional staff constitute 797 of the total of 2,514.

TABLE 4-2  Statistical Summary on the Status of Women
in UN Professional Positions, 2002

|  | MEN | WOMEN | PERCENTAGE WOMEN |
|---|---|---|---|
| LEVEL |  |  |  |
| Under-Secretary-General | 38 | 4 | 10.5* |
| Assistant Secretary-General** | 40 | 5 | 12.5 |
| CATEGORY |  |  |  |
| General Service | 6,694 | 4,227 | 61.9 |
| Security | 205 | 19 | 0.3 |
| Trades and Crafts | 190 | 6 | 3.5 |
| AGENCY |  |  |  |
| UN Population Fund |  |  | 50.4 |
| United Nations Children's Fund |  |  | 44.0 |
| The World Food Program |  |  | 42.9 |
| UN Educational, Scientific and Cultural Organization |  |  | 42.8 |
| United Nations Development Program |  |  | 39.7 |
| UN High Commissioner for Refugees |  |  | 38.9 |
| Joint UN Program on HIV/AIDS |  |  | 36.5 |
| UN Secretariat |  |  | 36.2 |
| International Maritime Organization |  |  | 35.0 |
| International Fund for Agricultural Development |  |  | 34.0 |
| International Labor Organization |  |  | 33.3 |
| World Health Organization |  |  | 33.2 |
| International Training Center for the ILO |  |  | 32.9 |
| World Intellectual Property Organization |  |  | 30.0 |

SOURCE: Status of Women at the United Nations, 30 March 2003, UN Office of the Special Adviser on Gender Issues and Advancement of Women.

*Compared with 2001, this represents a decline of 1.3 percent.

**At the ASG level a woman was appointed the first UN Ombudsman in 2002.

Initially, the principal basis for geographic distribution was budgetary contribution. In 1962 the General Assembly adopted a formula that took into account membership (one to five per member state regardless of other factors) and population, in addition to budgetary contribution. Desirable ranges for each country and region, derived from the formula, were to serve as a guide to the Secretary-General in the recruitment of staff. Since then, greater weight has been given to the membership factor, which now places the minimum desirable

TABLE 4-3    UN Staff in the Professional Category and above in Posts Subject
to Geographical Distribution by Region and Gender as of 30 June 1997

| REGION | WOMEN | MEN | TOTAL | PERCENTAGE WOMEN |
|---|---|---|---|---|
| Africa | 87 | 284 | 371 | 23.45 |
| Asia and the Pacific | 193 | 240 | 433 | 44.57 |
| Europe (Eastern) | 28 | 211 | 239 | 11.72 |
| Europe (Western) | 214 | 358 | 572 | 37.41 |
| Latin America | 76 | 129 | 205 | 37.07 |
| Middle East | 39 | 81 | 120 | 32.50 |
| North America & Caribbean | 261 | 247 | 508 | 51.38 |
| Others | 3 | 10 | 13 | 23.08 |
| Total | 901 | 1,560 | 2,461 | 36.61 |

SOURCE: UN Office of Human Resources Management, 1998.

range at two to fourteen. The majority of UN members, being small and poor, fall within this range. The distribution of such posts, by geographic region, is presented in Table 4-3. Most governments have come to regard the ranges as entitlements rather than guidelines, and some have generated great political pressure on the Secretary-General to conform. Even for regions within or very close to their desirable ranges, merely maintaining the balance is a drag on recruitment by merit, and individual countries continue to press the Secretary-General for the maximum number of posts. The Assembly has kept up the pressure by setting targets for the appointment of candidates from underrepresented countries. Ironically, the most grossly overrepresented countries are themselves from developing areas. This is possible because no hiring disadvantage is imposed on overrepresented states from underrepresented regions.

As might be expected, the developing countries have not been content with overall geographic equity but have sought a proportionate share of senior and policy-formulating posts as well. There is ample precedent for politicizing recruitment among top echelon UN administrators. The initial distribution of top-level posts was determined by informal agreement among the permanent members of the Security Council to have a national of each of them appointed as an Assistant Secretary-General. The Soviet Union was awarded the top post in political and Security Council affairs and held it until its demise, except for a few years in the mid-1950s. In 1992 this informal claim was transferred to Russia, but France, Britain, the United States, and China have also staked their respective claims to such positions at the highest administrative level.

Intimately related to geographic distribution is the problem of the long-term appointment to posts subject to geographic distribution. Short-term appointments are appropriate for positions at the highest levels where some rotation is desirable, for needed specialists who are not willing to make a career of UN service, and for posts that are temporary because of the nature of the work (for example, technical assistance projects). Nevertheless, a career service is the heart of the international civil service ideal. With the large-scale admission of new members after 1955, the career ideal was challenged by the principle of equitable geographic distribution. Many new member states did not possess large pools of trained candidates whom they could afford to lose permanently. Nonetheless, they wanted to be "represented," and they were willing to send people who would return after a short period, often more experienced because of their UN experience. Thus term appointments that range from one to five years became a tool for achieving desired geographic distribution of UN jobs. Not all short-term appointments are inconsistent, however, with a career system. A two-tier, five-year contract may provide a probationary period before a career appointment is granted. Some term appointments often develop into career appointments, and others become de facto career vehicles by virtue of periodic renewal. The result was an increase in the percentage of term appointments from about 10 percent in 1955 to about 25 percent in 1965 and 36 percent in 1985. A reversal of the trend began in the late 1980s, reducing the percentage of these term appointments to less than 25 percent.

The developing countries do not bear the sole responsibility for the large percentage of term appointments. Until recently East European states, with the exception of Yugoslavia, insisted on similar appointments for their nationals. They rejected the civil service ideal of placing loyalty to international organization above loyalty to country, and they were unwilling to run the risk that national ties might become attenuated through long residence abroad. They also opposed a career service on principle, insisting that international civil servants are less effective if they have lost touch with life in their own country. With the breakup of the East European bloc and the splintering of the former Soviet Union, these countries became more receptive to the principle of career appointments. The proportion of East European nationals with term appointments in posts subject to geographic distribution was reduced from 99 percent (1986) to 66 percent (1992). This was still more than twice as high as for Africa, the region with the second highest proportion of term appointments (25 percent).

Although the Secretary-General has ultimate responsibility for Secretariat recruitment, geographic considerations and government pressures often lead to the hiring of government-sponsored candidates with little effort to canvass the experience of available applicants. Announcements of vacancies are commonly sent to governments, universities, professional societies, and other agencies where people with needed requirements may be contacted. But if a department already has a particular person in mind for the job, the distribution of such announcements may be limited to UN permanent missions and a few international organizations. Some appointments are made with no circulation of a vacancy announcement at all.[2] This is more likely to be the case with senior posts. For positions at the lowest professional levels, candidate screening is frequently done through publicized national competitive examinations.

The recruitment of able personnel is also affected by conditions of service. Staff salaries thus far have been maintained above national levels, but large-contributor efforts to hold the line on budgetary increases have reduced career advancement prospects through periodic hiring freezes and staff reductions in some areas. UN pay rates, however, for matching grades at the professional level average higher than pay rates for comparable federal civil service positions in Washington, D.C. Recruitment of the most able candidates has also been hampered by the politicization of personnel decisions. Promotion prospects for the career civil servant are necessarily limited if many higher-level positions are satisfied from outside the organization in response to government pressures and geographic considerations. When extraneous factors of national origin and political pressure determine promotion, the whole concept of a career service is undermined.

## LOYALTY, INDEPENDENCE, IMPARTIALITY

The international civil service ideal requires that national loyalties be transcended by a primary professional loyalty to the international organization and the cause of international cooperation. In practice the ideal has not always been attained. Most UN personnel have put international interests above the interest of any single state or group of states. But some have not, and the UN record clearly demonstrates that observance of the international ideal declines when it is undermined by the conduct of member states.

The elements of international loyalty, set forth in Staff Regulation 1.4, are integrity, impartiality, and independence. From the viewpoint of individuals, *integrity* is the key. People of integrity will not be false to their own standards or their responsibility to others, including their oath to put the interests of the organization before everything else. *Impartiality* requires Secretariat workers to act neutrally toward all states, except as the interests and objectives of the United Nations dictate. Since appearances are important, impartiality embodies an element of prudence in not publicly taking sides on controversial matters. The ideal of impartiality probably goes no further than integrity requires, and it does not presume that international civil servants must or will free themselves from all cultural bias or previously developed political values and attitudes.

*Independence* in Secretariat officials is the ability to act without regard to political pressure from any national government or any group of countries. The UN Charter (Article 100) states that the Secretary-General and the Secretariat staff "shall not seek or receive instructions from any government or from any other authority external to the Organization." Members, on their part, undertake "to respect the exclusively international character of the responsibilities of the Secretary-General and the staff and not to seek to influence them in the discharge of their responsibilities." Independence is thus a two-way street. It requires determination by civil servants to be independent and a willingness of governments, particularly their own governments, to let them be independent.

Unfortunately, governmental pressures have sometimes been hard to resist. During the League days the governments of Nazi Germany and fascist Italy tried, with some success, to control their nationals on the Secretariat. Until the demise of the communist regimes in the Soviet Union and Eastern Europe, these states followed the same practice in the United Nations. Their policy of national control has now begun to change. Other states have also made inroads on the ideal of independence. From 1953 to 1986 the United States subjected its nationals to a loyalty check before their appointment to the UN Secretariat. The practice was discontinued after a federal court decision that the loyalty program violated the First Amendment rights of speech and association. A number of other governments screen their nationals informally, which is less obvious but equally incompatible with Secretariat independence.

Other practices may be even more inimical to Secretariat independence. Some governments make supplementary payments to their nationals on the Secretariat, in clear violation of the staff regulations, which prohibit acceptance of "any honor, decoration, favor, gift or remuneration from any Government excepting for war services." The dangers of creating dependence on the government making the payment are obvious. Independence is similarly threatened when an initial appointment or a subsequent promotion results from government intervention on behalf of the candidate.

The relatively large proportion of term appointments to key positions also has implications for staff independence because people with a career stake in the United Nations may have more incentive to serve the organization single-mindedly. Many term employees do in fact measure up to the international civil service ideal, and the threat to independence is probably more acute with seconded employees, that is, national civil servants on temporary duty with the United Nations who anticipate returning to government service when the UN appointment expires. Even in such cases, personal integrity and government respect for the Secretariat's role may preserve the civil servant's independence of action, but the risk of partiality and special pressure is undoubtedly increased by the nature of temporary status.

# THE UN SECRETARIAT IN THE POLITICAL PROCESS

Every aspect of international administration is affected by its political milieu, and the UN Secretariat is far more a creature than controller of its environment. Nevertheless, secretariats do affect political outcomes through initiative and leadership in the administration of programs, participation in the decisions of policy-making organs, and the practice of quiet diplomacy. The following pages will examine each of these avenues of involvement.

## POLICY THROUGH ADMINISTRATION

Administration is the process of carrying into action the commands of policy-making bodies. Some legislative commands are more direct than others, but nearly all leave room for administrative discretion in the application of rules to particular cases. On occasion, commands from UN institutions and agencies are stated so broadly that highly important decisions are left to Secretariat administrative officers. During the 1956 Suez-Sinai War and the 1960 Congo crisis, for example, Secretary-General Dag Hammarskjöld was given very wide latitude in creating and directing the operations of UN peacekeeping forces. Since the Hammarskjöld years, the Security Council has maintained closer control of the Secretary-General's political and security activities, but in many situations, including peacekeeping, a large amount of Secretariat discretion is unavoidable. In economic and social matters, broad mandates for the Secretary-General are quite common.

Administration also becomes entwined with large policy decisions in less-direct ways. Research studies and reports prepared by the UN Secretariat add to the information base for government policy. The monumental *Nutrition Report*—which called attention to the abysmally low levels of nutrition in most parts of the world—was issued in 1937 by a special committee of the League Assembly and had far-reaching effects on the attitudes of governments and private groups in many countries. A 1987 report, prepared by an independent commission established by the UN General Assembly, titled *Our Common Future,* also focused global interest. It dealt with the connection between environmental preservation and economic development.[3] Nearly every international organization can point to reports drafted by expert UN Secretariat personnel that were the basis for subsequent action by policy-making bodies.

Successful performance of assigned duties by UN Secretariat personnel can lead to requests for more of the same. The UN Emergency Force had to be built almost from the ground up when the Suez crisis arose in 1956, but that precedent made a peacekeeping force the logical UN response to subsequent outbreaks of violence in the Middle East, the Congo, Cyprus, Croatia, Central America, Cambodia, and elsewhere. It also is important to note that ineffective administrative performance may lead to a significant change or the abandonment of programs.

## SECRETARIAT PARTICIPATION IN DECISION MAKING

International civil servants participate directly in the decision-making processes of their governing bodies. Among existing international organizations, probably no secretariat enjoys greater importance than the staff of the World Bank, which not only frames the program for discussion by its executive directors and governing board, but generally secures their approval for what the bank President and President's staff recommend. Governments are of course closely consulted in the preparation of the recommendations. The UNESCO secretariat also prepares the agenda and presents a program of action for its governing body. Although the UNESCO General Conference is sometimes disposed to alter the program, the Director-General is undoubtedly the most important decision maker in the organization. The European Union represents yet a different relationship. By constitutional fiat, policy-making authority is divided between the Council of Ministers, which speaks for governments, and the Commission, which heads the administrative establishment. Decisions are often left to the Commission acting alone. But some decisions are rendered by the Council of Ministers, while others, of considerable importance, are made by the concurrent action of both. These organizations are to be contrasted with the UN General Assembly, where most agenda items are proposed by member states, or mandated by previous resolutions, and simply compiled by the Secretariat in a preliminary agenda. Although the Secretary-General may suggest additional items, he does not submit a legislative program, as is done in some other international agencies. However, most items represent continuing business from a previous session and are usually accompanied by a Secretariat report that helps shape consideration of the issue. Where the issue involves programs administered by the Secretariat, the recommendations of the Secretariat have considerable weight, especially because the views of member states are likely to have been solicited in formulating the Secretariat positions.

The Secretary-General also is responsible for the preparation of the biennial UN budget. These estimates are, for the most part, based on the amounts required for the United Nations to carry out programs already authorized by the policy-making bodies, but the choice of expenditures nevertheless involves discretion. The Secretary-General is normally required to defend his budget vigorously and usually loses something to the budget cutters. Large contributors put great pressure on the Secretary-General to produce a "no-growth budget," even though many smaller members would like to see continuing expansion of UN programs of special significance to them. In this tug-of-war, the more heavily taxed member states carry the greater weight. But the Secretary-General's negative-growth budget for 1998–99 also proposed a Revolving Credit Fund, while a new Office of Development Financing was designed to utilize a smaller member "Development Dividend" that would be drawn from resources heretofore used for other more generalized administrative purposes. As a consequence of such measures, expenditures during 2002 had been decreased and aggregate cash balances at the beginning of 2003 were higher than ever.

Whether or not the secretariat of an international agency has a large role in initiating program proposals, other avenues of participation in the policy process are open. Executive heads are usually authorized to take part in formal discussion and debate of agenda items. All UN policy-making organs have provision for hearing the Secretary-General. Other Secretariat members conduct their own lobbying operations with varying degrees of directness. National governments often consult individual civil servants because of their expertise in a subject, and they will certainly consult the Secretary-General if members are seriously considering the proposal of new functions or responsibilities for the Secretariat. On some questions the Secretary-General may be drawn into informal negotiating processes because he represents a relatively neutral and impartial viewpoint on an issue or because he can serve as a useful channel of communication. A case in point was the stated intention of the United States to establish a democratically elected government in Iraq in 2004, and the belated request by the occupation authorities to have the UN Secretariat smooth the path for a transition that reconciles Kurds as well as Sunni and Shia Arabs.

## The Practice of Diplomacy

International civil servants affect organizational policy and the larger international system in important ways by means of "quiet diplomacy." Here we refer to the Secretariat's role in promoting agreement among states through quiet discussion and reconciliation of differences, as contrasted with public discussion and voting.

Opportunities for quiet diplomacy are presented in a wide variety of situations. Continuing diplomatic activity is required for carrying out the programs of an organization and obtaining compliance with its resolutions. Establishing and maintaining a UN peacekeeping mission, for example, requires a pivotal role for the Secretary-General both as administrator and diplomat. He has responsibility for writing the operation's terms of reference, for appointing the commander, and for negotiating necessary arrangements with affected states. The Secretary-General also must deal with the many diplomatic problems that arise from the mission.[4] No peacekeeping activity can be launched without extensive negotiations with countries supplying the troop contingents and necessary matériel, as well as with the host country and any other country directly involved with the underlying threat to peace. No mission is maintained without continuing negotiation to resolve problems and differences as they arise. The same is true of other operating programs of international organizations. Every technical assistance project is the product of extensive and detailed interchange among governments and the responsible international agency. Programs for refugee relief often require negotiation among representatives of one or more international organizations, the host country, the countries supporting the refugee program, and private organizations that cooperate in the relief activities.

When UN resolutions call for government action rather than establishing operating programs, the Secretariat may perform a diplomatic function in seeking compliance from member states. The object of the negotiation is as varied as the subject matter of the resolutions—from urging financial contributions to support of UN development programs to the observance of human rights to the support of UN economic sanctions.

Another form of diplomatic activity is the resolution of controversy between states. The role of mediator, conciliator, and consensus-builder often appears in the quiet negotiations that occur behind the scenes of conference diplomacy. While government representatives often serve in that role, not a few compromises are embodied in a resolution that has been forged with the help of a timely suggestion or mediation services provided by the secretariat. The expertise, impartiality, and continuity of secretariats become especially important in negotiating issues that persist over a long period of time within the UN framework, such as arms control or economic development.

The UN Secretary-General and his staff may also mediate particular disputes between countries.[5] Frequently this involvement comes through a mandate from the Assembly or the Security Council. The diplomatic services provided by the Secretary-General, acting personally or through his representatives, have been enlisted by the Assembly or Council in numerous instances, including the Iran-Iraq war, Afghanistan and the Taliban, the Falkland Islands confrontation between Britain and Argentina, the Lebanese civil war, the Arab-Israeli dispute, the U.S. attack on Grenada, the killing fields of Cambodia, ethnic cleansing in Bosnia and Herzegovina and Kosovo, genocide in Rwanda and Burundi, the Guatemalan insurgency, the seizure of Kuwait by Iraq, the partition of Cyprus, the liberation of East Timor, armed insurrection in Ivory Coast and Senegal, and the brutal conflict in the Congo.

Sometimes Secretaries-General have not waited for the Council or Assembly to act but have tried a mediating role on their own initiative. Hammarskjöld's successful mediation effort in 1958 between Thailand and Cambodia and Pérez de Cuéllar's successful mediation through his emissary Diego de Cordovez in Afghanistan in 1988–89 are most noteworthy. Boutros-Ghali, de Cuéllar's successor, however, was not nearly as successful. Nevertheless, Kofi Annan has sustained the Secretary-General's practice of personal diplomacy, from his intervention in the politics of Angola to special efforts to bring about the reunification of Cyprus. The Secretary-General and his team of weapons inspectors worked arduously to avoid a renewal of the conflict between the United States and Iraq, and he has continued to emphasize the importance of the United Nations in his insistence on a UN role in the rebuilding of Iraq after the demise of Hussein government.

## THE SECRETARY-GENERAL AND POLITICAL LEADERSHIP

Political leadership and initiative cut across all avenues of secretariat involvement—administration, policy-making, and diplomacy. In the United Nations the focus of political leadership within the Secretariat must necessarily rest on the Secretary-General as the chief administrator of the organization. In contrast to all subordinate UN civil servants, the Charter makes his appointment subject to a uniquely political process. Under Article 97, he is "appointed by the General Assembly upon the recommendation of the Security Council." Since the Security Council recommendation is a nonprocedural matter, the recommendation is subject to all the hazards of great power politics. In practice, whenever the Security Council has been able to agree on a candidate, the General Assembly has hastened to add its formal approval.

Agreement in the Security Council has not always come easily. In 1950, when Trygve Lie's initial five-year term was about to expire, the Soviet Union vetoed Lester Pearson of Canada and Paul-Henri Spaak of Belgium, and the United States then threatened to veto any candidate other than Lie. During this impasse the Secretariat was prevented from going leaderless only by the constitutionally questionable expedient of extending Lie's term an additional three years by General Assembly resolution. Since then, the appointment of a Secretary-General has sometimes gone to several ballots in the Security Council, but disagreement has never forced such an extraconstitutional extension of tenure. In 1981 the Council was deadlocked for more than six weeks. Through sixteen straw ballots China vetoed Kurt Waldheim's bid for an unprecedented third five-year term, while the United States blocked his Tanzanian challenger, Salim A. Salim. When these two candidacies were finally withdrawn, Javier Pérez de Cuéllar was nominated on the first formal ballot from a list of nine Third World hopefuls. The process of selecting Pérez de Cuéllar's successor, Boutros Boutros-Ghali of Egypt, went more smoothly. In the Security Council the field was narrowed by a number of straw votes, which permitted Boutros-Ghali to be approved unanimously on the only formal vote taken by the Council. The General Assembly, as expected, gave its approval by consensus. Boutros-Ghali, however, was not allowed to seek another term. The United States had rated Boutros-Ghali a failure in dealing with the problems in Somalia and Bosnia. Washington also was unhappy with the Secretary-General's budget reforms. After a lengthy struggle, Boutros-Ghali's supporters were forced to acknowledge defeat, especially after the United States, using its prerogatives in the Security Council, cast the only vote in opposition to his reappointment. When Boutros-Ghali announced the suspension of his candidature, Kofi Annan received the unanimous support of the Security Council, and the General Assembly elected him the seventh UN Secretary-General. Annan's election to a second five-year term was done by acclamation in recognition of his special service to the United Nations during uncertain times.

Given the political considerations that surround the appointment of the Secretary-General, it is not surprising that all successful candidates have come either from small and generally neutral European countries or from the developing world (see Table 4-4).

Boutros-Ghali's appointment owed something to geography—in particular, the insistence of African states that the selection be made from their region. This claim had the backing of the Non-Aligned Movement, which reportedly agreed to vote in the General Assembly against any non-African candidate. The United States, Britain, and the Soviet Union were reluctant, however, to recognize any claim based on geography. They also questioned whether Boutros-Ghali might have the energy (at age sixty-nine) to handle the pressing problems of peace and security, economic development, the environment, and internal budget as well as the issues of complex administration that the Secretary-General must address. Ultimately, they found him acceptable, and Boutros-Ghali became the first African and Arab, although not a Muslim, to serve in the office. Annan sustains an even sharper focus on the African continent and gives particular attention to the much-troubled sub-Saharan region. Born in 1938, Annan was seen as possessing more energy than his predecessor, and as the first international civil servant to hold the post, he was perhaps more familiar with the operations of the United Nations than any Secretary-General preceding him. Annan also brought important academic credentials to the position, completing his undergraduate work in economics at Macalaster College in St. Paul, Minnesota, and having served as a Sloan Fellow at the Massachusetts Institute of Technology where he received a Master of Science degree in management. He also had undertaken graduate studies at the Institut Universitaire des Hautes Etudes Internationales in Geneva.

TABLE 4-4    UN Secretaries-General, 1946–2004

| SECRETARY-GENERAL | NATIONALITY | TERM OF OFFICE | PREVIOUS EXPERIENCE |
|---|---|---|---|
| Trygve Lie | Norway | 1946–53 | Norway Foreign Minister at time of appointment; head, Norway delegation to San Francisco Conference (1945); former Minister of Justice, Commerce; politician and trade union negotiator |
| Dag Hammarskjöld | Sweden | 1953–61 | Minister of State (Finance) of Sweden at time of appointment; former chairman, Bank of Sweden; high-level civil servant, academic (political economy) |
| U Thant | Burma (now Myanmar) | 1961–71 | Permanent representative of Burma to United Nations at time of appointment; former government press director, freelance journalist, high school teacher |
| Kurt Waldheim | Austria | 1972–81 | Permanent representative of Austria to United Nations at time of appointment; former foreign minister, ambassador to Canada, foreign service officer; unsuccessful candidate for president of Austria (1971) |
| Javier Pérez de Cuéllar | Peru | 1982–91 | Representative of UN Secretary-General in Afghanistan at time of appointment; former UN Under-Secretary-General; representative of UN Secretary-General in Cyprus; permanent representative of Peru to United Nations; ambassador to Switzerland, Poland, Venezuela; foreign service officer, professor of international law and relations |
| Boutros Boutros-Ghali | Egypt | 1992–96 | Deputy Prime Minister of Egypt at time of appointment; Egypt's minister of state for foreign affairs; diplomat, law professor, author, journalist |
| Kofi Annan | Ghana | 1997– | UN Under-Secretary-General for Peacekeeping Operations at the time of his appointment; he had served the UN as an international civil servant for more than thirty years, having served in UN offices in Addis Ababa, Cairo, Geneva, Ismailia, and New York City |

The Charter appointment process assures that the Secretary-General will have the support, or at least the acquiescence, of each permanent member, and a majority in Security Council deliberations. This is a political asset, but leadership demands that he continue to seek support wherever he can—primarily among governments, but also with private interest groups and the general public. Since governments are the principal clients of the Secretariat and the direct recipients of most of its service, earning their goodwill begins with trying to serve them well. It also requires careful counting of costs before taking action or assuming a public stance that will antagonize important members. Lie's outspoken endorsement of UN action in Korea alienated the Soviet support he had formerly enjoyed. Hammarskjöld's handling of the Congo crisis also enraged the Soviet Union, but his cultivation of Afro-Asian support paid off handsomely in that crisis. U Thant's efforts at mediation in the Vietnam War brought a cooling in his relations with the United States. His withdrawal of the UN Emergency Force from Egypt in May 1967, albeit under Egyptian pressure, brought severe criticism from many sides—especially after it proved a prelude to a costly war pitting Egypt and several Arab countries against Israel. Waldheim made no implacable enemies during his two terms, but his bid for an unprecedented third term was blocked by China's veto. The Chinese position revealed a strong preference for a Third World candidate rather than antagonism to Waldheim. Pérez de Cuéllar, entering a more hospitable political environment, concluded his service at the end of 1991 with general approbation from the world community he had served so well and so successfully.

Secretariat links with private groups can also be a source of support. Private groups supply helpful information, and some have area operations that can be harnessed to UN objectives in such areas as refugee and disaster relief or development assistance. Private groups may also lobby national governments and mobilize public opinion in favor of UN programs. The UN Department of Public Information maintains liaison with many national and international groups having an interest in the work of the United Nations. UN staff also try to inform and accommodate the numerous nongovernmental organizations that hold consultative status with the Economic and Social Council. Individual units and programs established by the United Nations, such as UNICEF, the UN Population Fund, the UN Environment Programme, and the UN Development Program, also maintain ties with national and international groups that may provide political support for their operations. UN specialized agencies and other intergovernmental organizations do the same.

The general public is cultivated as well. In New York and Geneva, busy information clerks and smartly uniformed tour guides minister to the throngs of people who visit the UN headquarters each year to see the sights and observe UN public meetings. The United Nations reaches out to a vast world audience through a constant stream of news releases from New York, Geneva, and international UN information centers. Publications range from documentary reports of proceedings and Secretariat research to slick brochures lauding the accomplishments of the United Nations and its related agencies.

The object of building a power base is to shape the affairs of the organization and the larger political community. Annan's eclectic abilities and his long domicile in New York City have sensitized him to the importance of a variety of groups and organizations, many of which are located in the private sector. His emphasis on civil society is symbolized by his convening a People's Millennium Assembly organized around the General Assembly session in 2000. Annan's central idea aimed at ensuring the greater participation of the world's ordinary people. From the beginning of his tenure as Secretary-General, Annan reached out to the business sector, whose assistance he sought in tackling the great issues of poverty and injustice. In response to this appeal, then-chairman of Time-Warner Ted Turner announced in September 1997 that he would contribute $1 billion of his personal wealth to the United Nations.

All incumbents have considered themselves spokesmen for the world community and have not hesitated to take positions in support of UN purposes and principles. Lie, as he later recalled in his memoirs, "was determined that the Secretary-General should be a force for peace." [6] Hammarskjöld also insisted on the right to take a stand on international issues whenever it could "be firmly based on the Charter and its principles." [7] Thant, Waldheim, Pérez de Cuéllar, Boutros-Ghali, and Annan have continued to defend the Secretary-General's right to speak out, whether the issue be Vietnam, Iran, Afghanistan, the Falklands, the Middle East, the Balkans, Somalia, or Iraq. No less so, human rights, economic development, the environment, and Secretariat staffing are also of important concern to the Secretary-General.

The Secretary-General's opinion carries more weight if the Secretariat has special expertise in the matter. The Secretary-General and his agents often are closer to the facts of an issue than are the representatives of most governments, and their arguments weigh accordingly. The same is true where the Secretary-General is engaged in mediation, either in person or through an appointed representative.

In taking political initiatives, the Secretary-General has certain formal powers on which to draw, such as enjoying the privilege of speaking to UN deliberative bodies or placing items on their agendas. Under Article 99 of the Charter, he is specially authorized "to bring to the attention of the Security Council any matter that in his opinion may threaten the maintenance of international peace and security." While this right has rarely been exercised—almost always some member state will raise an issue if it is appropriate for Security Council consideration—Article 99 clearly stamps the office of Secretary-General as one of political as well as administrative functions. A seemingly innocuous clause in Article 98, authorizing the Secretary-General to "perform such other functions as are entrusted to him" by the other major organs, has also been interpreted as an important grant of power. For Hammarskjöld it was a mandate to do whatever he found necessary to implement directives from the General Assembly and the Security Council relating to the Middle East, the Congo, and other problem areas.

Hammarskjöld went even further in defining the broad political responsibilities of the Secretary-General. When deadlock in the Security Council prevented enlargement of the UN Observer Group in Lebanon in the summer of 1958, the Secretary-General enlarged it on his own initiative. Explaining to the Security Council that under the Charter he "should be expected to act without any guidance from the Assembly or the Security Council," he argued that it was the Secretary-General's responsibility to act when neither Charter provisions nor traditional diplomacy could safeguard the peace. Hammarskjöld's assumption of such authority was bold, almost audacious, but in another perspective it was simply part of the ongoing process of Charter evolution, albeit through interpretation.

U Thant continued the practice of taking independent political initiatives. The UN temporary executive authority in West New Guinea (1962), the observer mission in Yemen (1963), and the UN plebiscite in North Borneo and Sarawak (1963) were instigated by Thant, although each action was subsequently approved by the General Assembly or the Security Council. At the height of the 1962 Cuban missile crisis, Thant's appeal for a voluntary suspension of Soviet arms shipments to Cuba and of U.S. quarantine measures provided a formula that helped avert a direct confrontation at sea. After 1964 he made various attempts, all unsuccessful, to assume a mediating role in Vietnam.

Pérez de Cuéllar also used the powers of Secretary-General as an international peacemaker. During his initial tenure, his attempts at peacemaking in Lebanon, the Falkland Islands, Iran and Iraq, and Grenada were largely unavailing, but his second term saw genuine progress. Internal changes in the Soviet Union, the coincident thaw in the Cold War, the unexpected Soviet embrace of the United Nations in 1987, and a somewhat more positive U.S. view of the United Nations that emerged near the end of the Reagan administration created a favorable setting for UN action. In the war between Iraq and Iran, weariness in both countries provided the ingredients for successful action, and in 1988, the Secretary-General and his aides were able to arrange an end to the eight-year-old war. That same year a second major diplomatic breakthrough was engineered when UN Undersecretary-General Diego de Cordovez finally persuaded the Soviets to withdraw their troops from Afghanistan. These achievements were followed by further mediation in Central America, Cambodia, and Western Sahara; in 1991, the United Nations negotiated the release of American and European hostages in Lebanon. Less successful were the Secretary-General's efforts to prevent the 1991 Persian Gulf War. The UN coalition that was led by the United States to liberate Kuwait from Iraqi control was clearly a Security Council operation.

Boutros-Ghali added to the precedent of political activism set by his predecessors. In the first year of his term he tried to get the warring Afghan factions to resolve their differences. He also took the initiative in trying to resolve continuing disputes in Cyprus and East Timor. He recommended new peacekeeping forces for Yugoslavia, Somalia, and Mozambique and proposed a wide-ranging overhaul of UN enforcement capabilities. Boutros-Ghali persistently urged stronger military measures in the Balkans and Somalia. The vigor with which he pursued his objectives was surprising to some observers, but it was consistent with his experience as a diplomatic troubleshooter in Africa and a key participant in the Camp David talks that led to the 1979 peace treaty between Egypt and Israel.

Annan followed in this same tradition. As UN Undersecretary-General for Peacekeeping Operations before his election as Secretary-General, he was already adept in the diplomatic arts. Annan was expected to bring his expertise to bear in the most urgent world crises, and he did not disappoint his supporters. Shortly after becoming Secretary-General, Annan revived the peace process in Israel and Palestine, Cyprus, East Timor, and Kosovo. The Secretary-General summed up his attitude toward diplomacy in noting, "it is not an event, but a process." An experienced international civil servant, Annan demonstrated remarkable calm under stress. Counseling patience and determination, he frustrated those in search of a quick fix to complex problems. Where some called for unconditional surrender, the Secretary-General cautioned compromise and the building of rapport between parties. Nowhere was Annan's style more exposed than in the winter of 1998 when, with Security Council approval, he went to Baghdad to head off a violent U.S. response to Iraqi provocations. Annan's discussions with Saddam Hussein were declared successful when the Secretary-General announced that Iraq would abide by all UN resolutions in return for a pledge from the United Nations not to undermine the country's sovereignty. How the one could be achieved without the other was not explained, but Annan insisted that even if the agreement was faulty, the process was working.

Annan's penchant for giving diplomacy a chance to develop was witnessed again in 2002 when Annan was instrumental in organizing another team of UN arms inspectors (UNMOVIC) to search for weapons of mass destruction in Iraq after pressure from the Bush administration. Unfortunately, before the inspectors had completed their work and despite the Secretary-General's beseeching Washington to allow them to continue, the U.S.-led coalition invaded Iraq. Unable to delay let alone prevent the action, Annan authorized his staff to draw up a plan for the rehabilitation and reconstruction of Iraq once the war had ended. But again, the Secretary-General ran into U.S. opposition, with the Bush administration arguing that it alone would determine the level of UN operations in Iraq after the defeat of Saddam Hussein. Once the war had ended, however, occupying troops came under daily attacks, and with time, the United Nations was once more viewed as the organization best equipped to deal with development programs. After considerable diplomatic pressure, on October 16, 2003, a unanimous Security Council approved a resolution authorizing assistance both in combat personnel and funds. The patient and persistent Annan cited this resolution as a positive step, but he also acknowledged the deep rift that had opened in both the Security Council and General Assembly. Citing the fear of a breakdown in international order over the unilateral U.S. action in Iraq, the Secretary-General insisted that "the United States and the United Nations need each other" and that no country alone can address the great issues of security and development. Never in the history of the United Nations, he added, was there greater need for collective action.

The Secretary-General's capacity for political initiative is now well established. Its limits, of course, are circumscribed by prevailing political realities. A more-restrained approach to political leadership is no doubt best in the circumstances after the Cold War and more importantly during an era of heightened terrorism. The Security Council can be expected to hold a tighter rein on the UN Secretary-General, and with more intense cooperation among the great powers, especially given the war on terrorism, fewer occasions are likely to exist for either the General Assembly or the Secretary-General to exercise broad discretionary powers. The events of September 11, 2001 placed the most powerful country in history at risk. With U.S. vulnerabilities exposed so dramatically and so tragically, Washington's reluctance to defer to the United Nations, let alone to a proactive Secretary-General, was understandable. Moreover, U.S. concern for its security is mirrored in the behavior of other states, large and small, all of which address their national prerogatives. The patient diplomacy of the Secretary-General of today and the future will be tested as never before.

Because the support of governments is so crucial to the successful outcome of mediation or other political initiatives, the Secretary-General takes a serious risk in making any major political move without consulting members of the Security Council, formally or informally. When the Secretary-General appeals for UN action (or stronger action) in a given situation, he may simply be calling members to a sense of their responsibilities to the global community. Without advance consultation, however, it may appear as carping, scolding, or criticizing the policies of governments whose support he needs. Boutros-Ghali's public statements regarding the Balkans, Somalia, and other problem areas crossed over the line long before September 11. The negative reaction of some of the larger states, especially the United States, reaffirmed the proposition that effective political leadership by the Secretary-General lies primarily in the area of quiet diplomacy. Annan meets this requirement, but the criticism directed against him by important members of the U.S. Congress is an indication of how difficult it is to satisfy so vast a constituency as the member states of the United Nations.

## THE BASIS OF SECRETARIAT INVOLVEMENT

International secretariats and their executive heads have extensive involvement in the political processes of international organizations. But involvement and effectiveness vary from one organization to another, and even within a single organization, over a period of time. What accounts for these differences? Although an adequate answer to that question would require a book in itself, some of the reasons will be summarized here.

### Legal Powers

The charter of an organization gives the executive head certain rights, powers, and duties that describe prerogatives and responsibilities. Other grants of authority may be conferred by action of the organization's governing bodies. The

UN Charter gives more authority to the Secretary-General than did the League Covenant. The constitutional grant of authority to the Commission of the European Union, as contained in relevant treaties, is still greater. Legal rights and legitimacy are at the source of this exercise of authority.

## An Administrative Organization

A secretariat is a working organization, often embracing hundreds or, in the case of the United Nations, thousands of employees. It can perform or withhold service. Its programs affect the welfare of people around the world. The ability to control such an organization is a source of power to the Secretary-General, or to whoever is in charge.

In some secretariats, perhaps most, the executive head is never fully in charge. This may be because he or she lacks the personal skills to administer effectively. In part it results from the complex nature of large bureaucracies. In some instances geographic distance from headquarters, or the support of governmental clients, or the strong personality of an able subordinate, may reduce the Secretary-General's control over particular units of the staff. Higher-level actors who owe their appointments primarily to the political leverage of their governments may feel some independence from the executive head. The General Assembly has created a number of special programs, for example, the UN Development Program, UNICEF, the UN High Commissioner for Refugees, and the UN Relief and Works Agency for Palestine Refugees in the Near East, over which the Secretary-General has little or no administrative responsibility. In addition, the Assembly frequently creates committees, consisting of national representatives, to carry out some of its mandates. The work of the staff assigned to these committees is subject to the control of the committee rather than of the Secretary-General. Bodies such as the Special Committee against Apartheid, the Committee on the Exercise of the Inalienable Rights of the Palestinian People, or the Special Committee to Investigate Israeli Practices Affecting the Human Rights of the Palestinian People and Other Arabs of the Occupied Territories often work at cross-purposes with the Secretary-General. Moreover, when an executive head lacks full control, his or her administrative power is diminished.

## Information

Many states rely on the Secretariat to provide reliable information and advice on a wide variety of subjects. This "information power" may result from the technical expertise of Secretariat personnel, continuity of service and depth of experience, or access to sources of information not directly available to governments. Sometimes the balance of power between government representatives and international civil servants hinges on relative expertise, particularly if the organization performs primarily technical functions. If government representatives possess the technical expertise, they will certainly dominate the policy process. If Secretariat staff is more technically able, their affect on policy will be greater.

## Neutrality

Achieving absolute neutrality in international affairs is almost impossible, and one source of Secretariat strength is its role as speaker for the whole community. A reputation for neutrality, impartiality, and integrity increases trust and thereby the prospect for successful mediation of disputed questions.

## Personal Qualities of the Incumbent

Executives bring their own talents and interests to the assignment. They may be good administrators or good politicians, or both, or neither. They may be interested in administration or in politics. They may be more or less adept at building coalitions of support among governments and private groups and at inspiring their staff to a sense of unity and purpose.

Albert Thomas, original Director-General of the ILO, was a promoter of causes and heavily involved in broad questions of organizational policy. This presumably mirrored his background as a politician, a trade unionist, a social campaigner, and a reformer. On the other hand, Sir Eric Drummond brought to the League of Nations the self-effacing anonymity of the British civil servant. While leaving center stage to others, Drummond exerted his authority through management, counsel, and negotiation behind the scenes. Trygve Lie, like Thomas, delegated administration to deputies and emphasized the political function of the UN Secretary-General both as a public personality and as a quiet negotiator. Dag Hammarskjöld appeared in many ways to combine the best aspects of both Lie and Drummond—concern for administrative detail, mastery of quiet diplomacy, and zealous advocacy of Secretariat initiative.

Hammarskjöld's successors have preserved the political functions of the Secretary-General although their personal qualities and their circumstances have dictated a less-assertive approach. U Thant by nature was calm, self-assured, and nonconfrontational. He spoke out on principle, however, and in fact offended the United States by his criticisms of the Vietnam War. Kurt Waldheim, whose reputation was later tarnished by revelations of his Nazi connections during World War II, was more polished, correct, and formal. He was less inclined to criticize member states in ways that would diminish his personal power. Pérez de Cuéllar, also in the quiet mold, was genuinely self-effacing. Integrity, persistence, optimism, and a sense of humor contributed to his success in the political arena.

Boutros-Ghali, the first Secretary-General to serve after the Cold War, was neither a successful administrator nor politician. Distancing himself from the career members of the Secretariat, he failed in his management of a complex international bureaucracy. In political matters, he often said the wrong thing in the wrong place, under the wrong circumstances. He clearly fell out with the UN's most prominent member, the United States, and he had the misfortune of running afoul of the U.S. Congress when it shifted from a Democratic to a Republican majority in 1994. Moreover, American isolationism reappeared with the passing of the Cold War, and isolationist policies had long been associated with Republicans. If President Clinton is credited with the undoing of Boutros-Ghali, his decision to withhold U.S. support for a second term was in major part prompted by political sentiment in the Congress and in the public at large that professed a diminished interest in international affairs.

Kofi Annan inherited the legacies of all the previous Secretaries-General, but none weighed upon him more than that of his immediate predecessor. With the United States playing the role of prominent UN monitor, Annan was under constant pressure to satisfy U.S. demands without compromising his role as the world's most important international civil servant. The award of the Nobel Peace Prize to Annan in 2001 was aimed at both elevating the profile of the United Nations and legitimating the Secretary-General's role as principal moderator and guide for the nations. Beholden to no single nation, the honor emphasized the Secretary-General's position as chief representative of all the world's people.

## The Organizational Task

The nature of the organizational task has important consequences for the Secretariat's role in policy-making. Highly technical tasks usually generate less controversy than broad political questions and hence provide safer subjects for Secretariat initiative. An organization that administers programs is likely to have greater staff input on policy than one that makes rules for state behavior or tries to settle international disputes. Within the United Nations one should expect more Secretariat effect on the form of technical assistance programs than on the outcome of resolutions dealing with rivalries in the Middle East. If task performance generates its own funding sources, as with the lending operations of the World Bank, the reduced dependence on member states for funds is almost certain to give the staff a larger policy role.

## The Political Environment

The political environment of an organization may be the most important variable affecting Secretariat activity and, indeed, every other aspect of international organization. One kind of environmental impact consists of unplanned events that may frustrate organizational goals or, contrarily, offer new opportunity for initiative and constructive accomplishment. Another is the persistent effect of government attitudes, preferences, and control of resources that set limits on any attempted Secretariat initiative. The environment, far more than the skills of the executive head, determines the support that may be available from governments and nongovernmental groups. Attitudes can of course change, and sometimes the process of participation precipitates change. But the political environment, even one that is changing, controls the organization, and not vice versa.

## REVITALIZING THE UNITED NATIONS

Confronted with the challenges of a new era, the United Nations is experiencing important restructuring of its Secretariat and associated institutions, agencies, and administrative units. Led by Secretary-General Kofi Annan, the 1998 General Assembly was described as the "Reform Assembly" and gave Annan a clear mandate in meeting the UN's twenty-first-century objectives. Determined to give concrete expression to the centrality of the United Nations in issues of concern to the international community, especially peace and security, Annan stressed making the peacekeeping operations more effective. Thus, in 1997–98 the peace process was revived in the Western Sahara, East Timor, Cyprus, Tajikistan, Afghanistan, and Angola. In Iraq, Annan obtained agreement from the Security Council to increase the oil-for-food program and pledged an end to UN-imposed sanctions once Baghdad had demonstrated full compliance with UN resolutions and had opted for peace with its neighbors. UN peacekeeping operations also successfully monitored elections in Liberia and in the Eastern Slavonia region of Croatia, where in January 1998 the United Nations completed handing over its administrative responsibilities to local authorities. The United Nations also completed peacekeeping operations in Haiti, where only a small contingent of police advisers remained to help fashion democratic institutions.

No less important was the restructuring of the UN administrative system. The General Assembly welcomed Annan's plan to create a Department of Disarmament Affairs in the UN Secretariat that would consider a reduction in conventional weapons and weapons of mass destruction. The Secretary-General also stressed the need to ban land mines and sought to override the lack of enthusiasm from some of the major world actors by drawing support from nongovernmental organizations. At the signing ceremony of the new Convention on the Prohibition of the Use, Stockpiling, Production, and Transfer of Anti-Personnel Mines and on Their Destruction in Ottawa in December 1997, Annan paid tribute to the "union of governments, civil society, and international organizations" for their acceptance of the Convention. Citing the spreading importance of NGOs in humanitarian affairs, the Secretary-General called for greater cooperation and coordination among all public and private institutions. Moreover, at his order the UN High Commissioner for Refugees, UNICEF, and the World Food Program were brought into intimate relationship with particular NGOs.

Annan has also given human rights abuses closer scrutiny. Citing a degree of helplessness in investigating human rights violations in the Democratic Republic of the Congo and the continuing slaughter of innocent people in Algeria, the Secretary-General reiterated the UN's commitment to people threatened by indiscriminate violence. Addressing the Organization of African Unity in Harare, he declared that "human rights are African rights, not an imposition or plot by the industrialized West." He followed this performance with a speech at the Tehran Conference on Human Rights Day, where he noted that "human rights are foreign to no culture and native to all nations, and lie at the heart of all that the United Nations aspires to achieve in peace and development." Noting the fiftieth anniversary of the Universal Declaration of Human Rights, Annan articulated a theme of "all human rights for all." Acting on this principle, the Secretary-General combined the Geneva-based programs on human rights into one office to ensure greater coordination and strength of purpose.

Annan's reorganization and upgrading of the different UN institutions drew people of special talent and experience to the many departments, agencies, and programs of the United Nations. High-level appointments were made in a number of agencies and programs, including the UN Environment Programme and the new Vienna-based Office of Drug Control. Experts were appointed to executive positions in Crime Prevention, in the Office of Emergency Relief Coordinator, and in the Office of the Special Representative for Children in Armed Conflict. Of special interest to the Secretary-General was the staffing of the newly created Department of Disarmament Affairs, the UN Human Resources Office, and a Special Adviser on Gender Issues. Annan's long experience with the United Nations convinced him that the work of the Secretary-General was more than one administrator could manage. Therefore he proposed, and the General Assembly approved, the new post of Deputy UN Secretary-General— an act long discussed but never pursued by other Secretaries-General. This new post was testimony to the Secretary-General's considerable negotiating skills. Louise Frechette, Canada's Deputy Minister of National Defense, was Annan's choice for the position.

Never in the history of the United Nations had so many high-ranking positions gone to women. In hiring matters, Annan emphasizes gender neutrality in his search for the best talent and most-committed people. This emphasis that was cited in a 2002 report of the Office of the Focal Point for Women in the United Nations, which revealed that the overall proportion of women in the "professional" and higher categories in the twenty-eight UN agencies rose from 33.5 percent in December 1999 to 33.7 percent at the end of 2000. Three of the twenty-six organizations with twenty or more staff members at the professional level employed more than 40 percent women. Another ten organizations employed between 30 and 40 percent professional women, and only twelve organizations employed less than 30 percent professional women overall. In 2002 gender balance was achieved in several UN Secretariat departments and offices (Budget and Accounts, Human Resources Management, Management, Program Planning, Public Information) as well as in the Undersecretary-General's Office for Management.

At the end of 2002, as a consequence of pressure exerted through the office of the Secretary-General, 9 of 191 government permanent representatives leading their delegations to the United Nations were women. Moreover, fifty-four of the member states had 50 percent or more female staff employed in the United Nations. Among the UN's own Regional Commissions, two of the five commissions had women serving as executive secretaries in 2002 (the Economic Commission for Europe and the Economic and Social Commission for

Western Asia); three had women as deputy heads (the Economic Commission for Africa and the Economic and Social Commissions for Asia and the Pacific, and for Western Asia). Women were also serving as the Deputy Special Representative of the Secretary-General in the Democratic Republic of the Congo and as the Deputy Head in the UN Mission for the Verification of Human Rights in Guatemala. In UN peace operations in 2002, however, women constituted only 24 percent of staff. Among twenty-eight peace operations, women accounted for 30–50 percent of staff in only six missions. In another six missions there were no women. Only one out of fifty-one special representatives of the Secretary-General or special envoys on peace support operations was a woman (the special representative of the Secretary-General in Georgia).

Annan had assumed the leadership of the United Nations at a time of high controversy, a period during which the United Nations had lost considerable stature and its major sponsor, the United States, had lost interest in the collective nature of the organization. With the United States behind in its payments to the world organization, the Secretary-General was compelled to cut administrative costs in order to secure more funds for development programs. Annan proposed the first negative-growth budget in the world organization's history in 1998–99 and collapsed the three departments involved in economic and social development into a single Department of Economic and Social Affairs. In fact, within a year of assuming his new responsibilities, Annan rearranged some thirty UN units, grouping them into four thematic areas for greater effectiveness and cost savings. These areas included peace and security, economic and social affairs, development operations, and humanitarian affairs. Moreover, all UN funds and programs, including development operations, were brought together in a UN Development Group that functioned on the basis of common goals (see Table 4-5).

The consolidation of conference support services into a Department of General Assembly Affairs and Conference Services dovetailed with the upgrading of the Department of Political Affairs and its linkage with the new Secretariat Department of Disarmament Affairs. The Secretariat also tightened its procurement services by streamlining procedures, by expanding electronic procurement and the use of documents in electronic form, and by developing a single service to provide information technology and telecommunications infrastructure. All this was accomplished with a reduced budget and a staff 25 percent smaller than the one Annan had inherited from his predecessors.

## TERRORISM AND THE UNITED NATIONS

The war on terrorism imposed new strains on the United Nations. More concerned with poverty and illiteracy, the UN Secretariat acknowledged its limitations in a global environment influenced by the perpetrators of terror. Nevertheless, it was obvious that the restructuring of the organization went far beyond the reformation of a world organization whose central activity was supposed to be a more cost-effective operation.

TABLE 4-5   Renewing the United Nations: A Program for Reform*

| PEACE AND SECURITY | |
|---|---|
| DPA | Department of Political Affairs |
| DPKO | Department of Peace-keeping Operations |
| DDAR | Department for Disarmament and Arms Regulation |

| UN DEVELOPMENT GROUP | |
|---|---|
| UNDP | United Nations Development Programme |
| UNICEF | United Nations Children's Fund |
| UNFPA | United Nations Population Fund |

| HUMANITARIAN AFFAIRS | |
|---|---|
| ERC | Emergency Relief Coordinator |
| UNHCR | United Nations High Commissioner for Refugees |
| WFP | World Food Programme |
| UNRWA | United Nations Relief and Works Agency for Palestine Refugees in the Near East |

| ECONOMIC AND SOCIAL | |
|---|---|
| DESA | Department of Economic and Social Affairs |
| Regional | Economic Commission for Africa |
| Commissions | Economic Commission for Europe |
| | Economic Commission for Latin America and the Caribbean |
| | Economic and Social Commission for Asia and the Pacific |
| | Economic and Social Commission for Western Asia |
| UNCTAD | United Nations Conference on Trade and Development |
| UNEP | United Nations Environment Programme |
| Habitat | United Nations Centre for Human Settlements |
| ODCCP | Office of Drug Control and Crime Prevention |
| UNU | United Nations University |

| GENERAL SERVICES | |
|---|---|
| OLA | Office of Legal Affairs |
| DM | Department of Management |
| GAACS | Department of General Assembly Affairs and Conference Services |
| DPI | Department of Public Information |
| OIOS | Office of Internal Oversight Services |

SOURCE: United Nations Web site (http://www.un.org/reform/track2/initiate.htm#newun).

*This chart places the various UN entities under the sector to which they principally contribute. A number of entities contribute to the work of more than one sector. Human Rights (composed of the Office of the High Commissioner and the Centre for Human Rights) is introduced in the chart as a distinct sector but also constitutes an integral dimension of all sectors.

In the wake of the September 11 tragedy, the Security Council approved Resolutions 1368 and 1373, creating the Counter-Terrorism Committee (CTC) and giving the UN Secretariat responsibility for assisting the committee in its work. The mandate centered on the formation of a global approach to counter-terrorism. Coordinating with the Association of Southeast Asian Nations, the

League of Arab States, the European Union, the Organization of American States, the Organization of the Islamic Conference, NATO, and Interpol, the CTC was declared the hub for action by UN member states. The UN role was described as being that of an "enabler" and not an operational agency. Hard security operations were the responsibility of individual states, but the United Nations could assist in coordinating actions between states. The CTC was described as conducting work that involved raising the capability of member states to deal with counterterrorism everywhere. It therefore was entrusted with monitoring all areas covered by the Security Council's resolution: setting global standards for dealing with counterterrorism, assisting regional and subregional organizations in strengthening global counterterrorism capacity, and determining the role of international and regional organizations in pursuing the war on terrorism.

The Policy Working Group on the United Nations and Terrorism was established at the order of the Secretary-General in October 2001. The purpose of the Working Group, chaired by the Undersecretary-General for Political Affairs, was to identify the longer-term implications and broad policy dimensions of terrorism for the United Nations and to formulate recommendations on the steps that the UN system might take to address the issue. The Working Group established eight subgroups to address the following concerns: (1) international legal instruments and international criminal justice issues, (2) human rights, (3) activities of the UN system, (4) weapons of mass destruction and other weapons and technology, (5) use of ideology (secular and religious) to justify terrorism, (6) the CTC, (7) media and communications, and (8) non-UN multilateral initiatives. The subgroups were composed of UN officials and outside experts who were encouraged to reflect diverse perspectives on the contemporary dilemma. Each subgroup prepared its own report and developed background information for the Working Group. Ultimately, the Working Group reported to the Secretary-General, who in turn reported the Group's findings to the CTC and the Security Council. More general reports were to be made by the Secretary-General to the General Assembly.

This subject of a United Nations challenged by international terrorism will be treated in subsequent chapters.

# NOTES

1.  F. P. Walters, *A History of the League of Nations* (New York: Oxford University Press, 1952), p. 76.
2.  Maurice Bertrand, "The Recruitment Policy of United Nations Staff," in *International Administration: Law and Management Practices in International Organizations,* ed. Chris de Cooker, for United Nations Institute for Training and Research (Dordrecht: Martinus Nijhoff, 1990), pp. I.2/3–4. See also Theodor Meron, *The United Nations Secretariat* (Lexington, MA: Heath, 1977), p. 57.
3.  *Our Common Future,* World Commission on Environment and Development (Oxford: Oxford University Press, 1987).
4.  For a good sketch of the Secretary-General's role in peacekeeping, see Kjell Skjelsbae, "The UN Secretary-General and the Mediation of International Disputes," *Journal of Peace Research* 28, no. 1 (1991): 112–13.
5.  See Indar Jit Rikhye, "Critical Elements in Determining the Suitability of Conflict Settlement Efforts by the United Nations Secretary General," in Louis Kriesberg and Stuart J. Thorson, eds., *Timing the De-Escalation of International Conflicts* (Syracuse, NY: Syracuse University Press, 1991), pp. 58–82.
6.  Trygve Lie, *In the Cause of Peace* (New York: Macmillan, 1954), p. 42.
7.  Dag Hammarskjöld, address in Copenhagen, May 2, 1959, reprinted in *United Nations Review* 5 (June 1959), p. 25.

# SELECTED READINGS

Barros, James. *Office without Power: Secretary-General Sir Eric Drummond, 1919–1933.* New York: Oxford University Press, 1979.

———. *Trygve Lie and the Cold War: The UN Secretary-General Pursues Peace, 1946–1953.* DeKalb: Northern Illinois University, 1989.

Bercovitch, Jacob. *Resolving International Conflicts: The Theory and Practice of Mediation.* Boulder, CO: Lynne Rienner, 1995.

de Cooker, Chris, ed. *International Administration: Law and Management Practices in International Organisations.* United Nations Institute for Training and Research. Dordrecht: Martinus Nijhoff, 1990.

Diehl, Paul F., ed. *The Politics of Global Governance: International Organizations in an Interdependent World.* Boulder, CO: Lynne Rienner, 2001.

Finger, Seymour M., and John Mugno. *The Politics of Staffing the United Nations Secretariat.* New York: Ralph Bunche Institute on the United Nations, 1974.

Fisher, Julie. *Nongovernments: NGOs and the Political Development of the Third World.* West Hartford, CT: Kumarian Press, 1997.

Gordenker, Leon. *The UN Secretary-General and the Maintenance of Peace.* New York: Columbia University Press, 1967.

Graham, Norman A., and Robert S. Jordan, eds. *The International Civil Service: Changing Role and Concepts.* New York: Pergamon Press, 1980.

Gunaratna, Rohan. *Inside Al-Qaeda: Global Network of Terror.* New York: Penguin, 2003.

Jordan, Robert S., ed. *Dag Hammarskjöld Revisited: The UN Secretary-General as a Force in World Politics.* Durham, NC: Carolina Academic Press, 1983.

Langrod, Georges. *The International Civil Service.* Leyden: Sijthoff, 1963.

Lie, Trygve. *In the Cause of Peace: Seven Years with the UN.* New York: Macmillan, 1954.

Loveday, Alexander. *Reflections on International Administration.* Oxford: Clarendon Press, 1956.

Marks, Edward. *Complex Emergencies: Bureaucratic Arrangements in the UN Secretariat.* Washington, DC: National Defense University Press, 1996.

McLaren, Robert I. *Civil Servants and Public Policy: A Comparative Study of International Secretariats.* Waterloo, Ont.: Wilfrid Laurier University Press, 1980.

Meron, Theodor. *The United Nations Secretariat: The Rules and the Practice.* Lexington, MA: Heath, 1977.

Mouritzen, Hans. *The International Civil Service, A Study of Bureaucracy: International Organizations.* Aldershot, UK: Dartmouth, 1990.

Pérez de Cuéllar, Javier. *Pilgrimage for Peace: A Secretary-General's Memoir.* New York: St. Martin's Press, 1997.

Pitt, David, and Thomas G. Weiss, eds. *The Nature of United Nations Bureaucracies.* Boulder, CO: Westview Press, 1986.

Ranshofen-Wertheimer, Egon F. *The International Secretariat: A Great Experiment in International Administration.* New York: Carnegie Endowment for International Peace, 1945.

Reymond, Henri, and Sidney Mailick. *International Personnel Policies and Practices.* New York: Praeger, 1985.

Rovine, Arthur W. *The First Fifty Years: The Secretary-General in World Politics, 1920–1970.* Leyden: Sijthoff, 1970.

Royal Institute of International Affairs. *The International Secretariat of the Future.* London: Oxford University Press, 1944.

Russett, Bruce, ed. *The Once and Future Security Council.* New York: St. Martin's Press, 1997.

Thant, U. *View from the UN.* Garden City, NY: Doubleday, 1978.

Urquhart, Brian. *Hammarskjöld.* New York: Knopf, 1972.

Urquhart, Brian, and Erskine Childers. *A World in Need of Leadership: Tomorrow's United Nations.* Uppsala, Sweden: Dag Hammarskjöld Foundation, 1990.

Weiss, Thomas G. *International Bureaucracy: An Analysis of the Operation of Functional and Global International Secretariats.* Lexington, MA: Heath, 1975.

Zacher, Mark W. *Dag Hammarskjöld's United Nations.* New York: Columbia University Press, 1970.

# 5

# SECURITY THROUGH COLLECTIVE ACTION

Safeguarding international peace and security was the primary reason for the establishment of the United Nations in 1945. The aspiration "to save succeeding generations from the scourge of war" is enshrined in the opening lines of the UN Charter. Maintaining peace and security appears first in the Charter's statement of purposes and principles. UN functions are not narrowly limited to promoting military security, but even the nonmilitary functions are framed in the Charter by their potential contribution to peace. The rationale for international economic and social cooperation, for example, as set forth in Article 55 of the UN Charter, is "the creation of conditions of stability and well-being which are necessary for peaceful and friendly relations among nations." Peace and security also appear prominently in Articles 73(c) and 76(a) for dependent territories and peoples.

The frequency of armed clashes since 1945 reveals that the UN security system has not worked as intended. Security is still the central concern of all states, but the United Nations has been less central to the security of its members than the Charter might indicate. States rely primarily on their own might and that of their allies to deter aggression against themselves and, should peace fail, to vindicate their interests by force of arms. Lack of centrality does not mean irrelevance, however, and the United Nations has in many situations affected the way states pursue their security interests. The UN role in the settlement of disputes, control of arms, and establishment of the economic and social foundations for peace will be discussed in succeeding chapters. This chapter will examine efforts through the United Nations to prevent and limit war and to organize coercive sanctions against states that violate Charter norms.

The UN war-prevention role has often been called "collective security," although in practice the United Nations has been largely an adjunct to the operation of local and global balances of power. Before examining UN activities in detail, this chapter will present a brief historical and theoretical analysis of the concepts of the balance of power and collective security. A second section will discuss the generally unsuccessful efforts of the United Nations to achieve the ideal of collective security. A third section recounts the evolution of UN "peacekeeping" as a means of war limitation that depends, not primarily on coercion, but on the willingness of the affected states to accept a pacifying UN presence. A fourth section examines the conditions that led to the calamity of September 11, 2001, and analyzes the Charter peace function during an era when individuals and small groups of bitter men and women, not states per se, threaten the essentials of the state system.

# BALANCE OF POWER AND COLLECTIVE SECURITY

## ALLIANCES AND THE BALANCE OF POWER

Historically, the most common security arrangement among independent political entities has been the military alliance. The book of Genesis gives accounts of alliances and wars among rival groups of kings in the days of Abraham. Thucydides' *History of the Peloponnesian War* is the story of alliances and counteralliances among contending groups of Greek city-states. The modern state system has followed the same pattern from its inception, and even today arrangements for military cooperation among two or more states—secret or open, simple or highly organized—maintain undiminished popularity.

*Balance of power* is the term usually applied to a system in which states rely on international alliances to promote their individual security interests. However, what is accepted as a balance of power system in a world of independent nation-states, each of whom is mindful of and in pursuit of exclusive national interests, is more a condition rather than an operative mechanism. Alliance arrangements are methods in the balance of power and generally give tangible form to a perceived balance, but the balance of power operates even in the absence of formal alliances, and oftentimes despite them. The outbreak of World War I was attributed to the failure of the balance of power, and politicians such as Woodrow Wilson argued for its abandonment as an instrument of state behavior. But it was not the balance of power that failed to sustain the peace in the second decade of the twentieth century. Rather, it was the changing assumptions and perceptions of those responsible for the making of critical decisions. The central premise of any balance of power system is the assumption of those involved with its operation that their adversary or rival has the capacity to do them particular damage and that prudence requires their dispelling conditions that might precipitate a costly confrontation. The mutual overestimation of the capability and will of one's adversary to engage in war, and the rational decision to avoid such entanglement, gives meaning to a balance of power system. In other words, if the balance of power is working effectively, what nations generally think is "peace" is really their capacity combined with a willingness to avoid war. Thus, the balance of power is not concerned with the righting of wrongs, or the perfection of political systems. To the contrary, if the balance of power is anything, it is the acceptance of the status quo by the state actors. The balance of power, therefore, is a diplomatic, not a military exercise. When diplomats no longer see the logic of "peace," the balance breaks down and soldiers make war. And as certain as peace follows war, still another balance is formed, and diplomats again grope for the limits of a new system that will better ensure that there will be no more war.

The outbreak of World War I, therefore, irrespective of those who argued its cause, was not a consequence of the balance of power system, but the gross failure of key European decision makers. Otto von Bismarck had demonstrated the successful use of the balance of power system. His dismissal by Kaiser Wilhelm, however, and the latter's determination to establish Germany as both a major land and naval power had elevated the threshold of threat to the reigning nations. The Kaiser's Germany provoked the guarantor of the early twentieth-century balance, notably Great Britain, to abandon its role as the "balancer" and engage itself in the crosscutting rivalries that eventually produced the Great War. If World War I had proved anything, it was the need for a more credible balance of power system, albeit for a more successful demonstration of international diplomacy.

The victors of World War I could not ignore the epic transformation in warfare that occurred during 1914–18. Citing the technological advances made in weapons and munitions and the terrible loss of life as a consequence of their almost casual employment, the politicians who assembled at Versailles to fashion a new world order were primarily concerned with preventing a repeat performance of this human tragedy. As they saw the situation, it was a matter of restricting the use of, or even eliminating, what then could be described as weapons of mass destruction. But disarmament was hardly a realistic pursuit when the political issues underlying the Great War had not been satisfactorily addressed. Some empires had been defeated and dissolved, but imperialism remained the central feature of international politics, and as time would demonstrate, national or popular imperialism was exponentially more aggressive than its traditional, aristocratic cum-commercial predecessor.

Unfortunately, the world leaders who met at Versailles to restore world equilibrium failed to grasp the realities of the time. Confronted with the dilemmas created by the Great War, and imposed upon by a U.S. president, whose armed forces had helped turn the tide of battle, the European leaders yielded to their transatlantic counterpart. The European victors of the "war to end all wars" agreed with Wilson that serious concern must be given to the creation of an international organization that ensured the continuance of the wartime alliance. Wilson fervently believed that this "world" organization would not act as a prop for the creation of a more formidable balance of power, but as a substitute for it! Thus too, the idea of collective security as the only workable substitute for the balance of power was introduced. But whereas the balance of power acknowledged the sovereign independence of the many nation-states, collective security called for a diminution in exclusive state behavior. Collective security in fact implied a commitment to matters of world concern that transcended the immediate interests of the individual sovereign states. The U.S. Senate's rejection of the Versailles Treaty, the League of Nations, and more so, of collective security, was not surprising given the Americans' fear of a loss of sovereignty, that is, a loss of national control over critical events. For the American senators who damned the League, the issues that the international organization could be called upon to address were judged too distant from U.S. national interests. The Americans therefore rejected the roles of both the balance of power and collective security. Collective security was virtually dead before it could be demonstrated, kept alive only by the more idealistic of the European leaders who had had enough of war and longed for an era of extended tranquility. A meaningless expression of the theory of collective security failed to prevent World War II. Moreover, in the absence of a resilient diplomacy that was capable of managing the much maligned balance of power, global struggle, buttressed by the breakthrough in weapons technology during World War I, was repeated with even more devastating results.

## THE ADVENT OF COLLECTIVE SECURITY

The task of creating a substitute for the balance of power was undertaken by the Paris peacemakers in 1919, under the prodding of President Woodrow Wilson. The available precedents for bringing two or more states within a common security system were not promising. The principal historical precedents were conquest, political federation, and, at a lower level of integration, military alliance. Conquest was a wholly unacceptable model, and voluntary extinction of separate sovereignties through political federation was not feasible, given deep-seated national sentiment. Global diversity in economic development, social organization, and political values also were too ingrained to overcome. Military alliances made little demand on national sovereignty, but as security systems they stood discredited by their inability to prevent World War I.

Another nineteenth-century precedent was the Concert of Europe, a loose-knit system of consultation among great powers spawned by the Napoleonic Wars and continued sporadically to the eve of World War I. The Concert was more a state of mind than an organized security system, and it was only indifferently effective. When the Serbian crisis arose in the summer of 1914, the Concert technique of great power consultation was not even called into play. In addition to the Concert, there was the legacy of the 1899 and 1907 Hague Conferences and the considerable experience of organized international cooperation in economic and social areas. Although suggestive of organizational forms and procedures, the international conference and the public administrative union were not security systems. The hard fact was that nothing in history constituted a working precedent for an effective system of security within a community of sovereign states.

The peacemakers thus were forced to innovate. They took the ideal of a universal security system, hitherto the domain of political dreamers, and fused it with nineteenth-century international organization. In the process, they used much of their own ingenuity to forge the essential compromises between ideals and realities. The result, emerging as the initial twenty-six articles of the Versailles Treaty, was the League of Nations Covenant—the world's first genuine experiment with "collective security."

## THE NATURE OF COLLECTIVE SECURITY

The rejection of the League of Nations by the United States, as well as the League's failure to meet its collective security obligations, heralded its end even before the outbreak of World War II. Nevertheless, as a concept, "collective security" survived the war, and the politicians of the post–World War II period, again led by a U.S. president, this time Franklin Delano Roosevelt, recognized the need to give the idea another try. The alliance forged during World War II to defeat the aggressive forces of fascism and ultranationalism, although composed of discordant actors, nevertheless acknowledged the need to sustain their association. Appalled by the horrors and destructiveness of modern warfare as well as their own capacity for unlimited and unrestrained violence, and arguably more realistic than their predecessors after World War I, the framers of the UN Charter were determined to avoid the pitfalls of the League. Indeed, they gave still another interpretation to the meaning of collective security. What it means, however, varies with the context.

The term *collective security* had been applied indiscriminately to almost any arrangement among two or more countries that involves the possibility of joint military action. After World War II it was used to describe military alliances, such as NATO, in order to give them more respectability. In this context it became a virtual synonym for a "good" or "defensive" alliance, as contrasted with a "bad" (someone else's) alliance, which might be used for offensive and hence "aggressive" purposes. Terms like *collective defense* or *collective self-defense* (see Charter Article 51), rather than collective security, have been applied to multilateral alliances aimed primarily at threats to security created by countries outside the coalition. In its more specialized and correct meaning, however, collective security is an arrangement among states by which all are committed to aid any country threatened with armed attack by any other country. The object is to deter aggression by confronting a potential aggressor with the power of an overwhelming coalition and, should war nevertheless occur, to bring the aggressor quickly to heel. A collective security system, while close to a balance of power system, alters conventional conceptions of alliances. While an alliance is geared to threats from foes of the alliance, collective security focuses on threats arising within the larger balance of power system. Among the states involved, there are no predetermined alignments. All of them, presumably, are "friends" or "associates" until one of them chooses to become an aggressor. That state then becomes the "enemy" of all the others, that is, until the threat of aggression has been removed.

As originally conceived, collective security was intended to be worldwide in scope. In theory, however, a collective security system might include any smaller number of states as long as preponderant power could be marshaled against any one of them. Some regional organizations have collective security aspects. The Inter-American Treaty of Reciprocal Assistance (the Rio Pact) makes explicit provision for resisting possible aggression by one Latin American country against another. NATO, the Organization of African Unity, and the Arab League all tried to deal with conflicts among their own members. The Commonwealth of Independent States that emerged from the breakup of the Soviet Union has not displayed a collective interest in a common security arrangement. NATO's enlargement in 1998, however, to include Poland, Hungary, and the Czech Republic, and in 2004, to extend membership to the Baltic States, the Slovak Republic, Slovenia, Bulgaria, and Rumania, raises the prospect that the CIS might yet consider a similar course. For the time being, however, CIS cooperation with the Organization of Security and Cooperation in Europe (OSCE) sustains at least the idea of a collective security dimension. Although these organizations and combinations fall short of the collective security ideal, they nevertheless are regarded as either collective security alliances or collective self-defense expedients. Indeed, their utility is demonstrated in the growing number of cooperative associations with UN peacekeeping operations.

The essential elements of an effective collective security system are *consensus, commitment,* and *organization.* At the minimum level of *consensus,* states must agree that peace is indivisible and that threats to peace anywhere are the concern of all. But more is required. There must be a *commitment* to act in accordance with the collective security principle. The commitment has both a positive and a self-denying aspect. States are duty bound to combine their forces to meet any threat to the security of the world community. They are also committed to refrain from unilateral use of force to achieve purely national objectives. Ideally, the commitments should be so binding and so widely embraced that attempts to change the status quo by violence are considered unlawful and are subjected to overwhelming force. Without this commitment, consensus remains a meaningless abstraction. But commitment, too, may fail in times of crisis if there is no *organization* to make it effective. Every such commitment is necessarily a generalized commitment until a crisis arises. If each state is then free to decide how and when its commitment will be honored, enforcement may be highly selective. An effective collective security system requires a central decision-making organ that is empowered to say how and when collective force is to be used, with adequate military forces available on call to carry out that decision.

For practical purposes collective security has a fourth prerequisite. Power should be widely enough dispersed that no state can hope to challenge all the others. The effectiveness of the system depends on its capacity to deter most potential violators and to defeat an actual aggressor in short order. If one state is substantially stronger than the rest, it may be willing to act unilaterally in clear defiance of the collective security system. The failure of the League of Nations as a collective security system was the failure of any of the members constituting the collective to take the necessary and timely action that would have thwarted the imperial and national ambitions of Germany, Italy, and Japan in the 1930s.

By contrast, the United Nations, although not better at acting collectively, was preserved by the decisions of the United States to become a member and of the Soviet Union to remain associated with the organization all through the Cold War. The fact that the two most prominent permanent members of the UN Security Council avoided direct confrontation, that is, never took the blood of the other on the battlefield, allowed the idea of collective security to remain, if in a moribund state. "Hot wars" during the Cold War were either proxy wars (conflicts waged by countries associated or aligned with one or the other superpower) or wars in which one superpower engaged in lethal combat while the other pretended to be aloof. The Korean War and the Soviet war in Afghanistan are two major cases in point. It was only in 1990, after the Iraqi invasion of Kuwait, that the UN principle of collective security was seriously employed. But the demise of the Soviet Union shortly thereafter raised new questions about the use of the UN collective security system in the future. Further questions were raised about the utility of collective security after the United States launched an unprovoked attack on Iraq in 2003 over the opposition of a majority of Security Council permanent members, a vast number of UN members, and even the Secretary-General. When one country dominates world events and holds a monopoly of world power, the system of collective security is doomed to failure.

## THE LEAGUE SECURITY SYSTEM

The League of Nations did not satisfy any of the conditions for effective collective security, except perhaps the last—that is, organization. Before World War II no country was strong enough to defy all the others if the others were united. But League members, and the United States as the major nonmember, were not adequately convinced that every war anywhere was a threat to them. And certainly they lacked commitment to use their combined force against any and every case of aggression, regardless of who the aggressor might be. The League Covenant did not even require such a commitment. In disputes coming before the League, the Covenant expressly permitted aggressive war against a state that refused to comply with recommendations unanimously endorsed by the Council and against any party to a dispute on which the Council was divided. These so-called gaps in the Covenant were widely deplored, but even more enfeebling was the absence of obligation to act when unauthorized aggression occurred. Article 10 of the League Covenant declared unequivocally that "the Members of the League undertake to respect and preserve as against external aggression the territorial integrity and existing political independence of all Members of the League." Yet Manchuria, Ethiopia, and ultimately a host of other members fell victim to violence without a shot being fired in their defense in the name of the League and without any state being obligated by the Covenant to fire such a shot.

Article 11 embodied both the necessary consensus and commitment in its grand assertion that "any war or threat of war, whether immediately affecting any of the Members of the League or not, is hereby declared a matter of concern to the whole League." It concluded that "the League shall take any action that may be wise and effectual to safeguard the peace of nations." But when the obligations were spelled out in greater detail, League decisions to take military action had only the force of recommendations (Article 16). Even the supposedly automatic "severance of all trade or financial relations" was vitiated by League resolutions adopted in 1921 emphasizing the right of each state to determine for itself how and when to apply economic sanctions. The League was also hampered by its rule requiring a unanimous vote for most decisions. Whenever the League was moved to action against threats to the peace during the troubled 1930s, it was almost always too little and too late. In short, the League system did not work well, not for any real fault in the Covenant but because the disposition of members to view their own security as separable from that of others was reinforced by weak legal commitments and ineffective decision-making procedures.

## THE UNITED NATIONS AND COLLECTIVE SECURITY

### THE CHARTER FRAMEWORK

The framers of the UN Charter were not willing to abandon the collective security concept of peace enforced by the community of nations. Although they recognized the need for some compromise with the ideal, they hoped that improved institutions and a new urgency to cooperate would succeed where the League had failed.

Influenced by the 1928 Pact of Paris that outlawed war as an instrument of national policy, the UN Charter commits all members to "refrain in their international relations from the threat or use of force against the territorial integrity or political independence of any state" (Article 2, section 4). Only four exceptions to the use of force were cited in the Charter. First, self-defense, whether individual or collective (Article 51); second, action against the "enemy" states of World War II—Germany, Italy, and Japan (Article 107); third, joint action by the Big Five (the United States, Soviet Union, Great Britain, France, and China) on behalf of the organization, pending the availability of troops under Article 43 (Article 106); and fourth, any other use of force authorized by the Security Council, including enforcement by regional organizations (Article 53). The Charter did not deal with the issue of internal armed revolt and civil wars, which, strictly speaking, are judged domestic matters and are not concerned with the use of force in "international relations."

Equally important was the attempt to put sharper teeth into the Charter. Instead of economic sanctions that were automatic in theory but discretionary in practice, the Security Council was given the right to impose nonmilitary sanctions, with all members obligated "to accept and carry out the decisions of the Security Council." In place of the League Council's right to recommend military sanctions, the Security Council was to have earmarked troops supplied by prior agreement with members and awaiting only the Council's call to action. Abandoning the requirement of unanimity, the Security Council was empowered to take military action by vote of seven of eleven (now nine of fifteen) members, including the concurring votes of the five permanent members.

The retention of a great power veto was, admittedly, a conscious compromise with the principle of collective security, but one dictated by common sense. Critics had constantly pointed out that collective security treated all wars as incipient world wars, with the practical danger of turning localized wars into global war if powerful forces were ranged on both sides. The veto was intended to prevent such an eventuality. With the great powers all committed to collective enforcement through the organization, the prospect of quickly squelching an outburst of violence would be very good indeed.

On paper the UN Charter seemed a reasonable approach to collective security, subject to the limitation of the veto. The Charter registered broad consensus that peace is indivisible and that any threat to international peace and security is the concern of all. Members were legally committed to accept and carry out Security Council decisions, and the Council could make binding decisions (not just recommendations) to impose both military and nonmilitary sanctions. Here, then, was consensus, commitment, and central decision-making machinery merged in a coherent collective security system.

## THE DEMISE OF MANDATORY MILITARY SANCTIONS

The Charter system did not work as intended. The root problem was lack of genuine consensus and commitment to match the responsibilities on paper. Even while the United Nations was being planned, leaders of the Big Three questioned the collective security concept or the operations of particular institutional arrangements. Roosevelt, Churchill, and Stalin all regarded new rivalries as inevitable. Churchill and Stalin hoped to stabilize international conditions by recognizing spheres of influence over areas of special interest to them—particularly the Balkans. Roosevelt looked more to a "Four Policemen" concept (that included reconstructed China) modeled after the old Concert of Europe as a means of providing order in the system. Great power cooperation, that is, the balance of power, not collective security, was the answer. Roosevelt ultimately accepted the UN concept, but the germ of his Four Policemen idea was preserved in the provision for permanent members of the UN Security Council.

Events subsequently reinforced President Roosevelt's judgment about collective security, if not his optimism about the prospects for East-West cooperation. Wartime collaboration quickly degenerated into the Cold War, revealing discordant national security interests that could not be harnessed to the collective security requirement of all for one and one for all. Soviet-U.S. rivalry was apparent in the Security Council, where a Western majority was held in check by the Soviet veto. But the veto was only a symptom. Fundamental divergence of interest was the underlying problem.

One of the early institutional casualties was the UN security force envisioned by Charter Article 43. The capacity of the Security Council to take military action on its own initiative depended on the subsequent negotiation of special agreements with member states to make standby military forces and facilities available to the Council at its call. Each such agreement required formal approval by the states concerned according to their respective constitutional processes. But this requirement only meant that member states, in accepting the Charter, had made a moral commitment to support UN military sanctions, while postponing to a later day any limitation on the right to control their own military forces. In fact, no Article 43 agreement ever reached the stage of national legal approval because the major powers could not agree on the size and character of their respective national contributions or on where the units should be based. The Security Council and its Military Staff Committee (Articles 46, 47) were never able to resolve their differences.

Without agreement on guidelines for UN military forces, no special agreements under Article 43 could be negotiated. The broad Charter commitment to collective security was not translated into a real commitment to supply troops and war-making matériel. Despite the intent of the Charter, members retained the right to decide for themselves, according to the circumstances of each case, how their military forces should be used. If collective military action were to be taken at all, it would be on a voluntary basis.

While the Security Council struggled with Article 43, the General Assembly embarked on the project that would legally define what was meant by "aggression." Nearly thirty years later, in 1974, the Assembly approved a compromise formula embodying a fair degree of international consensus but containing enough ambiguities to leave the specific declarations of aggression as still an ad hoc political act. The Assembly determined that an act of aggression must be considered "in light of all the circumstances of each particular case." Article 1 of the formula proscribes "the use of force against the sovereignty, territorial integrity or political independence" of another state and labels it "aggression." Article 2 makes "the use of force by a State in contravention of the Charter" prima facie evidence of aggression, subject to Security Council determination that the act in question did not constitute aggression. Article 3 lists several additional acts that may also be labeled as "aggression" subject again to Security Council decision to the contrary. Article 7, however, excludes from the description of aggression those acts by and in support of peoples struggling to achieve "self-determination, freedom and independence" from "colonial and racist regimes or other forms of alien domination."

## KOREA AND COLLECTIVE ACTION

Korea provided the initial major test of voluntary collective security under UN auspices. In a number of respects, the conditions for voluntary UN enforcement action were highly favorable. When war broke out in June 1950, a UN observation group already in South Korea was able to confirm that an armed attack by North Korean troops had in fact occurred. The absence of the Soviet delegate, in protest against the continued seating of Nationalist China, eliminated the prospect of a veto and allowed a quick Security Council endorsement of the U.S. request for military aid to South Korea. The United States had troops stationed in Japan and Okinawa that could be moved quickly to the scene of the conflict. Thus a "UN" action was introduced in Korea, relying almost totally on U.S. initiative and resources.

When the return of the Soviet delegate in August snuffed out the Security Council's capacity to act, the issue was removed from the Security Council to the General Assembly. The General Assembly usually was able to act on crucial issues with some dispatch. As the months wore on, however, Chinese intervention, military stalemate, and rising concern about touching off a third world war brought division and dissension among the members of the United Nations. Nearly all members therefore breathed a sigh of relief when a Korean Armistice was arranged in July 1953, ending the fighting. UN action helped preserve the independence of the Republic of Korea, but it brought no renewed enthusiasm for collective security, on a voluntary basis or otherwise. What was first seen as the rebirth of collective military action, the Korean War proved almost the opposite. The reasons are now fairly clear, and most of them speak to characteristics of the world and of the United Nations that persist today.

One reason is the ambiguous form in which armed struggle has occurred since Korea. Civil wars, revolutions, guerrilla warfare, clandestine penetration and subversion, and foreign intervention in the guise of assistance to contending domestic factions were the common forms of violence that ruptured the peace of the world before September 11, 2001. In such situations there often was no clearly discernible aggressor to be the object of a collective military response. Moreover, the probability that the Korean experience may have encouraged the subsequent use of more covert forms of aggression in place of overt military invasion does little to enhance the usefulness of collective military sanctions in meeting the kinds of threats that do exist. Even more so, with the advent of a more aggressive worldwide form of international terrorism, the use of traditional military strategies that include collective action to stem aggression appear even more questionable.

The Korean War highlighted basic defects of the United Nations as an instrument for launching collective military sanctions. Without consensus among its permanent members, the Security Council could not take decisive action in times of crisis. Only the absence of the Soviet delegate made the initial Security Council action possible, and the Security Council was immobilized by the Soviet return. When responsibility for decisions was then shifted to the General Assembly, that body proved too large, too unwieldy, and too divided in counsel to direct a military operation effectively. Korea further revealed the disadvantages of dependence on voluntary commitment of forces in times of crisis. Just twenty-two of the sixty member states offered military forces, and only sixteen of the offers were of usable size and quality. The United States contributed more than half of the ground forces, 85 percent of the naval forces, and nearly

95 percent of the air force contingents, with South Korea providing most of the remaining personnel. Less than 10 percent came from the other contributors. This means that the Korean War was largely an American operation. It was directed by a unified command, a euphemism generally understood to mean U.S. command. The unified command reported to the United Nations, but only what the United States saw fit to report. The United Nations undoubtedly provided a valuable political cover for U.S. operations in Korea, but a collective response so heavily dependent on a single great power, and so closely tied to its national interests, was a questionable kind of collective security.

If UN institutions and member response fell short of the collective security ideal, in one respect the Korean action exceeded the carefully delimited bounds of the Charter. The United Nations wielded arms against the interests of a permanent member of the Security Council, that is, China, with all the explosive potential for a third world war that the veto had been designed to prevent. Korea did not lead to a direct military confrontation between the Soviet Union and the United States and thereby to another world war, but at times the thread by which the Damoclean sword hung suspended seemed perilously slender. The enduring lesson of the Korean venture was not that it repelled aggression but that it was too risky to try again—at least in the absence of an agreement among great powers.

Korea also demonstrated the absence of a fundamental precondition for effective collective security: consensus on the kind of world that is to be made secure. Enforcement of peace in a national political system is possible because of general agreement on political goals and the existence of machinery for the peaceful settlement of most disputes as they arise. Collective security, by attempting to outlaw violent change, assumes that existing methods of peaceful change and dispute settlement are adequate to resolve international differences and satisfy legitimate national aspirations. The unreality of this assumption is well illustrated by the Korean War, where technically a state of war continued to exist decades after the Armistice, and the only settlement possible was an agreement to exchange prisoners and to stop fighting along a line roughly corresponding to the status quo ante. A divided Korea was perpetuated, and the underlying problems that precipitated the crisis remained unresolved. Without greater agreement on the kind of world that was to be made secure, the nations were not ready for collective security.

Nor was the Korean problem something that would simply go away. Two independent, very different Korean states separated only by a menacing demilitarized zone remained massively armed and in hostile postures. The United States, decades after the cessation of hostilities, was forced to maintain thousands of troops below the thirty-eighth parallel to guarantee the security of South Korea. Although remaining below the radar for much of the Cold War, the problem of a divided peninsula that both North and South still sought to unify was revealed again in the early 1990s. North Korea's earlier agreement to eschew the development of nuclear weapons, and its acceptance of the Nuclear Nonproliferation Treaty, was declared null and void when P'yŏngyang declared it intended to possess nuclear weapons after all. It also dedicated itself to the rapid development of advanced missile delivery systems. The Clinton administration, after hinting at a first-strike possibility against North Korea's nuclear facilities and the possible renewal of the Korean War, finally opted for a diplomatic solution that resulted in an agreed framework for a negotiated settlement between the two countries. North Korea accepted an agreement that would substitute U.S.-supplied light-water nuclear reactors solely for the generation of electricity in return for the dismantling of nuclear reactors capable of producing weapons-grade plutonium. Washington also pledged the transfer of substantial oil supplies to the North to compensate for the expected shortage in energy during the transition process. But that agreement came undone in October 2002 when P'yŏngyang announced to the world that it had been clandestinely working on a nuclear weapons program. North Korea followed by denouncing the Joint Declaration on the Denuclearization of the Korean Peninsula as well as the International Atomic Energy Agency's Safeguards Agreement. At the same time it declared that it was reactivating its plutonium facility in Yongbyon and expelling the IAEA inspectors stationed there to monitor compliance with the agreements.

Tensions between North Korea and the United States attained new levels after President George W. Bush declared North Korea to be a member of the tripartite "Axis of Evil" of Iraq, Iran, and North Korea, and even more so, after the United States led an assault on Iraq in March 2003. The destruction by U.S.-led coalition forces of the regime of Saddam Hussein, representing another member of the Axis, elevated concerns in P'yŏngyang that North Korea might be Washington's next target. North Korea insisted on direct one-on-one talks with the United States and a guaranteed nonaggression pact with Washington. The Bush administration, however, refused to negotiate with North Korean authorities, insisting that its government could not be trusted to keep an agreement. Washington also insisted that the matter was at the very least a regional one and any negotiations must include North Korea's neighbors, that is, South Korea, Japan, China, and the Russian Federation. Both P'yŏngyang and Washington could not agree to negotiate on the other's terms, but South Korean leaders visited the capital of North Korea. A meeting was also held in Beijing between U.S. and North Korean officials. None of these talks left any reason for optimism, however. In June 2003 P'yŏngyang formally declared that it considered nuclear weapons a "deterrent" and repeated its earlier warning that any attempt to sanction the country would be judged a hostile act. President Bush asserted that unlike his decision to remove Saddam Hussein, his objective in North Korea was not regime change but rather a multilateral effort to pressure North Korea to give up its nuclear weapons program. At the annual Asia-Pacific Economic Cooperation Conference in Bangkok in October 2003, President Bush reiterated the offer of a multilateral guarantee involving China, Japan, Russia, South Korea, and the United States. Pledging nonhostile policies in return for P'yŏngyang's decision to cease its pursuit of nuclear weapons, Bush was rebuffed by the North Koreans, who continued to insist on a nonaggression treaty between North Korea and the United States but nevertheless appeared to leave the door open to future negotiations. Not in the habit of developing nonaggression treaties, Washington continued to ignore that demand, but its call for multilateral diplomacy was nonetheless aimed at reducing some of the tension in the region. Indeed, China had become concerned with P'yŏngyang's bellicosity and was expected to play a more important role or face the possibility that Japan, and possibly Taiwan, would yet seek its own nuclear deterrents. The Six Nation Talks hosted by Beijing in February 2004 illustrated China's heightened interest in a diplomatic settlement over the issue of nuclear proliferation.

Collective security was at work here, but it was a form of collective security that opted for a diplomatic solution, not a renewal of the long dormant but unresolved Korean War. If there was a lesson in the Korean peninsula, it was the failure of genuine collective action that long ago should have ended the confrontation between North and South. Left in precarious limbo, the Korean dilemma shrouded all thoughts of peace in the Korean peninsula. Moreover, despite the passage of more than half a century, conditions in the region had not improved, and indeed the escalation of the rhetoric highlighted a situation that went well beyond northeast Asia.

One enduring institutional legacy of the Korean War, however, was the Uniting for Peace Resolution, adopted by the Assembly in early November 1950.[1] The resolution was a U.S. proposal intended to make the United Nations more effective in dealing with future threats to the peace. The UN system had worked reasonably well in repelling North Korean aggression (or so it appeared at the time), but only because of fortuitous circumstances (the Soviet boycott and nearby U.S. forces in Japan). The Uniting for Peace Resolution was the way the General Assembly responded to a crisis when the Security Council was unable to act. Given the General Assembly's prerogative under the Charter to recommend collective military action, a procedure was established for calling the General Assembly into "Emergency Special Session" by a vote of any seven (now nine) members of the Security Council, or on request of a majority of UN members. In addition, it created a Peace Observation Commission to send observers to tension-laden areas on request, authorized a Collective Measures Committee to study and report on methods of strengthening international peace and security, and urged members to earmark national military units for use by the United Nations. The last three provisions of the Resolution quickly fell into disuse, but the Emergency Special Session procedure survived and was invoked in the Suez and Hungarian crises of 1956, the Lebanon crisis of 1958, the Congo crisis of 1960, and the Suez War of 1967. After a period of disuse, it was revived again to deal with Afghanistan (1980), Palestine (1980, resumed in 1982), Namibia (1981), and the Occupied Arab Territories (1982). The Uniting for Peace system that evolved was originally sponsored by the United States to facilitate UN action in security matters when the Soviet veto immobilized the Security Council. Ironically, however, the last three Emergency Special Sessions of the Cold War were made possible by the votes of the Soviet Union and Third

World countries, over the objection of the United States. The Uniting for Peace Resolution, however, was no substitute for Chapter VII of the UN Charter.

The attempt to apply the full force of Chapter VII of the UN Charter in Korea and, in effect, to give genuine meaning to collective security failed in the first instance because of the ideological rivalry existing between the United States and the Soviet Union. The success of Chapter VII is read in an "all against the aggressor" principle that is the hallmark of collective security. And although North Korea was deemed to be an "aggressor" against the South, Cold War differences between Security Council members negated the unity necessary for meeting the high standards of collective security actions. The passage of Council responsibilities to the Assembly through the Uniting for Peace Resolution enabled the United States to sustain its military effort in Korea under the aegis of the United Nations, but the demands on UN member states were considerably reduced. Where the Security Council under Chapter VII provisions could "order" the full membership of the United Nations to assist in beating back an aggressor, once the matter was transferred to the General Assembly the capacity to "order" had been downgraded to a "recommendation." Thus, the member states were left to determine for themselves the extent of their commitment, and whether or not it was in their interests to pursue a war that not only involved North Korean forces, but in 1951, also those from Communist China. In sum: The UN General Assembly, after the Korean experience, found it possible to send forces into other emergency situations under the Uniting for Peace Resolution but with limited involvement from both the United States and the Soviet Union. Chapter VII of the UN Charter, therefore, could not be applied in its collective security mode during the decades of the Cold War, that is, until the 1990–91 action against Iraq's occupation of Kuwait. That conflict appeared to give new emphasis to UN collective security operations under Chapter VII provisions. It also returned responsibility for managing world equilibrium to the Security Council. The self-destruction of the Soviet Union shortly thereafter, however, raised new questions concerning the utility of the UN collective security system. Despite the collapse of one of the world's two superpowers and the end of the Cold War, the post–Cold War period revealed that old dilemmas persisted. Cooperation on military matters by major, and lesser, powers was still an illusive objective as the twenty-first century began. And as far as the Korean peninsula was concerned, China's, and to a large extent Russia's, different perception of North Korea's nuclear program did not even hint at collective action, at least not that stipulated in the provisions of Chapter VII of the UN Charter.

## WAR IN THE GULF—THE CONTINUING METAMORPHOSIS OF COLLECTIVE SECURITY

On August 2, 1990, an Iraqi army crossed the border into the Kingdom of Kuwait, quickly subdued its defenders, forced the exile of its ruler and government, and left the small country at the mercy of Iraq's leader, Saddam Hussein.

Kuwait was not only conquered by the Iraqi assault, it was eliminated as an independent, sovereign state and given new status as the nineteenth province of Iraq. Coming as it did, hardly two years after the end of hostilities between Iraq and Iran, this Iraqi aggression against a neighboring state was attributed to the machinations of Saddam Hussein, whose ambition, it was said, centered on dominating the Arab world, controlling its oil reserves, toppling its remaining monarchs, and eventually doing successful battle with Israel. Although the United States had earlier tilted toward Iraq in its war with Iran, Washington reacted most unfavorably to this act of aggression against a sovereign member of the United Nations. The Soviet Union, under the leadership of Mikhail Gorbachev, also condemned the Iraqi invasion and called upon Iraq to withdraw its troops or risk threatening the relationship forged between their two countries since the late 1950s. Given the effectiveness of the Iraqi military campaign, however, the only recourse was to bring the matter before the UN Security Council, which for the first time since the war on the Korean peninsula in 1950 appeared ready to apply the collective security provisions under Chapter VII of the UN Charter.

Unlike the Korean War, the United States had no substantial military forces in the area capable of offering serious resistance. In other respects, however, the conditions for UN action were favorable. The Iraqi invasion was readily judged a violation of the prohibition of the use of force in the UN Charter (Article 2, Paragraph 4) against "the territorial integrity or political independence" of another state. It was not cast in the ambiguous mold of clandestine activity and subversion or intervention in aid of a domestic rebellion. Still more important, the turnabout in Soviet foreign policy under Gorbachev had brought a Soviet-U.S. rapprochement that made the Security Council a workable instrument of collective action. Perhaps most important, as in Korea, the United States perceived its threatened interests in the Middle East (oil, pro-Saudi interest, Israeli security) as something worth confronting.

The Security Council reacted quickly. On August 2, the day the attack began, the Security Council condemned the invasion and demanded an immediate unconditional withdrawal, citing as authority Articles 39 (determining the existence of a breach of international peace) and 40 (provisional measures). Four days later the Security Council ordered mandatory economic sanctions, as provided in Article 41, barring all trade with Iraq except "supplies intended strictly" for medical and humanitarian purposes. Over the next five months the Security Council adopted ten additional resolutions to deal with the crisis, including a request for the Secretary-General to seek a diplomatic solution. Council action culminated in Resolution 678, adopted November 29, setting January 15, 1991, as a deadline for Iraq's withdrawal from Kuwait and authorizing member states "to use all necessary means" to force compliance if Iraq did not withdraw voluntarily.

While the Security Council was tightening the screws, the United States worked feverishly to build U.S. ground, air, and naval strength in the area, initially for the defense of Saudi Arabia and eventually for an assault on Iraqi positions in Kuwait. With equal fervor the United States moved to forge a military coalition against Iraq, particularly among states of the Middle East. All attempts at a negotiated withdrawal failed, including last-minute initiatives by the United States and the UN Secretary-General. On January 16, 1991, the day after the UN deadline, coalition forces began massive aerial and naval bombardment of Iraqi military targets in Kuwait and Iraq. An all-out ground offensive was launched on February 24; it had such devastating effectiveness that President Bush was able to proclaim a provisional cease-fire on March 6. At the beginning of the air attack, U.S. troops in the Persian Gulf region were estimated at 425,000. Before the buildup ended U.S. forces numbered 540,000. In addition to this massive U.S. contribution, twenty-seven countries contributed an additional 250,000 troops: Argentina, Australia, Bahrain, Bangladesh, Belgium, Canada, Czechoslovakia, Denmark, Egypt, France, Germany, Greece, Italy, Kuwait, Morocco, Netherlands, Niger, Norway, Oman, Pakistan, Qatar, Saudi Arabia, Senegal, Spain, Syria, United Arab Emirates, and the United Kingdom.

Ousting the armies of Saddam Hussein from Kuwait served to vindicate the United Nations in its stand against armed aggression and removed Iraq, at least temporarily, as a serious military threat to the stability of the Middle East. A UN Iraq-Kuwait Observation Mission (UNIKOM) was established to monitor a demilitarized zone along the boundary between the two countries. As a condition of a permanent cease-fire, the Security Council demanded the destruction of Iraqi chemical and biological weapons, long-range missiles, and facilities for producing nuclear weapons. UN inspection teams (UNSCOM) were sent to Iraq to monitor compliance.

Despite the defeat imposed on Iraq by the UN coalition, Saddam Hussein and his government remained and in fact had more than enough military capacity to crush both a Shiite Muslim rebellion in the southern area of the country and a Kurdish insurrection in the north. The Security Council decision to halt the conflict was in part predicated on the belief that Saddam would be swept aside by his Iraqi opposition, as well as the knowledge that the Americans, who carried major responsibility for the ground war, were reluctant to move on to Baghdad. Saddam, however, surprised the pundits. He not only survived the war, he appeared to gain in strength as his internal enemies were liquidated. Saddam's regime, however, suffered the embarrassment of surrender, and more important, the obtrusive scrutiny of UNSCOM. Moreover, until it could be demonstrated that Iraq was no longer a threat to its neighbors and the world, the UN-imposed economic sanctions remained in place. Furthermore, as a consequence of Baghdad's assault on the Kurds, the United Nations secured an enclave in northern Iraq where Kurds uprooted from their homes found relative security, and in time created an autonomous government. To protect the enclave from Iraqi air attacks, the United States, under UN authorization, established a no-fly zone in the northern region of the country, thus denying Iraqi aircraft use of airspace over a portion of their own country.

In the years that followed the war, the Iraqi government sought to reassert its sovereign power. In the south, it acted as though it would again invade Kuwait. Later, it also was disclosed that Baghdad plotted the assassination of former President Bush during a visit to liberated Kuwait. Bush was succeeded in the presidency by Bill Clinton in January 1993, and the new U.S. president ordered cruise missile strikes against a limited number of Iraqi targets when it was learned of the attempt on Bush's life. Clinton also extended the no-fly zone to include the southern Shiite area of Iraq. In the northern region, however, Iraq successfully took advantage of rivalry between Kurdish factions, and Saddam's forces moved into a portion of the UN-protected enclave unopposed by the Security Council. In fact, nothing was done to reverse the action. But given the continuing tug-of-war with Saddam, the UN punitive resolutions remained in place and the sanctions imposed on Baghdad prevented the country from selling its oil or entering into normal commerce with other nations. While Saddam's government weathered these limitations on its sovereignty and power, the Iraqi people, especially its children, confronted dire circumstances. Reports by international agencies, propagandized by the Iraqi government, cited the deaths of thousands of children as a direct consequence of the UN-imposed embargo. Bolstered by international opinion that argued for leniency in the acquisition of food and medicine, Baghdad ultimately was allowed to sell some of its oil on the open market, but at the same time it impeded the work of the UNSCOM inspection teams. Iraqi authorities blocked access to suspected sites and generally harassed the investigators. After six years of UNSCOM's intrusive behavior, the Iraqi government declared it had had enough and demanded an end to its activities.

Pressured by the United States, the Security Council insisted that UNSCOM's work had not been completed. Saddam's regime, it was said, continued to possess and could still manufacture weapons of mass destruction. Baghdad was warned to obey all the UN resolutions, which meant unfettered access to all suspected weapons sites, or face the consequences of a military response. Defying this threat, Baghdad ordered the U.S. members of UNSCOM to leave the country. The remaining UNSCOM inspectors also decided to quit the country. The United States again reinforced its military units in the region and attempted to exert new pressure on Baghdad, but the Security Council was no longer of one mind. With Washington threatening to take action outside the confines of the Security Council, the UN Secretary-General went to Baghdad in an effort to get the Iraqis to allow UNSCOM to resume its inspections. Meeting with Saddam Hussein and members of his cabinet in February 1998, Kofi Annan allegedly persuaded the Iraqi leaders to readmit the Americans and to open all sites to UNSCOM inspection. UNSCOM activities were revitalized soon thereafter, but in June, reporting to the Security Council on the mission's progress, the head of the UN operation questioned the Baghdad government's credibility and indicated that the work of the inspectors was not yet at an end. Nevertheless, Iraq continued to press for the termination of economic sanctions, for the withdrawal of UNSCOM, and for the full restoration of Iraq's sovereignty and territorial integrity.

If Saddam Hussein's strategy was to prevent the reformation of the 1991 coalition, he certainly succeeded in neutralizing almost all the Arab states. If he also sought to paralyze or fracture the Security Council, he had at least begun a process that revealed serious divisions among the permanent members of the Security Council. If he expected to gain international sympathy for the Iraqi people, he also achieved that objective. Saddam believed time was on his side. But what did the prolonged crisis in the Gulf mean to the United Nations?

At least a partial answer to that question was not long in coming. Despite the promises Kofi Annan made in Baghdad, on August 6, 1998, the Security Council again cited Iraq's failure to allow UNSCOM inspectors open access to the country's facilities deemed capable of producing weapons of mass destruction. Calling Baghdad's behavior "totally unacceptable," the Council appeared ready to force compliance with its resolutions. However, if that was the expectation, it was not to be realized. Russia and France, and to a lesser extent China, were more inclined to ease or even lift the sanctions against Iraq altogether, but the United States and Britain refused to support the other Security Council permanent members. Washington and London insisted on the need to again physically punish Iraq if it insisted on holding to its position. Observing and taking advantage of the division in the Security Council, Baghdad announced it would no longer cooperate with the arms inspectors and would allow only video and other technical surveillance to continue. In the face of this challenge, UNSCOM sent a letter to the Security Council that it no longer could verify Iraq had not restarted its prohibited weapons programs. Not since the Gulf War had Saddam Hussein taken such a clear step to block UNSCOM inspections. And as expected, the Iraqi parliament unanimously adopted a resolution calling for an immediate halt to the UN intrusion in Iraq's domestic affairs. Citing the failure of the United Nations and the United States to act forcefully against Saddam, a prominent American member of the UNSCOM inspection team, Scott Ritter, quit the organization to publicize his views. Embraced by members of the U.S. Congress, Ritter warned of dire consequences if Saddam was allowed to avoid intensive scrutiny. Describing Saddam's "breakout scenario," Ritter warned that Iraq would be able to reconstitute its biological and chemical weapons capability and deliver a weapon of mass destruction within six months from the end of the UN inspection program. Although Ritter was criticized for his outspokenness, his message could not be ignored. The U.S. Congress was galvanized to authorize funds for use in overthrowing the Iraqi regime, and in September the United States and Britain introduced a draft resolution to the UN Security Council that was aimed at punishing Iraq if UNSCOM operations were not allowed to continue. Still seeking to head off a U.S. air attack on Baghdad, the Security Council agreed to suspend its review of the 1991 sanctions, but otherwise, members continued to bicker over the course of action.

The tug-of-war between Iraq and the Security Council continued through October and into November 1998 when Baghdad abruptly declared it was severing all relationships with UNSCOM. The Council called Iraq's declaration a "flagrant violation" of its resolutions and with total disregard of promises made to Secretary-General Kofi Annan in February. The Council, however, insisted on pursuing the matter through diplomatic channels, and only the United States and Britain urged the need for a military response. With UNSCOM inspectors leaving Iraq, Baghdad demanded the firing of Richard Butler, the head of UNSCOM, accusing him of collaborating with U.S. and Israeli intelligence. By November 11 virtually all UNSCOM inspectors had been ordered to leave Iraq. The departure of UNSCOM caused a stampede among UN humanitarian workers, who also left the country. Appealed to by the UN Secretary-General and under threat of an immediate U.S. assault, on November 14 Saddam again backed down and once more invited the UNSCOM observers to return to the country. At this juncture President Clinton declared that he would refrain from using force but that if Iraq again impeded the work of UNSCOM, there would be no further resort to diplomacy. UNSCOM teams resumed their searches in mid-November, but Baghdad refused to submit documents on its biological weapons program. On December 10 an UNSCOM team sought admission to Iraqi Baath Party headquarters and was denied entry. This time, the crisis could not be avoided.

On December 17, 1998, the United Nations again having withdrawn its personnel from Iraq, the United States with cooperation from Great Britain—and despite criticism from Russia, France, and China—authorized Operation Desert Fox, a four-day intensive air campaign against targets described as central to Iraq's military establishment. Unmanned cruise missiles and bomber aircraft hit scores of Iraqi military installations, including several of Saddam Hussein's palaces as well as the barracks of his elite Republican Guard. Although the strike was capable of delivering a punishing blow to Saddam's weapons of mass destruction, it was decided to avoid hitting targets believed to house chemical and biological weapons because their destruction could release deadly toxins and microbes into the atmosphere. President Clinton declared the raids were aimed solely at the regime of Saddam Hussein and were not intended to cause more casualties among the Iraqi people. The attacks, however, ended UNSCOM's labors, and it appeared that UN inspectors would not again be allowed inside Iraq. Given this reality, Washington argued that UNSCOM had long been prevented from carrying through its mission and that in the absence of an assured UN monitoring institution, the United States was prepared to "contain" Saddam until that day when the Iraqi opposition deposed him.

Not yet prepared to yield to the increased U.S. pressure, Baghdad ordered the United Nations to cancel the stay of UN military observers, members of UNIKOM who since 1991 had patrolled the border between the two countries. Baghdad also audaciously renewed its claim to Kuwait. By the end of December, Iraq announced it would more aggressively challenge the no-fly zones patrolled by U.S. aircraft; almost immediately, Iraqi antiaircraft batteries began targeting U.S. planes. The U.S. reaction was immediate. Authorized to defend themselves, the patrolling aircraft attacked Iraqi antiaircraft sites and command centers, and thus began a train of events that followed through the remaining portion of the Clinton administration and into that of its successor. The administration of George W. Bush sustained the no-fly zones over Iraq, and U.S. aircraft continued to protect the free Kurdish enclave in the north of the country and dominated the skies over the south.

Citing the illegality of the U.S. actions, Saddam called upon his Arab neighbors for support in Iraq's effort to "regain its sovereignty." At the same time he lashed out against those Arab leaders, notably in Kuwait, Saudi Arabia, and Egypt, who he claimed worked in harmony with the Americans. Saddam's actions and statements calling for a U.S. overthrow were judged to be those of a desperate man, unable to put an end to his isolation. Nonetheless, on January 14, 1999, Iraq declared that all "Kuwaiti land and coastal regions belong to the Iraqi people" and that the border between the two countries was "a bombshell that may explode in the future." Almost simultaneous with this declaration, articles appeared in the U.S. press suggesting a conspiracy against Iraq by UNSCOM and Washington. Kofi Annan and Richard Butler denied the accusations, but the articles nonetheless were an embarrassment to the United Nations.

Saddam Hussein may have been wounded but remained fully in control of his government, and there were many indications that he planned a comeback.

## COLLECTIVE SECURITY IN TRANSITION

The Gulf War countered overt aggression. The forces invading Kuwait were defeated, and Iraq's capacity for further aggression was substantially reduced. The Security Council, immobilized by the veto during the Korean War, proved resolute, united, and effective. The Gulf War did not necessarily portend a greatly enlarged role for collective military sanctions, however. A forthright and overwhelming UN response was possible in 1991 because Saddam's open use of naked force against Kuwait's independence and territorial integrity was a clear, universally recognizable case of armed aggression. Iraq departed from the common postwar practice of using a neighbor's domestic upheavals as the cover for military intervention, resorting instead to old-fashioned military conquest. This stark, undisguised violation of the UN Charter permitted mobilization of an international consensus against Iraq that would not have been possible in a more ambiguous situation. Given the collective response, Iraq's experience was supposed to deter others from the more overt forms of aggression. To the extent that collective security encouraged potential aggressors to desist, rather than merely to modify their tactics, the result should be applauded, but the end of the Cold War indicated that more conventional forms of aggressive actions were a lesser possibility. Moreover, with the breakup of the Soviet Union, a formidable actor on the world stage disappeared. Only the United States remained as a superpower, and its mere presence was anticipated to deter more conventional forms of conflict.

Therefore, apart from the possible deterrence dividend of the Gulf crisis, the nature of the UN military response may justify only two cheers for this reincarnation of collective security. The economic sanctions were mandatory, on the authority of Article 41 of the Charter, but the military action remained voluntary. Without forces made available in advance under Article 43, the Security Council depended on volunteers. As the legal basis for Resolution 678 authorizing the use of "all necessary means" against Iraq, the Council referred to Chapter VII but cited no particular article. Chapter VII deals with "Threats to the Peace, Breaches of the Peace, and Acts of Aggression." Given the voluntary nature of the military coalition then being assembled in opposition to Iraq, and the nonexistence of any Article 43 forces, the Council must have been making a "recommendation" under Article 39. Presumably, also, it was authorizing the coalition to exercise "the inherent right of individual or collective self-defense" under Article 51.

As in Korea, the United Nations had to rely on a convergence of UN objectives with the national interests of states capable of supplying the necessary military power. In both instances the initiative and bulk of the power came from the United States. This is the same limited kind of collective security displayed in Korea. It may be comforting to the United States to know that such actions will not be undertaken without its approval, but that assurance was already embodied in the UN Charter in the form of the Security Council veto. The other side of the coin is more sobering: No major enforcement action will occur unless the United States is willing to shoulder the lion's share of the burden. But other states cannot be highly enthusiastic about a collective security that is invoked only when U.S. national interests are heavily engaged.

Nor is this the only problem implicit in the collective security decision process. During the Korean War, UN policy was formulated through the General Assembly's cumbersome and ultimately unmanageable process. UN decision making went more smoothly during the Gulf War because of close collaboration among the permanent members of the Security Council. This too, however, was a source of frustration to other UN members who felt inadequately consulted or entirely left out of consultation. Included among the frustrated states were the other ten members of the Council and developed countries such as Germany and Japan, which were expected to pay, and eventually did pay, a substantial part of the cost. Most other UN members (other than the coalition) were given no voice at all. The problem of broadening the consultative process while retaining the necessary speed and flexibility in decision making had yet to be resolved.

Still more disturbing to some was the free hand the United States exercised, with the acquiescence of other coalition members, in battlefield decisions. In effect, the authorization of "all necessary means" proved to be a blank check to be completed as necessary. Destruction of Iraq's infrastructure through massive aerial bombardment undoubtedly weakened its military capability. Iraq suffered heavy casualties, and a substantial array of weapons was destroyed with the foray into the southern section of the country. But the decision in 1991 by President Bush, not the UN Security Council, to refrain from destroying Saddam's regime was based on a number of scenarios. They ranged from the human cost in capturing and policing Baghdad to the breakup of Iraq, with its consequences on Turkey and its Kurdish minority or on Iran, which still had visions of spreading Shiite Islamic revolution. Reasons for leaving Saddam in power also included Saudi Arabia's fear that a power vacuum in the region could only benefit its nemesis, Iran, or that the Iraqi government, despite its aggressive record, was still a balance to other more radical forces rallying in the area. In any event, the U.S.-led coalition, under UN aegis, halted its actions before complete victory had been achieved. Had the military action against Iraq been a more chaste use of the UN Charter, the campaign might have ended differently. As it was, however, the war in the Gulf was tailored to the immediate objectives of the United States, namely, the liberation of Kuwait, the security of Saudi Arabia, and the assurance that oil would continue its flow uninterrupted from the region.

Thus, the United Nations was compelled to assume a protracted role in the Gulf. Saddam Hussein was left in power, but not to be trusted, and would have to be monitored by the international community. Iraq had used chemical weapons against both Iranian and Kurdish-Iraqi citizens, so its stockpiles of biological and chemical weapons were earmarked for destruction, lest they be used elsewhere. Moreover, Iraq's attempt at constructing nuclear weapons also had to be thwarted. With U.S. ground forces returning to the United States, and a lesser number repositioned in the Gulf region, the job of locating and destroying Iraq's weapons of mass destruction was made the responsibility of the United Nations. UNSCOM focused on biological and chemical concerns, and the IAEA assumed the charge of policing the nuclear issue.

UNSCOM therefore had the task of sustaining the collective security arrangements originally agreed to by the permanent powers at the end of the Gulf War. But the disbanding of the coalition soon after the war left only the threat of renewed collective military action should Iraq violate the earlier agreements. In reality, there was little possibility that so large a UN response would again be mounted. Iraq's efforts in the years that followed the end of the Gulf War were directed at bringing to a conclusion the UN intrusion. Moreover, the intrusion had become more and more associated with U.S. policy, a policy not necessarily shared by the other permanent members of the Council. Kofi Annan's meeting with Saddam Hussein in Baghdad in February 1998 was aimed at least in part at clarifying where the United Nations stood in challenging Iraq. Unlike the United States, which had targeted Saddam, Annan was more inclined to depersonalize the struggle, and in so doing, to pose the United Nations (with notable support from Russia, China, and France) as a disinterested party in the matter of how Iraq was governed or by whom. The United Nations's main consideration was the establishment of conditions that allowed for threat-reduction and confidence-building measures. The mission of the United Nations, noted the Secretary-General, was ensuring the peace, not making war.

In effect, the United Nations was foremost a diplomatic institution, and with Article 43 of the Charter in abeyance, only in the most critical circumstances could the world organization be judged a war-making body. Moreover, unlike the United States, which continued to insist that the Iraqi government could not be trusted, Annan believed he spoke for the majority of UN member states when he intimated that inspections should be ended as soon as UNSCOM verified that Iraq no longer possessed weapons of mass destruction. Annan's effort at bringing UN operations in Iraq to a satisfactory conclusion, however, was frustrated by Saddam Hussein, who never was content with the UN inspectors. By exploiting divisions within the Security Council, as well as the goodwill of the Secretary-General, Saddam hoped to bring a quick end to the UN intrusion on his sovereignty. And indeed, were it not for the determination of the United States, he would have succeeded in eliminating the UN sanctions imposed on his government. Saddam insisted on another test of wills when he forced UNSCOM inspectors to again leave Iraq, and this time the international community made no serious effort to have them return. While UNSCOM remained an organ of the Security Council, Saddam had read the divisions within the Security Council to his advantage. UNSCOM continued to exist, but only in technical limbo as it no longer functioned inside Iraq. Faced with this reality, France put forth an alternative program for a more remote monitoring of Iraqi military ventures.

An IAEA Iraq Action Team had been established by Security Council Resolution 687 in 1991 to uncover and dismantle Iraq's clandestine nuclear program. It also had been charged with developing and implementing an ongoing monitoring and verification system. Under its mandate the IAEA Action Team paralleled the work of UNSCOM in the nuclear area and reported directly to the Director General of IAEA. The name of the operation was changed in December 2002 to the Iraq Nuclear Verification Office (INVO), and unlike UNSCOM, it had resumed inspections in 2002. Twenty-nine on-site inspections were conducted during a limited period in 2002. In addition, INVO reported making fifteen hundred OMV (Ongoing Monitoring and Verification) inspections, using the same techniques and tools as on-site inspections. The information sent to the Security Council appeared to provide an adequate level of assurance that Iraq was not conducting activities prohibited by UN resolutions. In fact, IAEA/INVO reported in December 1998 that it had removed all known weapons-grade nuclear material, that is, highly enriched uranium and plutonium. It also had taken custody of all known remaining uranium compounds, had destroyed and rendered harmless all known dedicated facilities and associated equipment, and had monitored all known dual-use equipment. Inspections in 2002 had not indicated any change in the status of Iraq's nuclear program, which previously had been well funded and well staffed and aimed at the production of a small arsenal of nuclear weapons. As of December 2002 INVO had a staff of twenty-four members from thirteen countries. Funding for INVO came from funds made available by the UN-sponsored "oil-for-food" program that permitted Iraq to escape some of the sanctions imposed on it and to sell a portion of its oil production in return for food that its desperate population needed. Profits from the sale of such oil supplies were administered by the United Nations.

The United States, however, continued to emphasize its intention to "contain" Iraq and to hold it to all the resolutions previously approved by the Security Council. With assistance from Great Britain, the United States was left alone to police the UN resolutions concerning Iraq's disarmament. France and Russia instead worked to pressure the United States to relieve the economic sanctions that allegedly had taken a heavy toll on innocent Iraqis. Extensions of the oil-for-food program were about as far as this lobbying went, however, as Washington stood fast in its determination to persuade Saddam to yield his reported cache of chemical and biological weapons. Except for the persistent flights over Iraq's no-fly zones and the occasional bombing of Iraqi ground installations by U.S., and to a lesser extent, British aircraft, UN attention had generally shifted away from Iraq, with its interest in the Middle East again focused on the Palestinian quest for a homeland and Israeli efforts to guarantee their security. Afghanistan also was another UN concern, given the takeover of the government there in 1996 by the Taliban, an austere Islamic movement. In time, however, Iraq and the Taliban became entwined, and the United Nations could not avoid giving increased attention to the intensifying crisis in the Gulf region.

## TERRORISM, THE UNITED STATES, IRAQ, AND THE DOCTRINE OF PREEMPTION

As the only remaining superpower, the United States was ever more likely to take aggressive action in response to an assault on its national interests. The mainstay of the United Nations, the United States was also the glue that held the Atlantic community together and also the only country in the world with genuine global extension in the post–Cold War era. The prominence of the United States in the absence of countervailing power was of some consequence to friend and foe alike. France's growing distance from U.S. actions in the Security Council was in part a reflection of Paris's concerns about U.S. hegemony in Europe and throughout the world. French efforts in the creation of an independent European defense system, the strenuous methods Paris used in drawing a reunified Germany into its circle of valued partners, could not be lost on anyone familiar with the power equation in the years after the Soviet collapse. But even more so were the registered fears of those seriously opposed to U.S. influence in their very heartlands. In 1990, Saudi Arabia had called upon the United States to defend the kingdom against the ambitions of Saddam Hussein, who had already swallowed Kuwait. The stationing of U.S. troops on Saudi soil was an affront to many Saudis who believed the United States was the greater evil in the world. Moreover, religious issues came to the fore, as U.S. forces were close to holy sites of Islam, which were located in Saudi Arabia. Opposed to the monarchy, the royal family's critics saw the opportunity to exploit this dependence on the Americans to undermine the House of Saud. Central and most outspoken of these critics was Osama bin Laden, a scion of a wealthy Saudi family who had given up a life of leisure to help the Afghans resist the Soviet Army. Assisted by the United States and Pakistan, the Afghan Mujaheddin had fought a protracted war with the Soviet Union, during the course of which

Arabs like bin Laden had offered their services. In 1988, as a consequence of these combined efforts, the Soviet Union yielded to a UN-negotiated agreement that called upon the Soviet Army to withdraw from Afghanistan. The last Soviet soldier left Afghanistan in 1989, and bin Laden, like many other volunteers, returned to Saudi Arabia. On arrival, however, bin Laden was caught up in the Iraq invasion of Kuwait and the U.S. response. Believing that the Americans were the only ones standing between the monarchy's critics and the eventual overthrow of the Saudi government, bin Laden appealed to the more austere members of the religious community. He condemned the Saudi royal family, not only for its obvious weakness, but also for allowing unbelievers to enter and thereby pollute and desecrate the holiest of Muslim land.

Not only did bin Laden position himself among like-thinking antagonists of the Saudi monarchy, he also saw himself as central to a movement that had defeated the Soviet superpower in Afghanistan. He now believed that similar tactics, notably using a grand alliance of Muslims, could also defeat the remaining superpower. Bin Laden's objective therefore was to drive the United States from Saudi Arabia, from the Arab states, and ultimately, from the Islamic world. Toward that end he began to organize his private army of Muslim volunteers that in time became the terrorist network known as Al-Qaeda. Bin Laden's grand plan, however, required a base of operations in a location remote from and beyond the reach of the United States. Thus when the religious Muslim zealots known as the Taliban occupied Kabul in 1996, bin Laden returned to Afghanistan and was immediately embraced by their leader, the Mullah Omar. With the Taliban now largely in control of the Afghanistan government, Al-Qaeda began to work freely in the regions bordering Pakistan and southeastern Iran. The establishment of training installations for Al-Qaeda followed, with recruits coming not only from a variety of Arab countries but from Muslim countries as close as Pakistan, and countries as distant as Indonesia and the Philippines. From Afghanistan, Al-Qaeda operatives were trained and sent on missions to attack U.S. targets—civilian and military; indeed, the simultaneous destruction of the U.S. embassies in Kenya and Tanzania in 1998 was traced to Al-Qaeda. President Clinton's decision to retaliate and make cruise missile attacks on Al-Qaeda bases in Afghanistan was aimed at killing bin Laden, but instead the attacks proved more a stimulus for terrorists long at odds with the United States. Al-Qaeda continued to strike at U.S. targets of opportunity in Saudi Arabia and Yemen, but it was not until September 11, 2001, that the threat posed by bin Laden and his army of transnational terrorists exploded on the world and reverberated through the halls of the United Nations.

The hijacking of U.S. passenger aircraft by suicidal operatives, who proceeded to fly them into the twin towers of the World Trade Center in New York City and the Pentagon in Washington on September 11, bore the imprint of bin Laden's worldwide Al-Qaeda network. Like the Japanese attack on Pearl Harbor in 1941, which precipitated the U.S. entry into World War II, the September 11 attacks precipitated an American decision to go to war. But making war on transnational terrorists is not the same as making war on the nation of Japan. Nonetheless, President George W. Bush, the former president's son, decided to answer the terrorists by declaring war on terrorism. Bush's declaration was not just aimed at the perpetrators of the September 11 attacks but at governments and/or states that might harbor, fund, or supply terrorists or in any way demonstrate an intimacy or empathy with their program of mass violence.

In one day, the United States had gone from being the most formidable country on earth to feeling like the most vulnerable. The open borders and open society of the United States, formerly the nation's strength, had suddenly become its weakness. And although the United Nations declared its solidarity with the United States, it was clear that only the United States was in position to defend itself from still more attacks. Therefore, the U.S. decision to attack Afghanistan was not unexpected. By October 2001 Washington had marshaled adequate air, naval, and land forces to move directly against the Taliban government of Mullah Omar. With bases quickly established in Pakistan and Uzbekistan, and with naval forces in the Indian Ocean, the United States, without seeking UN approval, began a preemptive assault on the country that the Soviet Union had not been able to conquer in nine years of determined effort. However, in surprisingly little time the Taliban was forced to retreat to its main citadels in Kabul and Kandahar, and when these cities were overrun, to scatter to the mountains. Joined by European nations as well as Turkey and Australia, a new ad hoc Afghanistan government was assembled by the United States under Hamid Karzai, and King Zahir Shah, after twenty-nine years in exile, returned to his country to take up symbolic residence. An International Security Assistance Force (ISAF) was organized for deployment in Kabul without UN authorization, but on March 28, 2002, the UN Security Council approved Resolution 1401 creating the UN Assistance Mission in Afghanistan (UNAMA). UNAMA will be discussed in detail in another section of this chapter.

Unfortunately, U.S. success in ousting the Taliban did little to end the war on terrorism. Neither the Mullah Omar nor bin Laden was apprehended, and it was assumed that both men survived the assault and that bin Laden continued to plot the destruction of his enemies, in particular, the United States. The hunt for bin Laden and his followers continued, and the war on terror did not abate. President Bush made it clear that the war on terror would be protracted and burdensome. It became U.S. policy to move against states, unilaterally if necessary, if the security of the United States was deemed to be at risk from international terrorists. The events of September 11 confirmed a necessity for choice, that sovereignty was not absolute, and that preemption in the face of dire threat was an appropriate response.

In a climate mixed with fear and concern for the future, Washington again turned attention to Iraq and Saddam Hussein. Almost on the heels of September 11, letters laden with weapons-grade anthrax were sent to members of the U.S. government; several people handling the mail were exposed and subsequently died. The source, let alone the perpetrator, of this act of bio-warfare could not be identified, but Iraq was believed to have developed huge quantities of the substance. Washington's fear was that Saddam not only possessed such biological weapons, but that he was capable of using them or supplying them to Al-Qaeda or other terrorist organizations with agendas similar to his own. Thus in 2002 the Bush administration intensified its verbal attack on the government of Saddam Hussein. Citing the forced removal of UNSCOM inspectors, Washington tried to convince the world that Iraq was manufacturing and stockpiling biological and chemical weapons of mass destruction beyond the reach of the United Nations.

President Bush's speech to the General Assembly in September 2002 was a call to the United Nations to draw a conclusion that was obvious to him. He urged understanding that Iraq's noncompliance with UN resolutions was positive proof that Saddam's regime was in league with international terrorists and that together they planned a major attack against the United States, as well as other nations around the world. Bush earlier had authorized the expansion of U.S. military forces in the Gulf region, and as these ranks began to swell, the Security Council in November 2002, hesitatingly but unanimously, approved Resolution 1441 that offered Iraq one more opportunity to report its possession of weapons of mass destruction. The resolution declared that Iraq was in continued breach of its obligation to disarm and threatened the Hussein government with "serious consequences" if it failed to comply with this final warning.

With IAEA inspectors already in Iraq, the Security Council authorized and Baghdad accepted a return of UN chemical and biological weapons inspectors. UNMOVIC, the Security Council's answer to the defunct UNSCOM, had been created on December 17, 1999, under Security Council Resolution 1284. This, however, was UNMOVIC's first deployment. Within days of the Security Council order, the first detachment of chemical and biological weapons experts began arriving in Iraq. UNMOVIC was given responsibility for certifying the destruction of chemical and biological weapons, but it was also charged with eliminating Iraq's missiles with a range greater than 150 kilometers. In the course of their work, the inspectors destroyed several dozen such missiles. Secretary-General Kofi Annan appointed Swedish civil servant Hans Blix to act as UNMOVIC's Executive Chairman. The Secretary-General selected sixteen additional officers to serve on what was called a College of Commissioners, whose staff included weapons specialists, analysts, scientists, engineers, and operational planners. UNMOVIC was financed from money raised from the export of Iraqi oil in the oil-for-food program. With more than one hundred inspectors on the ground, UNMOVIC was to report every three months to the Security Council through its Executive Chairman.

The United States, joined by Great Britain and Australia, continued, however, to assemble forces in the Gulf region. In the meantime, the deployment of UNMOVIC inspectors passed through several stages as more equipment arrived to facilitate their work. In January 2003 Iraq provided UNMOVIC with a list of personnel associated with its weapons program, and Blix reported slow but steady progress to the Security Council. The UNMOVIC Chairman returned to Baghdad shortly thereafter and in late January cited some problems but also announced continuing progress. Blix's overall assessment was that Baghdad could facilitate the work of the inspectors by being more forthcoming. Indeed, Saddam's strategy was to cooperate with the inspectors but to slow the process. That strategy appeared to be paying off despite the steady coalition buildup of forces and the pressure the United States imposed on Baghdad and the United Nations. Blix requested more time for the inspectors to do their work, and members of the Security Council agreed, notably France and Germany (having just begun its two-year term). Soon joined by Russia, all insisted over U.S. opposition to provide the extension. Scott Ritter, despite his earlier warnings concerning Iraq's weapons capability, also made an about-face, concluding that Iraq no longer possessed weapons of mass destruction and joined the Europeans in opposition to a resumption of the Gulf War. The critics of Washington's motives were largely of one voice, all calling for more time and more inspectors on the ground. Despite the pressure, however, the Bush administration showed no patience for UN efforts. Iraq, Bush officials insisted, was playing for more time only to further divide members of the Security Council.

With European opposition to a new war in Iraq spreading throughout the western portion of the continent, and with widespread demonstrations in Europe's major urban centers, the Bush administration saw Saddam in a position to break the U.S.-Britain coalition. Furthermore, opposition at home insisted on some form of coalition to legitimize the operation. British Prime Minister Tony Blair found himself under extreme pressure from his own Labour Party that forced him to make one last appeal to UN Security Council members, with U.S. concurrence, calling for still one more resolution. Faced with high-level resignations from his party for throwing in his lot with the Bush administration, Blair's Security Council resolution aimed at ending the ambiguity in previous resolutions, especially Resolution 1441. The Prime Minister wanted a clear statement from the Security Council that Iraq must give up its weapons of mass destruction or accept the combined wrath of the United Nations. What followed was a feverish effort to get the permanent powers to agree to the Blair resolution, or at least to get the nine votes needed on the Security Council to avoid the possible use of the veto. U.S. Secretary of State Colin Powell made still another visit to the United Nations, this time to the Security Council. Powell came armed with audiovisual material that appeared to confirm the Bush administration's fear that Saddam was hiding massive stores of chemical and biological weapons. Behind-the-scenes diplomacy also was intense, with the United States and Great Britain trying to persuade Security Council members of the necessity of signing on to the British resolution fixing a certain date for making war on Iraq if Baghdad again refused to cooperate.

France and Russia, and to a substantial extent Germany, were just as active in their diplomatic efforts. With France leading the opposition, Paris announced it would veto the resolution under any circumstances. Russia subsequently followed the French lead. Realizing that the resolution would meet certain defeat, Great Britain withdrew its resolution, and it was never voted upon. By the end of February 2003, the Bush administration had mobilized almost 250,000 soldiers and air and naval personnel in the region. It became obvious that with or without the acquiescence of the United Nations, Washington would issue the order to begin hostilities. The UN collective security system never appeared weaker than at this juncture. The Security Council was hopelessly split, and the Bush administration was determined to move ahead with what it called a "coalition of the willing." Moreover, the coalition was less than what appeared on paper. Forty-nine countries gave their names to this new U.S.-led Iraqi war, but only the United States, Great Britain, Australia, and Poland would actually supply combat troops.

On March 17, 2003, the eve of the Iraq War, President Bush addressed his nation and the world, declaring that "intelligence gathered by this [American] and other governments leaves no doubt that the Iraq regime continues to possess and conceal some of the most lethal weapons ever devised." Secretary of Defense Donald Rumsfeld reinforced the words of his Commander in Chief: "We know where they are. They're in the area around Tikrit and Baghdad and east, west, south and north somewhat." Earlier, in his State of the Union address, President Bush claimed that Iraq possessed an active nuclear program despite the argument to the contrary by IAEA/INVO inspectors who were on the spot. Arguing that the Iraqi regime consorted with operatives of Al-Qaeda, Secretary of State Powell placed the matter before members of the Security Council, but this charge, like the others, was met with skepticism by a majority of the members. With the troops marking time in inhospitable desert conditions, the Bush administration no longer saw the need to win over the reluctant and the unwilling. Having made his decision to go it alone, even before his September 2002 speech to the UN General Assembly, Bush issued the final orders to his commanders and the second Gulf War was unleashed, not as a display of collective action but rather of preemption. Reports spoke of a U.S. strategy of "shock and awe" by which it was assumed that the United States would begin hostilities with an overwhelming assault from the air. The objective was more than the disarming of Iraq; the United States unambiguously announced that the goal was nothing less than the removal of Saddam Hussein and his regime. This war, unlike that in 1990–91, would not end with one side surrendering to the other. With the war judged to be an extension of the war on terror and with the United States committed to a policy of no negotiation with a terrorist enemy, nothing short of strategic or unconditional surrender would suffice.

Thus, along with an air campaign of historic proportions, the U.S. troops were ordered to cross into Iraq from their bases in Kuwait and begin the run to Baghdad. British troops were sent in the direction of Iraq's only port city, Um Qasr, and Basrah, with its heavy Shiite population. From the outset of the land campaign, the troops met with little formal resistance, and one town after another either fell to the invading army or was bypassed on the road to Baghdad. The anticipated Iraqi use of chemical weapons did not materialize. Nor did the Iraqis demonstrate anything resembling a weapon of mass destruction. In the Iraqi north, free Kurdish forces quickly enveloped the major cities of Kirkuk and Mosul. There was little attempt and even less success at torching oil installations in the south and north. With U.S. special forces in the northwestern sector of the country, Iraq was also deprived of missile launching sites; hence, even if attacks on Israel were contemplated, they could not be realized. Even the urban fighting anticipated for Baghdad did not materialize. The capital city yielded to the U.S. force that broke through its outer perimeter, seizing the international airport and quickly occupying the downtown area. This was no replay of the Gulf War of 1991. The absence of a real Iraqi defense hinted at the possibility that Saddam had been killed in the early air raids, or possibly had fled the country.

The Iraq War did not formally end because there was no government to surrender. Washington was intent on establishing a new government in Baghdad, and President Bush indicated that the United States would be responsible for Iraq's reconstruction. Indications from Secretary-General Kofi Annan that this was perhaps the appropriate moment for the United Nations to take over, to play a major role in Iraq's reconstruction, were not acceptable to Washington, which wanted a free hand in any future Iraq. U.S. forces, military and civilian, were to take up the responsibility of governing occupied Iraq, and Washington alone, not the UN Security Council, was to determine where and when the United Nations might be needed. Given the justification of the war as the imminent threat posed by Iraq's weapons of mass destruction, and having found none during the hostilities, the United States was determined to seek them out. Washington rejected the UN Secretary-General's offer to send its team of UNMOVIC weapons inspectors back into the country, although Washington did allow limited access to one site for IAEA experts. President Bush and his government continued to assert that weapons of mass destruction were in the country and would be uncovered, no matter the time or cost required. Hans Blix publicly questioned the U.S. effort and intimated that the evidence the United States claimed it had in making its original case to the Security Council lacked credibility.

The American-led war against Iraq had soured relations between the United States and other major powers as never before. Divisions within the Security Council were deep and could be expected to dissipate only with time. Washington argued that Iraq had never lived up to the terms of the 1991 ceasefire or Resolution 1441 of 2002 and that the use of force was valid, as in fact it had been judged to be by the Security Council in Kosovo in 1999. The opposition to the war, however, was unconvinced. Their collective judgment was that the United States had violated international law in attacking a country without provocation. In the final analysis, Washington had no justification for making war against a sovereign nation. Moreover, if Washington intended to make the war a UN action, the Blair resolution should not have been withdrawn before the Security Council could vote on it. But that was so much history. Although the formal military campaign had ended, the search for Iraq's weapons of mass destruction began in earnest. The legitimacy of the doctrine of preemption was still in doubt. So too was the occupation of Iraq, which proved to be a much larger task than Washington planners had originally contemplated. U.S., and to a lesser extent, British forces found themselves under constant attack by elements believed to be connected with and loyal to Saddam Hussein. Volunteers from other Arab countries also allegedly targeted coalition units, most significantly, Americans. By the summer of 2003, the number of U.S. military dead surpassed the number killed during the formal hostilities, and no end was in sight to the hit-and-run tactics. Some U.S. generals indicated a need for additional troops.

Initially, Saddam's whereabouts remained a mystery although his sons had been killed in a firefight, and most of his closest advisers had been found and apprehended. Arab radio and television stations periodically aired audiotapes allegedly made by Saddam calling upon Iraqis to sustain the pressure on the Americans and asserting that Washington's resolve could be broken by the increased casualties. Saddam was eventually captured near his hometown of Tikrit in January 2004, but this did not end assaults on coalition forces, and the frequent use of roadside bombings took an increasing toll.

Guerrilla and terrorist tactics and the sustained losses incurred in rebuilding Iraq proved psychologically much more damaging to the Americans than the toll of dead during the preemptive war. Although the Bush administration had indicated it could pursue the war without the assistance of others, especially the United Nations, in the difficult aftermath of the war, some members of Congress urged the administration to seek international assistance. Preemption had its limits, and collective security remained an important option. The Bush administration was forced to acknowledge that it had not calculated the level of commitment required once the Hussein regime had been removed. Efforts to rehabilitate the Iraqi infrastructure had run into obstacles. The oil industry suffered more damage than initially realized and required huge investments before it could be transformed into a useful profitable utility. Moreover, pipelines and installations were frequently sabotaged. Power and clean water were in short supply, and security was a major problem both for the occupying forces and for Iraqis. Given the need for greater security and the consequent increasing pressure on U.S. forces, as well as the rising cost in managing and reconstructing Iraq, the Bush administration was forced to reconsider the option of collective security and renew the role of the United Nations.

Collective security had failed the League of Nations when the United States decided not to participate. UN collective security, never a perfect vehicle for remedying difficult situations between states, suffered a grievous blow during this latest of Gulf wars, and again the United States had inflicted the blow. The implications for the future, especially given the cooperation required in the ongoing war on terrorism, were difficult to know. The G-8 summit meeting of the world's economic and financial powers in Evian, France, on June 1, 2003, offered the opportunity for President Bush to discuss differences with his counterparts, particularly the French, German, and Russian leaders. Bush, however, had much on his plate and left the meeting early in order to meet with Arab leaders in Egypt before sitting down with Israeli and Palestine Authority decision makers in Jordan. A final stop in Qatar to review the troops rounded out his tour. If a healing process was in the offing, any degree of success rested on developments in Iraq. On May 22 the UN Security Council adopted Resolution

1483, proposed by the United States, that granted wide interim governing powers to the United States and its coalition partners in Iraq. With the United States agreeing to a role for a UN Special Representative to work with the Iraqi provisional authority, the Council agreed, though reluctantly, to lift the sanctions imposed on Iraq thirteen years before. The resolution, cosponsored by Great Britain and Spain, allowed for the full resumption of oil sales in order to restore economic activity for reconstruction. The resolution also accepted the establishment of a U.S.-controlled authority for Iraq. The vote was fourteen to zero, with Syria not participating. So as not to suggest that the Security Council had become a rubber stamp for Washington, the Secretary-General quickly selected the UN Special Representative to be Sergio Vieira de Mello, the UN Commissioner for Human Rights. De Mello was authorized to work "intensively with the [American-led coalition] Authority, the people of Iraq, and others concerned to advance efforts to restore and establish national and local institutions for representative governance . . . leading to an internationally recognized representative government of Iraq." The resolution also extended the Secretary-General's authority to run the UN oil-for-food program an additional six months. The Secretary-General also had the power to prioritize shipments for billions of dollars of already signed contracts in the humanitarian pipeline before remaining activities were handed over to the provisional authority. The United Nations therefore acknowledged U.S. power, but it also demonstrated that it was still an active player in issues of significant moment and no nation could ignore its presence. Perhaps to demonstrate their distaste for the UN's subordination to U.S. demands, on August 19, 2003, terrorists detonated a car bomb outside of UN Headquarters in Baghdad. Almost two hundred people were in the building at the time of the attack. Many UN officials died in the blast, including de Mello, who was deeply mourned at UN Headquarters in New York and around the world. After this episode UN and other aid-dispensing agencies were reluctant to place their workers in harm's way without reasonable assurances of security. The inability of coalition forces to provide protection for international aid workers, despite the capture of Saddam Hussein, forced the United Nations to pull back its personnel to safer environments. It established a unit to monitor circumstances in Iraq from Cyprus.

In September 2003 President Bush again addressed the UN General Assembly, and his administration acknowledged the need for international assistance. Still another resolution was placed before the Security Council requesting both troops and money for the pacification and reconstruction of Iraq. While claiming to be sympathetic to the U.S. request, Security Council members registered serious reluctance. The French were most outspoken in calling for an earlier deadline for returning self-government to the Iraqi people than that projected by Washington. Declaring France's plan "unrealistic," the Bush administration continued to press for cooperation but argued that it would not be swayed from its course. In October the Security Council unanimously approved a resolution authorizing the Secretary-General to establish a multilateral force, but authorization did not ipso facto mean compliance by member states. France, Russia, and Germany, despite their outward show of support for the resolution, persisted in their view that Iraq should be returned to full sovereignty as quickly as possible and hence before the creation of a peacekeeping force. Undaunted, Bush held to his original position and subsequently asked the Congress for an additional $87 billion for U.S. operations in Iraq (a portion of which was meant for Afghanistan). It was obvious, however, that even this sum would be insufficient and far more would be needed over a longer period.

In mid-September President Bush had been pressured by a report from his chief investigator to announce that Iraq's weapons of mass destruction had not been found. He later also noted that Saddam's connection with the events of September 11, 2001, could not be verified. The Security Council therefore persisted in its demand that the U.S. occupation should be ended and a duly elected Iraqi government be installed. Washington's request for financial assistance met the same general reaction. The convening of a seventy-eight-country conference in Madrid to help the United States fund the rebuilding of Iraq garnered some money from Japan, the International Monetary Fund, and the World Bank, but nothing from France, Germany, or Russia. Moreover, the European Union, save Britain and Spain, also was reluctant to make available the huge sum of money deemed necessary for Iraq's rehabilitation. The sustained division within the United Nations and the larger world community over the U.S. occupation of Iraq appeared to reinforce the Iraqi resistance. In late October and early November, guerrillas raised the tempo of their assaults on U.S. troops as well as the suicide bombings of targets such as the headquarters of the International Red Cross.

## The Uncertain Future of UN Enforcement Action

The U.S.-led war on Iraq raised new questions about the UN's ability to satisfy the central features of the Charter, which in effect state that the United Nations is chiefly responsible for the maintenance of world peace. Although claiming it had acted under the authority of previous Security Council resolutions, and in fact was furthering the UN mandate, Washington could not escape its unilateral exhibition or its desire to set the pace for the world body to either follow its lead or step aside. Washington did not threaten to abandon the United Nations, but its actions and the statements of some of the Bush administration's more avid supporters appeared to indicate a tendency in that direction. The United Nations, in the opinion of many Americans inside and outside the government, either would assume a more aggressive posture in the protracted war on terrorism or would have to confine itself to vaccinating the needy and policing the world's waste-disposal projects. The UN record in the area of global security was not a positive one, and it remained to be determined how the organization, if it was to become more militarily effective, could be reformed.

The problem of ensuring UN control over UN enforcement actions could undoubtedly be overcome by negotiating Article 43 agreements and assigning real responsibility to the UN Military Staff Committee as provided in Article 47. The Secretary-General proposed such action in June 1992 (to the applause of some states but with a cool reception by the United States and some

European powers). If the agreements were actually concluded they would, pre-sumably, solve the problem of ready availability because Article 43 provides for "armed forces, assistance, and facilities" to be made "available to the Security Council, on its call." On the other hand, the existence of an Article 43 force would not guarantee small states a voice in their utilization, nor would it do anything to alter the reality that UN military sanctions would still be exercised only at the behest of a Security Council dominated by major powers.

Other questions also arise regarding the use of such a force. The United Nations could act quickly, but under what circumstances would it and should it act? The Article 43 force, as proposed by the Secretary-General, would not have been large enough to respond to a threat of the magnitude posed by the Taliban and Al-Qaeda, let alone to another regional Saddam Hussein deter-mined to overrun weaker neighbors. Given such events the United Nations would be thrown back on the model of the Korean War or earlier Gulf War.

The most likely occasions for the use of a ready enforcement capability would be UN intervention to suppress violent internal civil wars or to prevent gross violations of human rights (such as the mass killings in Cambodia during the 1970s). Another use would be as in Somalia in the 1990s, to combat inter-nal chaos that threatened widespread death and suffering to civilian popula-tions. The targets would ordinarily be small power states with little effective global reach. Except in the most unusual circumstances, large states could not feasibly be the objects of military intervention by the United Nations. Even with small states, forcible intervention would be fraught with peril. Military set-backs could occur, creating a need for reinforcements and escalating strife be-yond what was originally contemplated. UN forces would in any event incur persisting hostility among factions on the other side. Assuming that initial mil-itary objectives were achieved, the UN force could still face sporadic fighting with irregular forces should the intervention prove unpopular with large ele-ments of the local population. If violence is related to ethnic issues, for exam-ple, as in Bosnia and Kosovo, and also is rooted in centuries-old antagonisms, any abrupt departure of UN forces could lead to renewed violence. Moreover, a substantial political and economic rebuilding task would remain on comple-tion of formal military operations. The problems of achieving internal stability would seem no less if the purpose of the intervention were to halt government oppression of its own citizens as in the former Yugoslavia, in Liberia, or in the Congo.

These and other questions surrounding the coercive use of force by the United Nations describe an issue that is complex and far from resolved. They also suggest that the decision to authorize the use of UN military force, with or without Article 43 agreements, will continue to be decided on a case-by-case basis and as the particular interests of different Security Council states dictate. The post–Cold-War system does not promise more agreements than before about the kind of world to be made secure. Many obstacles to a functioning collective security system remain. Most prominent among them is the question of contemporary terrorism. Do Article 43 provisions apply here, or does the current genre of terrorism preclude that Chapter VII provisions will ever be invoked by the United Nations? Whereas the Charter writers focused on states aggressively challenging other states, the Charter was quickly made adaptable to internal conflict and civil war. The Charter also appeared adaptable to more isolated regional problems that were not likely to transform into global threats. In such contests the central issue remained the compatibility, or lack thereof, of the sovereign nation-states. Since the UN's founding, the Palestinian issue has perhaps received the most attention from UN members because it did not fit either of these elusive categories. The intractable nature of the Israeli-Palestinian dispute, its tendency to move away from the idea of reconciling state rivalries, and its current, more abstract manifestation as a religious or quasi-religious phenomenon, will test Article 43 expectations well into the foreseeable future.

## NONMILITARY SANCTIONS

Like the League Covenant, the UN Charter provides for nonmilitary sanctions against states that threaten the peace. Article 41 authorizes the Security Council to enforce its decisions through "complete or partial interruption of economic relations and of rail, sea, air, postal, telegraphic, radio, and other means of communication, and the severance of diplomatic relations." Moral condemnation is also available as a sanction for noncompliance.

Moral condemnation, although frequently invoked, has seldom been very effective in encouraging states to comply with UN directives, at least in the short run. In the longer term the mobilization of shame can sometimes have productive results, as in the Human Rights Commission. Certainly, alleged violators do their best to tone down or eliminate phraseology that condemns their behavior. States may sometimes act with an eye to avoiding UN condemnation, but UN scolding after the fact is more likely to harden positions than evoke repentance. Israel has been the constant object of UN railing, with little discernible effect on its policies. China was totally undeterred by the "aggressor" label attached to its Korean intervention, and UN censure did nothing to hamper either Soviet suppression of the 1956 Hungarian revolt or Soviet repression in Afghanistan. Nor has the United States responded penitently to UN disapproval of its support for Israel or such ventures as the 1983 invasion and occupation of Grenada, the December 1989 invasion of Panama, or the 2003 occupation of Iraq.

Diplomatic and economic sanctions have had somewhat greater effect when kept in place over a long period of time, but they have seldom had the desired political effect in the short run. The more notable examples of UN nonmilitary sanctions include actions taken against Rhodesia, South Africa, Iraq, Libya, and Serbia.

### Sanctions against Rhodesia

Modest success might be claimed for UN efforts to topple Ian Smith's white minority regime in Rhodesia though the use of nonmilitary sanctions. The initial Security Council response to Rhodesia's 1965 unilateral declaration of independence from Britain was to apply a limited range of voluntary economic and diplomatic measures. This was followed in 1966 with the first-ever UN *mandatory* sanctions under Chapter VII of the Charter. Although limited in its initial stage to an embargo of arms, oil, and motor vehicles and a boycott of Rhodesian exports, the sanctions were expanded in subsequent years to include a ban on most economic intercourse with Rhodesia. The sanctions contributed to Rhodesia's economic deterioration, despite nonobservance by a number of states. They were lifted in 1980 when power was transferred to the black majority and Rhodesia was renamed Zimbabwe. This outcome was attributable primarily to the pressures of internal civil war, combined with persistent British efforts to promote a settlement, but the UN sanctions linked with general delegitimization of the Rhodesian regime by the world community undoubtedly had some effect.

### Sanctions against South Africa

South Africa had been the most frequent target of UN nonmilitary sanctions, which were aimed at altering its racial policies and securing the independence of Namibia. With Namibian independence achieved in 1990 and the repeal of apartheid laws in 1991, some success for the sanctions policy can be claimed. The process required more than three decades, however—not exactly a quick fix. Beginning in 1962 the General Assembly repeatedly called for severance of economic and diplomatic relations as well as an embargo on arms and war materials. The arms embargo was endorsed as a voluntary measure by the Security Council in 1963 and eventually made mandatory under Chapter VII in 1977. The UN sanctions were not well observed during those years and did not substantially affect the economic and military strength of South Africa or its racial and colonial policies. South Africa occasionally made modest concessions to satisfy its Western friends but was quite contemptuous of the UN majority.

South African relations with the world entered a new phase in 1985 and 1986 when the white government's stern reaction to internal dissent induced a number of countries to take a hard look at their own policies toward South Africa. The Security Council at last endorsed voluntary economic sanctions, and a number of countries—including the United States and other important trading partners of South Africa—adopted new or strengthened sanctions. Private multinational corporations also moved toward divesting themselves of assets in South Africa under the watchful eye of UN monitoring groups.

The combined effects of internal troubles and increased external economic pressures induced a substantial weakening of the South African economy, and this was a factor in South Africa's decision at last to seek fundamental change. In December 1988, with U.S. prodding, South Africa signed a protocol on the independence of Namibia leading to the creation of the new state in March 1990. Dismantling of apartheid was a little slower in coming, but in early 1990, under the leadership of its new President F. W. de Klerk, South Africa began a gradual process of healing internal divisions and eliminating discriminatory practices. In December 1991 the UN General Assembly responded by voting to restore international sporting, cultural, scientific, and academic ties with South Africa. The Assembly also suggested that states might consider lifting other restrictive measures as South Africa moved toward a new multiracial government and a democratic constitution. Many influences, both external and internal, were at work, but the salutary changes in South Africa undoubtedly owed something to the weight of economic sanctions. However slow in achieving their result, the sanctions imposed by the United Nations achieved their most positive result when Nelson Mandela, leader of the African National Congress, was released from an imprisonment that had extended over twenty-eight years. Moreover, apartheid was formally abandoned in 1994, and that same year, in South Africa's first general election, Mandela was elected president of the country, ending a sustained period of all-white rule.

## Sanctions against Iraq

Iraq's invasion of Kuwait triggered the most extensive economic sanctions yet imposed by the United Nations. Beginning in August 1990 the Security Council ordered a mandatory trade and arms embargo (with exceptions for medical supplies and humanitarian foodstuffs) and severance of all financial relations with Iraq. It subsequently authorized member states to cut off maritime shipping to and from Iraq and imposed a cargo-related air transport embargo. The sanctions received general compliance and had a severe effect on the Iraqi economy, which depended heavily on proceeds from oil exports. The sanctions also had serious economic repercussions in countries having close economic relations with Iraq and Kuwait. Jordan, Lebanon, and Yemen were especially hard hit, along with several states of South Asia that supplied migrant laborers to the Gulf region and in turn received substantial remittances from them. Twenty-one countries claimed economic hardship resulting from the sanctions and exercised their right under Article 50 of the UN Charter to seek Security Council assistance in alleviating the problem. In most instances, no extensive relief was available.

Although widely observed, the economic sanctions did not achieve their intended effect of securing Iraqi troop withdrawal and restoring the independence of Kuwait. Military action was required for that. Whether economic sanctions would have succeeded over a longer period of time is uncertain. Rhodesia took fifteen years, South Africa thirty. Withdrawal from Kuwait by the year 2020 would scarcely be a vindication of UN sanctions. The sanctions against Iraq were more comprehensive than previous efforts, and Iraq was more vulnerable, but Saddam Hussein was both durable and obdurate. After the military operations were terminated in 1991, the economic sanctions remained in effect. This was necessary because Iraq, even in military defeat, was slow to comply with UN demands to accept liability for the damage it caused by invading Kuwait. Moreover, Iraq was ordered to submit to nuclear, biological, and chemical weapons disarmament.

The lifting of the UN sanctions became a major objective of the Iraqi government in the years after the Gulf War. Although Iraq claimed that the embargo denied it the opportunity to meet the basic needs of its citizens and asserted that the sanctions had caused the death of thousands of Iraqi children, the United Nations struggled to sustain the restrictions. Efforts by some UN members to at least reduce the harshness of the sanctions were somewhat effective. Oil-for-food arrangements were pressed through the Security Council in 1997 and again in 1998. Baghdad, however, was not pleased with such UN contrition, and it continued to demand the lifting of all the sanctions. When it was not successful in this effort, Iraq displayed its dissatisfaction by blocking the work of UNSCOM inspection teams. Whereas members of the Security Council began to waver, the United States and Great Britain increased their resolve, and the sanction policy was perpetuated. Baghdad's decision to force all UNSCOM inspectors to leave the country in 1998 did not resolve the problem to anyone's satisfaction. Sanctions remained in place in the years that followed, driving Iraq into deeper economic depression. The renewal of hostilities in Iraq by the U.S.-led coalition ended the regime of Saddam Hussein in April 2003, but not the UN sanctions. Members of the Security Council, opposed to the war, refused to lift the sanctions when the U.S. government made the formal request. The main argument of those holding to the sanctions was that they had been imposed in major part to force Iraq to give up its weapons of mass destruction. But with the war at an end, and the Hussein regime no longer functioning, the weapons of mass destruction had not yet been found. Hence, Russia argued that the sanctions should remain. The United States, now the occupying power, argued for the lifting of the restrictions so that Iraq's economy could be restarted. Here too, however, there was resistance to the U.S. request because lifting the sanctions also confirmed the United States as the ruling authority in Iraq. Only after considerable debate and diplomatic pressure was Washington successful in having the sanctions terminated.

## Sanctions against Libya

In April 1992 the United States, Britain, and France persuaded the Security Council to impose mandatory sanctions on Libya, consisting of a ban on air traffic and arms sales and a reduction in the size of Libyan diplomatic missions abroad. The sanctions went into effect when Libya refused to surrender for trial two suspects in the December 1988 bomb explosion on board Pan American 103 over Lockerbie, Scotland, which resulted in the death of 288 people. Libya attempted to nullify the sanctions by an appeal to the International Court of Justice. The Court, however, concluded that the Security Council sanctions took precedence over any rights Libya might claim under the 1971 Montreal Convention for the Suppression of Unlawful Acts against the Safety of Civil Aviation, under which the two men might be tried in Libya. Libya subsequently called for direct negotiations with the United States, Britain, and France about a possible compromise location for a trial of the two suspects. In 1998, however, with the sanctions still in force, the International Court of Justice agreed

to hear a Libyan complaint concerning the venue for the trial of the alleged perpetrators of the Pan Am bombing. Subsequently, with an agreement developed
by Libya, the Netherlands, the United Kingdom, and the United States, Tripoli
in April 1999 transferred the suspects for trial in the Netherlands, but under
Scottish law. The UN-imposed sanctions against Libya were suspended but not
entirely lifted until September 2003. The UN action was prompted by the Libyan government's announcement that it would pay compensation to the families of the victims of the Lockerbie bombing as well to the relatives of those
killed in a 1989 bombing of a French airliner. The United States abstained when
the vote was taken to lift the sanctions, arguing that Libya remained in violation of human rights and continued to pursue the development of weapons of
mass destruction. (France also abstained on more technical grounds that the
deliberations over compensation for the 1989 action had not been formally
completed. In January 2004, however, the French government announced that
the Libyan government had agreed to pay a substantial sum to the families of
the victims of the tragedy and that Paris would forthwith drop all sanctions imposed on Tripoli.) In a surprise statement in December 2003 the Libyan government declared that it had abandoned the development of all weapons of
mass destruction—nuclear, chemical, and biological. Within days of the announcement, UN International Atomic Energy Agency officials were allowed to
inspect Libya's facilities, and observers believed that the Tripoli government
was sincere in seeking to normalize its relations with the international community. Statements by Prime Minister Tony Blair and President George Bush in reaction to the Libyan declaration hinted at the inevitable lifting of all sanctions
against Libya.

*Sanctions against Serbia*

The dissolution of Yugoslavia in 1991 provoked war between Serbia and Croatia that spilled over into Bosnia-Herzegovina and presented Europe with its first
episode of a major bloodletting since the end of World War II. Serbia and Montenegro were the only units of the old federation to cling together, while the
Serb inhabitants of the other states found themselves in a struggle for survival.
Belgrade's attempt to assist these distant remnants of "greater Serbia" provoked violent clashes among the different ethnic groups, especially in Bosnia
where the Serb population tried to seize a portion of the territory in a campaign
that came to be described as "ethnic cleansing." In the quasi–civil war that ensued, more than two hundred thousand casualties were recorded and Europe
was again confronted with a vast and complex human tragedy. The UN Security Council as early as September 1991 imposed a general and complete embargo on all deliveries of weapons and military equipment to all the regions
of the former Yugoslavia. In 1992 another resolution reaffirmed the arms embargo and applied it to all areas of the collapsed state. By May 1992, it was determined that the Federal Republic of Yugoslavia (FRY), comprising Serbia and

Montenegro, was the principal purveyor of violence in the Balkans and a full trade embargo was imposed. The FRY also was denied participation in all international sporting and cultural events, and in November 1992 a further resolution blocked the shipment through the FRY of petroleum, coal, steel, and other products. In April 1993 these latter sanctions were strengthened, and in September 1994, Bosnian Serbs were singled out when their leaders were prohibited from traveling to other states. The same resolution curtailed trade with the Bosnian Serbs and froze Bosnian-Serb assets held abroad. In 1994, the Security Council suspended sanctions against the FRY for an initial period of one hundred days when it was reported that Serbia had closed its border with the Bosnian Serbs. The lifting of the sanction permitted the resumption of civilian air flights to and from Belgrade, allowed for the reinstatement of ferry services to Italy, and canceled the ban on participation in international events. In 1995 and 1996, following the Dayton Accords and the establishment of a cease-fire under NATO supervision, the Security Council removed the arms embargo and other sanctions that had been imposed on all the parties. When the Organization of Security and Cooperation in Europe (OSCE) approved the September 14, 1996, elections in Bosnia-Herzegovina, all sanctions against the FRY and the Bosnian Serbs were terminated.

Given the 1998 extension of NATO's mandate in policing the Bosnian cease-fire, efforts were made at restoring normalcy in the region, but conditions in Kosovo, claimed by Serbia as an integral part of FRY territory, deteriorated. Kosovo's overwhelmingly Albanian population expressed sentiments of self-determination, and a Kosovo Liberation Army (KLA) assaulted the Serb minority in the province. Belgrade's response was immediate and violent, with regular FRY forces ordered to clear a western strip of the separatist region. The killing of several hundred Kosovars and the flight of still more refugees caused the European Union and the United States to impose new sanctions on Serbia in June 1998. Serbia called these sanctions arbitrary and unjustified because according to Belgrade Kosovo was an integral portion of Serbia and the government had a duty to quell civil unrest. The Serbs were even more incensed that the sanctions had been directed against them and not the FRY as a whole. Judged a more explosive problem than that in Bosnia, it was feared that the Kosovo conflict could spread to Albania and Macedonia, and if not contained, to Greece, Bulgaria, and possibly Turkey. And because it was the NATO intervention, not the sanctions, that brought a semblance of peace to Bosnia, few believed the sanctions would work in the matter of Kosovo. Serbia's suppression of the KLA had had a spillover effect on the civilian population, and Serbian "ethnic cleansing" operations raised new, more fearful questions for the European community. Fearing genocide, NATO's Supreme Commander General Wesley Clark met with Slobodan Milošević in Belgrade in October 1998. General Clark warned the Serbian leader that NATO was poised to take military action in Kosovo. Milošević promised General Clark that he would withdraw his forces, but by January 1999 atrocities recurred. Clark again met with Milošević, but this time the Serbian leader refused to yield to pressure, and even Kofi Annan was forced to acknowledge NATO's right to use force against Serbian positions.

Confronted with an intensifying dilemma, the Contact Group, which included the United States, Russia, and the major European powers, insisted on a conference between the leaders, or their representatives, of the Belgrade government and the KLA. Under considerable pressure from NATO, whose planes were prepared for an assault on Serbian forces, the parties grudgingly agreed to a meeting in Rambouillet, France, in February 1999. The deliberations, which included the U.S. Secretary of State, were protracted. Several deadlines were allowed to pass to give the participants more opportunity to accept the terms of the Contact Group and the major NATO actors. The Contact Group's plan envisaged an autonomous but not independent Kosovo, policed by NATO forces similar to those in Bosnia. The draft agreement was a take-it-or-leave-it proposition, however, and the deliberations at Rambouillet were without result. The Serb delegation, under orders from Belgrade, rejected the introduction of NATO troops in Kosovo, arguing that such a force would violate Serbia's sovereignty. The Kosovar delegation, under pressure, eventually accepted the Rambouillet draft, but Belgrade used the hiatus provided by the deliberations to reinforce its military units in the province. Determined to obliterate the KLA, the Serbs resumed their campaign of ethnic cleansing, defying repeated NATO warnings. Forced to follow through on its threats, in March 1999 NATO aircraft struck Serbian military infrastructure and installations. The Serbs responded by accelerating their actions against the Kosovars, and NATO, reluctant to use ground forces, did not prevent the forced removal of hundreds of thousands of ethnic Albanians from Kosovo. The Belgrade government not only ignored the renewed sanctions imposed upon it, it also refused to yield to NATO's increasingly deadly bombing campaign.

Belgrade's brutal operations in Kosovo ultimately triggered NATO ground intervention. Russia tried to protect Serbia by breaking off relations with NATO and expelling NATO information officers from Moscow. Notably, however, Russia's military cooperation in Bosnia, also a NATO operation, was not affected. By June 1999 Yugoslav military commanders representing Serbia and Montenegro surrendered to NATO forces and a Military Technical Agreement was signed between NATO and the Yugoslav army. The UN Security Council quickly followed with Resolution 1244 of June 12, establishing the basis for an international security presence in Kosovo, and a NATO Kosovo Force (KFOR) was created. Russia accepted the NATO role in a separate agreement signed in Helsinki, Finland. An interim administration was established for Kosovo by the international community and was protected by a NATO force of forty thousand. Under terms of the UN resolution, working in tandem with KFOR, a limited number of Yugoslav personnel were allowed back into Kosovo to clear minefields and provide for a Serb presence at patrimonial sites and border crossings. A UN Mission in Kosovo (UNMIK) was authorized by the Security Council to work with local authorities and KFOR in rebuilding the government; managing and paying teachers, railway and municipal workers, judges, and prosecutors; and training the new civil administration. The codeployment arrangement developed between NATO and the United Nations provided Kosovo with the distinction of being an internationally administered province within the sovereign state of Yugoslavia. It was not long, therefore, before the Serb population questioned how they could have allowed Milošević to so humiliate and divide the old Yugoslavia. What followed was a general uprising that drove Milošević from power and gave Yugoslavia an opportunity to develop democratic institutions. With only two republics remaining in the federation, in 2002 the new Yugoslav parliament approved a broad plan for provincial autonomy with a single federal presidency. Milošević eventually was sent to the International Criminal Court in The Hague for trial, and the new state of Serbia and Montenegro was born on January 1, 2003, with Yugoslavia fading into history. UN sanctions were lifted with the beginning of the country's democratization program.

*Sanctions against Afghanistan Related to Al-Qaeda*

The Taliban government of Afghanistan was recognized by three Muslim governments—those of Pakistan, Saudi Arabia, and the United Arab Emirates (UAE). Declaring itself the government of the Emirate of Afghanistan, its stated intention was the creation of a theocratic state founded in the Islamic religion and functioning under the most austere version of Islamic jurisprudence. The Taliban originated during the Soviet invasion of Afghanistan from among the displaced Afghan population, hundreds of thousands having found refuge in Pakistan. After the Soviet Army withdrew from Afghanistan, the movement became a paramilitary force capable of imposing its will on most of Afghan territory. The Pakistan army was instrumental in the success of the Taliban, given the swelling of Taliban ranks by thousands of Pakistani volunteers. When the Taliban seized Kabul and consolidated their gains in 1996, its leader, Mullah Omar, invited Osama bin Laden and his nascent Al-Qaeda organization to establish their operations in his country. The Taliban and Al-Qaeda shared similar interests and goals, and while the Taliban continued their campaign to dominate the country, Al-Qaeda plotted and carried out external attacks, notably against U.S. targets.

The destruction of the U.S. embassies in Kenya and Tanzania was traced to Afghanistan and the machinations and direction of Osama bin Laden. The United Nations called upon the government of Mullah Omar to turn over bin Laden to international authorities; Afghanistan defied the request, and the Security Council approved Resolution 1267 in 1999 imposing sanctions on the country. The resolution ordered a flight ban on any aircraft owned, leased, or operated on behalf of the Taliban, as well as a freeze on funds directly or indirectly owned or controlled by the Taliban. In 2000, the Security Council approved Resolution 1333 demanding that the Taliban comply with the earlier resolution. It also imposed an embargo on the direct or indirect supply, sale, and transfer to Afghanistan of arms and related matériel of all types, including weapons and ammunition, military vehicles and equipment, and paramilitary equipment and spare parts. Furthermore, the resolution made it mandatory that states not to provide technical advice, assistance, or training related to military activities; and countries maintaining military ties with the Taliban government, such as Pakistan, were ordered to withdraw their missions. In like fashion, states with offices in Taliban territory were told to close them. Funds and other financial assets, especially those belonging to Osama bin Laden and individuals associated with him, also were frozen. Chemicals that could be used in the making of high explosives were banned. And no flights from Taliban-held territory were to be permitted landing rights in other countries.

An Afghanistan Sanctions Committee was authorized and initially chaired by Chile. Resolution 1363 of 2001 authorized the UN Secretary-General to establish a mechanism to monitor the implementation of sanctions against Afghanistan. A Monitoring Group was created in New York City, and an Enforcement Support Team was located in states bordering the country. The U.S.-led attack on the Taliban produced Resolution 1388, which was adopted on January 15, 2002, by the Security Council. It terminated the sanctions applying to Ariana Afghan Airlines, noting that it was no longer owned, leased, or operated by the Taliban and was essential to the running of a newly installed Afghan government. The next day, however, Resolution 1390 sustained the remaining sanctions despite the scattering and displacement of the Taliban by U.S. and Afghan forces from the Northern Alliance. On January 17, 2003, the Security Council declared its intention to improve by 2004 those measures found in the original sanctions, and the Monitoring Group was called to issue periodic reports on improvements in the situation. Clearly, the defeat of the Taliban had not yet meant the capture of Osama bin Laden or Mullah Omar. Moreover, lawlessness was an ongoing problem throughout Afghanistan where local warlords harbored private militias and paid little heed to the provisional government in Kabul, headed by Hamid Karzai. UN aid and associated workers were easy targets for an array of guerrilla elements, making the country's rehabilitation even more difficult. Sanctions therefore were not entirely lifted.

## SANCTIONS: A SUMMARY

Collective sanctions failed during the era of the League of Nations, and the United Nations has compiled only a slightly better record. Despite the numerous sanctions imposed on Iraq, Baghdad did not alter any of its policies. Unilateral sanctions have had no better record. The U.S. grain embargo against the Soviet Union in 1980 did not force Moscow to withdraw from Afghanistan, nor have strenuous efforts aimed at pressuring Cuba to change its political ways resulted in the desired result. Sanctions are often circumvented by governments or undermined by business interests in the pursuit of profits. In this regard, economic sanctions can sometimes do more damage to local commercial interests than to the targeted country. Generally speaking, the UN Security Council has been reluctant to use sanctions, and in the initial forty-five years of the United Nations only two sanctions regimes were imposed. Both were against white governments in Africa—Southern Rhodesia (now Zimbabwe) in 1966 and South Africa in 1977. Both were subsequently withdrawn. More stringent sanctions were brought to bear against South Africa outside the United Nations during the 1980s, and in 1989, the U.S. Congress approved a sanctions bill that the Bush administration opposed. Nevertheless, U.S. maritime and longshoremen unions, in cooperation with UN agencies, helped to expose corporations doing business with the apartheid government, and in time many were pressured to cease their operations in the country. It is believed that these economic sanctions, unlike those imposed on other nations, reduced South Africa's gross national product by approximately 5 percent and therefore played a role in forcing the regime to end its racial practices and introduce democratic reforms.

Of the more than 125 cases of sanctions since 1914, the United States has initiated about 70 percent, but less than 15 percent have been applied in a collective manner. In fact, it was only during the 1990s that the United Nations adopted sanctions as a major instrument in dealing with international questions. Starting with Iraq in 1990, the Security Council authorized sanctions against the former Yugoslavia in 1991; Libya, Somalia, Haiti, and Angola in 1993; Rwanda in 1994; Liberia in 1995; Sudan and Burundi in 1996; Sierra Leone in 1997; Ethiopia and Eritrea in 1998; and Afghanistan in 1999, 2000, 2001, and 2002. Pressure on the United Nations brought by the United States to sanction India and Pakistan for their tests of nuclear devices in 1998 did not succeed. Even U.S.-imposed sanctions raised complaints from domestic agricultural interests that forced the U.S. Senate to exempt food exports, the most painful economic penalty that Washington had imposed. Cuba, however, was a different story. The United States imposed unilateral sanctions there that went into effect in 1962 and were further embellished in 1996 when the Helms-Burton Act imposed penalties on third parties doing business with the island nation. Many of the world's leading nations had condemned the United States for its original action, and the Helms-Burton legislation embittered Canada, Mexico, and the European Union, which lodged a formal protest with the World Trade Organization. The Organization of American States declared that the legislation was "not in conformity with international law." Following the OAS action, in 1996 the UN General Assembly condemned the U.S. embargo of Cuba and the Helms-Burton Act by a vote of 117 to 3, with 38 abstentions. The Red Cross also has condemned the use of sanctions, especially those directed at Iraq, which it argued harmed only the people least responsible for Baghdad's policies. The United Nations probably will be reluctant to use economic sanctions against its members in the future. The practice will of course remain, but it is ever more likely to be an instrument used more by individual countries than by the world organization.

Overall, the Security Council has tried to improve sanctions policy in recent years. Steps have been taken toward improving the design of sanctions, applying more selective measures, strengthening monitoring and enforcement, and prioritizing humanitarian concerns. The dominant trend in UN policy-making has been the shift away from general trade sanctions toward more selective measures. Financial sanctions, travel bans, arms embargoes, and commodity boycotts have replaced general trade embargoes. The counterterrorism measures adopted in Security Council Resolution 1373 in 2001 continued this trend.

## The Regional Alternative

The UN Charter places primary responsibility for international peace and security on the Security Council, with regional organizations playing a secondary role. The principal proponents of regionalism at the San Francisco Conference were delegates from the American states who wished to preserve the developing inter-American security system; the relevant provisions, Articles 51 to 54, are a compromise. These provisions focus on three central issues: peaceful settlement, self-defense, and enforcement action (the use of diplomatic, economic, or military sanctions). Regional associations are expressly encouraged to take the initiative in settling local disputes (Article 52). Article 51 recognizes an "inherent right of individual or collective self-defense" against armed attack, but all action taken in self-defense must be immediately reported to the Security Council and that body retains authority to take any concurrent action it deems necessary. The Security Council's predominance with respect to enforcement action is even more forcefully established in Article 53. With the exception of measures against the enemy states of World War II, the Charter states categorically that "no enforcement action shall be taken under regional arrangements or by regional agencies without the authorization of the Security Council."

In practice, the roles were reversed. Because of bitter East-West rivalries, the Security Council never acquired its military capability, and members used Article 51 to expand collective self-defense arrangements out of all proportion to the puny enforcement arm of the general system and, in some instances, to justify outright aggression. The United States led the stampede to regional security and autonomy. From the Pact of Rio de Janeiro (1947) to NATO (1949) to ANZUS (security pact between Australia, New Zealand, and the United States, 1951) to the Southeast Asia Treaty Organization (SEATO, 1954) to the Baghdad Pact (1955) and the latter's transformation to the Central Treaty Organization (CENTO, 1959), as well as numerous bilateral military pacts, the United States became the hub of the most complex and extensive system of alliances the world had ever known. Other states followed suit in a more modest way with such arrangements as the Arab League, the Warsaw Pact, the Organization of African Unity, and a host of bilateral alliances.

Much of the U.S.-led system disintegrated during the Cold War. The Baghdad Pact came apart with the overthrow of the Iraqi monarchy in 1958, SEATO was formally abandoned in 1977, and CENTO in 1979. New Zealand's participation in ANZUS was effectively suspended in 1986 because of that state's refusal to let U.S. nuclear-powered or nuclear-armed ships into its ports. The Rio Pact experienced severe strains because of revolutionary regimes in Cuba and Nicaragua, U.S. support of Britain in the Falklands War, and other sources of disunity. On the other hand, the Warsaw Pact was dissolved in 1991 with the breakup of the Soviet Union and the defection of its East European satellites. While East-West alliances were generally considered casualties of the end of the Cold War, the Arab League was a casualty of another kind of war. The Gulf War of 1990–91 and again of 2003 pitted Arab against Arab and thereby damaged the quest for Arab unity.

Although alliance systems appeared less functional with the end of the Cold War and the dissolution of the Soviet Union, NATO, judged destined for the ash heap of history, dramatically took on new importance. NATO operations in war-torn Bosnia were necessitated by the failure of the UN peacekeeping mission there. NATO operations in Kosovo in 1999 were undertaken without approval from the UN Security Council and without reference to Article 51 of the Charter, but with the full sanction of the alliance. The U.S. action against Iraq in 2003 and the forced removal of an established government by a Washington-inspired coalition hinted at the reformation of classic alliances—that is, not alliances in perpetuity as with NATO, but ad hoc alliances assembled to deal with something related to an older casus belli and certainly not related to Article 51. Nevertheless, Article 51 of the Charter retains some relevance, and the NATO alliance enjoys a life after the Cold War. The United Nations neither has the forces nor the strategy to regulate contemporary civil wars. But NATO and ad hoc organizations do, as was the case with Australia leading a small coalition of forces against Indonesia in 2000 to defend the independence of East Timor. Moreover, NATO's role, whether in Bosnia or in Kosovo, illustrated the continuing functionality of both formal and informal alliances. Not to be overlooked is the Partnership for Peace that was formed in 1994 linking the former Warsaw Pact countries with NATO. NATO's enlargement in 1998 and again in 2004 developed out of the Partnership for Peace and attests to NATO's sustained utility and importance in the overall UN security system. Alliances of one kind or another, whether constrained or defined by Article 51 of the UN Charter, have a role in the twenty-first century.

## THE PEACEKEEPING ALTERNATIVE

Collective security as envisioned by the Charter never became a reality, and even the voluntary version of military enforcement action has been attempted sparingly. Nevertheless, the United Nations has found other ways to remain a relevant force in the control of international violence. The most important and innovative is UN peacekeeping. In a UN context, the term *peacekeeping* was first used to describe the work of the UN Emergency Force (UNEF), created by the General Assembly during the 1956 Suez War to take temporary control of the Suez Canal area. Its aim was to encourage the withdrawal of invading Anglo-French and Israeli forces from Egyptian territory, but since that time it has become the generic term for a UN noncombatant operation. Peacekeeping usually involves military and civilian personnel, who are charged with maintaining or restoring peace in an area of conflict.[2]

Peacekeeping, as heretofore practiced, contrasts sharply with the collective military sanctions contemplated by Article 41. Instead of acting to deter or defeat an aggressor, the UN peacekeeping mission is deployed with the notion that it has no enemy. Assuming there is a peace to oversee, its purpose is to help maintain peace when tension is high but parties are reluctant to engage in violent contests. Peacekeepers observe border violations, police cease-fire or truce lines, serve as buffers between hostile forces, supervise troop withdrawal, and help monitor elections or add a sense of decorum during periods of transition. A peacekeeping force is deployed only with the consent of the sovereign of the territory where it operates, and usually with the consent or acquiescence of all major parties. While large UN peacekeeping forces are normally armed, military observer units commonly are not. If weapons are carried, they are to be used only in self-defense and not to enforce the UN will on any of the contending parties. In practice, UN peacekeeping operations have seldom been large enough to enforce order against serious military opposition. The largest UN forces thus far have served in the Congo (20,000), Cambodia (19,500), and Yugoslavia (23,000).

Secretary-General Dag Hammarskjöld, at least in retrospect, viewed UNEF as part of a UN strategy to prevent local disputes or power vacuums from becoming extensions of or inciting escalation of the Cold War. This concept, which he fathered and nurtured, became known as "preventive diplomacy." During the Cold War era most UN peacekeeping missions embodied a large element of this preventive diplomacy, which was explained as filling power vacuums with a calming UN presence.

Over the years, preventive diplomacy has acquired a broader meaning and now commonly connotes any diplomatic action aimed at preventing potential or actual conflicts from getting worse. In a report issued in June 1992, Secretary-General Boutros-Ghali characterized preventive diplomacy as a means "to ease tensions before they result in conflict—or, if conflict breaks out, to act swiftly to contain it and resolve its underlying causes." The Secretary-General's report gave new prominence to the concept of preventive diplomacy. It called for an ambitious program of measures aimed at building confidence between contending states (such as exchange of military missions and monitoring of arms agreements). It also called for a system for the early warning of potential threats to peace. The report was rooted in the belief that preventive deployment of UN forces could forestall the outbreak of violence and create demilitarized zones before armed conflict arises.

UN peacekeeping forces were generally deployed after hostilities had occurred. But in 1997, the combined efforts of the member states, the Secretary-General, and the Department of Peacekeeping Operations (DPKO) acknowledged the need for more rapid and more effective deployment. By Security Council resolution, a Standby High Readiness Brigade (SHIRBRIG) was authorized to address the question. SHIRBRIG aimed at improving the Secretariat's reaction capacity, while DPKO was provided with a Mission Planning Service, a Standby Arrangements System, and a Rapidly Deployable Mission Head-quarters. According to its sponsors, SHIRBRIG's ready-alert status enabled the international community to intervene swiftly and effectively in a crisis be-fore it became critical. Organized outside the auspices of the United Nations, SHIRBRIG fell under Chapter VI of the Charter. It was to include a headquar-ters of its own, ready infantry battalions, reconnaissance units, engineer and lo-gistics support, and a common pool of military instruments, weapons, and vehi-cles. Established formally in Denmark, the Nordic countries committed between four thousand and five thousand troops to its operation. SHIRBRIG in fact fol-lowed the 1994 creation of a Standby Arrangements System for DPKO, to which approximately seventy countries authorized a total of eighty-eight thou-sand troops for future peacekeeping missions. The latter provided DPKO with a database that gave the UN body important information about the availabil-ity of personnel and equipment for future missions. Essential to DPKO's oper-ation was its capacity to respond quickly to a crisis. Thus, the Mission Planning Service was created and charged with the constant study of potential problem areas. Past and present UN peacekeeping missions—their size, function, and duration—are shown in Table 5-1. A brief description of each peacekeeping mission follows.

## EARLY UN EXPERIMENTS

Early UN experiments with a noncombatant military presence occurred in Greece, Indonesia, Kashmir, and Palestine. Two of these missions, in Greece and in Indonesia, were never included in UN lists of UN peacekeeping opera-tions because they were not organized and administered by the UN Secretariat. Nevertheless, these initial missions became the forerunners of those that fol-lowed. From 1947 to 1952, a UN Special Committee on the Balkans (UNSCOB) kept a small observer team (up to thirty-six members) along the northern fron-tiers of Greece to monitor border violations by Soviet bloc states in support of leftist Greek rebels. In Indonesia, from 1947 to 1951, UN military observers as-sociated with the UN Commission for Indonesia (UNCI) and its predecessor Good Offices Committee aided Security Council peacemaking efforts in the In-donesian war for independence from the Netherlands and observed the subse-quent repatriation of Dutch forces.

Two observer missions dating from the pre-UNEF period proved to be more than temporary. The UN Truce Supervision Organization (UNTSO) was established in 1948 to police a truce between Israel and its Arab neighbors. It grew to nearly 600 in number before armistice agreements were concluded in 1949. The size of UNTSO has since fluctuated with events, but lack of perma-nent peace in the area has made its continuance necessary. In 2003, UNTSO maintained 154 observer personnel, supported by 101 international civilian personnel and 111 local civilian staff, to monitor situations in Lebanon with the UN Interim Force in Lebanon (UNIFIL), in the Golan Heights with the UN

Table 5-1 Principal UN Peacekeeping Missions, 1947–2003

| Mission | Date | Peak Force Size | Force Size December 2003 | Function |
|---|---|---|---|---|
| UNSCOB | 1947–52 | 36 | — | Monitor violations of Greek border |
| UNCI | 1947–51 | 63 | — | Observe Indonesian cease-fire and Dutch troop withdrawal |
| UNTSO | 1948– present | 572 | 169 | Report on Arab-Israeli cease-fire and armistice violations |
| UNMOGIP | 1949– present | 102 | 42 | Observe Kashmir cease-fire |
| UNEF I | 1956–67 | 6,073 | — | Observe, supervise troop withdrawal and provide buffer between Israeli and Egyptian forces |
| UNOGIL | 1958 | 591 | — | Check on clandestine aid from Syria to Lebanon rebels |
| ONUC | 1960–64 | 19,828 | — | Maintain order in the Congo, expel foreign forces, prevent secession and outside intervention |
| UNSF | 1962–63 | 1,576 | — | Maintain order during transfer of authority in New Guinea from Netherlands to Indonesia |
| UNYOM | 1963–64 | 189 | — | Supervise military disengagement in Yemen |
| UNFICYP | 1964– present | 6,411 | 1,197 | Prevent internal conflict in Cyprus, avert outside intervention |
| DOMREP | 1965–66 | 2 | — | Report on cease-fire between domestic factions |
| UNIPOM | 1965–66 | 96 | — | Observe India-Pakistan border |
| UNEF II | 1973–79 | 6,973 | — | Supervise cease-fire and troop disengagement, control buffer zone between Egypt and Israel |
| UNDOF | 1974– present | 1,450 | 1,032 | Patrol Syria-Israel border |
| UNIFIL | 1978– present | 7,000 | 4,473 | Supervise Israeli troop withdrawal, maintain order, help restore authority of Lebanese government |
| UNGOMAP | 1988–90 | 50 | — | Monitor Geneva Accords on Afghanistan and supervise Soviet withdrawal |
| UNIIMOG | 1988–91 | 399 | — | Supervise cease-fire and mutual withdrawal of forces by Iran and Iraq |
| UNAVEM I | 1989–91 | 70 | — | Verify withdrawal of Cuban troops from Angola |
| UNTAG | 1989–90 | 4,493 | — | Assist Namibia's transition to independence, ensure free and fair elections |

TABLE 5-1    *(continued)*

| Mission | Date | Peak Force Size | Force Size December 2003 | Function |
|---|---|---|---|---|
| ONUVEN | 1989–90 | 120 | — | Monitor Nicaraguan elections |
| ONUCA | 1989–92 | 1,098 | — | Verify compliance by Costa Rica, El Salvador, Guatemala, Honduras, and Nicaragua with agreement to disarm and neutralize irregular forces in the area |
| ONUVEH | 1990–91 | 260 | — | Observe elections in Haiti |
| UNIKOM | 1991–2003* | 1,440 | — | Monitor demilitarized zone between Kuwait and Iraq. Removed with the occupation of Iraq by an American-led coalition. (Small observer group remains, but technically nonfunctioning and awaiting Security Council action)* |
| UNAVEM II | 1991–95 | 476 | — | Verify compliance with Peace Accord to end civil strife in Angola |
| ONUSAL | 1991–95 | 1,003 | — | Monitor cease-fire and human rights agreements in El Salvador's civil war |
| MINURSO | 1991–present | 375 | 283 | Conduct referendum in Western Sahara on independence or union with Morocco |
| UNAMIC | 1991–92 | 380 | — | Assist Cambodian factions to keep cease-fire agreement |
| UNPROFOR | 1992–95 | 21,980 | — | Encourage cease-fire in Croatia and Bosnia-Herzegovina, protect relief programs |
| UNTAC | 1992–93 | 19,500 | — | Demobilize armed forces of Cambodian factions, supervise interim government, conduct free elections |
| UNOSOM I | 1992–93 | 550 | — | Monitor cease-fire between Somali parties, protect shipments of relief supplies |
| ONUMOZ | 1992–94 | 7,500 | — | Supervise internal peace accord in Mozambique, disarm combatants, establish a non-partisan army, hold national elections, conduct humanitarian program |
| UNOMIG | 1993–present | 120 | 120 | Verify cease-fire agreement, with Abkhazia, observe CIS peacekeeping force |
| UNOMUR | 1993–94 | 100 | — | Observer mission in Uganda-Rwanda, monitor arms shipments |
| UNOSOM II | 1993–95 | | — | UN mission in Somalia, peacemaking operations |

*(continued)*

Table 5-1    *(continued)*

| Mission | Date | Peak Force Size | Force Size December 2003 | Function |
|---|---|---|---|---|
| UNAMIR | 1993–96 | 5,500 | — | Stop the massacre of the defenseless population of Rwanda, assist refugees, report atrocities |
| UNMIH | 1993–96 | 900 | — | Mission in Haiti, pacification and monitor elections |
| UNOMIL | 1993–97 | 91 | — | Observer group in Liberia monitor OAS peacekeeping |
| UNASOG | 1994 | 25 | | Observer group in Aouzou Strip, Libya-Chad border |
| UNMOT | 1994– 2000 | 24 | — | Investigate cease-fire violations and work with OSCE and CIS missions in Tajikistan |
| UNMIBH | 1995– 2002 | 1,584 | — | Monitor law enforcement in Bosnia and Herzegovina |
| UNPREDEP | 1995–99 | 1,150 | — | Preventive deployment force Former Yugoslav Republic of Macedonia |
| UNCRO | 1995–96 | 20 | — | Confidence restoration in Croatia |
| UNAVEM III | 1995–97 | 5,560 | — | Angola verification Mission of the Peace Accords (1991), the Lusaka Protocol (1994), and relevant Security Council resolutions |
| UNMOP | 1996– 2002 | 28 | — | Monitor demilitarization in Prevlaka Peninsula, Croatia |
| UNTAES | 1996–98 | 5,257 | — | Facilitate demilitarization in Eastern Slavonia (Croatia) |
| UNSMIH | 1996–97 | 1,549 | — | Support Mission in Haiti |
| UNTMIH | 1997 | 300 | — | Transition Mission in Haiti |
| MINUGUA | 1997 | 155 | — | Verification Mission in Guatemala |
| MIPONUH | 1997– 2000 | 290 | — | Civilian Police Mission in Haiti |
| MONUA | 1997–99 | 5,560** | — | Observer Mission in Angola and a follow-on to UNAVEM III |
| MINURCA | 1998– 2000 | 1,350 | — | Help maintain and enhance security and stability in the Central African Republic |
| UNAMSIL | 1998– present | 109 | 41 | To observe and report to the Security Council military conditions in Sierra Leone |
| MONUC | 1999– present | 5,537 | 4,420 | Monitor cease-fire agreement, provide humanitarian assistance Democratic Rep. of the Congo |
| UNMIK Kosovo | 1999– present | 40,000 (KFOR) | 40,000 (KFOR) | Combines effort in pacification of Kosovo with KFOR/NATO forces, essentially humanitarian assistance |

TABLE 5-1    *(continued)*

| MISSION | DATE | PEAK FORCE SIZE | FORCE SIZE DECEMBER 2003 | FUNCTION |
|---|---|---|---|---|
| UNMEE Ethiopia and Eritrea | 2000– present | 4,300 | 4,034 | Monitor cessation of hostilities |
| UNAMA Afghanistan | 2002– present*** | 450 | 443 | Not technically a peacekeeping mission, works with International Security Assistance Force, provides humanitarian aid |
| UNMISET East Timor (Timor Leste) | 2002– present | 5,000 | 3,484 | Transitional Security for the new Timor Leste government |
| MINUCI | 2003– present | 0 | 26 | Oversee implementation of Linas-Marcoussis Agreement with ECOWAS and French troops |
| UNMIL | 2003– present | 15,000 | 3,500 (Oct. 2003) | Oversee implementation of the cease-fire and peace agreement, provide police training and assist in formation of a new restructured military |

SOURCE: United Nations Peacekeeping Operations, *Police, Troops and Military Observers—Contributors by Mission and Country,* UN Peacekeeping home page, December 2002; Center for International Relations, *Current UN Peace-Keeping Operations,* Zurich, Switzerland, PKO webmaster, Jan. 1998.

*Still in force by UN records.

**Not judged a UN peacekeeping force.

***The force identified with UNAVEM III is the same force operating under MONUA.

Disengagement Observer Force (UNDOF), and in the Sinai area. UNTSO maintains offices in Beirut and Damascus with headquarters in Jerusalem. The UN Military Observer Group in India and Pakistan (UNMOGIP) has experienced a similar longevity. Set in operation in January 1949 to help curb fighting in Kashmir, it continues to monitor the cease-fire line that was a consequence of the first Indo-Pakistan War (1947–49). Nevertheless, it has never persuaded the parties to resolve their differences diplomatically, nor has it prevented them from attacking one another. War erupted in 1965 when Pakistan tried to take the mountain state by force. In 1971 India attacked Pakistan in eastern Bengal, but it also struck blows all along the West Pakistan frontier. None of these actions reinforced UNMOGIP's credibility, and its helplessness in the face of renewed unrest in the Kashmir valley did not serve the cause of the international community. By the late 1990s, Indian army and paramilitary units, estimated at several hundred thousand, were unleashed against rebellious Kashmiris, who, New Delhi insisted, were aided by the Pakistan government. The small UN observer force, which had been reduced from a peak of 102 several decades earlier to 44 military observers by 2003, is supported by 24 international civilian personnel and 47 local civilian staff and continues to monitor the situation. UNMOGIP has witnessed intense fighting in Kashmir, especially since the uprising against Indian rule began there in 1989. Periodic clashes by Indian and Pakistani troops have several times precipitated the mobilizing of larger army formations. In 2002 the two sides mobilized more than one million troops in the region, and nuclear threats by both sides caused Great Britain and the United States to send some of their highest ranking officials to Islamabad and New Delhi in an effort to calm the situation. Acts of terror in Kashmir are common, and thousands of innocent Kashmiris, Muslim and Hindu, have been victimized. Almost all of the violence since the turn of the century has been linked to radical Islamic organizations with ties to the Taliban and Al-Qaeda, and given Pakistan's decision to support the United States in the war on terrorism, Islamabad has banned most of them. Nevertheless, Pakistan continues to maintain that wars of national liberation are not to be confused with acts of terror. India, however, judges all violence in Kashmir as acts of terror. Diplomatic efforts in January 2004 by Pakistani and Indian leaders called for a cessation of hostilities in the region and improved communications and trade between the neighbors. New Delhi subsequently toned down its accusations that Pakistan organized, trained, and directed guerrilla movements in Kashmir. Islamabad nevertheless continued to insist on the Kashmiri right to self-determination. In this new, somewhat more flexible diplomatic climate, it was left to UNMOGIP to observe and report to the Security Council if the parties seriously entertained resolving their long-standing dispute.

## UN EMERGENCY FORCE (UNEF I)

The first UNEF, extending from November 1956 to June 1967, like the earlier observer missions, was a noncombatant UN military presence designed to help bring international violence under control. The violence in this case was precipitated by an October 1956 Israeli invasion of Egypt launched in coordination with Anglo-French seizure of the Suez Canal, which Egypt had nationalized the previous July. Security Council action was prevented by a British and French veto, but the General Assembly, responding to an initiative by Canadian Foreign Minister Lester Pearson, called for a cease-fire and authorized Secretary-General Hammarskjöld to prepare a plan for an international emergency force. Because of the large hostile armies and the extent of the area to be patrolled, UNEF I went far beyond any previous UN peacekeeping operation in size and function. UNTSO at its largest had numbered less than six hundred; UNEF I represented six thousand troops from ten countries. Earlier missions had been concerned largely with observation and reporting. UNEF I was intended not only to observe, report, and supervise troop withdrawal but also to serve as a buffer between the contending forces and to keep order in the areas under its control.

With Israeli strategists primarily concerned with neutralizing the Sinai location of Sharm al-Sheikh astride the Gulf of Aqaba, any Israeli withdrawal from the Sinai was predicated on Tel Aviv's claim to transit the Gulf of Aqaba to the Israeli port of Eilat. Heretofore, Egyptian forces had blocked the waterway. Now, however, Israel insisted on its sovereign right to use this only outlet to and from the Red Sea. UNEF I forces were therefore stationed at Sharm al-Sheikh in return for the Israeli promise of withdrawal from the Sinai, which it did in March 1957. During the next ten years Israel used the UNEF I presence to expand its port operations at Eilat, and the city became central to the nation's trade with Asian countries insofar as Israel was still prohibited from using the Suez Canal. Secretary-General U Thant's decision in 1967 to acquiesce when Egypt's leader Gamal Abdel Nasser demanded the removal of UNEF I from Sharm al-Sheikh therefore created an instant crisis. U Thant took the action without consulting the Security Council or the General Assembly, and Israel, sensing a major challenge to its security, quickly mobilized its forces and attacked Egyptian air and army installations and again sent its forces into the Sinai peninsula. Despite the renewed hostilities, UNEF I had demonstrated its importance, and what was learned from the 1967 experience would be applied to other peacekeeping operations in the years that followed. Among the more important principles learned were the following:

1. A peace force should be established only by authorization of the General Assembly or the Security Council.
2. While responsible to the organ that established it, the force should be administratively integrated with the UN Secretariat under the political control of the Secretary-General.
3. Troops from the great powers should not participate in the force.
4. The force should remain politically neutral in relation to the various contending parties.
5. The force should be limited to noncombatant functions—those that could be performed with the consent or acquiescence of all the governments concerned—but weapons might be used in self-defense.
6. Troop-supplying states should pay the costs that would be incurred if the military units remained in national service; all other costs should be borne by UN members in accordance with the normal UN scale of contributions.

These principles have continuing validity with two principal exceptions: (1) UN assessments for the more costly peacekeeping missions are now based on a scale that minimizes contributions from the developing country, and (2) with the decline of East-West antagonisms, troop contributions from the United States and Russia are no longer excluded. The last peacekeeping force acting under General Assembly authorization was the UN security force in West New Guinea, created in 1962. Since then the establishment of peacekeeping missions has become the prerogative of the Security Council.

## THE CONGO (ONUC AND MONUC)

When the first Congo crisis erupted in July 1960, the United Nations turned without hesitation to the UNEF model even though conditions in the Congo were quite different from conditions in the Middle East. The Congo had achieved independence from Belgium on June 30 with obviously inadequate preparation for statehood. Widespread rioting, tribal disorders, and mutiny in the Congolese army broke out almost immediately, and Belgium intervened militarily on July 8 to protect the lives and property of its nationals. Three days later the mineral-rich province of Katanga seceded to form an independent state with economic ties to Belgium. Faced with a breakdown of internal order, outside intervention, and secession, the government of the Congo appealed to Secretary-General Hammarskjöld for UN military assistance. The Security Council authorized Hammarskjöld to prepare a plan for military and technical aid and thereafter approved his proposal for a UN Operation in the Congo (ONUC, using the French acronym). The ONUC peacekeeping force eventually involved twenty thousand troops from twenty-nine countries, cost more than $400 million in its four-year existence, and, with its massive civilian aid component, helped restore a measure of internal stability to the Congo. ONUC functioned from July 1960 to June 1964.

In the chaotic situation of the Congo operation, several of the UNEF rules for peacekeeping were bent or broken. The U.S.-Soviet consensus that permitted initial authorization of ONUC quickly evaporated, and responsibility shifted from the establishing organ to the General Assembly. Political neutrality also suffered. A fair degree of neutrality with respect to outside powers was maintained (the Soviet Union thought otherwise), but internal factions were not treated evenhandedly. Early actions of the force tended to favor an anti-Soviet faction over a leftist faction striving for control of the central government. Later, ONUC supported the central government in its struggle to prevent the secession of Katanga. Support for the government also meant abandonment of ONUC's noncombatant role because the Katanga secessionists and their foreign mercenaries could be suppressed only by the use of force. Throughout the Congo operation the principle of financing by assessment of all UN members was maintained, but the Soviet Union, France, and some other countries refused to pay. The severe funding shortfall brought with it financial and political problems, and the United Nations was forced to withdraw prematurely before stability had been restored.

Whatever its shortcomings, ONUC had notable accomplishments. The Belgian troops, mercenaries, and foreign military advisers were gone; the secession of Katanga and other areas of the Congo had been forestalled; and a modicum of law and order had been created. The civilian side of the operation had kept essential public services in operation—transport and communication, health, education, public administration—while providing needed technical training for Congolese personnel and supplying emergency relief throughout the country. The threat of intervention by foreign governments was substantially reduced, and the Congo was insulated from the worst effects of Cold War rivalry. UN intervention nevertheless was costly. Among the casualties in the campaign was UN Secretary-General Dag Hammarskjöld, who died when his aircraft crashed during a mission to the war zone.

The Congo was again in crisis during the late 1990s (when the country was known as Zaire) after the overthrow of the twenty-five-year dictatorship of Mobutu Sese Seko. An insurgency led by Laurent Kabila was successful in establishing a new government, but elements loyal to Mobutu and external interests made Kabila's consolidation of power virtually impossible. After several years of vicious rivalry, Kabila was assassinated and succeeded by his son, Joseph Kabila, who had no more success in establishing a stable order. The Security Council sought to reconcile the different contenders, which included the Congolese government, the rebel Congolese Rally for Democracy, and several African states. The Security Council in August 1998 acknowledged that the conflict, if not checked, constituted a threat to regional peace. Foreign forces were ordered to leave the Congo so that the different political organizations could find grounds to settle their differences. Secretary-General Kofi Annan appointed a Special Envoy to the Congo in April 1999 who was approved by the Security Council under Resolution 1234. In the same resolution, the Council criticized the presence of foreign forces, describing their behavior as contrary to the principles of the UN Charter. Reaffirming its commitment to preserving the territorial integrity and political independence of all states in the region, the UN body called upon the parties to participate with equanimity and flexibility. In August 1999, the Security Council authorized the deployment of 90 UN military liaison personnel along with necessary civilian staff to work through agreements with the reconciling states. In November that mandate was extended, but the work of the UN team was obstructed by malcontents. The Secretary-General then called for the creation the UN Organization Mission in the Democratic Republic of the Congo (MONUC), and the Security Council approved a resolution formally establishing the force. Since then, the force has grown and its responsibilities extended into other areas, such as human rights, child protection, and medical and administrative support. By 2003, 8,700 military personnel were in the Congo supported by specialists in a variety of areas. Among this number were 3,805 fully armed soldiers under a force commander from the Senegalese army. Fifty-three countries were represented in the MONUC force.

Despite this substantial effort, the strife in the Congo continued. South African president Thabo Mbeki tried to reconcile the parties in 2002 but could not achieve a settlement. The British and French Foreign Secretaries also attempted mediation but failed. Congolese President Joseph Kabila privately arranged to meet with the principal rebel leader who controlled much of the northern Congo, offering his rival the role of Prime Minister, but even that offer was flatly rejected. An agreement with Rwanda in July 2002 aimed at getting the Rwandan forces to leave the Congo in return for the repatriation of Hutu Rwandans who had taken refuge in the Congo. Kabila also tried to strike a deal with Uganda, which promised to pull its forces from the Congo if Kabila could prevent the rebels from threatening Uganda's western border. None of the rebel groups had been privy to these negotiations, however, nor did Kabila have the forces to neutralize the guerrillas. Moreover, the officers commanding the foreign armies were reaping high profits from the exploitation of the Congo's vast resources, and they were disinclined to withdraw their forces. Nonetheless, on July 30,

2002, Rwanda signed an agreement with the Congo that called for withdrawal, as well as the disarming and dismantling of the rebel forces. Secretary-General Annan hailed the agreement as a milestone that would pave the way for a settlement of one of Africa's longest and most costly conflicts.

But matters in the Congo remained in a desperate condition. In the spring and summer of 2003, when tribal warfare broke out in Bunia between the Hema and Lendu militias, gross atrocities were reported, precipitated by feuds that had been held in check by a Ugandan army that had withdrawn its 6,000 troops under the 2002 agreement. Nothing in the Congo appeared to work as anticipated. It became obvious that MONUC required reinforcements if the UN presence was to have any meaning. In June 2003, therefore, the UN Security Council and the European Union agreed that more than 2,000 combat troops would go to Bunia to reinforce a beleaguered 750-man UN contingent. The EU force was not to be attached to MONUC, nor would it operate under UN command. Made up initially of French soldiers, the operation was described as another instance of codeployment, and like NATO in Bosnia and Kosovo, would function as a combat force, not as a peacekeeping force. The introduction of French forces was the beginning of an effort by European countries to demonstrate their solidarity with the United Nations, as well as their capacity for out-of-area operations. If initially successful, the French force was likely to be joined by troops from Canada, South Africa, Senegal, Nigeria, and Pakistan.

## UN FORCES IN WEST NEW GUINEA AND CYPRUS

The UN Security Force (UNSF) in West New Guinea (West Irian) from October 1962 to April 1963 and the UN Peacekeeping Force in Cyprus (UNFICYP) (begun in March 1964 and still deployed in 2004) were both initiated while the Congo operation was still in progress. They followed the UNEF/ONUC organizational pattern in most respects, with some differences in force composition. Of some 1,600 UNSF personnel in West Irian, more than 1,500 were Pakistani troops and the others were drawn from U.S. and Canadian air force personnel. The latter were assigned to an air contingent for supply and liaison activities. The Cyprus force was much larger, about 6,400 in the initial stages. It was more widely international in composition, but the largest contribution came from one of the large powers—the United Kingdom—for reasons of direct interest and immediate availability. Both UNSF and UNFICYP departed from precedent in their mode of financing, in recognition of the growing impasse over the funding of peacekeeping forces by mandatory assessment on the regular UN budgetary scale. The Netherlands and Indonesia—the two parties directly involved in the West Irian dispute—agreed to share all UN expenses equally. UNFICYP, by contrast, has been financed by countries supplying troops for the mission, the government of Cyprus, and voluntary contributions, largely from countries of the Atlantic Community.

UNSF, unlike the other peacekeeping forces, came into being as the result of prior political settlement between the disputants. After years of dogged resistance to Indonesian claims, the Dutch government finally agreed to give up West Irian and to use the United Nations as a convenient mechanism for the transfer. An August 1962 agreement committed the Netherlands to turn over the administration of the territory to a UN Temporary Executive Authority (UNTEA) on October 1. UNTEA, in turn, was to transfer governmental authority to Indonesia after May 1, 1963, subject to the right of the native Papuans to determine their own political fate by a plebiscite before the end of 1969. UNSF was created by the General Assembly to maintain the authority of UNTEA and supplement existing Papuan police in preserving law and order.

UNFICYP was created to cope with rivalry between Greek and Turkish communities in Cyprus and the threat of military intervention by Greece and Turkey. A British dependency since 1878, Cyprus was granted independence in 1960 under a constitution drafted as a compromise minimally acceptable to the United Kingdom, Greece, Turkey, and the local Cypriot leaders. Under the constitution, majority rule—which would have meant rule by leaders of the Greek Cypriots constituting 80 percent of the island's population of six hundred thousand—was modified by placing a legislative veto in the hands of the Turkish minority. In the absence of good faith, goodwill, and rational behavior, all of which were in short supply, the constitution was scarcely workable. And without consent of the Turkish minority and of the British, Greek, and Turkish governments, it could not lawfully be amended.

Not surprisingly, the machinery of government stalled, the Greek Cypriot majority set about to amend the constitution unilaterally, and domestic violence ensued. Bloodshed and the formation of rival terrorist groups on Cyprus brought Greece and Turkey to sword's point once more, with Britain in the middle as mediator, peacemaker, and police. Unable to quell the violence, Britain turned to the Security Council, which established UNFICYP in March 1964.

The UN force has been on duty in Cyprus ever since, though its initial strength of 6,400 has been scaled down to a present force of fewer than 1,245 uniformed personnel in 2003. The initial function of UNFICYP was to create a buffer between Greek and Turkish communities in Cyprus but not to interfere with freedom of movement throughout the island. Subsequently, its functions included resolving local conflicts between the two groups, adjudicating local disputes, and, with the assistance of a special UN civilian police force, helping to maintain local order. A new crisis erupted in 1974 when a military coup in Cyprus and the prospect of closer military ties between Greece and Cyprus prompted Turkey to invade the island. UNFICYP became involved in the fighting and suffered a number of casualties before a cease-fire could be arranged. The result was a de facto territorial division strongly favoring the Turkish community, followed by a resumption of UNFICYP functions along a now distinct dividing line.

UNFICYP has competently performed its mandate to curb violence and contribute to the maintenance of law and order. But the mandate for the peacekeeping force was running out and the Security Council was disinclined to extend the mission. Negotiations therefore were intense, and in 2002, the UN Secretary-General became directly involved in seeking a formula that could end the impasse. Diplomatic activity focused on the EU's decision to admit the Greek portion of the island as a full member of the European Union. Annan and the other negotiators tried to leverage a deal that would merge the two regions and admit Cyprus to the EU as a total entity. Annan's talks with Greek and Turkish Cypriot leaders in February 2003 eventually broke down, with the EU's refusal to admit Turkey to its ranks an important factor. The future of the UNFICYP mission waited on still another order from the Security Council.

## Observer Missions after UNEF

The invention of the large peacekeeping force did not make small observer missions obsolete. Besides perpetuating UNTSO and UNMOGIP, the United Nations deployed new observer teams during the 1958 Lebanese crisis and in Yemen and India-Pakistan during the mid-1960s. A token UN observer presence was also sent to the Dominican Republic in 1965 to report on U.S. military intervention there and observe a cease-fire agreement between internal factions.

The largest of the three small observer missions was the UN Observation Group in Lebanon (UNOGIL), a mission of six hundred troops that was established in June 1958 at Lebanese request to check on clandestine aid from Syria to rebel groups in Lebanon. UNOGIL reported only minor infiltration of Lebanon, but in July the border problem was overshadowed by a violent pro-Soviet coup in Iraq that raised fears of a similar upheaval in Lebanon. UNOGIL appeared wholly inadequate to cope with this new threat, and fourteen thousand U.S. troops were rushed to Lebanon at the request of the Lebanese president. In retrospect, the U.S. intervention was an overreaction; threats to Lebanon's territorial integrity had been exaggerated, as domestic strife had declined markedly after the July 31 election of a new president. UNOGIL's presence, however, continued to serve a useful purpose by providing a diplomatic rationale for the early withdrawal of U.S. troops. The UNOGIL mission was terminated in December, having played an important role in relieving a potentially serious crisis.

The UN Yemen Observation Mission (UNYOM) had a more-challenging mandate to satisfy. It was established in July 1963 to observe a military disengagement agreement between parties to Yemen's civil war, which posed a serious international threat due to Egyptian and Saudi Arabian competing interests. UNYOM's small team, never more than 189 observers, exerted a modest restraining influence on the parties. Repeated violations of the disengagement agreement, however, led to its withdrawal in September 1964.

Political conditions permitted a better conclusion to the work of the UN India-Pakistan Observation Mission (UNIPOM), which supplemented UNMOGIP in observing a cease-fire between India and Pakistan from October 1965 to February 1966. The Tashkent Agreement of January 1966 led to mutual troop withdrawal and to the disbanding of UNIPOM, with its work successfully completed. Of the three observer missions, UNIPOM and UNOGIL were funded by regular budget assessments. UNYOM expenditures, however, were borne by Saudi Arabia and Egypt.

The Mission of the Representative of the Secretary-General in the Dominican Republic (DOMREP) consisted of a three-person team sent at the request of the Security Council to report on the prevailing situation. No more than two observers were on duty at one time, and DOMREP's role was very limited because of noncooperation by the United States and other parties. DOMREP confirmed the proposition that UN peacekeeping during the Cold War was unlikely to be viable if it came within the regional sphere of a superpower.

## PEACEKEEPING FROM THE 1970S INTO THE NEW MILLENNIUM

From 1965 to 1973, no new peacekeeping missions were established, although UNTSO, UNMOGIP, and UNFICYP continued to function under repeated extensions of their mandates. In 1973 an attack on Israel by Egypt and Syria made UN peacekeeping again seem a necessary collective response to crisis. The Security Council authorized a UN Emergency Force (UNEF II) of seven thousand troops to supervise a cease-fire and troop disengagement on the Egyptian front and subsequently to control a UN buffer zone between the combatants. On the Syrian front military action persisted until May 1974, when a disengagement agreement was signed at Geneva by Syria and Israel, with provision for a UN peacekeeping force. Pursuant to the agreement, the Security Council established a UN Disengagement Observer Force (UNDOF) of approximately 1,450 to supervise disengagement and patrol the border area. UNEF II and UNDOF initiated the practice of peacekeeping missions being paid through a specially scaled budgetary assessment designed to reduce the proportionate share of developing countries.

Both UNEF II and UNDOF performed their assignments successfully and kept hostile incidents to a minimum. Warming relations between Egypt and Israel culminated in the 1978 Camp David accords and the March 1979 peace treaty, the first political settlement between Israel and any Arab country. The treaty included agreed withdrawal of Israeli forces from the Sinai, to be completed by April 1982. Both parties requested the reconstitution of UNEF II to serve within the framework of the peace agreement, but Soviet and Arab opposition to the treaty made continued UN involvement impossible. UNEF II was terminated in 1979 through nonrenewal of its mandate, leaving a few UNTSO observers as the only UN presence in the Sinai. The gap was bridged temporarily by expanding the duties of the U.S. Sinai Field Mission (staffed by civilians, most under private contract), which had been established in 1976 to monitor two strategic passes, heretofore within the UNEF II buffer zone, by means of highly sophisticated electronic surveillance equipment. In 1982 a Multinational Force and Observers (MFO) was created outside the United Nations to monitor the final stages of Israeli troop withdrawal and to serve as a continuing border watch. Its force of twenty-five hundred has included troops from the United States and ten other countries, with 60 percent of the cost defrayed by the United States.

UNDOF, established in June 1974, was not a precursor of a Syria-Israel settlement, but it continues to keep peace by patrolling a forty-seven-mile-long corridor separating opposing forces in the Golan Heights area. The tenuous peace between Israel and Syria has survived the Syrian occupation in 1981 of large parts of Lebanon. Syrian missile batteries located in Lebanon's Bekaa Valley continue to pose a threat to Israel. Israel therefore annexed the Syrian Golan Heights and shows little inclination of negotiating its return to Damascus. Israel's invasions of Lebanon in 1978 and 1982 led to the creation of a six-mile-wide "security zone" in southern Lebanon in 1985, and Syria, with assistance from Iran, positioned guerrilla-type forces in southern Lebanon to force the Israelis to withdraw. After numerous military incidents initiated by both Israel and Lebanese military groups loyal to Israel, counterattacks launched by guerrillas/terrorists, notably Hesbollah, elevated tensions in the region. Israel withdrew from southern Lebanon in 2001, but this gesture did not stop the fighting or reduce the number of Hesbollah attacks on northern Israel. UNDOF has confined its activities to the Golan Heights and continues to supervise the area of separation between Israeli and Syrian forces. Monitoring the area, UNDOF also assists the International Committee of the Red Cross with facilities for mail and the safe passage of individuals through the region of separation. And UNDOF provides medical treatment to the local population on request. The mission has marked minefields and provides mine-awareness programs to the area's inhabitants. There appears little chance that UNDOF will be disbanded before an Israeli-Syrian peace treaty is established.

A third peacekeeping force involved in the Israeli-Arab conflict is the UN Interim Force in Lebanon (UNIFIL), created in March 1978. A Security Council response to the 1978 Israeli invasion of Lebanon, UNIFIL was given the job of "confirming the withdrawal of Israeli forces, restoring international peace and security, and assisting the Government of Lebanon in ensuring the return of its effective authority in the area." This mission proved impossible for its seven thousand troops to carry out. Although Israel eventually withdrew under heavy international pressure, UNIFIL lacked the resources to maintain order among the numerous armed Christian and Muslim groups or to restore government control over southern Lebanon. Israel complained that UNIFIL was unable to prevent continued PLO raids across its border, while Israel continued to make retaliatory strikes against PLO forces both within and beyond the UNIFIL area. UNIFIL troops frequently came under fire, suffered many casualties, and—though a "defensive" force—sometimes had to initiate preventive military action against one or another of the domestic military groups.

Israeli forces ignored UNIFIL in their June 1982 invasion of Lebanon. At the conclusion of the 1982 hostilities, non-UN Multinational Forces (MNFs) consisting of British, French, Italian, and U.S. contingents were established to monitor withdrawal of PLO forces from Beirut (MNF I) and to help maintain domestic order (MNF II). MNF II was unable to remain neutral in the ensuing civil war. American, and to a limited extent, French troops found themselves fighting not only in self-defense but in support of the Lebanese army against Druze, Shiite, and Palestinian militias. Their position proved untenable, as illustrated by the October 1983 truck bombings that killed 299 U.S. and French troops. MNF II withdrew in early 1984, unable to provide for even its own security.

UNIFIL, however, remained in place through numerous civil and cross-border skirmishes as well as random acts of terror. UNIFIL's force level has varied from more than eight thousand to just over two thousand troops in 2003. Its presence in the region was extended, and the mission was authorized by the Security Council to work in close harmony with the Lebanese government. The Israeli government on April 17, 2000, notified the UN Secretary-General that its force would be withdrawn from southern Lebanon by July, declaring that it was prepared to work in full compliance with UN authority. UNIFIL monitored the withdrawal and assumed responsibility for securing the peace. From July to October 2000 the situation in the UNIFIL area was relatively calm. But an effort by Palestinians to cross from Lebanon to Israel and rocket attacks by Hesbollah on Israeli settlements broke the peace. Lebanese army units moved into the region but also left a place for Hesbollah along the "Blue Line" separating the country from Israel. UNIFIL made strenuous efforts to encourage the Lebanese to police the border; when Beirut hesitated to take action, UNIFIL moved in its troops. Having forced the Lebanese government's hand, the Beirut government ordered its forces to relieve the UN forces. UNIFIL then withdrew and returned to its work in identifying and removing mines from the border region.

Successful in pressuring the Lebanese government to take more direct action, the UNIFIL force was reduced by several thousand in January 2001 and continued to drop through 2002. The Lebanese military establishment, however, was no substitute for the UN peacekeeping force. Never in control of Hesbollah, it allowed the terrorists to control the Blue Line. Hesbollah also took on the character of a quasi-government in the area, and Kofi Annan complained to the Security Council that the organization had interfered with the work of UNIFIL. UNIFIL, however, had been reduced to the size of an observer force and could only place slightly more than two thousand troops between Hesbollah and the Israelis. Nonetheless, it could not be withdrawn and was extended to July 2002. Indeed, in that same month, the most serious breach of the peace occurred when Hesbollah attacked settlements in northern Israel and the Israelis retaliated with air strikes deep into Lebanese territory. The Secretary-General's Personal Representative to southern Lebanon sought to defuse the tense situation, and UNIFIL was ordered to increase its patrols, but the strikes and counterstrikes continued. The Beirut government maintained an inflexible position, arguing that it would not demilitarize the Blue Line until such time as a comprehensive peace was achieved. Moreover, the lawlessness on the Blue Line was demonstrated when UNIFIL observers were prevented from making their regular patrols and Hesbollah operatives beat members of the lightly armed force with rifle butts. UNIFIL withdrew some of its contingents, and although the Security Council renewed its mandate and called upon the parties to provide the mission full freedom to carry out its program, the peacekeeping force was less able to oversee the cease-fire line. With UNIFIL scarcely a viable force, Israel was left to ponder its decision to withdraw from Lebanon. Clearly, the maneuver did not bring an extended calm to the region.

## SUCCESSES AND FAILURES OF UN PEACEKEEPING

After the creation of UNIFIL in 1978, a decade elapsed before the United Nations authorized another peacekeeping mission. This was the low tide of UN fortunes, the nadir of UN prestige. Although a half-dozen peacekeeping operations were launched during this period and the world did not lack situations appropriate for UN peacekeeping, the United Nations was not called in. Hobbled by East-West and North-South divisions, and a general image of ineffectualness, the organization awaited better days.

The better days arrived, perhaps to be dated from Mikhail Gorbachev's September 1987 address to the General Assembly announcing a new (and as it turned out, genuine) commitment to the United Nations and to "the idea of a comprehensive system of international security."[3] The extent of the internal changes then underway in the Soviet Union were not yet fully appreciated, but Soviet leaders had clearly come to grips with the cost, danger, and futility of the ruinous Cold War competition. Shifts in U.S. policy were less dramatic, but President Ronald Reagan experienced a notable softening toward the United Nations during the closing months of his administration. His successor, George Bush, already had a concept of UN possibilities based on his earlier service as U.S. Ambassador to the United Nations from 1971 to 1973. Bill Clinton, Bush's successor, likewise had an interest in bolstering UN peacekeeping activity. But Clinton was left with an ongoing U.S. operation in Somalia, as well as a UN peacekeeping force that had followed the American lead. The new U.S. President quickly ran into a firestorm of criticism for his handling of the Somali operation, notably after a number of Americans were killed and whose fate at the hands of a Somali mob were dramatized on television around the world. U.S. critics targeted both the United Nations and its Secretary-General. Clinton was pressured to withdraw the American force, and the United Nations, after a brief effort at nation building, also retired from the Somali scene. Humiliation was heavy in Washington, and the United Nations was subjected to verbal assaults that came to reflect general public opinion in the United States. Anti-UN sentiment continued to rise in the American countryside, and when George W. Bush assumed the presidency in 2001, there was little desire in the new administration to operate U.S. foreign policy through the world organization. But that is not the way it was elsewhere in the world, and certainly not in the Russian Federation that succeeded the Soviet Union. Moscow even before the end of the Cold War was inclined to lean more heavily on the United Nations in matters that threatened regional, let alone global, equilibrium.

Under the leadership of Gorbachev, the Soviet Union began to pay its peace-keeping assessment arrearages, and the UN Good Offices Mission in Afghanistan and Pakistan (UNGOMAP) was created in May 1988 to monitor Soviet troop withdrawal from Afghanistan. This was soon followed by a major peace initiative in the stalemated war between Iran and Iraq, leading to a cease-fire and establishment of the UN Iran-Iraq Military Observer Group (UNIIMOG) in August 1988.

Most UN operations were relatively small observer missions with a staff of five hundred or fewer, but all had important assignments. UNGOMAP was commissioned to help implement the Geneva Accords of 1988 that brought an end to more than eight years of Soviet military intervention in Afghanistan and aimed at, even if unsuccessful, reducing tensions between Afghanistan and Pakistan. Pakistan had provided a haven to an estimated three million Afghan refugees and, with U.S. assistance, had channeled military aid to Afghan guerrillas (Mujaheddin) fighting the Soviet-supported Kabul government. UNGOMAP's fifty military observers successfully monitored Soviet troop withdrawal and somewhat less successfully kept watch on unauthorized Afghan-Pakistani border crossings. When UNGOMAP withdrew in March 1990, the internal strife still continued but the international tensions were greatly reduced. In 1992, after the demise of the Soviet Union, the communist regime in Kabul was defeated and an Afghan government composed of the different resistance groups was attempted, but it too came apart when opposed factions began making war. Pakistan's interest in one of these factions, coupled with the departure of the United States, left Islamabad with a free hand to meddle in Afghan affairs. Into this scenario came the Taliban, very much supported by the Pakistan army, who with the latter's assistance began to conquer much of the country. UN aid workers could only look on as the fighting intensified between Afghan tribal and ethnic elements, as well as between the regions. The United Nations never acknowledged the Taliban when it seized control of Kabul in 1996 and declared that it was now the government of the Emirate of Afghanistan. But these were the events that led to the link between Al-Qaeda and the Taliban, eventually leading to the events of September 11, 2001. None of this could have been forecast when the Soviet Union self-destructed and when it was hoped the world could more directly embrace the ideals of the world organization.

The UN Iran-Iraq Military Observer Group, authorized in August 1988 and ending its mission in February 1991, was also a response to major armed conflict. It helped bring an end to a devastating war that took nearly one million lives and lasted almost eight years. The combatants had repeatedly rebuffed UN efforts to mediate their war, but in 1988 the new unity on the Security Council, the U.S. tilt in favor of Iraq, and general war weariness on both sides provided a setting for peaceful intervention. UNIIMOG's 399 military observers faithfully patrolled the 850-mile cease-fire line until 1991 when the exigencies of the war in Kuwait led Iraq to make a formal peace settlement with Iran. UNGOMAP was small enough to be financed as a part of the regular UN budget; however, UNIIMOG was funded from the special peacekeeping account raised by assessments falling more heavily upon the wealthier states and the permanent members of the Security Council.

Two observer missions were required to deal with Angola's troubled domestic and international situation. After gaining independence from Portugal in 1975, Angola became a base for the South West Africa People's Organization (SWAPO) to carry on its armed struggle against South African authorities in Namibia. At the same time, South Africa was giving aid to the National Union for the Total Independence of Angola (UNITA), an armed insurgent group within Angola. The picture was further complicated by fifty thousand Cuban troops stationed in Angola since 1975 to prop up its left-leaning government. The international aspects of the situation were resolved by a U.S.-engineered agreement between Cuba, Angola, and South Africa in December 1988, linking Cuban troop withdrawal with a South African commitment to accept Namibia's independence. The UN Angola Verification Mission (UNAVEM I), utilized seventy military observers to verify the withdrawal of Cuban troops from Angola over two years from 1989 to 1991.

This left Angola with a serious internal problem that was addressed by UNAVEM II, a force of 350 military observers and 126 police observers enlisted to monitor a peace settlement between the Angolan government and UNITA. UNAVEM II began operation in June 1991. Its size was temporarily augmented by some 400 civilian observers, which watched over the general election of September 1992. UNAVEM II was supposed to be disbanded after the election, but UNITA cried fraud following electoral defeat, and the United Nations was faced with the task of negotiating a new cease-fire.

Having assisted in reconciling UNITA with the elected Angolan government, the work of UNAVEM II was completed in February 1995. Almost immediately, however, differences again developed between the parties, and UNITA forces once more struck at government positions, disrupting the country's governance. Again the United Nations was called upon to intervene between the warring parties, and UNAVEM III was authorized to pick up where UNAVEM II had left off. UNAVEM III was composed of troops from thirty-two countries, and in 1997, 5,560 police, military personnel, and observers, including more than 4,900 armed soldiers, were deployed in Angola. UNAVEM III was transformed into the UN Observer Mission in Angola (MONUA) in June 1997. MONUA helped the government of Angola and UNITA to consolidate peace and national reconciliation on the basis of the peace accords of 1991 and the Lusaka Protocol of 1994. Unlike UNAVEM III, MONUA was altered from a verification force to an observer mission. It also was authorized to monitor the normalization of state administration throughout the country, observe and verify the activities of the Angolan National Police, oversee security for UNITA leaders, investigate offensive troop movements, monitor the dismantling of checkpoints and UNITA command posts, and promote human rights. Deeply concerned by the failure of UNITA to comply with its obligations and Security Council resolutions, the Council imposed travel restrictions on UNITA personnel in August 1997. This sanction was extended and expanded to include the closure of UNITA offices. After UNITA forces shot down two UN aircraft, however, the Security Council decided against putting unarmed observers at continuing risk, and in February 1999 the peacekeeping mandate was allowed to expire. MONUA was liquidated and the Secretary-General was authorized to work with the Angolan government on how the United Nations might maintain a presence in the country.

The death of UNITA leader Jonas Savimbi in a firefight on February 22, 2002, brought a virtual end to the long civil war that had brutalized Angola since 1975 when Angola achieved its independence from Portugal. On March 15 the government offered the rebels a cease-fire and amnesty in return for their integration into the Angolan army. With assistance from the UN Secretary-General and the leaders of South Africa, the United States, and Portugal, an end to the hostilities was signed in Luanda on April 4, 2002. The long war and two years of drought had taken its toll on Angola's infrastructure, agriculture, and industry. It was a time for reconstruction, and one of the first organizations to answer the call for assistance was the UN World Food Program, which tried to help the estimated half million Angolans suffering from starvation and one million others who depended entirely on outside food aid.

Quelling the civil war in Liberia was the responsibility of the UN Observer Mission in Liberia (UNOMIL), which was sent in 1993 to monitor a cease-fire agreement and the Cotonou Peace Agreement. The latter called for an embargo on the delivery of arms, in addition to the disarmament and demobilization of combatants. It was also authorized to train engineers from the Economic Community of West African States Monitoring Group (ECOMOG) to clear mines and remove unexploded bombs. When the parties to the civil war made it impossible for these responsibilities to be carried out, UNOMIL was assisted by forces from the Organization of African Unity and the Economic Community of West African States (ECOWAS), which subdued some of the fighters but nevertheless could not provide an environment in which UNOMIL could pursue its mandate. The UN peacekeepers were withdrawn in September 1997, leaving the policing of Liberia to the OAU and its ECOWAS forces. The OAU, however, was unable to quell the violence, and the civil war, which abated in 1999, flared again in 2000. Then in 2002, the Liberian armed forces were engaged in a vicious struggle with the rebel movement Liberians United for Reconciliation and Democracy. The success of the rebel offensive forced Liberia's president, Charles Taylor, to declare a state of emergency. Given the intensity of the fighting, thousands fled the country to nearby Sierra Leone, Ghana, and Guinea. Hundreds died and peace talks collapsed immediately as President Taylor criticized UN sanctions imposed in 2001. But Taylor, in turn, had been charged with war crimes by a UN-authorized tribunal in Sierra Leone. Accused of playing a major role in destabilizing West Africa, Taylor was disinclined to permit another UN peacekeeping force to enter Liberia. The United Nations was left with no choice but to ban the purchase of Liberian diamonds, deny travel to senior Liberian officials, and create an embargo on weapons to Monrovia. Relief agencies were prevented from doing their work, and most left Liberia to help refugees in nearby countries. The fighting spilled over into 2003, and with defections in his government and army, Taylor declared that he would resign his office and possibly accept exile. In June 2003, however, he changed his mind and remained president. Under continuing pressure, Taylor indicated in July that he might accept exile in Nigeria if the war crimes charges against him were lifted. In the meantime, UN efforts were directed at assisting the Liberian and other West African refugees and encouraging all the countries and movements in the region to implement the Linas-Marcoussis cease-fire of January 2003. The intensification of fighting in Monrovia between rebel and Taylor forces compelled the UN Security Council to authorize the establishment of a security force to help restore order. The U.S.-backed resolution called for a multinational force spearheaded by Nigeria through ECOWAS to deploy in the Nigerian capital until calm was restored. Under renewed pressure to leave the country once the first contingent of Nigerian troops arrived, Taylor finally resigned his office and left Liberia on August 11, 2003. The warring camps almost immediately lay down their arms, and although Washington was reluctant to deploy its own combat forces, it did send a small contingent of marines to help reestablish civil order and to protect the U.S. embassy. With Taylor no longer present the parties to the conflict entered into a fragile peace agreement, and in October 2003 the new National Transitional Government of Liberia was inaugurated. In September the Security Council established the UN Mission in Liberia (UNMIL). The resolution called for a force of fifteen thousand soldiers to be drawn from Bangladesh, Benin, Gambia, Ghana, Guinea-Bissau, Mali, Nigeria, Senegal, and Togo to implement the cease-fire and peace agreement and support the UN staff of almost sixteen hundred police and development specialists. A Special Representative of the Secretary-General was made Head of the Mission, which was mandated to run through September 2004.

On another front, the UN Mission in the Central African Republic (MINURCA) had been authorized by the Security Council to take over peacekeeping responsibilities from the Inter-African Mission to Monitor the Bangui Agreements (MISAB) in the Central African Republic in March–April 1998. MINURCA again demonstrated the UN commitment to Africa. In addition to maintaining security, MINURCA was called upon to train local police and security forces as well as monitor the elections of August–September 1998. It completed its work and was withdrawn in February 2000.

Another emergency triggered by the unrest and sustained civil strife in Liberia developed in the Ivory Coast in May 2003. The UN Security Council acted quickly to send a peacekeeping force to supervise the Linas-Marcoussis Agreement (which also involved Liberia). The UN Mission in Côte d'Ivoire (MINUCI) peacekeeping force was constituted with the help of the UN Secretariat, and in June Kofi Annan appointed a brigadier general from Bangladesh to lead the mission. Other officers recruited for the operation came from Austria, Benin, Ghana, India, Ireland, Jordan, Kenya, Moldova, Nepal, Niger, Pakistan, Paraguay, Poland, Senegal, Tunisia, and Uruguay. Among other details, the Linas-Marcoussis Agreement, brokered by the French in January 2003, called on the Ivory Coast government, and by inference also the Liberian government, to share power with rebel groups and the political opposition until elections could be held, believed to be in 2005 for the Ivory Coast. The Ivory Coast principal rebel groups were the Patriotic Movement of Côte d'Ivoire, the Movement for Justice and Peace, and the Ivorian Popular Movement of the Great West. France was to play the major role in bringing peace to the Ivory Coast, and French troops were agreeable to a working exercise with ECOWAS and the Ivory Coast regular army. Countries contributing to MINUCI were Benin, Togo, Senegal, Niger, and Ghana.

Called to manage dilemmas in Tajikistan, where civil strife had erupted soon after it achieved independence in 1991, the UN Observer Mission to Tajikistan (UNMOT) was mandated to accomplish similar peacekeeping tasks. A joint commission composed of the representatives of the Tajik government and the Tajik opposition was to monitor an agreement entered into in 1994 and to investigate reports of cease-fire violations. UNMOT was created to work parallel with the Joint Commission and to report to UN Headquarters on the progress made in providing good offices. Here as elsewhere the UN peacekeepers were called upon to work with other international organizations that had committed considerable resources to ease the suffering of the innocent. Given the strife in Georgia and Abkhazia, the Commonwealth of Independent States, and particularly Russia, was committed to mollifying the parties. The Organization of Security and Cooperation in Europe (OSCE) also became involved. Nevertheless, UNMOT's mandate was extended by the Security Council in 1997 with the expectation that the peacekeepers would be successful in getting the United Tajik Opposition to accept integration into the Tajik armed forces, to break contact with the Taliban, and to give up their bases in Afghanistan. UNMOT's mandate was terminated in May 2000 after President Imomali Rakhmonov entered into an agreement with various warring factions that generally ended the civil war. Tajikistan found itself in desperate need for assistance, and the United States was a principal aid giver. How closely tied Tajikistan had become to the United States was witnessed after the events of September 11, 2001, when Rakhmonov allowed the United States to deploy military personnel in the country. The fall of the Taliban in some form was attributed to the support received from Dushanbe, which profited from the changed situation in Afghanistan. Attention now turned to the reconstruction of Tajikistan, and the UN Development Program was introduced into the country. The World Bank and the Asian Development Bank also offered significant funding for the country's new infrastructure. Tajikistan also established an air link with Kabul and offered to help train Afghan troops. Tajikistan still had to contend with the threat posed by the Hizb-ut Tahrir, an extremist Islamic order with the objective of transforming Tajikistan into a medieval-type Islamic caliphate. Rakhmonov's order in 2002 closing 33 mosques (of 152) in the rebellious northern province of Isfara was aimed at preventing the spread of the radical Islamic message. In such matters, there was little room or opportunity for UN peacekeeping.

The UN Advance Mission in Cambodia (UNAMIC) was established in No-

vember 1991 with a staff of 380 military and civilian personnel to prepare the
ground for a much larger UN peacekeeping operation projected for 1992. The
larger objective was to assist contending Cambodian factions to end years of
civil strife and foreign intervention, punctuated by unspeakable atrocities, and
erect a government that all could live with. In satisfying its mandate, UNAMIC
provided a line of communication between the military headquarters of each of
the contending Cambodian parties, monitored cease-fire violations, and conducted a mine-awareness program to help the public avoid injury from hidden
mines and booby traps. It was terminated in 1992 when UNTAC (see below)
became operational.

Two additional missions, having at least a kinship with peacekeeping, were
established for the purpose of observing national elections in Nicaragua and
Haiti. The UN Observer Group for Verification of Elections in Nicaragua
(ONUVEN) and the UN Observer Group for Verification of Elections in Haiti
(ONUVEH) completed their tasks without serious incident and ceased opera-
tions in February 1990 and January 1991, respectively.

The UN Mission for the Referendum in Western Sahara (MINURSO), established in September 1991, originally involved 375 military and civilian observer experts. This number was reduced to 283 in 1997 but was expected to
increase again if the long postponed referendum on the status of the Western
Sahara can be conducted. MINURSO's task in the interim was to monitor
the cease-fire between Morocco and the Polisario Front, which sustained its
demand for self-determination and independence for the region. A settlement
agreed to in 1988 had promised a reduction of Moroccan forces in the Western
Sahara. MINURSO was authorized to monitor compliance, ensure the release
of political prisoners, oversee the exchange of prisoners of war, and register voters and organize and ensure a free referendum. MINURSO was given responsibility for proclaiming the results of the election, but the divergent views and
different interpretations of key elements contained in the settlement plan made
conforming to an earlier timetable impossible. The 1998–99 timetable was not
any more realistic. Nevertheless, James Baker, former U.S. Secretary of State
during the Reagan administration, assumed the role of a UN special envoy in
2001 and presented a proposal to Kofi Annan that resulted in a four-option
plan to bring peace to the warring parties. In the expectation that a settlement
could be reached, the Security Council extended MINURSO's mandate for an
additional six months. When all the posted alternatives failed to achieve an end
to the hostilities, another six months were tacked on in 2002. Rabat's rigid policy in the Western Sahara, insisting that the region was an integral part of Morocco and therefore not negotiable, produced more intense fighting, and reports of atrocities were issued by Western Sahara human rights organizations
to the United Nations.

Two larger observer missions were established in Central America. The UN
Observer Group in Central America (ONUCA) was created in November 1989
to help verify implementation of the Esquipulas II Agreement dealing with border violations affecting Costa Rica, El Salvador, Guatemala, Honduras, and

Nicaragua. The border problems had resulted from activities of the Nicaraguan Resistance (Contras) and, to a lesser extent, from the Salvadoran civil war. The Agreement bound the parties to prevent arms traffic in the area, cease aid to insurrectionist forces, and deny use of each state's territory for attacks on another state. ONUCA consisted of 260 military observers, in addition to an air wing and a naval unit. The observer corps was expanded to a peak of nearly 1,100 in May 1990 when its mandate was extended to include assistance with the voluntary demobilization of the Contras. The termination of hostilities in Nicaragua and the establishment there of a democratically elected government brought a substantial reduction in border violations, and ONUCA was disbanded in January 1992.

The remaining ONUCA observers, about 160 in number, were transferred to the UN Observer Mission in El Salvador (ONUSAL). ONUSAL was created in July 1991 as part of a UN-brokered attempt to end a protracted civil war between the Salvadoran government and the insurgent Frente Farabundo Martí para la Liberación Nacional (FMLN). With an initial strength of 135 military and civilian staff, ONUSAL's task was to help reduce human rights abuses through monitoring human rights activities, investigating particular complaints, and making recommendations to eliminate violations. By the end of the year its staff had grown to 260, and in January 1992 the Security Council authorized a force of 372 military personnel and 631 police to monitor a cease-fire to take effect on February 1. Besides monitoring the separation of forces and cease-fire, and continuing to check on human rights violations, ONUSAL was given the complex assignment of supervising the creation of a new national police force to administer even-handed protection free from past antagonisms. ONUSAL's success allowed the Security Council to withdraw the observers and terminate the mission in April 1995.

A third large observer mission, subsequently reduced in size, was a product of the 1991 Gulf War. The UN Iraq-Kuwait Observation Mission (UNIKOM) was moved into position in April 1991 to monitor the Khawr' Abd Allah waterway between Iraq and Kuwait and to deter violations of a demilitarized zone established along the Iraq-Kuwait land boundary. At its inception the force included 1,440 troops and unarmed military observers. The troops were withdrawn in June 1991, leaving 300 observers to patrol the area. Given the tenuous situation in the region, the United Nations continued to augment its UNIKOM force. In February 1993, given renewed threats from Iraq, the Security Council again added a military component and extended its terms of reference to include a capacity to take physical action to prevent violations of the demilitarized zone and of the newly demarcated boundary between Iraq and Kuwait. With the addition of a mechanized infantry battalion, UNIKOM assumed a combination of patrol and observer missions in 1995–96. Operations included ground and air patrols, vehicle checkpoints, roadblocks, and investigation teams. By March 1997 UNIKOM was staffed with a small-unit detachment of 891 soldiers drawn from thirty-three countries. One hundred and ninety-seven observers were also assigned to the operation, which was paid for from assessments in respect of the UN special account. In February 2000, UNIKOM expanded to include the Khawr' Abd Allah waterway monitoring project, which was concerned with monitoring the larger Al Faw peninsula. UNIKOM had the forces and the mobility to move anywhere in the demilitarized zone and blocked all aggressive threats. The situation in the region was essentially tranquil, that is, until the United States mobilized its forces in the area for an assault on Iraq in 2002–03. On March 17, 2003, in advance of the military campaign against the Baghdad government by the U.S.-led coalition, Secretary-General Kofi Annan suspended UNIKOM's operations and the mission was withdrawn, although not officially ended. A small headquarters consisting of thirteen military officers and twenty civilian staff moved to Kuwait City from Um Qasr; the residual peacekeeping force, at the Secretary-General's request, was maintained until July 6, 2003. The Security Council concurred with the Secretary-General's request. Technically, UNIKOM was sustained, but the mission ceased to have significance in light of the coalition's occupation of Iraq and the termination of the threat posed to Kuwait.

### UN Forces in Namibia and Cambodia

In addition to observer teams ranging in size from 50 to as many as 1,400, peacekeeping operations also were numerous. Of these the UN Transition Assistance Group (UNTAG) was the most obviously successful. It had the responsibility of supervising Namibia's transition from South African colonial rule to independent statehood; this was accomplished in thirteen months from February 1989 to March 1990. At peak strength, the mission consisted of approximately 4,500 troops, 1,500 civilian police, and 1,000 election observers. Although its basic mandate was to ensure a fair election process, the need to create preconditions for free and uncoerced choice involved UNTAG in a variety of tasks, including some not usually associated with peacekeeping missions. It observed the cease-fire between South African forces and those of SWAPO and supervised not only the November 1989 elections but also the registration process. It presided over South African military withdrawal, monitored the conduct of South West African police, and encouraged SWAPO forces to honor their agreement to remain in designated base areas. It also assisted the return of large numbers of refugees, ensured the repeal of racially discriminatory laws, and generally attempted to create an atmosphere in which people subjected for one hundred years to repressive and discriminatory colonial rule might exercise a genuine act of self-determination. UNTAG's mission was accomplished when Namibia declared its independence as a new sovereign entity on March 21, 1990. The total cost was $383 million, assessed to member states according to the special scale for peacekeeping.

A larger peacekeeping force began operation in March 1992 when the initial contingents of UN troops arrived in Cambodia. Preparations for the UN Transitional Authority in Cambodia (UNTAC) had been laid by the 380 military liaison officers and civilian staff of UNAMIC, established the previous October to help maintain the cease-fire between warring factions in Cambodia. UNTAC at full strength included 21,900 troops, 3,600 police monitors, and 2,400 civilian administrators. The largest UN peacekeeping force since the Congo operation, UNTAC had the mammoth task of preserving order and providing transitional governance until a new freely elected government could assume control. In addition it had to disarm the military forces mobilized by the four warring domestic factions in Cambodia. Elections were initially scheduled for April 1993 and the dissolution of UNTAC by July 1993. Led by Yasushi Akasi, UNTAC was to be a catalyst for the assembly of a government of reconciliation. It also was slated to operate at least five of Cambodia's ministries, but faced with resistance, UNTAC reduced its tasks to providing basic medical services and distributing food. Unable to bring the different factions together, and no match for lawless businesspeople, let alone the Khmer Rouge, the UN mission was closed down on schedule. The venture cost the international community approximately $2 billion between 1992 and 1993, but there was little to show for it given the worsened social conditions, the enormous peasant displacement, and widespread government corruption. Cambodia was left to its own designs, and although a formula was initially found to bind the competing groups in common endeavor, shared responsibility was not Cambodia's strong suit. In 1997, the government divided again, and although the country confronted renewed fighting, a relative calm prevailed that allowed for the holding of new elections in the summer of 1998. Cambodia entered a twilight period in the years that followed, stalked by its violent past. The UN Secretary-General tried to get the Phnom Penh government to address the issue of war crimes, not to seek punishment as much as to bring healing to the groups still bearing the scars of internal war. With the government generally controlled by Prime Minister Hun Sen in disarray, and with the monarchy confronting inner crisis, the World Bank refused to extend the payments needed to keep the country in equilibrium. The UN Commissioner for Human Rights visited Cambodia in 2002 to impress upon Hun Sen the need to come to grips with the nepotism and corruption that had brought more distress to the nation. Working in tandem with the World Bank, the Human Rights Commission finally moved the Hun Sen government. In April 2003 the Cambodian government removed its opposition to the establishment of an international tribunal to try perpetrators of atrocities committed by the Khmer Rouge during the 1970s.

## UN Forces in the Former Yugoslavia and Somalia

The initial mission of the UN Protection Force (UNPROFOR) in Croatia was to supervise a cease-fire between Croats and Serbs, the latter supported by the Serb-dominated Yugoslav army. But UNPROFOR's authorized force of 14,400 troops, police, and observers found the cease-fire hard to maintain in the face of the underlying ethnic struggle. When fighting also broke out in neighboring Bosnia-Herzegovina, the Security Council was reluctant to authorize another large, expensive peacekeeping force. However, on the understanding that countries supplying the troops (primarily Britain, France, Italy, and Canada) would pay the additional costs, UNPROFOR was expanded to more than 23,000 (up from the original authorization of 21,980) by the end of the year, making it the largest UN peacekeeping force at that time. Irrespective of its size UNPROFOR was not a success story for UN peacekeeping. The bulk of the force was stationed in Bosnia and made responsible for protecting humanitarian agencies that were involved in the distribution of food and medicine. The force had air support provided by NATO, as well as airlift capability for food and medicine drops in battle areas cut off from normal supply routes. These airdrops were described as the most ambitious in history. UNPROFOR was supposed to interpose itself between the warring factions, its lightly armed status meant to convince the combatants of its peaceful intentions. Not called upon to take sides, UNPROFOR was supposed to slow and reduce the level of combat so that the peace process might go forward. The largest contingents for the peacekeeping operation were drawn from France (3,493), Britain (3,283), Pakistan (2,973), Malaysia (1,539), the Netherlands (1,485), Turkey (1,468), Spain (1,402), and Bangladesh (1,239). Ten other countries also contributed forces.

Despite its declared neutrality and peaceful representation, UNPROFOR was attacked militarily, politically, verbally, and psychologically. Spread over a vast area and operating in small units, the troops were easy targets for the warring groups, especially the Serbs, who in 1995 seized more than three hundred UNPROFOR troops and declared them to be prisoners of war. UNPROFOR could neither protect itself nor the victims of indiscriminate aggression and ethnic cleansing pogroms. Moreover, the mission took a considerable number of casualties, and the Security Council was forced to consider withdrawing the troops before more were killed. Sensing an opportunity to be rid of the UN presence, in 1995 Bosnian Serbs threatened a bloodbath on UN forces. But no longer prepared to stand by defenseless, without UN authorization, France, Britain, and the Netherlands organized a Rapid Reaction Force of ten thousand fully armed combatants. Deploying this force as security for UNPROFOR, the Europeans insisted that they were not taking sides, merely trying to protect their troops in UNPROFOR. The United States remained somewhat hesitant, refusing to become more involved in what Washington believed was a European problem. With the exception of the NATO airlift, to which it was a major contributor, the United States practiced a hands-off policy. Moreover, Washington, claiming strict neutrality, had refused to arm the Bosnian Muslims who were challenged by a far better equipped Bosnian-Serb army.

The seizure of UNPROFOR hostages, however, did register among Americans, and President Clinton ordered some very limited air strikes against select Serbian targets. These strikes were deemed to be of token value, and the United States again hesitated when the areas delimited as "safe havens" were made free-fire zones by the Bosnian Serbs. Seldom had so many large nations been so humiliated by so few renegades. In fact it was only when Croatian forces scored a series of victories against Serbian units in the Krajina region of Croatia that the United States galvanized a NATO response to what Washington now judged was unacceptable Serbian aggression.

A large-scale NATO air campaign began on August 30, 1995, and was slated to continue until the Serbs had removed their artillery from around Sarajevo and the other safe havens. Given the ferocity of the bombing, in October 1995 the Bosnian Serbs agreed to accept cease-fire terms. Diplomatic negotiations went forward under arrangements pressed by the United States. UNPROFOR's role was made dysfunctional, and the force was quickly phased out. In its place was a sixty-thousand-person NATO force fully armed and ready to do battle with those who would restart the war. Unlike UNPROFOR, the NATO force was composed of mainline U.S. units that were totally removed from UN control. Thus, with NATO providing a counterweight to the Bosnian Serbs, other UN peacekeeping missions were authorized for Bosnia-Herzegovina (UNMIBH) and the Former Yugoslav Republic of Macedonia (UNPREDEP), both in 1995; Eastern Slavonia, Baranja, and Western Sirmium (UNTAES) and Prevlaka (UNCRO) in 1995; and Prevlaka again (UNMOP) in 1996. All of these missions were in one way or another related to the conflict in the former Yugoslavia. UNMIBH was made responsible for monitoring the reestablishment of political and juridical activity in Bosnia. It was called upon to train police personnel and help develop and improve law enforcement institutions.

The introduction of NATO forces gave the United States a more direct role in pacifying the region. Washington also engineered the Dayton Peace Agreement between the presidents of Serbia, Bosnia, and Croatia, but the United Nations was given responsibility for developing an International Police Task Force. UNPREDEP was the preventive deployment force that was sent to monitor conditions in Serbia's neighbor, the former Yugoslav Republic of Macedonia. Fear that the civil unrest in Serbian Kosovo province might spill over into Macedonia prompted the UN action. Included in the six-hundred-person military unit that was dispatched to Macedonia were three hundred U.S. troops. Worsening conditions in Kosovo in 1998, and Washington's demand that Serbia end its brutal repression of the majority Albanians living in Kosovo, gave importance to the region. The bloodletting in Kosovo, however, also revealed the precarious nature of the UNPREDEP mission. Indeed, at a time when conditions in Macedonia were even more disturbed by the movement of thousands of Kosovar refugees seeking safe havens in the neighboring state, UNPREDEP lost its mandate when China cast a veto in the Security Council. The vote to extend the United Nations's first preventive peacekeeping force was thirteen to one, with Russia abstaining. Although China argued its vote was in opposition to a mission that it believed had completed its task, the underlying reason for the negative vote was Beijing's dissatisfaction with Macedonia over its recognition of the Republic of China (Taiwan).

The Security Council authorized UNCRO and its successor UNMOP to monitor the demilitarization of the Prevlaka peninsula in Croatia; UNTAES performed a similar role in another area of Croatia that had been won from Serbia. It supervised and oversaw the voluntary return of refugees and displaced persons to their original homes in Eastern Slavonia and contributed to the maintenance of peace and security in a region inhabited by Croats and Serbs. UNTAES also organized elections to local bodies of government and monitored compliance with prior commitments those governments had made to respect the highest standards of human rights and fundamental freedoms, irrespective of ethnic origin. De-mining programs were also included. The success of UNTAES was read in its withdrawal from the region in 1998 and demonstrated that the United Nations, unlike earlier failures, was capable of satisfying its mandate given the relative goodwill of parties involved. Nevertheless, in December 1997 the UN Security Council authorized a Police Support Group (UNPSG) to assume the task of UNTAES. The function of UNPSG, formally instituted in January 1998, was to continue monitoring the performance of the Croatian police in the Danube region and especially to monitor the return of displaced persons. The 114-strong force was drawn from eighteen countries, including the United States, Russia, Finland, and even Switzerland, which was not yet a UN member. In October 1998 UNPSG completed its mission and its responsibilities were assumed by the Organization for Security and Cooperation in Europe (OSCE). UNCRO was authorized to operate from March 1995 to January 1996, after which UNMOP assumed a similar charge.

Functioning under the security umbrella provided by NATO in Bosnia, UNCRO and UNMOP monitored compliance with the cease-fire agreement of 1994 and an economic agreement also arranged in 1994. Especially concerned with checking the movement of weapons and military personnel across the Serbian, Croatian, and Bosnian frontiers, the missions continued humanitarian assistance to Bosnia-Herzegovina. Thirty-eight countries provided personnel for UNCRO and UNMOP, which for all intents and purposes had replaced UNPROFOR, but with a vastly reduced force. UNCRO was short-lived and phased out in January 1996, and UNMOP assumed the overall burden in the Prevlaka Peninsula. UNMOP was concerned with border disputes between Croatia, Bosnia, Serbia, and Slovenia, especially territorial boundaries around the Bay of Piran. Croatia was admitted into NATO's strategic plan and initialed its formal application in May 2002, but continuing instability prevented its admission to the alliance or the European Union. Nevertheless, the UN Security Council deemed it necessary to terminate UNMOP's mandate in December thus restoring Croatia's sovereignty over all its territory.

UNPROFOR's lack of success was somewhat masked by the relative achievements of UNMIBH, UNCRO, UNMOP, and UNTAES. But UNMIBH had the larger responsibility before it too was phased out at the close of 2002. UNMIBH was the most extensive effort of reform and restructuring in the history of UN peacekeeping. The major focus of the UNMIBH mission was police reform and reorganization. Operating in Bosnia-Herzegovina, it reduced police personnel from forty thousand in 1996 to less than eighteen thousand in 2002. It administered compulsory basic training courses in human dignity, community policing, and specialized matters related to drug control, organized crime, crowd control, and senior management. UNMIBH established a fully multiethnic police service, helped introduce disciplinary codes, and enhanced professionalism and accountability. It investigated more than thirteen thousand cases of human rights abuses by law enforcement, eleven thousand of which were successfully resolved. UNMIBH streamlined police organization, advanced institution-building and interpolice cooperation, heightened public/police awareness, and even participated in similar work in East Timor. UNMIBH made full freedom of movement possible throughout Bosnia-Herzegovina by securing the region and by issuing a policy of common license plates. In 2000 sixty-seven thousand refugees returned home, and in 2001 the number returning eclipsed ninety-two thousand. The reconciliation of ethnic and religious differences made this possible. None of UNMIBH's successes, however, could hide Bosnia-Herzegovina's continuing political, economic, and social dilemmas. Nevertheless, in October 2002 national elections were held without international supervision for the first time since war had broken out in 1992. The Bosnian-Serb republic, however, insisted on maintaining its aloofness from the greater territory in fear that Serbs would be overwhelmed by the Muslim population; indeed, Bosnian-Serb leaders did not attend a ceremony in Srebrenica to memorialize the eight thousand Muslims massacred by the Serbs in 1995. Moreover, for all of UNMIBH's solid performance, accused war criminals General Ratko Mladic and Radovan Karadžić remained at large, secreted in the Bosnian-Serb enclave.

The relative success of UN peacekeeping in the Balkans, albeit with significant help from NATO, could not remove the blemish the United Nations suffered in Somalia. The Somalian story began in April 1992 when the Security Council created the small UN Operation in Somalia (UNOSOM I) of fifty unarmed military observers to monitor a cease-fire in Somalia's civil conflict. Several hundred Pakistani soldiers were assigned responsibility for protecting the distribution of food and medicine to a population cut off by the fighting between local warlords. Their failure to manage this charge, however, caused the United States to send a major military force into the country, with the objective of feeding and caring for a people facing famine conditions. The earlier overthrow of the long-time ruler of Somalia, Muhammad Siad Barre, had caused turmoil in the country, and ultimately anarchy. Armed bands of thugs, led by regional leaders, struggled over the spoils of the dismembered government, and in the absence of a credible police infrastructure, only UN forces were left to deal with the lawless criminal elements. Without a government or any kind of law and order, the people of Somalia suffered abuse, neglect, and in time mass starvation.

President George Bush, moved by photo reports of Somalia's despair, took the unprecedented step of ordering U.S. forces into the country on what was called a humanitarian mission. A U.S.-led Task Force (UNITAF) forced open the principal port of Mogadishu and its airport, and a relief program was set up. With the hope of gaining compliance from the warring parties, a conference of reconciliation was held in 1993, and UN Secretary-General Boutros Boutros-Ghali, sanctioned by Security Council resolutions, expanded the UNOSOM I mission to UNOSOM II. UNOSOM II involved a major change from peacekeeping to peacemaking. Boutros-Ghali, apparently impressed by UNITAF's initial success, urged the United Nations to take up the task of creating a government for Somalia. To pursue this objective, the Secretary-General called for the disarming of the militias. As the U.S. presidency passed to Bill Clinton, who was more willing to work with the United Nations, in May 1993 UNITAF was subsumed under UNOSOM II.

Somali gang leaders, however, believing that they should have the opportunity to determine the country's future, opposed the more blatant UNOSOM II role. Clashes between armed Somalis and the international force therefore were inevitable. In June 1993 a major act of violence was directed at UN forces, and twenty-three Pakistani members of UNOSOM II were ambushed and killed while attempting to search a weapons depot controlled by the militia of Mohammed Farah Aidid. In response to the attack, the Security Council called for the arrest and punishment of the Somali leader; however, Aidid was no easy target, and his forces answered the UN threat by attacking a unit of U.S. soldiers sent to capture those implicated in the violence against the Pakistani troops. In the action that ensued, a U.S. helicopter was shot down and U.S. troops on the ground were overwhelmed by armed mobs. Engaged in a battle they could not win, the soldiers fought valiantly, but eighteen were nonetheless overrun and killed, and one dead man's naked body was dragged through the streets of Mogadishu before television cameras. The U.S. public, appalled by this video, initially wanted to avenge their dead. U.S. and UN forces mounted a combined campaign to locate Aidid, but the effort failed. In the meantime, heavy congressional criticism was directed at the Clinton administration, which, it was said, had succumbed to the UN's increasing involvement in nation-building. Clinton also was accused of placing U.S. soldiers at undue risk by not providing sufficient firepower for the Somali mission.

Under pressure from his many critics, and with public opinion in the United States raging against the United Nations and the Somalis, President Clinton decided to end the U.S. presence in Somalia. What had started as a humanitarian mission by President Bush had metamorphosed into a humiliating and tragic defeat. Aidid eluded his would-be captors. The UNITAF mission was disbanded, and the troops returned to the United States. Washington tried to put a positive face on the affair, noting that the humanitarian mission had in fact succeeded, famine had been stemmed, and the Somali people were on the road to managing their own affairs. Contrary to UN Secretary-General Boutros-Ghali's wishes, however, Washington declared that it was not interested in nation building and would not play a role in the creation of a new Somali government. Without the U.S. involvement that had placed the United Nations in Somalia, the United Nations also lost interest. After the U.S. withdrawal, the Security Council passed a resolution calling for UNOSOM II to be disbanded; it ended operations in Somalia in March 1995.

UN peacekeeping and peacemaking had suffered a grievous setback in Somalia, and the humiliating retreat from the East African nation would have consequences for other UN missions. The experience in Somalia also altered Americans' perception of the United Nations. American policy about U.S. responsibility in matters not directly concerned with the country's national interest was to be reevaluated. Subsequent U.S. reluctance to meet its financial obligations to the United Nations and Washington's insistence that Boutros-Ghali be denied an additional term as UN Secretary-General were only two of the more immediate costs of the Somali fiasco.

## Proliferation of Peacekeeping Missions from the 1990s

The Security Council granted the Secretary-General's request to establish yet another large peacekeeping force—the UN Operation in Mozambique (ONUMOZ)—to assist Mozambique's transition to internal peace. After years of civil war, a peace accord between the government and the Renamo insurgent group was signed, and the United Nations was invited to supervise the implementation of the agreement. The UN agenda included demobilizing troops on both sides, helping to establish a new nonpartisan army, organizing elections by the end of 1993, and carrying on a large-scale humanitarian program. A force of some seventy-five hundred, plus civilian staff, was projected to accomplish these tasks. ONUMOZ completed its work successfully and was disbanded on schedule in 1994.

The extent and geographic range of UN peacekeeping had broadened remarkably after 1988. One notable feature was the focus on internal conflict rather than conflict between sovereign states. Of the thirty-five missions authorized from 1988 through 1998, only five dealt exclusively with interstate conflict—UNIIMOG (Iran-Iraq), ONUCA (Central America), UNIKOM (Iraq-Kuwait), UNOMUR (Uganda-Rwanda), and UNASOG (Libya-Chad). UNGOMAP was concerned with withdrawal of Soviet troops from Afghanistan and also with incidents along the Pakistan border, but the roots of the problem, as noted previously, lay in the continuing Afghan civil war. The UNAVEM I mission in Angola was aimed at both internal and external warfare. The withdrawal of Cuban troops from Angola was South Africa's price for ceasing military aid to UNITA as well as a precondition to moving ahead with Namibian independence.

The UN Observer Mission in Georgia (UNOMIG), authorized in 1993, was mandated to verify compliance with the cease-fire agreement between Georgia and breakaway Abkhazia. Called upon to investigate reports of violations, it was also instructed to mediate the parties. With a force of 120 observers, UNOMIG operated in the midst of a Commonwealth of Independent States peacekeeping force that was primarily responsible for separating the armies and limiting their weapons deployment. UNOMIG was called to monitor protection for the city of Sukhumi and to verify the withdrawal of Georgian troops from the Kodori valley. It was required to make regular reports to the Secretary-General, who in turn kept the Security Council informed of developments in the war-stricken region. The Georgian government of Eduard Shevardnadze, however, was accused of breaking its promise to withdraw its troops from the strategic Kodori Gorge, and the Abkhaz leadership refused to work with UNOMIG or engage in further talks with the Tbilisi government. Nevertheless, the Georgian parliament acknowledged its inability to crush the rebellious elements, and in October 2002 Abkhazia was declared an autonomous republic. UNOMIG's mandate was scheduled to end in December 2002, but after the events of September 11, 2001, Georgia opened its borders to U.S. forces operating in Afghanistan. Complicity between Georgian radicals (including Abkhaz) and Chechens, as well as indications of networking between Islamist radicals in the Caucasus and Afghanistan, led to air strikes against rebel strongholds in Georgia, especially in the Pankisi Gorge region. Russian Federation President Vladimir Putin also saw a threat to his interests in breakaway Chechnya emerging from the Pankisi region, and he too declared a willingness to strike at the guerrilla camps. Activity in Georgia after September 11, as elsewhere in the Caucasus and Central Asia, had changed the nature of the game, and ONOMIG seemingly had lost its relevance with the influx of Americans and Russians. UNOMIG had a force of 117 military observers, 91 international civilian personnel, and 175 local staff by the close of 2002.

The UN Observer Mission to Uganda-Rwanda (UNOMUR) was also authorized in 1993 and yielded to the UN Assistance Mission in Rwanda (UNAMIR) the following year. Charged with monitoring the Ugandan border with Rwanda, UNAMIR was supposed to confirm that Uganda was not being used to funnel weapons into Rwanda. Three African nations (among a group of eight) provided observers for a mission that did not total more than one hundred peacekeepers. After the killing of the Presidents of Rwanda and Burundi on April 6, 1994, militant members of the Hutu majority in Rwanda launched attacks against the Tutsi minority, moderate Hutu politicians, and UNAMIR positions. When major contributors began withdrawing their contingents, the Security Council elevated UNAMIR to a combat unit, and the Secretary-General requested a force of fifty-five hundred soldiers from member states. Member states, however, showed little willingness to provide the necessary troops. Given this indifference, the Hutu-induced massacres in Rwanda continued unabated and UNAMIR was paralyzed by a lack of capacity to respond. France's willingness to deploy its troops, but outside the UN orbit, ended some of the carnage. French actions also downgraded the UNAMIR mandate, which was now relegated to providing assistance to Rwandan refugees. Although thirty-nine countries later gave UNAMIR the force that the Secretary-General had originally requested in 1994, the peacekeeping operation was judged a failure. UNAMIR never quite provided the necessary security for the city of Kigali, but it did monitor the cease-fire agreements and assisted in land mine clearance and the repatriation of Rwandan refugees as well as their resettlement. It also investigated reports of atrocities and aided the United Nations in the establishment of an international tribunal to try people accused of genocide. UNAMIR was terminated in 1996 after a Tutsi-led coalition successfully routed the Hutu perpetrators of the massacres and established a government of reconciliation. The plight of the Hutu refugees, however, remained a complex matter that continued to burden UN and NGO relief workers and in the late 1990s undermined efforts to stabilize conditions in neighboring Congo.

In November 1994 the UN Secretary-General appointed a Special Envoy to work with the Organization of African Unity (OAU) and the Economic Community of West African States (ECOWAS), which were seeking to mediate a peaceful resolution between rival factions in Sierra Leone. Parliamentary and presidential elections were held in 1996, and Ahmed Tejan Kabbah was made president of the country. The election results, however, were not accepted by the Revolutionary United Front (RUF), which had been insisting on its right to govern Sierra Leone since 1991. Nevertheless, an agreement was reached between the parties through the good offices of the Ivory Coast, the United Nations, the OAU, and the Commonwealth, and it was anticipated that life in Sierra Leone could be normalized. In May 1997, however, high-ranking army officers led a coup d'état against the government, and an Armed Forces Revolutionary Council was formed. Citing the overthrow of an elected government, the UN Security Council imposed sanctions and an oil embargo on the country and authorized ECOWAS to ensure their strict implementation. Shortly thereafter an agreement was arrived at with the junta, and ECOWAS dispatched a Military Observer Group (ECOMOG) to the area and called upon it to work with the UN military observers already in the country. At this juncture a large, heavily armed ECOMOG force launched an attack on rebel units, and after gaining the advantage, it returned President Kabbah to office. The Security Council welcomed the change in events and lifted the sanctions and the embargo. RUF and former members of the military junta were not satisfied, however, and by the spring and summer of 1998 they had succeeded in brutalizing the populations coming within their sphere of operations. The rebel campaign led to the displacement of approximately 450,000 people, many of them having to flee to neighboring Ivory Coast, Gambia, Senegal, Guinea, and Liberia. The UN Observer Mission in Sierra Leone (UNOMSIL) was thus authorized by the Security Council to work with ECOMOG in the effort to restore a semblance of normalcy to that country. At a summit meeting in London in October-November 1998, the UN mission declared its intention to work in tandem with ECOMOG, but despite these efforts the security situation in Sierra Leone did not improve. Moreover, the government's execution of twenty-four ranking military officers for alleged complicity in the coup only added to the struggle. Atrocities and massacres of the innocent in those regions occupied by the RUF could not be stopped, and despite their considerable number and dedication, ECOMOG forces were hard-pressed to maintain order. The peacekeepers nonetheless were not ready to yield to the insurgents. In January 1999 the Security Council extended the mandate of UNOMSIL to October 1999 and urged the parties to seek a way out of their impasse.

After UNOMSIL, the UN Assistance Mission to Sierra Leone was established in October 1999 and called upon to cooperate with government and other parties in implementing the Lome Peace Agreement, disarmament activities, the demobilization of rebel forces, and the reintegration of breakaway territories. In February 2000 the Security Council revised UNAMSIL's mandate and expanded the size of the mission. In March 2001 it was reauthorized, as it was again in 2002 and 2003. A huge mission for the United Nations, UNAMSIL was authorized to have 17,500 military personnel, including 260 military observers and 90 civilian police personnel. At the end of 2002 it had a force of 16,042 military personnel, most of those being combat troops. UNAMSIL also employed 552 local civilian staff and 298 international civil servants. With assistance from UNAMSIL the civil war that had plagued Sierra Leone since 1991 was declared over in January 2002. More than 45,000 RUF rebels turned in their weapons, peace was formalized, and the United Nations lifted the ban on trade in rough diamonds that had been so much a part of the conflict. In the April 2002 elections Kabbah was returned to office, defeating the rebel leader Pallo Bangura by a wide margin. Given the relative calm that settled over the country, Sierra Leone became the destination of choice for thousands of refugees fleeing renewed fighting in Liberia. UNAMSIL therefore was not disbanded, and in fact its higher force levels were sustained into 2003 lest the country be again destabilized. Pressing on with its need for reformation, Sierra Leone established a Truth and Reconciliation Committee and judges were appointed to a UN tribunal that was to handle the proceedings.

The United Nations was pressed into service in behalf of Western Hemispheric interests in 1993. The elected president of Haiti, Jean-Bertrand Aristide, had been ousted from the presidency by a military coup shortly after his inauguration. Disturbed by this act of undemocratic behavior in a region of vital importance to the United States, Washington used considerable diplomatic pressure to force the junta to meet with Aristide, who was in exile in the United States. Washington tried to return the president to his country and to a resumption of his duties; the Governor's Island Agreement was a consequence of this effort. The junta pledged to the United States on the matter of Aristide's return and reinstatement, but subsequent violation of the agreement caused the United States to threaten military force. Only when air strikes were readied and a U.S. invasion force was poised for attack did the military leaders of Haiti relent. Discredited, the junta agreed to leave the country for exile. With the junta's departure from the country seemingly assured, Aristide was allowed to return. The United States sent several thousand troops to the island to assure his reinstatement, but it was the United Nations that was called upon to assume responsibility for revitalizing the country through the UN Mission in Haiti (UNMIH).

The U.S. military disassembled the army/police organization that had dominated the country and terrorized its population, but UNMIH was given responsibility for stabilizing the political environment, retraining the Haitian armed forces, forming a new police establishment, and arranging for free and fair elections to succeed Aristide, who was prevented from seeking another term. UNMIH was supposed to consist of six thousand soldiers and police, twenty-five hundred drawn from the United States and thirty-five hundred from Pakistan, Bangladesh, Nepal, France, Canada, Honduras, Algeria, Argentina, Austria, Benin, Belize, Antigua and Barbuda, and the Bahamas. It never attained this strength, however, and had to function with far fewer forces. Nevertheless, UNMIH was given an initial six-month mandate that was subsequently extended to almost three years, during which time the United States withdrew most of its forces but left a small force in place to deal with untoward events.

In 1995 Haiti experienced new elections, and in 1996 UNMIH was dissolved in favor of the UN Support Mission in Haiti (UNSMIH). Combat forces were removed from the island and replaced by three hundred civilian police personnel and six hundred troops who were charged with overseeing the development of police and economic institutions. Given the need to eliminate its peacekeeping presence, UNSMIH was phased out in July 1997 and in August the UN Transition Mission in Haiti (UNTMIH) was authorized by the Security Council to focus exclusively on upgrading the Haitian National Police.

UNTMIH provided the necessary protection for UN personnel, and the mission was ended four months later. Military personnel were drawn from Canada and Pakistan, while civil police trainers came from Argentina, Benin, Canada, France, India, Mali, Niger, Senegal, Togo, and the United States. UNTMIH was composed of 250 civilian police and 50 military personnel for security purposes. It was authorized to assume all the assets of UNSMIH. The transition to greater Haitian self-government centered on economic rehabilitation and the reconstruction of the Haitian government. Moreover, as the poorest country in the Western Hemisphere, Haiti depended desperately on international assistance. With the end of UNTMIH's mandate in November 1997, still another mission, the UN Civilian Police Mission in Haiti (MIPONUH), was authorized in December of that same year. MIPONUH, described as a follow-on mission to UNTMIH, was directed to work with the government of Haiti in the further development of its National Police. The training of special units and the monitoring of police performance were major concerns. Moreover, unlike previous missions, MIPONUH was not to undertake patrolling missions. Composed of 290 police officers, including a 90 person special police unit to protect mission personnel and installations, MIPONUH members were further authorized to carry personal weapons. The mandate was for one year and drew personnel from Argentina, Benin, Canada, France, India, Mali, Niger, Senegal, Togo, Tunisia, and the United States. Although the UN peacekeeping operations had come a long way in a relatively short period, Haiti's problems were legion. Nevertheless, the several missions seemed to have accomplished what they could in a country that had only recently become self-governing and was still desperately impoverished. MIPONUH completed its mission and was withdrawn in March 2000. Haiti continued to hold the bottom position in the UN register of country living conditions. Almost 25 percent of its children younger than five years of age were malnourished, and barely more than one-third of the population had access to clean drinking water. One of every twelve Haitians was believed infected with the virus that causes AIDS. Aristide had been returned to the Haitian presidency and remained a popular figure, but even he could do nothing to relieve Haiti's suffering without foreign aid. Moreover, much of that aid had been suspended over election irregularities in 2000, and conditions in the country had gone from worse to desperate. The United Nations gave what assistance it could; however, the Security Council saw no need for further peacekeeping, despite rebellions in 2002 and the overall political instability that plagued the country in 2003.

The United Nations, however, was nevertheless called to answer the plight of the Haitian population in February 2004. Violent opposition to Aristide's government spread across the country and eventually caused Aristide to seek exile in Africa. The United Nations was again called to mount an aggressive peacemaking operation as U.S. and French troops arrived in the country to help restore law and order. The UN Security Council approved a resolution calling on the United Nations, the Caribbean Community and Common Market (CARICOM), and the Organization of American States to "promote the rebuilding of democratic institutions" and combat poverty in the country. In March a new Haitian government was sworn in and immediately welcomed international intervention, at least as long as the country was lifted from anarchy and promised foreign economic assistance.

Haiti, of course, was not the only country in Latin America to draw UN assistance. A UN Observer Group (ONUCA) had functioned in wide-ranging activities in Central America from 1989 to 1992. In a 1960s mission, DOMREP, a representative of the Secretary-General, had been sent to the Dominican Republic to oversee the stabilization of the country after the conflict that provoked the United States to invade the island. ONUSAL had also performed the task of helping restore stability to El Salvador after many years of civil strife. Then too, there was the UN Verification Mission in Guatemala (MINUGUA), created in January 1997 and terminated in May. MINUGUA was called upon to monitor the Comprehensive Agreement on Human Rights that had been signed by the government of Guatemala and the Unidad Revolucionaria Nacional Guatemateca in Mexico City in March 1994. The agreement required the Guatemalan authorities to follow up complaints of human rights violations and to carry out thorough investigations in accordance with human rights norms. Both sides had agreed to a cease-fire and had requested that the United Nations deploy military personnel to verify implementation of their agreement. MINUGUA had the distinction of becoming a full peacekeeping operation under the terms of the agreement. When its mandate ended in May 1997, it nevertheless remained in place, although it ceased being a responsibility of the United Nations. At its height, MINUGUA was authorized a force of 155 military observers and requisite medical personnel.

Eritrea had gained its freedom in 1993 in a protracted struggle with Ethiopia, but there was no peace between the two countries. Fighting erupted in earnest in May 1998 over a disputed border, and Secretary-General Annan contacted the two countries in an attempt to prevent a major clash. Annan arranged for his Special Envoy in Africa to work with the Organization of African Unity (OAU), hoping that a total effort would avert a renewal of old animosities. The two countries met at an OAU summit in July 1999 and accepted plans for the implementation of an OAU framework agreement calling upon Eritrea and Ethiopia to redeploy their forces. A neutral commission was to determine the precise location for the warring forces so that their common border could be demilitarized. Eritrea complied with the arrangement but Ethiopia hesitated, triggering another round of hostilities and the displacement of more people. A special mission from the Security Council visited both African capitals in May 2000 and entered into talks aimed at finding a permanent solution to the conflict. Despite these efforts, however, fighting resumed. The Security Council, sensing a breach of East African peace, indicated a willingness to assist the people caught in the middle of the struggle. On May 17, 2000, the Security Council adopted a resolution calling for sanctions that would deny both countries access to weapons or arms-related assistance. The Council also called for the immediate resumption of peace talks under the auspices of the OAU.

By March 2000 it was estimated that 370,000 Eritreans and 350,000 Ethiopians had been affected by the conflict. The region had suffered from extreme drought conditions, and although UN emergency food aid had been sent, the hostilities prevented supplies from going through. Kofi Annan appointed the director of the UN World Food Program to investigate the situation and explain to the parties that their sustained conflict had put hundreds of thousands of people at risk. Annan also set up a special task force to examine developments in the Horn of Africa, and its findings indicated that timing was essential if a humanitarian disaster was to be averted. The parties to the dispute, however, turned a deaf ear to all entreaties, and it took a diplomatic understanding, orchestrated by the OAU, to finally get the respective governments to reconsider their options. An agreement was arrived at with the help of the Algerian President, the Personal Envoy from the presidency of the European Union, and President Clinton's personal associate, Anthony Lake. To secure the agreement for an immediate cessation of hostilities, on June 31, 2000, the Security Council authorized the UN Mission in Ethiopia and Eritrea (UNMEE). Although a small token force was authorized initially, by December 2002 the military personnel in UNMEE totaled 4,034, with combat forces put at 3,832. Approximately 200 military observers rounded out the force, and support was provided by 227 international civil servants. The UNMEE mandate was extended to March 15, 2003, and after the parties promised to end hostilities, the process began to delimit and demarcate the ambiguous colonial treaty border, to establish a Claims Commission, and to examine the origins of the conflict. In 2002, the Court of Arbitration in The Hague delimited the border, which both countries initially found acceptable, but then Ethiopia registered a complaint when the Ethiopian town of Badme wound up in Eritrean hands. The decision was made, however, to wait on de-mining of the frontier before grievances could be aired. Tensions between Ethiopia and Eritrea had abated but not disappeared, notably because prisoners of war had not yet been exchanged. UNMEE therefore still had work to do.

### The Changing Form of Peacekeeping

Kosovo had presented a different kind of peacekeeping experience. Although the United Nations had been embedded in the peacekeeping design there, UN operations depended on a NATO presence to separate and disarm the parties, end the hostilities, and establish a successful ad hoc administrative apparatus.

UN Security Council Resolution 1244 of June 12, 1999, established the ground-work for the creation of an interim administration for Kosovo. This resolution, the Military Technical Agreement on the withdrawal of Yugoslav forces from the province, and NATO's Operation Joint Guardian formed the foundation for KFOR's role in Kosovo. Together, the joint UN/NATO deployment was aimed at (1) deterring renewed hostility and threats against Kosovo by Yugo-slav and Serb forces; (2) establishing a secure environment and ensuring public safety and order; (3) disarming the KLA; (4) providing support for the interna-tional humanitarian effort; and (5) coordinating and supporting the interna-tional civil presence, that is, UNMIK. Under the terms of the Military Techni-cal Agreement signed by both NATO and Yugoslav commanders on June 9, 1999, the Yugoslav Army and Interior Ministry Police withdrew from both Kosovo and a five-kilometer-wide Ground Safety Zone between the province and the rest of the Federal Republic of Yugoslavia. The Agreement governed the relationship between NATO's KFOR and Yugoslav forces. In addition, the presence of some forty thousand fully equipped and well-trained NATO troops in the region acted as a powerful deterrent to renewed hostilities. UN peace-keeping capabilities could not have managed the Kosovo problem alone. More-over, because of KFOR's overwhelming presence, it was possible for the return of an agreed number of Yugoslav military and police personnel to be permitted for specific purposes and tasks, such as clearing minefields and providing a Serb presence at patrimonial sites dear to the Serb people. The gesture went a long way in easing the Kosovo transition from Yugoslav/Serb dominance to a neu-tral international administrative regime. UNMIK, for its part, managed the po-lice work and interfaced with KFOR's military role. KFOR alone conducted be-tween 500 and 750 patrols each day and stood guard over five hundred key sites. A stronger police force would have reduced KFOR's burden, but UNMIK faced a shortage of funds from the beginning of its mission, and it has not had the manpower or expertise to deal effectively with criminal elements or to se-cure minority activity. Nevertheless, KFOR and UNMIK work in tandem, and the latter has assumed responsibility for humanitarian issues, such as opening schools, treating medical problems, and setting up civil administration. Since September 11, KFOR and UNMIK have also engaged in antiterrorist operations.

Afghanistan, heretofore the central base for Al-Qaeda, was the scene of sig-nificant fighting, precipitated by the United States in pursuit of Osama bin La-den and his followers after September 11, 2001. The U.S.-led assault that be-gan in October 2001 brought down the Taliban government of Mullah Omar and replaced it with a provisional Afghan government under the leadership of Hamid Karzai. While U.S., British, Canadian, and Australian Special Forces continued their campaign to destroy the Al-Qaeda operation in Afghanistan and their Taliban supporters, the Karzai government diligently sought to re-store a degree of normalcy in the country. Karzai was made responsible for everyday administration and was protected by an International Security Assis-tance Force (ISAF) authorized by the Security Council but not controlled by the

United Nations. The unsettled nature of the country after more than two decades of brutal conflict, however, was made even more fragile by the prominence of regional leaders equipped with personal militias and often at odds with one another.

With the border areas harboring Al-Qaeda and the Taliban, and with local warlords refusing to accept Karzai's authority, the task of reconstructing a national infrastructure proved daunting. Moreover, with ISAF confined to Kabul, the Afghan countryside was essentially lawless. In March 2002 the UN Security Council authorized the UN Assistance Mission to Afghanistan (UNAMA), which had the task of helping the Karzai government meet its obligations to the Afghan people and integrate all UN activities in Afghanistan. Sixteen UN agencies were established in Afghanistan to work with the Karzai administration, and all UN programs were to lend support to the transition process. UNAMA's mandate therefore lay in promoting national reconciliation, in meeting the responsibilities entrusted to the United Nations in the Bonn Agreement that paved the way for the creation of the new government, and in promoting human rights, the rule of law, and equality for women. Overall, UNAMA was responsible for humanitarian, relief, recovery, and reconstruction activities, while U.S. Special Forces and ISAF contributing countries engaged in fighting terrorism and building the necessary military and police establishments for the new Afghan government. UNAMA's administrative division administered a budget for 2003 of nearly $38 million and employed 443 staff members that included 175 international aid workers and 268 Afghan nationals. Unlike ISAF, however, UNAMA operated in different regions of the country at great risk to the UN workers and their employees. Regional offices were located in Bamiyan, Gardez, Herat, Jelalabad, Kandahar, Kunduz, and Mazar-i-Sharif, scenes of some of the most vicious fighting. UN liaison offices also were opened in Islamabad (Pakistan) and Teheran (Iran). UNAMA functioned on the basis of Afghan needs and priorities. Its goal was to relieve the expatriates and in time staff all operations with Afghan personnel.

UNAMA strives to inculcate values of good governance, law and order, and security. Considerable emphasis is given to increasing employment by paying for services in cash that can be immediately reintroduced into the Afghan economy. With Resolution 1444 the Security Council authorized an extension of ISAF's tenure to run through December 2003. UN member states were authorized to contribute personnel, equipment, and other resources to the force and to make contributions to the Trust Fund established through Resolution 1386 (2001), which defined ISAF's authorization. Great Britain assumed charge of ISAF in its initial phase; this was followed by Turkish and then joint German and Netherlands leadership. On August 10, 2003, ISAF became the responsibility of NATO, representing the first time in the history of the organization that it extended its operations beyond Europe. Present for the dramatic turnover was Afghan President Hamid Karzai, German Defense Minister Peter Struck, and NATO's Supreme Commander General James Jones. NATO's succession to the leadership of ISAF symbolized the international commitment to Afghanistan's transformation to a peaceful state. It also ended the arduous task of searching every six months for a new "lead nation" to manage ISAF.

The thirty-nation ISAF force created in December 2001 to stabilize the Afghan capital consisted of approximately five thousand troops, 90 percent of them drawn from NATO countries. The troops provided by the fifteen non-NATO countries, though representing a small segment of the force, were also slated to remain. ISAF and UNAMA personnel, however, are targets for insurgents, and numerous members of both organizations have lost their lives trying to restore equilibrium to a war-torn country that has not seen the last of the Taliban or Al-Qaeda. A heavy loss of life among ISAF forces occurred in June 2003 when a suicide bomber killed four German soldiers and wounded twenty-nine others. But despite continuing attacks, Kabul is considered a relatively safe island in a sea of disorder and insecurity.

Rival warlords operate freely in most areas of the country. A vast area along the eastern and southern border with Pakistan is home to warring tribes still loyal to the Taliban and Al-Qaeda, and U.S. Special Forces are heavily committed to the neutralization of that region. With NATO a somewhat permanent fixture in Afghanistan, it became possible to respond more positively to Karzai's request that ISAF be expanded to function in other parts of the country, especially with general elections in Afghanistan scheduled for June 2004. But with NATO also involved in peacekeeping roles in Bosnia and Kosovo, NATO's European members were reluctant to expand ISAF operations. In October 2003, however, the UN Security Council approved establishing ISAF units in other parts of Afghanistan.

The fate of East Timor was placed on the UN General Assembly's agenda in 1960 when the territory was added to the UN list of Non–Self-Governing Territories. Portugal originally held East Timor within its colonial empire, but in 1974, in an effort to give the country its freedom, a provisional government was established. Not all of East Timor's inhabitants welcomed the Portuguese decision, notably those who wanted the territory to be made part of Indonesia. A civil war resulted when opposing groups could not be reconciled. Portugal then decided to abandon the former colony and allow the warring parties to determine their future without its participation. Indonesia, however, filled the power vacuum left by the Portuguese, and in 1976 it absorbed the area and declared it to be its twenty-seventh province. The United Nations refused to recognize the Indonesian action and demanded their withdrawal. Indonesia, however, refused to accept the order, and in 1982 the UN Secretary-General went to both Portugal and Indonesia to determine the future of the East Timor. Although Indonesia insisted that East Timor was an integral part of the archipelago nation, in time the Indonesian government modified its position. In 1999 the United Nations finally received Indonesia's acquiescence to an agreement that efforts would be made to ascertain whether the Timorese wished to acquire special autonomy status within the Republic of Indonesia. Resolution 1246 (1999) of the Security Council authorized the UN Mission for East Timor (UNAMET) to oversee the transition period pending implementation of the results of the polling. In August 1999, 78.5 percent of Timorese voters rejected autonomy and insisted on their independence. Violence and accompanying atrocities committed by those in opposition to the vote as well as elements of the Indonesian Special Forces caused havoc throughout the island. The UN Secretary-General and Security Council engaged in strenuous diplomatic efforts to restore order. By Resolution 1264 the Security Council set up a multinational force led by Australia. The International Force in East Timor (INTERFET) was authorized to establish peace and security in East Timor and to protect and support UNAMET in carrying out its humanitarian tasks.

INTERFET's arrival, with heavily armed Australian troops, was met by an Indonesian decision to withdraw its military forces and administrative personnel. An agreement between Indonesia and Portugal was then reaffirmed transferring authority over East Timor to the United Nations. Another UN Security Council resolution called for the creation of the UN Transitional Administration in East Timor (UNTAET), which was an integrated and multidimensional peacekeeping operation responsible for the full administration of East Timor until political, civil, and social responsibilities could be transferred to the local Timorese population. In February 2000, INTERFET military operations were folded into UNTAET. On August 30, 2001, more than 91 percent of East Timor's eligible voters elected an eighty-eight-member Constituent Assembly for the purpose of writing a constitution for the territory. Transitional governments were created in preparation for East Timor's independence as a sovereign state, and the country's first constitution came into force in March 2002. Xanana Gusmao was elected President of East Timor by an overwhelming margin, and the constituent assembly was transformed into the country's parliament in May 2002. With the inaugural session of the parliament, East Timor became an independent country on May 20, 2002. UN Secretary-General Kofi Annan was on hand with three hundred foreign dignitaries to celebrate the creation of a new sovereign nation. East Timor's request for membership in the United Nations was made directly to the Secretary-General at that time.

The United Nations, however, was not yet done in East Timor. In order to assure stability and security, the Security Council unanimously authorized a UN Mission of Support in East Timor (UNMISET) for an initial period of twelve months to provide assistance to core administrative structures critical to the viability and political stability of the country. UNMISET was also called upon to provide interim law enforcement and public security, as well as to assist in developing the East Timor Police Service. As another cautionary step, UNMISET was made responsible for the country's external security until a Timorese army could be raised. UNMISET was administered by a Special Representative of the Secretary-General and was to be composed of more than 8,000 people, including civilian police, combat-ready soldiers, international civilian staff, experts for the Civilian Support Group, locally recruited staff, and UN volunteers. In 2003 that number was somewhat reduced, but the mission nonetheless was a sizable one. Twenty-nine countries supplied military personnel, and thirty-three sent civilian police experts. Finances for UNMISET came from a UN special account, and the estimated cost of the operation through June 2003 was placed at $305.2 million. East Timor officially became Timor-Leste (the Portuguese spelling of the name) in 2002 and was known by that name when it became the 191st member of the United Nations on September 27, 2002.

## THE UN PEACE FORCE: RETROSPECT AND PROSPECT

In a world overshadowed first by the Cold War and now by the protracted war on worldwide terrorism, the UN peacekeeping force has evolved as a creative alternative to the coercive enforcement action contemplated by the UN Charter. During dangerous periods, UN peacekeeping enables the United Nations to play a constructive role in matters of global security, especially when the larger powers see a common interest in bringing an end to hostilities and maintaining order. Despite U.S.-Soviet hostility during the Cold War, violence was curbed through UN intervention in such diverse places as Indonesia, the Middle East, Kashmir, and Cyprus, without resort to international military sanctions. When Soviet and U.S. interests converged, the UN-authorized international peace force proved a highly useful instrument for performing local police functions, especially during the settlement period. Moreover, it often was in the interest of the superpowers to encourage restraint and to work at separating combatants in volatile situations, even if permanent settlement proved elusive.

Lack of the requisite Soviet-U.S. cooperation, and/or U.S. disenchantment with the United Nations, often left UN peacekeeping in a holding pattern. Military conflicts occurred in many parts of the world—Afghanistan, the Congo, Cambodia, the Falkland Islands, Grenada, Panama, and Iran-Iraq—but the United Nations was hardly irrelevant. Even in such conflicts the United Nations played a role, even if at best a marginal one. UN mediation in the Soviet-Afghanistan matter was important in gaining the Soviet withdrawal, even though a UN force interposed between the parties was unthinkable. The United Nations could not prevent the terrible loss of life in Cambodia, but in due course the world body was instrumental in reviving a shattered polity. Neither Iran nor Iraq would listen to voices of reason that urged an end to hostilities, but the conscience of humanity could not be ignored, and it reminded the combatants time and again of their mutual responsibilities to bring an end to their bloodletting.

Judged in terms of political feasibility, the future of peacekeeping appears ever more important. Despite a record of peacekeeping setbacks, there are successes too, and cooperation among major powers in the Security Council can allow for timely and forthright decisions. Since the end of the Cold War, states in crisis seem more willing to accept UN assistance, in part because the organization continues to represent universal moral and political standards. This also is because the world organization reflects, even if not clearly articulated, the overwhelming desire of the world's population for peace and security. This hardly removes the significant political obstacles to effective UN peacekeeping, such as the problem of obtaining cooperation from rival ethnic, tribal, and religious groups. Moreover, the global threat posed by transnational terrorism requires innovative thinking and collective response. UN peacekeeping establishes the conditions for feasible political debate; the dilemma of contemporary terrorism appears to lie in terrorists' lack of willingness to reason or place limits on their violent actions. There is also the implicit understanding that sovereign nation-states cannot negotiate, let alone compromise, with terrorists. Finding solutions to the modern predicament wherein groups, and even individuals, threaten humankind will test UN peacekeeping as never before.

Financial feasibility, of course, remains an ever-present constraint. In the past the funding problem was in large part a political problem resulting from disagreement over the establishment, control, and functioning of peacekeeping operations. Today the issue is primarily one of spending priorities—how much are governments willing to spend on UN peacekeeping in relation to other domestic and international demands on their resources? The costs have escalated. In 1987 UN peacekeeping assessments totaled $233 million; in 2002 peacekeeping assessments totaled $2.25 *billion*. In recent years, given the expansion of tribunals and the need to meet their costs, the acquisition of funds from member states has been difficult, requiring a transfer of money from the peacekeeping to the tribunal budget. Peacekeeping payments to contributing countries also have been a constant problem, with money owed to member states made dependent on payments received from states with significant arrears. Nevertheless, the General Assembly in 2002 decided there should be no further borrowing from active peacekeeping missions, and a resolution provided that the peacekeeping reserve fund may be used only for the requirements of new and expanded peacekeeping operations, pending the receipt of assessed contributions. Accordingly, only cash balances in inactive missions could be drawn to meet temporary cash shortfalls in other accounts. The budgeting complications for peacekeeping are a reflection of the uncertainties in every mission. Missions are designated in times of crisis without a complete understanding of their financial cost. The needs of the different missions cannot be known in advance. Faced with reluctant contributing states, the Secretariat preparing peacekeeping budgets tries to hold expenditures to a minimum, but the best of intentions are not usually enough and member states do not always pay their share. By 2002 peacekeeping arrears were $1.34 billion, with the United States owing $536 million, or 40 percent. Nine of 14 major contributors to peacekeeping operations owed another $494 million, or 37 percent, and 161 others owed a total of $305 million, or 23 percent. Improvements in U.S. payments in 2003 reduced outstanding contributions further. By May 31, 2003, peacekeeping arrears were about $1.15 billion.

As of June 2003, fifty-six peacekeeping operations had been organized since 1948, and thirteen were ongoing. The peacekeeping budget for 2002–03 was $2.63 billion, with approved budgets for 2003–04 of $2.17 billion. As of May 2003, a total of 34,941 military personnel and civilian police from eighty-nine countries were working in peacekeeping operations, along with more than

3,000 international civilian personnel and approximately 6,500 local civilian employees.

The total estimated cost of UN peacekeeping operations from 1948 to June 2003 was approximately $28.73 billion. The UN Secretary-General has suggested that member states treat peacekeeping costs as part of their defense budgets, not as foreign affairs expenditures. Typically, national defense budgets are much larger than the budgets of foreign ministries, and contributions to UN peacekeeping could rationally be regarded as serving the interests of national security. If adopted (and national defense establishments may resist a new demand on their resources), this alteration in national budgetary practice could make it politically more acceptable for some countries to allot funds to UN peacekeeping. Generally, domestic support is greater for "national defense" than for "foreign aid" or "international organizations." By comparison with amounts governments spend on their national defense, usually in the many billions, the few hundred millions spent each year by UN peacekeepers is a very small price in the effort to build international cooperation, as well as to ensure peace and security.

Nevertheless, with the United States reevaluating the cost of peacekeeping, and Russia seriously stressed in meeting its assessed peacekeeping budget, UN peacekeeping must continually confront the issue of financial feasibility. The peacekeeping expertise of the UN Secretariat and its cadre of peacekeepers is a valuable international asset under any circumstances. In past years this resource was underutilized. In the United Nations of the new millennium, however, the demands for UN peacekeeping services can be greater than the members are willing to support. With limited resources, the United Nations cannot intervene everywhere it is invited, or everywhere serious violence is threatened. It must make choices, which means that setting priorities and guidelines for future UN peacekeeping is one of the more compelling questions now facing the organization. This is particularly true in view of proposals to use peacekeeping forces in situations where the consensual basis for the UN mission breaks down, or perhaps never existed, and military force must be used. Peacekeeping undoubtedly plays a central role in the UN security system of the twenty-first century, but the challenge to adapt to changing needs remains.

Peacekeeping is not only difficult, it also is often a thankless activity—and dangerous. Since the United Nations began assisting nations challenged by extreme deprivation, insecurity, threat, and aggressive intent, almost two thousand peacekeepers have lost their lives. Often in harm's way, with little to protect them other than the blue beret that marks their impartiality, peacekeepers are at the mercy of those who have created the conditions they seek to temper. In fifty years of UN peacekeeping, more than 750,000 military and civilian police personnel, and thousands of civilians, have given their services. (See Table 5-1 and Figure 5-1.)

It is important to note that while the Secretary-General is usually at the center of each peacekeeping operation, it is the Security Council that sets each one in motion. Given the veto power of the permanent members, a mission can

Figure 5-1    United Nations Peacekeeping Operations

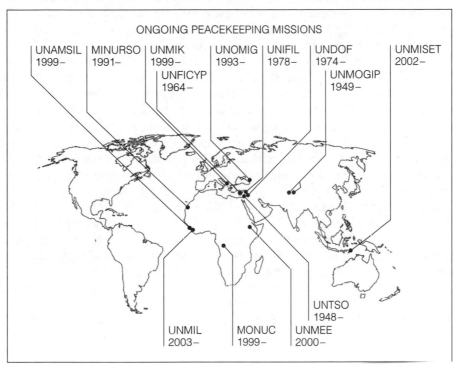

ONGOING PEACEKEEPING MISSIONS

| UNAMSIL | MINURSO | UNMIK | UNOMIG | UNIFIL | UNDOF | UNMISET |
| 1999– | 1991– | 1999– | 1993– | 1978– | 1974– | 2002– |

UNFICYP 1964–

UNMOGIP 1949–

UNTSO 1948–

| UNMIL | MONUC | UNMEE |
| 2003– | 1999– | 2000– |

Peacekeeping operations since 1948                                                        56
Current operations                                                                          13

### Personnel (31 December 2003)

Military personnel and civilian police serving in peacekeeping operations          45,732
Countries contributing military personnel and civilian police                          94
International civilian personnel                                                       3,269
Local civilian personnel                                                              6,369
Total number of fatalities in peacekeeping operations since 1948                      1,821

### Financial Aspects

Approved budgets, 1 July 2003–30 June 2004                          c. $2.81 billion
Estimated total cost of operations, 1948–30 June 2004              c. $31.54 billion
Outstanding contributions to peacekeeping, 31 December 2003         c. $1.07 billion

Source: Map 4000(E) Rev. 23, United Nations Department of Public Information, Cartographic Section (October 2003). Available on UN Web site (http://www.un.org/Depts/dpko/dpko/home.shtml), posted 10 January 2004; prepared by the United Nations Department of Public Information, Peace and Security Section, in consultation with the Department of Peacekeeping Operations and the Peacekeeping Financing Division, Office of Programme Planning, Budget and Accounts.

Note: The term "military personnel" refers to military observers and troops, as applicable. Fatality figures include military, civilian police, and international and local personnel in United Nations peacekeeping operations only.

be rejected by any one of them. Similarly, ultimate command and control of a nation's designated force of peacekeepers remains with the contributing government, and that government can withdraw a force at any time and for any reason. Up to 2003, 110 nations had contributed personnel to UN missions. The countries contributing the largest number of peacekeepers during the 1990s were Pakistan, Bangladesh, Jordan, Poland, the Russian Federation, and Canada, in that order. Moreover, the island of Fiji and Canada have taken part in virtually every UN peacekeeping operation.

Having noted that peacekeeping is linked more to diplomacy than to warfare, the activity rests on a foundation of good faith, not military capability. Thus peacekeeping must be separated from and contrasted with the enforcement that is so often confused with it. Peacekeeping requires the consent of all parties, that is, the peacekeeping contributors, and most important, the countries where the forces are deployed. Enforcement procedures do not require consent, and the United Nations has used it sparingly, for example, in Bosnia, Somalia, Rwanda, Haiti, and Iraq. Clearly, contributing governments are more prepared to provide forces for peacekeeping than for enforcement purposes. For example, considering the threat posed to the "safe havens" in Bosnia, UN efforts that were aimed at raising the necessary force to protect them were unsuccessful. Instead of the thirty-five thousand troops authorized by the Security Council, only seventy-six hundred were made available, and that smaller number took a whole year to assemble. Similarly, genocide was not unanticipated in Rwanda, and the Security Council was unanimous in its call for fifty-five hundred troops to avert the tragedy. Nevertheless, it took six months to mobilize the needed force, and by the time it was deployed the bloodletting had already run its course.

Chastened by these tragic events, the United Nations of the twenty-first century will stress the need for cooperation with regional organizations. Co-deployment with other international organizations is now a matter of normal activity. The Organization of American States (OAS), the African Union (formerly the Organization of African Unity), the Economic Community of West African States (ECOWAS), the Organization of Security and Cooperation in Europe (OSCE), the Commonwealth of Independent States (CIS), and the North Atlantic Treaty Organization (NATO) now function alongside the United Nations. Operations such as the Implementation Force (IFOR) and Stabilization Force (SFOR) in Bosnia-Herzegovina, the Kosovo Force (KFOR), and the International Security Assistance Force (ISAF) in Afghanistan; the use of the Australian-led INTERFET in Timor-Leste; the European/African action led by the French in the Congo and Ivory Coast; and the British role in Sierra Leone all point to different applications of Chapter VII Charter responsibilities. A case in point was Australia's response to the turmoil in the Solomon Islands in June 2003. The Australian government acknowledged the lawless situation in the Solomons, a near neighbor, and publicly declared its intention to intervene. Declaring that sovereignty was not an absolute right of state independence and that the doctrine of preemption in the war on terrorism was valid and germane,

Australia saw no need to ask for UN permission to act in a matter that concerned its vital national interests. If in fact Australia reinforced the U.S. view that unilateral action in military matters is an available option to individual nation-states, the implications for UN collective security operations were significant. UN peacekeeping in the future will more than likely focus attention on matters requiring the largely even-handed nature of Chapter VI Charter provisions, rather than Chapter VII enforcement requirements. Finally, it bears mentioning that while UN peacekeepers are often criticized for being inept or unprepared for the task assigned them, the appearance of ineptness is more a consequence of an international organization laboring to do the world's work in an arena of particular and exclusive nation-states.

## NOTES

1. General Assembly Resolution 377 (V), November 3, 1950.
2. The United Nations has defined peacekeeping as "an operation involving military personnel, but without enforcement powers, undertaken by the United Nations to help maintain or restore international peace and security in areas of conflict." United Nations, *The Blue Helmets: A Review of United Nations Peacekeeping* (New York: United Nations Department of Public Information, 1990), p. 4.
3. Mikhail Gorbachev, "Realities and Guarantees for a Secure World," reprinted in Richard A. Falk, Samuel S. Kim, and Saul H. Mendlovitz, eds., *The United Nations and a Just World Order* (Boulder, CO: Westview Press, 1991), p. 13.

## SELECTED READINGS

Ayoob, Mohammed. *The Third World Security Predicament: State Making, Regional Conflict, and the International System.* Boulder, CO: Lynne Rienner, 1994.

Benton, Barbara, ed. *Soldiers for Peace: Fifty Years of United Nations Peacekeeping.* New York: Facts on File, 1996.

Bowett, D. W. *United Nations Forces: A Legal Study.* London: Stevens and Sons, 1964.

Boyd, Gavin. *Regionalism and Global Security.* Lexington, MA: Heath, 1984.

Claude, Inis L., Jr. *Power and International Relations.* New York: Random House, 1962.

Damrosch, Lori Fisler, and David J. Scheffer, eds. *Law and Force in the New International Order.* Boulder, CO: Westview Press, 1991.

Daniel, Donald C. F., et al. *Coercive Inducement and the Containment of International Crises.* Washington, DC: U.S. Institute of Peace Press, 1999.

Dinan, Desmond. *Encyclopedia of the European Union.* Boulder, CO: Lynne Rienner, 1998.

Doxey, Margaret P. *International Sanctions in Contemporary Perspective.* New York: St. Martin's Press, 1987.

Durch, William J., ed. *UN Peacekeeping, American Politics, and the Uncivil Wars of the 1990s.* New York: St. Martin's Press, 1996.

Durch, William J., and Barry M. Blechman. *Keeping the Peace: The United Nations in the Emerging World Order.* Washington, DC: Henry L. Stimson Center, 1992.

Finkelstein, Marina S., and Lawrence S. Finkelstein, eds. *Collective Security.* San Francisco: Chandler, 1966.

Goodrich, Leland M., and Anne P. Simons. *The United Nations and the Maintenance of International Peace and Security.* Washington, DC: Brookings Institution, 1955.

Gordenker, Leon, and Thomas G. Weiss, eds. *Soldiers, Peacekeepers and Disasters.* London: Macmillan, 1991.

Hampson, Fen Osler, and David M. Malone, eds. *From Reaction to Conflict Prevention: Opportunities for the UN System.* Boulder, CO: Lynne Rienner, 2002.

Higgins, Rosalyn. *United Nations Peacekeeping, Documents and Commentary.* 4 vols. London: Oxford University Press, 1969–81.

Ishiyama, John T., and Marijke Breuning. *Ethnopolitics in the "New Europe."* Boulder, CO: Lynne Rienner, 1998.

James, Alan. *Peacekeeping in International Politics*. London: Macmillan, in association with the International Institute for Strategic Studies, 1990.

Lepgold, Joseph, and Thomas G. Weiss, eds. *Collective Conflict Management and Changing World Politics*. Albany, NY: SUNY Press, 1997.

Mackinlay, John. *The Peacekeepers: An Assessment of Peacekeeping Operations at the Arab-Israeli Interface*. London: Unwin Hyman, 1989.

Mills, Susan R. *The Financing of United Nations Peacekeeping Operations*. Occasional Paper No. 3. New York: International Peace Academy, 1989.

Murphy, John F. *The United Nations and the Control of International Violence: A Legal and Political Analysis*. Totowa, NJ: Allanheld, Osmun, 1982.

Otunnu, Olara A., and Michael W. Doyle. *Peacemaking and Peacekeeping for the New Century*. Lanham, MD: Rowman and Littlefield, 1998.

Pugh, Michael, and Waheguru Pal Singh Sidhu, eds. *The United Nations and Regional Security: Europe and Beyond*. Boulder, CO: Lynne Rienner, 2003.

Rhodes, Carolyn. *The European Union in the World Community*. Boulder, CO: Lynne Rienner, 1998.

Rikhye, Indar Jit. *The Theory and Practice of Peacekeeping*. London: C. Hurst for the International Peace Academy, 1984.

Rikhye, Indar Jit, and Kjell Skjelsbaek, eds. *The United Nations and Peacekeeping: Results, Limitations and Prospects—The Lessons of 40 Years' Experience*. New York: St. Martin's Press, 1991.

Rosner, Gabriella E. *The United Nations Emergency Force*. New York: Columbia University Press, 1963.

Royal Institute of International Affairs. *International Sanctions*. London: Oxford University Press, 1938.

Skogmo, Bjorn. *UNIFIL: International Peacekeeping in Lebanon, 1978–1988*. Boulder, CO: Lynne Rienner, 1989.

Sriram, Chandra Lekha, and Karin Wermester, eds. *From Promise to Practice: Strengthening UN Capacities for the Prevention of Violent Conflict*. Boulder, CO: Lynne Rienner, 2003.

United Nations. *The Blue Helmets*. 2nd ed. New York: UNDPI, 1990.

———. *The United Nations and the Maintenance of International Peace and Security*. United Nations Institute for Training and Research. Dordrecht: Martinus Nijhoff, 1987.

Urquhart, Brian. *A Life in Peace and War*. New York: Harper & Row, 1987.

Wainhouse, David W. *International Peace Observation: A History and Forecast*. Baltimore: Johns Hopkins University Press, 1966.

Weiss, Thomas. *The United Nations and Civil Wars*. Boulder, CO: Lynne Rienner, 1995.

Weiss, Thomas G., and Jarat Chopra. *United Nations Peacekeeping: An ACUNS Teaching Text*. The Academic Council on the United Nations System, Reports and Papers 1992–1.

Wesley, Michael. *Casualties of the New World Order: The Causes of Failure of UN Missions to Civil Wars*. New York: St. Martin's Press, 1997.

White, N. D. *The United Nations and the Maintenance of International Peace and Security*. New York: Manchester University Press, 1990.

# 6

## The Settlement
## of International Disputes

Collective security was never seen as the answer to all global problems of peace and security. Whatever the deterrent effect of UN enforcement machinery, the underlying sources of international tension and conflict would still exist. Countries would continue to have disputes with one another, with the ever-present possibility that some controversies might escalate into a violent exchange. The UN Charter acknowledges this problem by encouraging states to use existing methods of peaceful settlement and by providing additional options found throughout the UN system.

Before examining the UN role in the pacific settlement of disputes, this chapter will describe the traditional settlement procedures and practices that have become an accepted part of international law and through which most disputes are settled. We will then look at the UN contribution to see what world organization has added to the procedures and machinery already available. This includes understanding and appraising in general the work of the International Court of Justice, which technically is a principal organ of the United Nations but renders decisions independent of the other organs. A subsequent section will examine a sampling of disputes that have come before the General Assembly and Security Council to illustrate how the system operates in practice, including its capabilities and limitations. A concluding section will render judgment on the UN's performance in dispute settlement, on efforts to hold government officials responsible for human rights violations, and the formation of institutions that modify the principle of absolute state sovereignty.

## PROCEDURES FOR SETTLING
## INTERNATIONAL DISPUTES

The international norm of peaceful settlement is set forth in Article 2, Paragraph 1, of the UN Charter, which states, "All Members shall settle their international disputes by peaceful means in such a manner that international peace and security, and justice, are not endangered." On its face the injunction to settle disputes appears obligatory, but in fact no UN organ has authority to require states to settle a dispute or to accept any particular form of settlement. A dispute could go unresolved indefinitely without constituting a Charter violation. The obligation, rather, is to *try* peaceful settlement and, in any event, not to seek resolution of a controversy by the use of violence.

Most of the common procedures for settlement of international disputes are listed in Article 33, Paragraph 1, of the Charter:

> The parties to any dispute, the continuance of which is likely to endanger the maintenance of international peace and security, shall, first of all, seek a solution by negotiation, inquiry, mediation, conciliation, arbitration, judicial settlement, resort to regional agencies or arrangements, or other peaceful means of their choice.

All of these techniques of dispute resolution were embodied in international law and practice well before the advent of the United Nations. The Charter merely recognizes their existence and encourages their use. The procedure of "good offices," to be discussed shortly, is another time-honored approach to dispute settlement. Unlike the procedures listed in Article 33, which parties to a dispute are urged to use, good offices depends entirely on the initiative of third parties.

Except for negotiation, each of the procedures requires the assistance of third parties, that is, people not directly involved in the dispute. Most are also *political* rather than *judicial* modes of settlement, in the sense that parties are left free to accept or reject proposed settlements, as their interests dictate and their capacities permit. Third-party assistance is concerned primarily with finding some common ground where agreement can be reached. Arbitration and judicial settlement, however, are in the judicial mode because (1) the basis of decision is supposed to be international law rather than national interest and power, and (2) the decisions are legally binding on the parties that accept these settlement procedures in a particular case.

*Negotiation* among parties to a dispute is older than the state system and is the most common method of settlement. It involves direct discussion by appointed representatives of the states concerned for the purpose of reaching agreement on matters at issue. Successful negotiation normally requires a good faith effort on the part of the negotiators to achieve compromise solutions that serve the national interests of all parties.

*Good offices* (not mentioned in Article 33) is the name given to friendly assistance rendered by a third party for the purpose of bringing disputants together so that they may seek to reach a settlement. Good offices may be offered by a state through an official representative or by a group of states. Good offices also can be associated with an individual of international stature, such as the UN Secretary-General. The procedure involves a third-party representative meeting separately with each party to a dispute, and the representative may, with the consent of the parties, convey messages between them. Technically, good offices are limited to facilitating negotiation by the states directly concerned and do not include discussion of substantive issues. Good offices are particularly useful where the disputing parties have broken off diplomatic relations or where negotiations have been interrupted and neither side takes the initiative to resume them, possibly out of pride, or then again, out of fear that such action would be an indication of weakness.

*Mediation* occurs when a third party actively participates in the discussion of substantive issues and offers proposals for settlement. If the disputants are not speaking, the mediator may also tender good offices as a prelude to mediation. The mediator may meet with the parties either separately or jointly and is expected to maintain an attitude of impartiality throughout. The mediator can expect little success unless he or she enjoys the confidence of all parties. The mediator's proposals are suggestions only, with no binding force on any party. Disputants are of course free to reject an offer to mediate.

*Inquiry,* or *enquiry,* may be used when the disputing parties are unable or unwilling to agree on points of fact relating to a controversy but are willing to let an impartial commission investigate and report on the facts. The parties need not accept the findings of the inquiry, but they usually do. The inquiry is limited to matters of fact and does not include proposed terms of settlement. Many international disputes hinge on disputed questions of fact, and inquiry may be a means of lowering tensions as well as reducing the area of disagreement.

*Conciliation* is a procedure for settling a dispute by referring it to a commission, or occasionally a single conciliator, charged to examine the facts and recommend a solution that the parties are free to accept or reject. Conciliation is more formal and not as flexible as mediation. Whereas mediation is a continuing process of assisting negotiations among parties to a dispute, conciliation involves formal submission of the dispute to a conciliation body in anticipation of a final report containing the conciliator's findings and recommendations for settlement. The boundaries between the two tend to blur in practice because the conciliator usually confers informally with the parties, hoping to arrive at an area of agreement. Moreover, in UN parlance, such terms as mediation, conciliation, and good offices are frequently used without careful reference to the legal distinctions among them. Thus a UN conciliator may in reality be a mediator who also finds it necessary to render good offices and never has occasion to publish a formal recommendation for settlement.

*Arbitration* is a procedure by which disputants agree to submit a controversy to judges of their own choosing, who render a legally binding decision based on principles of international law. Commonly, each side names one or two arbitrators, and those two or four designate one additional arbitrator to complete the panel. The essential characteristics of arbitration are (1) free choice of judges (arbitrators), (2) respect for international law, and (3) obligation to comply with the award. The parties frequently stipulate in the arbitral agreement (*compromis*) the particular rules of law or equity, or even special rules, that are to be applied. The parties are relieved of their obligation to accept or carry out the award only if the arbitrators disregard instructions laid down in the *compromis*. Arbitration is at least as old as the ancient Greek city-states, and within the modern state system it enjoyed a substantial renaissance during the nineteenth and early twentieth centuries. Since 1945 arbitration has been used extensively in resolving trade and investment disputes but less frequently to resolve political disputes between states. Some exceptions may be noted, however. The Rann of Kutch arbitration between India and Pakistan in 1965–66 brought a peaceful end to a violent confrontation over a swampy borderland near the Arabian Sea. Iran's seizure in 1979 of the U.S. embassy in Tehran and the incarceration of its staff for forty-four months caused a severe rupture in the relations of the two nations. The release of the American hostages in 1981, however, led to the establishment of the U.S.-Iran Claims Tribunal, which subsequently arbitrated hundreds of claims. By 1990, the Tribunal had awarded more than $6 billion to U.S. citizens, corporations, and banks, while more than $1 billion was paid to the government of Iran and its citizens. Still another contentious dispute between Chile and Argentina was resolved through a Vatican-assisted arbitration when in 1984 Argentina accepted Chilean sovereignty over islands in the Beagle Channel. Chile in turn yielded to Argentina's claim on the Atlantic side of Cape Horn, thus ending their one-hundred-year-old controversy.

*Judicial settlement* or *adjudication,* like arbitration, produces legally binding awards or judgments based on rules of international law. Unlike arbitration, judges are not chosen by the contesting parties but are members of a preconstituted international tribunal. Judicial settlement of disputes between states involves the voluntary acceptance by the parties themselves. States agree either through advance agreement to accept the jurisdiction of the court in special types of cases or through agreement when the dispute is submitted for adjudication. The same is generally true of arbitration. The International Court of Justice (ICJ) and its predecessor from League of Nations days, the Permanent Court of International Justice, provide the principal examples of judicial settlement at the global level. The League Court was not widely used, and the ICJ docket has until recently been even less crowded. Decisions have generally been carried out, but no effective means have been available to enforce Court decisions against recalcitrant states that have ignored their obligation to comply. Noncompliance is most common in cases involving controversies over the Court's jurisdiction. At the regional level the Court of Justice of the European Union has been extensively used and is a highly successful organ of judicial settlement.

# UN PRACTICE

The Charter provides broad authorization for UN involvement in any dispute serious enough to threaten international peace and security. Although the Security Council is given preeminence, the General Assembly is also authorized to consider questions of peace and security. The Assembly may not, however, make any recommendation as long as the Security Council is exercising jurisdiction over a question. A dispute may be submitted to the Council or the Assembly by one of the parties, by any member of the United Nations, or by the

Secretary-General. Neither body can *impose* a final settlement on any party to a dispute, but the Charter places no limits on UN organs in *recommending* procedures or terms of settlement.

UN organs utilize most of the traditional techniques of dispute settlement, and submission of a dispute to the Security Council or the Assembly has something in common with the procedure of conciliation. The United Nations becomes a third party that examines the facts of the dispute and renders a decision that the parties are free to accept or reject. But the UN political setting and procedures make the process considerably different from traditional forms of conciliation. Recourse to conciliation generally assumes that both sides are willing to submit the dispute to an impartial commission in hope of reaching an acceptable compromise. Most disputes before the United Nations, however, come not as agreed submissions but as complaints brought by one party against another or by a third state without necessarily obtaining the consent of either party to the dispute.

The United Nations, moreover, is not always impartial toward the disputes brought before it. Its members are not free from being partisan and are often bitterly divided. Nations frequently take complaints there not for the purpose of seeking an agreed compromise but to legitimize the position of one side or another. The parties themselves participate in the discussion and may be more interested in scoring debating points before the bar of world opinion than in honestly seeking common ground for agreement. One example is the ICJ's decision to hold three days of hearings, prompted by a resolution in the General Assembly, on Israel's construction of what it considered a security barrier that separated Israelis from West Bank Palestinians. The Israeli government declined to participate in the debate before the Court but nevertheless lodged a formal brief protesting interference with its sovereign right to protect its citizens. Such exchanges may widen the gulf between parties, harden their positions, and do more harm than repair relations. The public nature of UN debate facilitates the appeal to world opinion but often at the expense of viable compromise that might emerge from the privacy and quiet deliberation of traditional conciliation.

The UN process thus is sui generis, a new approach to dispute settlement having strengths and weaknesses. The public debate pattern is only part of the picture, and even that is not wholly negative. Public debate makes UN members aware of rival positions and sometimes helps clarify facts. Although speeches and supporting documentation submitted by the parties are mostly self-serving versions of a case, they can be informative as well. Public debate also provides governments with a way to "blow off steam," particularly in situations where an objectionable act has been committed, no redress is in sight, and retaliation is not feasible. When Soviet troops occupied Afghanistan, and when Soviet aircraft shot down a South Korean civilian airliner over the Sea of Japan, denunciation in the United Nations was a way for the United States to express outrage, uphold principle, and score a few propaganda points at little cost or risk. When the USS *Vincennes* mistakenly downed an unarmed Iranian passenger aircraft over the Strait of Hormuz, Iran had the satisfaction of publicly excoriating the United States before the Security Council. Giving and receiving public denunciation is of course not limited to large states.

On a more positive note, UN consideration serves the further purpose of legitimizing the involvement of other states that may sometimes be able to exert a moderating influence on the disputants. In the early decades of the United Nations an anticolonial majority was automatic, with the United States frequently using its influence in the world organization to steer parties to a dispute away from extreme positions.

## THE SECURITY COUNCIL

The Security Council has established its preeminence among UN organs in the area of peace and security. During the early postwar years the United States was the prime mover in an effort to enhance the security role of the General Assembly as a means of overcoming the Soviet veto in the Security Council. The effort was so successful that during the early 1950s the Council sometimes went months without discussing a substantive question. The shift of activity away from the Council was only temporary, however. The growing numbers and solidarity of Third World countries undermined U.S. dominance in the Assembly and made the Security Council a relatively more attractive forum for the United States. It became clear that U.S. as well as Soviet interests might require the protection of the great power veto. These developments paved the way for the reemergence of the Security Council as the central security organ of the United Nations. This resurgence was hastened by the Council's inherent advantages over the Assembly that stemmed from its smaller size, its capacity to function continuously, and the primacy assigned to it by the UN Charter.

Although the United Nations appears to thrive on the high visibility of public debate, the more important work of the organization is conducted in quiet consultation and negotiation, and this is certainly true in the case of the Security Council. The delegates tend to follow working procedures that involve prudent and careful preparation, and the day-to-day contact between members allows for a range of interactions that are both formal and informal. Moreover, the assistance provided by staff and senior members of the Secretariat, sometimes even by the Secretary-General, has proved vitally important in the conduct of effective diplomacy. Much of the Security Council's work involves such quiet diplomacy, and if the parties to a dispute are prepared to seek counsel, they generally find Council members agreeable to procedures that are aimed at avoiding embarrassment and maximizing results.

The Security Council is not obligated to discuss every complaint that a state chooses to submit to it, and potentially raucous debate may sometimes be avoided by prior consultation and informal decision not to place an item before the Council. Occasionally the Council has discussed a proposal to put an item on its agenda but failed to obtain the necessary votes to do so. It is important to note that a decision by the Security Council to discuss a matter of peace and security is considered a "procedural question" and thus not subject to the veto.

When the Security Council decides to consider a dispute or threatening situation, numerous techniques are available for dealing with it. Whatever is said in the debating chamber, members of the Council usually approach the parties quietly to explore the possibilities for agreed settlement. Sometimes debate is adjourned, at least temporarily, while exploratory discussions are conducted. Quick agreement on a solution to the underlying substantive dispute is uncommon, but an understanding is frequently reached as to the appropriate limits of Security Council action. The understanding may be that the Council will adjourn without adopting a formal resolution, or will simply urge the parties to seek a solution by negotiation or other peaceful means. However, this was not done following India and Pakistan's testing of nuclear weapons in May 1998. The Security Council met in an emergency session almost immediately after the tests, and it ignored all the subtleties of diplomacy when it demanded, by unanimous vote, that both India and Pakistan refrain from further testing. The Council also called for a halt to the two countries' weapons programs and demanded they sign with due haste the nuclear control agreements, that is, the Nuclear Nonproliferation Treaty and the Comprehensive Nuclear Test Ban Treaty. Moreover, the Security Council resolution denied both India and Pakistan legal status as nuclear powers, hence preventing the two countries from acquiring the legal and formal status as such powers under terms of the 1970 Nonproliferation Treaty. India's indignation was obvious when it quickly denounced the Security Council resolution, calling it "coercive and unhelpful." The Indian foreign ministry said the Security Council action was "grotesque," and it questioned how an organ of the United Nations could address the proud and sovereign state of India in such a condescending manner. The Pakistani government was no less outspoken, accusing the major powers of using the nuclear treaties "to legitimize their own possession of huge nuclear arsenals," but denying others the same sovereign right. The Pakistani delegation informed the Council that nonproliferation is no longer an issue in South Asia. The "real danger" now, was not proliferation but "nuclear conflict," and no amount of "sermonizing and lamentations can rectify or reverse" what was now a reality. Although approving the resolution, a number of nonnuclear states were moved to support the argument made by the South Asian nations that it was time for the permanent members of the Security Council, all of whom were nuclear weapons powers, to seriously reduce their own stockpiles. Seldom had the Security Council been so challenged as a whole. Nor could it be lost on all the major actors that the entire system of global nuclear controls was threatened and that an arms race more unpredictable and more terrifying than any experienced during the Cold War was a possibility. In the superheated environment, the Pakistan ambassador to the United Nations insisted that his country reserve the right to deter aggression through conventional or unconventional means, and the Security Council was urged to accept the existing worldwide power equation and alter its procedures to accommodate the new reality.[1]

Sometimes more than discussion and resolutions is called for by a situation or demanded by members of the Council. The Secretary-General can be authorized to appoint a mediator or to consult with parties and intercede himself as circumstances permit. The Council may occasionally create a special commission of inquiry or conciliation body to deal with a problem. Alternatively, a dispute may be referred to an appropriate regional organization, such as the Organization of American States or the European Union. If hostilities seem imminent, the Council or its President may urge parties to refrain from taking any action that might aggravate a dispute. Should fighting break out, the Council will in all likelihood issue an order for a cease-fire. If one party has occupied the territory of another, the cease-fire order may be accompanied by an order for troop withdrawal. In a number of situations the Security Council has authorized peacekeeping forces and observer missions (discussed in Chapter 5) to help police a cease-fire and avoid renewed violence.

When the Security Council speaks, disputants do not always listen. In his 1982 report on the work of the United Nations, Secretary-General Pérez de Cuéllar lamented that the Council's resolutions "are increasingly resisted or ignored by those that feel themselves strong enough to do so." [2] Although respect for the Council's authority ebbs and flows, this lament still has substance. Israel, perhaps the most frequent target of Security Council censure, has repeatedly disregarded Council resolutions that run counter to its national interests. South Africa did the same for many years, as have many other countries determined to safeguard their independence. For example, in the spring of 1982 Argentina ignored a Security Council demand for a cease-fire in the Falkland Islands; and until 1988, Iraq and Iran persistently flouted Council requests to terminate hostilities. In the 1990–91 Gulf crisis, Iraq rejected numerous Security Council calls for withdrawal from Kuwait, and it yielded only to the use of superior military force. Security Council demands for the cessation of hostilities in Liberia and the Congo in 2002 and 2003 were acknowledged only when the parties saw their interests enhanced, but given sustained instability, the tranquillity achieved soon gave way to more intense fighting. Making peace has proved far more difficult than promoting conflict, and the Security Council is under no delusions about its capacity to ensure lasting compliance with its wishes.

Nevertheless, disregard of Security Council recommendations is not undertaken lightly. According to a former Director-General of Israel's Foreign Ministry, Israeli actions in times of crisis have been heavily influenced by anticipation of what the Security Council might do. In his words:

> Throughout the thirty years of conflict the estimated timing of intervention by the Security Council in the fighting had engaged the closest attention of the military planners of both sides. Strategists and field commanders planned and conducted their campaigns virtually with an eye on the ticking of the United Nations clock. They accelerated the advance or slowed down the retreat of their forces in synchronization with the movements of the clock's hands. The ringing of the Security Council bell was never absent from their mind, because they knew that military means would not finally decide the outcome of the conflict. [3]

Israel's concern was no doubt a response to the history of Security Council intervention in the Middle East, as well as Israel's dependence on U.S. support, which might be alienated if Israel ignored Council actions taken with the approval of the United States. Argentina, Iran, and Iraq, on the other hand, anticipated that Council intervention in their wars would go no farther than harsh words. With regard to Kuwait, Iraq proved to be badly mistaken. And certainly, words alone would never have dislodged Saddam Hussein from Kuwait in 1991. Baghdad's noncompliance with Security Council resolutions calling for Iraq's disarmament, especially in the area of weapons of mass destruction, was designed as a waiting game. In 2003, Iraq played for time in order to divide the Security Council and hence to prevent it from enforcing its own directives. Saddam's miscalculation was only in his failure to read the limits of U.S. power. Judging the actions of the Security Council therefore is a much more complicated task, especially in the current era of global terrorism. Terrorists admit to no constraints save those they impose on themselves; therefore, conventional thinking about avoiding the disapproval of the international community no longer has relevance. Unlike states, terrorist organizations are not in the least concerned with their place in the world community.

## THE GENERAL ASSEMBLY

The General Assembly has also been extensively involved in disputes among UN members, but because it is a very large public forum, its debates and decisions are better adapted to legitimizing the position of one side or another than to promoting a negotiated settlement. During the first ten years of the United Nations, the Assembly overshadowed the Security Council as a forum for airing disputes and threats to the peace. This enhancement of the Assembly's security role occurred mainly as a U.S.-led response to Soviet vetoes in the Security Council. Even then, the most obvious function of the Assembly was legitimizing U.S. and Western positions rather than promoting agreed settlement of issues.

Although the Assembly has since relinquished its primacy to the Security Council, security questions still make up a substantial part of its agenda. In the early years, issues relating to the Middle East and South Africa predominated. But subsequently, conflicts in Cambodia, Grenada, Central America, the Falkland Islands, Afghanistan, Bosnia, Croatia, Kosovo, and an array of African countries have found their way to the Assembly as well as to the Security Council. Since the 1970s, however, the Assembly tends to reflect the foreign policy positions of the more recently independent states, particularly those emerging from colonialism in the post–World War II era. By sheer weight of numbers in the General Assembly their voice has become the legitimating expression of UN activity. The changed character of the Assembly therefore not only mirrors the dominant role played by the developing nations, it also accounts for their repeated opposition to U.S. positions on a variety of issues. It is important to note that whereas the older European nations have learned to accommodate the General Assembly majority, the United States has difficulty in accepting direction from Third World nations. The legitimacy found in numerical judgments, in conditions where the veto does not apply, is noted in Washington's adverse reaction to Libya heading the Commission on Human Rights or Saddam Hussein's Iraq chairing the UN Disarmament Committee, both in 2002.

Dispute settlement, whether indulged in by the Security Council or the Assembly, is often more than a propaganda exercise or display of explosive oratory. If consensus is high, the offending party may look for ways to bring its conduct more in line with the views of the majority without compromising its vital interests. Numerous disputes arising out of the decolonization process have been considered by the Assembly. The substantial progress made by states in achieving their independence and self-government can be traced to diplomatic pressures exerted in the General Assembly.

Occasionally the Assembly has been able to play a third-party role extending beyond legitimization. It authorized peacekeeping operations that helped defuse the 1956 Suez crisis. It also facilitated West Irian's transition from Dutch to Indonesian rule in 1962–63. It took over control of the UN Congo force in 1960 when the Security Council became deadlocked. It deployed a border watch team in Greece from 1947 to 1952, as well as in Korea before the outbreak of the Korean War. Since the West Irian mission in the 1960s, however, the authorization of missions for security purposes has become the exclusive province of the Security Council.

The Assembly can enlist the services of the President of the Assembly or one of its members in promoting quiet negotiations among disputing parties. It can formally appoint a UN mediator to help parties reach agreement, as it did in the early stages of the Arab-Israeli conflict, although mediation is now more likely to be undertaken by the Secretary-General and the Security Council. Like the Security Council, the Assembly has authorized and supported the Secretary-General's peacemaking efforts in the Falklands War, Afghanistan, the Iran-Iraq War, southern Africa, Cyprus, Palestine, Lebanon, Ethiopia and Eritrea, Sierra Leone, Liberia, the Congo, and numerous other places. The convening of the General Assembly each year also provides occasion for high-level diplomatic representatives to gather in New York and, if they choose, to meet privately for an exchange of views and even on some occasions for the resolution of differences.

## THE SECRETARY-GENERAL

The Secretary-General is a very important resource for UN dispute settlement—at the direction of the Security Council or the General Assembly, on his own initiative, or at the request of a disputing party. His operations as a third-party intermediary, acting personally or through a special representative or a special mediator, are generally carried on without the disadvantages of great publicity and public debate. His purposes are also more exclusively focused on settlement, in contrast to the substantive biases that frequently motivate governmental representatives to UN bodies. Where there is genuine room for agreement, the Secretary-General can perform an effective third-party role. The political role of the Secretary-General has already been discussed in Chapter 4.

## THE UNITED NATIONS AND REGIONAL DISPUTE SETTLEMENT

The United Nations was not expected to handle every international dispute that might endanger international peace and security. Article 33 of the Charter urges parties to a dispute to first "seek a solution" through "peaceful means of their own choice," including "resort to regional agencies or arrangements." Since 1945 regional organizations have become an important supplement to UN procedures for pacific settlement. A 1987 study found that four regional agencies—the Organization of American States, the Organization of African Unity, the Arab League, and the Council of Europe—had dealt with 90 disputes from 1945 to 1984, compared with 159 for the United Nations during the same period.[4]

There are no clear guidelines for determining whether a dispute should be handled by a regional organization or by the United Nations. A dominant state within a region might prefer to have intraregional disputes settled locally, where it has greater control, but one of the parties often sees a political advantage in appealing to the United Nations. Until the mid-1960s the United States had considerable success in keeping hemispheric disputes within the Organization of American States. Thereafter inter-American controversies began to appear frequently on UN agendas, but usually over U.S. objections. Since 1988, the United States has accepted a greater UN role in the Americas and supported the establishment of UN observer missions in Central America. The Arab League has always had trouble keeping its quarrels at home because the issues are generally quite divisive. The split in the Arab world over making war on Iraq, especially in 2003, and the earlier decisions by Egypt and later Jordan to make peace with Israel, are just two of the more prominent examples. The Organization of African Unity (renamed the African Union in Durban, South Africa, on June 28, 2002), embracing the vast expanse of the African continent, also finds consensus elusive. Nevertheless, in October 2002 the African Union established an African Economic Council to increase economic integration. It also drafted a Nuclear Weapons–Free Zone Treaty to prohibit nuclear weapons in the African continent.

The techniques of dispute settlement used by regional organizations do not differ from those used by the United Nations. Good offices, inquiry, informal mediation, conciliation, formal debate, adoption of resolutions, cease-fire pleas—all approaches are available. Regional organizations have even resorted to various forms of peacekeeping by a military presence. The Organization of American States authorized a peacekeeping force in the 1965 Dominican crisis, although the OAS action was largely a post hoc ratification of U.S. military intervention. The Arab League established a peacekeeping force in Kuwait from 1961 to 1963, mostly composed of Egyptian and Saudi Arabian troops, to ward off the threat of an Iraqi attack. In 1976, the Arab League legitimized Syrian intervention in Lebanon's civil strife by creating an Arab League force dominated by Syrians. Since 1991 Syria has been the dominant influence in Lebanon, and along with Iran, a principal supporter of Hesbollah, the terrorist organization dedicated to the destruction of Israel. In 1980, the Organization of African Unity authorized a peacekeeping force to operate in Chad for two months. In 1981 and 1982 another force was used for six months but was withdrawn with no appreciable effect on the shifting tides of revolution and outside intervention in that African country. In 1990 the Economic Community of West African States sent a peacekeeping force of seven thousand to curb the violence of Liberia's civil war. ECOWAS and the Organization of African Unity continued to operate alongside UN peacekeeping observers from 1993 to 1997, when the latter mission was phased out. ECOWAS and the OAU became similarly engaged in trying to control the bloodletting in Sierra Leone in 1998 and in the Central African Republic in 1999. When fighting flared again in Liberia in 2003, the African Union sought to pacify the situation. Forces from the Commonwealth of Independent States were deployed in Georgia and Tajikistan after the breakup of the Soviet Union and the subsequent civil strife that consumed those new republics. Given the volatility in Georgia and Tajikistan, a CIS, and notably a Russian presence has been perpetuated. Perhaps the most noted intervention by a regional organization, however, was NATO's replacement of the UNPROFOR mission in 1995. NATO's sustained role in Bosnia-Herzegovina provided the security needed for rebuilding the devastated country. NATO's parallel role in Kosovo not only ended the fighting there, but also led to regime change in Belgrade. The promise of a more peaceful Balkans as a consequence of the sustained NATO intervention cannot be minimized. The emergence of a nascent democratic state as well as democratic practices in the former Yugoslavia (renamed Serbia and Montenegro on January 1, 2003) was dramatized not only by the fall of Slobodan Milošević but by his forceful transfer to the International Criminal Court for trial. Still another dividend of the NATO intervention was the December 2002 signing of an agreement between Yugoslavia and Croatia ending their ten-year dispute over the commercially important Prevlaka Peninsula.

## JUDICIAL DISPUTE SETTLEMENT

As noted in Chapter 2, the International Court of Justice is one of the six principal organs of the United Nations. The ICJ budget is included within the regular UN budget, and its fifteen judges are selected by action of the Security Council and General Assembly. All UN members are ipso facto parties to the ICJ Statute. The Court nevertheless performs its judicial duties independently of the other UN organs and is guided in its decisions by international law rather than international politics. Although its decisions apply only to disputing parties and do not constitute precedents binding on others, its opinions—like those of the League of Nations Court before it—have been recognized as important statements of existing international law. Only states may apply to and appear before the Court; all UN member states (numbering 191 in 2004) are entitled to use its legal services.

The procedure the Court follows in contentious cases is delineated in its

Statute and in Rules of the Court that have been adopted under the Statute. The Rules currently in force were adopted in April 1978. Court proceedings include a written phase in which the parties to a dispute file and exchange pleadings, and an oral phase consisting of public hearings at which agents and counsels address the Court. Because the Court functions in two languages (English and French), whatever is written or presented orally must be translated into one or the other. After the oral proceedings, the Court deliberates privately and later delivers its judgment in a public proceeding. The Court's judgment is final and without appeal, and a state or states that fail to comply may have the matter of their noncompliance brought before the Security Council by the party favored by the judgment. The Court operates as a full Court, but at the request of the parties it may establish a special chamber. The Court constituted a special chamber in 1982 for the first time, and followed with another in 1985, two more in 1987, and two more in 2002. Each year, the Court elects a Chamber of Summary Procedure in accordance with the Court's Statute. In July 1993 the Court also established a seven-member Chamber to deal with any environmental cases falling within its jurisdiction.

In the twenty-five years of its existence, 1921–46, the League Court rendered decisions in thirty-two cases and gave twenty-seven advisory opinions at the request of League organs. This was not a heavy caseload, and the ICJ has been no busier. From 1946 through 2002, the Court delivered just seventy-six judgments in "contentious" cases (actions by one state against another). Thirty-four cases were decided from 1947 to 1960, but only twelve more in the next twenty years. A modest resurgence occurred after 1980, with thirty additional judgments between 1981 and December 2002. Court judgments center on disputes concerning inter alia land frontiers and maritime boundaries, territorial sovereignty, the nonuse of force, noninterference in the internal affairs of states, diplomatic relations, hostage-taking, the right of asylum, nationality, guardianship, rights of passage, and economic rights. In January 2003 one case was being heard and twenty-four cases were pending before the Court.

In addition, since 1946 the Court has been called to issue twenty-four advisory opinions at the request of UN agencies. The advisory procedure is open solely to international organizations, and the only bodies currently authorized to request advisory opinions are the six principal organs of the United Nations and the specialized agencies of the UN system. Requests for advisory opinions can be made in writing or orally, and the Court's procedures follow that used in contentious cases, as well as applicable law. Unlike judgments in contentious cases, the Court's advisory opinions are consultative and hence not binding. Advisory opinions can be made binding, however, if the instruments or regulations that call for the advisory opinion contain specific advance notification. The Court had rendered twenty-four advisory opinions up to 2003. They have included admission to UN membership, reparation for injuries suffered in the service of the United Nations, the territorial status of South-West Africa (Namibia) and the Western Sahara, judgments rendered by international administrative tribunals, expenses of certain UN operations, and the applicability of the

UN Headquarters Agreement. Two advisory opinions were made in July 1996. One was in response to a request made by the World Health Organization on the "Legality of the Use by a State of Nuclear Weapons in Armed Conflict," and another by the UN General Assembly on the "Legality of the Threat or Use of Nuclear Weapons."

The Court's opinions are varied, as was the one rendered in 1998 that unanimously called upon the United States to postpone the execution of a Paraguayan citizen who had been sentenced to death in Virginia. The argument was that the defendant's government had not been consulted and thus the Paraguayan citizen was denied the opportunity to provide legal counsel under terms of established international treaty law. The United States and the state of Virginia, although acknowledging that the government had *not* complied with the Vienna Convention aimed at protecting nationals charged with crimes in other countries, ignored the ruling and proceeded with the execution. A somewhat similar case was brought before the Court by the government of Germany in March 1999. Germany charged the United States with violations of the Vienna Convention on Consular Relations (1963) after the state of Arizona executed a German national and was about to put another, a brother of the deceased, to death. The two brothers had been charged with and found guilty of killing a bank manager in the course of a robbery in Arizona. Germany maintained that the two men were tried and sentenced without being advised of their rights to consular assistance, as required by the Vienna Convention. Germany argued that the failure to provide the required notification precluded it from protecting its nationals' interests in the United States at both the trial and the appeals level in the state courts. Although the German action did not spare the life of the second brother, who was executed on schedule, the German government insisted on pressing its case against the United States. The German government cited Article 1 of the Vienna Convention's Optional Protocol, which states the ICJ had the jurisdiction to resolve the dispute between the United States and Germany on the interpretation or application of the Convention.

The Court has been used sparingly in part because of its limited jurisdiction. Only states—not individuals or organizations—can be parties to a dispute before the Court. Private claimants cannot be represented there unless they can persuade their own governments to plead their cause. Requests for advisory opinions may be submitted only by the General Assembly, the Security Council, or another UN organ or specialized agency previously authorized by the Assembly to make such requests on legal questions pertaining to their activities. Thus the number of entities entitled to invoke the jurisdiction of the Court is strictly limited.

A still more stringent limitation on use of the Court is the requirement that all parties consent to the Court's jurisdiction. The complaining state (the "applicant") notes consent by its act of submitting the dispute to the Court, and the respondent state may of course consent at that time by special agreement or by filing a response accepting jurisdiction. But agreed submissions to the Court after a dispute has arisen are not numerous. Few defendants in a civil suit would appear in national courts if they were not required to appear, and very few plaintiffs would file lawsuits if the courts could not compel the defendant to respond. Lacking any general compulsory jurisdiction, the ICJ is in precisely that position: few applications are filed because the country complained against can usually ignore the Court if it wishes.

The docket would be even shorter if the Statute did not provide for methods of consent conferring a limited degree of compulsory jurisdiction on the Court. This is done by permitting states to give consent *before* a dispute has occurred, through treaty or other agreement accepting the Court's jurisdiction for a particular class of cases that might arise in the future. For example, an optional protocol to the 1961 Vienna Convention on Diplomatic Relations provides that disputes arising out of the interpretation or application of the Convention fall within the compulsory jurisdiction of the Court. Any party to the protocol may invoke the jurisdiction of the Court against any other party in that class of cases. This optional protocol allowed the Court in 1979 to entertain the U.S. claim that Iran had violated the Vienna Convention by holding U.S. diplomatic personnel hostage in their Tehran embassy. Iran denied the Court's jurisdiction at the time of the U.S. application, but the Court nevertheless took jurisdiction because of Iran's prior consent in ratifying the protocol. The United States also claimed jurisdiction for the Court under a bilateral treaty between the United States and Iran because the treaty included a dispute settlement clause, conferring jurisdiction on the Court. Other bilateral or multilateral treaties similarly confer jurisdiction on the Court, although they are seldom invoked.

The ICJ Statute provides a further avenue for states to grant compulsory jurisdiction to the Court by depositing a declaration to that effect with the UN Secretary-General. Because no state is required to do so, this provision (Article 36, Section 2) is commonly known as the "optional clause." It applies only between states that have made the optional declaration, but for them it extends the Court's jurisdiction to a very broad range of cases. In the words of the Statute, it includes

all legal disputes concerning
a. the interpretation of a treaty;
b. any question of international law;
c. the existence of any fact, which, if established, would constitute a breach of an international obligation;
d. the nature or extent of the reparation to be made for the breach of an international obligation.

As of 2003, the requisite declaration was in force for sixty-three parties to the Statute.

In accepting the optional obligation, many states have given with one hand and taken away with the other by attaching reservations that substantially limit the scope of the jurisdiction accepted. The most common reservation is to exclude disputes within the domestic jurisdiction of the state concerned. An extreme form of this reservation is illustrated by the U.S. declaration of acceptance in 1946, which excepted "disputes with regard to matters that are essentially within the domestic jurisdiction of the United States *as determined by the United States of America.*" This italicized phrase, added by the U.S. Senate, was the so-called Connally Amendment, which greatly weakened U.S. acceptance. It allowed the United States rather than the Court to determine the existence of domestic jurisdiction. Because of the reciprocity principle recognized by the Court, other states could invoke the same exception against the United States if the United States brought an action against one of them. Several other countries have adopted similar "self-judging" reservations. For the United States, the reservation became moot on April 7, 1986, when it withdrew its declaration of acceptance following a six-month notice of termination. Its withdrawal was prompted by the Court's decision to entertain Nicaragua's complaint of U.S. intervention in support of the Nicaraguan Contras.

Another reason for the Court's scanty caseload is the expensive, time-consuming, and highly public nature of the Court's proceedings. Settling a dispute by quiet negotiations between parties is much preferred. If the ICJ is involved, the parties can expect at least a two-year wait between submission of the case and the Court's judgment. Legal action entails the time and expense of preparing memorials (legal briefs), exhibits, counter-memorials, replies, and supporting documents, as well as conducting a formal hearing with witnesses, expert testimony, and oral argument. The parties may then wait many months for the Court to render its decision. If preliminary decisions on jurisdictional questions or provisional orders are necessary, this argumentation process may occur more than once. The costs of legal counsel can run high, especially when—as is commonly done—private counsel is hired to assist with an ICJ proceeding. Common sense suggests settling in some quicker, cheaper way if possible. In recognition of these legal and material obstacles, the UN Secretary-General in 1989 established a trust fund to aid states lacking funds to employ expert legal counsel. On the other hand, even if the money is available to press a case, if the dispute is not already a matter of serious public concern, submission to the Court may still be an unnecessarily costly venture. It also could further disadvantage the state making the submission, especially if the controversy is between otherwise friendly states.

In the decades immediately after World War II, Third World states and the former communist-bloc countries had additional reasons for avoiding the Court. International law evolved to accommodate the needs of a state system that was dominated by Europe and oriented to the status quo. Many new states believed that the international legal system inherited from European practice did not adequately reflect their needs and perspectives. The distinction was probably less one of geography than one of vested interests. Law tends to protect established rights and thus to work against demands for change by states in a less favored position. Most cases brought before the Court during its first three decades were initiated by Western states, but since that period, it has been Third World nations that have found the Court an important instrument in their dealings with other, sometimes more powerful, states. The contentious cases brought before the Court since 1976 by Third World countries far exceeds those originating with more developed countries. The importance of this reversal in the use of the Court was dramatized in 1998 when the Court agreed to hear the complaint registered by the government of Libya. Libya had resisted a U.S. and U.K. interpretation and application of the 1971 Montreal Convention arising from the aerial incident that caused the destruction of Pan Am flight 103 over Lockerbie, Scotland, in December 1988. The United States and the United Kingdom, concerned with a loss of control over the decision process, and already pressing the international community to sustain sanctions against Libya for its failure to yield for trial the people accused of causing the incident, were clearly disturbed by the Court's action. Because important interests are in conflict between disputing states, and because the stakes are usually judged to be very high, governments are most unwilling to risk an unfavorable decision by the Court. Although the ICJ continued to register the Libyan case on its docket, in April 1999 Tripoli agreed to yield the people accused of perpetrating the bombing. A prior compromise agreement between Libya, the United Kingdom, the Netherlands, and the United States allowed the men to be tried in the Netherlands by Scottish jurists, operating under Scottish law. In 2003 the Libyan government agreed to pay compensation to the families of the victims in the Lockerbie bombing.

Prolonging a dispute may be preferable to a settlement on unsatisfactory terms. In nonlegal approaches to dispute settlement, the parties remain the judges of settlement terms, and matters of primary national interest are not compromised. In legal settlements, a majority of the judges make the decision, which is binding on the parties. In extreme circumstances a state might reject the award of the Court, but given the legal obligation to comply with the decision, this can be done only at considerable diplomatic cost by any state that wishes to be known as law-abiding.

The unpredictability of judicial decisions is one aspect of the problem. Not all international law is uncertain, but the disputes most likely to be brought before an international court are those in which the relevant law or facts are uncertain. The numerous dissenting opinions mirror a wide divergence of opinion on the Court in many cases. Moreover, uncertainty in the law increases the probability that a judge, consciously or unconsciously, may be influenced by political considerations. If uncertainty discourages advance acceptance of the Court's jurisdiction, certainty as to the applicable law may also discourage submission by the side with the weaker legal position. In either situation, loss of control over the outcome of the dispute, and consequent risk of injury to important interests, discourages submission to the Court. Under these circumstances the limited use of both the ICJ and its League predecessor is wholly understandable.

Given such formidable deterrents to the use of the Court, one may reasonably ask why it is used at all. A close look at the cases submitted since 1945 reveals that the motivations are almost always intensely practical, having to do with specific questions of national interest rather than generalized allegiance to the ideal of a world governed by law. Recourse to the Court is often merely an incident in a larger process of bargaining and political conflict. A strong legal position can give the application some deterrent or harassment value against an antagonistic state, even if the Court ultimately fails to establish jurisdiction. This probably helps explain U.S. resort to the Court in three aerial incidents of the 1950s in which the Soviet Union twice and Bulgaria once were charged with illegally shooting down foreign aircraft. Undoubtedly, it was also a factor in Nicaragua's 1984 decision to seek ICJ action on its complaint against the United States for mining Nicaraguan harbors and aiding Nicaraguan rebels, although the Court subsequently found jurisdiction in that case and, indeed, ruled in favor of Nicaragua.

Among friendly states, recourse to the Court may be a means of isolating a dispute to prevent it from tainting otherwise cordial relations. Australia and New Zealand had this consideration in mind when they asked the Court in 1973 to declare that French atmospheric nuclear testing in the South Pacific was illegal. That objective was largely achieved, even though France never admitted the competence of the Court to hear the case. France continued its testing during 1973 and again in 1995 before announcing its compliance with the Comprehensive Nuclear Test Ban Treaty of 1996.

The outcome of the nuclear testing cases suggests another reason for initiating litigation—to encourage a negotiated settlement. Resort to the Court by Australia and New Zealand came only after ten years of unsuccessful bilateral negotiation and UN debates on the subject. A similar motivation has accompanied numerous other applications to the Court. The United Kingdom and West Germany, for example, brought suit against Iceland in 1972, primarily to communicate the seriousness of their determination to resolve their long-standing dispute over Iceland's unilateral extension of its fishing boundaries. The Court rendered a judgment favoring the applicants' position, but a more important effect of the litigation was to encourage subsequent negotiation among the parties. In 1973 Pakistan found the Court helpful in breaking a stalemate with India in negotiations over the release of Pakistani prisoners of war taken during the hostilities in East Pakistan (now Bangladesh) in 1971. The application was filed in May, negotiations were resumed in July, the case was withdrawn from the Court in December, and a final agreement for release of the prisoners was signed in April 1974.

A variety of other reasons may enter into the calculations of an applicant state in deciding for judicial settlement. If settlement of a dispute among friendly states is slow in coming, the bargaining process may reach a point where finding a settlement is more important to both sides than striking a particular kind of bargain. In the North Sea continental shelf cases (1967–69) pitting Denmark and the Netherlands against West Germany, the controversy was submitted by agreement of all the parties because just such a plateau had been reached. The Court decision broke the deadlock over the division of the oil-rich shelf, although resolution of all the disputed issues required still further negotiation and a compromise settlement. One additional motive for the agreed submission, at least on the part of Denmark, was to "save face" with domestic public opinion. If territorial concessions were the price of settlement, a Court judgment would make them more politically acceptable.

Much more than saving face was involved in the Belgrade government's decision in April 1999 to bring ten separate but joined cases against the NATO countries most involved in the war against it. Eight of those cases were still on the Court's docket in 2003. (See Table 6-1.) The Yugoslav cases were based on Article 36, Paragraph 2 of the ICJ Statute, with Belgrade charging ten NATO countries with violating international obligations banning the use of force against another state. Included in this list of state obligations are the following: (1) the obligation not to intervene in the internal affairs of another state; (2) the obligation not to violate the sovereignty of another state; (3) the obligation to protect the civilian population and civilian objects in wartime; (4) the obligation to protect the environment; (5) the obligation related to free navigation on international rivers; (6) the obligation regarding fundamental human rights and freedoms; (7) the obligation not to use prohibited weapons; and (8) the obligation not to deliberately inflict conditions of life calculated to cause the physical destruction of a national group.

# CASE STUDIES IN UN CONFLICT RESOLUTION

Disputes before the United Nations have had a variety of causes, but during the several decades of the Cold War they involved controversies between the East and West, conflicts produced by the decolonization process, questions relating to territory and boundaries, and disputes arising from intervention by one or more states in the internal quarrels of another. In the post–Cold War world, the United Nations has been asked to resolve disputes stemming primarily from internal conflict rather than external intervention. Terrorism also has begun to draw the attention of the legal fraternity. Seeking damages for pain inflicted by acts of terror is usually an indirect process, however, such as the legal cases addressed to the Saudi Arabian government by the families of the victims of September 11. Because many of the perpetrators of the tragedy were Saudi subjects, the Saudi government was deemed to have culpability. The following are case studies illustrating the range and difficulty of the disputes placed on UN agendas throughout the history of the organization.

## SOUTH AFRICA AND THE UNITED NATIONS

South Africa's racial policies dominated UN discussions and debates more than any other issue through the 1980s. Some twenty UN offices, committees, or funds were centered solely on South African issues. In one General Assembly session in the 1980s, antiapartheid agitation occurred in 62 of 111 plenary

TABLE 6-1  2003 Docket of the International Court of Justice

| ISSUE | PARTIES |
|---|---|
| 1. Avena and other Mexican nationals | Mexico v. United States of America |
| 2. Questions of interpretation and application of the 1971 Montreal Convention arising from the aerial incident at Lockerbie | Libyan Arab Jamahiriya v. United Kingdom |
| 3. Questions of interpretation and application of the 1971 Montreal Convention arising from the aerial incident at Lockerbie | Libyan Arab Jamahiriya v. United States of America |
| 4. Oil platforms | Islamic Republic of Iran v. United States of America |
| 5. Application of the Convention on the Prevention of the Crime of Genocide | Bosnia and Herzegovina v. Yugoslavia |
| 6. Gabcikovo-Nagymaros Project | Hungary v. Slovakia |
| 7. Ahmadou Sadio Diallo | Republic of Guinea v. Democratic Republic of the Congo |
| 8–15. Legality of the use of force | Yugoslavia v. Belgium, Canada, France, Germany, Italy, Netherlands, Portugal, United Kingdom |
| 16. Armed activities on the Territory of the Congo | Democratic Republic of the Congo v. Uganda |
| 17. Application of the Convention on the Prevention and Punishment of the Crime of Genocide | Croatia v. Yugoslavia |
| 18. Maritime delimitation between Nicaragua and Honduras in the Caribbean Sea | Nicaragua v. Honduras |
| 19. Application for the revision of the Judgment of 11 July 1996 in the case concerning application of the Convention on the Prevention and Punishment of the Crime of Genocide Preliminary objections | Bosnia and Herzegovina v. Yugoslavia<br><br>Yugoslavia v. Bosnia and Herzegovina |
| 20. Certain property | Liechtenstein v. Germany |
| 21. Territorial and maritime dispute | Nicaragua v. Colombia |
| 22. Frontier dispute | Benin v. Niger |
| 23. Armed activities on the Territory of the Congo (New application 2002) | Democratic Republic of the Congo v. Rwanda |
| 24. Application for the revision of the Judgment of 11 September 1992 in the case concerning the land, island, and maritime frontier dispute (El Salvador v. Honduras: Nicaragua intervening) | El Salvador v. Honduras |

SOURCE: Registry of the Court Web site (http://www.icj-cij.org/icjwww/idocket.htm).

meetings. Moreover, the white South African government was made the target of criticism in one-fifth of all UN resolutions adopted during that period.

South Africa's discrimination against minorities first came before the General Assembly in 1946. The complaint was brought by India, alleging South African violation of the Capetown Agreements of 1927 and 1932, which guaranteed equality of treatment for each other's resident nationals. The Indian complaint was never resolved, and it was a perennial subject of Assembly discussions and resolutions until it was merged in the 1950s with a broader attack on South African racial discrimination, focusing on the policy of apartheid, or separation of whites from the nonwhite majority.

The major objective of sustained UN condemnation of apartheid was to isolate South Africa from the world community, and ultimately, to force the Afrikaner government to abolish the practice. In 1962 the Assembly created a Special Committee against Apartheid to gather information about apartheid and make sure the issue remained a priority in the Assembly and the world at large. When South Africa persistently refused to heed Assembly demands to abandon its apartheid policies, the Assembly responded with increasingly bitter denunciations, repeatedly urging members to cut all political and economic ties with South Africa and calling on the Security Council to impose mandatory sanctions. In 1973 an International Convention on the Suppression and Punishment of the Crime of Apartheid was opened for signature, and in 1976 the Assembly began explicitly to advocate "armed struggle" in South Africa as a means of eradicating the evil.

Action on apartheid by the Security Council was more restrained because harsh measures were subject to U.S. and British vetoes. The Council addressed the apartheid issue in 1960, criticizing South African behavior in the Sharpesville incident in which police killed sixty-seven people during an antiapartheid demonstration. Three years later the Council called for a voluntary embargo on the sale of arms to South Africa, and in 1977 it made the embargo mandatory. The 1977 resolution also banned nuclear cooperation with South Africa. Third World and East European states called for much stronger measures, including a total severance of economic relations with South Africa, but the Western members of the Council were never quite ready to do the same. In 1985, with Britain and the United States abstaining, the Security Council recommended nonmandatory economic sanctions against South Africa. In 1986 the U.S. Congress adopted economic sanctions over a presidential veto, and the European Community also decided to impose economic sanctions, including an oil embargo. Furthermore, many private multinational businesses undertook a voluntary withdrawal of investment activity in South Africa.

Through the decade of the 1980s the apartheid system remained largely intact. In 1982, in response to growing external pressures, South Africa introduced modest reforms, including a tri-cameral legislature with separate chambers for whites, Indians, and "coloreds" (people of mixed race). The changes gave no political rights to blacks and left the white minority in control. Meanwhile the government used the full force of criminal law, including the death penalty, against internal opponents of apartheid. Members of the antiapartheid African National Congress (ANC) were the most frequent targets. Externally, South African forces periodically raided neighboring countries harboring ANC guerrillas and unabashedly gave aid to insurgents seeking the overthrow of leftist governments in Angola and Mozambique. During all these years South Africa remained a perpetual affront to UN ideals and majority interests and adamantly defended its policies of racial separation.

The first major crack in the South African wall came in December 1988 with an agreement to accept Namibian independence in exchange for the withdrawal of Cuban troops from Angola. Other hopeful signs followed. In February 1989 P. W. Botha was succeeded by F. W. de Klerk as head of the ruling Afrikaner-dominated National Party. De Klerk, though conservative, was seen as more open to change. In March the Dutch Reformed Church, the largest denomination in South Africa and traditionally a supporter of racial separation on biblical grounds, publicly reversed its position and condemned apartheid as contrary to Christian teaching. These events occurred against the background of severe economic decline, induced in part by the international sanctions and domestic unrest. Taking hope from these developments, the UN General Assembly held a special session in December 1989 to enunciate guidelines for negotiating a peaceful dismantling of apartheid.

The initiative came at the right moment. F. W. de Klerk, now President of the Republic, had seen the light and was prepared to embark on a course that would change the history of South Africa. In February 1990 he lifted the country's political ban on the ANC and other antiapartheid groups. Within days he ordered the release of ANC leader Nelson Mandela, who had been in prison for twenty-eight years. This was followed by the release of other political prisoners and, in the ensuing months, the repeal of most antiapartheid legislation. The new policy brought vocal protest from internal opponents of change, but in a national referendum of white voters held in March 1992, a majority of 68.7 percent gave de Klerk their support. Though uncertain and even fearful of the future, South Africa's white population preferred integration and sharing power with a black majority to the alternative prospect, that is, renewed international isolation, civil war, and economic collapse. The way was thus cleared for the most difficult task of all—negotiating a new constitution for a democratic, multiracial society.

The world reaction was approving but cautious. The UN General Assembly removed a ban on South African participation in international sporting, scientific, and cultural activities and advised members to consider ending other sanctions as circumstances warranted. The European Community scrapped its oil embargo, and the United States ended restrictions on economic contact with South Africa.

Sustained diplomatic pressure and economic sanctions were deemed successful when political reforms were introduced in the country that permitted elections in which each adult South African, white and black, voted in 1994 for a government of his or her choice. Nelson Mandela's victory and his inauguration as president of South Africa marked the end of a long, tedious ordeal. The UN role in the political and social transformation of South Africa was pivotal. The end of sanctions and the recognition of the new government of South Africa by all UN members marked a new era for the country. It also was a major milestone in the maturation of the international organization. South Africa's emergence as a prominent actor in the developing world was symbolized by the peacemaking role in West and Central Africa played by Mandela's successor, Thabo Mbeki. His advocacy for the New Partnership for Africa's Development at the World Economic Forum in Durban in June 2002, as well as South Africa's hosting of the UN World Summit on Sustainable Development in August 2002, pointed to a new history for the once-isolated nation.

## NAMIBIA

Closely related to apartheid was the issue of South African rule in Namibia. Large (half the size of Europe), arid, rich in uranium, and small in population (about 1.5 million), Namibia borders South Africa to the northwest. A German colony before World War I, the territory (known as South West Africa until the late 1960s) was invaded and occupied by South Africa in 1915 and governed by South Africa as a League of Nations mandate after 1920. Unlike other holders of League mandates, South Africa refused to accept UN supervision under the trusteeship system at the end of World War II but instead took steps to integrate the territory with South Africa and impose its apartheid system there.

The General Assembly responded to these developments with alarm, criticism, attempted negotiation, and legal action against South Africa. A 1950 advisory opinion of the International Court of Justice ruled that the South West African mandate should be subject to UN supervision, but South Africa ignored this opinion. Subsequently the Assembly encouraged Ethiopia and Liberia, as former League members, to file an ICJ action against South Africa to obtain a binding legal decision on the former mandate. This effort failed when the Court in 1966 determined that Ethiopia and Liberia lacked the necessary legal interest to pursue the claim. According to the Court, the right to sue in such a cause belonged to the League, as distinct from its individual members, which left no legal remedy since the League had ceased to exist.

The General Assembly then acted unilaterally to terminate the mandate and declare Pretoria's continued occupation of Namibia illegal. This position was subsequently endorsed by the Security Council and by advisory opinions of the ICJ. In 1967 the Assembly created an eleven-member Council for South West Africa, subsequently renamed the UN Council for Namibia, to take over administration of the territory from South Africa. The Council for Namibia was never permitted to serve in that capacity, but it became a center for constant UN agitation against South African occupation of Namibia. Many UN members blamed the failure of UN efforts on the United States and its Western allies because their vetoes in the Security Council prevented tougher sanctions against South Africa.

In addition to external UN pressures, South Africa faced growing opposition within Namibia. The principal opposition organization, the South West Africa People's Organization (SWAPO), was formed in 1960 and began guerrilla warfare in 1966. In 1973 the General Assembly recognized SWAPO as the "authentic" representative of the Namibian people.

For years, hostility between South Africa and the UN majority disabled the United Nations from serving as an effective third party or a forum for negotiations. The Secretary-General was designated as a UN representative to negotiate with Pretoria, but his role was barely acknowledged. In 1977 the five Western members of the Security Council, called the "contact group," succeeded in promoting dialogue between South Africa and SWAPO. This led to a proposal for Namibian independence that was accepted by both South Africa and SWAPO and subsequently embodied in Security Council Resolution 435 (1978). The UN Secretariat prepared an elaborate plan for a UN Transition Assistance Group (UNTAG) including a seventy-five-hundred-strong peacekeeping force to supervise elections and oversee the transition to independence. South Africa persistently balked at the details for implementation, however, and beginning in 1981 the issue was further complicated by the efforts of the United States and South Africa to link a Namibian settlement to agreement for withdrawal of the fifty thousand Cuban troops stationed in neighboring Angola. This linkage was not totally without factual underpinning, as Angola was providing a haven for SWAPO guerrillas, but most UN members regarded the linkage as a ploy to postpone settlement.

The long-awaited break in the impasse occurred in December 1988 against a background of increased U.S.-Soviet cooperation. South Africa agreed to cease hostilities against Angola and grant Namibian independence, while Angola and Cuba agreed that Cuban troops would be withdrawn from Angola. In addition to great power pressure for a settlement, the cost to South Africa of continued presence in Namibia, including military operations that extended into Angola, had come to exceed the benefits. With Angola a sanctuary for SWAPO units and Cuban troops supporting the Angolan government, the prospects for victory were slim. On the rebels' side, war weariness was taking its toll, and signs were clear that Soviet support of the Angolan war effort would be reduced.

The December 1988 protocol on the independence of Namibia was a signal for the activation of UNTAG, heretofore a paper force in the files of the UN Secretariat. The first troops arrived in April 1989; the last departed in March 1990, leaving behind an independent Namibia with SWAPO leader Sam Nujoma the duly elected President. The settlement had been long in coming, and not wholly peaceful, but the United Nations played a critical role in bringing it to a conclusion. Namibia's fortunes as an independent state were intertwined with that of its SWAPO leader, Sam Nujoma, who remained the dominant force in the country into the new millennium. It was not until November 2001 that Nujoma declared he would leave the presidency with the end of his current term in March 2005. The President's extended stay in the executive mansion had the effect of transforming Nujoma into a dictatorial figure, and it was not a surprise when he embraced a neighboring dictator, Robert Mugabe, President of Zimbabwe. Like Mugabe, Nujoma extended a contract to North Korea to build a memorial and adjoining presidential complex—supposedly a symbol of his lasting place in the history of southern Africa. Also like Mugabe, Nujoma ordered the seizure of 192 farms belonging to white landlords. Although the white population of Namibia represented less than 5 percent of the population, they owned more than 70 percent of Namibia's farmland.

## ARAB-ISRAELI AND ISRAELI-PALESTINIAN CONFLICTS

The Arab-Israeli and Israeli-Palestinian conflicts have been a perennial concern of the United Nations almost from the inception of the organization. To briefly trace the origins of the problems: Diaspora Jews, living mostly in Eastern Europe, formed the World Zionist Organization under the leadership of Theodor Herzl toward the close of the nineteenth century. Calling for a Jewish homeland or state where Jews could practice their traditions free from persecution, the movement centered its attention on a "return to Zion," that is, to the biblical source of Jewish identity, in modern times often referred to as Palestine. A Jewish agency was organized to purchase land from absentee Arab landlords in the territory, then long under Ottoman Turk occupation and administration. Before World War I, and under Turkish rule, the region was known as Greater Syria. World War I proved the catalyst for the crystallization of the Zionist dream. The Ottoman defeat in the war meant that the European armies could seize control of the Ottoman's Middle East empire and transform it into European colonies. Ultimately, the British and French completed that task. Contemporary "Palestine" was re-created as a separate entity during this time and became a British mandate that was consecrated by the League of Nations. Transjordan, also a part of the original Palestine mandate, subsequently assumed separate status as still another British mandate and would in time metamorphose into the Kingdom of Jordan.

In 1917, the British declared their intention to establish a formal Jewish homeland in Palestine (the Balfour Declaration), and with the war over, the Zionists anticipated that the British would honor their commitment. But the British had also promised Arab leaders that after the war the Arabs would be granted rule over the territories previously dominated by the Turks. These two promises could not be reconciled, especially in the case of Palestine, where Jewish settlements appeared to negate the creation of an independent Arab state. With the Jewish settlers of Palestine caught between rival Arab aspirations and British imperial machinations, the period after World War I was turbulent and costly to all concerned. World War II further aggravated the situation. The British, under pressure from the Arabs, denied the further settlement of Jews in Palestine at a time when Nazi Germany had launched an all-out campaign to destroy European Jewry. The Zionists of Palestine tried to save as many European Jews as they could, and both during and after the war, they struggled against what they judged to be the inhumane tactics of the British Palestine Authority. The Jewish settler community demanded unlimited immigration to Israel for those Jews surviving the German Nazi Holocaust. A number of Arab states, however, had become independent before World War II and reacted adversely to this idea. The British were pressured to reject all Zionist demands for a separate Jewish state. Unable to stem the flow of Jewish refugees to Palestine from Europe, and lacking the will to reconcile the parties, the British quit the mandate and turned it over to the United Nations in 1947.

The UN General Assembly recommended partition of the Palestine mandate into separate Arab and Jewish states, each politically independent but forming an economic union. Arab opposition thwarted the peaceful implementation of this partition plan, however, and after a military struggle, the Palestinians were defeated and Israel was established in May 1948. The independent Arab states, however, within moments of the Israeli declaration of independence, attacked the new country. Surprisingly, Israel prevailed over the invading Arab states and extended its control and ultimately its sovereignty over a broader area than that described in the original UN resolution. Subsequently, a UN mediator was able to secure a cease-fire and a truce. Later, four armistice agreements were concluded.

Since that time no annual session of the General Assembly has been free from the conflicts between Arabs, Jews, and Palestinians. The issues confronting the United Nations have all centered on the aftermath of Arab defeats in their several wars with Israel. Prominent among them have been refugee relief and resettlement, claimed Arab property rights in Israel, Israeli human rights violations, and after 1967, Israeli occupation of Arab territories, especially the West Bank, Gaza Strip, and Syrian Golan Heights. Also important has been the status of Jerusalem, the creation of an independent Arab Palestinian state, and a host of security questions stemming from terror tactics employed by Arab states and organizations against the Jewish state.

The Security Council also has been heavily involved in the Arab-Israeli and Israeli-Palestinian conflict; major hostilities have erupted during nearly every decade since the 1948–49 war for Israeli independence. In 1956 Egyptian nationalization of the Suez Canal provided the occasion for an invasion of Egypt by Britain and France (the Suez-Sinai War) and subsequently by Israel. In 1967 (the Six-Day War) Israel launched a crushing military strike against Egypt to remove the threat to its security from Egyptian-supported guerrillas and to maintain use of the Gulf of Aqaba for its trade and commerce. A UN force stationed at Sharm al-Sheikh after the 1956 war to guarantee Israeli use of the Gulf of Aqaba had been removed abruptly by UN Secretary-General U Thant. In the 1967 war, Israel occupied the Sinai up to the Suez Canal. Jordan lost control of the West Bank territory it had seized in the 1948–49 war, and Syria was pushed off the Golan Heights. In 1973 (called the Yom Kippur War by Israelis and the Ramadan War by Arabs) Egypt and Syria struck the initial blow against Israel in hope of regaining territory lost in the 1967 war. In 1978 and again in 1982, Israeli forces initiated major hostilities in Lebanon in response to Palestinian raids into Israel over the Lebanese border.

Security Council resolutions have established certain principles to which all the participants repeatedly refer in Middle East negotiations. Security Council Resolution 242, adopted unanimously on November 22, 1967, in the aftermath of the Six-Day War, is by far the most important. Its two cardinal principles are (1) Israeli withdrawal "from territories occupied in the recent conflict" and (2) "respect for and acknowledgement of the sovereignty, territorial integrity, and political independence of every State in the area and their right to live in peace within secure and recognized boundaries." The two points were intended to be mutually dependent. Unfortunately, agreement in the Security Council in 1967 did not produce agreement among the parties to the conflict, and Israel interpreted the withdrawal provision of Resolution 242 as though it read "some but not all" occupied territories.

The Six-Day War established Israel as a formidable actor in Middle Eastern affairs, and Arab declarations about destroying the country ceased to carry the weight of earlier years. Israeli military prowess registered on Anwar al-Sadat, President of Egypt after Gamal Abdel Nasser's death. Sadat initiated the 1973 war against Israel, but his objectives were directed more at achieving diplomatic leverage than at making a knockout blow. Just a few years after that war, Sadat flew to Jerusalem, and for the first time since Israel's self-proclaimed independence, an Arab leader acknowledged the need to find a diplomatic settlement acceptable to both sides. Sadat's action angered and frustrated the other Arab states, especially because Egypt represented the most important Arab nation and had shouldered the major burden in all the Arab wars with Israel. Shouts of betrayal, however, failed to deter Sadat, who, with the good offices provided by U.S. President Jimmy Carter, met with Menachem Begin, his Israeli counterpart, at Camp David in the United States. The outcome of those meetings in 1978 was the Egypt-Israel Peace Treaty of 1979. Sadat's peacemaking efforts were little appreciated back home, however, and in 1981 he was assassinated while viewing a military parade. Sadat was succeeded by another military leader, Hosni Mubarak, and the treaty with Israel was sustained, but it was also paralyzed by Israel's assault on PLO positions in Lebanon in 1982.

The UN General Assembly failed to reflect these dramatic turns in the Arab-Israeli conflict. Over the years the role of the General Assembly had changed from that of a relatively evenhanded third party to that of a shrill partisan of the Arab cause. With the passing years, the Third World nations increased their leverage in the United Nations, and the General Assembly was more inclined to substitute condemnation of Israel for any genuine attempt at peaceful settlement. With the Assembly abdicating its role as peacemaker, what headway could be made was largely accomplished outside the United Nations. The ending of the Cold War did not change the equation. The Assembly continued its assault on Israeli policies and actions, and the intifada movement, or uprising of Palestinian youth, on the West Bank and in the Gaza Strip only provided more fuel for passionate speeches in the General Assembly.

The United Nations continued to mirror the views of the Arab states that rejected the existence of an independent Israel. The Persian Gulf War in 1990–91, pitting some Arab states against others, however, offered new opportunities for resolving the Arab-Israeli conflict. Iraq's aggression against Kuwait divided the Arab world; it also made it possible for the United States to pressure the General Assembly to repeal its 1975 resolution that equated Zionism with racism. In December 1991 the Assembly voted to withdraw that resolution. Moreover, the Palestine Liberation Organization, led by Yasir Arafat, found itself on the losing side in the Gulf War, and one immediate consequence was the loss of its financial support from the Arabian states, especially Saudi Arabia and Kuwait. Sensing its isolation, and unwilling to abdicate its role as the leader of the Palestinian Arabs, the PLO in October of 1991 was forced to join the Madrid Conference, convened by the United States, with the Soviet Union a cosponsor. Attended by Egypt, Syria, Lebanon, the PLO, and Israel, the conference expanded the Middle Eastern dialogue and set the stage for secret meetings between high representatives of the PLO and Israel in Oslo, Norway. These meetings, known as the Oslo Accords, produced something resembling a breakthrough. In September 1993, Arafat entered into an agreement with Israeli Prime Minister Yitzhak Rabin, and the Israelis turned over the administration of the Gaza Strip and Jericho in the West Bank to PLO administration. In return, Arafat promised to end violence against Israel. In the aftermath of these understandings, in 1994 Jordan also entered into a peace treaty with Israel. Still another accord between Israel and the PLO was entered into in September 1995 when Israel agreed to withdraw from six additional West Bank cities as well as 450 towns and villages. The subsequent formation of a Palestinian Ruling Council, and Arafat's election as President of the Palestinian Authority, transformed the PLO into a quasi-government. The prospect for an independent Arab Palestine was in the offing.

Dissatisfaction with the agreements on both the Israeli and Arab sides, however, led to more violence, especially after Yitzhak Rabin was assassinated. Rabin was succeeded by Shimon Peres, a staunch liberal peacemaker of the Israeli Labor Party. But Peres's tenure was brief, and the Israeli public shifted to more conservative politicians, led by a Likud Party leader, Benjamin Netanyahu. Conservatives were reluctant to follow the lead of the Labor Party, and the peace process was further delayed. Arafat became trapped between Arab extremists on the one side and his disaffected brethren on the other. Under the circumstances, there was little the United Nations could do but monitor the situation.

Undaunted, however, U.S. government envoys did not allow the parties to forget their peacemaking pledges, and Washington maintained its pressure, especially on Prime Minister Netanyahu. Nevertheless, like Arafat, Netanyahu had to answer to a constituency that sustained his authority. And although the Israeli leader associated himself with the peace process, indeed cited its irreversibility, and had withdrawn Israeli troops from sensitive areas such as Hebron, he was equally adamant on Jerusalem's status as the Israeli capital. He also refused all demands to forego construction of Israeli settlements in Arab Jerusalem. Although the peace process had shown progress, the prominent issues—the permanent security of Israel, the status of Jerusalem, the total withdrawal of Israeli forces from the West Bank, Israeli acceptance of Palestinian self-determination, and Israel's return of the Golan Heights to Syria—were far from resolved. Moreover, the UN General Assembly's decision in July 1998 to elevate the PLO from its long-standing observer status to "near membership" further complicated the peace process. Given Israeli reluctance to yield to Palestinian demands, and fearing that more delay would only complicate matters, President Bill Clinton pressured the principals to reinvigorate their peacemaking efforts. Clinton arranged a meeting in Wye, Maryland, not far from Washington, in October 1998. Prime Minister Netanyahu and President Arafat agreed to attend but again failed to reach an understanding. Obviously in need of good offices, President Clinton asked King Hussein of Jordan to enter the negotiations, which he agreed to do. The U.S. president and King Hussein, working together, convinced the parties that an accord was in everyone's interest, and on October 24, their efforts were crowned by an agreement that the four leaders signed in the White House. The Wye River Accord provided for a series of intricately linked steps over three months, including Israeli withdrawal from an additional 13 percent of West Bank territory. In return, the Palestinian Authority agreed to abrogate that section of the Palestinian National Covenant calling for the destruction of Israel. Arafat also pledged a crackdown on alleged Palestinian terrorists. The central purpose at Wye had been the building of confidence between the parties. The accord, however, also left in question the Palestinian Authority's threat to unilaterally declare an independent Palestinian state by May 1999, something Israel adamantly opposed. Moreover, Arafat still claimed Jerusalem as the Palestinian capital and insisted on the closing of all Israeli settlements on the West Bank, the return to the West Bank of Palestinian refugees living in other Arab nations, and the division and joint control of the region's freshwater supply.

Unable to neutralize opposition to the Wye agreement in both Israel and the West Bank, and with acts of Arab terror and protest unabated, the Netanyahu government failed to meet the January 1999 deadline for withdrawal from the West Bank that had been detailed in the accord. The Palestinian Authority's response was to release from its prisons known terrorists, and Arafat also made gestures toward proclaiming the independence of Palestine. The death of Jordan's King Hussein on February 7, 1999, only added to the instability in the region. Even the funeral of the king, attended by more than forty heads of state, including President Clinton, Prime Minister Netanyahu, and Yasir Arafat, did not improve the atmosphere or move the major participants to compromise their positions. Israel, however, conducted new elections in May 1999, and to the surprise of many, the Israelis chose a disciple of Yitzhak Rabin and a former chief of the Israeli Defense Forces, Ehud Barak, to succeed Netanyahu. Israel's new Prime Minister insisted that his main task was the reinvigoration of the peace process, and Clinton, who had a little more than a year remaining in his second term, made working with Barak his principal foreign policy gambit. Barak's progressive style promised a new opportunity for finding a solution to the Arab-Israeli conflict, which now had been transformed into an Israeli-Palestinian contest.

Clinton saw in Barak's election an Israeli public opinion mobilized for a renewed peace effort. In July 2000, he called Barak and Arafat to Camp David for a two-week effort to reconcile the leaders and to find a path that both were prepared to follow. Clinton placed on the table the celebrated UN Resolution 242 and the subsequent reaffirming Resolution 338 and made them the framework for a comprehensive settlement. Under Clinton's prodding, Barak agreed to transfer 92 percent of the West Bank and all of the Gaza Strip to the Palestinian Authority and ultimately its sovereign control. Barak also agreed to dismantle most of the Israeli settlements in the West Bank and to concentrate the bulk of Jewish settlers inside the 8 percent of the West Bank to be annexed by Israel. East Jerusalem was to be declared the capital of the new Palestinian state, with Arab neighborhoods assuming functional autonomy. Palestinian sovereignty was to be established over the Muslim and Christian quarters, and a Palestinian "custodianship," though not Palestinian sovereignty, was to be secured over the Temple Mount. Palestinian refugees in other lands were to be provided with the right of return to the new Palestinian entity, but not to Israel proper. Led by the United States, the international community was to be mobilized for a massive aid program to facilitate refugee rehabilitation. In return, Israel called for an end to violence and for a demilitarized Palestine.

To Clinton's consternation, Arafat's response was a flat rejection. He insisted on not 92 percent but 100 percent of the West Bank and demanded all of Jerusalem and recognition of a sovereign Palestinian state. Furthermore, Arafat wanted Israel to open its frontiers and territory to the Palestinian refugees who insisted on returning to lands abandoned in 1948. Barak had gone as far as he could in conceding to the Palestinian demands. If opened to the migration of the millions of Palestinians, many claiming the right to possess Israeli territory, Israel would be in an untenable situation. It would cease being a majority Jewish state and would be exposed to eventual absorption by Arab Palestine. Barak therefore would not budge from his original proposals.

Given the impasse, Arafat publicly rejected the Barak plan, and within weeks a new intifada erupted in the West Bank. Clinton, however, persisted, submitting revised peace proposals to the parties in December 2000. Israeli-Palestinian talks were resumed, and Israel agreed to withdraw from 95 percent of the West Bank. But the Palestinian negotiators responded with a map conceding only 2 percent of the West Bank to Israel and continued to insist on the "right of return" of the Palestinian refugees to Israel and sovereignty over all of Jerusalem. Clinton worked on the Palestinian question through his remaining days in the White House, but Arafat, rebuffed him on almost every point. Israel's response to this last effort by Clinton was just as intransigent. Israeli negotiators were not about to allow the Palestinian Authority to gain at the conference table what they could not achieve on the battlefield. Israel refused to listen to the Palestinian demands, and the Palestinian intifada continued, with terrorist attacks on Israeli civilians. Israel again responded with counterattacks against Palestinian installations and targeted killings of alleged Palestinian extremists. All expectations for a settlement were dashed in the renewed fighting. Clinton ran out of time, leaving the dilemma to his successor.

Convinced that Arafat and the Palestinian Authority were determined to liquidate the sovereign state of Israel, and aware that sympathies in Europe and elsewhere were with the Palestinian cause, Israelis dug in their heels. Barak was the first casualty of the failed peace efforts, succeeded by the Likud Party's most conservative leader, Ariel Sharon. In the United States, President George W. Bush refused to invest his political capital in another vain effort at resolving Israeli-Palestinian differences. Nor was Bush inclined to negotiate with Yasir Arafat. But without the good offices or mediation of the United States, mayhem in the region intensified.

Sharon's visit in September 2000 to the Temple Mount had set off a firestorm. Palestinians rioted and paramilitary forces of the Palestinian Authority unleashed violent assaults on Israeli targets. Although the international media framed the visit as a blatant attempt by Sharon to intimidate the Palestinian Authority, the visit was more directed at Israeli public opinion. Sharon wanted it understood that the days of Barak's appeasement were coming to an end. Once in office, Sharon and his government decided a harder line was necessary in dealings with Yasir Arafat.

In April 2002, in retaliation for the Palestinians' increased use of suicide bombers, Sharon launched Operation Defensive Shield. Israeli troops seized control of several cities, and Arafat was sealed in his offices and prevented from leaving the building or the area. Israeli Defense Forces killed or arrested numerous Palestinian operatives of organizations allegedly connected to the ongoing violence. In June, Israel struck again in a campaign called Operation Determined Path. As a consequence of stepped-up terrorist attacks, Israeli civilian losses rose to new levels and the Bush administration acknowledged Israel's right to retaliate. By this time, the United States was itself engaged in the war against terror, and Washington was more likely to see the terrorist organizations assaulting Israel as no different from those striking the United States. Israeli targeting of terrorist leaders was cast in a similar light with U.S. assaults on the Taliban and Al-Qaeda bases in Afghanistan.

But whatever Israel gained in U.S. opinion, it lost in Europe. European criticism of Sharon's tactics had even moved a Belgian official to lodge a formal indictment against the Israeli Prime Minister with the International Criminal Court. Israeli superior military prowess was depicted in European cities and media as Nazi-like, and Jewish commercial and religious establishments in Europe became targets for vigilante elements, many of them resident Muslims. For the most part, European authorities were slow or seemed reluctant to protect the lives and property of their Jewish citizens. Israel was accused of a massacre in the West Bank town of Jenin, but a UN report subsequent to the Israeli operation in the town disputed the charge. Nonetheless, the United Nations accused Israel of denying humanitarian aid to Palestinians. Sharon's election victory in January 2003 was sufficient to ward off the domestic threat to his government, but the Prime Minister still faced a determined foe. Perhaps more significant, however, was the fact that George W. Bush, who earlier had become the first U.S. President to call for the establishment of a sovereign Palestine state, now began showing renewed interest in brokering a peace settlement.

As the Bush administration was preparing for an invasion of Iraq, presidential advisers were ever more cognizant of the need to tackle the Palestinian issue. Still determined not to deal with the Yasir Arafat, however, the United States urged the Palestinians to choose a new leader. At the end of this process, Abu Mazen (also known as Mahmood Abbas), Arafat's long-time associate, was selected to be the Palestinian Authority's Prime Minister. Arafat, however, remained the Authority's President and power behind the scene. In order to bolster Abu Mazen's power, the United States along with the United Nations, the European Union, Russia, and key Arab leaders, developed what was called the Road Map to Peace. With President Bush reiterating the goal of an independent Palestinian state, side by side with Israel, the U.S. Secretary of State pressed the Road Map on both Israel and the Palestinians. In May and June 2003 the pressure on the parties intensified, and Bush met with both Sharon and Abu Mazen in Jordan after his earlier visit in Egypt with Arab leaders to discuss Israeli-Palestinian issues. Bush formally presented the Road Map, and Abu Mazen and Sharon indicated their compliance with its step-by-step program. Israel was to begin by dismantling a number of outposts in the West Bank, pulling back its forces from West Bank cities and ending its military operations against the Palestine Authority. In concert with these activities, Abu Mazen was called to rein in the terrorist organizations, most notably Hamas and the Islamic Jihad. The two leaders furthermore agreed to end the thirty-three-month intifada. On June 29, 2003, Hamas and the Islamic Jihad declared a three-month cease-fire, and the Bush administration announced its intention to stay involved until a real and permanent settlement had been achieved. At a July meeting, the adversaries agreed to resume joint patrols in new security zones. The United States, with the concurrence of the United Nations, planned to deploy peacekeepers from European and several Arab states. Indeed, a small team of U.S. monitors was already on the ground to oversee the implementation of the Road Map, and more U.S. monitors arrived throughout the summer. The Palestinian Authority called an end to the intifada, and Abu Mazen and Sharon publicized their intentions to work together.

In the thirty-three months of the intifada 2,414 Palestinians had lost their lives, along with 806 Israelis. The Palestinian figure included at least 99 suicide bombers and 60 suspected informers for Israel killed by Palestinian militants. Thirteen Israeli-Arabs had been killed in pro-Palestinian riots, as well as a British UN worker, an American peace activist, an Italian and a British journalist, and a German resident of the West Bank. The Israeli figure included 14 foreign workers, two UN international observers, one Swiss and one Turkish citizen, and a Greek monk killed in a roadside shooting. Also included in the Israeli losses were 35 Americans, many of them dual citizens. One Palestinian-American was also among the victims.

The promise of peace was dashed, however, almost before the first steps could be taken. Suicide bombers again struck at Israeli targets, and once more Sharon ordered his forces to retaliate. Arafat was again singled out as the problem. Unwilling to turn over Palestine Authority security forces to Abu Mazen, Arafat blocked every attempt by Abu Mazen to reach a compromise formula with Sharon. Abu Mazen was also pressured to accuse Israel of tokenism and of failing to meet the initial requirements laid out in the Road Map. Concluding that the meager understandings developing between the Israeli and Palestine Authority Prime Ministers were of little value, the terrorist organizations ignored their own declarations for an end of hostilities and unleashed more assaults on Israeli citizens. Israel accused Abu Mazen of failing to live by his promises, and in late summer Israeli missile strikes were directed at Hamas leaders in the Gaza Strip. Under increasing pressure from all sides, but most notably from Arafat, Abu Mazen resigned in September. Arafat quickly named another member of his inner circle, Ahmad Qureia, to succeed to the position. Israel's response was the bombing of the Gaza Strip home of Sheikh Ahmad Yessin, the founder and spiritual leader of Hamas. Yessin was slightly wounded, but there were a number of deaths and Hamas representatives declared a renewal of the intifada.

The Road Map to Peace appeared to be a dead letter although President Bush continued to insist his government would press on. In mid-September 2003 the Israeli government publicly declared that it reserved the right to remove Arafat from the West Bank or kill him if necessary. Arguing that Arafat remained the principal obstacle to any peace plan, Sharon declared it futile to believe progress could be achieved as long as Arafat remained in control on the West Bank. The United Nations immediately condemned the Sharon government. Syria pressed a resolution at the Security Council condemning Israel, but the United States vetoed it, not because it sanctioned an Israeli action against Arafat but because it declared the resolution flawed for its failure to condemn sustained terrorist attacks on Israel. Failing to get UN Security Council acquiescence, the Arab countries brought the matter before the General Assembly where the resolution was approved overwhelmingly. None of these developments, however, pointed in the direction of the Road Map to Peace. Nor was Qureia able to wrest from Arafat the authority needed to consolidate his power. In October he threatened to resign the position he had not yet begun to fill. Also in October Israel launched punitive raids into the Gaza Strip. Despite UN condemnation, the Sharon government continued to build a security barrier that sealed off some Palestinian communities, preventing the continuity of a Palestinian state. Israel also raided what it alleged was terrorist bases in Syria, threatening an escalation of the hostilities and possibly another Israeli-Arab War.

## INDIA-PAKISTAN

Territorial and other disputes between India and Pakistan have been a periodic feature of the UN landscape. The India-Pakistan issue originally came before the Security Council in January 1948 at the complaint of India. When the two countries gained independence in August 1947, more than five hundred princely states of the subcontinent were given the choice by the British government of joining one or the other of the new states. The option to remain apart and declare independence was also on the table for the princes. For most, the choice was made on the basis of the dominant religion and especially the geographic proximity to India and Pakistan. In India's case, New Delhi had no intention of allowing the princes to remain apart from the Indian Union. Literally hundreds of princely states were absorbed, forcibly where necessary, and the princes were retired with an annual government stipend. The princely state of Kashmir (organized as the state of Jammu and Kashmir), however, with its Hindu maharaja presiding over a predominantly Muslim region, but with geographic contiguity to India and Pakistan, decided to remain independent. But invading tribal people from Pakistan's northwest frontier challenged this decision. The maharaja's army was no match for the invading Muslim tribes, and the Hindu ruler was forced to send a plea for help to New Delhi. New Delhi demanded the maharaja's accession to India in return for this support and his safe removal. The maharaja complied with that demand, and Indian troops moved to protect what they considered a new member of the Indian Union. Pakistani forces thereupon formally entered the fray, and Kashmir became a region of combat between India and Pakistan from that day forward.

The Security Council appointed a UN Commission on India and Pakistan (UNCIP) to investigate and mediate the Kashmir dispute. After months of negotiation, UNCIP was able to secure a truce and cease-fire, effective January 1, 1949, and an acceptance in principle of a plebiscite to resolve the accession question. A UN military observer group (UNMOGIP) was established to supervise the cease-fire. The proposed plebiscite was never held, however, primarily because India occupied the larger part of Kashmir and regarded this fait accompli as preferable to a free vote in which the Muslim majority would in all likelihood opt for union with Pakistan. The United Nations therefore refused to acknowledge India's claim to Kashmir, and the region was judged in dispute and made subject to continued negotiations. The United Nations sent U.S. mediators to the region, first Admiral Chester Nimitz and then Senator Frank Graham, both of whom were deputized to find a solution to the problem. Neither was successful. India was determined to make Kashmir, although its only dominant Muslim state, an integral part of its domain. Thus, New Delhi moved to unilaterally annex the state in 1957, over the objections of Pakistan and in defiance of the United Nations.

In August 1965 renewed fighting shattered the truce in Kashmir, but prompt Security Council action, offers of mediation by the Secretary-General, and especially the good offices provided by the Soviet Union brought a cease-fire in September. In fact the United States was Pakistan's sole supplier of weapons, and even though Pakistan had committed itself to the American-led alliances in SEATO and the Baghdad Pact (later CENTO), President Lyndon Johnson refused to resupply Pakistani forces. Pakistan had no choice but to accept the cease-fire. And under pressure from his generals, Pakistan's President Muhammad Ayub Khan agreed to accept a Soviet invitation to meet with his Indian counterpart, Prime Minister Lal Bahadur Shastri, in Tashkent in Soviet Central Asia. With Ayub and Shastri accepting the Tashkent Agreement and hence the line of control between their forces, the UN observer group also assisted where it could in making the cease-fire effective. But the Kashmir dispute had become protracted. Pakistan had been prevented from seizing the region in two wars, and India refused to negotiate a settlement in peace. Pakistan continued to use the United Nations to berate New Delhi for failing to hold the UN-demanded plebiscite, and India refused to budge on the idea that the Kashmir dispute had ended with India's annexation of the territory. In 1971 war again broke out between India and Pakistan, although the major hostilities this time were in East Pakistan, where Indian armies intervened in support of Bengali separatists who had declared their independence from Pakistan. The Soviet Union, prone to side with India, vetoed a Security Council order for a cease-fire. A similar resolution by the General Assembly was ignored. India thus was in position to dismember Pakistan and to play midwife to the creation of independent Bangladesh.

UNMOGIP was organized in 1949 to monitor the cease-fire line in Jammu and Kashmir, not to do diplomacy. Indeed, UN diplomatic efforts in the region were virtually nonexistent after 1958. Nor did the Indo-Pakistani wars of 1965 or 1971 cause the United Nations to take more aggressive action to resolve the Kashmir dispute. Thus, by the 1990s, nongovernmental diplomacy tried to fill the power vacuum. Confronted by renewed fighting in Kashmir and sensing a lack of will in New Delhi and Islamabad, let alone in the United Nations, university academicians and working journalists tried to breathe life into an almost expired peace process. Representing the intelligentsia from both countries, they engaged in conversations that were aimed at finding a solution for the decades-old problem. They were described as the "Third Generation" and were detached from the traumatic events of their elders, so their deliberations seemed to point to the rebirth of diplomacy in the region. By August 1997, several "summer school" meetings had been arranged, notably in Sri Lanka and the United States. This effort at freelance diplomacy was just beginning to show positive results when in May 1998, New Delhi, without warning, tested several nuclear devices. Moreover, the Indian Prime Minister's public declaration that his country now possessed the "big bomb" was not intended to ease the work of the informal negotiators. Nor was Pakistan intimidated by the Indian action. Within weeks, Pakistan demonstrated that it too possessed nuclear weapons. With the two governments exchanging verbal threats, and now brandishing their weapons of mass destruction, the UN Security Council was forced into Emergency Session. The Council called upon both governments to cease their tests, and more important, to accept the terms of the Nonproliferation Treaty as well as the Comprehensive Nuclear Test Ban Treaty. Attention was also given to the Kashmir dispute, but in the course of the debate none of the Council members appeared ready to engage in serious diplomacy. Sanctions were also discussed, but here too there was no agreement, and individual countries were left to implement their own policies. It did appear, however, that IMF and World Bank assistance would be hard to obtain. Fearing that renewed fighting in Kashmir could escalate into a nuclear exchange, the Security Council acknowledged the need to encourage conversations between the two governments. But India held to its position that Kashmir was a permanent unit within the Indian Union, and the government of Pakistan continued its demand that the 1949 UN resolution calling for a plebiscite in Kashmir be honored. In effect, despite the serious escalation in tension and the threat of a tragic encounter, the Kashmir question was no nearer to a solution at the end of the century.

What did change, however, was the proliferation of terrorist organizations, largely based in Pakistan, and the increased carnage in Kashmir. Linked to the Inter Service Intelligence branch of the Pakistan Army, terrorists daily penetrated the porous frontier between the two countries. India expanded its army in the state to deal with the assault, but a toll was taken, and the assault did not end. New Delhi argued that Washington must include Pakistan on the State Department's list of terrorist states, and although Washington seemed to lean in that direction, it did not satisfy the Indian demand. September 11, 2001, however, changed the equation. The unprecedented attack on the United States prompted Washington to seek out the perpetrators of the action, who were based next door to Pakistan in Afghanistan. Moreover, to strike at Afghanistan, the United States needed Pakistan. Pakistan, now under the leadership of Pervez Musharraf, was pressured to carry the fight to the terrorists secreted in the mountains of the neighboring state. Musharraf's decision to stand with the United States as it unleashed an attack on the Taliban and Al-Qaeda forces in Afghanistan settled the matter of Pakistan assuming the status of a terrorist state. Pakistan in fact was inundated with terrorist organizations, including Al-Qaeda, but Musharraf ordered his armed forces to neutralize the extremists long nurtured by the Pakistan Army. U.S. air bases were opened on Pakistani soil and Pakistan became a full-fledged member of the coalition in the U.S.-declared war on terrorism. Musharraf at first indicated that Kashmir was not a part of that war and that the actions against the Indian occupiers were solely an act of liberation. It was not long, however, before Musharraf had to back off on that distinction. Nevertheless, the terrorists were not prepared to yield. In 2001 they attacked the Kashmir legislature, indicating that no target was off-limits to their assaults. Emboldened by this action, by the end of the year they made an even more dramatic assault on the Indian parliament in New Delhi. India's response was the massing of troops on the Pakistan frontier, especially in the Kashmir area. For several months in 2002 more than 1 million troops stood ready to make war in the subcontinent. Moreover, the threat of nuclear war hung over the region, prompting visits from the British Prime Minister and high-placed U.S. officials to both Islamabad and New Delhi. Only when Musharraf began working closely with the Americans and his forces began to capture and turn over to them several high Al-Qaeda operatives did India relax its posture on the frontier. Musharraf banned the terrorist organizations and ordered the arrest of many of their leaders.

To assist Musharraf, the United States agreed to reopen the Kashmir dispute and to pressure India to consider high-level talks over the disposition of the region. At no time did India indicate a willingness to relinquish dominion over Kashmir, but even New Delhi was confronted with the need to find a way out of the impasse. In the meantime the daily intrusions into Kashmir continued. Pakistan claimed it had blocked many of the infiltrators, but it also had to acknowledge that it could not prevent repeated assaults on Indian positions, let alone the attacks that continued to take a toll on the innocent. Diplomacy, whether organized by the United Nations or independent of it, was still limited by events, and there was little promise that a solution to the problem of Kashmir would be found. Nevertheless, despite continuing assaults in Kashmir by terrorist organizations, a breakthrough of sorts occurred in January 2004 when the Pakistani President and the Indian Prime Minister met in Islamabad and agreed to a formal cease-fire in Kashmir. The two leaders agreed to conduct high-level negotiations on Kashmir as well as seek ways to normalize communications and commerce between their two countries.

## UN DISPUTE SETTLEMENT

For more than forty years the United Nations existed in a Cold War environment that severely hampered its peacemaking role. Since 1987 a fundamental transformation has occurred in the conditions of global politics that may make the United Nations more successful in dispute settlement. Some of the successful efforts during the Cold War period are presented in the cases that follow.

### The U.S. Airmen

The release of U.S. air force personnel imprisoned by China in violation of Korean Armistice arrangements is an early instance of successful UN dispute settlement from the Hammarskjöld era. The issue arose in November 1954 when the Peking government unexpectedly announced that eleven crewmen of a B-10 bomber shot down near Korea in January 1953 had been tried by a military tribunal and sentenced to long prison terms for espionage. Four U.S. jet pilots had been similarly detained. The United States immediately appealed to the General Assembly, which in this case proved surprisingly effective. At the request of the Assembly, Dag Hammarskjöld departed for Beijing in early January, and shortly after his visit, Beijing announced that relatives of the airmen would be permitted to visit China. Four months later, in a letter to the Secretary-General sent through the Swedish ambassador in Beijing, the Chinese government informed Hammarskjöld that the four jet pilots would be deported. In August the eleven crewmen were freed. Whatever the motivation of the Chinese, the United Nations played an important mediating role in obtaining the release of the airmen.

### Thailand-Cambodia, Equatorial Guinea, Bahrain, and Greenpeace

In 1958–59 and again in 1962–64, a representative of the Secretary-General was instrumental in resolving border disputes and hostile incidents between Thailand and Cambodia. The representatives were sent at the request of both parties, which undoubtedly helps explain the success of the missions. The second UN mission remained on the scene for two years, with expenses jointly shared by the two governments. The Secretary-General's Personal Representative was also successful in assisting the peaceful withdrawal of Spanish troops from Equatorial Guinea (a former Spanish colony) in the spring of 1969. Again, the assistance was requested and received with cooperation by the parties.

A potentially much more explosive situation was defused by a representative of the Secretary-General in the 1970 controversy over the status of Bahrain, a small oil-producing British protectorate off the coast of Saudi Arabia in the Persian Gulf. Iran claimed sovereignty over Bahrain but Great Britain disputed the idea, and the good offices of the Secretary-General were enlisted to help resolve the controversy. All of the parties subsequently agreed to a report by the Personal Representative of the Secretary-General. It was further reinforced by UN consultation in Bahrain and determined that the islands should become independent. The final report was accepted unanimously by the Security Council. Bahrain assumed independence and became a member of the United Nations the following year.

Considerably less threatening to international peace, but nevertheless irritating to the parties involved, was an incident involving Greenpeace, an international environmental organization. In this case Secretary-General Pérez de Cuéllar successfully mediated a controversy between France and New Zealand arising from the clandestine bombing of the Greenpeace ship *Rainbow Warrior* by French agents while the ship was in Auckland harbor. Greenpeace had planned to use the ship to protest French underground nuclear tests on a South Pacific atoll. One life was lost as a result of the incident, and a New Zealand court convicted two French agents of manslaughter. The agreed settlement, announced in July 1986, called for $7 million compensation to New Zealand, an apology by France, and the lifting of a French embargo on the import of food from New Zealand. New Zealand, in return, released the two agents on the condition that they be transferred to a French military garrison in the South Pacific for three years.

## The Cuban Missile Crisis

The United Nations played a modest part in the resolution of the 1962 Cuban missile crisis, potentially one of the most serious East-West confrontations of the postwar period. The crisis arose from the presence of Soviet missiles and jet bombers in Cuba that were discovered by a U-2 surveillance mission over Cuba in the fall of 1962. Agreement on dismantling the missile sites and removing the missiles and bombers from Cuba was reached primarily through great power negotiation, but the UN contribution is not to be discounted.

The UN link most obvious at the time was U.S. use of the Security Council as a forum to display evidence that missiles were indeed being installed in Cuba. Aerial photographs presented to the world body by the United States made Soviet denials no longer credible. The United Nations also had a part in the less public negotiation processes. Both superpowers used their UN ambassadors to channel informal suggestions and semiofficial messages that supplemented more direct communication. At various times during the crisis, Secretary-General U Thant served as an intermediary. After the acute stage of the crisis had passed, the United Nations was the site of extensive negotiations on the means of verifying the weapons withdrawal. At this stage U Thant was the principal point of contact between Cuban leader Fidel Castro and the superpower representatives in New York.

Another important UN contribution to settlement was a face-saving formula that gave Soviet Premier Nikita Khrushchev an excuse to call for the return of Soviet freighters bearing additional missiles to Cuba and ultimately to agree to the withdrawal of all missiles and equipment. At a crucial moment in the dialogue between Khrushchev and President John F. Kennedy, Secretary-General U Thant offered a proposal for a voluntary suspension of Soviet arms shipments to Cuba in return for a voluntary suspension of the U.S. naval quarantine around the island. Khrushchev quickly accepted this suggestion. Moreover, the Soviets had their excuse for Soviet freighters, already under way with a missile cargo and a submarine escort, to steer clear of the quarantine fleet. And even though Kennedy's reply to Thant made suspension of the quarantine contingent on removal of offensive weapons already in Cuba, the understanding had already been arrived at. At this point the UN role may have been crucial. Kennedy could scarcely have made such a public proposal, and if he had, Khrushchev could not easily have accepted it. But Thant, as impartial spokesman for a community of states, was able to elicit a degree of restraint from the parties that neither could have exercised under pressure from the other.

*Decolonization*

The United Nations has been involved in numerous disputes arising from the now completed decolonization process. The important UN contribution to the overall process of decolonization is examined in Chapter 8. The end of Namibia's colonial status has already been discussed as a post–Cold War UN success story, but much earlier the United Nations played a third-party role in colonial disputes that ultimately turned out well. Indonesia was one of the first countries to elicit extensive UN involvement. During the course of the Indonesian struggle for independence from the Netherlands (1945–49), a Security Council Good Offices Committee (later reconstituted as the UN Commission for Indonesia) arranged a cease-fire in the region, maintained a small truce observation team, and assisted with negotiations. At UN Headquarters, debates and resolutions kept continual pressure on the Dutch to grant Indonesian independence. When the United States took sides in the controversy, the United Nations helped legitimize U.S. diplomatic and economic pressures on the Dutch. The agreement on independence, in December 1949, owed much to UN involvement. As noted in Chapter 5, the subsequent controversy over Western New Guinea (West Irian, now Irian Jaya), which the Netherlands refused to relinquish to Indonesian rule in 1949, was also resolved with UN assistance when the Dutch were ready to deal. The terms of the transfer of West Irian to Indonesia were arranged by a UN mediator and executed with the help of the UN Temporary Executive Authority and a UN Security Force.

The United Nations also peacefully resolved the fate of the former Italian colonies of Libya, Eritrea, and Italian Somaliland. France, the Soviet Union, the United Kingdom, and the United States had agreed in the World War II treaty of peace with Italy to let the UN General Assembly decide the future status of the colonies if the powers were unable to agree among themselves by September 1948. Disagreement prevailed, and the decision fell to the Assembly. The question occupied several sessions of the Assembly, but ultimately Libya was granted independence (proclaimed in December 1951), and Somaliland was placed under Italian trusteeship until independence was achieved in 1960. Eritrea was associated in a federal arrangement with Ethiopia but broke away and achieved independence in 1993. Subsequent border disputes between Ethiopia and Eritrea were covered in Chapter 5.

### Cold War–Era Efforts at and Obstacles to Dispute Settlement

UN successes in dispute settlement sometimes came after the outbreak of violence between parties, and some of the partial successes in curbing violence left the controversy still unresolved. Other conflicts, often entailing death and destruction of major proportions, seemed impervious to UN settlement attempts. Although UN attempts at dispute settlement will not be examined in detail here, they should be mentioned to keep the UN role in perspective. They include the two most devastating international wars of the period—the Vietnam War and the Iran-Iraq War. The Vietnam War, largely because of the U.S. attitude, proved totally resistant to UN attempts at mediation. The Iran-Iraq War eventually succumbed to persistent UN mediation but only after eight years of war and the onset of the Cold War thaw. Soviet military intervention in Afghanistan created another major crisis that could not be resolved during the Cold War. But the United Nations persisted in its mediation of the conflict, and in 1988 the UN-negotiated settlement led to the Soviet withdrawal in February 1989. Military actions on a lesser scale that eluded UN efforts at mediation included the Argentine attack on the British-held Falkland Islands, U.S. intervention in Grenada, and Nicaragua's struggle with U.S.-backed insurgents and the neighboring states that harbored them. Among the serious internal wars that resisted settlement was civil strife in Cambodia, where the Khmer Rouge reign of terror during the late 1970s took the lives of an estimated one to three million Cambodians. UN persistence did not relieve the suffering, but here too it paid off in subsequent years as peace was restored to Cambodia through UN aegis, and indeed in 2003 Cambodia agreed to try former members of the Khmer Rouge as war criminals, again under UN auspices.

### Afghanistan

UN-monitored Soviet troop withdrawal from Afghanistan was one of the first tangible fruits of the Cold War thaw. In December 1979 the Soviets sent 85,000 troops into Afghanistan, later increased to 115,000, to ensure that a factional struggle there would not bring an anti-Soviet government to power. The Soviet Army bolstered the communist government in Kabul and tried to crush resistance to its rule. Although Washington did not become directly involved in the conflict, it began channeling aid to Afghan Mujaheddin or resistance fighters through Pakistan. In time, the internal fighting expanded into a full-scale guerrilla war against the communist Afghan government and its Soviet backers. Early in 1980 the General Assembly issued the first of many unheeded calls for Soviet troop withdrawal, and the following year UN Secretary-General Kurt Waldheim appointed Javier Pérez de Cuéllar as his Personal Representative to seek a diplomatic solution. When Pérez de Cuéllar became Secretary-General in 1982, he named UN Undersecretary-General Diego de Cordovez as his successor in that assignment.

Through skill and persistence de Cordovez kept the negotiations alive year after year until a fundamental change in Soviet leaders and foreign policy goals dictated an end to the intervention. Agreement was reached in April 1988 through the Geneva Accords, which committed the Soviet Union to early troop withdrawal under UN supervision. The United States and Pakistan, along with the Soviet Union, also agreed to cease intervention in the Afghan civil war. By this time the Soviet Union had come to recognize that the war could not be won without a heavier commitment of forces. The subsequent reconsideration of the costs of its aggressive foreign policies undoubtedly played an important part in the Soviet decision to end its involvement in Afghanistan.

## The Iran-Iraq War

The continuation of the war between Iran and Iraq, like Soviet intervention in Afghanistan, represented a failure of pre-1988 UN peacemaking. Like the intervention in Afghanistan, it also was brought to a halt in the changed world climate of 1988.

Iraq began the war in September 1980 in the aftermath of the Iranian revolution. Baghdad anticipated a quick victory that would nullify Iran's support for a Shiite revolution in Iraq, gain control of the Shatt al-Arab waterway and access to the Persian Gulf, and establish Iraqi dominance over the region's oil supply. Iraq miscalculated. Although the tides of battle periodically shifted, the overall result was a stalemate. After years of futile struggle, Iraq was ready to call an end to the war, but the conflict had caused hundreds of thousands of casualties, material losses running to billions of dollars, severe economic damage, and a drastic reduction in oil production. Iran, led by the religious cleric Ayatollah Khomeini, refused to quit, declaring the conflict a struggle against the forces of secularism. Moreover, the U.S. tilt toward Iraq convinced the Ayatollah of the righteousness of his cause.

Iran therefore repeatedly rejected Security Council calls to end the fighting. Several mediation missions by a representative of the Secretary-General, acting under the Security Council's authorization, proved fruitless. A fact-finding mission sent by the Secretary-General in May 1983 was praised by Iran for its objectivity, but it too brought the war no closer to an end. The General Assembly also called for an end to the fighting, but Iran refused to support any resolution that did not brand Iraq an aggressor. In June 1984, in response to an appeal by the Secretary-General, the two combatants agreed to stop deliberate attacks on civilian population centers. That agreement was generally, if imperfectly, observed. Conciliation efforts by the Organization of the Islamic Conference, the Gulf Cooperation Council (formed during the conflict by Saudi Arabia and five small Arab states bordering the Persian Gulf), and the Non-Aligned Movement were fruitless.

Years of war sapped the military and economic capabilities of both sides, however, and in 1987 the United Nations undertook a renewed effort. In July the Security Council unanimously adopted a resolution offering a new peace plan and repeated its demand for a cease-fire, with the implicit threat of a mandatory arms embargo against any party that refused to comply. The threat was primarily aimed at Iran, however, the more recalcitrant of the belligerents. The United States also had indirectly intruded itself into the conflict when it decided to fly the U.S. flag on Kuwaiti-owned tankers and U.S. naval escorts followed their paths through stormy Gulf waters. The U.S. military presence in the Gulf was aimed at keeping the oil flowing, but it also was introduced to intimidate Iran. Indeed, several incidents involving U.S. or U.S.-flagged vessels resulted in U.S. attacks on Iranian naval craft and oil installations. The accidental shooting down of an Iranian passenger aircraft by a U.S. warship near the Strait of Hormuz in 1988 ultimately led to a change in Iranian policy.

With the perception of closer U.S.-Iraqi collaboration, Ayatollah Khomeini decided to allow the United Nations to play a hand. UN Secretary-General Pérez de Cuéllar conducted negotiations with the two warring countries, and the costly conflict was brought to an end in August 1988 with an agreed cease-fire supervised by a UN peacekeeping force (UNIIMOG). Comprehensive peace negotiations between the parties were begun in Geneva and mediated by the Secretary-General, but a conclusive settlement proved elusive. Neither side had anything positive to show for the heavy sacrifice in lives and national treasure. Nevertheless, both the Iraqi dictatorship and the Iranian theocracy survived the conflict. Moreover, neither was chastened by the experience, and each continued to insist that they represented the future in the Middle East and throughout the Islamic world. A peace agreement between Baghdad and Teheran came only in February 1991, and only after Iraq had suffered defeat at the hands of a U.S.-led coalition that liberated Kuwait and penetrated southern Iraq.

## Central America

In one respect the most remarkable UN peacemaking ventures in the new era occurred in Central America. The United States has traditionally regarded security in this area as Washington's responsibility and, with the major exception of the Cuban missile crisis, has treated UN involvement as superficial at best. Nevertheless, when the Sandinista government in Nicaragua decided to make peace with the Contras and agreed with four neighboring states on the need for UN assistance in policing the arrangement, the United States went along.

There, as elsewhere, until the parties were ready to stop fighting, the United Nations could do little. In 1989 the parties were ready. Nicaragua was overwhelmed by civil war, its economy was in shambles, and aid from its erstwhile Soviet patron was shrinking as a result of new Soviet policies. The Sandinistas wanted peace and were willing to pay for it with free and fair UN-monitored elections. Nicaragua's neighbors also were tired of the border violations and ready to end them. The Bush administration, impressed with recent UN peacemaking success and perceiving growing domestic opposition to its Contra policy, acquiesced. ONUCA was sent to patrol the border areas and demobilize the Contras, while ONUVEN observed the elections from which the Sandinistas emerged as the minority party. The ONUCA mission was phased out in January 1992.

One success was followed by another. With the barriers to UN peacemaking in the Americas removed, the Secretary-General was encouraged to try his hand in El Salvador, where both sides in the civil war were growing weary of the struggle and were sickened at the human consequences of their deeds. Through a Personal Representative, the UN Secretary-General negotiated an agreement in July 1990 to end human rights violations. After months of further negotiation, the parties agreed to a UN observer mission to monitor the human rights agreement. ONUSAL's 135 observers took up their positions in July 1991. The civil war continued sporadically, but in late December Pérez de Cuéllar personally negotiated a cease-fire agreement as the last act of his administration. ONUSAL was subsequently enlarged to monitor the cease-fire and help maintain internal order as the Salvadorans pursued the business of creating a new constitution and government.

ONUSAL's success was demonstrated in its dissolution in April 1995, leaving only the MINUGUA peacekeeping mission in Guatemala in 1997, which oversaw compliance with a peace agreement entered into by the disputing parties in December 1996. Already involved in policing human rights violations, MINUGUA was given responsibility for monitoring the demobilization of the combatants, a task that was accomplished under a sixty-day deadline. In the brief period it operated in Guatemala, MINUGUA helped improve the electoral system and permit wider citizen participation. Although originally scheduled for termination in May 1997, a scaled-back version of MINUGUA was extended to the year 2000. Similar UN activity occurred in Nicaragua, where, with the cooperation of the government, the United Nations sustained its efforts at disarming the combatants and promoting social and economic reintegration after long years of civil strife.

UN successes in Central America were echoed in the UN operations during the 1990s in Haiti discussed in Chapter 5. The UN began its task in Haiti after U.S. intervention on behalf of an elected government that it forcefully reinstated despite the efforts of a military junta to dominate the country. The several UN missions (UNMIH, UNSMIH, UNTMIH, and MIPONUH) stabilized the political environment, helped reorganize the Haitian armed forces, and organized free elections. Acknowledging the need to maintain law and order in an atmosphere of general mistrust and a lack of popular support in traditional institutions, the task of the United Nations was hardly a simple one but was nonetheless assumed with considerable enthusiasm and purpose. Enthusiasm aside, however, conditions in Haiti were not improved sufficiently to provide the country with the tranquillity necessary to tackle an array of problems. In early 2004, the United Nations, along with the United States and France, was again called to deal with difficult circumstances.

## Cambodia

In 1990 the United Nations assumed the task of bringing peace to Cambodia. Achieving independence from France in 1953, Cambodia was governed by the neutralist Prince Norodom Sihanouk until 1970 when he was overthrown in a right-wing coup led by Lon Nol. Despite substantial aid from the United States, the Lon Nol regime was in turn ousted by Marxist Khmer Rouge forces under Pol Pot in 1975. Incident to Pol Pot's brutal Marxist and anti-Western reforms, an estimated one to three million Cambodians were killed by disease, starvation, and mass execution. Khmer Rouge military forays into Vietnam led to a Vietnamese invasion of Cambodia in December 1979. The Vietnamese defeated Pol Pot and installed a new government styled the People's Republic of Kampuchea (PRK). This action did not end the fighting in Cambodia. In the unsettled conditions a civil war erupted pitting the Vietnam-backed government against several resistance groups, including the Khmer Rouge, which was militarily the strongest.

War and civil strife continued until the late 1980s when the Soviet Union, in the process of reducing its financial commitments to leftist movements around the world, began to encourage the PRK to resolve its civil war by sharing power with the insurgents. In August 1989 the various Cambodian factions convened a Paris International Conference on Cambodia, while contemporaneously Vietnamese forces were withdrawn from the country. When the parties were unable to reach a compromise settlement, however, hostilities were renewed.

In early 1990 the permanent members of the Security Council decided to assume a more active part in the peacemaking. Drawing on Secretariat expertise, they drafted proposals for a settlement that became the basis for discussion when in mid-1991 the five permanent members succeeded in again bringing the opposing domestic factions to the peace table. These talks led to a cease-fire agreement, to the creation of UNAMIC to monitor the cease-fire, and to the subsequent establishment of UNTAC to facilitate the establishment of a new constitutional system. UNAMIC completed its mission in March 1992 and UNTAC was withdrawn in September 1993, but Cambodia's problems did not end. Despite the limited success in establishing a government of national reconciliation, conflict between Hun Sen, a leftist ideologue, and his copremier, the monarchist Prince Norodom Ranariddh, produced still another clash. In 1997,

their mutual antagonism degenerated into open warfare, with Hun Sen prov-
ing to be the stronger of the two. Ranariddh was forced to seek refuge in the
Cambodian hinterland from where he sustained his attacks on the government.
Although Pacific-Asian nations made efforts to moderate the dispute, in March
1998 Hun Sen's high court sentenced Ranariddh, in absentia, to thirty years'
imprisonment. The continuing rivalry between Cambodia's key political personalities was only somewhat muted by the subsequent death of Pol Pot, who
had successfully evaded punishment for his major role in the "killing fields" of
the 1970s. The demise of Pol Pot nevertheless marked an end to the long period
of civil strife. In the new circumstances, and although differences between the
major Cambodian actors had not been reconciled, the parties, including Hun
Sen, agreed to hold a new round of popular elections. Moreover, given the presence of scores of international observers, the elections that were conducted in
July 1998 seemed to promise a new beginning for the beleaguered nation. Hun
Sen and Ranariddh were not reconciled, but the sentence imposed on the latter
was lifted, and both men again indicated a desire to work toward improving
conditions within Cambodia. New elections in February 2002 for local com-
munes resulted in a resounding victory for Hun Sen's Cambodian People's
Party. Prince Ranariddh's chances in the 2003 national election were considered slim at best. King Sihanouk, old and ailing, was estranged from his son,
and in matters of succession he seemed to favor the appointment of Queen
Monineath as regent. In the meantime, Hun Sen favored a successor to the king
who would be apolitical and subordinate to the elected leadership.

### The Balkans

The 1990s focused particular attention on the Balkans, and especially the
events leading up to and following the disintegration of Yugoslavia. The self-
declared independence of Croatia and Slovenia in 1991 received instant recognition from a newly unified Germany while other Western European states hesitated to certify an action that had such explosive potential. Indeed, Serbia,
seeking to perpetuate the Yugoslavian federation, was propelled into a war with
Croatia, a war that quickly spilled over into Bosnia-Herzegovina. No longer
able to sustain the unity of the old Yugoslavia, Serbia attempted to make the
most of the situation by moving against areas of Croatia and Bosnia. These actions caused the different ethnic groups to form themselves into rival armies,
with the most intense fighting occurring in Bosnia-Herzegovina.

The United Nations was among a number of international bodies that
sought to prevent the spread of the fighting and in 1992 sent the UNPROFOR
mission of several thousand troops drawn from countries around the world.
UNPROFOR was authorized to interpose itself between the warring parties.
While UNPROFOR was deployed in the most conflicted regions, diplomatic efforts were launched through the good offices of the United Nations, the European Union, and the Organization of Security and Cooperation in Europe. All
these efforts failed amid the viciousness of the combat, which had become
known as "ethnic cleansing." Serbia was judged the principal culprit in the pro-

longation of the fighting, and pressure was brought to bear on Yugoslavia's leader, Slobodan Milošević, to end his country's military involvement. At the same time, Milošević was ordered to restrain the Bosnian Serbs, who seemed determined to carve out a separate Serb state from Bosnia-Herzegovina.

In 1995 the leaders representing Serbia, Croatia, and Bosnia-Herzegovina were invited to participate in a peace conference in Dayton, Ohio, by President Bill Clinton. Although the Dayton Accords did not bring an end to all the fighting, the scene had been set for the introduction of NATO ground forces. UNPROFOR was dissolved and a UN International Police Task Force (UNMIBH) took its place alongside NATO troops.

The UN Transitional Administration for Eastern Slavonia, Baranja, and Western Sirmium (UNTAES) also helped demilitarize Serb forces and facilitate elections in April 1997. Moreover, a UN Preventive Deployment Force (UNPREDEP) was sent to the former Yugoslav Republic of Macedonia to protect that state from the spillover effects of the conflict in Bosnia. Kosovo could not be pacified, and the plight of its Albanian population provoked NATO to take still more forceful action against Serbia. The outcome of that clash was NATO's occupation of Kosovo in the form of KFOR, the establishment of an autonomous government for the region, the ultimate fall from power of Slobodan Milošević, and Serbia's attempt to transform itself into a workable democracy.

### Caucasus and Central Asia

The United Nations sent peacekeeping forces to the Caucasian state of Georgia, which had previously been a republic within the Soviet Union. But Georgia's territorial integrity and national unity were tested soon after it declared its independence. Abkhazian citizens of Georgia declared their desire to establish a separate state, and in the ensuing conflict, Russia led a Commonwealth of Independent States (CIS) peacemaking force into the new nation. UNOMIG was authorized to work with the CIS in monitoring compliance with a cease-fire agreement of 1993, and a separation of forces agreement was signed in Moscow in 1994. Given the volatility of the situation in Georgia, UNOMIG was destined to remain there, and it remained on station in 2004. A similar disturbance destabilized newly independent Tajikistan, and in 1994 the United Nations was called upon to monitor a 1994 agreement entered into by the government and the Tajik opposition. Here too the CIS sent a sizable military force, while a mission from the OSCE attempted to mediate the dispute. Nevertheless, it was the UN mission known as UNMOT that played an important role in inducing the parties to sign a peace agreement.

### Africa

UN efforts at achieving peaceful settlements in Africa after the end of the Cold War have not been easy. The several missions sent to Angola between 1989 and 1997 were largely responsible for the restoration of civil order. Indeed the verification missions—of which UNAVEM III was the last in a series—were re-called when the parties indicated that they could form a government and rec-oncile their differences. Renewed fighting, however, between the government and the forces of Jonas Savimbi destabilized the government in 1998, and a smaller mission (MONUA) sustained the UN presence and was authorized to help bridge factional differences as well as monitor violations of human rights. Savimbi, heavily supported by the United States during the Cold War years, still believed he was the only genuine representative of the Angolan nation. Savim-bi's forces were accused in December 1998 and January 1999 of shooting down two transport aircraft of the UN mission in Angola. The mortal danger this posed to MONUA members illustrated the desperate conditions in the region and questioned the feasibility of leaving MONUA in an exposed position. The mission therefore was phased out in February 1999. It was not until the death of Savimbi in a military skirmish on February 22, 2002, that this chapter in An-golan history came to an end. A cease-fire in March and blanket amnesty to Sa-vimbi's UNITA fighters led to a conference and peace agreement pressed by the UN Secretary-General and signed in Luanda in April 2002.

The situation in Liberia was perhaps worse because it involved anarchic conditions, similar to those that overwhelmed Somalia, and civil war of un-known proportions. UNOMIL operated in Liberia from 1993 to 1997, and in conjunction with Organization of African Unity (OAU) and ECOWAS peace-keepers it sought to restore a semblance of order to the war-torn nation. Liberia was unable to secure a government to unify the many tribes and factions that surfaced after the destruction of the long-standing regime of William V. S. Tub-man. As Liberia was a source of instability in western Africa, neighboring states made it their responsibility to correct the situation, and the OAU orchestrated an agreement that the United Nations tried to reinforce. Promising humani-tarian relief and seeking a return of the refugees that had inundated adjoining countries, the United Nations offered assistance in disarming the combatants, clearing mines, and removing unexploded bombs and artillery shells. Absorb-ing the demobilized fighters into a more congenial system proved extremely tedious, however, and it was with mixed emotions that the UN peacekeeping operation was ended after elections in the summer of 1997. After Septem-ber 1997, the ongoing problem of Liberia was made the exclusive concern of ECOWAS and the OAU, and matters were generally held in check, that is, un-til Charles Taylor, the President of Liberia, began exploiting strife in neighbor-ing Sierra Leone and Ivory Coast. Seeking personal gain, Taylor's forces and mercenaries sought to exploit the riches of the region. In the meantime, a rebel movement of Liberians United for Reconciliation and Democracy launched at-tacks in Monrovia and the hinterland. Much of the country came under rebel control, but Taylor pulled his forces back to Monrovia and prepared them for a protracted struggle. Liberia was plunged into chaos in 2001 and 2002, and the indiscriminate nature of the fighting took its toll on thousands of innocent civilians. Liberians again took flight, seeking asylum in neighboring countries as the civil war intensified. Taylor offered to negotiate with the rebels, but they flatly refused, insisting that he had to resign and leave the country. Faced with an unconditional demand, the war raged on. In June 2003 Taylor announced he had decided to give up the presidency. The call went out for an international peace force to intrude itself in the struggle. The United States was called upon to follow the example of France in the Congo and Britain in Sierra Leone, but Washington was not interested. Arguing that the African Union could handle the matter and that Nigerian forces trained by the United States could answer the call, the United States indicated that it could not answer calls of distress in every part of the world.

If Angola and Liberia were something less than outstanding as UN achievements, the bloodletting in Rwanda in 1996–97 was a disaster. Although UNOMUR had been sent to police the Ugandan border with Rwanda in 1993, no one was prepared for the genocide that the Hutus visited upon the Tutsi. Pleas by the UN Secretary-General to member states to help thwart the slaughter went unanswered, and were it not for the French intervention, there is no telling how many more tens of thousands would have lost their lives. Although the military situation in Rwanda was subsequently the responsibility of indigenous African forces, and a Tutsi-dominated government assumed power in the country, the United Nations offered technical assistance, refugee relief, and training for the judiciary and communal police through UNAMIR.

Somalia was still another publicized setback for the United Nations. The intervention there was prompted by the United States, which had cited a humanitarian emergency to save hundreds of thousands of innocent Somalis who were threatened by famine. The United Nations was enlisted in this effort and thus began the deployment of UNOSOM and UNOSOM II, the last of which represented a force of some twenty-eight thousand military and police personnel. Functioning with a budget of more than $1.6 billion, it assumed the tasks of UNITAF, the multinational force organized by the United Nations earlier. Authorized to use "all necessary means" to establish a secure environment for humanitarian relief operations, UNOSOM II also was mandated to rebuild the political, economic, and social life of Somalia. Compelled to make war on local militias blocking the formation of a central government, UNOSOM's humanitarian resettlement operations became demonstrations of force.

UN peacekeepers also operated in the Aouzou Strip between Chad and Libya, where a small staff of nine military observers and six civilians oversaw the withdrawal of Libyan forces. A coup in Sierra Leone in 1997 ousted the elected government, but the Security Council hesitated in responding to that problem. A resolution of concern was voted on February 26, 1998, but it did little to relieve the situation. Seizing the initiative, ECOWAS, and especially Nigeria, sent troops into Sierra Leone. They forced the coup leaders to leave the country, after which they also reinstated the original government. Tranquillity, however, did not come to Sierra Leone. Rebel forces continued to contest the ECOWAS force, now known as ECOMOG, and despite the latter's determined efforts, the violence continued. The UN Security Council authorized the dispatch of an observer force, UNOMSIL, in 1998 and gave its support to ECOMOG, but the fighting did not end. Although UNOMSIL was to be withdrawn by the end of 1998, given sustained turbulence in the East African nation, its mandate was renewed until October 1999. The civil war in Sierra Leone did not end until January 5, 2002, when the Revolutionary United Front turned in their weapons and the United Nations lifted the ban on the country's trade, especially its diamonds. In August 2002, however, the United Nations sent seventeen thousand peacekeepers to Sierra Leone, in major part to deal with the problems affecting the country from the Liberian civil war. The UN mission was extended because of the heavy influx of refugees and the need to maintain law and order in a country itself just months removed from civil mayhem.

## South Pacific

UN concerns for the people of East Timor were somewhat reduced when Indonesia's post-Suharto government ceased its aggressive campaign against the Timorese people. In the summer of 1998, Jakarta removed its troops and agreed to conduct elections in an effort to restore tranquillity and self-government to the island. Seizing the opportunity to press for a resolution of the Timorese problem, Secretary-General Kofi Annan named a Personal Representative on East Timor to work with the parties. In March 1999 the Representative, Jamsheed Marker, reported progress in his negotiations, and an agreement to hold a direct ballot in Timor was obtained from the Indonesian government. In effect, the people of East Timor were to be given the option of accepting or rejecting a proposal of autonomy. Secretary-General Annan cited his continuing concern but welcomed the positive atmosphere of the negotiations as well as the statements by the parties that their objective was peace and stability on the island. The election results indicated the heavy preference of the East Timorese for independence. Those opposed to the move, however, were not to be reconciled. Fighting broke out that required an international force led by Australia. In the ensuing battles, the Indonesian forces gave up the fight, and in due course peace was restored but at a considerable price in death and destruction. UNMISET was sent to the island in May 2002 to help guide the new state, now officially known as Timor-Leste.

## Perspective and Looking Ahead

The end of the Cold War did not eliminate the political, economic, and sociological roots of conflict, nor did it enable the United Nations to settle every dispute brought before it. The Middle East is still a volcano waiting for the next eruption. In Cyprus the underlying rivalry between Greek and Turkish sections remains unresolved after nearly three decades of UN settlement efforts. In Croatia, Bosnia-Herzegovina, Kosovo, Azerbaijan, Armenia, Georgia, Uzbekistan, Afghanistan, Kashmir, and elsewhere, political and cultural ambitions combine with ancient ethnic antagonisms to produce continuing threats to the peace. In a number of Third World countries, of which Somalia is one example and Liberia another, internal divisions and lack of governmental institutions provide a setting for persisting violence and disorder.

Citing the problems in making UN peacekeeping operations more effective as well as less expensive, and also noting the greater likelihood in the post–Cold War era of other organizations being involved in peacekeeping, Secretary-General Kofi Annan called for a reexamination of the co-deployment principle. Georgia, Tajikistan, Liberia, Sierra Leone, and the former Yugoslavia provided insight for the development of doctrine and guidelines that might better prepare the United Nations for more frequent partnerships with regional organizations. Annan digressed on the need to ensure that humanitarian strategies as well as longer-term development aims are fully integrated in an overall, sustainable peacekeeping program. The building of a collective security system in the twenty-first century, he noted, should center on preventive diplomacy and the avoidance of armed struggle. The UN system, as never before, must learn to meld its activities with regional IGOs as well as purposeful NGOs concerned with military security, civil law and order, human rights, refugees and displaced persons, elections, local administration, public utilities, health, education, finance, and reconstruction as well as the creation of civil society. All international institutions are important and all must be enlisted in the cause of peace and development, he opined, but no organization demonstrated more experience or greater scope and universality than the United Nations. Thus, despite the obvious weaknesses and shortcomings of the United Nations, the Secretary-General left little doubt that there was no real substitute for the UN system.

## SETTLING INTERNATIONAL DISPUTES AND HUMANITARIAN LAW

In settling international disputes, it should come as no surprise that the United Nations gives credence to the question of international humanitarian law. Drawing on the experience at the Nuremberg War Crime Trials after World War II, in May 1993 the Security Council established the International Criminal Tribunal for the Former Yugoslavia (ICTY) at The Hague. In November 1994, it created still another juridical agency, the International Criminal Tribunal for Rwanda (ICTR) in Tanzania. Citing "crimes against humanity," the violation of the four 1949 Geneva Conventions, as well as the 1948 Convention on the Prevention and Punishment of the Crime of Genocide, the United Nations was authorized by the member states to apply international humanitarian law to those responsible for violating fundamental human rights.

The ICTY was mandated to prosecute people responsible for serious violations of international humanitarian law committed in the territory of the former Yugoslavia from 1991 to 1995. Eleven judges were drawn from several countries, along with a chief prosecutor and deputy prosecutor. The tribunal began its work in 1995, and by 2003 it had rendered indictments against seventy-four individuals. Twenty voluntarily surrendered, nineteen were apprehended by international forces, and thirteen by national police. Several were under-going formal trial, fifteen having been sentenced to terms in prison and five hav-ing completed their time. In 2002, citing a lack of resources needed to manage the tribunals, the Secretary-General's office renewed pressure on the member states to pay their arrears. Faced with this dilemma, the ICTY had no alterna-tive but to withdraw charges against a number of Bosnian Serbs. In the past many years the ICTY could pursue cases only against those individuals for whom the evidence reveals "exceptionally brutal or serious offenses." Never-theless, since its inception the ICTY has become a fully operational legal insti-tution rendering judgments and setting important precedents of international criminal and humanitarian law. Legal issues now adjudicated by the court have not been considered since the Nuremberg and Tokyo trials after World War II. Examples of important legal decisions made by the ICTY include clarifications of the application of the Geneva Conventions, the further development of the doctrine of command responsibility, and the interpretation of rape as a form of torture and a crime against humanity.

The Rwandan tribunal was linked with the formation of a UN Human Rights Force (HRFOR) that functioned in concert with the UN High Commis-sioner for Refugees (UNHCR). Facing a more complex situation on a larger scale than that of the former Yugoslavia, the ICTR was concerned with not only bringing to justice the perpetrators of the 1994 genocide (in which an estimated one-half million to one million lives were lost) but also addressing the contin-uing assaults on refugees and displaced persons. HRFOR assisted the tribunal by identifying those connected with the bloodletting, a momentous task, given the detention of approximately ninety-two thousand people who were believed responsible for the slaughter. By 1997 HRFOR had more than 130 human rights observers deployed in Rwanda. The vastness of the undertaking is seen in the eleven HRFOR branches that covered all the prefectures of Rwanda. The mills of the Rwandan Criminal Court ground ever so slowly, however, and by 2003 total detainees were listed at sixty-one, with six serving sentences upon conviction. On trial were another eighteen, while thirty-one were awaiting ju-dicial proceedings against them.

Somewhat spurred by the creation of the courts for Rwanda and the for-mer Yugoslavia, but nevertheless in train since the end of World War II, a con-ference was convened in Rome from mid-June to mid-July 1998 for the ex-pressed purpose of giving reality to a global Nuremberg principle. The time was right for the creation of a permanent International Criminal Court where in-dividuals accused of atrocities and genocide could be tried and punished, ir-respective of the safeguards provided by their official positions. Attending the conference were delegations from 160 countries, seventeen intergovernmental organizations, fourteen specialized agencies and funds of the United Nations, and 124 NGOs. In the course of the month-long conference, debate swirled around the issues of jurisdiction and accountability, with the United States ea-ger to rein in the proposed court's broad powers of prosecution. The United States argued the need to try as war criminals personalities such as Pol Pot of Cambodia and Saddam Hussein of Iraq, but it refused to provide the court with unlimited powers to charge and prosecute U.S. citizens. Washington's greatest concern was the protection of its soldiers, sailors, and air personnel who served in stations around the world and who might be accused of war crimes. During the Iraq War in 2003, for example, General Tommy Franks, the U.S. commander of coalition forces, was accused of crimes against humanity and threatened with trial before the International Criminal Court.

The United States, originally joined by China, Russia, and France, insisted on the Security Council having the final say in all prosecution judgments. But despite major power opposition, fully one-third of the participants argued in favor of the Court's total independence. Supporting these nations were NGOs and human rights associations, many of them U.S.-based, who argued most forcefully for an unrestricted criminal court. In the course of the month-long discussions, numerous concessions were made, and delegates were called upon to alter their positions with each innovation. The United States, however, could not be accommodated. Efforts by the United States to seek more time, and to delay a vote on the issue, failed to receive any of the necessary support. On July 17, 1998, 120 countries overwhelmingly approved the statute that formally established the Court; the vote was 120 for and only 7 against, with 21 nations abstaining. At the request of the United States, the vote was listed as nonrecorded, however.

The formal title of the finished document was the Rome Statute of the International Criminal Court. The Statute and the Final Act of the Conference were opened for signature at the headquarters of the Food and Agriculture Organization, and subsequently at a ceremony hosted by the Mayor of Rome. The new International Criminal Court was slated to begin operations in The Hague as soon as the structure and personnel were in place. Established as an autonomous organ, the tribunal was made independent of the United Nations and therefore could act even when the international community was divided on a matter. Having been denied veto powers, the United States did not join the Court.

The creation of the International Criminal Court was a long time in coming, although its arrival was notably different from that envisaged by the Nuremberg trials. Nevertheless, the International Criminal Court was intended to be a permanent court with the power to investigate and bring to justice individuals who commit the most serious crimes of concern to the international community. And while the Court had its origin in World War II, it was only in 1992 that the UN General Assembly had directed the International Law Commission to elaborate a draft statute for an International Criminal Court. The Security Council's establishment of the criminal tribunals for the former Yugoslavia in 1993 and for Rwanda in 1994 accelerated this work. In December 1994, the Assembly formed an ad hoc committee of all the member states and members of specialized agencies to review the International Law Commission's draft statute. In December 1995, the Assembly created a Preparatory Committee for the purpose of discussing the substantive and administrative issues involved in the creation of the Court. Initial sessions of the Preparatory Committee were held in 1996, and the General Assembly extended its mandate, setting

1998 for the international conference. The Preparatory Committee's draft consisted of thirteen parts and 116 articles, which generated controversies on no fewer than fifteen hundred matters. The adoption of the statute, therefore, was no small accomplishment. And while many delegations acknowledged that the document was far from perfect, most conceded that it represented a major international achievement.

The International Criminal Court became a reality on July 1, 2002, sixty days after sixty states became parties to the Statute of the Court. The Court's mandate was to try individuals rather than states and to hold them accountable for the most serious crimes of concern to the international community, including genocide, war crimes and crimes against humanity, and eventually, the crime of aggression. The Court's jurisdiction extends only over crimes committed after July 1, 2002, when the Statute went into force. Genocide has been defined as a list of prohibited acts, such as killing or causing serious harm, committed with intent to destroy, in whole or in part, a national, ethnic, racial or religious group. Crimes against humanity include crimes such as the extermination of civilians; enslavement; torture; rape; forced pregnancy; persecution on political, racial, national, ethnic, cultural, religious, or gender grounds; and enforced disappearances as a systematic attack directed against a civilian population. Crimes against humanity do not include random acts of violence. War crimes include grave breaches of the Geneva Conventions and other serious violations of the laws and customs that apply to international armed conflict. Concern is with crimes committed as part of a plan or policy on a large scale. On the matter of aggression, the parties to the Statute must adopt a definition of aggression and the conditions under which the Court can exercise its jurisdiction. Terrorism was not included in the Rome Treaty, as the General Assembly was in the process of drafting a comprehensive convention against terrorism. There will be a later effort to add the crime of terrorism to the Court's jurisdiction. Working with the principle of complementarity, the Criminal Court will seize jurisdiction only in cases where the national courts have not acted. The International Criminal Court does not terminate the jurisdiction of national courts in individual states, but where national governments do not take the initiative in egregious cases, the International Criminal Court can act. The International Criminal Court is an entity separate from the United Nations. According to its Statute, its expenses will be funded by assessed contributions made by states that are parties to the Statute and by voluntary contributions from governments, international organizations, individuals, corporations, and other entities. In special circumstances, the United Nations can fund Court cases, but this is subject to the approval of the General Assembly.

## GLOBAL SECURITY AND THE UNITED NATIONS

In the fall of 1961, the United States submitted to the General Assembly a plan for "General and Complete Disarmament." An integral part of the plan was a proposal to build a "United Nations peace force" strong enough, ultimately, to "deter or suppress any threat or use of force in violation of the purposes and principles of the United Nations." In the final stage of disarmament, the force would be so strong that no state would have the military power to challenge it. The proposal was breathtaking, to say the least, if it could be taken seriously. It went much farther along the road to settling disputes through the collective will of international organizations than anything the peace architects of Versailles and San Francisco had dreamed of. The proposal created a noticeable ripple on the UN diplomatic pond, but the reaction was in no way commensurate with the drastic alteration of the conditions of international life that it contemplated. Most observers regarded it as lip service to international cooperation that would bring no more practical result than preceding proposals. This episode illustrates the paradox of global security today. People cherish the ultimate ideal of an orderly, peaceful world made secure by force wielded in the common interest, but their actions often negate the notion of a common interest.

The United Nations has often been characterized as similar to the mythological Sisyphus, forever commanded to roll a stone uphill and never permitted to reach the top. But perhaps the plight of world organization is not so eternally void of hope as that of Sisyphus. No one can feel confident about getting to the top, but occasionally the stone is rolled upward to a new plateau that marks a gain over previous efforts to promote world peace and security. The establishment of the League of Nations was such an advance, for all the League's inability to stave off aggression and a catastrophic world war. If international security arrangements had changed very little from the days of Abraham to the assassination of the Austrian Archduke at Sarajevo, the creation of the League of Nations nonetheless interjected a new and lasting element into the international system. The League symbolized widespread acceptance of the principle of common interest in the maintenance of peace and security, and it was an institutional embodiment of the principle. Even World War II could not wipe out this concept; the United Nations reflected the same sense of common interest.

This development, of course, is no more than a step toward world order. If international organization at the end of the twentieth century marked a plateau in the ascent toward world peace and security, it is still very far from the top. Note, for example, the end-of-the-century war between NATO and Serbia over Kosovo, and even more so, the twenty-first-century terrorist attacks of September 11, 2001. It is all too obvious that international organizations whose goals are the formation of a more integrated and tranquil planet must still manage in a world where armaments, alliances, and some form of balance of power remain the chief reliance of states in their quest for security. Or, how do international organizations function when angry people with access to weapons of mass destruction threaten the larger global system, and sovereign states determine that only self-defense, namely, the course of preemption, is a feasible option? What may pass for a global balance of power, or for setting limitations on the power of contemporary terrorism, however, remains dependent on the services provided by international organizations, and not the least, the United Nations. The United Nations promises enhanced communication, balanced mediation, judicious mentoring, and rational approaches to a world burdened by global crisis. Contemporary events have demonstrated that internal as well as external conflict may yet be ameliorated by a pacifying UN presence. Resolving conflict indeed has merit in itself, notably in humanitarian matters. The promotion of domestic stability more often than not also makes regional and global systems more stable and better prepared to cope with the challenges of a new and unsettled age. Therefore, an ever-increasing convergence of security interests among the larger powers through international organization is essential. Signs that the world has reached a higher plateau in the ascent toward peace and universal understanding are emerging, but clearly the work of building world order is still in its infancy.

## CONCLUSIONS ON DISPUTE SETTLEMENT

Most states settle most of their disputes with one another most of the time without resorting to force and needing assistance from third parties. The bulk of day-to-day transactions between nationals of different countries and their governments are mutually beneficial, and all parties have an interest in peacefully resolving differences that may arise. Most differences between governments are settled by diplomatic negotiation without recourse to courts, the United Nations, or complicated procedures and pose no threat to international peace and security. The United States alone concludes perhaps two hundred treaties and executive agreements with foreign governments every year, each of which settles some disputed question. Major states annually settle scores or even hundreds of disputed matters with other states through letters and memoranda, without resorting to the formality of a treaty. If one could identify and count all of the disputes between governments that have been peacefully resolved, the statistical evidence in support of peaceful settlement as an international norm would be overwhelming.

By contrast, the UN record of peaceful settlement is statistically not strong. Although people may reasonably differ in their judgment of UN effects on particular disputes, knowledgeable observers agree that during the Cold War era the United Nations contributed to the settlement of many fewer than half of the disputes brought before it. Table 6-2 presents the findings of Ernst Haas in a study of disputes considered by the United Nations from 1945 to 1984. During that time, by his methods of calculation, 137 disputes were referred to the United Nations for settlement. Of this number, the United Nations helped settle just 32. In 11 of the disputes, the organization's contribution to settlement was judged substantial; in the other 23 the United Nations was important but nevertheless modest in relation to other influences working toward settlement. An additional 42 disputes, for a total of 74, were in some degree ameliorated because of UN efforts at conflict management. Conflict *management,* as Haas defines the term, includes not only settling disputes but also abating a conflict (reducing its intensity), isolating a conflict (inhibiting third parties from intervening diplomatically or militarily in support of disputants), and stopping armed

TABLE 6-2   UN Success in Conflict Management, 1945–1984

| TIME PERIOD | NUMBER OF DISPUTES REFERRED TO UNITED NATIONS | GREAT UN SUCCESS | | LIMITED UN SUCCESS | | GREAT OR LIMITED UN SUCCESS | |
|---|---|---|---|---|---|---|---|
| | | NUMBER | PERCENTAGE | NUMBER | PERCENTAGE | NUMBER | PERCENTAGE |
| 1945–50 | 20 | 8 | 40.0 | 5 | 25.0 | 13 | 65.0 |
| 1951–55 | 12 | 3 | 25.0 | 1 | 8.3 | 4 | 33.3 |
| 1956–60 | 16 | 6 | 37.5 | 6 | 37.5 | 12 | 75.0 |
| 1961–65 | 26 | 5 | 19.2 | 5 | 19.2 | 10 | 38.5 |
| 1966–70 | 14 | 4 | 28.6 | 5 | 35.7 | 9 | 64.3 |
| 1971–75 | 12 | 3 | 25.0 | 2 | 16.7 | 5 | 41.7 |
| 1976–80 | 24 | 3 | 12.5 | 13 | 54.2 | 16 | 66.7 |
| 1981–84 | 13 | 0 | 0 | 5 | 38.5 | 5 | 38.5 |
| Total | 137 | 32 | 23.4 | 42 | 30.7 | 74 | 54.0 |

SOURCE: Ernst B. Haas, "The Collective Management of International Conflict, 1945–1984," in *The United Nations and the Maintenance of Internal Peace and Security,* United Nations Institute for Training and Research (Dordrecht: Martinus Nijhoff, 1987), tables 5, A, E, and F, pp. 63, 67–68.

hostilities. UN success in conflict management was characterized as "great" in 32 cases and "limited" in the other 42. If the concept of pacific settlement is expanded to embrace Haas's definition of conflict management, the UN success level through 1984 rises to just 54 percent, including cases in which the organization made only a limited contribution.

No similar study has covered the period since 1984, but the cases discussed in connection with UN peacekeeping and dispute settlement indicate that UN performance has not improved. The United Nations would undoubtedly do better if it had the legal right and practical capability to enforce settlements. In this respect the United Nations mirrors the shortcomings of the larger international system, which lacks an adequate sense of community for supporting central coercive institutions. In peacefully settling most of their bilateral disputes with one another, states also operate within the constraints of the existing system, but that is an unfair comparison because the United Nations never deals with routine disputes susceptible to ready compromise. Bilateral negotiation has already failed in most disputes brought to the United Nations, and parties have often resorted to the threat or use of force. In many UN cases, one or more of the parties is willing to settle only for the complete capitulation of the other side. Not all UN disputes are this intractable, but generally, the disputes that reach the United Nations are the most difficult to resolve. Viewed in this light, the spotty UN settlement record is understandable. Given the nature of the disputes that come to the United Nations, one may conclude that a contribution to the settlement of any of them is noteworthy.

The UN's ability to settle disputes has always been closely correlated with the existence within the United Nations of a consensus having links with effective centers of power outside the organization. At the inception of the United Nations, the necessary consensus in the Security Council was available only on the rare occasions when Soviet and U.S. interests converged. For a number of years U.S. leadership was able to engineer the needed consensus in the General Assembly on many issues, and that consensus was given practical effect by U.S. global stature. The organization was seldom effective in resolving conflicts between opposing Cold War coalitions, but promoting settlement between an aligned and a nonaligned state was often possible. The United Nations was quite effective in dealing with decolonization disputes, perhaps the typical case of aligned versus nonaligned.

After 1960 U.S. leadership in the Assembly was replaced by Third World dominance. The new majority readily mustered a united front on issues of Western colonialism, on Israel and South Africa, and usually on opposition to superpower military interventions. But the remaining vestiges of vanished colonial empires became a declining portion of the UN agenda, and when a superpower opposed the consensus, the prevailing majority lacked the power to carry out its mandates. This often led to name-calling and denunciation in place of a genuine search for settlement. Other serious quarrels and threats to peace occurred within the Third World, and here the requisite consensus was often lacking. Thus, whereas Israel, South Africa, and the remaining colonial enclaves evoked strong UN disapproval, the Third World majority was much less decisive in dealing with disputes between the nonaligned. Some examples of the latter are Indian aid to secessionist Bangladesh in 1971, Indonesian seizure of East Timor in 1975, Vietnamese military occupation of Cambodia, China's incursion into Vietnam in 1979, and the Iraqi attack on Iran in 1980.

Since 1987 U.S.-Soviet and now U.S.-Russia cooperation has brought new consensus to the Security Council. Remarkably, China—sometimes grudgingly or by abstention—goes along. The introduction of a new level of terrorism also demands increased cooperation among the greater of the world's powers. Peaceful settlement procedures with terrorists determined to destroy the contemporary nation-state system have yet to be proved germane. Terrorism reveals all the conditions of unremitting violence, and some believe that it is only the language of counterviolence that applies to such situations. Peaceful settlement revolves around compromise, but with global terrorism the practice of compromise ceases to have meaning. More than ever before, a UN consensus is linked with effective centers of world power. The Charter framers at San Francisco never contemplated that the United Nations would abolish differences of interest among states. They certainly never imagined the forces of anarchy challenging the major representatives of global power. Their beliefs and thoughts centered on international disputes and how they could be kept within peaceful bounds. They saw that the United Nations could help with this task. In this they were not wrong or mistaken. Peaceful settlement of international disputes between states is still a most worthy goal, and the United Nations has been and will continue to be a helpful adjunct to other settlement techniques. It is important to note in this age of substantial uncertainty that no war of global extent, no conflict severe enough to threaten the system of independent states has emerged since the United Nations was established. To this conflict containment, the United Nations has made a noble contribution. The persistence of unresolved disputes and the occurrence of numerous local wars, especially those that give rise to terrorist movements, however, still leave the world far short of the ideal of peaceful settlement. One can no longer regard such conflict at the periphery as a reasonable price to pay for stability at the center because the periphery has become the center. But if the framers of the UN Charter were right in believing that any war must be avoided, preventing war in the era of global terrorism represents an even greater challenge.

# NOTES

1. *New York Times,* June 6, 1998.
2. "Report on the Work of the Organization," *UN Chronicle* 19, no. 9 (October 1982), p. 2.
3. Gideon Rafael, *Destination Peace: Three Decades of Israeli Foreign Policy* (New York: Stein & Day, 1981), p. 235. This subject is elaborated in Istvan S. Pogany, *The Security Council and the Arab-Israeli Conflict* (Aldershot, UK: Gower, 1984).
4. Ernst B. Haas, "The Collective Management of International Conflict, 1945–1984," in United Nations Institute for Training and Research, *The United Nations and the Maintenance of International Peace and Security* (Dordrecht: Martinus Nijhoff, 1987), pp. 58–59, note 3.

# SELECTED READINGS

Annan, Kofi. *Prevention of Armed Conflict: Report of the Secretary-General.* New York: United Nations Publications, 2003.

Art, Robert J., and Patrick M. Cronin, eds. *The United States and Coercive Diplomacy.* Washington, DC: United States Institute of Peace, 2003.

Bailey, Sydney D. *How Wars End: The United Nations and the Termination of Armed Conflicts, 1946–1964.* 2 vols. New York: Oxford University Press, 1982.

———. *The Procedure of the U.N. Security Council.* 2nd ed. New York: Oxford University Press, 1988.

Berridge, G. R. *Return to the UN: UN Diplomacy in Regional Conflicts.* New York: St. Martin's Press, 1991.

Boudreau, Thomas E. *Sheathing the Sword: The U.N. Secretary-General and the Prevention of Inter-Nation Conflict.* Westport, CT: Greenwood Press, 1991.

Boyd, Andrew. *Fifteen Men on a Powder Keg: A History of the United Nations Security Council.* New York: Stein & Day, 1971.

Brus, Marcel, Sam Muller, and Serv Wiemers, eds. *The United Nations Decade of International Law: Reflections on International Dispute Settlement.* Dordrecht: Martinus Nijhoff, 1991.

Childers, Erskine, ed. *Challenges to the United Nations: Building a Safer World.* New York: St. Martin's Press, 1995.

Deng, Francis M., and I. William Zartman. *Conflict Resolution in Africa.* Washington, DC: Brookings Institution, 1991.

Diehl, Paul. *The Politics of Global Governance: International Organizations in an Interdependent World.* Boulder, CO: Lynne Rienner, 1996.

Hillen, John. *Blue Helmets: The Strategy of U.N. Military Operations.* Washington, DC: Brassey's, 1998.

Jones, Dorothy. *Toward a Just World: The Critical Years in the Search for International Justice.* Chicago: University of Chicago Press, 2002.

Lall, Arthur S. *Multilateral Negotiation and Mediation.* New York: Pergamon Press, 1985.

McWhinney, Edward. *Judicial Settlement of International Disputes: Jurisdiction, Justiciability, and Judicial Law-Making on the Contemporary International Court.* Dordrecht: Martinus Nijhoff, 1991.

Merrills, J. G. *International Dispute Settlement.* 2nd ed. Cambridge, UK: Cambridge University Press, 1991.

Nicol, Davidson. *The United Nations Security Council: Towards Greater Effectiveness.* New York: UNITAR, 1982.

——, ed. *Paths to Peace: The UN Security Council and Its Presidency.* New York: Pergamon Press, 1981.

Niedermayer, Oskar, and Richard Sinnott, eds. *Public Opinion and Internationalized Governance.* New York: Oxford University Press, 1995.

Peck, Connie, and David A. Hamburg. *Sustainable Peace: The Role of the UN and Regional Organizations in Preventing Conflict.* Lanham, MD: Rowman and Littlefield, 1998.

Price, Richard, and Mark Zacher, eds. *The United Nations and Global Security.* New York: Palgrave, 2004.

Roberts, Adam, and Benedict Kingsbury. *United Nations, Divided World.* Oxford: Clarendon Press, 1988.

Rosenne, Shabtai. *The World Court: What It Is and How It Works.* 4th rev. ed. Dordrecht: Martinus Nijhoff, 1989.

Singh, Nagendra. *The Role and Record of the International Court of Justice.* Dordrecht: Martinus Nijhoff, 1989.

United Nations. *The United Nations and the Maintenance of International Peace and Security.* United Nations Institute for Training and Research. Dordrecht: Martinus Nijhoff, 1987.

Urquhart, Brian. *A Life in Peace and War.* New York: Harper & Row, 1987.

Weiss, Thomas G., and James G. Blight, eds. *The Suffering Grass: Superpowers and Regional Conflict in Southern Africa and the Caribbean.* Boulder, CO: Lynne Rienner, 1992.

Woodhouse, Tom, Robert Bruce, and Malcolm Dando, eds. *Peacekeeping and Peacemaking: Towards Effective Intervention in Post-Cold War Conflicts.* New York: St. Martin's Press, 1998.

Yost, David S. *NATO Transformed: The Alliance's New Roles in International Security.* Washington, DC: U.S. Institute of Peace Press, 1999.

# 7

## DISARMAMENT AND ARMS CONTROL

Although the UN Charter does not include disarmament in its statement of purposes and principles, arms control negotiations have been a UN concern since they came into being. For decades the results were meager. A few limited arms control measures were agreed to, but the growth of national armaments and the development of new and more destructive technologies continued apace. Hundreds of proposals and thousands of meetings brought disarmament no closer to being a reality. It was always a mirage—visible at a distance but fading away on close approach.

Then the Cold War ended. The world communist threat dissolved. The Warsaw Pact was terminated, unilateral actions to reduce armaments were undertaken in Eastern Europe, and NATO reciprocated by a reduction in forces. The collapse of communist economic theory and the breakup of the Union of Soviet Socialist Republics (USSR) into fifteen independent states made continued arms competition with the West totally unfeasible. These developments engendered hope that at last the much-mentioned East-West disarmament might become a reality. Expectations for worldwide peace and security, however, were short-lived. The specter of nuclear proliferation, the burgeoning arms trade to less developed states, and the aggressive posturing of global terrorists meant that states would continue to center attention on national defense and the acquisition of still more deadly and sophisticated weapons.

This chapter nonetheless explores the prospects for disarmament. The history of arms negotiations is reviewed and efforts are made to evaluate the progress to date. The chapter also analyzes the obstacles to successful arms control and examines a number of possible approaches to the continuing disarmament problem. This broad-based analysis of the theory and practice of arms control is necessary to place UN actions in their global and historical contexts and to identify both the promise of disarmament and the realities of the international situation.

# DISARMAMENT IN HISTORICAL PERSPECTIVE

Pursuit of disarmament through international negotiation is largely a phenomenon of the twentieth century. In centuries past, visionaries such as Immanuel
Kant, Jean-Jacques Rousseau, and William Penn had postulated the ideal of a
completely disarmed world, but these utopian notions had little effect except in
intellectual circles. Through most of the nineteenth century, various proposals
for arms reduction by European leaders aroused little interest. The only real
success of that period was the Rush-Bagot Agreement of 1817 by which the
United States and Great Britain limited naval armaments on the Great Lakes
and established an open and unfortified frontier across the North American
continent. The first major conference to focus attention on disarmament was
called by Tsar Nicholas of Russia and it convened at The Hague in 1899. The
Russian Tsar's action was motivated by a desire to reduce the economic burden
of armaments and to keep Russia's rivals from equipping their armies with new
and improved artillery. The conference was attended by virtually all the great
imperial powers of that day. Although no agreement was reached on the limitation of armaments and war budgets, the first Hague Conference codified
some of the laws of war and produced a Convention for the Pacific Settlement
of Disputes. Eager to pursue the matter further, the conferees agreed to hold a
second Hague Peace Conference in 1907. At this conference there were some
minor victories, but Europeans did nothing to slow the arms race, which in a
few short years climaxed in the maelstrom of World War I.[1]

## DISARMAMENT EFFORTS DURING THE LEAGUE YEARS

The Covenant of the League of Nations followed the prescription advocated by
Woodrow Wilson in one of his Fourteen Points. It provided that armaments, as
a recognized cause of war, should be "reduced to the lowest point consistent
with national safety" but retained in sufficient quantities to provide for "the enforcement by common action of international obligations." Implementation of
Covenant provisions awaited general agreement on arms limitation, but Germany was immediately subjected to disarmament under the terms of the Versailles Treaty that formally ended World War I. The German Rhineland was occupied by the French and completely demilitarized, and Germany was denied
the right to build a formidable military presence. Other limitations on German
power also were imposed, that although effective in the short term, caused Germans to demand the rescinding of the Versailles Treaty. Neither the League nor
the allied powers that had defeated Germany were prepared to enforce the
treaty provisions, and Germany had no reason to limit its military program.
Moreover, the war reparations imposed on Germany had destroyed its fragile
economy. It also lit the fuse for the Great Depression that shook the world in
the late 1920s. With economic dislocation and political instability undermining the peace in numerous countries, Germany defied the imposed restrictions,

and no one among the former allies was prepared to make an issue of it. Adolf Hitler's election as Chancellor of Germany in 1933 was a direct consequence of these events, and when the German Fuehrer ordered the remilitarization of the country, no European power was prepared to test Hitler's will. Moreover, the Americans, no longer guided by Wilson, used their geographic location to project a policy of isolation, and Washington indicated that it did not object to German actions, or at least would not challenge them. European militarism was again in vogue, this time in the guise of fascism and communism. The League of Nations continued its quest for disarmament, but by the mid-1930s that goal only reminded observers of the idealism that briefly flourished at the end of World War I.

It is important to recount the League of Nations' efforts at realizing a disarmed world. The horrors of World War I were still vivid when the several disarmament conferences were organized under provisions of the League Covenant. The first major postwar conference to limit arms by voluntary agreement, because of U.S. participation, took place outside the League framework. The United States had declined membership in the League, but it was keenly interested in disarmament and hosted the first major attempt at reducing the arms stockpiled during the Great War. In 1921 the Washington Naval Conference—called by the United States and attended by representatives of Britain, France, Italy, and Japan—set the pace for arms limitation negotiations. The deliberations in Washington extended beyond a full year, and at the close of the conference a treaty was signed that limited the size of capital warships, the most awesome weapon of the period. The treaty restricted the construction of battleships and aircraft carriers for ten years, and limited new construction thereafter by a ratio agreement (the United States, 5; Britain, 5; Japan, 3; France, 1.67; and Italy, 1.67). The treaty also imposed limitations on naval bases on Pacific islands. The ink on the treaty was hardly dry, however, when some of the parties violated the spirit of the treaty, and others the letter of the treaty. Britain and the United States engaged in a "cruiser race"; Japan devised ingenious variations of the prohibited vessels to nullify the intent of the treaty; and France refused to implement any limit in the absence of a general European security arrangement. The record of violations and subterfuge that followed the Washington Naval Arms Limitation Treaty, and the countermeasures undertaken in response to evasions, call attention to the failure of implementing a disarmament agreement without international inspection and enforcement machinery in place. Moreover, Germany, which was denied the right to build any battleships, maneuvered around the prohibition by constructing fast, maneuverable, and lighter vessels but with the same firepower of a capital ship.

The League was even less successful in its efforts to promote a general reduction in armaments. A Temporary Mixed Commission of nongovernmental experts, appointed by the Assembly to formulate a plan for consideration by the Council, labored from 1921 to 1924 without producing an acceptable proposal. In 1925 the Assembly decided to try the world conference approach and established a Preparatory Commission composed of governmental representatives to lay the groundwork for an agreement. After five years of sporadic effort, in 1930 the Commission prepared a Draft Convention that demonstrated only the inability of its members to reach accord on limiting their armed forces. The main provisions of the Draft Convention called for the reduction of military budgets, modest reductions in naval armaments, and the establishment of a Permanent Disarmament Commission. The Preparatory Commission's experience did not augur well for arms limitation agreement, although the deepening worldwide economic depression raised the possibility that the struggle to preserve fiscal solvency might force some states to curtail arms production unilaterally.

A World Disarmament Conference was convened at Geneva in 1932, with sixty-one states represented. Each of the major nations in turn offered its scheme to a skeptical group of delegates. The French plan envisaged a comprehensive security system that included limited disarmament, an international control system, compulsory arbitration, and an international police force under League jurisdiction to guarantee security. Britain offered a plan that would outlaw the use of "offensive" weapons through a reinforced League security system, provide for disarmament by stages over a five-year period, and outlaw weapons of mass destruction. Germany demanded equality with France in any disarmament program, and the United States proposed a uniform reduction in forces but with a view to the same arms ratio existing before the agreement.

There was never much chance for agreement, but the last bit of idealism was extinguished in 1933 when Hitler became Chancellor of Germany and withdrew his country from the disarmament conference, and subsequently, from the League of Nations. The conference, immobilized almost from the start by the conflict between German demands for arms equality and the French insistence on arms superiority over Germany, adjourned in 1934 without agreement on an arms limitation treaty. The conference may have been a useful learning experience, however. There had been agreement on broad principles. Though never formalized, there was general revulsion against the use of chemical and bacteriological weapons. There also was consensus on arms reduction, as well as agreement that military budgets must be curtailed. The general acceptance of the idea that an international authority should be established to supervise any disarmament agreement also was a step forward. All the debates in the global conference and in the League's Assembly, though protracted and ultimately fruitless, nevertheless helped prepare the world for the next round in the disarmament cycle under the aegis of the United Nations.

## THE UNITED NATIONS AND DISARMAMENT

Disarmament negotiations since 1945 have been more persistent than during the League era and have been driven by a greater sense of urgency. The explosion of an atomic bomb over Hiroshima just six weeks after the signing of the UN Charter alerted the world to the potential of a calamity far greater than the destructiveness of World War II. The ensuing Cold War, accompanied by full-scale rearmament, rival alliances, perpetual crises, and the development of intercontinental missiles with thermonuclear warheads—all occurring within a setting of ideological hostility—forged a link in some minds between disarmament and sheer survival. Third World peoples, silent during the 1930s, joined the disarmament chorus not only from fear of nuclear destruction but in the hope that resources diverted from armaments might be channeled to economic development.

The Charter framers did not assign disarmament a prominent role in pursuing the primary goal of peace and security. In the Charter scheme, the use of collective force against international lawbreakers, rather than disarmament, was the key to maintaining a peaceful world. Specific mention of the word "disarmament" in the Charter occurs only twice. Under Article 11, the General Assembly is authorized to consider and make recommendations concerning "the general principles of cooperation in the maintenance of international peace and security, including the principles governing disarmament and the regulation of armaments." The other reference appears in Article 47, which authorizes the Military Staff Committee to advise the Security Council on "the regulation of armaments and possible disarmament."

The failure of the UN framers to stress the need for disarmament can be ascribed in part to their ignorance of the atomic device that scientists were secretly preparing to test at the very time the Charter was being written. Moreover, the frustrations that combined with League failure gave new emphasis to the need for an international army to maintain peace and security through community applied force. But even the quest for an international army was hardly the objective of the nations emerging from a war that had challenged all their ideas for a new, more amicable world order. Simply put, the post–World War II period did not succumb to the idealism that had surfaced after World War I. Disarmament was hardly judged a realistic program in an age of ballooning nation-states.

Unlike the League Covenant, which had called for an outright *reduction* in arms, the Charter merely proclaims the objective of arms *regulation*. Regulation implies the need for a strategically balanced ceiling on armaments so that the collective security machinery of the United Nations can function in a world not obsessed with fear of an imminent and massive attack. The close relationship between the two objectives—arms regulation and collective security—led the framers to assign responsibility for both functions to the Security Council aided by the Military Staff Committee (Articles 26 and 46, respectively). Giving the same bodies the responsibility of formulating plans for arms regulation *and* the use of military forces offered no contradiction for the framers, who considered progress in both areas essential to the maintenance of peace and security.

Despite the difficulty encountered in the area of disarmament during the years of the Cold War, the United Nations never lost sight of its goal of a world less prone to arms races. The General Assembly established six committees dealing exclusively with disarmament and international related issues, of which the First Committee, consisting of all member states, focuses on disarmament and security questions and recommends draft resolutions to the Assembly. The Disarmament Commission is another body that addresses key areas, notably nuclear-free/weapon-free zones and the reduction and limitation of conventional weapons. The Secretary-General also was made responsible for overseeing activities concerned with arms reduction, especially in the matter of weapons of mass destruction. A UN Institute for Disarmament Research (UNIDIR) was established in Geneva and made an integral part of the UN Secretariat. In 1978, an Advisory Board on Disarmament Matters was created by action of the General Assembly and made functional in 1982. This Board advised the Secretary-General on various aspects of research in the area of arms limitation. It also served as the Board of Trustees for UNIDIR and assisted in the dissemination of the UN Disarmament Information Program.

In 1997 the Board examined the reorganization of the UN disarmament sector proposed by Kofi Annan and cited the new security challenges facing the world body in the twenty-first century. The 1997 conference focused attention on both weapons of mass destruction and conventional arms and emphasized the need to have member states register conventional arms in their arsenals. It also called for the establishment of norms in the implementation of agreements related to weapons of mass destruction. A most important action of the UN disarmament organs was the 1995 Nuclear Nonproliferation Treaty conference, which was convened at UN Headquarters in New York City for the purpose of extending the 1970 NPT indefinitely. After twenty-four days of difficult negotiations, agreement was achieved when the acknowledged nuclear powers— the United States, Russia, China, Britain, and France—assured the nonnuclear states that a comprehensive test-ban treaty would be entered into during the following year. The nuclear powers also expressed a determination to reduce their nuclear stockpiles over a twenty-year period. On the subject of conventional weapons, notably those described as "excessively injurious" or having "indiscriminate effects," the United Nations sought to outlaw the use of blinding laser weapons and land mines. The success of these ventures was illustrated in protocols calling for their abandonment in 1995, 1996, and again in 1997. (See Table 7-1.)

The UN Department for Disarmament Affairs (DDA) was reestablished in January 1998 by a General Assembly resolution after having been discontinued in 1992. The DDA promotes the goal of nuclear disarmament and nonproliferation and the strengthening of disarmament regimes in respect to other weapons of mass destruction, that is, chemical and biological weapons. It also promotes disarmament in conventional weapons, especially in regard to land mines and small arms. DDA provides organizational support for setting norms in disarmament through the work of the General Assembly and its First Committee, the Disarmament Commission, the Conference on Disarmament, and other bodies. It fosters preventive disarmament measures, including transparency and confidence building on military matters. It also encourages regional disarmament. DDA is responsible for the implementation of practical disarmament

TABLE 7-1    Major International Instruments on Disarmament and Related Issues

| DATE | INSTRUMENT |
| --- | --- |
| 17 June 1925 | Protocol for the *Prohibition of the Use in War of Asphyxiating, Poisonous or Other Gases,* and of Bacteriological Methods of Warfare |
| 12 August 1949 | *Geneva Convention (I)* for the Amelioration of the Condition of the Wounded and Sick in Armed Forces in the Field |
| 12 August 1949 | *Geneva Convention (II)* for the Amelioration of the Condition of Wounded, Sick, and Shipwrecked Members of Armed Forces at Sea |
| 12 August 1949 | *Geneva Convention (III)* Relative to the Treatment of Prisoners of War |
| 12 August 1949 | *Geneva Convention (IV)* Relative to the Protection of Civilian Persons in Time of War |
| 14 May 1954 | Convention for the *Protection of Cultural Property* in the Event of Armed Conflict; *Final Act* of the Intergovernmental Conference on the Protection of Cultural Property; *Protocol* |
| 1 December 1959 | The *Antarctic* Treaty |
| 5 August 1963 | Treaty Banning Nuclear Weapon Tests in the Atmosphere, in Outer Space, and Under Water (*Partial Test Ban Treaty*) |
| 27 January 1967 | Treaty on Principles Governing the Activities of States in the Exploration and Use of *Outer Space,* including the Moon and other Celestial Bodies |
| 14 February 1967 | Treaty for the Prohibition of Nuclear Weapons in Latin America (*Tlatelolco Treaty*) |
| 1 July 1968 | Treaty on the *Non-Proliferation of Nuclear Weapons* |
| 10 April 1972 | Convention on the Prohibition of the Development, Production, and Stockpiling of *Bacteriological (Biological) and Toxin Weapons* and on Their Destruction |
| 26 May 1972 | Treaty between the United States of America and the Union of Soviet Socialist Republics on the *Limitation of Anti-Ballistic Missile Systems* |
| 3 July 1974 | Protocol for Limitation of Anti-Ballistic Missile Systems Treaty |
| 3 July 1974 | Treaty Between the United States of America and the Union of Soviet Socialist Republics on the Limitation of Underground Nuclear Weapon Tests (*Threshold Test Ban Treaty*); Protocol |
| 10 December 1976 | Convention on the Prohibition of Military or Any Other Hostile Use of *Environmental Modification Techniques* |
| 8 June 1977 | Protocol I Additional to the Geneva Conventions of 12 August 1949, and Relating to the *Protection of Victims of International Armed Conflict* |
| 8 June 1977 | Protocol II Additional to the Geneva Conventions of 12 August 1949, and Relating to the *Protection of Victims of Non-International Armed Conflict* |
| 21 September 1977 | Guidelines for Nuclear Transfers Adopted by the 15-Nation Nuclear Suppliers' Group (*London Guidelines*) |
| 18 December 1979 | Agreement Governing the Activities of States on the *Moon* and other Celestial Bodies |
| 10 October 1980 | Convention on Prohibitions or Restrictions on the Use of Certain *Conventional Weapons* Which May be Deemed To Be Excessively Injurious or To Have Indiscriminate Effects |
| 12 October 1995 | Additional Protocol (IV) on *Blinding Laser Weapons* |

TABLE 7-1    *(continued)*

| DATE | INSTRUMENT |
|---|---|
| 6 August 1985 | South Pacific Nuclear Free Zone Treaty (*Treaty of Rarotonga*) |
| 13 January 1993 | Convention on the Prohibition of the Development, Production, Stockpiling, and Use of *Chemical Weapons* and on their Destruction |
| 3 April 1992 | Guidelines for Transfers of Nuclear-Related Dual-Use Equipment, Material, and Related Technology (*Warsaw Guidelines*) |
| 1 April 1993 | Guidelines for Nuclear Transfers (*Revision of NSG London Guidelines* of 1977) |
| 11 May 1995 | Decisions and Resolution Adopted by the 1995 *Review and Extension Conference* of the Parties to the Treaty on the Non-Proliferation of Nuclear Weapons |
| 15 December 1995 | Treaty on the Southeast Asia Nuclear-Weapon-Free Zone (*Bangkok Treaty*); Annex; Protocol |
| 11 April 1996 | Treaty on the Nuclear-Weapon-Free Zone in Africa (*Pelindaba Treaty*); *Cairo Declaration* |
| 10 September 1996 | Comprehensive *Nuclear-Test-Ban Treaty* |
| 5 September 1997 | Joint Convention on the Safety of Spent Fuel Management and on the Safety of Radioactive Waste Management (IAEA) |
| 18 September 1997 | Convention on the Prohibition of the Use, Stockpiling, Production, and Transfer of Anti-Personnel Mines and on their Destruction (*Ottawa Convention*) |
| 12 January 1998 | United Nations International Convention for the Suppression of Terrorist Bombings |
| 17 July 1998 | Rome Statute of the International Criminal Court |
| 15 December 2000 | United Nations Convention against Transnational Organized Crime |

SOURCE: UN Website (http://www.unog.ch/disarm/distreat/warfare.htm).

measures after a conflict that includes disarming and demobilizing combatants and helping them to fit themselves back into civil society.

The DDA is structured into five branches: the Secretariat and Conference Support Branch; the Weapons of Mass Destruction Branch; the Conventional Arms Branch; the Regional Disarmament Branch; and the Monitoring, Database, and Information Branch. In 2003 the Secretary-General appointed Nobuyasu Abe to succeed Jayantha Dhanapala to become Undersecretary-General for Disarmament Affairs. Not the least of DDA concerns is the issue of transparency in arms transfers. Without substantive and accurate disclosure, confidence building and security among member states is impossible. With this need in view the General Assembly agreed in 1992 to establish the UN Register of Conventional Arms. The arrangement encourages governments to provide information on a voluntary basis, especially arms transferred to other states. Among the major weapons to be accounted for are battle tanks, armored combat vehicles, large-caliber artillery systems, combat aircraft, attack helicopters, warships and missiles, and missile launchers. Data collected are published annually by the United Nations as official documents and are made available to any interested party. Discussion continues on weapons of mass destruction, small arms, and additional information on procurement through national production and military holdings. Regional and subregional registers, especially of small arms, are also under review for inclusion.

Considering the detailed work of the DDA along with the General Assembly First Committee, the Disarmament Commission, and the Conference on Disarmament, it is obvious that the United Nations has come a long way on the road to disarmament since the days of the League of Nations. The determination of those who pursue these tasks, despite the obstacles and the handicaps, has never flagged. It is clear that progress along the road to a more settled condition among the states begins with the development of a sensitivity to critical issues and an awareness that remedies to world problems can be found outside the traditional circles of arming and rearming.

# THE UN AND ARMS NEGOTIATIONS IN THE NUCLEAR ERA

## THE BEGINNING OF THE NUCLEAR ARMS RACE

Real disarmament began with the creation of the UN Atomic Energy Commission (AEC) in January 1946. The Commission for Conventional Armaments was created the following year. With the devastating consequences of the atomic explosions over Japan still fresh in every mind, control of atomic weapons was given the higher priority. In recognition of the great potentialities for peaceful uses of atomic energy, as well as grave dangers for all of humanity, the Assembly rather than the Security Council was chosen by the great powers to create and empower the AEC. In its initial order to the AEC, the General Assembly called on the Commission to develop "with the utmost dispatch" a plan to provide for (1) the exchange of scientific knowledge for peaceful purposes, (2) the control of atomic energy to limit its use to peaceful purposes, (3) the elimination of atomic and other weapons of mass destruction, and (4) the establishment of an inspection and enforcement system to prevent state evasions.

At the first meeting of the AEC, the United States, then with a monopoly on atomic weapons, offered a plan that would make it possible for nations to share atomic secrets under a system of strict international controls. The proposal, based on recommendations made in the Acheson-Lilienthal Report, was presented by elder statesman Bernard Baruch, an adviser and friend to former President Franklin Roosevelt. In its fundamentals the Baruch Plan provided for a transition to peaceful atomic control in a series of stages, with each stage dependent on the successful implementation of the preceding one. The Baruch Plan called for the creation of an International Atomic Development Authority that would operate an elaborate inspection and control system under Security Council direction, but unhampered by the veto power of the permanent members. All atomic weapons were to be destroyed once the control system became operational. The manufacture of new atomic bombs was to be outlawed. The Authority was to exercise exclusive ownership of atomic raw materials, control all atomic activities, encourage their use for the benefit of all nations, hold a monopoly on research and development in weapons-grade atomic material, and license national atomic research for peaceful purposes. In sum, the plan would establish a world federal government in the area of atomic energy.

The Soviet Union emphatically rejected the U.S. proposal, calling instead for the immediate outlawing of all atomic weapons followed by the establishment of a minimum system of control. In the Soviet view, each state was to accept responsibility for the peaceful development of atomic power and for the policing of the prohibition against atomic weapons within its borders, subject to periodic oversight by an international authority. Enforcement action was to be undertaken by the Security Council against violators, but only with the agreement of all permanent members. This sharp difference between the U.S. plan and the Soviet rejoinder was the first indication that a system of atomic inspection and control would not be an easy one to agree upon. The creation of a supranational agency to control and monitor nuclear development was judged an unwelcome interference in the domestic life of the sovereign nation-states on both sides of the ideological divide. Moreover, if power were granted to an agency outside the purview of the states, how could the states sustain their exclusive jurisdiction over matters of critical importance to them?

The Soviets, placed on the defensive by the Baruch Plan and outnumbered on the AEC, tried to retrieve the initiative by proposing to the 1946 General Assembly a plan for "general and complete disarmament," including both conventional and nuclear weapons. The proposal apparently was an effort to overcome the propaganda advantage gained by the United States in offering to relinquish its atomic monopoly and to contribute its know-how to the peaceful development of atomic power for humanity. The Soviet Union obviously preferred to discuss the broad, innocuous subject of general disarmament while carrying on a crash program to develop an atomic bomb to offset the U.S. advantage. In 1949 the Soviets tested their first atomic bomb, killing the Baruch Plan forever. Thereafter, the arms race was converted into a race between the superpowers, each seeking nuclear superiority.

The inexorable development of new technologies produced new complexities and dangers. In 1952, the United States exploded a hydrogen bomb, a fission-fusion device whose output of explosive power was measured in megatons or millions of tons of TNT equivalents, many, many times more devastating than the atomic bombs that destroyed Hiroshima and Nagasaki. In 1953, the Soviets successfully exploded a similar hydrogen bomb, and the U.S.-Soviet nuclear arms race was on in earnest. This dangerous competition produced not only new and more powerful nuclear warheads, but in rapid time, new delivery systems as well, including new types of manned bombers, intercontinental ballistic missiles, and missiles with multiple warheads capable of striking multiple targets (the MIRV, or multiple independently targeted reentry vehicle). U.S.-Soviet rivalry also extended to short-range delivery systems, down to the level of artillery shells with nuclear devices. Despite repeated attempts at negotiation and occasional agreement on subsidiary issues, the nuclear rivalry continued almost unabated through the 1980s. Disarmament had been all but forgotten.

## THE SEARCH FOR EFFECTIVE FORUMS

Early failures, however, did not end the discussion of arms control issues, although legitimization of national positions rather than agreed limitations often appeared to be the primary objective. With disarmament a virtual impossibility, the states centered attention on arms control, a more realistic approach to the threat posed by weapons of mass destruction. The arms control dialogue, however, was carried on through a succession of specialized disarmament forums created in an attempt to reconcile the needs of effective negotiation with political demands for self-defensive measures.

### UN-Related Forums

From 1946 to 1952 the principal negotiating bodies were the twelve-member UN AEC, including the eleven Security Council members and Canada, and an eleven-member Commission for Conventional Armaments. In 1952 these were combined into a single twelve-person Disarmament Commission. From 1954 to 1957 the main negotiating body was a five-member Subcommittee of the Disarmament Commission, consisting of the United States, the Soviet Union, the United Kingdom, France, and Canada. Beginning in 1957 the Soviet Union boycotted the Disarmament Commission and its subcommittee, demanding that communist-bloc states gain representation on the committee in equal numbers with the West. In hope of luring the Soviet Union back to the table by steps short of East-West parity (which the United States opposed in principle for any UN body), in 1958 the UN General Assembly enlarged the Commission to twenty-five members. In 1959, a decision was made to include the entire membership of the General Assembly in the body. Thus enlarged, however, the Disarmament Commission became too unwieldy for serious negotiation. As a consequence, it almost never met.

The impasse was ultimately resolved by creating disarmament bodies ostensibly outside the framework of the United Nations, where the United States was more inclined to accept parity of representation. Thus in 1958 two conferences of experts were convened to deal with the technical problems of detecting nuclear testing (four Western states and four Soviet-bloc states) and guarding against surprise attack (five Western, five Eastern). Beginning in 1958 the United States, Britain, and the Soviet Union began three-nation nuclear test-ban talks at UN Headquarters in Geneva. In 1959 a Ten-Nation Committee on Disarmament (five Western, five communist) was established by agreement among the foreign ministers of the Big Four (the United States, the Soviet Union, Great Britain, and China). In 1961, under pressure from the Third World for its failure to achieve disarmament results, the ten-nation body was enlarged into an

Eighteen-Nation Disarmament Committee (ENDC) by the addition of eight nonaligned countries. Third World representation was further increased in 1969 when the ENDC was replaced by a twenty-six-member Conference of the Committee on Disarmament (CCD).

In 1979, at the request of the General Assembly, the CCD was expanded to forty in the hope that additional members could apply greater pressure on the nuclear powers to reach agreement. The body was reduced to thirty-nine members in 1991 with the reuniting of the two Germanys and is currently called the Conference on Disarmament (CD). It meets in Geneva about six months a year as a forum for the negotiation of multilateral arms control and disarmament issues. The CD, like its predecessors, preserves the fiction of independence from the United Nations, even though the question of parity has lost all relevance with the ending of the Cold War. In practice, the CD functions almost as a UN sub-organ, utilizing UN conference services at UN expense (a Personal Representative of the UN Secretary-General serves as secretary-general of the conference), reporting regularly to the Assembly and accepting general guidance from it.

The Disarmament Commission, which had not held a meeting since 1965, was revived in 1978 by the General Assembly's first Special Session on Disarmament as a means of involving more member states in the arms control dialogue and generating world public pressures for disarmament. Unsuited for negotiation because of its large size, it was intended to be a forum for consciousness-raising and the elaboration of ideas. The Commission now holds annual meetings of two to four weeks to discuss general issues of disarmament and makes recommendations to the General Assembly.

Items regularly brought to the attention of the General Assembly by the Disarmament Commission included notification of nuclear tests, the prohibition or restriction of certain conventional weapons (notably land mines), the establishment of nuclear-weapon-free regions, the reduction of military budgets, and the development of programs for weapons transparency. In addition to these continuing efforts, the Commission scored an important achievement in December 1997 when the CD, meeting in Ottawa, Canada, signed the Convention on the Prohibition of the Use, Stockpiling, Production and Transfer of Anti-Personnel Mines, and on Their Destruction.

Although a priority item in matters before the United Nations, disarmament in the form of arms control has been more successfully performed by states in direct relations with one another. Special disarmament sessions of the General Assembly were called in 1978, 1982, and 1988. Each extended over a period of approximately five weeks, but they did little more than encourage member states to give greater consideration to the urgency of arms reduction. The 1982 session in fact provoked a World Disarmament Campaign that energized disarmament activists who proceeded to demonstrate against the sustained emphasis on weapons dependency. Similar reactions greeted the 1988 session. The questionable results of these special conferences, especially the platform they provided for pacifist propaganda, made governments reluctant to hold subsequent meetings. The Disarmament Commission has been unable to reach agreement for the holding of still another General Assembly Special Session on disarmament despite the concern registered over North Korea's and Iran's nuclear programs in 2003. This point was made by outgoing Commission Undersecretary-General Dhanapala in March 2003 when he cited the difficult times that had beset the body, which could not even schedule a substantive session in 2002, the year of its fiftieth anniversary. Disagreements over the role of force in international relations, as well as the questions raised concerning the value of multilateralism to peace and security, and indeed, the relevance and role of the United Nations in serving a gamut of global norms, had cast a dark cloud over their proceedings. Moreover, the obstacles facing the Disarmament Commission were similar to those faced by the world organization in other areas; no one could hide from the fact that global military expenditures had been projected to exceed $1 trillion in 2003. Not since the depths of the Cold War had there been such a rush to acquire more and more deadly weapons systems.[2]

### Non-UN Forums: SALT and START

From the beginning of UN arms control efforts, there has been a general recognition that little progress was possible without agreement among the major powers. Many of the key issues were essentially bilateral in nature and not well suited to negotiation in a large, cumbersome forum. In 1969 at Helsinki, the United States and the Soviet Union recognized this fact by initiating the Strategic Arms Limitation Talks (SALT). The original SALT negotiations were envisaged as a series of agreements in which incremental reductions in nuclear weapons production and deployment would eventually produce levels that were less threatening and less costly to the rival superpowers. The success of SALT I led to SALT II, but SALT II proved stillborn. The U.S. Senate cast the treaty aside after the Soviet Union's invasion of Afghanistan in 1979. Ronald Reagan and his Soviet counterparts reenergized the process some years later as the Strategic Arms Reduction Talks (START), but a START treaty was not approved until July 1991. Under its terms, stockpiles of strategic weapons (numbering about 10,000 each) were to be reduced to approximately 8,550 for the United States and 6,450 for the Soviet Union. Other provisions cited specific categories of strategic weapons and established an extensive system of verification. Treaty ratification was delayed by the abortive anti-Gorbachev coup, however, as well as the subsequent collapse of the Soviet Union. In May 1992 the United States signed a protocol with the government of Russia and the new republics of Belarus, Ukraine, and Kazakhstan, making them all parties to START I. Ratification for START I was subsequently acquired from all the states. In addition, all four sovereign states agreed to accede to the Nuclear Nonproliferation Treaty that had been signed in 1968 and put into force in 1970. Furthermore, Belarus, Ukraine, and Kazakhstan opted for the dismantling of their nuclear weapons and the transfer of their warheads to Russia. These states subsequently renounced their status as nuclear powers when the United States and

Russia guaranteed their security. Moreover, the United States helped all three countries liquidate their nuclear capabilities.

Seizing upon what was believed to be an opportune moment, on January 3, 1993, the United States and the Russian Federation signed a START II agreement that was aimed at further reducing their land-based, strategic nuclear weapons stockpiles. START II reduced the United States stockpile of strategic weapons to 3,500 and Russia's to 3,000 in 2003. The Russian parliament (Duma), had originally registered alarm with START II, asserting that it placed Russia at a gross disadvantage vis-à-vis the United States. Russia's parliamentary leaders indicated a desire to extend the START II time frame beyond 2003 so that the country's nuclear weapons need not be withdrawn before they reached the end of their designed life cycles. The Russians also showed displeasure that the disarmament agreement had not reduced sea-based weapons where the United States was perceived holding a distinct advantage. Nor did START II apply to the Chinese, British, and French nuclear arsenals. Finally, the Duma was suspicious of U.S. maneuvers that called for the enlargement of NATO, and Russian legislators cited U.S. congressional actions in 1998 approving NATO admission for Poland, the Czech Republic, and Hungary. Russia still held some 7,000 strategic weapons, to 8,000 for the United States. France was said to possess 482 weapons, while China had 284 and Britain 100. To highlight that the world was still a very dangerous place after the Cold War, it was noted that Russia and the United States continued to hold an additional several thousand theater-type or tactical nuclear weapons. Moreover, the United States decided in January 1999 to proceed with the development and deployment of an antimissile defense. Noting the conflict with the existing antiballistic missile (ABM) treaty, a throwback to the early years of the Cold War, the decision to deploy an ABM system seemed to make it even less likely that the Duma would agree to ratify START II.

The matter carried over into the new administration of George W. Bush. Bush not only pressed for the early deployment of an antimissile system, he also declared his intention to unilaterally abrogate the ABM treaty. True to his word, in June 2002 President Bush announced the official U.S. withdrawal from the ABM treaty. The next day Moscow declared it would no longer be bound by its START II commitments, ending almost a decade of U.S.-Russian efforts to bring the 1993 treaty into force. To a large extent, however, START II had become superfluous. Washington and Moscow had entered into a different nuclear arms accord on May 24, 2002. Described as the Strategic Offensive Reductions Treaty (SORT) or Moscow Treaty, it committed the United States and Russia to reduce deployed strategic arsenals to 1,700 to 2,200 warheads by December 31, 2012, going further than START II's target of 3,000 to 3,500 warheads by December 2007. SORT, however, did not include START II's prohibition against deploying MIRVs on intercontinental ballistic missiles.

It should be noted that START II was ratified by the U.S. Senate in January 1996, but a 1997 protocol extending the treaty's implementation waited action. The protocol for START II would have shifted the deadline for completion of the START II reductions from January 1, 2003, to December 31, 2007. In May 2000, Russian President Vladimir Putin had signed a resolution of ratification for START II, its extension protocol, and the 1997 ABM-related agreements. Russia's ratification legislation made exchange of START II's instruments of ratification contingent on U.S. approval of the extension protocol and the ABM agreements. The U.S. Congress never voted to ratify the entire package. The SORT treaty not only made START II moot, it also eliminated the need for START III that envisaged further reductions in nuclear arsenals. The original START treaty, however, remained in force between the United States, the Russian Federation, Belarus, Kazakhstan, and Ukraine. START's verification regime was to provide the foundation for transparency and predictability regarding implementation of the new SORT treaty. Moreover, at the time of the SORT signing ceremony, the parties also issued a Joint Declaration on the New Strategic Relationship and pledged to continue discussions to further enhance transparency. The SORT treaty and declaration appeared to lay aside Russian hostility to U.S. actions abrogating the ABM treaty and cleared the way for further nuclear arms reduction.

# DISARMAMENT AND ARMS CONTROL—
# A BALANCE SHEET

The pursuit of security in a dangerous nuclear world over six decades has produced no assurance to the global community that Armageddon can be avoided. Yet progress has been made in a number of arms control and related fields. These fields include (1) achieving demilitarization and denuclearization of specific geographic areas, (2) halting nuclear proliferation, (3) banning nuclear weapons tests, (4) avoiding a nuclear weapons race in outer space, (5) limiting or reducing nuclear warheads and delivery systems, (6) developing confidence-building and communication measures to avoid accidental war, (7) banning chemical and biological weapons, (8) reducing tension through economic and political policies, and (9) banning antipersonnel mines. Each of these fields will be examined.

## DEMILITARIZATION AND DENUCLEARIZATION

If global disarmament is beyond reach in the contemporary world, disarmament within specific geographic areas may still be possible. The first arms control agreement to emerge after World War II provided for the complete demilitarization of the Antarctic continent. The Antarctic Treaty of 1959, signed by twelve governments, developed into the Antarctic Treaty System (ATS), which subsequently included more than forty countries, representing 70 percent of the world's population. Larger than China, India, or the United States and Mexico combined, Antarctica accounts for 10 percent of the planet's land surface and 30 percent of all the land in the Southern Hemisphere. Because Antarctica is believed to possess vast mineral deposits, especially in platinum, petroleum, and natural gas, a protocol on environmental protection established a permanent ban on their mining and exploitation. ATS sought to maintain the frozen continent as a region open to all nations that wish to join in its preservation and scientific discovery. The treaty centers on the following provisions:

1. The use of the region for military activities of any kind is forbidden.
2. Each signatory has the right to inspect the installations of the others to ensure that no treaty violation has occurred.
3. Territorial claims on the continent remain unrecognized, and no new claims may be made.
4. No nuclear explosions or dumping of radioactive wastes is permitted.
5. Disputes under the terms of the treaty will be settled peacefully.
6. The signatories will cooperate in scientific investigations in the region.

The Antarctic Treaty provides a model for the potential demilitarization of other regions in the world. No known violations have occurred, and the right of national inspection has been fully acknowledged. Although no joint arrangements exist for governing the area, Antarctica is at least partially "internationalized" by the voluntary system.

Other proposals aimed at reducing the threat of nuclear war through denuclearization of various regions of the world have since been presented in the General Assembly or developed by regional groups. Third World scholars and diplomats have demonstrated a continuing concern about the impact of a great power war on the peoples of Africa, Asia, and Latin America and have frequently called for demilitarization and denuclearization of their regions (without, however, showing much concern for reducing their own national armaments).

The prototype nuclear-weapons-free zone was concluded in the Treaty of Tlatelolco in 1967. This Treaty on the Prohibition of Nuclear Weapons in Latin America was signed by the representatives of twenty-one countries. By 1980, twenty-five had signed the treaty, and in 1995, Cuba also became a signatory to the treaty. The treaty created an operational body known as OPANAL (Agency for the Prohibition of Nuclear Weapons in Latin America), which oversees enforcement of treaty provisions. Two protocols supplement the treaty and guarantee that the region will remain denuclearized. It also offers assurances that the United States, Russia, Britain, China, or France will not deploy nuclear weapons in the region.

Other regions also have tried to establish nuclear-weapons-free zones. A resolution adopted by the General Assembly in 1961, for example, requested all countries to "consider and respect the continent of Africa as a denuclearized zone." The Organization of African Unity, now the African Union, followed up by adopting a Declaration on the Denuclearization of Africa, which led the General Assembly to call for an African nuclear-weapons-free zone. The result of this diplomacy was the Treaty of Pelindaba, which established Africa as a nuclear free zone. The treaty prohibits the research, development, manufacture, stockpiling, acquisition, testing, possession, control, or stationing of nuclear explosive devices in the territory of parties to the treaty. It also prevents dumping of radioactive waste in the African zone by treaty parties. Furthermore, the treaty prohibits any attack against nuclear installations in the zone by treaty parties and requires them to maintain the highest standards of physical protection of nuclear material, facilities, and equipment that are to be used exclusively for peaceful purposes. The treaty was open for signature in April 1996.

In 1987, a number of states, including Australia, New Zealand, Indonesia, the Soviet Union, and several island nations in the South Pacific, notably Fiji, signed the Treaty of Rarotonga, which declared the South Pacific to be a nuclear-free zone. The United States did not sign the treaty, nor did France, which maintained a nuclear test site near Tahiti. Although the treaty declared the region off-limits to nuclear weapons deployment and testing, U.S. nuclear-armed vessels continued to operate in the area (even though denied port calls in New Zealand), and in 1995, Paris resumed testing of nuclear weapons, defying provisions of the Rarotonga Treaty. Despite threats of economic and political retaliation from Australia and New Zealand, France proceeded with its testing program, arguing that it would be the last of its kind. Only a month earlier France had agreed to the indefinite extension of the Nuclear Nonproliferation Treaty, and this action by Paris disturbed and angered nations around the world.

The 1995 Treaty of Bangkok also declared Southeast Asia to be a nuclear-free area. So too the Central Asian states, meeting in Uzbekistan in September 1997, notified Kofi Annan of their intentions to establish a nuclear-free zone. The Uzbekistan conference noted that more than one hundred UN member states were parties to such agreements. Each of these zones and agreements has its own regional characteristics and concerns, but their experience and examples have served as guideposts for the establishment of nuclear-weapons-free zones in other parts of the world. Agreement on nuclear-free zones is a boon to regional security cooperation, has contributed to nuclear nonproliferation and disarmament, and has represented a major step in the direction of a nuclear-free world.

## NUCLEAR PROLIFERATION

### The Growing Brotherhood of the Bomb

Opposite to the concept of denuclearization is the issue of nuclear proliferation, a problem that was born in 1949 when the Soviet explosion of an atomic device ended the U.S. postwar monopoly on atomic weapons. Three years later Britain exploded a fission bomb, followed by France in 1960 and China in 1964. Each member of the "nuclear club" also exploded test fusion warheads thousands of times more powerful than the Hiroshima bomb. India became the first Third World country to join the brotherhood of the bomb in 1974, when it successfully tested a "peaceful nuclear explosive." At least ten nations have the scientific and technological capability to join the nuclear club, and as many as ten additional nations may in time have that capability. A number of European countries and Canada, Australia, New Zealand, and Japan have the capability to develop nuclear weapons but have refrained from doing so. Several nations, such as North Korea and Israel, have secretly developed nuclear weapons capability. In 2002, however, North Korea revealed that it was in violation of the Nuclear Nonproliferation Treaty and that it intended to restart its nuclear reactor capable of producing weapons-grade plutonium. Israel on the other hand has never revealed the extent of its nuclear capability although it is believed to have a sizable arsenal of nuclear weapons.

Long-standing efforts to create a nuclear-weapons-free zone in South Asia have done little to dissuade the major countries of the region from proceeding with the development of nuclear weapons. India's detonation of a nuclear device in 1974, ostensibly as a signal to China, registered more particular impact upon neighboring Pakistan, which was prompted to accelerate its efforts at developing similar capabilities. Although the world seemed to little notice India's nuclear program, Pakistan received special scrutiny. The United States was especially concerned with the possibilities of a nuclear arms race in South Asia because of the sustained hostility between the subcontinent's two most prominent states. Neither India nor Pakistan accepted the Nuclear Nonproliferation Treaty, and they again refused to become signatories after the treaty's extension in 1995. In 1996 neither country agreed to sign the Comprehensive Nuclear Weapons Test-Ban Treaty. Moreover, despite strenuous U.S. efforts at dissuading other nations from assisting Pakistan's nuclear program, by 1997 various intelligence circles had concluded that Pakistan was nuclear capable. Thus, when India shocked the world by exploding five additional nuclear devices in May 1998, few were truly surprised when Pakistan followed with six tests of its own, not three weeks later. Although India again said its actions were meant to balance the threat posed by nuclear China, Pakistan now cited the threat to its security from its immediate neighbor. The Indo-Pakistani actions reminded the world how fragile the peace was in the years after the Cold War. More important, the nuclear tests had seriously damaged UN efforts at preventing the proliferation of nuclear weapons.

The nuclear explosions in South Asia also resonated in the Middle East. Arab-Israeli hostility was undoubtedly the principal reason for the failure to ensure a nuclear-weapons-free region there. Israel began developing atomic weapons in the 1950s and by the 1990s was believed to possess a formidable nuclear arsenal. Several Arab countries had also been eager to develop nuclear weapons programs, but none more so than Iraq. In 1981, Israel made a surprise and daring raid on Iraq's nuclear facility at Osirak, destroying it before it was ready to manufacture nuclear weapons. Although a violation of international law and Iraqi sovereignty, as well as an audacious act that was without precedent, Israel's action had nonetheless delayed Baghdad's quest for the bomb. Iraq's attempt to develop atomic weapons was sustained through the 1980s, but its invasion of Kuwait in 1990 again exposed its nuclear facilities, this time to the U.S.-led coalition. Baghdad's surrender to the coalition in 1991 opened Iraq to UN inspection teams, which were authorized to identify and destroy the country's facilities for the development and deployment of all weapons of mass destruction, whether nuclear, chemical, or biological. A UN Special Commission (UNSCOM) was set up to implement the nonnuclear provisions of a 1991 Security Council resolution and to assist the International Atomic Energy Agency (IAEA) with its nuclear inspections.

### Coerced Disarmament: Iraq, North Korea, and Iran

Coerced disarmament is one way to help prevent the proliferation of weapons of mass destruction. UNSCOM was mandated by the Security Council to carry out on-site inspections of Iraq's biological, chemical, and missile capabilities and to seize and render harmless all such weapons as well as all stocks of agents and related components used for their research, development, support, and manufacturing. Furthermore, UNSCOM was required to verify Iraqi compliance and Baghdad's agreement not to use, develop, construct, or acquire any items connected with weapons of mass destruction.

UNSCOM's work proved to be a protracted affair (see Chapter 5), and despite the Commission's success in destroying important stores of Iraqi weapons and facilities between 1991 and 1997, its mandate was not ended. Inspectors returned to the country in 1998 during a period of high tension. With traditional diplomacy at an impasse, it was only the decision of Secretary-General Kofi Annan to go to Iraq that offered the possibility of avoiding a violent showdown. Meeting with Saddam Hussein and members of his government in Baghdad in February, Annan negotiated an arrangement that permitted UNSCOM unfettered access to all sites. A report was later issued declaring Iraq free of nuclear weapons or their development although it was felt that Baghdad was still active in developing chemical and biological weapons.

Baghdad was incensed over the report, arguing that it had complied with all UN resolutions and demands. By the fall of 1998 Saddam Hussein's soldiers again impeded UNSCOM operations and tensions again rose, particularly as the United States threatened Iraq with air attacks. Washington declared that it would hold its hand as long as it could confirm Iraq's full compliance with UNSCOM operations. In December 1998, judging that Iraq had not complied, the United States, supported by Great Britain, launched an intense four-day air campaign against Iraqi military installations. Although unable to defend the target areas, Baghdad remained defiant and refused to readmit UNSCOM. The Commission was declared unwelcome by the Baghdad government, and the entire operation was closed down and the inspectors forced to leave the country. Although UNSCOM had ceased to be a factor, forcibly disarming Iraq remained a stated goal of U.S. administrations. UNSCOM was credited with the destruction of more Iraqi weapons of mass destruction and their delivery systems than were accomplished by the U.S.-led coalition in the 1991 Gulf War, but coercive disarmament remained a questionable method in the attempt to further the cause of disarmament and nonproliferation.

In 2003 South Korea and Iran became flash points of interest as nuclear or would-be nuclear weapons states. In 2002 President George W. Bush had named Iraq, North Korea, and Iran as members of an "Axis of Evil," so it is not surprising that the United States should have an interest in disarming these states.

North Korea had engaged in nuclear weapons development over an extended period. Although President Clinton had negotiated an arrangement in 1994 that was believed to have alleviated the concern that North Korea would develop or export nuclear weapons (discussed below), in 2002 North Korea announced that it had been in violation of the 1994 agreement and that it intended to revive and expand its nuclear weapons program. In December 2002 the P'yŏngyang government forced IAEA inspectors to remove their monitoring instruments and leave the country, and in 2003 reports circulated in the world press that North Korea was the recipient of nuclear weapons technology from Pakistan. These reports were confirmed in February 2004 when Pakistan's chief nuclear scientist was exposed and subsequently confessed that he had transferred nuclear technology not only to North Korea but to Iran and Libya. Despite these revelations, the North Korean government continued to insist that it had not been the recipient of clandestine Pakistani nuclear assistance. Declaring that its nuclear weapons program was a defensive measure, North Korea's representative to the UN Disarmament Commission had earlier answered all criticism of his government's nuclear policy by claiming that the nuclear program was directly related to the security of the Korean nation. The problem, it was noted, was the hostile policy toward his country held by the United States. North Korea sustained the argument that it reserved the right to defend itself, and only nuclear weapons could deter the United States. Earlier, the North Korean ambassador to the United Nations had announced that his country would interpret the imposition of sanctions by the United Nations or individual nations as an act of war against the Korean nation and that his government would not yield to any pressure exerted by the United Nations or the United States.

Iran, the third member of Bush's Axis of Evil, insisted that its nuclear facility, built in collaboration with the Russian Federation, was meant solely for peaceful purposes. This, however, was not the judgment of the United States, and IAEA reports in June 2003 and March 2004 declared that Iran had failed to report certain nuclear material and activities to IAEA inspectors. IAEA Director-General Mohamed El Baradei indicated that Iran must be more forthcoming with its nuclear program. IAEA had wanted to take environmental samples at a location allegedly the site for enrichment activities, and Iran had refused that request, heightening concern that it had something to hide. The IAEA wanted to continue to pressure the Teheran government on its uranium conversion and enrichment program, but the Bush administration registered skepticism and a lack of patience. Washington continued to insist that Iran open its facilities to full inspection, and U.S. intelligence reported that Iran would be capable of producing nuclear weapons in no more than two years.

It is obvious that both North Korea and Iran, while fearing U.S. intervention, are determined to proceed with their nuclear programs. In fact, some observers argue that the more the United States presses its cases against the two countries, the more those countries are likely to proceed with their weapons programs.

## The Threat of Proliferation

What happens if the number of nuclear states expands to fifteen or to twenty-five? Would the threat of a major war be greater, or would nuclear proliferation reduce the danger of nuclear war? What role should the United Nations play in reducing or stopping the expansion of the nuclear club? Could an international control system help prevent additional states from "going nuclear"? While the answers to such questions are not altogether clear, there is general agreement that nuclear proliferation does pose a threat to world peace and security.

The Stockholm International Peace Research Institute and the U.S.-based Natural Resources Defense Council each noted the availability worldwide of 30,000 nuclear weapons in 2002, despite the Nuclear Nonproliferation Treaty that has been in force since 1970. This number reveals a net reduction of only 1,353 weapons over the life of the treaty, a rate of only 42 per year. At this rate, hundreds of years would be required for the promise of NPT to be fulfilled. States are devising new rationales and doctrines for expanding the circumstances under which they opt for nuclear weapons and determine their use. Doctrines that threaten preemptive nuclear strikes, even against states that do not have nuclear weapons, and that reaffirm the great value of such weapons in advancing key security interests have whetted the appetites of not a few international actors to become nuclear powers. This is especially so among those that claim the absence of a guaranteed nuclear umbrella provided by another state.

The debate over proliferation has tended to polarize. One group regards nuclear diffusion as an obvious danger that will increase the possibility of nuclear war, probably more than proportionally to the addition of each new state. The other group views the dissemination of nuclear weapons as dangerous but inevitable and wants major consideration given to the problem of how to manage a multinuclear world.

The process of expanding the nuclear club tends to be self-propelling as is witnessed in the Indian and Pakistani test explosions in 1998. Both countries justified their behavior on national security grounds, but it was New Delhi that was most outspoken on its right to possess nuclear weapons as long as the United States, Russia, China, Britain, and France did not destroy their own stockpiles. India in effect argued that either the world should be totally nuclear free or India had every reason to expect an equal position alongside the other nuclear states. Such argument was fuel for still other would-be nuclear powers, and India and Pakistan's intrusion into the "select" nuclear club obviously strengthened the political and strategic motivations of other states to follow their example.

As the nuclear club expands, nuclear weapons may be increasingly viewed as an acceptable means for waging war, and the probability that they will be used by design or accident mounts when a new finger is added to the trigger. States caught up in the nuclear race will also find it far more difficult to meet other priorities, such as funding economic development. The result may be a growing internal instability and a proneness to revolution in developing states that could encourage rash or even irrational actions by their leaders. Worst of all, a "catalytic war" could be touched off by a small power that surreptitiously uses an atomic bomb to destroy a major U.S., Russian, Chinese, British, or French city. This is unlikely, but in the nuclear age all dangerous possibilities must be recognized and collective efforts undertaken through UN machinery to deal with such threats.

Terrorism only adds to this dilemma. Whereas established states with stakes in their own survival may hesitate before pressing the nuclear trigger, what can be said about non-states, with no particular concern for territoriality, and sometimes with no concern for individual life, even their own? Thus far, suicide attackers have used only conventional weapons, but the events of September 11 showed how far such attacks can go, and the possibility that such attackers could obtain and use weapons of mass destruction raises serious questions about the world's security and how the community of states should, or can, respond. The community of states continues to labor over safeguards that can prevent the use of weapons of mass destruction, but no institutions or procedures are in place to deter people from committing horrific deeds. More and more state nuclear programs and arsenals do not help the situation. On the contrary, they open the possibility that by theft or transfer or sale, weapons of mass destruction can fall into the hands of those who are committed only to destruction.

## Efforts to Halt Nuclear Proliferation

Despite the end of the Cold War and its positive effects on the arms race, the problem of nuclear proliferation remains real and urgent. Indeed, with the breakup of the Soviet Union and the loss of central control over weapons located in the former Soviet republics, the dangers of proliferation have increased.

The principal multilateral approach to the problem, the Treaty on the Nonproliferation of Nuclear Weapons, was approved by the General Assembly in 1968. A product of seven years of debate and negotiation in the Eighteen-Nation Disarmament Committee and the Political and Security Committee of the General Assembly, the treaty aimed to solve the problem of proliferation by preventing it. The main provisions of the eleven-article treaty are found in the first two articles, which assign obligations to nuclear and nonnuclear states as follows:

### Article I

Each nuclear-weapon State Party to this Treaty undertakes not to transfer to any recipient whatsoever nuclear weapons or other nuclear explosive devices or control over such weapons or explosive devices directly, or indirectly; and not in any way to assist, encourage, or induce any non-nuclear-weapon State

to manufacture or otherwise acquire nuclear weapons or other nuclear explosive devices, or control over such weapons or explosive devices.

Article II

Each non-nuclear-weapon State Party to this Treaty undertakes not to receive
the transfer from any transferrer whatsoever of nuclear weapons or other nuclear explosive devices or of control over such weapons or explosive devices directly, or indirectly; not to manufacture or otherwise acquire nuclear weapons
or other nuclear explosive devices; and not to seek or receive any assistance in
the manufacture of nuclear weapons or other nuclear devices.

The treaty also obligates each nonnuclear state to enter into an agreement
with the IAEA to provide safeguards, through verification by the Agency, to
prevent any diversion of nuclear energy from peaceful uses to nuclear weapons.
Other provisions of the treaty call for cooperation in the development of nuclear energy for peaceful purposes and for the nondiscriminatory transfer of nuclear explosive devices to nonnuclear states for peaceful purposes. Each of the
parties to the treaty also agrees "to pursue negotiations in good faith on effective measures relating to cessation of the nuclear arms race."

The major obstacle to the treaty in General Assembly debates had been the
fear prevalent among nonnuclear states that renouncing their right to acquire
nuclear weapons might leave them open to nuclear blackmail. To meet this
problem, three of the nuclear powers—Britain, the Soviet Union, and the
United States—in Article 6 of the Nonproliferation Treaty agreed to guarantee
the security of nonnuclear states against such actions or threats. The Security
Council underwrote this guarantee. The Council adopted a resolution affirming the decision of three of the four nuclear powers on the Council to provide
"immediate assistance to any non-nuclear-weapon State . . . that is a victim of an
act or an object of a threat of aggression in which nuclear weapons are used." [3]

More than 140 states ratified the original Nonproliferation Treaty, although
France and China—two of the five original nuclear powers—did not agree to
sign the document until 1991. A number of states, including Argentina, Brazil,
India, Israel, North Korea, and Pakistan, originally refused to adhere to it; subsequently, however, Argentina and Brazil entered into a Joint Safeguards Agreement with the IAEA that provided comparable safeguards against diversion of
fissionable materials to military uses.

The dissolution of the Soviet Union presented a new problem of nuclear
proliferation. With Moscow no longer at the pinnacle of the command and
control system, the use and disposal of such weapons now devolved upon the
leaders of numerous independent units not necessarily subject to the constraints
previously observed by the Soviet government. While Russia attempted to
reduce the uncertainties through negotiation and agreement with the former
Soviet republics, the United States also offered assistance. Recognizing the urgency of the problem, the U.S. Congress in 1991 enacted the Soviet Nuclear
Threat Reduction Act of 1991 to make financial and technical aid available to
the new states in regard to the handling and disposal of their nuclear weapons.
The program dealt with the storage, transport, and destruction of nuclear war-

heads and the creation of safeguards against proliferation among the newly independent states of the Soviet Union. It also addressed the need to protect against sales of nuclear weapons, critical materials, and technological know-how to other nations.

Nuclear weapons originally stored and deployed in Belarus, Ukraine, and Kazakhstan were dismantled in accordance with a series of agreements, and their warheads were transported to the Russian Federation where the United States was a party in their destruction. Nevertheless, rumors continued to circulate that nuclear warheads and delivery systems had found their way to third countries, and the fear persisted that some weapons may have been acquired by would-be terrorists. The problem of how to control the spread of nuclear weapons proved to be far more complicated with the end of the Cold War. U.S. Defense Secretary William Perry had stated that "the fewest nuclear weapons in the fewest hands" was a central objective of his government, and that even the use of one nuclear bomb, by miscalculation, by terrorists—whether state-sponsored or transnational—was intolerable. In the quest for a truly nuclear-free world, the nuclear powers, especially the United States, Russia, and China, required a common policy. Deterrence, that is, the threat to inflict overwhelming damage on a nuclear-armed enemy, no longer sufficed.

After India's decision to demonstrate its nuclear capability, followed by Pakistan's, in 1998, there was no longer room to maneuver based on exclusive national interest. The time seemed to call for a new international security structure, a structure that had adequate confidence-building measures, and above all, that centered on total transparency. Meanwhile the votes each year on nuclear disarmament resolutions in the General Assembly's First Committee remained deeply divided. The Conference on Disarmament has been unable to make any progress on nuclear disarmament for many years. Early in April 2003, the UN Disarmament Commission, after three years of deliberation, adjourned its session without any consensus on ways and means to achieve nuclear disarmament. Even the Strategic Offensive Reductions Treaty between the United States and the Russian Federation speaks of "deployed" missiles but not the destruction of a single warhead or delivery system. From the perspective of the other NPT states there is virtually no transparency in these reductions and no independent verification. The existing nuclear weapons states continue to resist efforts by states, such as Canada and Germany, to address the transparency problem through improved reporting requirements. Moreover, Pakistan's repeated denials and then admission that its nuclear scientists were major participants in the sale of nuclear weapons technology was a major setback in the UN's efforts for promoting nuclear disarmament.

## ELIMINATING NUCLEAR TESTING

Elimination of nuclear testing has been high on UN agendas for many years, but to date the principal limitation on testing remains the Limited Test-Ban Treaty of 1963. Although underground nuclear testing is still permissible, the 1963 treaty has been well observed and has been a notable contribution to a safer environment. The treaty was a product of years of negotiation and became possible only when conditions had so ripened that the three negotiating parties—Britain, the United States, and the Soviet Union—regarded it as fully complementary to their respective national interests. Both the United States and the Soviet Union had exploded bombs of immense power and had perfected sophisticated devices for strategic and tactical nuclear weapons. The bombs had reached such a magnitude of power that testing more powerful ones had become dangerous and nonsensical. Levels of radioactive fallout from Soviet and U.S. tests in the early 1960s had reached proportions that might pose a health threat to present and future generations. In addition, the rising clamor of world opinion demanding an end to nuclear testing had become increasingly difficult to ignore. This was a setting for agreement.

Under the 1963 treaty, each state adhering to the treaty agrees

> to prohibit, to prevent, and not to carry out any nuclear test explosion, or any other nuclear explosion, at any place under its jurisdiction or control . . . in the atmosphere; beyond its limits, including outer space; or underwater, including territorial waters or high seas.

Because of the seismological problem of detecting underground nuclear tests and distinguishing them from natural earth tremors, subsurface tests were not prohibited by the 1963 agreement. The Soviet Union and the United States carried out numerous underground tests after the treaty took effect.

Although there was a clear implication that the "limited" nature of the test ban would be made complete as soon as technology had advanced to the point of ensuring the detection of all nuclear tests, negotiations lagged behind scientific advances. The treaty was also "limited" in another equally important respect: Two nuclear powers—France and China—did not sign it, and both powers conducted atmospheric tests. In 1991 China declared a moratorium on further testing, as did France the following year, but China subsequently broke the moratorium in 1992 and France did likewise in 1995 by conducting major atmospheric tests.

UN disarmament bodies continued to press for agreement on a Comprehensive Nuclear Test-Ban Treaty. But the United States had taken a position against such a treaty on the grounds that it would not be possible to assure the safety and reliability of existing nuclear stockpiles without periodic testing. Russia in 1991, however, came out unequivocally in favor, and in 1990 both countries ratified agreements limiting underground testing and other nuclear explosions to devices not exceeding a yield of 150 kilotons.

The 1963 Limited Test-Ban Treaty was an acknowledgment by the three major nuclear states that the dangers of an uncontrolled arms race outweighed the risk that someone might not honor the agreement. At the time it represented a substantial compromise of the U.S. position against entering into any disarmament or arms control agreement without the safeguards of inspection, verification, and control. Although the treaty did not seriously restrict either side's military efforts in the arms race, it greatly reduced the level of radioactive fallout around the globe. With the subsequent Russian decision to unilaterally suspend all testing, increasing pressure was placed on the United States to follow suit.

The United States agreed to follow the Russian example with the indefinite extension of the Nuclear Weapons Nonproliferation Treaty in 1995. Linked to that extension, and in order to meet the concerns of the nonnuclear states, Washington was the first of 149 nations to sign the Comprehensive Nuclear Test-Ban Treaty in 1996. On doing so, President Clinton announced that the United States had ceased testing all nuclear weapons. The treaty created a Comprehensive Nuclear Test-Ban Treaty Organization (CTBTO), and on November 19, 1996, the original signatory states established a Preparatory Commission to oversee the treaty's implementation. In 1997, the Preparatory Commission appointed an Executive Secretary and established a Provisional Technical Secretariat in Vienna, in the same physical complex that housed the IAEA. The Technical Secretariat was given full responsibility to form a global verification system to guarantee compliance. Neither the UN agency nor the U.S. detection services, however, were successful in forecasting the Indian explosions of 1998, and the elaborate machinery available for such purposes proved inadequate in the face of a determined effort by a nuclear weapons state to defy the international community. India's action appeared to make a mockery of efforts by major powers to forego and prevent future tests. The precedent was not lost on Pakistan, nor was it likely to escape the attention of other states with similar ambitions.

Suspicions among the nonnuclear states persist despite the declarations in the 2000 NPT Review Conference that the goal of the treaty was total nuclear disarmament. The final document of the Conference reaffirmed that "total elimination of nuclear weapons is the only absolute guarantee against the use or threat of use of nuclear weapons." But despite this grandiose statement, the challenge to the NPT remained the issue of enforcement. Moreover, the 2003 war in Iraq gave this issue new importance. Enforcement concerns are long-standing, but the inability of the Security Council to reach consensus on a common approach to enforce Iraq's disarmament had profound implications for the NPT, for the rule of law, and for the entire world. Questions persisted on whether the Iraq War served as a deterrent to future proliferation or whether it merely encouraged states to seek their own nuclear capability. Moreover, there was concern that the war had affected future multilateral inspections, perhaps the major instrument in dealing with proliferation risks. Also is the need to re-examine the issue of multilateral sanctions, up to and including the use of force, especially when the Security Council is divided, as it was with the matter of Iraq. Kofi Annan's assertion that civil society must act where the states are reluctant to do so is significant. The Secretary-General would envision civil society as "the new superpower," the source of popular sovereignty from which the states draw their authority. The dilemma here is that the credibility of the NPT cannot rest on civil society in an era when states accrue even more power and still display sufficient capacity to deflect or influence civil society.

## PEACEFUL USES OF OUTER SPACE

The launching of the first satellite in 1957 by the Soviet Union added another dimension to the disarmament problem—that of preventing military exploitation of outer space. The General Assembly took an initial action the following year when it established a Special Committee on the Peaceful Uses of Outer Space to draft a set of principles governing national conduct in the new environment. After early failures and a long deadlock over legal issues, the United States and the Soviet Union reached agreement within the Committee. In 1961, the General Assembly unanimously adopted the Committee's draft in the form of a Declaration of Legal Principles Governing the Activities of States in the Exploration and Use of Outer Space. The declaration enunciated major principles to guide states in using and exploring space: outer space and celestial bodies were "internationalized"; international law was made applicable to them; states were made internationally responsible for their activities in outer space; and the responsibility of rendering emergency assistance to astronauts and their vehicles and of returning them safely to their country of origin was proclaimed. The declaration also endorsed the exchange of scientific information on space programs and the establishment of a world "weather watch" under the sponsorship of the World Meteorological Organization.

From 1958 to 1963, the General Assembly adopted six other resolutions relating to outer space. These resolutions affirmed several additional guidelines for space activity:

1. The exploration and use of space should be "only for the betterment of mankind."
2. All states, regardless of their scientific or economic development, should benefit from space activities.
3. The United Nations should serve as a center for coordinating space activities and for the exchange of information regarding such activities.
4. International cooperation in space activities will foster closer relations between nations and peoples.

Space cooperation between the United States and the Soviet Union got off to a good start with bilateral agreements in 1962 and 1964 that provided for a coordinated weather satellite program and for joint satellite communications tests. Subsequent activities by both countries pointed to the potential military use of space and dramatized the need for agreement on a space treaty. In December 1966 a consensus was achieved and a draft treaty was approved by the General Assembly without a dissenting vote. The following year, a decade after the launching of the Soviet *Sputnik*, the Outer Space Treaty came into force, with the United States and Soviet Union included among the eighty-four signatory nations.

The main provisions of the treaty (1) prohibit placing nuclear or other weapons of mass destruction in orbit or on the moon and other bodies in outer space, (2) ban military bases on the moon and the planets, (3) reject all claims of national sovereignty in outer space, (4) require that explorations and uses of outer space benefit all countries, and (5) provide for international cooperation in exploring space, in rendering assistance to astronauts and space vehicles, and in exchanging scientific information. The treaty culminated ten years of negotiations aimed at avoiding a military space race and achieving the internationalization of space.

The Outer Space Treaty succeeded only partially in its basic objective of avoiding a military space race. Both the United States and the Soviet Union sought to develop antisatellite weapons that could destroy each other's orbiting communication and reconnaissance systems, opening a new and dangerous phase of the superpower arms race. For many years efforts by the General Assembly to mitigate the more hostile aspects of the space race found neither the United States nor the Soviet Union particularly receptive. In 1983 President Ronald Reagan gave new impetus to the space race with his Strategic Defense Initiative (SDI, popularly known as "Star Wars") aimed at the development of new laser and other weapons into an ultimate outer space defense system. After the dissolution of the Soviet Union, Russian leader Boris Yeltsin called for joint development of outer space defense systems and suggested bilateral cooperation in research and development for SDI. Although the Yeltsin initiative remained dormant, the U.S. Congress, still concerned with the threat of nuclear weapons, in 1999 authorized the continuing development of a modified SDI program, thus heightening the suspicions of Russia and other governments. The development of an antiballistic missile system by the United States received even greater support from President George W. Bush, who unilaterally abrogated the ABM treaty and called for the deployment of the missile defense system even before it had proved its reliability. Arguing that even a partial defense system was better than none after September 11, Bush went forward with construction of radar detection and launch sites despite opposition from domestic and international critics.

## CONTROL OF NUCLEAR WARHEADS AND DELIVERY SYSTEMS

### Confidence Building

One important outcome of the post–Cold War condition was the improvement in communications between the United States and the Russian Federation and their changed attitudes toward arms control and something approaching eventual nuclear disarmament. But this greater receptivity for arms control was somewhat diminished when George W. Bush replaced Bill Clinton in the White House. The Bush position on arms control was more negative than positive, especially given Bush's heavy reliance on an independent defense posture, particularly after the events of September 11, 2001.

Nevertheless, during the first forty-five years of disarmament negotiations, the biggest obstacle to agreement had been verification. In the 1990s, by contrast, that problem had been reduced to a relatively minor one. The Russians, in fact, requested technical and financial help in dismantling their nuclear weapons, and U.S. technicians were invited to participate in the on-site process. In effect, Russia requested that the two former rivals become active partners in the process of destroying weapons. Such cooperation was welcomed, but realism demanded a degree of caution. The new vulnerability of the United States after September 11 revealed a different future than that contemplated with the demise of the Soviet Union.

Furthermore, that demise had led to new economic woes. Russia adopted the free market and posed itself as a new, if budding, democracy; nevertheless, there was concern that the country's military leaders, scientists, and technicians—suffering a diminution or loss of livelihood—could be tempted to sell their know-how and even their weapons to countries aspiring to achieve nuclear weapons capability. Russia itself, in need of business clients, was inclined to sell much of its technical knowledge to start-up countries intent on developing nuclear capacity. Such countries ostensibly were interested in the peaceful uses of nuclear energy, but the capacity for nuclear weapons production could not be ignored in circumstances of dual use. Few Russians addressed the matter of government policy in assisting countries like Iran to develop their nuclear industry, but informants were not reluctant to speak of those within the scientific community who could be induced to sell to the highest bidder.

One serious effort by Washington to purchase its way out of a nuclear weapons problem occurred in 1994. A 1993 CIA report revealed that North Korea had violated its earlier acceptance of the Nuclear Nonproliferation Treaty. North Korea was believed to have developed several atomic weapons and had demonstrated its missile delivery capability. Faced with the urgency of the matter, the Clinton administration believed it best to press for a diplomatic solution. When the IAEA tried to investigate alleged treaty violations, North Korean authorities refused them entry. With tensions on the rise, and with the threat of a renewed war on the Korean peninsula, the United States advanced a proposal that eased the confrontation. In 1994, an agreement between the United States, North Korea, South Korea, Japan, and Russia offered North Korea financial and material assistance in return for P'yŏngyang's willingness to dismantle its fuel-enrichment facilities. When the North Koreans declared they needed the nuclear plants to generate needed energy, Clinton offered to replace the enrichment plants with light-water nuclear facilities for energy generation. Japan and South Korea, with assistance from the United States, pledged to construct the new plants, and until they could be placed on line, the United States agreed to transfer to the North, free of charge, 500,000 tons of heavy oil annually. After the signing of the agreement, the first shipment of fuel oil began arriving in North Korea. Seoul and Tokyo agreed to pay the major cost of the operation—a small price for a nuclear-free region.

In 1995, North Korea also promised to halt development of its graphite-moderated reactors and dismantle those already in operation. Although North Korea retained its nuclear weapons inventory, the realization that further bomb making would cease was judged a breakthrough in confidence building. The agreement not only hinted at a change in attitude in the North Korean government after the death of Kim Il Sung, it also created conditions in which to restart the peace and unification talks between North and South Korea. Peace prospects as well as the conditions needed for a tranquil peninsula were the anticipated dividends from this act of diplomacy. Moreover, it was just at this time that crop failures in North Korea's agricultural sector forced the government to seek substantial assistance from South Korea, Japan, and the United States. Several million people were at risk in the affected area, and all three aid-giving countries acknowledged the humanitarian character of the North Korean request. But what had been judged a success also had its drawbacks. Subsequent developments in late 1998 and 1999 threatened the improved diplomatic atmosphere. North Korea continued to test longer-range ballistic missiles, firing some of them over Japan. P'yŏngyang also sustained its bellicose posturing on the peninsula, and it continued to raise serious questions about the efficacy of confidence building in the area. Confidence building seemed to be further cast aside when North Korea rescinded its support for the Nuclear Nonproliferation Treaty and publicized its intention to restart its nuclear weapons program.

## AVOIDING ACCIDENTAL WAR

Atomic weapons were exploded over Hiroshima and Nagasaki in August 1945 to hasten the end of World War II. Since then nuclear weapons have not been used, and a primary function of such weapons has been deterrence. Because of the prospect of mutual destruction, a nuclear attack against another nuclear power or one of its allies has been viewed as an irrational action. Over the years each superpower suspected that the other was developing a first-strike capability, but in fact no nuclear weapons were ever used. For whatever reasons, the possessors of nuclear weapons since World War II have been deterred from using them.

Although first use of nuclear weapons has never been invoked as a viable strategy, the fear has persisted that nuclear war may come about by a means other than a planned attack—by misinterpretation of the other side's actions, by electronic or mechanical error, or by human derangement. The 1962 Cuban missile crisis dramatized the need in the nuclear age for some means of direct and rapid communication between the leaders of states possessing nuclear weapons. To reduce the possibility of a great power clash through miscalculation, accident, or failure of communication, the two governments in 1963 set up a Teletype system, called the "hot line," directly linking the Kremlin in Moscow to the White House in Washington. Subsequently, hot lines were established between Paris and Moscow and between London and Moscow. Most observers hailed this communications link as a major step forward in reducing the threat of accidental war, at the same time that they expressed amazement that no such precautionary arrangement had existed between the two governments during years of major crises. At the height of the Cuban missile crisis, for example, President Kennedy had to fall back on commercial facilities to communicate with the Kremlin.

The changed atmosphere of the 1990s diminished the likelihood that either Russia or the United States would mistake an accidental missile flight as the first shot in a planned nuclear attack against the other. Recognition of the dangers led members of the Commonwealth of Independent States to negotiate among themselves regarding nuclear security, and it also led to unilateral actions aimed at avoiding accidental war. An earlier Bush administration, for example, quietly ended what for twenty-nine years had been referred to as "doomsday flights" of Air Force planes equipped to direct a nuclear war if a Soviet attack on the United States occurred. Doomsday planes had been in the air continuously since the crisis in 1961 that led to the building of the Berlin Wall. The decision to discontinue such flights was based on budgetary considerations as well as the thaw in the Cold War. But that was a time when two state actors dominated the international scene.

Accidental nuclear war is still a consideration and concern among the chief nuclear powers, but it appears to be a lesser concern of nuclear-armed countries that have emerged since the end of the Cold War. India and Pakistan speak less in terms of accidental threat than in terms of strategic interests. Terrorist activity directed against India in Kashmir spilled over into India in 2002, and both countries mobilized their armies for what appeared to be imminent war. Both countries also publicized their willingness to defend their territorial integrity, with nuclear weapons, if necessary. Pakistan was especially outspoken, indicating that it could not expect to repulse a massive Indian attack with conventional arms. When after months of high tension both countries agreed to pull back from the abyss, Pakistani leaders attributed the Indian decision to withdraw to Pakistan's nuclear deterrent. Certainly, many of the world's leaders were fearful that a nuclear exchange could become a reality in the subcontinent, and their diplomatic efforts were never more feverish in persuading the two governments that it would be better to find a solution to their rivalry at the conference table.

North Korea does not use the language of accidental war either; nor does Israel. Both countries believe that they have the necessary safeguards in place, and if ever they use nuclear weapons it would be because they believe that they have no other alternative. Iraq's nuclear capabilities were stunted by UN inspections, and finally, the program became a victim of the Iraq War in 2003. The decision by Ukraine, Kazakhstan, and Belarus to forego their nuclear arsenals removed these countries as a source of accidental nuclear war, but it remains to be seen whether porous frontiers in the Caucasus and Central Asia raise new questions about the monitoring of nuclear weapons and/or technology.

In the changed circumstances after September 11, a new doctrine of preemption has been introduced that limits further the possibility of accidental war but also makes war, even nuclear war, an optional but serious instrument of national power. This doctrine cannot be minimized. With the fear that nuclear weapons could fall into the hands of terrorists, the use of force against nuclear facilities has taken on greater credibility. The thought that international law protects the sovereignty of states, indeed permits them to function with impunity in all matters within their domestic jurisdiction, no longer has the same import. Despite the unaltered wording of the UN Charter protecting the sovereignty of states, in a world where terror exists everywhere and can strike anywhere, states reserve the right to strike the first blow. Clearly, the doctrine of preemption is about survival, not necessarily winning an "arms race." In the world of the contemporary terrorist, there is no understanding of accidental nuclear war, and states are ever more likely to act first and question later.

## BANNING CHEMICAL AND BIOLOGICAL WEAPONS

Ever since chemical weapons were used with devastating results in World War I, the world community has sought to ban these odious devices. This objective was achieved in the Geneva Protocol of 1925, which incorporated a legal ban on the *use* of chemical and biological or bacteriological weapons. Although most existing states ratified the Protocol during the interwar years, the United States and Japan rejected it. Japan, however, accepted it after World War II and the United States tardily gave approval in 1975. Despite the treaty, both the United States and the Soviet Union were able to build and maintain substantial stockpiles of chemical agents, since the Geneva Convention prohibited their first use but not their production or stockpiling. The United States no longer produces "offensive" biological weapons but continues to develop counteractive defensive agents.

Since 1969 the issue of chemical and bacteriological or biological weapons has been included annually on the agenda of the UN General Assembly, with the two types of weapons considered separately since 1971. As a result of UN efforts, a Convention on the Prohibition of the Development, Production, and Stockpiling of Bacteriological (Biological) and Toxin Weapons and on Their Destruction was signed in 1972 and entered into force in 1975. The United States accepted the convention in that same year. Previously, U.S. objections to both the 1925 Geneva Protocol and the Biological Convention had been based on the position that outlawing these particular weapons should be part of a general disarmament treaty rather than treated separately. Banned by the treaty are pathogenic agents, such as bacteria and viruses, and toxins from microbes, plants, and animals.

In 1972 the General Assembly urged the drafting of a treaty that would also ban the development, production, and stockpiling of chemical weapons, as well as their use, and that would require the supervised destruction of existing stockpiles and production facilities. Although the United States and the Soviet Union had by far the largest supplies of chemical weapons, the problem became increasingly widespread as the technology for chemical weapons began to find its way to the Third World. In 1984 the Security Council issued a declaration condemning the use of chemical agents in the Iran-Iraq War. Evidence made it clear that Iraq had used such weapons against Iran and its own citizens, whose loyalty had been questioned by Saddam Hussein's regime. Iraq's continued development and stockpiling of chemical agents was scrutinized and confirmed by UNSCOM inspectors after the Gulf War.

Throughout the 1970s and 1980s mutual suspicion of the superpowers, along with reluctance to relinquish the chemical weapons bargaining chip, prevented serious progress in UN-sponsored negotiations on a new chemical weapons treaty. These roadblocks dissolved with the decline of East-West hostility and the new urgency afforded the issue by Iraq's possession and use of chemical weapons. As a result the Conference on Disarmament was able to approve a treaty outlawing the production and stockpiling (as well as use) of chemical weapons. The treaty also provided a stringent system of on-site, short-notice inspection. The General Assembly approved the treaty in 1992. In January 1993, the Secretary-General opened the convention for signature. In 1996, Hungary became the sixty-fifth country to ratify the Convention on the Prohibition of the Development, Production, Stockpiling, and Use of Chemical Weapons and Their Destruction, and it entered into force on April 29, 1997, 180 days after Hungary deposited its instrument of ratification. The chemical weapons ban was given unlimited duration and included an extensive verification system. The treaty represented the first multilateral disarmament agreement that intended to eliminate an entire category of weapons of mass destruction. A technical headquarters was established at The Hague and it was given responsibility for carrying out the verification provisions of the Convention.

Unfortunately, as experience with Iraq and UNSCOM has shown, international conventions without enforcement cannot prevent the manufacture, stockpiling, or use of chemical and biological weapons in a world where non-states as well as states believe they still serve a purpose.

## TENSION REDUCTION THROUGH POLITICAL AGREEMENT

A variety of agreements and policies have contributed to a lessening of tension among the chief or older nuclear powers. The expansion of East-West trade and the opening of China to Western trade, including the granting of most-favored-nation status to China, have clearly contributed to better relations, although other irritants have frequently tended to negate the gains achieved from closer economic ties.

Perhaps the main instrument of East-West tension reduction during the Cold War years was the Conference on Security and Cooperation in Europe (CSCE) in the 1970s and the Helsinki Accord or Final Act that it produced in 1975. Divided into four sections or "baskets," the Helsinki Final Act included provisions for (1) security in Europe, including the development of confidence-building political and military measures (Basket I); (2) cooperation in economics, science and technology, and the environment (Basket II); (3) cooperation in promoting human rights, cultural exchanges, education, and the free flow of people, ideas, and information throughout Europe (Basket III); and (4) the holding of review conferences "to continue the multilateral process initiated by the Conference" (Basket IV).

The Helsinki Accord included no provisions for disarmament or arms control, but it was a major effort to reduce hostility between the East and West by encouraging all the nations of Europe plus the United States to accept the post–World War II status quo in Europe. Programs of cooperation and understanding, it was believed, would engender a relaxed atmosphere that would encourage good relations and perhaps promote demilitarization in Europe. Although the Final Act was a diplomatic agreement and not a binding lawmaking treaty, the signatories were expected to honor the spirit as well as the letter of the agreement. Periodic review conferences aimed at goading them into meeting that expectation. With the Cold War ended, the CSCE became an important forum for fostering cooperation among all the countries of Europe, East and West, but notably for Russia and the East European states. Reformed as the Organization for Security and Cooperation in Europe in 1996, the OSCE assumed the role of a formal organization whose central purpose was the alleviation of social and political pressures that were likely to culminate in conflict. Alongside peacekeeping forces from the Commonwealth of Independent States, OSCE has helped ease tensions in Georgia, Armenia, Azerbaijan, and Tajikistan in Central Asia.

## BANNING ANTIPERSONNEL MINES

The Convention on the Prohibition of the Use, Stockpiling, Production, and Transfer of Anti-Personnel Mines and on their Destruction was completed in Oslo on September 18, 1997, and entered into force on March 1, 1999. By the end of February 2003, 131 states had formally accepted the convention, including 45 mine-affected countries. Of the total of 48 states that did not sign the treaty, most prominent were the United States and Russia. China, Iran, North Korea, Iraq, and Pakistan also did not sign. The Convention prohibits the production, use, or transfer of antipersonnel mines and requires that each state party to the treaty destroy existing stockpiles within four years of the Convention's entry into force. As of mid-2003, 55 states had completed destroying national stockpiles or were in the process of doing so. Italy and Japan destroyed more than two million mines between them. If all the states now party to the Convention destroy their mine holdings, the total destroyed will exceed 32 million. The states not signatory to the Convention were requested to consider its humanitarian purpose, but countries like the United States believed situations continued to exist that demanded the use of such weapons. One case cited was the demilitarized zone dividing North and South Koreas, which was judged to be the most heavily mined region in the world.

# OBSTACLES TO DISARMAMENT

The UN objective in seeking disarmament through agreement—in contrast to the more pragmatic objectives of arms control—is to build a peaceful world by ridding it of weapons of war. This solution is so simple, so obvious, and so preferable to its alternative that an impartial observer from another planet might think that only a dedicated warmonger or a potential aggressor could resist its logic. Yet the historical record of efforts to achieve disarmament through agreement reveals appallingly few and mostly short-lived examples. Why have the United Nations and its members failed to achieve this almost universally acclaimed objective? There are many reasons—some technical, others related to the nature of the state system, and still others rooted in human nature. What follows is an analysis of some of the major problems that help explain the disarmament impasse.

## SECURITY QUESTIONS

The difficulty of securing disarmament can perhaps be understood best if it is related to the question of why nations arm in the first place. If an arms race causes war, what causes the arms race? Obviously, the building of weapons of war is related to the objectives of states, especially national survival. Nations arm for security to protect their existence, but they also arm to pursue political and economic objectives. For centuries arms have provided the means for states to carry out national policies. As long as leaders regard military capacity as essential to fulfilling their states' vital interests, the abandonment of that capability through international agreement is unlikely. Some, such as many ethnic groups in the former Soviet Union and Yugoslavia, have found that lack of military preparedness in today's world can spell disaster when they are attacked by a rival ethnic group. Similarly, current conditions in East and Central Africa address the same point, if in fact, the issue is more tribal antagonism than ethnic differences.

The pursuit of security through the arms race is based on the ancient Roman maxim *Si vis pacem, para bellum* (If you seek peace, prepare for war). In today's nuclear world, however, efforts to increase security by building more and more deadly weapons tend only to produce greater insecurity. Therein lies the paradox of UN efforts to end the contemporary arms races in different parts of the world. Too many countries in all regions of the globe are feverishly developing new weapons systems and bolstering older ones in their search for security. The idea of security through a general disarmament remains only a theoretical abstraction.

## SOVEREIGNTY AND NATIONALISM

The search for explanations of the failure to achieve disarmament leads to the heart of the disarmament dilemma. Controversies over means and details are only symptomatic of the basic contradiction between international needs and national prerogatives that has stymied most disarmament efforts. Two forces that emerged early in the history of the modern state system—state sovereignty and nationalism—constitute the major legal and emotional barriers to the idea of reaching agreement with "foreign" elements. A disarmament agreement, by its very nature, would limit the sovereign power of a state to exercise full control over the area most vital to its security. Ardent nationalists resent the access, free movement, and "snooping" within their states that must accompany a disarmament enforcement system in the form of on-site inspections.

An effective disarmament arrangement in the contemporary world must be based on some form of effective international control. For example, in formulating the Acheson-Lilienthal proposals that became the basis for the Baruch Plan, Dean Acheson insisted that inspection would be inadequate if the production of fissionable materials remained under national control and that enforcement would be insufficient unless a veto-free international body could punish a violator. The question of the feasibility of disarmament essentially boils down to this: is the world ready for a measure of world government? The answer seems clear: there is as yet no consensual support for it in any country. The sovereign state system may be obsolete when it is objectively evaluated within the context of intercontinental missiles and thermonuclear weapons systems, but in the minds of human beings nationalism and sovereignty still offer the best approach to security.

## Vested Interests

Disarmament in today's world must take into account the armaments that nations already possess. How can the arms race be reversed in a world in which enormous amounts of money are spent each year for military purposes, millions of people serve in the armed forces, and other millions are engaged in military production? There may well be too many vested interests in the world of armaments and the military services to challenge the status quo successfully.

The economic consequences of disarmament are viewed ambivalently in some states. Total disarmament would permit states to devote the huge savings to economic betterment. Many observers, however, fear that it would result in a loss of jobs and profits or a dislocation of the national economy. Communists used to argue that capitalism depended on the artificial stimulus provided by arms production and war. Although little evidence existed to substantiate that charge, many Americans even today react adversely to the closing of defense plants and the cancellation of military procurement contracts. The military-industrial complex continues to function as a powerful force to challenge any disarmament proposal that threatens a loss of status or income. Any successful disarmament plan, therefore, would have to take economic consequences into account.

## Threats of Deception

The technological revolution that has dramatically changed the mode of warfare has also increased the difficulty of disarmament. Arms reduction in a world of conventional weapons might mean that one side could achieve an initial advantage through deception. Though this advantage is not likely to be decisive, a violation in these circumstances could give the attacking state a significant edge. With the spread of thermonuclear, chemical, and biological weapons, however, treachery in a disarmament agreement could be decisive. Moreover, the ability to deceive has increased; it is far easier to hide a few intercontinental rockets and their thermonuclear warheads than to conceal several divisions of troops or a flotilla of battleships. Even more subject to concealment are chemical and biological weapons, the poor nation's doomsday weapon. Fear of deception has led the United States to insist that an effective system of on-site inspection be operational *before* any disarmament measures are implemented.

Deception may also relate to intentions and the fear of a surprise attack. The world has not yet forgotten the immediate military advantages enjoyed by the armies of Germany in their June 1941 invasion of the Soviet Union, or by the Japanese attack on Pearl Harbor in December 1941. Although both attacking armies were eventually defeated, the advantage of surprise was great and the war no doubt protracted and hence more costly.

## IDEOLOGICAL AND ETHNIC RIVALRY

A world of colliding values offers a poor milieu for reaching agreement on disarmament. When one side in an ideological or ethnic struggle becomes convinced that the other is bent on conquest or destruction, any proposal for a reduction in arms is regarded as a devious inducement for a nation to weaken itself, providing the enemy with an opportunity to attack. Any disarmament agreement must depend on some minimal amount of good faith and a belief that the other side will live up to its terms. But a deep gulf between ideological and ethnic enemies makes trust a rare commodity.

During most of the postwar years, ideological hostility between the Soviet Union and the United States tended to create a "deaf man's dialogue" in disarmament negotiations. Both sides favored the reduction of arms and proposed various schemes to accomplish it, but each side was wary of the proposals of the other because it feared a trap. Each believed its plan was logical and responsible and that if the other side were sincerely interested in disarmament, it would have ceased its diversionary tactics and accepted the plan. In the early 1990s, the ideologies of communism and state socialism were replaced by those of democracy and capitalism in the independent states that were formerly parts (republics) of the Soviet Union. Immediately, the long-stalled negotiations for major disarmament agreements became a meaningful exercise.

Ethnic rivalry, however, provided a new and very uncertain challenge, especially within the former republics. A noteworthy case was Chechnya, an unwilling extension of the Russian Federation. Chechens had suffered discrimination at the hands of Russians over decades, and during World War II they were thought to be allies of the Germans. Punished with banishment from their homeland by Joseph Stalin, after the dictator's death they were allowed to reestablish their settlements. With the breakup of the Soviet Union, the Chechens assumed the time was right for their declaration of independence, but Russia was not about to yield the territory. What ensued has been a high-cost guerrilla war that stretches all the way to Moscow where Chechen terrorists have numerous times caused havoc and taken a toll on innocent Russians. In the meantime, without any sign of achieving their objective, the Chechens have paid a high price in thousands of lives lost and cities and towns razed. This has not been a conflict that the United Nations can address. Moreover, Chechens have joined with other Muslim terrorists from the Middle East and Central Asia in their assault on Western targets. Other ethnic wars have been waged in the states of the former Yugoslavia. The struggle to free Bosnia-Herzegovina from Serbian control caused a million casualties; perhaps as many as two hundred thousand were dead before the conflict subsided with NATO intervention. The battle for Kosovo was also costly, and as in Croatia, Macedonia, and Serbia and Montenegro there is no indication that disarmament takes precedence over military preparedness.

## FULL PARTICIPATION NEEDED

A meaningful world disarmament agreement requires the participation of all affected states. If one or several states with sizable military strength were not included, the delicate balance of power provided by a carefully worked-out schedule of arms reductions would be in constant danger of being upset. It is no simple task to get all the major powers to support disarmament, because one or several may prefer an independent policy or may regard the existing power distribution in the world as favorable to their national interests. For example, in the years between World War I and World War II, France was interested in maintaining arms superiority over Germany; it was not inclined toward general disarmament. Both China and France refused for many years to participate in nuclear disarmament negotiations. It is doubtful that the United States and Russia will enter into treaties calling for deeper cuts in nuclear weapons without the participation of all nuclear powers. Nonetheless, the nuclear nonproliferation treaty has been ratified by 188 states, more countries than have entered into any other arms limitation and disarmament agreement. The NPT represents the only binding multilateral commitment by the nuclear weapon states to the goal of nuclear disarmament. The Comprehensive Nuclear Test-Ban Treaty, adopted by the UN General Assembly in 1996, bans all nuclear explosions for military and civilian purposes. It has not been as readily accepted by the states despite its connection to the indefinite extension of the NPT.

## THE PROPAGANDA BARRIER

The appeal of disarmament to millions of people has made it a prime subject of psychological warfare. Diplomats, knowing that countries will reject their schemes for general disarmament, are free to advance radical proposals designed to make their countries appear to be creative in their search for peace. In the United Nations both the East and West often drafted their proposals to appeal to the great mass of nonaligned states rather than to the negotiators sitting across the table. Sweeping Soviet proposals for general and complete disarmament, with control machinery to be established later, were often matched by U.S. plans providing for a maximum of elaborate international inspection and enforcement but deemphasizing such problems as overseas bases and German rearmament, which were central to Soviet security considerations.

Pressures for great power agreement on disarmament emanated regularly from the majority of the states in the General Assembly, challenging both sides to find new platitudes they could safely endorse while tabling concrete proposals "for further study." Each side tried to preserve its image—that of a peaceloving, humanitarian, but horrendously powerful nation that would gladly lay down its arms and contribute the savings to economic development but for the intransigence and uncompromising hostility of the other side. It is noteworthy that one of the most important agreements in the arms control field during the past forty years, the Limited Nuclear Test-Ban Treaty of 1963, was reached through closed negotiations among U.S., British, and Soviet diplomats. SALT I and SALT II agreements and the first START treaty also were the products of bilateral great power negotiations. The end of the Cold War, however, saw a great diminution in this global propaganda war. More cooperation between Russia and the United States, along with the rejection of communism and the furthering of democracy, has muted much of the war of words and improved the climate for exchanges on arms control and reciprocal reductions in the development of weapons of mass destruction. But as the war on terrorism suggests, there have been and will continue to be a need for newer and more sophisticated weapons. If people yearned for a peace dividend with the end of the Cold War, the war on terrorism has dashed any hope that an end to global violence is near.

## THE SPEED OF CHANGE

An increasingly important factor working against consensus to end the global arms race is the realization that much scientific research and development for peaceful purposes can be related to weaponry; hence no disarmament agreement can really stop progress in military technology. The development of a decisive new weapon that could upset the agreed balance of arms is a potential danger that both sides would have to assume in any arms control or disarmament agreement. No inspection or control system could offer full protection against such an eventuality. In an age of intensive exploration of the atom and of new ventures with particle beams and lasers in outer space, any disarmament agreement could be rendered obsolete within a short time unless it provided for periodic updating. It may be that the day has already passed when disarmament through agreement is rationally practicable.

Over the years disarmament negotiators have faced a basic dilemma: As scientific knowledge grows and technology changes with revolutionary speed, disarmament agreements become increasingly dependent on trust; but trust is vitiated by the fear of new, secret weapons spawned by advancing technology.

Science and technology, the very forces that have made it necessary to end the arms race in order to save the human race from destruction, paradoxically are the same forces that make agreement to disarm too dangerous for national security interests.

## Timing Problems

There is a pervasive tendency for nations caught up in an arms race to procrastinate in the belief that the future will offer a more propitious time for entering into a disarmament agreement. That right moment never seems to occur. Instead, new weapons, military confrontations and other crises, and burgeoning military capabilities increase the need for disarmament but decrease its likelihood. The Western-Soviet arms race of 1945–90 illustrates the point. When the military rivalry began, both sides had just ended a major war and were faced with critical problems of recovery. The Soviet Union had suffered the destruction of its cities and calamitously high civilian and military casualties. The United Sates had a monopoly on nuclear weapons that it offered to sacrifice in return for a world security system. In retrospect, the first few years after World War II appear to have been an ideal time for disarmament, yet negotiations fostered by the United Nations failed. Thereafter, the Cold War led to new alliance systems and a wide-open arms race. Military bases were established in strategic locations around the planet. New weapons of mass destruction were perfected. Both the United States and the Soviet Union became peripherally or directly involved in local wars (for example, Korea, Vietnam, and Afghanistan), and the state of almost constant belligerence fostered a climate for the acquisition of nuclear weapons and their delivery systems. The grounds for insecurity and fear were no longer hypothetical or based on a future potentiality. Mass extermination became a proximate danger. Nevertheless, the Americans and the Soviets continued for forty-five years after World War II to manufacture nuclear "overkill" capacity in a vain effort to achieve a preferred position in disarmament negotiations.

The cycle of more and better armaments was finally broken with the self-destruction of the Soviet Union. Since 1992 the East-West arms race is no longer a constant reminder of the ideological divide that prompted it. But the arms merchants are neither silent nor inactive. The states of the world still spend more of their resources on armaments than on any other item. Arms races are visible on virtually every continent. It does not require a cynic to note that the time is seldom right for real disarmament without fundamental changes in human attitudes and conditions.

## Ratio Problems

During any arms control negotiations, the future power relationship among the parties becomes a matter of grave concern. Each nation, in any prospective agreement, seeks a minimum goal of maintaining parity, and, if possible, a maximum advantage of arms superiority. Because power and security are never absolute but always relative, each proposal must be carefully weighed for determining its potential effect on all the parties. The result is an unending series of calculations by military tacticians who prefer to err on the conservative side, in keeping with their general distaste for disarmament as a security objective. The problem of balancing different categories of forces (strategic versus tactical, air versus naval, nuclear versus conventional) provides an additional complication.

General and complete disarmament supervised by the United Nations or a system of enforcement by regional police forces might overcome the fear of giving advantage to another state, but it would raise a new threat to national freedom of action from the global police force. Even if the world government implications of UN-enforced general disarmament could be accepted, the not inconsiderable difficulty of phasing out arms through stages would remain. At each stage, no party can be left relatively weaker than at an earlier point as each strives to compare more favorably with its power rivals. Since it is impossible for complete parity to be achieved, each state must be led to believe that it will be advantaged by successive stages of disarmament. The conundrum in successfully pulling off this sleight-of-hand maneuver is evidenced by the forty-five-year disagreement between the United States and the Soviet Union over the numbers and types of forces to be disarmed at each stage and the ratio of forces that would remain.

The problem of ratios is central to any disarmament scheme but is not simple to resolve. When the United States argued for more delivery systems in the 1960s, it was with the awareness that the Soviet Union was a landmass three times the size of the continental United States. When the Soviets made their pitch for a ratio of nuclear weapons in their favor, it was with the understanding that U.S. missiles were more accurate and many were aboard undetectable submarines at the bottom of the world's oceans. When multiple-warhead missiles were deployed, the United States had to acknowledge the greater lift capacity of Soviet missiles, and hence their capacity to hold ten warheads to only three for the smaller U.S. missiles. In the end, ratio questions may be important in arms control situations, but they do more to enhance armaments than to eliminate them. How, for example, can ratios be applied in the stockpiling of weapons of mass destruction when the number of states involved are more than two, or even more than five? How many nuclear weapons and delivery systems should North Korea, or Iran, or Israel possess compared with China, let alone the United States or the Russian Federation? And what about the question of sufficiency in the nuclear standoff between India and Pakistan? At what point is the one deemed to be a threat to the other, and indeed, is it really a matter of numbers? By the same token, what sort of ratio applies to other weapons of mass destruction, that is, biological and chemical. Clearly, there is no answer to this issue of ratios in the post-superpower era. With any country in a position to develop and/or acquire some weapon of mass destruction, it is impossible to speak of security in number counts. In effect, arms control is unreliable in contemporary times, and the only security to be achieved is in a fail-safe disarmament regime that purges weapons of mass destruction from the planet.

## Inspection and Enforcement

From the earliest postwar discussions of the Baruch Plan in 1946, disarmament talks have been centered on issues of "inspection and control." U.S. proposals consistently offered to exchange arms reduction for a verifiable system of safeguards against clandestine arms buildup and surprise attack. During most of this period the Soviet Union accepted the general proposition that inspection and control are necessary, but attempts to work out the details often resulted in little more than an exchange of recriminations. The detailed inspection provisions of the START treaties, with their comprehensive multiple systems of onsite inspection, reveal how far Russia was prepared to move in reducing its nuclear stockpile. The sacrifice of START II safeguards by the George W. Bush administration in favor of a missile defense system apparently brought an end to START deliberations even though Russia was prepared to engage in START III negotiations. START III clearly would have promised even greater cuts in the nuclear arsenals of both Russia and the United States. Russia warned the United States that its unilateral abrogation of the ABM treaty would spark another nuclear arms race, but the Bush administration, convinced that it was providing more security, proceeded with its plans.

To be effective, an inspection system to verify disarmament must resolve the following issues: (1) the extent of access to each country's territory; (2) the frequency of on-the-spot surveillance; (3) the timing—whether inspection arrangements are to go into effect before or after the disarmament measures that they will verify; (4) the nature of aerial and ground reconnaissance to guard against the possibility of a surprise attack; (5) the means of detecting weapons in outer space; (6) the determination of what constitutes a weapon or a potential weapon; (7) the selection of the areas to be included in a progressive territorial demilitarization; and (8) the composition, powers, and number of inspection teams required to do the job. In addition to discouraging treaty violations, proper verification could make it more difficult for a future government to reverse the disarmament agreement, inhibit efforts of insurgent forces to gain control of weapons in their territories, limit the possibility of nuclear materials and other high-tech weapons finding their way into Third World states, and establish confidence essential to future arms reductions.

The technical aspects of detecting violations lead to a second and equally difficult set of issues that involve the political and military consequences of a violation once it has been found. To what extent, for example, will world opinion contribute to enforcement and sanctions? What role should the injured state or states play if they detect an evasion? What kind of enforcement mechanism should be set up, and what should be the nature of its sanctions? Should the injured state be entitled to undertake "restorative measures" after a violation to restore the military balance that would have existed without a disarmament agreement? Arms control agreements are entered into, presumably, on the theory that parties will honor their commitments. But realistically, the possibility of violations must be taken into account in framing any agreement. Moreover, it is the lingering belief that disarmament agreements will not be honored that is the fundamental justification for the continuing arms race. States will continue to enter into agreements not out of altruism, or even out of common sense, but because they compensate for the weaknesses inherent in all states. No state is omnipotent, and all are in one way or another dependent on others. But this interdependency, if acknowledged at all, is still not enough to encourage states to seek avenues other than the use of force to protect their national interests.

## APPROACHES TO THE DISARMAMENT PROBLEM

Arms and security are inseparably intertwined, but they frequently exhibit a catch-22 relationship. Nearly all states regard armaments as essential to their national security. But when one state's armaments are perceived as a threat to the security of another state, the second state may resort to an arms program that threatens the security of the first. This is not a necessary consequence of national armaments. Canada, for example, does not view the huge U.S. military establishment as a threat to its own security. Undoubtedly, a history of peaceful relations and a long-term disarmed boundary contribute to this happy situation. The catch-22 is readily apparent, however, in India-Pakistan relations, the Middle East, and most of the postwar history of East-West dealings. In these and other situations where arms and security are in tension with one another, the challenge is to make arms reduction compatible with the security of each state. A small sampling from the profusion of approaches offered by politicians and scholars to overcome the dilemma or afford a partial remedy will be examined here.

### The Direct Approach

Identifying a useful approach to disarmament starts with the question of whether the major effort should be placed on reducing arms or on developing security. Those who advocate a "direct" approach regard the arms race itself as the main source of fear and insecurity. The solution they offer is simple: "The way to disarm is to disarm." These words have reverberated through the chambers of the League and the United Nations on many occasions. As arms are reduced, so holds the theory, the familiar cycle that produces the upward spiral in the arms race (increased arms produce greater fear and insecurity, which, in turn, produce greater expenditures on arms, and so on) will be reversed. Reduced international tensions will follow in the wake of disarmament, encouraging agreement in other areas of controversy. Most Third World nations have been vocal proponents of the direct approach during the UN era, for others if not for themselves. The United States and Britain, which supported the direct approach during the League of Nations period, have changed since 1946 to the indirect approach.

## THE INDIRECT APPROACH

Proponents of an indirect approach regard armaments as a reflection of the deep insecurities of the state system. Disarmament, therefore, should be recognized for what it is—a fundamentally *political* problem that involves the totality of relations among the nations caught up in the arms race. Disarmament becomes the secondary, not the immediate, objective. Major political conflicts must first be ameliorated, an effective collective security system must be established, and carefully planned inspection, verification, and sanctions arrangements must be made operational. Disarmament cannot be feasible, therefore, until there is a convergence of national policies on these issues.

The 1990s offered some assurance that the indirect approach to disarmament can work. The end of the Cold War and the resulting improved relations between Russia and the United States appeared to breathe new life into arms control negotiations. Deliberations between the two powers were expected to continue and to produce positive results if the two governments focused their attention on confidence-building measures. But the more conservative posture of the George W. Bush administration, its early preference for unilateralism, and its general disdain for the United Nations created new tensions with Russia as well as other states. Moreover, the Al-Qaeda terrorist attacks of September 11, 2001, elevated these tensions and caused the declaration of a protracted war on terrorism. The Cold War was all but forgotten as the United States was geared to meet a new, and in many ways more unpredictable, enemy. The war on terrorism also negated both the direct and indirect approach to disarmament, which had lost its practical utility.

## UNILATERAL DISARMAMENT

Discourse on unilateral disarmament appears out of place in an age challenged by the perils of terrorism, but it is still a matter requiring some elucidation. Some disarmament advocates offer this novel strategy of one-sided initiative to secure an arms reduction breakthrough. Once such an action has started the disarming process, reciprocation would theoretically give it the motive power necessary to accelerate its momentum. Underlying unilateral disarmament theories is an assumption that the reduction of arms is really a matter of common interest but that inertia, tension, mistrust, fear, and habit make it appear to be beyond realization.

Several religious groups advocate a complete unilateral disarmament. If the other side uses the opportunity to impose its control, a Gandhian passive resistance would be employed against the conqueror. While no one can be certain that utopian schemes of this nature would fail, they are impracticable because neither side in the arms race would be likely to place its national security or way of life in the hands of its opponent.

Disarmament theoreticians have worked out unilateral schemes that depend on reciprocal initiatives and responses rather than on the complete surrender of retaliatory power. Unilateral initiatives are not posited as a substitute for bilateral negotiations but only as a "psychological primer" to reverse the trend of the arms race by demonstrating good intentions. If the other side fails in due time to reciprocate or tries to take advantage of the unilateral reductions or withdrawals, such plans call for a return to a hard-line policy.

Although partial unilateral disarmament would be unlikely to threaten the security of a state that has the power to destroy its opponent many times over, it violates the injunction not to encourage a potential aggressor through signs of weakness. The history of the superpower arms race presents evidence both for and against the efficacy of voluntary restraint. Neither participant strained its capabilities to the utmost in developing its arsenal, preferring some semblance of balance to an all-out drive for massive superiority. Moreover, periods of lessened tension during the Cold War reduced the rate of growth in arms on both sides. On the other hand, new crises had a tendency to boost the rate of arms production in both the United States and the Soviet Union to more than counterbalance previous cuts. The Soviet Union on several occasions stopped testing nuclear weapons for several years and invited the United States to do the same. The United States, however, was never willing to stop its testing program.

Unilateral arms control initiatives by Soviet President Mikhail Gorbachev and Russian President Boris Yeltsin contributed to a relaxation of tensions and paved the way for the conclusion of important arms reduction treaties. A notable example was Russia's unilateral decision in 1992 to cease nuclear targeting of U.S. cities and military installations.

Experience of the postwar period suggests that unilateral disarmament initiatives are more likely to be reciprocated during periods of low rather than high international tension. Although unilateral disarmament schemes may be rational enough in their inherent logic, in most high-tension arms race situations neither side is willing to accept the risk of taking the first step. If one side does, the other may be too suspicious or too fearful to reciprocate. During periods of decreasing threat, however, unilateral initiatives appear less risky and may invite reciprocation because they appear more genuine to the other side.

## TOTAL DISARMAMENT

At differing times during the Cold War era both the United States and the Soviet Union presented proposals to the United Nations for "general and complete disarmament." There is little evidence that either side either wanted or expected the outcome they were proposing. Various commentators, however, have seriously advocated total disarmament, and in particular total nuclear disarmament, as the only real hope for human survival.

That contemporary weapons of mass destruction offer at least the possibility of human extinction can no longer be doubted. At the Hiroshima kill-ratio of approximately four deaths per ton of explosive power, the billions of tons of TNT equivalent in the combined nuclear arsenals of the United States and Russia have the capability to destroy the entire population of the earth many times over. Even if all stages of START had been reached, the capability would still exist to destroy the world. When the deadly effects of radioactive fallout and of chemical and biological weapons of mass destruction plus the nuclear weapons capability of other states are added to this estimate, only the most imperturbable optimist can talk about a meaningful aftermath should a nuclear war occur.

Although cataclysmic global destruction is a possibility not to be disregarded, state behavior since the dawn of the nuclear age does not indicate that this is a likely, let alone a probable, consequence of state possession of nuclear weapons.[4] The "balance of terror" was an effective mutual deterrent during the Cold War years, and nuclear weapons undoubtedly continue to figure in the deterrence calculus of states possessing them in the current era. Total elimination of all nuclear weapons would by hypothesis remove the possibility of nuclear war, but nuclear technology would still remain widely available and some nuclear weapons are relatively easy to hide. The present nuclear powers will be quite reluctant to destroy all nuclear weapons knowing it might leave them at least temporarily vulnerable to a rogue nation, terrorist, or insurgent group that had managed to acquire, secrete, or clandestinely construct nuclear devices.

The impossibility of total disarmament does not gainsay the desirability of reducing armaments far below current levels, or placing more stringent controls on their production and dissemination. For Russia and the United States, a case for massive disarmament could be made on economic grounds. Everywhere in the world the diversion of resources from military uses to the production of economic wealth would bring a substantial increase in human welfare. With verified mutual reductions it could also enhance security. The dramatic changes in global politics after the Cold War augured well for this possibility of more accommodating state relationships, especially between the former rival superpowers. But the challenge to peace and security in the new millennium does not point to major clashes or contests between the world's most prominent actors. Rather, the world's attention has shifted to the underside of the global divide where people with little stake in a future designed by others present a different kind of challenge.

## Disarming Terrorists?

On September 11, 2001, terrorism ceased being described as a form of low-level warfare. The terrorism phenomenon is certainly not new. During the years of Cold War, terrorists sought to get the attention of the superpowers, whose rivalry they believed could be turned to their advantage. The immediate purpose of terrorists was to focus world attention on their objectives and to publicize their mistreatment, which they also felt justified their adopting unconventional means to dramatize their predicament. Political leverage, not military victory, was their objective. It mattered little that the victims of terrorism were not the true targets. Terrorist hijacking of commercial aircraft, and in some instances cruise vessels, belonging to other nations or the destruction of other people's life and property was calculated to impress governments, to get them to consider their pain, and ultimately to espouse their cause.

State sponsors of terrorism abounded and multiplied from the 1970s onward, and armed terrorists grew in number and boldness in the years just before the end of the Cold War. Although terrorist organizations were well rooted in dozens of states around the world, Al-Qaeda came to epitomize the contemporary terrorist, dedicated to reaping violence on unsuspecting targets anywhere and everywhere. In the mind of "true believers" all things are possible, and none of the underpinnings of the modern world are of concern to them. Indeed, all the systems and institutions, all the procedures and processes of the prevailing state system are alien to them.

The United Nations was forced to acknowledge after the events of September 11 that "terrorism is a global threat with global effects and its consequences affect every aspect of the United Nations agenda—from development to peace to human rights to the rule of law."[5] A Policy Working Group on the United Nations and Terrorism was established at the order of the Secretary-General in October 2001. Its purpose was to identify the longer-term implications and broad policy dimensions of terrorism for the United Nations. Most important, discussions in the Policy Working Group centered on the terrorists accessing and potentially using weapons of mass destruction. None of the international norms constrained the terrorists; no intermediary was available to press upon them the need for negotiations. Bargaining with global terrorism was not an option. Dealing with and potentially disarming terrorists remains one of today's biggest challenges for individual states and for the United Nations.

# CONCLUSION

The problem of controlling armaments is fundamentally a problem of creating a secure world. Any general disarmament agreement must operate within some broader framework for maintaining global security. The major nuclear powers have shown a proclivity to return to the UN framers' concept of collective security to keep the peace in a disarmed world, but states are unlikely to give up their arms without some alternative guarantee of national security. And this does not, of course, address the new problems of disarmament posed by contemporary terrorism.

Disarmament is a problem that cannot be isolated from the development of universally acceptable international legal, political, economic, and social systems. Armaments will become obsolete, if ever, only when the bonds of world community, which depend on progressive evolution in each of these areas, become strong enough to moderate the conflicts and rivalries that make armaments and armed actions seem necessary. The transformation of international relations from a system exuding power, tension, fear, and conflict to one of cooperation, understanding, and common action may be an impossible undertaking. But small gains are better than nothing, and managing armaments more rationally, even in an age of terrorism, can be a step in that direction.

# NOTES

1. A lively account of the personalities and issues involved in the two Hague Peace Conferences can be found in Barbara W. Tuchman, *The Proud Tower* (New York: Macmillan, 1962), pp. 229–88. For a more detailed discussion of arms limitations efforts in the century before World War I, see Merze Tate, *The Disarmament Illusion* (New York: Macmillan, 1942).
2. See "Statement by the Undersecretary-General for Disarmament," United Nations Press Release DC/2859, March 31, 2003.
3. For a verbatim copy of the treaty and an extensive record of the process leading up to the writing of the treaty and its adoption, see the documentary work published by the U.S. Arms Control and Disarmament Agency titled *Arms Control and Disarmament Agreements—Texts and Histories of the Negotiations,* 1990 edition, pp. 89–106.
4. Kenneth E. Boulding, in a provocative and widely circulated 1962 essay, insisted that it was: "I believe the present international system to be one which has a significant probability built into it of irretrievable disaster for the human race. The longer the number of years we contemplate such a system operating, the larger this probability becomes. I do not know whether in any one year it is one per cent, ten per cent, or even fifty percent. I feel pretty sure, however, that it is of this order of magnitude, not, shall we say, of the order of magnitude of .01 per cent." Boulding, "The Prevention of World War III," *Virginia Quarterly Review* 38, no. 1 (winter 1962), pp. 1–12, reprinted in Richard A. Falk and Saul H. Mendlovitz, *The Strategy of World Order* 1 (New York: World Law Fund, 1966), p. 5. As a solution Boulding advocated not only total national disarmament but world government as well.
5. UN Department for Disarmament, "Weapons of Mass Destruction Branch, Department for Disarmament Affairs: Summary Report," 2002, http://disarmament2.un.org/wmd.

# SELECTED READINGS

*Arms Control and Disarmament Agreements—Texts and Histories of the Negotiations.* Washington, DC: United States Arms Control and Disarmament Agency, 1990.

Caldwell, Dan. *The Dynamics of Domestic Politics and Arms Control: The Salt II Ratification Debate.* Columbia: University of South Carolina Press, 1991.

Cohen, Roberta, and Francis M. Deng. *Masses in Flight: The Global Crisis of Internal Displacement.* Washington, DC: Brookings Institution, 1998.

Cortright, David, and George A. Lopez. *Sanctions and the Search for Security: Challenges to UN Action.* Boulder, CO: Lynne Rienner, 2002.

———. *The Sanctions Decade: Assessing UN Strategies in the 1990s.* Boulder, CO: Lynne Rienner, 2000.

Craig, Paul P., and John A. Jungerman. *Nuclear Arms Race—Technology and Society.* New York: McGraw-Hill, 1986.

Crocker, Chester A., and Fen Osler Hampson, eds. *Managing Global Chaos: Sources of and Responses to International Conflict.* Washington, DC: U.S. Institute of Peace Press, 1996.

Elliot, Jeffrey M., and Robert Reginald. *The Arms Control, Disarmament, and Military Security Dictionary*. Santa Barbara, CA: ABC-CLIO, 1989.

Falk, Richard A., and Saul H. Mendlovitz, eds. *The Strategy of World Order*. Vols. 1–4. New York: World Law Fund, 1966.

Glynn, Patrick. *Closing Pandora's Box: Arms Races, Arms Control, and the History of the Cold War*. New York: Basic Books, 1992.

Harris, John B., and Eric Markusen, eds. *Nuclear Weapons and the Threat of Nuclear War*. New York: Harcourt Brace Jovanovich, 1986.

Jacobson, Harold Karan, and Eric Stein. *Diplomats, Scientists, and Politicians: The United States and the Nuclear Test Ban Negotiations*. Ann Arbor: University of Michigan Press, 1966.

Kanet, Roger E., and Edward O. Kolodziej, eds. *The Cold War as Cooperation: Superpower Cooperation in Regional Conflict Management*. Baltimore: Johns Hopkins University Press, 1991.

Larsen, Jeffrey A. *Arms Control: Cooperative Security in a Changing Environment*. Boulder, CO: Lynne Rienner, 2002.

Larsen, Jeffrey A., and Gregory J. Rattray, eds. *Arms Control Toward the 21st Century*. Boulder, CO: Lynne Rienner, 1996.

Levine, Herbert M., and David Carlton. *The Nuclear Arms Race Debated*. New York: McGraw-Hill, 1986.

Levine, Robert A. *Still the Arms Debate*. Brookfield, VT: Dartmouth Publishing Company, 1990.

Lund, Michael S. *Preventing Violent Conflicts: A Strategy for Preventive Diplomacy*. Washington, DC: U.S. Institute of Peace Press, 1996.

Malone, David M., and Yuen Foong Khong, eds. *Unilateralism and U.S. Foreign Policy: International Perspectives*. Boulder, CO: Lynne Rienner, 2003.

Myrdal, Alva. *The Game of Disarmament*. New York: Pantheon Books, 1982.

Ravenal, Earl C. *Designing Defense for a New World Order: The Military Budget in 1992 and Beyond*. Washington, DC: CATO Institute, 1991.

Smoke, Richard. *National Security and the Nuclear Dilemma*. Reading, MA: Addison-Wesley, 1984.

Sokolski, Henry. *Fighting Proliferation: New Concerns for the Nineties*. Washington, DC: U.S. Government Printing Office, 1997.

Van Creveld, Martin. *The Transformation of War*. New York: Free Press, 1991.

Woolsey, R. James, ed. *Nuclear Arms—Ethics, Strategy, Politics*. San Francisco: ICS Press, 1983.

# 8

## THE REVOLUTION
## OF SELF-DETERMINATION

Since the end of World War II and the founding of the United Nations, both in 1945, the international system has been transformed from one of imperial and colonial design to another of independent, sovereign nation-states. Nothing has been more dramatic or significant than the proliferation of self-governing countries. The retreat from empire and the dissolution of the colonial world has spawned a vast array of political actors that promises greater freedom and expression across a broad spectrum of human experience. But just as independence is a celebration, it is also a responsibility that has not always been grasped by those succeeding to leadership in the new states. Self-determination is a quest that once realized imposes burdens on the liberated. It means choosing a path that is most likely to satisfy the yearnings of millions of people. It also brings with it the need to understand and to explain the limits of the development experience. Nations are not born equal, and especially in previously colonial territories there is much to be said for the scarcity of resources and the deficiencies in human capital. Independence is intoxicating but it is not a panacea for the woes that burden people who must fit themselves into a world they had no part in creating. A transfer of power from colonial overlords to indigenous leaders does not promise good government. Nor does independence usher in a time of plenty or guarantee the instant formation of civil society. There is much to be said for making one's own future, but it cannot be said that the national state, imposed from above, is always suited to the needs of a particular people. Moreover, the material as well as physical distance between the older, more established states and those of the newly independent presents obstacles that cannot be mastered by emotional displays or passionate oratory. At best, self-determination is an achievement, but it is not the end-all or the be-all of human expression.

More than ninety countries whose peoples before World War II were formerly under colonial rule are now members of the United Nations. In addition, many other territories have achieved self-determination through political association or integration with other independent states. In this display of liberation, the United Nations has usually played an important role. While the League of Nations was content to exercise minimal supervision over the administration of a few ex-enemy territories after World War I, the United Nations became an advocate of self-government for colonial peoples everywhere. Indeed, if the purpose of the United Nations was the maintenance of international peace and security, the would-be world organization had to support the peaceful liberation from colonial control of those colonies that were the possessions of the victors as well as the vanquished of World War II. Observers to this process believe that decolonization would have come in time without the involvement of the world body, but they are also quick to point out that the United Nations was present to reinforce the anticolonial trend and to hasten the transition process. Although decolonization is largely history, the subject nevertheless provides a case study of the effect of international institutions upon state behavior. This chapter traces the development and evolution of self-determination and explores some of the issues raised above.

## MANDATES UNDER THE LEAGUE

At the end of World War I, the European imperial system was still alive and well and an energetic force that shaped the times. Despite an earlier wave of anticolonial revolution in North and South America, and more gradual emancipation in Canada, Australia, New Zealand, and South Africa, European powers still held fast to vast territories in distant lands inhabited almost exclusively by native peoples. Settlers of European stock were few, but they were ubiquitous and domineering. The empires of the European Allies emerged intact from World War I, and as the victors of history's first total war, they could expect to extend their rule to German and Turkish possessions by right of conquest. Some of the Allies, even during the war, had concluded secret wartime agreements to this effect. For example, Britain and France entered into the Sykes-Picot Agreement in 1915 wherein they divided the Ottoman Middle East territories between them, despite various promises to leaders in those areas.

Disposition of the defeated enemies' colonies was not a simple matter. Direct annexation was not acceptable, particularly given the repeated claims that the war had been fought for the rights and freedoms of peoples, as well as for the defense of democracy. Outright seizure of territory proved untenable, and a way had to be found to satisfy the desire for greater empire while at the same time offering benefits to those contributing to the war effort. It was not long before a formula was enshrined in and given legitimacy within the League of Nations Covenant.

In the waning months of the war, the British Labour Party and the French Socialist Party had publicly urged that German colonies be placed under the trusteeship of the proposed League of Nations. More important was the position of President Woodrow Wilson at the Paris Peace Conference. Determined that the war his country had fought for principle should not now appear as an imperialist venture, he steadfastly opposed the outright territorial annexation that the other leading Allies preferred. Of course, another option, the restoration of the conquered territories to their former leaders, was not acceptable to any of the Allies.

There was also a general belief that the former enemy territories were simply not ready for self-government. The situation called for inventiveness, and a proposal by Jan Smuts, the leader of South Africa, reflected a touch of political genius. The territories could be and eventually were parceled out among the victors, but control of the different regions was made subject to League of Nations supervision. Article 22 of the Covenant declared that the "well-being and development" of the peoples in the liberated territories was "a sacred trust of civilization" accepted by certain "advanced nations" serving as mandated powers on behalf of the League. This doctrine had something in common with the still more patronizing notion of rule during the Roman Empire, but the recognition of an international trust for conquered territory undoubtedly represented a step forward from the days of the older imperialism. For the first time in the history of the state system, the relationship between some imperial powers and their subject peoples were made subject to international supervision.[1]

The effect of compromise is also evident in the classification of the conquered territories into three groups, subsequently known as Class A, B, and C mandates, on the basis of their political development, geographic location, economic conditions, and "other similar circumstances." The relative political sophistication of the Arabs, and British wartime commitments to them, made the former Turkish administrative zones candidates for the Class A mandate. According to Article 22, their status as independent nations could be "provisionally recognized subject to the rendering of administrative advice and assistance by a Mandatory until such time as they are able to stand alone." The tutelage stage lasted longer than the local peoples desired, but Iraq gained independence in 1932 and the other mandated areas of the Middle East achieved full statehood in the wake of World War II without undergoing a period of UN trusteeship (see Table 8-1).

At the other extreme were the Class C mandates—South West Africa and Germany's South Pacific colonies—which were to be "administered under the laws of the Mandatory as integral portions of its territory." Sparse population, small size, and "remoteness from the centres of civilization" were mentioned in the Covenant as reasons for this classification. Unmentioned was the political constraint built into Class C mandates. In effect, the maximum degree of internationalization that imperialists in Australia, New Zealand, and South Africa (the mandatory states) would gracefully accept was determined by the level of cultural and political status of the mandated territory. Class C mandates therefore were linked directly to the government of the mandatory power. Moreover, under the terms of the mandate system, C category peoples were not regarded as subjects for self-government anytime in the foreseeable future. The remaining German territories in East and West Africa suffered a different fate when they were placed in Class B. These mandates were not to be administratively annexed but nevertheless were to be governed as colonies without explicit provision for ultimate independence or self-government.

TABLE 8-1  Territories Placed under League Mandate and UN Trusteeship

| TERRITORY | CLASS OF MANDATE | ADMINISTERING AUTHORITY (LEAGUE OF NATIONS) | ADMINISTERING AUTHORITY (UNITED NATIONS) | PRESENT STATUS |
|---|---|---|---|---|
| Iraq | A | United Kingdom | — | Independent (1932) |
| Palestine | A | United Kingdom | — | Independent, Transjordan (Jordan) (1946), Israel (1948) |
| Syria and Lebanon | A | France | — | Independent, Syria (1946), Lebanon (1946) |
| Cameroons | B | France | France | Independent, Cameroon (1960) |
| Cameroons | B | United Kingdom | United Kingdom | Part merged with Nigeria, part with Cameroon (1961) |
| Ruanda Urundi | B | Belgium | Belgium | Independent, Rwanda (1962), Burundi (1962) |
| Tanganyika | B | United Kingdom | United Kingdom | Independent (1961); merged with Zanzibar as United Republic of Tanzania (1964) |
| Togoland | B | United Kingdom | United Kingdom | Merged with Gold Coast as Ghana (1957) |
| Togoland | B | France | France | Independent, Togo (1960) |
| Nauru | C | Australia, New Zealand, United Kingdom | Australia, New Zealand, United Kingdom | Independent (1968) |
| New Guinea | C | Australia | Australia | Independent, Papua New Guinea (1975) |
| North Pacific Islands | C | Japan | United States | Independence for Marshall Islands (1991), Micronesia (1991); commonwealth status for Northern Marianas (1991); independence for Palau (1994) |
| South West Africa | C | South Africa | — | Mandate terminated (1966); independent, Namibia (1990) |
| Western Samoa | C | New Zealand | New Zealand | Independent (1962) |
| Somaliland | — | — | Italy | Independent, merged with British Somaliland as Somalia (1960) |

The means of enforcing Covenant obligations were minimal. Article 22 provided for a "permanent Commission . . . to receive and examine the annual reports of the Mandatories and to advise the Council on all matters relating to the observance of the mandates." This Permanent Mandates Commission consisted of nine (subsequently ten) people appointed by the League Council as private experts rather than governmental representatives. A majority of commission members were drawn from nonmandatory states, but nearly all came from countries with colonial possessions, which supposedly better enabled them to understand the problems confronting the mandatory countries. Mandate administrators, for the most part, were able people who took their responsibilities seriously.

Being only advisory, the Commission had no power to affect the policies of the mandatory states other than through persuasion and publicity. Its principal means of supervision consisted of reviewing annual reports submitted by the mandatory powers and making recommendations to the Council. The Commission developed comprehensive questionnaires to facilitate uniform and complete reporting, and a representative of each mandate participated in all Commission discussions regarding its status. Written petitions were also entertained, but petitions from indigenous inhabitants had to be routed through the mandatory and all other petitions were sent to the mandatory for comments. The majority of petitions, however, came from mandates in Class A.

The Permanent Mandates Commission made its recommendations to the Council rather than directly to the mandatory. Although the Council usually agreed with the Commission, it was a political body not prone to giving needless offense to the mandatory powers, and in any event, it had no more legal authority than the Commission to coerce a mandatory that failed to honor its "sacred trust." The Assembly, without any special authorization in the Covenant, also developed the practice of making recommendations each year on some aspect of mandate administration. Like the Commission and the Council, it too was limited to exhortation and the sanction of publicity.

The political milieu governing the emergence of the League's system of mandated territories influenced its record of accomplishment, and that record was bound to be spotty. Its greatest achievement probably lay in establishing the principle of international accountability for dependent territories. It is doubtful that prevailing attitudes toward the treatment of colonial peoples would have been altered so rapidly in the past half century without the conditioning effect of the League's mandate system. Administration of the conquered territories was also improved in some details as a result of suggestions made by the Commission. The mandatory powers, for example, generally refrained from mass naturalization of mandate peoples and did not enlist them for general military service—two practices particularly disapproved by the Commission. The mandate system may have fallen short of idealistic hopes and expectations, but there is wide agreement that the League's methods of friendly persuasion helped center attention on the welfare of indigenous peoples. It also created a standard of administration that ushered in the inevitable period of independence.

# THE EFFECT OF WORLD WAR II

The League's mandate system was a symbol of change in world attitudes toward colonialism, but it left European imperialism untouched in most parts of the world. The great catalyst for change was World War II, which destroyed the political balance that had made imperialism viable. World War II severely weakened the colonial powers and for a time brought total or partial severance of contacts with their overseas possessions. The war also stimulated the growth of existing native nationalist movements.[2] The quick collapse of Belgium, the Netherlands, and France, and Britain's hurried retreat to a beleaguered island, destroyed at a stroke Europe's long-standing image of invincibility in the eyes of colonial peoples. The immense loss of respect for Europe was most apparent in Southeast Asia, where the ease of the Japanese conquest revealed the weakness of the former white masters and exploded the myth of racial superiority. The Japanese victory was clear proof that the West no longer enjoyed a monopoly of technological and military potential that had been the basis of its preeminence.

Japanese occupation physically eliminated European administrative and economic personnel and systematically destroyed existing colonial institutions. Japan did not encourage nationalist aspirations for autonomy, but the necessity of entrusting high administrative responsibilities to local leaders, which previously had been systematically confined to lower-grade positions, provided training for independence. At the close of the war, native nationalists in Indonesia and Vietnam took advantage of the sudden collapse of Japan to seize control of abandoned ammunition stocks and proclaim independence. Independence, however, did not come to Indonesia until 1949 and to Vietnam until much later. In both cases the liberation from colonial status came after considered sacrifice, and only after a protracted struggle with the former colonial powers, the Dutch and the French. But the nationalist movements would not be denied.

The end of World War II also speeded decolonization in areas not occupied by the Japanese. The Philippines had been overrun by Japan early in the war, and its scheduled independence under terms of the 1934 Tydings-McDuffie Act was delayed but nevertheless granted by the United States on July 4, 1946. Moreover, one colony, namely India, received special treatment and status when, in recognition of its contribution to the war effort, it was invited to participate in the 1945 San Francisco Conference as a founding and charter member of the United Nations even before it achieved its independence. Made an original member of the United Nations in 1945, India did not achieve independence until August 1947. Pakistan, however, which was also cut from Britain's Indian colony, and gained independence at the same time with India, followed the normal procedural channels in becoming a member of the United Nations. The independence of Britain's other South Asian colonies, that is, Burma (Myanmar) and Ceylon (Sri Lanka), also followed this imperial recessional.

In the Middle East, wartime pressures and Arab nationalism brought an early end to the British and French mandates. Syria, Lebanon, and Jordan (at the time known as Transjordan) became independent in 1946. Syria and Lebanon had been the responsibility of France, whereas Transjordan was a creation of the British. In 1923 the British split their Palestine mandate along the Jordan River, the eastern unit becoming the Emirate of Transjordan and the western region along the Mediterranean being the Palestine mandate with its mixed Jewish and Arab population. After achieving full independence, Transjordan joined other Arab states in the 1948–49 war aimed at destroying the Israeli state in its infancy. Relatively successful where the other Arab states failed, in 1950 Transjordan annexed the West Bank of the Jordan River, including Jerusalem, and assumed a different posture as the Kingdom of Jordan. Israel, which had its origin in a UN resolution of 1947, declared itself independent in 1948 when that resolution was rejected by the Arab states, who refused to consider a Jewish state in their midst. In the war that ensued between Israel and its Arab neighbors, Israel won by force of arms the remaining area of the former British mandate of Palestine, especially in the Negev Desert region and the area around the Sea of Galilee. The Gaza Strip, situated along the Mediterranean, and also a part of the original Palestine mandate, was seized by Egypt as an extension of the Sinai.

Still another consequence of World War II was the development of nationalist movements in French North Africa. In 1956 Morocco and Tunisia gained their independence from Paris, but Algeria was denied the same independent status. The French considered Algeria a metropolitan district of France, and a large French community had settled there. Paris had no intention of yielding to the indigenous demands for self-determination, and the result was a protracted and bloody encounter. Beginning in 1955, the struggle did not end until 1962, when the French acknowledged the futility of their effort to cling to empire. Algeria's independence came with the French retreat.

World War II also elevated nationalist fervor and accelerated demands for self-determination in sub-Saharan Africa. The first black African country to achieve independence was Ghana in 1957. Guinea followed in 1958, and sixteen more African countries acquired their independence and became members of the United Nations in 1960. The decolonization movement by this time had become worldwide and was acknowledged to be irreversible.

# UN TRUSTEESHIP

## TRUSTEESHIP AT SAN FRANCISCO

At the UN San Francisco Conference, meeting in April 1945, the new currents were being felt but were not fully appreciated. Although no state seriously objected to continuing the League mandate system in some form, proposals to extend the principle of trusteeship to the whole colonial system met with vehement opposition from Britain, France, Belgium, the Netherlands, and South Africa. The United States, so enthusiastic for self-determination in 1919, wavered in support of international supervision, in part because of a growing security interest in the Japanese-mandated Pacific Ocean islands.

Other forces, however, compensated for the foot-dragging of the colonial powers and the waning of Wilsonian zeal in the United States. At San Francisco the anticolonial viewpoint had new and vigorous supporters from Egypt, Syria, Iraq, India, and other former dependencies who loudly trumpeted the cause of fellow nationalists whose nations were still under colonial domination. The Soviet Union was not represented at Versailles after World War I, but after World War II, its prominence in the formation of the United Nations made it another forceful anticolonialist voice. Whereas leaders like India's Mahatma Gandhi forcefully projected the humanitarian cause of decolonization, clearly Moscow's interest centered on the elimination of what it believed to be a major source of capitalist power. Despite these different interests there was no gainsaying the capacity of the anticolonials to form a united front. The pressure that this combination of influence brought to bear on the colonial issue cannot be minimized. Even the United States was compelled to give up its opposition and to acknowledge that the trusteeship cause was connected to the belief that the just treatment of colonial peoples and their evolution toward self-government were connected with the maintenance of international peace and security. In the League Covenant the "well-being and development" of colonial peoples provided the rationale for League action. In the UN Charter, by contrast, the objective of the trusteeship system was "to further international peace and security."

As the Cold War had enveloped international relations in the years after World War II, so too the it created the context for decolonization. As the major principals in the postwar years, the United States and the Soviet Union struggled to achieve the leadership of the nations not yet free, as well as those whose independence had been achieved but whose needs could only be met by one or the other superpower. Decolonization therefore was not simply the recognition that the time had come for the dissolution of empire. It also became a contest that tested the declared goals and purposes of two very different, divergent ideological systems. Both Moscow and Washington invested heavily in the changing scene. Each sought to identify with the forces of liberation and to woo the new states through their gestation periods. Each became a source of inspiration and material support for those seeking self-determination. Indeed, the Cold War was fought not in a traditional manner as a power test between the principals, but rather on the margins of political interest where people seeking separation from their colonial overlords were enticed to adopt the one or the other superpower as their mentor and guide.

The trusteeship system was born and nurtured in these circumstances. Moreover, it was soon acknowledged that states supporting UN decolonization efforts also achieved an increase in their power and influence. A strengthened trusteeship system therefore replaced the League of Nations mandate system, and a declaration on non–self-governing territories committed members to submit economic and social information on all of their colonies. A greater departure from the League Covenant was the announced goal of ultimate "self-government or independence" for trust territories and "self-government" for all other dependencies. Although the consequences of these changes may not have been fully anticipated in 1945, they constituted the opening wedge for what subsequently became a broadside attack in the United Nations on colonialism in all its manifestations.

## THE NATURE OF THE TRUSTEESHIP SYSTEM

Despite the shift in goals, the new machinery of trusteeship made full allowance for the interests of the administering powers. The Trusteeship Council, as successor to the Permanent Mandates Commission, was composed of government representatives instead of private experts, with equal representation for administering and nonadministering states (UN Charter, Article 86). Each trust territory was to be brought within the system by an agreement drawn up by the administering member and approved by the General Assembly. Although the Assembly could reject a proposed agreement, the alternative was no trusteeship at all. Once the trusteeship was agreed on, both the Assembly and the Trusteeship Council were limited to information gathering, discussion, and recommendation, with no legal powers of coercion.

The Trusteeship Council was given means of inquiry into the conduct of trust administration superior to those of the League system. The practice of the annual report, based on a comprehensive questionnaire, was borrowed from the Permanent Mandates Commission. To this was added the right to receive petitions directly, without relying on the administering power as intermediary, and the right to send visiting missions to gain first-hand knowledge of conditions in trust territories. The administering powers thus matched their effective control of the trust territories against the organization's capacity to publicize, criticize, and mobilize the weight of diplomatic opinion.

The United States obtained an additional safeguard against UN interference with its administration of the Pacific Islands trusteeship. If an administering authority, in the trusteeship agreement, chose to designate all or part of a trust territory as a "strategic area," all matters relating to the area became the responsibility of the Security Council, where the veto could forestall any adverse recommendation. The Trust Territory of the Pacific Islands under U.S. supervision was so designated.

## THE FUNCTIONING OF TRUSTEESHIP

The Class A mandates were not candidates for trusteeship because they were scheduled for early independence, but all of the Class B and C mandates except South West Africa were placed under trusteeship through agreements approved in 1946 and 1947. The Charter also made trusteeship an option for territories "detached from enemy states as a result of the Second World War," as well as any other colonies a state might choose to place within the system. No state accepted the latter invitation, although Italian Somaliland, which had been taken from Italy during the war, was given a period of trusteeship under Italian administration. The legal evolution of the territories placed under mandate and trusteeship is shown in Table 8-1.

By 1975 ten of the eleven trust territories had achieved the promised independence or were united, on the basis of UN-approved plebiscites, with an adjoining independent country. Only the Trust Territory of the Pacific Islands, with 150,000 inhabitants scattered over 2,141 islands and atolls, remained within the system. Composed of four separate political entities—the Northern Mariana Islands, the Federated States of Micronesia, the Marshall Islands, and Palau—it also was beset by the winds of self-government. In 1975 the Northern Marianas voted to become a commonwealth within the United States when the trusteeship was ended. In 1983 the other three jurisdictions, through UN-sponsored plebiscites, approved association agreements providing local autonomy while leaving defense responsibilities with the United States. The plebiscites in Micronesia and the Marshall Islands ultimately became the basis for independence, but the Palau plebiscite was ruled invalid by the Palau court because the association agreement permitted the stationing of nuclear weapons on the island in violation of the Palau constitution. A proposal to remove this prohibition from the constitution failed for lack of the required 75 percent majority. In six subsequent plebiscites through 1991, support for the amendment ranged as high as 73 percent, but it was always short of the required constitutional majority. In November 1992, however, the voters of Palau approved a proposal to reduce the constitutional majority from 75 percent to 50 percent. Palau, the last of the trust territories, was declared independent in 1994.

The Charter's goal of independence or self-government for trust territories has been reached—an achievement for which the United Nations may claim considerable credit. Criticism in the Trusteeship Council and the General Assembly spurred the administering authorities to put the best possible face on their conduct of territorial affairs. This in turn affected administration of the territories, as policies were formulated with an awareness that the United Nations was watching. Occasionally government practices were altered in response to Security Council recommendations.

Petitions and visiting missions permitted detailed scrutiny of trust administration and thereby increased the pressure on administering authorities to justify their policies. At the height of its activity, the Trusteeship Council received several hundred written petitions annually and considered as many as 250 in a session, besides granting an occasional hearing to an oral petitioner. Aside from the informational function, the petitioning procedure made administering authorities more alert to the legitimate grievances of the local populace and sometimes resulted in direct relief to the complainant. In one instance two inhabitants of the Pacific Islands accomplished through oral petition what three years of direct negotiation with the United States had failed to achieve—a settlement of their claim against the government for property taken without just compensation.

Visiting missions, conducted every three years, also proved a valuable source of information as well as an outlet for native views and grievances. Reports of the visiting missions appeared to receive serious attention from the administering authorities and in some instances foreshadowed policy changes. Australia, for example, took steps to give the New Guinea territorial legislature an elective majority in response to the recommendations of a 1962 visiting mission. In several territories the United Nations sent plebiscite teams and election observers during the last stages of preparation for self-government, which increased the international acceptability of the regimes thereby established.

Considered as a whole, trusteeship helped raise standards of administration in the trust territories and hastened the coming of independence. Suggestions and criticisms from the Trusteeship Council and the Assembly strengthened progressive elements within the administering authorities and kept them mindful of their obligations to the peoples of the territories. Trusteeship encouraged more articulate native demands for national independence and may have fostered some increased readiness for self-government. Given the growth of nationalism, the changes in power relationships wrought by two world wars, and the increasing economic liabilities of the colonial system, independence would have come to most of these areas without the intervention of the United Nations. Indeed, in its rivalry with the Soviet Union, the United States became an outspoken proponent of decolonization, and on one noteworthy occasion President John Kennedy berated the French for their forceful actions against Algerian self-determination. Overall and by contrast, the UN trusteeship system provided a more orderly and peaceful process of change, and in none of the trust territories was the transition to independence marked by serious violence.

Trusteeship must be seen in perspective as but one aspect of a much wider movement for decolonization. Several African and Asian dependencies of France and Britain became independent before any of the trust territories achieved that status in 1960. While ten trust territories were gaining independence from 1960 to 1975, several times that number of former colonies underwent the same transformation outside the trusteeship system. Trusteeship contributed to a climate of world opinion congenial to decolonization, but the system itself was swept along in the broader current.

The trusteeship system never achieved the scope that its more enthusiastic supporters at San Francisco had envisioned. Except for Somaliland, it did not expand territorially beyond the League mandates, and South West Africa (now Namibia), because of South African intransigence, never came within its purview. The UN Charter's option of placing other dependent territories under trusteeship appears never to have been seriously considered by any colonial power. In meeting the larger problem of colonialism, the United Nations has consistently turned to other means.

# THE UNITED NATIONS AND TOTAL DECOLONIZATION

Unlike the League Covenant, the UN Charter went beyond prescribing conditions for mandated territories and extended its concern to dependent peoples everywhere. In the Declaration regarding Non–Self-Governing Territories contained in Chapter XI of the Charter, the colonial powers acknowledged a "sacred trust" to promote the well-being and self-government of all their dependencies. They were not willing to make independence a goal for their colonies or to accept international supervision, but they agreed to submit data "of a technical nature relating to economic, social, and educational conditions in the territories" for "information purposes." There was general accord at San Francisco that the declaration embodied only moral commitments, dependent on the good faith of the colonial powers for their fulfillment and involving no UN right to intervene in what the colonial powers regarded as a matter of domestic jurisdiction.

Today the picture is drastically altered. Independence has become not merely a goal but an accomplished fact for most of the colonial peoples of 1945. The original assumption in the UN Charter "that each colonial power should at its own discretion and in an unhurried way lead its dependent peoples to well-being and self-government" soon gave way to a more declarative expression. The new proposition held that colonialism was "an intolerable and illegitimate abuse to be done away with as speedily as possible by the international community." [3] Changes in ideology were accompanied by an organizational assault on the whole structure of colonialism that erased any essential distinction between trust territories and other non–self-governing areas. The change mirrored new global realities, but it amounted to a Charter amendment without the procedure of securing ratification.

## THE COMMITTEE ON INFORMATION

The initial step toward establishing UN responsibility for all dependent territories occurred in 1946 with the establishment of a Committee on Information from Non–Self-Governing Territories. Its purpose was to examine the information transmitted by the administering authorities and make recommendations to the Assembly. In composition it was modeled on the Trusteeship Council, having an equal number of administering and nonadministering members. It had no provision for permanent representation of the Big Five, however, and the Soviet Union and China generally did not hold membership on it. Like the Trusteeship Council, the committee prepared a questionnaire to guide members in reporting.

With the built-in moderation arising from its composition, the Committee on Information was not an aggressive instrument of anticolonialism. Its original terms of reference debarred it from examining "political" information. A few countries, however, voluntarily submitted such information. Even on economic and social matters, the Committee could make recommendations of general application but could not single out individual territories. It was not given the right to accept petitions or send out visiting missions.

Because of the Committee's limited powers, the anticolonial initiative remained largely with the General Assembly and its Fourth Committee, which soon requested governments to include political information in their annual reports. Later the Assembly began to demand that administering authorities submit adequate information on constitutional changes in the territories to enable it to determine whether self-government had in fact been attained. The Assembly's right to make such a determination was a much more sensitive issue than its demand for information, however, and the colonial powers vehemently rejected the idea.

The admission of Spain and Portugal to UN membership in 1955 raised the related question of who decided when and whether new members must begin to transmit information. The question was far from academic because Spain and Portugal, both of which had overseas dominions, assured the United Nations that they had no non–self-governing territories. In 1960 the Assembly resolved the question by informing both states of their obligation to transmit information. Spain capitulated to the pressure, but Portugal stubbornly refused to comply.

## SELF-DETERMINATION AND POLITICAL CRISIS

While the Assembly was attempting to turn all non–self-governing territories into quasi-trusteeships, the United Nations also was faced with a series of political crises arising from the breakup of colonial empires. During the early years the alignment of colonial and anticolonial forces was not sharply drawn, and the issues were sometimes perceived as having a complexity inconsistent with the taking of doctrinaire positions. The question of Palestine came before the United Nations in 1947 at the initiative of a harassed mandatory power that was no longer willing to bear the burden of reconciling Arab and Jewish claims to the area that it itself had prompted and then aggravated. Britain had promised both parties what it could not deliver, and only after acknowledging its misadventure did London try to cut its losses by leaving the matter to the nascent world organization. For the United Nations, therefore, the issue was not whether self-determination should be granted, but how and by whom it should be exercised. Israel resolved its part of the problem by its unilateral declaration of independence when the Arab states rejected the General Assembly's solution. The Arabs have struggled with the question ever since. In the Indonesian struggle for independence from the Netherlands, mediated in part by the Security Council from 1947 to 1949, but by the United States in particular, the continuation of colonial rule was more clearly at issue. Nevertheless, the Security Council's major concern was the threat the struggle posed to international peace and security. Assembly debates on the former Italian colonies of Libya, Eritrea, and Somaliland, from 1949 to 1951, were also relatively free from the kind of anticolonial diatribe that came to characterize UN debates on colonial questions in later years.

Assembly debates on Morocco and Tunisia brought the anticolonial position more sharply into focus during the early 1950s, but a two-thirds majority was never available for anything stronger than a call for "free political institutions" and continued negotiations among the parties. Both states were granted independence from France in 1956.

The emergence of serious and animated anticolonial displays in the United

Nations is illustrated by its handling of the Algerian question. The General Assembly considered Algeria each session from 1955 through 1961. In 1955 no action was taken; in 1956 the Assembly expressed the hope that a peaceful, democratic, and just solution in conformity with the Charter would be found; in 1957 the Assembly went so far as to urge negotiations; but in 1958 and again in 1959 no recommendation commanded a two-thirds majority. This stalemate demonstrated the unwillingness of the anticolonial bloc to support a weak statement against France, as well as its inability to obtain a strong one. In 1960, with the admission to UN membership of seventeen former colonies, the inhibitions of the earlier period vanished. The right of the Algerian people to self-determination was vigorously asserted despite Paris' bitter objection to discussing the matter at all. A year later the Assembly demanded nothing less than full "self-determination and independence." These resolutions may have had no greater influence on the French decision to grant Algerian independence in 1962 than on the granting of independence to Morocco and Tunisia in 1956, but the temper of the Assembly was obviously different.

## ANTICOLONIALISM TRIUMPHANT

By 1960 the anticolonial revolution was rapidly approaching its zenith. Four decades of mandate and trusteeship had established the principle of international accountability for the administration of a select group of territories, with independence as the ultimate goal. Fifteen years of gradually expanding activity under the Charter Declaration Regarding Non–Self-Governing Territories had gone far to establish the principle of international accountability for the well-being and self-government of all colonial peoples. Repeated recourse to the United Nations in crisis situations had established at least a prima facie connection between colonialism and the periodic outbreak of violence. Within the world community the day of colonialism was virtually at an end. A majority of the territories that had achieved full independence since 1945 were now members of the United Nations. Most other dependencies of any substantial size had moved toward and achieved independence, remarkably with the consent and cooperation of their colonial overseers.

### An Anticolonial Manifesto

Amid these signs of a revolution well on its way to completion, the General Assembly in 1960 took a step of unusual symbolic importance. In previous years the anticolonial forces had been forced to compromise in their attack on the old colonial order. With domination of the Assembly now assured, the newly independent states turned the organization into an instrument for the complete legitimization of their cause. In a historic Declaration on the Granting of Independence to Colonial Countries and Peoples, the General Assembly proclaimed that the subjection of any people to alien domination was a denial of fundamental human rights, contrary to the UN Charter, and an impediment to world peace and that all subject peoples had a right to immediate and complete independence. The General Assembly thereupon approved Resolution 1514 (XV) of December 14, 1960, which formally declared the following: (1) alien domination is contrary to the UN Charter; (2) all peoples have rights to self-determination; (3) inadequacy of political, economic, social, or educational preparedness is no excuse for delaying independence; (4) all repressive measures against dependent peoples must cease so that they can freely exercise their right to complete independence; (5) all powers of government should be transferred to remaining dependent peoples; and (6) disruption of national unity or the territorial integrity of a country is contrary to the UN Charter. The power of the resolution was read in the fact that not a single member state voted in opposition to the declaration. It is important to note, however, that nine countries abstained, and included among them were some of the world's more prominent colonial powers: Australia, Belgium, the Dominican Republic, France, Portugal, Spain, South Africa, Great Britain, and the United States. The old imperial order that had resisted Woodrow Wilson's call for the self-determination of peoples after World War I was forced to sound its final retreat in the years after the end of World War II. By the 1960s, the once all-consuming age of colonialism had given way to a vibrant and exuberant new age of worldwide national independence. Moreover, given the admission of numerous former colonial states to membership in the United Nations, the work of the world organization became more centered on anticolonial issues. The General Assembly, therefore, unlike the Security Council where the major powers remained dominant, mirrored more and more the concerns of the newly independent countries.

As long as colonial rule prevailed in any territory, the declaration provided a rationale for efforts to undermine or overthrow it. The anticolonial principle was carried to its logical conclusion when India, on invading the Portuguese enclave of Goa in December 1961, assured the Security Council that the invasion was an "embodiment of the principles" in the declaration and a "new dictum of international law." Some Western states were unconvinced that an Assembly resolution, which was legally binding on no country, could create international law that overrode express Charter prohibitions on the use of force. But the basic issue, as the Indian representative admitted, was moral, not legal. In effect, Portugal's centuries-old occupation of Goa, deemed by New Delhi to be Indian, constituted "permanent aggression," and India was justified in "getting rid of the last vestiges of colonialism—Charter or no Charter, Council or no Council."[4] Like the U.S. Declaration of Independence, the Declaration of 1960 was an appeal to a higher law to which all lesser claims were subordinate.

## The Special Committee

Within the United Nations the declaration presaged a more vigorous assault on the last bastions of colonialism. In 1961 the Assembly expanded the role of the Committee on Information by authorizing it to discuss political information and to make recommendations centering on particular regions. The Fourth

Committee also broke new ground by granting a hearing to petitioners from two non–self-governing territories.

Of considerably more importance for the future was the creation of a Special Committee on the Situation with Regard to the Implementation of the Declaration on the Granting of Independence to Colonial Countries and Peoples. Known as the Committee of Seventeen (increased to twenty-four in 1962), it was assigned to study the declaration and make appropriate recommendations for its implementation. Parity of representation was discarded as the Assembly packed the Special Committee with an anticolonial majority. For its terms of reference, the Committee was given a blank check—a mandate to do whatever it was able to do in implementing the 1960 declaration. Under this broad grant of authority, the Committee assumed powers to hear petitions, send missions to the different regions, and make recommendations directed at particular territories—powers that the Trusteeship Council had exercised but that had been denied to the Committee on Information. By 1963 the Committee of Twenty-Four had so plainly overshadowed the Committee on Information in its systematic harassment of the colonial powers that the latter was formally abolished.

## The Demise of the Old Colonialism

The United Nations was able to launch its massive assault on colonialism because colonialism was already in full retreat. The Committee of Twenty-Four was engaged mainly in a mopping-up operation. In its 1963 report to the Assembly, the Committee listed sixty-four colonies, mandates, and trust territories that had not yet achieved self-government. Only ten of these could claim as many as one million inhabitants, and the total population of all sixty-four was less than fifty million. Forty of the sixty-four were British, consisting, as one writer put it, mostly of "little islands scattered about the face of the globe, representing the days when Britain was an indefatigable collector of scraps of empire." [5]

Rhodesia (Zimbabwe), Namibia, and the Portuguese African colonies of Angola, Mozambique, and Guinea were exceptions to the "scraps of empire" characterization. Rhodesia's white minority government unilaterally declared independence from Britain in 1965 and endured fifteen years of international ostracism, UN economic sanctions, and internal strife before accepting majority rule in 1980 and receiving admission to the United Nations as the state of Zimbabwe. Portugal's hard-line policy collapsed in 1974 under the weight of colonial wars that had absorbed nearly half of the Portuguese national budget. The dictatorship of Marcello Caetano fell victim to an internal coup, and Portugal's African policy fell with it. Portuguese Guinea (now Guinea-Bissau) became independent in 1974, and Mozambique and Angola followed in 1975. Namibia, the former South West Africa mandate, achieved independence in 1990.

At the century's end the Special Committee's list included seventeen dependencies, the majority being small islands with tiny populations (see Table 8-2). In a more controversial category were Gibraltar, Western Sahara, and

TABLE 8-2    Territories to Which the Declaration on the Granting of Independence to Colonial Countries and Peoples Continues to Apply

|  | TERRITORY | ADMINISTERING AUTHORITY | AREA (SQ. KM) | POPULATION (EST.) |
|---|---|---|---|---|
| Africa | Western Sahara | Spain | 266,000 | 147,000 |
| Atlantic and | Anguilla | United Kingdom | 96 | 7,200 |
| the Caribbean | Bermuda | United Kingdom | 53 | 59,000 |
|  | British Virgin Islands | United Kingdom | 153 | 12,400 |
|  | Cayman Islands | United Kingdom | 260 | 25,900 |
|  | Falkland Islands (Islas Malvinas) | United Kingdom | 12,173 | 2,000 |
|  | Montserrat | United Kingdom | 103 | 12,000 |
|  | St. Helena | United Kingdom | 412 | 5,500 |
|  | Turks and Caicos Islands | United Kingdom | 430 | 13,500 |
|  | U.S. Virgin Islands | United States | 343 | 103,200 |
| Europe | Gibraltar | United Kingdom | 6 | 29,700 |
| Pacific and | American Samoa | United States | 197 | 39,900 |
| Indian Oceans | Guam | United States | 540 | 127,700 |
|  | New Caledonia | France | 19,103 | 164,200 |
|  | Pitcairn | United Kingdom | 5 | 60 |
|  | Tokelau | New Zealand | 12 | 1,700 |

East Timor (an island territory of fifty-seven hundred square miles). Britain has been engaged in continuing negotiations with Spain on the future of Gibraltar, but the "rock" at the gateway to the Mediterranean remains solidly in British hands. Western Sahara, relinquished by Spain in 1975, was almost immediately plunged into controversy pitting Moroccan claims to sovereignty against those of an indigenous nationalist movement called the Polisario Front. Unable to mediate a settlement between the parties, the United Nations sent a peace-keeping force (MINURSO) to the region in April 1991 to oversee a cease-fire and a referendum that ultimately would enable the people of the Western Sahara to determine their own future. Repeated breakdowns in the agreement and Moroccan reluctance to yield the territory has resulted in a protracted UN presence that in 2003 involved 229 military personnel, 25 civilian police, and 167 international civil servants with an approved budget for 2003–04 of more than $43 million.

East Timor presented still another difficult problem. In 1976 East Timor, a former Portuguese colony, was annexed by Indonesia after the latter's intervention in a civil war. The civil war proved to be more a pretext for Indonesia's seizure of the territory than an act of mercy, and the annexation failed to receive UN sanction. Indonesia, however, insisted on establishing permanent control, ignored UN complaints, and proceeded to consolidate its hold. Given domestic opposition to the takeover, the Indonesians dealt harshly with the Timorese and showed virtually no respect for human rights. The United Nations responded to Indonesian repression by continuing to recognize Portugal's role as the administering power, but this only made the Indonesian government more determined to absorb the territory. It was only after Indonesia's long-time leader Suharto was forced to leave office in 1998 that a successor government agreed to look favorably on the Timorese demand for self-determination. Renewed efforts by the UN Secretary-General in March 1999 brought Jakarta to consider granting the Timorese a choice of either autonomy within Indonesia or independence. That effort eventually produced a decision that allowed a vote to be taken to determine East Timor's future. When the referendum was held the East Timorese voted overwhelmingly for independence, but pro-Indonesian elements refused to accept the results, and with assistance from units of the Indonesian army, they launched an attack on the East Timor population as well as the area's infrastructure and business establishments. Only the intervention of a heavily armed force led by Australia persuaded the Indonesian government to quit the region. In May 2002 East Timor finally became independent, but a UN peacekeeping force (UNMISET) was sent to the new country to help build a democratic government and society.

Puerto Rico has also been before the Special Committee with great regularity. Puerto Rico is technically not on the list of non–self-governing territories. The vote of the U.S. Congress in 1998 to offer the island future statehood appeared to close off UN debate on its status, that is, pending a decisive referendum of the Puerto Rican people. On August 12, 1998, the House of Representatives agreed to a local referendum to decide whether the island should become the fifty-first state or keep its commonwealth status. On December 13, the people of Puerto Rico voted to hold to their current status, defeating the other options that ranged from independence to independence with free association to statehood. Passing into the new millennium Puerto Rico remained a self-governing commonwealth in association with the United States, with a governor as head of government and the U.S. president as head of state. The United States maintained approximately three thousand active-duty military personnel on the island in 2004.

## THE UN ROLE: AN APPRAISAL

Decolonization, after more than four hundred years of colonial rule, was one of the great revolutions of the twentieth century. Since the founding of the United Nations, nearly 750 million people had exercised their right of self-determination. More than eighty once-colonized territories had gained their independence. At the time the United Nations was established there were seventy-two non–self-governing territories and eleven trust territories. By 1994 all the trust territories had achieved independence and only a handful of non–self-governing territories remained, most of them expressing content with their situations. International organization, however, was more the catalyst than the actual cause for the success of self-determination. In most instances, the empires simply ran out of time, and their antiquated nature could not be adapted to modern conditions, nor could the aspirations of people for self-government be ignored in an age of technological change and enlightenment. But the League of Nations and the United Nations nonetheless contributed to the speed and direction of the movement toward independence. In a number of instances international organization was hardly passive, and in not a few cases it helped promote a more peaceful transition to independence and self-government than might otherwise have been possible. The League gave respectability to the principle of international accountability in a limited area of colonialism and moderated some of the worst abuses of the system. After 1945 the United Nations did far more: it provided the forum where anticolonial supporters could articulate their positions; it greatly expanded the principle of international accountability; and it developed more effective instruments for international supervision of colonial administration. Above all, it gave an element of legitimacy to independence movements everywhere in the world. By holding aloft the standard of self-determination, the United Nations served as a reminder to Western colonial countries that such demands were basically consonant with enduring values in their own political traditions. When violence occurred, the United Nations sometimes intervened to curb hostilities, as in Indonesia, East Timor, the Western Sahara, Cyprus, Sierra Leone, Ivory Coast, and the Congo. Where possible, the United Nations hastened acceptance of the new order by legitimizing its tenets.

The UN record on colonial problems has not been without blemishes. In some instances the United Nations at least inadvertently encouraged a resort to violence by native nationalists who felt that creating a threat to peace and security was the best way to gain the attention of the organization. The 1960 Declaration has frequently been used to justify violence, including India's attack on Goa in 1961 and Argentina's abortive attempt in 1982 to seize the Falkland Islands from Great Britain by force.

A good case can also be made that the United Nations pushed many territories to premature independence and encouraged independence for mini-states with questionable viability. Statehood and full membership in the United Nations were attained by a number of new nations woefully lacking in trained personnel to administer government and economic institutions. In most of the new states, independence was not followed by hoped-for gains in economic welfare. This led many former colonies to complain that the old colonial system had merely been replaced by neocolonialism in the form of economic exploitation by the developed countries.

The benefits of decolonization were unquestionably oversold, although the United Nations can be held only partly responsible for that. Independence was in principle a good thing, and it brought immediate opportunities to those who were able to seize the levers of political and economic power in the new states. But removal of the foreign master did not everywhere bring greater respect for democratic values and individual rights. Indigenous leaders often adopted techniques of government as repressive and demeaning as those formerly attributed to colonialism. Racial, tribal, and political minorities have sometimes fared ill at the hands of new rulers. A notable example is the "killing fields" of Cambodia under the regime of the Khmer Rouge. Another is that of Zimbabwe. Robert Mugabe's one-party rule began when he became the country's president in December 1987. Mugabe tolerated no opposition and deflected assaults on his administration by a land-grab policy that forced white plantation owners from their lands. In 2002 Zimbabwe was suspended from membership in the Commonwealth as Mugabe strained to destroy any challenge to his absolute authority. In the meantime, Zimbabwe, a producer of surplus agriculture, experienced severe shortages that Mugabe promptly attributed to European actions on behalf of the dispossessed white farmers. Unlike Rhodesia earlier, the United Nations, given the strength of the African bloc, avoided imposing sanctions on the Mugabe government.

Dictatorships dominated many of the states that achieved independence after World War II. From Mugabe in Zimbabwe, to Charles Taylor in Liberia, to Mobutu Sese Seko in the Congo, the record of democratic government is a sorry one. Nor has decolonization done much to bring peace and security to former colonial domains. The preindependence era was marked by armed conflict in many dependent areas, but the era of independence also has witnessed internal wars and rebellions, outside interventions, and outright military aggression in many of these same lands. Civil war in Nigeria and Pakistan—the former unsuccessful in the creation of an independent Biafra and the latter successful, albeit with help from India, in bringing self-determination to Bangladesh—are but two of many cases that illustrate the rocky road following independence.

The United Nations did not create all the ills of decolonization any more than it produced all the benefits, but a fair appraisal requires recognition that decolonization has its down side as well as its positive aspects. In retrospect, the most important UN contribution in the arena of decolonization may be the UN's capacity to encourage acceptance of a new order before relations between colonial masters and subject peoples became impossibly embittered.

## SELF-DETERMINATION
## IN THE TWENTY-FIRST CENTURY

Self-determination is far from a completed process, and all indicators point to a new round of demands that carries into the twenty-first century. On one side, the United Nations stands at the center of such developments, while on the other, state sovereignty continues to argue a hands-off policy. Events in Kosovo in 1997–99 illustrate the former, while those that overwhelmed Chechnya in 1996–97 represent the latter. Kosovo's autonomous status within the Yugoslav Federation was withdrawn when Slobodan Milošević won control of the country in 1989. By 1998, given Serbian efforts at crushing the Kosovar Albanian culture and forcing thousands of Kosovars to flee to neighboring states, a Kosovo Liberation Army (KLA) emerged to challenge the Serbian forces. The KLA's call for self-determination had few outside supporters, but the fighting was too intense to be ignored. Aware of a maturing problem and fearing that the conflict could destabilize southeastern Europe, the United Nations, the European Union, and the OSCE all tried to restore order to the region. When they failed to temper hostilities, NATO was energized. It was only when NATO's diplomacy failed that the alliance began its bombing campaign against Serbian targets. Serbia argued that the Kosovar matter was an internal problem and therefore outside NATO's area of jurisdiction. NATO did not dispute Kosovo's inclusion in the Yugoslav Federation, but it made the counter argument that Belgrade's sovereignty had been compromised by the atrocities committed against its own citizens. NATO insisted it was not promoting self-determination for the Kosovar Albanians, but its actions clearly demonstrated that it had placed human rights over sovereign rights. On the other hand, Chechnya's declaration of independence from the Russian Federation had been met by a swift and violent response from Moscow. The intensity of the fighting and the heavy loss of life and property in Chechnya did not produce the same reaction from NATO, which opted not to become involved. Indeed a distinction was made between what was judged a civil war in Chechnya and what was considered "eth nic cleansing" in Kosovo. The distinction, no matter how tenuous, explained Russia's support for Serbia in its war with NATO. It did not clarify what other out-of-area missions NATO might undertake in the future, and it certainly did not clarify the issue of self-determination in the twenty-first century.

Furthermore, the breakup or threatened dissolution of established states is perceived differently in postcolonial and post–Cold War conditions. And whereas some may express sympathy to those peoples who continue to reach for independence, such as the Kashmiris, Kurds, Abkhaz, or Basque, the fervor with which nations earlier supported secessionist movements has diminished. More inclined to guarantee human rights and political stability, UN peacekeeping missions are concerned with sustaining the status quo rather than offering unrestrained encouragement to separatist movements. Thus, in 1997 the United Nations called for the creation of a Rapidly Deployable Mission Headquarters that could focus attention on regions of instability before UN peacekeepers were authorized to take up a cause. In the meantime, given the many requests for UN intervention, a logistics depot was opened in Brindisi, Italy. An easier procurement of supplies for ongoing and new missions was developed with nearly seventy countries pledging to allocate approximately eighty-eight thousand soldiers and technical experts for a UN standby force. Such actions by the United Nations revealed new thinking on the subject of self-determination. Could it be that even self-determination has its limits? Although some new states will be formed as a consequence of breakaway movements, the United Nations seems more inclined to help create the necessary conditions for disputing parties to find a way to reconcile their rival moral claims without going as far as self-determination. Giving credence to a shift in the UN attitude toward self-determination were the complicated arrangements that promised peace in Cyprus, in Bosnia-Herzegovina, and in Northern Ireland. All were examples of a more aggressive use of diplomacy that fell short of recognizing self-determination as an absolute right.[6]

## TERRORISM AND SELF-DETERMINATION: NEW DIRECTIONS?

How does global terrorism influence self-determination? Having cited situations in Kosovo and Chechnya, it is important to note that both have been connected with contemporary patterns of violence that are equated with terrorism. Kosovo, however, has submitted to the localization of its aspirations, whereas Chechnya has been caught up in a global network of arbitrary violence that both mutes its plea for self-determination and imposes a heavy burden on its population. While the Kosovars appear to accept the working relationship with the post-Milošević government in Belgrade and have set themselves the task of restoring civil society, Chechnya continues to suffer a harsh fate, and Chechen tactics are not aimed at realizing the self-governing state. For global terrorists, the retreat from empire is a mirage and the end of colonialism is still a goal to be striven for, even if it means denying that which gives meaning and purpose to the cause of self-determination.

# NOTES

1. A standard treatment of the League mandate system during its first decade is in Quincy Wright, *Mandates under the League of Nations* (Chicago: University of Chicago Press, 1930).
2. See "The Immediate Consequences of the War (1939–1945)," in Henri Grimal, *Decolonization: The British, French, Dutch, and Belgian Empires, 1919–1963,* trans. Stephan De Vos (Boulder, CO: Westview Press, 1978), pp. 113–37.
3. Rupert Emerson, "Colonialism, Political Development, and the UN," *International Organization* 19, no. 3 (summer 1965), p. 486.
4. UN Document S/PV/988, December 18, 1961, pp. 9, 15.
5. Emerson, "Colonialism, Political Development, and the UN," p. 498.
6. See Gidon Gottlieb, *Nation Against State.* New York: Council on Foreign Relations Press, 1993.

# SELECTED READINGS

Carpenter, Ted Galen, ed. *Delusions of Grandeur: The United Nations and Global Intervention.* Washington, DC: Cato Institute, 1997.

Carter, Gwendolyn M., and Patrick O'Meara, eds. *African Independence: The First Twenty-five Years.* Bloomington: Indiana University Press, 1985.

Danspeckgruber, Wolfgang, with Sir Arthur Watts. *Self-Determination and Self-Administration: A Sourcebook.* Boulder, CO: Lynne Rienner, 1997.

Dore, Isaak I. *The International Mandate System and Namibia.* Boulder, CO: Westview Press, 1985.

Emerson, Rupert. *From Empire to Nation.* Cambridge, MA: Harvard University Press, 1960.

Gottlieb, Gidon. *Nation Against State: A New Approach to Ethnic Conflicts and the Decline of Sovereignty.* New York: Council on Foreign Relations Press, 1993.

Grimal, Henri. *Decolonization: The British, French, Dutch, and Belgian Empires, 1919–1963.* Trans. Stephan De Vos. Boulder, CO: Westview Press, 1978.

Gurr, Ted Robert. *Minorities at Risk: A Global View of Ethnopolitical Conflicts.* Washington DC: U.S. Institute of Peace Press, 1993.

Hall, H. Duncan. *Mandates, Dependencies, and Trusteeship.* Washington, DC: Carnegie Endowment for International Peace, 1948.

Hey, Jeanne A. K., ed. *Small States in World Politics: Explaining Foreign Policy Behavior.* Boulder, CO: Lynne Rienner, 2003.

Hoffmann, Stanley. *The Ethics and Politics of Humanitarian Intervention.* Notre Dame, IN: University of Notre Dame Press, 1996.

Holland, R. F. *European Decolonization, 1918–1981.* New York: St. Martin's Press, 1985.

Hutchinson, John, and Anthony D. Smith, eds. *Ethnicity.* Oxford, UK: Oxford University Press, 1996.

———. *Nationalism.* Oxford, UK: Oxford University Press, 1994.

Jackson, Robert H. *Quasi-states: Sovereignty, International Relations and the Third World.* Cambridge, UK: Cambridge University Press, 1990.

Martin, Ian. *Self-Determination in East Timor: The United Nations, the Ballot, and International Intervention.* Boulder, CO: Lynne Rienner, 2001.

Murray, James N., Jr. *The United Nations Trusteeship System.* Urbana: University of Illinois Press, 1957.

Oakley, Robert B., Michael J. Dziedzic, and Eliot M. Goldberg, eds. *Policing the New World Disorder: Peace Operations and Public Security.* Washington, DC: National Defense University Press, 1998.

O'Neill, William G. *Kosovo: An Unfinished Peace.* Boulder, CO: Lynne Rienner, 2002.

Pomerance, Michla. *Self-Determination in Law and Practice: The New Doctrine in the United Nations.* The Hague: Martinus Nijhoff, 1982.

Reinicke, Wolfgang H. *Global Public Policy: Governing Without Government.* Washington, DC: Brookings Institution Press, 1998.

Sparks, Donald L., and December Green. *Namibia: The Nation after Independence.* Boulder, CO: Westview Press, 1992.

Stedman, Stephen J., Donald Rothchild, and Elizabeth M. Cousens, eds. *Ending Civil Wars: The Implementation of Peace Agreements.* Boulder, CO: Lynne Rienner, 2002.

Urquhart, Brian. *Decolonization and World Peace.* Austin: University of Texas Press, 1989.

Wainhouse, David W. *Remnants of Empire: The United Nations and the End of Colonialism.* New York: Harper & Row, 1967.

Wright, Quincy. *Mandates under the League of Nations.* Chicago: University of Chicago Press, 1930.

# 9

# SOCIAL AND TECHNICAL COOPERATION

Violence on the international scene commands world attention wherever it occurs, but economic and social programs command the major portion of resources in the day-to-day operations of international organizations. Article 55 describes the UN Charter provisions related to economic and social cooperation and calls for "the creation of conditions of stability and well-being" that are deemed necessary for peaceful and friendly relations among nations. Agencies within the UN system are responsible for many such programs. So too are several hundred global and regional intergovernmental organizations. Although these activities are supported primarily because of their contributions to economic and social well-being, they are also recognized for their contributions to a more peaceful world. Organizations for international economic and social cooperation are commonly called *functional organizations,* and people who advocate this approach to global peace are known as *functionalists.*

This chapter and the one following will evaluate the activities of the United Nations in a number of functional areas. This chapter focuses attention on human rights, international communication, health, the law of the sea, the environment, education and information, international relief programs, and aid to refugees. International organization for economic development is reserved for Chapter 10. Functional cooperation has been accompanied by the development of a unique body of ideas that justify and explain it. We therefore will preface the discussion of particular UN activities in social and technical cooperation with a brief review of functionalist theory.[1]

## FUNCTIONAL COOPERATION
## IN THEORY AND PRACTICE

### FUNCTIONALIST THOUGHT

Students of international organizations have used a variety of theories and approaches that are borrowed from studies of other social institutions. Functionalism does not fit this pattern. Although clearly connected to general intellectual explorations, functionalism is almost unique as a body of prescriptions, explanatory concepts, and predictions in its application to international organization. As empirical explanation and prediction, functionalist thought has its shortcomings and weaknesses, but it nevertheless demonstrates in its prescriptive aspects a continuing vitality.

Functionalist thought achieved currency in the early twentieth century as writers began to generalize about the multitude of international organizations centered on economic and social cooperation emerging even before the great wars of the twentieth century.[2] The functionalist persuasion subsequently was given increased impetus by the two world wars. Sensitive scholars and politicians expressed much frustration that the League of Nations could not develop successful mechanisms of collective security. World War I had been a painful exercise in national ambitions, and keeping the peace held the highest priority for these thoughtful individuals. The functionalist idea was embraced by these thinkers with the prospect that their "peace by pieces" was a way to overcome previous shortcomings. Not inclined to imagine a quick fix in some grand all-encompassing program, they centered their interest on particular functional areas where incremental steps could result in more significant outcomes. Grandiose military schemes had failed repeatedly in keeping the peace. They also were reluctant to press visionary schemes that could not be translated into the experience of the people for whom they were meant. Peace, they argued, was less likely to occur through the construction of global or regional political federations, not that the mission was unworthy, but rather because it was unfeasible in the ongoing circumstances.

As elaborated by its various supporters, functionalism was first a prescription for more international cooperation in dealing with economic and social problems. Since most people recognize the desirability of cooperative activity, this aspect of functionalism has few critics. Functionalists also assert that cooperation in "nonpolitical" matters will promote world peace. This too has a ring of self-evident truth. To the extent that needs are met and problems resolved by cooperation, there will be that much less to argue about. Deprivation and inequality generate frustrations and find outlets in international strife. By providing the means for solving such problems on a global basis, functional activities help eliminate the sources of tensions that lead to war.

The asserted link with peace extends well beyond this commonsense assumption, however, to embrace a theory of individual and social learning. Its key element is the belief that the workshop setting of functional activities provides a school for learning cooperative behavior. As individuals and governments work together for their mutual benefit, they can develop habits and attitudes conducive to further cooperation. One successful venture leads to another, and the result is an ever-widening circle of shared interests. The genius of this approach is its avoidance of major challenges to state sovereignty and strongly entrenched national interests. Particular functions—health, mail service, telecommunications, and the like—become the subject of international cooperation only as the shared interests are recognized. The process is gradual and pragmatic, and it involves searching out areas of mutuality while binding together those interests that are overlapping. As world community is constructed piece by piece, the roots of political conflict can be expected to wither and the whole area of international relations becomes infused with learned habits of cooperation.

Functionalists also have argued that performing needed functions at the international level is more efficient because it permits a global attack on problems, and permits the transcending of national boundaries. Moreover, technical activities can proceed in an environment of relatively low controversy. Politicians are more willing to delegate decision making to experts and professionals, whose main concern is the efficient performance of their tasks. As a side effect, by providing useful services to people around the world, functional organizations do not replace national governments; rather, they supplement the efforts of government, and in so doing enjoy increasing popularity and respect.

On the negative side, not all of functionalist assumptions can be confirmed in practice. Perhaps most important, international discussion of economic and social problems does not necessarily generate goodwill and cooperation. Some international issues are undoubtedly more controversial than others, but economic and social issues are not always low in controversy. Dispute has raged over Third World attempts to establish a new international economic order, despite their social or economic character. The history of recent adventures in functional cooperation is replete with instances of political wrangling. The process of authoritative value allocation has proved to be inherently political, whether the values are economic, social, or "political" in their content. The technical nature of an activity does not banish the need for value choices or the primacy of self-interest. Nor does the involvement of bureaucrats, however expert or professional, eliminate the push and shove of contending interests, including an interest in building bureaucratic empires. Replacing politicians with bureaucrats may simply be a means of reducing popular control.

Other functionalist assumptions also are questioned. The functionalist explanation of war, at best, overlooks multiple causative factors. Although social inequality and economic deprivation are contributing causes of some wars, they are not alone an adequate explanation. Experience also raises doubt that cooperative habits learned in one functional context will necessarily be transferred to another, or that a widening sphere of functional cooperation will lead to the elimination of violent conflict in the political sphere. While it can be said that functional cooperation has increased, conflict and the threat of it have not undergone a corresponding decrease. Time may yet vindicate the functionalist thesis, but recent history offers no assurance that it will. In fact, often-sounded complaints about "politicization" of economic and social agencies suggest that political controversy is more likely to hinder functional cooperation than to be mellowed by it.

Nor has the proliferation of functional activities thus far been accompanied by noticeable transference of loyalties from states to international institutions. The European Union, with its relatively high level of economic integration, has had only a modest effect on national loyalties. As for global agencies, it is almost ludicrous to suggest that the World Bank, the International Monetary Fund, UNESCO, or the World Intellectual Property Organization are the focus of human loyalties (except perhaps for their paid secretariats). With so many international agencies now emphasizing assistance to less developed countries, functional organizations clearly are engaged in promoting the viability of states rather than diverting loyalties from them.

Functionalism nevertheless retains relevance for the real world of international organizations. Despite its obvious weaknesses, the theory offers useful insights. Learning from past experience is undoubtedly a growth accelerator, and successful functionalist ventures have provided models for new applications. If national loyalties remain strong, functional cooperation is successful where it is perceived serving individual and national interests.

Notably, the functionalist prescription is closely attuned to the facts of international life. With time and space compressed by technology, states are constantly faced with new opportunities to promote welfare by joint action and to confront new challenges created by their closer proximity to one another. Interdependence is an inescapable fact. In such a world, the functional approach makes sense as a practical endeavor, whatever its theories of institutional development or its contributions to peace.

## THE ORGANIZATION OF FUNCTIONAL COOPERATION

The nineteenth-century system of international economic and social cooperation unfolded without plan or means of central coordination. The result was a patchwork of international institutions tending toward common structural forms, but each was legally and politically separate. Such unplanned growth is a common condition of national societies. A nation, however, has a central government that can undertake reorganization when its administrative structure grows too cumbersome. The international system has no central authority capable of rationalizing the random growth of its institutions. As a consequence, the pattern of decentralization has continued largely unabated to the present day.

The effect of the League of Nations on nineteenth-century organizational patterns was to multiply institutions and activities without providing effective overall coordination. The League Covenant (Article 24) extended its sheltering arms to existing "international bureaus established by general treaties" if the parties to the treaties consented, and it also provided that any international bureaus or commissions thereafter established were to be "placed under the direction of the League." Only a half dozen or so of the existing agencies chose to accept League direction.

Despite the problems of coordination, League functional programs were widely recognized as being vigorous, constructive, and worth preserving, and this opinion was reflected in the later copious UN Charter prescriptions for economic and social cooperation. The effect of League experience was also evident in the establishment of the Economic and Social Council as a special coordinating organ. This followed closely the report of the 1939 Bruce Committee (chaired by Stanley Bruce of Australia), *The Development of International Co-operation in Economic and Social Affairs,* which recommended the creation of special organs to supervise the work of League committees in economic and social areas.

The principle of decentralization was accepted, however, in the overall system of postwar economic and social collaboration. The UN Charter abandoned the League Covenant's vain hope that all international bureaus and commissions would be placed under the direction of the general organization. Instead, the various "specialized agencies" were authorized to maintain cooperative relationships with the Economic and Social Council and to accept such coordination as might emerge from consultation and recommendation.

In practice, decentralized control has characterized many of the UN functional activities established within the United Nations. Agencies such as UNICEF, the UN Environment Programme, the UN Relief and Works Agency for Palestine Refugees, and the UN Development Program, though subject to the general supervision of the Assembly, have separate governing boards, or advisory bodies, and depend heavily on voluntary contributions to support their programs. Their staffs also respond to mandates of their respective governing bodies and the needs of the governments and other agencies that make up the constituencies they serve. Perhaps the very extent and variety of the economic and social programs administered on a global scale preclude truly effective central coordination. Repeated unsuccessful efforts at coordination launched in the Economic and Social Council certainly suggest drawing such a conclusion.

Efforts were made to cope with and coordinate ever more complex social issues at the World Summit for Social Development, which met in Copenhagen in 1995. The conference addressed numerous social issues, notably the intensity and magnitude of worldwide poverty caused by rural and urban drift. Urban poverty was judged the most intractable problem, but it nevertheless received less attention than the agrarian scene. The Summit also failed to address forcefully the matter of women's rights, and the NGOs monitoring the proceedings concluded that the conference was too weighted on the intergovernmental side. Acknowledging the need for a follow-up conference, and prodded by the Group of 77, a Special Session of the General Assembly on the Implementation of the Outcome of the Summit was planned for the year 2000 in Geneva. In May 1998, the Preparatory Committee for the Special Session cited the need to invite all organs and agencies of the UN system. This included the Bretton Woods institutions, the World Trade Organization, the UN Development Program, the International Labor Organization, and NGOs accredited by the Economic and Social Council to attend UN special conferences and summits.

## The Millennium Summit

In August 2000, UN members agreed to discuss four themes—poverty and development, conflict prevention, environmental problems, and strengthening the role of the United Nations in international affairs—at what now was described as the Millennium Summit. Although the conference was broad in scope, the Secretary-General focused attention on the 1.2 billion people in the world who live on less than one dollar a day and the concrete steps needed to alter their plight. Eight goals were established:

1. Eradicate extreme poverty and hunger.
2. Achieve universal primary education.
3. Reduce child mortality.
4. Promote gender equality and empower women.
5. Improve maternal health.
6. Combat HIV/AIDS, malaria, and other diseases.
7. Ensure environmental sustainability.
8. Develop a global partnership for development.

A strategy also was adopted for the attainment of these goals. Called the UN Strategy for the Millennium Development Goals, they included the following:

1. The Millennium Project. The Plan called for the examination of policy options toward the achievement of millennium goals.
2. The Millennium Campaign. A call for the mobilization of political support for the Millennium Declaration.
3. Country-Level Monitoring. The need to monitor progress toward the achievement of millennium goals.
4. Operational Country-Level Activities. The need to coordinate across agencies through the UN Development Group to assist individual countries in implementing policies connected with the millennium development goals.

Secretary-General Kofi Annan presented the major address before the Millennium Summit. Noting the dramatic changes in the fifty-five-year history of the world organization, Annan described his vision as practical (functional) and centered attention on the need to make globalization more inclusive, to create opportunities for all, and to raise the hundreds of millions of the earth's inhabitants from abject poverty. In this massive undertaking the Secretary-General believed it imperative that the discussion should include many of the world's civil society organizations, and toward that end NGOs organized a Millennium Forum under UN aegis.

Overwhelmed by the events of September 11, 2001, the Millennium Summit took a back seat to the question of terrorism and the need for human security. UN Security Council Resolution 1373, which called on all member states to take immediate action to suppress terrorism, shifted attention away from the lofty goals of the Millennium Summit. Nevertheless, under authorization of the General Assembly, a World Summit on Sustainable Development was held in Johannesburg, South Africa, in 2002. Following ten years after the 1992 Earth Summit in Rio de Janeiro, Johannesburg reinvigorated sustainable development activities in the wake of still deeper poverty and environmental degradation. New goals were established and new commitments were made, but in the end, it was acknowledged that only practical and sustained efforts could begin to approach the enormity of the problems facing the world community. Less inclined to seek new treaties or to express grand objectives, the people most concerned with developmental questions saw progress only in their ability to coalesce and to form partnerships for specific projects.

## WHAT FUNCTIONAL ORGANIZATIONS DO

The things functional organizations do can be described in a number of ways. The substantive function of an organization—human rights, health, telecommunications, and so on—is a common, even unavoidable, method of classification. Organizational functions can also be usefully classified by reference to the nature of the policy product. Here we will focus on three types of policy output: *rules and standards* for state conduct, *operating programs* that provide services to states and their peoples, and *informational,* including *promotional activities.* Most functional organizations engage to some extent in all three, although some are oriented more toward one activity than another.[3]

*Rule-making* takes a variety of forms. In the broadest sense it includes recommendations and standards that depend on voluntary acceptance as well as international treaties having the force of law and authoritative rule-making by the few agencies empowered to bind their members by majority action. Organizations that make rules also attempt to secure some degree of compliance. Most of the implementation takes the form of publicity and moral pressures, or technical assistance to states whose noncompliance springs from lack of technical capacity rather than lack of will. Functional organizations generally have little power to enforce compliance through coercive sanctions, although noncompliance may in some instances be grounds for expulsion or loss of organizational benefits (such as future eligibility for loans and grants).

*Programs* to provide services, such as refugee relief or development aid, depend on funds and other resources available to the organization. The influence of secretariats on operating programs is usually substantial because they have responsibility both to prepare proposals and to administer the approved programs and, being more permanent than national delegates, are repositories of an "institutional memory." Secretariats are typically in league with recipient states because both have an interest in expanded programs, whereas donor states set the ultimate limits by their willingness—or unwillingness—to contribute the resources.

*Informational and promotional activities* involve the gathering, analysis, and dissemination of information as well as the airing or propagation of points of view. All organizations have personnel who perform these functions. Organizations also provide forums for state representatives and other participants to exchange views and information. Some of this communication is intended simply to inform, but much is intended to persuade and promote programs, causes, or points of view.

The discussion that follows will make reference to these functions in examining a number of important social and technical activities within the UN system.

# HUMAN RIGHTS RULE-MAKING

The rights of people have traditionally been matters of domestic jurisdiction and concern. International protection of individuals has not been completely absent from the law and practice of the modern state system, but until World War II such protection was limited to special groups—primarily diplomatic representatives, consular personnel, and aliens—whose status involved the interests of a foreign sovereign. From time to time, states have also undertaken treaty obligations with respect to their own nationals, as evidenced by the various European treaties from the sixteenth century onward guaranteeing freedom of worship to religious minorities. As another example, in 1890 the Brussels Conference produced a treaty providing effective measures to end the slave trade.

In the twentieth century the peace architects of Versailles required new states and defeated countries of Eastern Europe to assume treaty guarantees of the linguistic, educational, and other rights of ethnic minority groups incorporated within their territories. Neither the earlier religious guarantees nor the minorities treaties were very effective in securing the rights of individuals, and their strictly limited nature underscored the general freedom of a state to deal as it wished with those living within its jurisdiction. The League Covenant went a bit further in concept, if not in effectiveness. It made the "well-being and development" of subject peoples in mandated territories (Article 22) a matter of international concern and in committing members to "secure just treatment of the native inhabitants" of all their dependent territories (Article 23).

Against this background the UN Charter's emphasis on the promotion of human rights, induced in large part by reaction to Nazi atrocities, constitutes a sharp break with tradition. No less than seven references to human rights are found in the Charter. Human rights are stressed in the Charter's Preamble; they are also cited in Article 1 (purposes and principles), in Article 13 (responsibilities of the Assembly), in Article 55 (objectives of economic and social cooperation), and in Article 56 (members "pledge" to take action for the achievement of the purposes set forth in Article 55). Also important are Article 62 (functions and powers of ECOSOC), Article 68 (a commission to promote human rights), and Article 76 (objective of the trusteeship system). The new approach may not have taken the form of specific legal obligations, but it certainly asserted a significant international interest in the rights of individuals.

Since 1945 proponents of international action have waged a continuing battle with the conservative forces of national sovereignty, although few countries have been consistent in their support of either camp. Positions on humanitarian principles have often been tinged with political expediency. The Soviet Union, before its demise, consistently displayed a double standard in favor of socialist states, while the United States during the Cold War sometimes attempted to shield the questionable conduct of authoritarian states, for example, Chile and Iran, in the Western camp. Many Third World countries have persistently condemned the human rights violations of some countries while overlooking transgressions in other parts of the world. Surveying the record in his 1991 annual report, Secretary-General Pérez de Cuéllar probably struck an accurate balance when he pointed to a "certain dichotomy" in the area of human rights. On one hand, instruments and procedures for the international protection of human rights have multiplied; on the other, countless "human wrongs are committed in systematic fashion and on a massive scale," with the United Nations often "a helpless witness rather than an effective agent for checking their perpetration."[4]

Kofi Annan repeated this theme, citing difficulties in mounting consistent human rights investigations in Zaire and the successor post-Mobutu Democratic Republic of the Congo. He lamented the helplessness of the international community in preventing terrorist killings of innocent people in Algeria. He acknowledged the need to improve the machinery trying war criminals in the former Yugoslavia and Central Africa, and he underlined the responsibility of the United Nations in protecting human rights in all regions of the world. At the annual summit of the Organization of African Unity he declared that "human rights are African rights." Celebrating Human Rights Day in Tehran in December 1997, he underscored his belief of "all human rights for all" and declared it to be the theme of the fiftieth anniversary celebrations of the Universal Declaration of Human Rights.[5]

The UN record in dealing with human rights must be assessed in relation to the capacity of international organization to affect the conduct of states in this sensitive area. States, not international agencies, are the primary guarantors of individual rights. Unlike sovereign states, the United Nations has no courts of its own to hear the complaints of individuals. Even the International Court of Justice permits only states to be parties to contentious cases brought before it. If a violation is found, the United Nations has no means of providing redress other than negotiation, censure, or, in extreme cases, the levying of sanctions. The Charter authorizes economic and military sanctions only in cases of threats to peace and security, and as discussed in Chapter 5, the consensus required to use them has, until recently, seldom existed.

The recently established International Criminal Court functions as an instrument for the general redress of grievances against individuals allegedly responsible for violations of human rights. Only in rare circumstances can human rights violators such as Slobodan Milošević be charged with crimes against humanity. Accused of such crimes, including the crime of genocide in Kosovo, Milošević was brought to trial in The Hague in February 2002, and the proceedings were extended into 2004 without an end in sight. A speedier result was achieved, however, when Bosnian-Serb president Biljana Plavsic pleaded guilty to crimes against humanity before the criminal court and was expected to offer testimony in cases involving others accused of similar crimes. But the wheels of justice grind slowly, and in Rwanda fifty-three suspects awaited trial in 2002, years after their alleged commission of atrocities. Despite the difficulties in creating a tribunal to hear war crimes cases in Cambodia, the Cambodian government and the United Nations reached agreement in 2003 for the establishment of a criminal court similar to those in Rwanda and the former Yugoslavia. Nor did it require U.S. prodding for the newly assembled Iraqi governing council in July 2003 to make as its first gesture its intention to try Saddam Hussein for atrocities committed during his several decades of brutal rule. Thus, despite the hesitation and less-than-perfect machinery, some progress is being made in holding high individuals responsible for war crimes and crimes against humanity.

A key difficulty in international tribunals is the inevitable disagreement among states on the nature of the rights to be protected and on the priorities among them. Western industrialized democracies have emphasized political and civil rights, such as freedom of speech, religion, and the press, and freedom from arbitrary arrest and imprisonment. Third World states give priority to economic, social, and cultural guarantees—the right to decent food, shelter, clothing, humane working conditions, and education. Many economic and social rights depend for their realization not on political will but on adequate resources and efficient economic organization. Others—for example, equal rights for women—may challenge deeply ingrained social custom. Different societies have different values, and the right to food may seem far more important to hungry people than the right to an uncensored press. For these reasons, states guard their sovereign authority and their right to define individual rights and decide what protection shall be emphasized.

Of particular note is the U.S. decision in May 2002 to withdraw its signature from the treaty establishing the International Criminal Court. Fearing that its soldiers and citizens stationed in countries around the world could be charged with war crimes as a consequence of their duties, Washington not only insisted on remaining aloof from the court, it also declared its intention to punish countries that attempted to try its nationals. To counter the operations of the ICC the United States sought bilateral agreements with more than 150 countries that would pledge them to provide immunity from ICC prosecution to Americans abroad. By October 2002 more than a score of countries agreed to enter into such agreements. The European Union also gave its members permission to negotiate accords with the United States, but only in the case of officials and soldiers, and only then if Washington agreed to pursue prosecution in U.S. courts. The George W. Bush administration expressed its dissatisfaction with the European action and continued to insist on unconditional immunity, especially for its military personnel. It is important to note that Britain entered into an agreement with the Afghan government that protected the troops of its own and other nations connected with the International Security Assistance Force stationed in Kabul.

Given such disagreements, the UN role is concerned mainly with formulating standards, encouraging conformity to them, and occasionally condemning egregious lapses—at least with respect to civil and political rights. This is not "enforcement," but it does encourage greater observance. Supplying information and providing forums for exchange of views is one way of encouraging conformity, and technical assistance may be appropriate for a state that desires to achieve a higher standard but lacks experience and the necessary institutional infrastructure. Economic "rights" may also be promoted by technical assistance and financial aid channeled through international organizations. Aside from economic aid and some services rendered directly to individuals in need, the United Nations has only an indirect role in promoting human rights. Even the treaty guarantees formulated through the UN system and by other international organizations are not directly enforceable over a state's objection. However, patterns for monitoring compliance established under some of the treaties have provided significant incentive for states to honor their treaty obligations. To the extent that human rights treaties become part of the domestic law of the signatories, they then become enforceable through internal legal processes.

In a somewhat different context, UN peacekeeping may have a very practical effect on human rights by helping to eliminate the depredations that accompany violent conflict. Namibia, Cambodia, El Salvador, and other beneficiaries of UN peacekeeping undoubtedly enjoy a higher level of well-being because of it. These UN activities have been discussed in Chapters 5 and 6 but deserve mention here to emphasize the multifaceted character of human rights and their protection.

## SETTING VOLUNTARY NORMS

Voluntary norms are commonly those set by an international forum through the declaration of generally applicable rules of behavior. Declaring the rule produces no legal obligation; it simply expresses a goal, an aspiration, a guide to conduct, and perhaps a moral imperative. The most celebrated such statement in the area of human rights is the Universal Declaration of Human Rights, approved by the General Assembly on December 10, 1948, by a vote of forty-eight to zero, with eight abstentions (six Eastern European members, Saudi Arabia, and South Africa). Its thirty articles encompass a broad range of civil, political, economic, social, and cultural rights and mirrored the differing aspirations and values that had to be reconciled in order to secure wide agreement for its adoption. In the Declaration, the political and civil rights of the old liberalism are joined with the economic and social ideals of the new. At the same time, all are hedged with the right of the sovereign state to limit individual rights and freedoms as necessary to meet "the just requirements of morality, public order and the general welfare in a democratic society." Although the practical application of some of the enumerated economic and social rights might require more government control than is consistent with some of the political rights, and others depend on the availability of adequate economic resources, the Declaration is an admirable and appealing distillation of universal human aspirations.

Other human rights declarations approved by the Assembly since have dealt with more specific subjects such as the rights of children, racial discrimination, territorial asylum, discrimination against women and disabled people, torture, religious discrimination, rights of aliens, and discrimination against minorities. In addition to declarations, which are formalized statements of general principles, the UN General Assembly has adopted a number of resolutions on some aspects of human rights that are broadly defined. Many deal with economic and social conditions, but some are addressed to particular violations of civil and political rights. Such declarations and resolutions have unquestionably influenced the way governments talk about human rights. Moreover, governments are prone to cite them as standards of behavior. This is certainly the case when criticizing other governments, and so much lip service is paid to them both in and out of the United Nations. Declarations of human rights have probably brought increased observance of human rights as well, although the effect is not simple to measure. In the short run, most countries do not remedy their conduct in response to UN criticism, and UN action sometimes heightens intransigence. Chile, for example, reacted to UN criticism during the 1970s by holding a national plebiscite to endorse the regime of Augusto Pinochet, which had been accused of gross human rights violations. Only later, when Pinochet no longer held the reins of power, did the issue of human rights emerge to a critical level. The human rights picture has seen some change, as in South Africa where, after decades of UN criticism, the country abandoned its apartheid policies and has since elected black African presidents. Seeking to bind the wounds caused by the apartheid decades, South Africa also led the nations in its establishment of a Truth and Reconciliation Commission and found another way of dealing with the human rights violations of its immediate past. Although these developments may have had more to do with social, economic, and political factors than General Assembly resolutions, they nonetheless pointed to a more enlightened era in the matter of human rights.

Other responses to UN declarations suggest that the long-run effects could eventually be substantial. Many of the principles of these declarations have passed into the law of individual countries through embodiment in constitutions, statutes, and judicial decisions. The Universal Declaration, in particular, has been cited in numerous decisions of domestic courts, has served as a model and inspiration for domestic legislation, and has been mentioned or partially incorporated into more than fifty extant national constitutions. A U.S. federal court has cited the Universal Declaration as evidence that torture committed by officials of a foreign government against one of their own nationals was a violation of international law. Another U.S. court declared the Universal Declaration "a powerful and authoritative statement of the customary international law of human rights."[6] References to human rights declarations in statutes, constitutions, and judicial decisions nevertheless may be mere window dressing in some countries. In the United States and many other countries, they often are not. Frequent citation does not prove that human rights are being better observed than before. The sustained human rights violations, for example, in West and Central Africa that demand constant UN involvement continue to burden this subject. But despite these all too common episodes, the incorporation of UN declarations into legal instruments and judicial decisions does mean that they are acquiring legal status and that in the future they could raise respect for human rights to a still higher level.

## LAWMAKING TREATIES

The United Nations has not been content to let the Universal Declaration become part of national legal systems through the slow and uncertain process of exhortation, example, and action by individual states. When the Declaration was adopted in 1948, it was regarded as preliminary to the drafting of a multilateral treaty that would translate its precepts into binding legal obligations. Since that time the organization has drafted multilateral treaties on a variety of special topics. It also has drafted two omnibus covenants—the International Covenant on Civil and Political Rights and the International Covenant on Economic, Social, and Cultural Rights—generally paralleling the Universal Declaration.

The process of preparing such treaties is lengthy. Typically, it involves initial consideration in the ECOSOC Commission on Human Rights, reconsideration by the ECOSOC parent body, a third detailed examination in the Third (Social, Humanitarian, and Cultural) Committee of the General Assembly, and final approval by the Assembly in plenary meeting. Alternatively, the United Nations has sponsored special conferences to draft lawmaking treaties, including some in the area of human rights. Treaties take effect when a specific number of states individually sign and ratify the documents in accordance with their respective constitutional requirements.

A number of shorter, special purpose treaties pass through the UN pipeline more quickly than the two general covenants noted above. These include the conventions on slavery, refugees and stateless persons, genocide ("acts committed with intent to destroy, in whole or part, a national, ethnical, racial, or religious group, as such"), the political rights of women, the nationality of married women, the rights of children, and racial discrimination. A UN convention on Elimination of All Forms of Discrimination against Women took effect in 1981, and a convention proscribing torture was entered into force in June 1987. Another convention on the rights of children came into force in September 1990, and still another in 2003 on the protection of the rights of migrant workers and members of their families. Table 9-1 lists the principal UN human rights treaties and their current ratification status.

The two general covenants were not approved by the Assembly until December 1966, eighteen years after the adoption of the Universal Declaration, and both remained inoperative until 1976 when the requisite thirty-five states ratified them. Originally the provisions of the two covenants were proposed as a single document, but the United States and some other Western countries viewed as inappropriate and impractical the effort to convert economic and social goals into legally enforceable obligations. The traditional freedoms of speech, press, worship, assembly, security of person and property, political participation, and

TABLE 9-1    UN Human Rights Conventions

| CONVENTION (GROUPED BY SUBJECT) | YEAR OPENED FOR RATIFICATION | YEAR ENTERED INTO FORCE | NUMBER OF RATIFICATIONS, ACCESSIONS, ACCEPTANCES (DEC. 2003) |
|---|---|---|---|
| GENERAL HUMAN RIGHTS | | | |
| International Covenant on Civil and Political Rights | 1966 | 1976 | 140 |
| Optional Protocol to the International Covenant on Civil and Political Rights | 1966 | 1976 | 93 |
| Second Optional Protocol to the International Covenant on Civil and Political Rights, Aiming at the Abolition of the Death Penalty | 1989 | 1991 | 31 |
| International Covenant on Economic, Social and Cultural Rights | 1966 | 1976 | 137 |
| RACIAL DISCRIMINATION | | | |
| International Convention on the Elimination of All Forms of Racial Discrimination | 1966 | 1969 | 150 |
| International Convention on the Suppression and Punishment of the Crime of Apartheid | 1973 | 1976 | 101 |
| International Convention against Apartheid in Sports | 1985 | 1988 | 57 |
| RIGHTS OF WOMEN AND CHILDREN | | | |
| Convention on the Political Rights of Women | 1953 | 1954 | 110 |
| Convention on the Nationality of Married Women | 1957 | 1958 | 66 |
| Convention on Consent to Marriage, Minimum Age for Marriage and Registration of Marriages | 1962 | 1964 | 47 |
| Convention on the Elimination of All Forms of Discrimination against Women | 1979 | 1981 | 161 |
| Convention on the Rights of the Child | 1989 | 1990 | 191 |
| Optional Protocol to the Convention on the Elimination of Discrimination against Women (see above) | 2000 | | |
| SLAVERY AND RELATED MATTERS | | | |
| Slavery Convention of 1926, as amended in 1953 | 1953 | 1955 | 87 |
| Protocol Amending the 1926 Slavery Convention | 1953 | 1953 | 59 |

TABLE 9-1    *(continued)*

| CONVENTION (GROUPED BY SUBJECT) | YEAR OPENED FOR RATIFICATION | YEAR ENTERED INTO FORCE | NUMBER OF RATIFICATIONS, ACCESSIONS, ACCEPTANCES (DEC. 2003) |
|---|---|---|---|
| **SLAVERY AND RELATED MATTERS** | | | |
| Supplementary Convention on the Abolition of Slavery, the Slave Trade, and Institutions and Practices Similar to Slavery | 1956 | 1957 | 117 |
| Convention for the Suppression of the Traffic in Persons and the Exploitation of the Prostitution of Others | 1950 | 1951 | 72 |
| **REFUGEES AND STATELESS PERSONS** | | | |
| Convention Relating to the Status of Refugees | 1951 | 1954 | 131 |
| Protocol Relating to the Status of Refugees | 1967 | 1967 | 131 |
| Convention Relating to the Status of Stateless Persons | 1954 | 1960 | 44 |
| Convention on the Reduction of Statelessness | 1961 | 1975 | 19 |
| **OTHER** | | | |
| Convention on the Prevention and Punishment of the Crime of Genocide | 1948 | 1951 | 124 |
| Convention on the Non-Applicability of Statutory Limitations to War Crimes and Crimes against Humanity | 1968 | 1970 | 43 |
| Convention against Torture and Other Cruel, Inhuman or Degrading Treatment or Punishment | 1984 | 1987 | 104 |
| International Convention on the Protection of the Rights of All Migrant Workers and Members of Their Families | 1990 | 2003 | 21 |
| International Convention for the Suppression of the Financing of Terrorism | 1999 | not yet in force | |

SOURCE: United Nations Human Rights Web site (http://www.unhchr.ch/html/menu3/b/a-ccpr.htm).

procedural due process are prohibitions against unreasonable and arbitrary governmental action. Guarantees of an adequate standard of living, education, social security, full employment, medical care, holidays with pay, and a right to leisure are invitations to a vast expansion of governmental functions with no guarantee that the goals will in fact be attained. It was argued that several states were willing to accept treaty obligations for the promotion of political rights would refuse to ratify a treaty including economic and social rights. The answer, over the objections of some, was to write two covenants instead of one.

The United States, spurred by the enthusiasm and dedication of its best-known human rights delegate, Eleanor Roosevelt, played a leading part in drafting the Universal Declaration. Domestic controversy, fueled by fears that UN treaties might override U.S. laws in the area of civil rights, precluded a similar role for the United States in the covenant-drafting process. Some domestic opponents of human rights treaties feared that they would water down cherished U.S. rights. Others believed that international economic guarantees might hasten the growth of socialism in the United States. Still others were concerned that international treaty commitments might outlaw racially discriminatory laws and practices then common in many states. To head off a proposed U.S. constitutional amendment (the Bricker Amendment) limiting the President's treaty-making power, the Eisenhower administration assured the Senate that the United States would not sign or ratify the UN human rights covenants. This assurance had its desired domestic effect but at the price of diminished U.S. prestige and leadership in the international protection of human rights.

Although discriminatory laws that earlier were operative in the United States have been eliminated by judicial decision and legislative action, the United States has never regained its place in the forefront of international human rights activity. Of the principal UN human rights treaties, the United States by 1986 had ratified only a Supplementary Convention on Slavery and a related protocol, the Convention on the Political Rights of Women, and a protocol relating to the Status of Refugees. The U.S. policy of hostility or indifference to UN human rights treaties was reversed in the executive branch by President Jimmy Carter, who submitted several treaties to the Senate in 1977, urging consent to their ratification. The new interest in human rights survived the Carter administration long enough for the Senate to approve the Genocide Treaty in 1988. This was followed by the International Covenant on Civil and Political Rights in 1992, and the UN Convention Against Torture in 1994, as well as the International Convention on the Elimination of All Forms of Racial Discrimination, also in 1994. The United States also approved the Convention on Consent to Marriage, Minimum Age for Marriage and Registration of Marriages (1962); the Convention on the Political Rights of Women (1976); the Protocol Relating to the Status of Refugees (1968); the International Covenant on Economic, Social and Cultural Rights (1977); the Convention on the Elimination of All Forms of Discrimination Against Women (1980); the Convention on the Rights of the Child (1995); the Optional Protocol on Armed Conflict (2003); and the Optional Protocol on the Sale of Children (2003).

## IMPLEMENTING HUMAN RIGHTS

Any discussion of human rights implementation must take account of the global power structure within which the United Nations operates. International organizations provide important linkages within the system, but the principal centers of power are sovereign states. Whether individual rights are violated or vindicated in the territory of a given state depends mainly on decisions made within that state. A state may legitimately complain if its own nationals are mistreated by foreign governments and sometimes succeed in obtaining redress. But under traditional international law, states have been largely free to treat their own citizens as they will—and this is the source of the most persistent and flagrant human rights violations. The new law of human rights, arising from both treaty and custom, offers people more protection against their own governments, but the tradition of national autonomy remains strong. Pressures by one state on another for better observance of human rights generally stop short of coercive action. The reluctance of states to do more reflects the realities of an international system made up of sovereign entities. If states are thus inhibited, the United Nations is still less able to *enforce* individual rights against the wishes of a recalcitrant state.

Useful things can still be done through international action, however. One helpful, and generally inoffensive, way is to supply information and technical assistance. The United Nations has for years conducted a program of seminars, fellowships, and advisory services for countries requesting special help. The world organization also circulates information about human rights through UN meetings and through studies, reports, and other publications. UN discussions of human rights are all too frequently dominated by political polemics, but on some subjects they serve a useful informational function. It is quite probable, for example, that the ECOSOC Commission on the Status of Women has contributed to the extension of political rights to women through its efforts to gather information and exchange views and experiences. In other areas of concern, discussion has been enlightened by special UN studies on such topics as forced labor, slavery, torture, disappearances, summary and arbitrary executions, religious intolerance, protection of people with mental illnesses, and discrimination in education, employment, and political rights. In addition, national reports on human rights observance are periodically discussed in the ECOSOC Commission on Human Rights.

In dealing with alleged violations of human rights, the United Nations has relied on investigation, discussion, publicity, and censure. These have occurred in a variety of forums, including the General Assembly and its Third Committee, the Economic and Social Council, the Commission on Human Rights, and the Subcommission on Prevention of Discrimination and Protection of Minorities. In a few instances, where marginal national interests have been involved and UN action has been conciliatory, states have reacted favorably to such pressure. Most attempts by the organization to remedy specific violations of human rights have not been efficacious, at least in the short run. Viewed as a deterrent, UN censure seldom outweighs the domestic motivations that lead to rights violations.

Nevertheless, UN organs have persisted in exerting the moral pressure of discussion and recommendation and have strengthened their procedures for doing so. For years the Commission on Human Rights was debarred from taking any action on complaints that particular states were denying human rights.

This limitation was altered in 1967 when the Commission was authorized to examine information and make studies of situations revealing gross violations of human rights. The procedure was regularized in 1970 with the adoption of ECOSOC Resolution 1503, permitting the Commission to investigate "particular situations that appear to reveal a consistent pattern of gross and reliably attested violations."

The "1503 procedure" has since become the usual means of dealing with the thousands of letters and reports received each year at the United Nations, mainly from private individuals and groups, containing complaints of human rights abuses. Through the screening process most complaints are never acted on because the procedure restricts the Commission to matters referred by its Subcommission on Prevention of Discrimination and Protection of Minorities, which in turn acts only on a recommendation from a working group of five of its members. Even so, Resolution 1503 has been a step toward more effective UN scrutiny. All such matters remained private until 1978, when the Commission began to divulge the names of countries that it had discussed in closed sessions. Since 1980 the Commission has publicly disclosed reports of its investigations or discussions in a number of cases, including complaints against Equatorial Guinea, Bolivia, Cambodia, El Salvador, Guatemala, Nicaragua, the Soviet Union (in Afghanistan), Poland, Romania, Cuba, Iran, the Congo, Sierra Leone, and Liberia. Such "mobilization of shame" has become important in the Commission's compliance procedures.

Nongovernmental organizations have been especially active in support of improved UN human rights procedures. While many individuals and groups have communicated with the United Nations from time to time, some of the more active groups have their own operations independent of the United Nations. These include Amnesty International, the International Commission of Jurists, the International League for Human Rights, the International Federation for Human Rights, and the World Council of Churches. Amnesty International, established in London in 1961, has become widely known for its efforts to publicize and secure the release of political prisoners and to eradicate torture. It is respected as a source of information as well as for its persistence in mobilizing public opinion and encouraging government action to vindicate fundamental human rights.

Some of the human rights treaties have their own provisions for implementation, but most use the same procedures of complaint, investigation, discussion, and censure used by UN bodies outside the treaty framework. Under the International Covenant on Civil and Political Rights, an eighteen-member Human Rights Committee of specialists elected by the parties is empowered to receive reports from states on measures adopted to implement the covenant. The Committee studies the reports and transmits its comments to the parties and the Economic and Social Council. In addition, states may authorize the Committee to receive and consider communications from other parties alleging noncompliance with treaty obligations. No state may bring such a complaint unless it has made an appropriate declaration subjecting itself to the procedure.

The Committee's powers are limited to discussion and reporting, supplemented by a conciliation procedure with consent of the parties. By accepting an optional protocol to the treaty, states have empowered the Committee to consider complaints from private individuals within their jurisdiction. Any views expressed by the Committee have only the force of recommendation.

## SUMMARY OF GOALS AND STANDARDS IN THE UN HUMAN RIGHTS TREATY SYSTEM

Despite the obstacles and sustained violations of human rights in various parts of the world, there has been a marked acceptance of procedures related to the protection of human rights. What started with a handful of sensitive people is now a global phenomenon of entitlements that seek to protect the victims of abusive elements, whether states or groups. States are more and more inclined to voluntarily accept the strictures of the international community. The obligations of human rights treaties have been freely assumed, and it is their legal character that places them at the center of the international system of human rights protection. Moreover, rights generate corresponding legal obligations on states to protect against human rights violations, as well as to remedy them when and where they occur. International standards to determine human rights compliance within states are found in seven major treaties:

1. International Convention on the Elimination of all Forms of Racial Discrimination (in force since 1969)
2. International Covenant on Civil and Political Rights (in force since 1976)
3. International Covenant on Economic, Social and Cultural Rights (in force since 1976)
4. Convention on the Elimination of All Forms of Discrimination Against Women (in force since 1981)
5. Convention Against Torture and Other Cruel, Inhuman or Degrading Treatment or Punishment (in force since 1987)
6. Convention on the Rights of the Child (in force since 1990)
7. Convention on the Protection of the Rights of Migrant Workers (in force since 2003)

These treaties link with seven treaty committees that have the responsibility for monitoring the implementation of treaty obligations. All treaty bodies are formed from members elected by the states that are parties to the treaty, or through the UN Economic and Social Council. Committee members are experts who have independent functioning capacities. Treaty bodies meet periodically, review reports from states, and are free to comment on the adequacy of state compliance with the treaty. Several of the treaty bodies will also hear complaints, can make visitations, and generally contribute to the development and understanding of international human rights standards. Numerous instances of state legal reform have resulted from the treaties. Moreover, NGOs and human rights organizations have cited treaty standards as their particular point of reference. Treaties also have been incorporated into national law and have had direct application in constitutional provisions, or been used to interpret domestic law.

## REGIONAL INSTITUTIONS

A perspective on UN efforts to promote human rights throughout the world may be gleaned from an examination of the regional approaches to human rights in the Americas and Western Europe. The Organization of American States was seven months ahead of the United Nations when it adopted the American Declaration of the Rights and Duties of Man in Bogota, Colombia, in April 1948. The American Declaration was the first international human rights instrument of a general nature, and it led to the creation in 1959 of the Inter-American Commission on Human Rights (IACHR), which held its inaugural session in 1960. From that time through 1997, the Commission convened ninety-seven sessions at its headquarters in Washington, D.C., or in different countries of the Western Hemisphere. In 1961, the IACHR began site visits, observing human rights situations in a number of countries and launching investigations where conditions revealed violations of the Declaration.

In 1965, the IACHR became authorized to examine complaints or petitions regarding specific cases of human rights violations. By 1998 the Commission had received thousands of petitions, which resulted in twelve thousand cases being processed or ordered for processing. The published reports of the IACHR regarding these individual cases are found in the Annual Reports of the Commission or are released independently. In 1969, members of the Organization of American States adopted the American Convention on Human Rights, and it went into force in 1978. As of August 1997, it had been ratified by twenty-five countries. This Convention defines human rights and created the Inter-American Court of Human Rights. It is the responsibility of the IACHR to order the Court to issue "provisional measures" in urgent cases that involve a danger to individuals even when a case has not been submitted to the Court. It also submits cases to the Inter-American Court and appears before that body in the litigation of cases. Finally, the IACHR may request advisory opinions from the Court regarding questions of interpretation of the American Convention. In 1997–98, the Commission was charged with processing eight hundred individual cases to determine whether all domestic remedies had been exhausted and whether there was still reason to believe justice had not been done. The IACHR may seek to address a case itself, but on occasion it will transfer the case to the Inter-American Court. The Court, composed of seven judges who are elected by the states that are parties to the Convention, is located in Costa Rica and is considered an autonomous institution of the Organization of American States. Judges serve six-year terms and may be reelected to a second term. The Organization of American States also established an Inter-American Juridical Committee, which consists of eleven judges who function out of Committee headquarters in Rio de Janeiro. Its major task is the codification of international law.

Undoubtedly the most effective arrangement for the international protection of human rights is the European Convention on Human Rights, drafted under the auspices of the Council of Europe and in force since 1953. The Council's members have accepted the Convention and thereby agreed to submit certain types of human rights controversies to the binding determination of an international body. These states have also approved an optional provision granting individuals and private associations the right to complain. The emphasis is on quiet negotiation to find a "friendly solution" among the parties involved. For states that have ratified an optional protocol conferring jurisdiction on the European Court of Human Rights, the final decision is left to the Court.

The successful operation of the Convention has rested on a number of circumstances. First, it has been limited to traditional civil and political rights already widely guaranteed in Western European countries. Second, the legal systems of the parties have adequate homogeneity to produce similarity in interpretation and application of the treaty guarantees. Third, the emphasis throughout is on quiet negotiation of settlement, utilizing a judicial or quasi-judicial body as the ultimate arbiter and at no stage providing a public forum for political harassment of one state by another. Fourth, states have seldom used the machinery in their dealings with one another, with the great majority of complaints issuing from individuals. Fifth, petitions by individuals are carefully screened to rule out frivolous or insubstantial complaints.

The maintenance of European Council standards in the immediate post–Cold War era presented important but not insurmountable problems. The former Eastern bloc nations became members of the Council of Europe shortly after the demise of the Soviet Union, and the Russian Federation was made the organization's thirty-ninth member in February 1996. All pledged adherence to the principles safeguarding human rights and to the organs and procedures responsible for assuring compliance. But Russian problems with secessionist Chechnya, and the vicious ethnic wars that followed the breakup of the Yugoslav Federation, raised questions that could only be answered with force. What had been a positive record in human rights safeguards in Europe was weakened by these and other human rights incidents in the Baltic states, where minorities had been placed at substantial risk. With the inclusion of the East European states in the Council of Europe, violations of the European Convention on Human Rights escalated, and in the years immediately after the fall of the Iron Curtain, the East European states demonstrated a definite ignorance in human rights matters. With the passage of time, however, the termination of hostilities in the Balkans and Eastern Europe's deeper integration with the West took hold. It was not long before national reforms in virtually all the states brought them abreast of prevailing conventions. Thus, with Bosnia and Kosovo pacified, the Czech Republic, Poland, and Hungary were inducted into NATO before the end of the twentieth century, and seven more states were tapped to join the alliance in the early years of the new millennium. So too, the East Europeans demonstrated a capacity for economic and financial reform, and the European Union was prepared for their inclusion as full members. The elevation of human rights in the states of Eastern Europe turned out to be one of the more notable achievements of the UN human rights system.

## THE DECLARATION OF HUMAN RIGHTS REVISITED

By 1998, fifty years had elapsed since the Universal Declaration of Human Rights was adopted. The Declaration was the first time in history that a document considered to have universal value was formalized by an international organization. It also was the first time that human rights and fundamental freedoms were formulated in detail and inscribed in an international document. Moreover, the broad-based support for the Declaration hinted at a different future for the more threatened of the world's humanity. Cited as the "Magna Carta" for all the people of the planet, its contents ranged from civil to cultural, economic to political issues, as well as the gamut of social issues. Amplifying the first words of the UN Charter that were addressed to "We the Peoples," it was celebrated at the World Conference on Human Rights convened in Vienna in June 1993. Attended by 171 nations, a Vienna Declaration and Program of Action was adopted at the Conference to better integrate the human rights work of governmental organizations and NGOs. The conferees at Vienna reiterated the goals of the original Declaration as well as subsequent conventions aimed at the elimination of racial discrimination, discrimination against women, and the exploitation of children. Calling for a more proactive effort, the fiftieth anniversary of the Declaration provided a forum and an occasion for the condemnation of human rights abuses, as well as for a new interpretation of national sovereignty. Arguing the human condition to be more significant than the right of states, the Conference placed governments on notice that their sovereign status no longer protected them from international scrutiny, or even intervention.

The celebration of the Declaration of Human Rights fell within the Decade of Human Rights Education (1995–2004), and although the document had been translated into two hundred languages, additional language versions were judged essential. But more than words, the fiftieth anniversary was used to mobilize civil society and NGOs in the struggle to achieve basic human rights. National committees were formed in scores of states, and grassroots movements energized communities to higher awareness. In accordance with recommendations stemming from the 1993 World Conference on Human Rights for increased coordination within the UN system, Secretary-General Kofi Annan reiterated the organization's commitment to the complex issues that involved peacekeeping, protecting the rights of labor and children, and safeguarding health and the provision of appropriate education. If there was a core issue around which the United Nations was brought into existence it was the matter of human rights. Moreover, although progress since 1948 could be cited, the fiftieth anniversary celebration of the document was also a painful reminder that people everywhere remained at risk and too often were confronted by the most dire circumstances.

The plight of people at risk in fact had been noted in the proclamation that established 1993 as the International Year of Indigenous People and subsequently the period 1995–2004 as the International Decade of the World's Indigenous People. Noting the disproportionate effect of poverty on indigenous people in countries like Bolivia, Guatemala, Mexico, and Peru, Latin American community organizations deplored the failure to provide even the most minimal health services. Using a similar theme, the Australian Institute of Health and Welfare revealed the desperate conditions of aboriginal children in central Australia that produced an unconscionably high rate of infant mortality. In New Zealand the focus was on Maori males, who were twice as likely as non-Maori males to be affected by heart disease, pneumonia, chronic respiratory problems, and infections of the skin. And although regional organizations were more likely to report shortcomings in the area of human rights, the global character of the problems facing indigenous people did not go unnoticed. Much of the difficulty was traced to uncontrolled industrial development and its resultant environmental damage, especially water pollution; the loss of important sources of nutrition, such as fish; and the exposure to high levels of contaminants. Indigenous people also were deprived of property rights, experienced high unemployment, and suffered cultural genocide. Native Americans in the United States continued to live out impoverished lives on reservations. Brazil brutalized Indian communities that blocked lucrative mining interests. And the Chiapans of Mexico formed the Zapatista National Liberation Army and took up arms and terror in an effort to protect their domains from encroaching exploiters.

The above examples show that the adoption of the Universal Declaration of Human Rights more than fifty years ago did not end the abuses people suffer around the world. The UN system is mindful of its responsibilities, but beyond shedding light on grievances, publicizing salient questions, or prodding nations to improve their performance, it cannot make right the many complex wrongs. With the United Nations committed to the cause, the next fifty years must address the implementation of national development programs that are directed at correcting the inequities and gross displays of intolerance that are found in all societies. Only with the forging of new relationships based on mutual respect and recognition can the profound intentions of the Universal Declaration be realized. The UN system exists to promote that ideal, and if the organization's past dedication is a measure, its member states can anticipate even greater pressure to meet their stated goals.

## HUMAN RIGHTS, NATO, AND KOSOVO

Nowhere at the end of the twentieth century was the issue of human rights more dramatically or more tragically illustrated than in the plight of the Kosovar Albanians. And nowhere were the senseless struggles that pitted one portion of humanity against another more expressive of the shallowness of civilization than in Kosovo in 1999. In 1999, threatened populations stretched from the Adriatic to the Caucasus and into Russia, through the Mediterranean to Mesopotamia and Africa, eastward to the Asian subcontinent, and onward to Southeast, East, and Pacific Asia. But it was in an area nestled between Serbia, Albania, and Macedonia that the flash point for still another violent intercontinental contest manifested itself. Blind expressions of nationalism, nourished by ancient ideas and myths of territoriality, culture, and identity, fueled the fear and loathing between Serb and Kosovar Albanians. Although called to accept a common political order, Serbs and Albanians shared little except their mutual hate for one another. Their passions held in check during the decades of leadership by Josip Broz Tito that followed World War II, the great leader's death in 1980 left a power vacuum that no successor could fill. Moreover, Yugoslavia was once a reputed federation managed by strict communist rules of decorum, but the repudiation of European communism in 1989–90 further complicated the country's feeble efforts at the formation of a nonnational state.

By the 1980s Yugoslavia's ethnic claimants to power had stoked the furnaces of separatism and exclusivity. Generations of intermingling, however, had also intertwined the peoples of the different republics. Furthermore, a diplomatic separation of the various political units with clear territorial boundaries was never attempted. As a consequence, Yugoslavia's breakup provoked the disastrous ethnic wars that initially enveloped Croatia and Serbia and then spilled over into Bosnia. In that conflict, the efforts made to form a greater Serbia were matched by those determined to establish a greater Croatia. Bosnia was squeezed between them, and after several years of bloodshed it could only be rescued by the intervention of the NATO alliance led by the United States.

The transatlantic attempt to douse the flames of indiscriminate tribal warfare in the former Yugoslavia was aimed at restoring tranquillity to an expanding Europe as much as it was meant to promote and protect human rights in the Balkans. Therefore, NATO was called in to work its magic under these new and different circumstances, as its mere presence was believed sufficient to guarantee European stability and security. Moreover, Europe's deeper integration and democratization programs depended on the alliance's continued success in muting the nationalistic drives of its members. Transcending the national frontiers of the member states, NATO shifted its gaze from the protection of state boundaries to the protection of human rights. NATO was no longer simply a military alliance; its social-political role legitimized the organization in the post–Cold War years and justified its interventionist role in Bosnia. Performing at a virtual supranational level in Bosnia, NATO, in the absence of a more formidable United Nations, assumed a posture that arguably challenged the sovereignty of individual nations.

Hence NATO let it be known it could not ignore the conflict in Kosovo involving Serb forces and those of the Kosovo Liberation Army (KLA). Challenged by the Universal Declaration of Human Rights, and also fearing that the escalation of civil war in Kosovo could provoke a wider European war, NATO again demanded that the Serbs cease and desist and begin a process of reconciliation between Serbs and Albanians.

With tensions on the ascendant, NATO governments convened a conference in France in February 1999 between members of the KLA and the Milošević government. Although the KLA hesitatingly accepted the peace formula drafted by the alliance, a formula that left Kosovo an integral part of Serbia, Belgrade rejected it out of hand because it also called for the stationing of a NATO security force in the province. Milošević made the fateful decision to accelerate a program of ethnic cleansing, that is, the forced removal of the Kosovar Albanians from the territory.

What followed was Serbia's clear violation of the Universal Declaration of Human Rights, now a centerpiece for European integration and democratization. NATO warned Belgrade, as it had in October 1998, that it was prepared to use force if the Serbs persisted in their ethnic cleansing campaign. In fact, tens of thousands of Albanian Kosovars already had been forced from their homes when NATO reissued its warning in February 1999. Milošević and his government remained defiant, however, and in fact stepped up the campaign to change Kosovo's demographic character once and for all. With NATO's credibility on the line, and with the fear that a great human tragedy was about to occur, NATO repeated its warning to Belgrade. But neither that threat or last-minute diplomatic efforts could budge the Milošević government from its declared intention to rid the province of Albanian Kosovars.

NATO argued that it could no longer stand by while helpless Kosovars were brutally uprooted and murdered, so in March 1999 NATO air power was directed against Serbia and Montenegro, the latter still an actor in what remained of the Yugoslavian state. NATO air strikes were intended to bring the Serbs back to the conference table, but instead they propelled the Belgrade government to move even more rapidly with its program to eliminate the Albanian population.

Albanian refugees told countless stories about crimes against humanity, and given the new emphasis on the protection of human rights, NATO along with other agencies collected data on war crimes for transmission to the International Criminal Court. Of those to be listed as war criminals, the first on the list was Slobodan Milošević. Thus, although attention was riveted on the immediate plight of the Albanian Kosovars, the plan to punish the perpetrators of Europe's foremost human tragedy since World War II went forward.

Clearly involved in the Kosovo drama was the elevation of human rights over state rights. Moreover, NATO prevailed over Serbian arms and although Kosovo technically remained an integral part of the Serbian sovereignty, Kosovar autonomy was reestablished and assured by NATO occupation forces. Refugee Kosovars returned to their homes after Belgrade's surrender. The province came under KFOR scrutiny, a NATO-led force monitored by the United Nations, and Milošević was forced from power and transported to the International Criminal Court in The Hague to be tried as a war criminal.

NATO celebrated its fiftieth anniversary in April 1999. The Washington

Summit was attended by the alliance's heads of state or governments who collectively acknowledged their mutual responsibilities in preventing a repetition of the tragedy in Kosovo. KFOR remained in place to police conditions in the wake of the hostilities, and the forces were still there in 2004.

## IMPROVEMENT OF LABOR STANDARDS

Closely related to UN action in the area of human rights are the efforts of the International Labor Organization to upgrade labor standards around the world. The ILO has been a force for higher labor standards since its creation in 1919, when Allied diplomats, responding to labor pressures and honoring their wartime commitments to trade union groups, drafted the Constitution of the ILO as Part XIII of the Versailles Treaty. An annex to the Constitution came from the Declaration of Philadelphia of 1944, which embodies the following principles:

1. Labor is not a commodity.
2. Freedom of expression and of association are essential to sustained progress.
3. Poverty anywhere constitutes a danger to prosperity everywhere.
4. All human beings, irrespective of race, creed, or sex, have the right to pursue both their material well-being and their spiritual development in conditions of freedom and dignity, of economic security, and equal opportunity.

In 1998, the International Labor Conference in Geneva adopted the ILO Declaration on Fundamental Principles and Rights at Work and its Follow-up. It reaffirmed the commitment of the international community "to respect, to promote and to realize in good faith" the rights of workers and employers to freedom of association and the effective right to collective bargaining. It also expressed the continuing need to work toward the elimination of all forms of forced or compulsory labor, the effective abolition of child labor, and the elimination of discrimination with respect to employment and occupation. The Declaration emphasizes that all member countries have an obligation to respect the fundamental principles involved, whether or not they have ratified the relevant conventions.

Since its founding, the ILO has been marked by a vigorous secretariat, known as the International Labor Office, and a unique form of tripartite representation for employer, worker, and government interests in its policy-making bodies. Each member state sends two government delegates—one employers' delegate and one workers' delegate—to the annual meeting of the International Labor Conference, and the same tripartite distribution is found in its fifty-six-member governing body (twenty-eight governments, fourteen employers, and fourteen workers). Ten of the government seats are permanently held by states of chief industrial importance, namely, Brazil, China, France, Germany, India, Italy, Japan, the Russian Federation, the United Kingdom, and the United States.

The other government members are elected by the Conference every three years. Employer and worker members are elected in their individual capacity.

Like the United Nations in its human rights programs, the ILO functions by setting standards, giving advice, facilitating the exchange of information, and mobilizing world opinion in support of higher standards. Standards are set through legally binding conventions, subject to state ratification, and through recommendations voicing goals and aspirations that are beyond the reach of some states and hence not proper subjects for lawmaking treaties. The conventions and recommendations taken together are referred to as the International Labor Code. From 6 conventions and 6 recommendations adopted by the first International Labor Conference in 1919, the number had grown to 183 conventions and 191 recommendations by 2002. The Code extends to nearly every aspect of working conditions—hours, wages, the right to organize and bargain collectively, employment discrimination, workers' compensation, employment security, vocational guidance and training, and occupational safety and health, among others. A number of the conventions and recommendations deal with special abuses, such as slavery and forced labor, or with special categories of workers—women, children, miners, seamen, dock workers, and sharecroppers.

States vary widely in their ratification of conventions. France has ratified more than one hundred, the United States fewer than twenty. The ILO, however, has unusually well developed techniques for encouraging compliance with the Code. This is done by a searching annual review of member states' reports, a judicious use of the ILO's powers of investigation, and a procedure for hearing complaints in particular cases. The ILO has seldom been hesitant in pointing out instances of noncompliance and making specific recommendations for remedial action.

In addition to rule-making and implementation, the ILO carries on extensive informational activities through publications, conferences, seminars and fellowships, and technical experts. Its *Yearbook of Labor Statistics* and its quarterly *Official Bulletin* have long been important sources of data on international labor conditions. A monthly *International Labor Review* and numerous special publications provide information on current problems and conditions.

Programs of technical assistance are used to help countries conform to the Code as well as to promote economic development as a means of providing a social and economic base for improved labor standards. Assistance is provided in areas of ILO interest and expertise, such as vocational training, social security services, occupational health and safety, and labor statistics. Some ILO technical assistance is funded from its own budget, but a larger share draws on resources of the UN Development Program.

The ILO operates in the same world environment as the United Nations, and it has suffered the effects of political battles between East and West and between North and South. In 1977 the United States withdrew from the organization, after having held continuous membership since 1934. The U.S. dissatisfaction sprang from a number of causes. The United States saw the tripartite principle threatened by delegations from the Soviet bloc and some other states whose employer and labor representatives were, for practical purposes, government representatives under a different label. The United States also objected to what it saw as selective concern for human rights, especially as reflected in actions of the International Labor Conference that pilloried friends of the United States and ignored violations in some other countries. Excessive politicization was also alleged, particularly in using the forum to penalize Israel for actions that had little to do with labor standards and in granting observer status to the PLO in 1975. As early as 1970 the AFL-CIO, with its strong anticommunist tradition, had been seriously alienated by the appointment of a Soviet national as an ILO Assistant Director-General.

Loss of the U.S. financial contribution, amounting to 25 percent of the regular budget, caused severe temporary curtailment of ILO programs. But the United States returned in 1980 after some signs that the ILO would behave more circumspectly. An Arab proposal to condemn Israel was defeated, labor rights violations in Eastern Europe were given more attention, and procedures were adopted to bolster employer and worker autonomy within the organization. Perhaps more important, the United States concluded that working from within was a more effective method of influencing labor standards and ILO programs than remaining outside the organization. Since returning the United States has maintained a more sympathetic involvement with the organization and in 1988 ratified ILO conventions on forced labor and labor standards in maritime shipping. Two other conventions, dealing with tripartite consultation on international labor standards and labor statistics, have since been ratified. The forced labor treaty was the first ILO convention to be accepted by the United States in thirty-five years.

The International Labor Office is a permanent secretariat of the ILO and the focal point for overall activities that it prepares under the guidance of the governing body and the Director-General, who is elected for five-year renewable terms. The Office employs approximately nineteen hundred officials from 110 countries at its Geneva headquarters. It also has forty field offices around the world. In addition, about six hundred experts are enlisted for missions to any region of the world, through programs of technical cooperation.

## RULES IN OTHER FUNCTIONAL SETTINGS

Human rights and labor standards are matters of domestic concern that have traditionally been regulated by individual states. By contrast, many areas of functional cooperation involve interstate contacts that fall beyond the jurisdiction of any single state and must be regulated by international action if they are to be regulated at all. In recognition of this fact, states have submitted a number of their functional relationships to the regulative processes of international organization. Its growth does not necessarily justify the functionalist premise that economic and social cooperation leads to peace, but it does demonstrate that states will subject themselves and their citizens to a degree of international regulation in limited functional areas when self-interest requires it. Some of the more significant ventures in the regulation of international contacts will be examined here.

## POSTAL SERVICE

Among the best-observed international regulations are those of the Universal Postal Union (UPU), an organization dating from 1874. Under its authority letters can be delivered anywhere in the world by the most expeditious route at a modest uniform cost and in accordance with generally uniform procedures. The technical nature of UPU functions is conducive to consensus, and consensus on broad objectives provides the foundation for majority rule within the organization when the goal of complete unanimity cannot be attained. Revisions of the UPU constitution, initiated at meetings of the Congress of the Postal Union, held every five years, become effective upon ratification by two-thirds of member countries. Changes in the rules and regulations governing letter post are effected by a simple majority of the membership, without need for formal ratification. Between congresses, proposals for amendments to the postal rules are circulated by the bureau (secretariat) and take effect when enough affirmative replies are received. Compliance with the rules is obligatory from the time of their entry into force, with loss of membership privileges as the sanction. Formal approval of changes is not necessary as long as a state in fact observes the regulations. Compliance is generally forthcoming because the benefits of participation outweigh the burdens of compliance.

## TELECOMMUNICATIONS

The International Telecommunication Union (ITU) is unique among international organizations in that it was founded on the principle of cooperation between governments and the private sector. The climate in which the ITU operates today is very different from the one in which it was founded approximately 135 years ago. In the past twenty years, telecommunications have grown from a tool that facilitated person-to-person communication to the foundation that underpins a huge number of human activities, from international trade and commerce to health, and increasingly, to education. Fast, reliable telecommunication networks are now a vital aspect of the transborder delivery of services in banking, transportation, tourism, online information, and electronic home shopping. Most noted is the convergence of communication computing and audiovisual entertainment. Moreover, the liberalization and deregulation of the telecommunication sector in many countries has prompted ITU members to look to the ITU to provide new services that place greater emphasis on policy development and regulatory guidance. The ITU therefore has dramatically changed to remain relevant in the twenty-first century.

Covering all aspects of telecommunications, from setting standards that facilitate the seamless interworking of equipment and systems on a global basis to adopting operational procedures for the vast and growing array of wireless services, the ITU is most concerned with the improvement of telecommunication infrastructure in the developing world. Each of the three ITU sectors—radio communication, telecommunication standardization, and telecommunication development—works through conferences and meetings where members negotiate the agreements that serve as a basis for the operation of global telecommunication services. Study groups made up of experts drawn from leading telecommunication organizations worldwide carry out the technical work of the Union. The ITU therefore is concerned with terrestrial and space-based wireless services and systems and seeks to develop operational procedures. ITU experts prepare technical specifications for telecommunications systems, networks, and services. In 2003 there were twenty-four study groups spanning the Union's three sectors that together produced about 550 new and revised recommendations annually. ITU recommendations are nonbinding, and all are judged to be voluntary agreements. Each sector has its own bureau that ensures the implementation of the sector's work plan and coordinates day-to-day activities.

The older, more traditional work of the ITU is in many respects analogous to that of the UPU, especially its efforts to create a homogeneous global communication system by joint regulation of telegraph, telephone, and radio-telegraph services. The two organizations' methods of legislating and enforcing compliance are also broadly similar. The ITU conference meets at intervals of five to eight years to make general policy and initiate amendments to the ITU convention. Decisions are reached through unanimous agreement if possible but by simple and qualified majorities when necessary. A state is permitted to ratify amendments with reservations and still remain in good standing, but the penalty for nonratification is loss of its vote in ITU organs after a two-year grace period. As a practical matter, from the date of their entry into force, amendments are treated as provisionally applicable even to nonratifying states. In a number of technical matters, including the important function of radio-frequency regulation, the ITU assigns tasks to specialist, "nonpolitical" experts instead of to negotiating conferences composed of government representatives. This approach differs from that of the UPU and is possible because of the highly technical nature of the tasks.

Compliance with ITU rules, a product of necessity and convenience, has been very high except in the special problem area of radio broadcasting, where the ITU has sometimes faced defiance by countries refusing to be limited to the use of frequencies allotted by the ITU's International Frequency Registration Board. If a recalcitrant member broadcasts on a frequency not assigned to it, the ITU may punish the offender by freeing other states to use its assigned frequencies. Interference with authorized radio signals, otherwise known as radio jamming, is another special problem. The practice is clearly in violation of ITU regulations, but it is so entwined with the vital interests of states that ITU sanctions are unable to curb it. When faced with a complaint of radio jamming, the ITU has generally resigned itself to the fact that retaliation through release of frequencies would only add to the confusion and further impair radio transmission. With the end of the Cold War, however, the systematic radio jamming conducted by Eastern European states was discontinued and is essentially no longer a concern.

## CIVIL AVIATION

In the area of air transportation, international efforts to promote safety, regularity of transport, uniformity, and nondiscrimination are centered in the International Civil Aviation Organization (ICAO). Rule-making functions are largely the responsibility of the organization's thirty-three-member council. Standards approved by a two-thirds vote of the council become effective at a date prescribed by the council unless a majority of states indicate their disapproval during the intervening period. The organization distinguishes between binding *standards,* which are necessary to the safety or regularity of international air navigation, and nonbinding *recommended practices,* which represent desirable goals.

A state that cannot conform to a new standard may notify the council within the time period established for raising objections and be released from its legal obligation. If the standard relates to the airworthiness of aircraft or the competence of personnel, however, other states are free to close their airspace to the aircraft of the noncomplying state. The ICAO convention commits all members to the principle of nondiscrimination against the aircraft of any country, but noncompliance with standards revives the discretionary rights of one state against another that would prevail under the rules of customary international law. Compliance with ICAO rules is widespread, and most instances of noncompliance appear to be rooted in lack of economic and technical resources rather than willful disregard of the norms.

ICAO regulation is primarily technical, relating to such matters as air traffic control, communication and navigational aids, safety standards for aircraft, and rules of the air. The organization has not been given the authority to regulate the commercial aspects of civil aviation, including access to the passenger and cargo markets of individual countries. A right jealously guarded by states, the granting of commercial privileges still occurs through bilateral agreement between states.

## HEALTH

Health problems have long been a subject of international regulation. International health councils were established during the nineteenth century in seaport cities of North Africa, the Middle East, and Southeastern Europe, usually at the behest of the more powerful European states. These bodies represented an early form of international action to improve sanitary conditions and prevent the spread of epidemics along the channels of commerce. Later the councils were supplemented by multilateral conventions that established rules for quarantine, and other precautionary measures to be taken in ports, and prohibited vessels from leaving port without a clean bill of health. Exchange of information through conferences was put on a more systematic basis in 1907 with the establishment of the International Office of Public Health in Paris, and League health machinery subsequently forged ahead with direct efforts to fight disease and improve world levels of health.

The World Health Organization (WHO), which came into being in 1948 as a specialized agency of the United Nations, has combined and expanded international cooperation in all of these areas. The WHO is a regulatory body with effective rule-making power in several limited but important areas, including: (1) sanitary and quarantine regulations applicable to ground, sea, and air travel; (2) standardization of medical nomenclature; (3) standards for diagnostic procedures; (4) standards on the safety, purity, and potency of biological and pharmaceutical substances passing in international commerce; and (5) advertising and labeling of such products. When approved by the World Health Assembly, health regulations come into force for all members after a specified period of notice, except for states that object or enter reservations. The WHO constitution gives the Assembly the right to make law by treaty, subject to ratification by member states, but the WHO prefers the regulation approach because it speeds up the process and permits rules to take immediate effect for all member states, barring a formal objection. Beyond these special areas, the WHO may make recommendations on any health-related subject. Research, collection and dissemination of information, and expert advice are also used extensively to upgrade health standards around the world.

The WHO also has extensive programs of health services and technical assistance to developing countries, including a number of successful campaigns against disease. A concentrated effort to combat malaria, beginning in the mid-1950s, led to its eradication from most of Asia, much of the Americas, and all of Europe. Permanent eradication of malaria in Africa could not be achieved until basic health services were improved. The WHO's success in fighting smallpox was even more spectacular. An immunization campaign in the late 1960s and early 1970s reduced the incidence of smallpox to a rare occurrence in most parts of the world, and in 1979 the WHO declared the disease eradicated.

An Expanded Program on Immunization (EPI), launched in 1974, provides immunization for children against diphtheria, measles, pertussis (whooping cough), poliomyelitis, tetanus, and tuberculosis, all of which are major causes of death and disability in developing countries. Although not fully successful, the proportion of immunized children worldwide rose from less than 20 percent in the late 1970s to more than 70 percent in the 1990s. The worldwide struggle against disease is also aided by the WHO's epidemiological intelligence network, which receives reports from member governments immediately upon the outbreak of any case of smallpox, cholera, plague, or yellow fever and transmits the information to health authorities throughout the world by means of daily broadcasts.

A global strategy in support of a "Health for All by the Year 2000" campaign, adopted by the WHO assembly in 1981, had the goal of promoting a world level of health that would permit all people to lead socially and economically productive lives. Specific objectives included safe water within fifteen minutes' walking distance of every home, immunization against the six EPI diseases, local health care within an hour's travel, and trained personnel to attend childbirth and to care for pregnant mothers and for children up to at least one year of age. These goals, however, could not be reached by the year 2000 because neither the WHO nor the poorer countries had the resources to do the job.

The Joint UN Program on HIV/AIDS (UNAIDS) published an epidemic update in December 2002 that described the pandemic nature of the disease. Already judged the worst pandemic in world history, more than 3.1 million people were said to have died from AIDS in 2002 alone, and more than 5 million additional people were in need of immediate treatment. Estimates pegged HIV-infected people at 42 million worldwide, with 45 million more expected to contract the disease by 2010. The worst affected areas and countries were the regions and states of the former Soviet Union, Africa, Central Asia, China, and India. New incidences of the disease were highest in Russia, Ukraine, Latvia, and Estonia. The African continent was the hardest hit, with 29.4 million affected, roughly 70 percent of the worldwide total. A special Global Fund to Fight AIDS, Tuberculosis and Malaria was established after a plea by Secretary-General Kofi Annan was made to the nations of the world. Answering that call was the European Union, the World Bank, and especially the United States. In his 2003 State of the Union address, and again in his trip to Africa in July 2003, President George W. Bush pledged $15 billion over ten years for the war on HIV/AIDS.

The WHO program gathers and reports international statistics, supports national information and education programs, and provides training for medical personnel in member countries. It also seeks to improve national facilities for screening and protecting blood supplies and encourages the establishment and expansion of laboratory facilities for diagnosis and treatment of HIV/AIDS.

In addition to its general health functions, the WHO cooperates with the United Nations and related agencies for the control of narcotics and limiting their use to legitimate medical and scientific needs. Systematic efforts at international control date from The Hague Convention of 1912. International cooperation in this area was expanded by the League and further systematized under UN auspices. The present international regime is based on the Single Convention on Narcotic Drugs, adopted in 1961 to replace a number of earlier treaties and amended by a 1972 protocol, a 1971 Convention on Psychotropic Substances, and the 1988 UN Convention against Illicit Traffic in Narcotic Drugs and Psychotropic Substances. Under the treaties, an International Narcotics Control Board sets acceptable limits for the manufacture and importation of controlled drugs and monitors treaty compliance. The effectiveness of regulation depends largely on the ability and willingness of states to enforce treaty provisions, but international agencies help states remain sensitive to their obligations.

An ECOSOC Commission on Narcotic Drugs is an important forum for discussion of international narcotics problems, and the United Nations maintains research laboratories in several countries. The WHO's role is to advise other international agencies on drugs likely to produce addiction and to sponsor research and technical assistance relating to the prevention and treatment of drug addiction. Such was the case with tobacco, now considered a narcotic, when the WHO launched a "Tobacco or Health Program" aimed at educating people about the harmful effects of smoking.

At the end of February 2003 the WHO was confronted with still another dilemma when an atypical pneumonia of unknown etiology—called severe acute respiratory syndrome, or SARS—was identified in the Far East and in quick order determined to have arisen in China. The WHO was immediately involved in searching out the nature of and treatment for the disease in coordination with the Global Outbreak Alert and Response Network. The latter is a technical collaboration of existing institutions and networks that pool human and technical resources for the rapid identification of, confirmation of, and response to outbreaks of international importance. The organization contributes toward global health security by combating the international spread of outbreaks, ensuring that appropriate technical assistance reaches affected states rapidly, and contributing to long-term epidemic preparedness and capacity building. The Global Outbreak Alert and Response Network brings together medical and surveillance teams from UN organizations such as UNICEF and UNHCR, the Red Cross and Red Crescent Societies, and international humanitarian agencies and NGOs, such as Doctors Without Borders and the International Rescue Committee. Participation is open to all institutions and networks in a position to contribute to an immediate response. The activities of the WHO and the Global Outbreak Alert and Response Network are credited with the rapid detection of SARS, its isolation, and its early treatment.

Epidemics and newly emerging infections are threatening people around the world and affecting travel and trade in the global market. Globalization, climate change, the growth of megacities, and the increase in international travel have increased the potential for the rapid spread of infections. Deforestation and urban sprawl have brought humans and animals into closer contact, allowing animal pathogens to pass more easily to humans. Diseases that have been well-managed, such as cholera and meningitis, have reappeared and threaten to cause pandemics. Yellow fever has overwhelmed urban life in developing countries, along with drug-resistant tuberculosis and malaria. In 2001 the World Health Assembly, recognizing the threats to public health posed by epidemic-prone and emerging infections, adopted a resolution on global health security and epidemic alert and response that made specific recommendations to the WHO and its member states. Communicable Disease Surveillance and Response (CSR) was a consequence of this effort. CSR's strategy was aimed at working with partners to reach global health security, and in its initial stage it formulated International Health Regulations that focused on poverty-associated diseases such as cholera, dysentery, influenza, meningococcal meningitis, plague, viral hemorrhagic fevers (Ebola, Lassa), "mad cow" disease, anthrax, and others. The Regulations are intended to help speed up the response time when a deadly disease occurs and to facilitate intelligence gathering on it as well as its early diagnosis and treatment.

## THE ENVIRONMENT

When the UN Conference on the Human Environment met in Stockholm in June 1972, environmental concerns were barely visible on the international horizon. Only two government prime ministers attended. By June 1992, when the UN Conference on Environment and Development (UNCED) convened in Rio de Janeiro, the presence of heads of state or government from more than one hundred nations attested to the fact that problems of the global environment had achieved high priority on the international agenda.

The current salience of environmental concerns owes much to the 1972 conference. It adopted a Declaration on the Human Environment, setting forth twenty-six principles and 109 action recommendations that still serve as guidelines for UN environmental activities. Perhaps equally important, preparation for the conference induced some ninety states to create new governmental entities, bureaucracies, and intragovernmental consultative mechanisms to deal with the problems to be discussed at Stockholm.[7] Many governments responded affirmatively to the conference and thus gave environmental concerns an emphasis they had not previously enjoyed.

The 1972 conference also proposed the establishment of a UN Environment Programme (UNEP) as a permanent UN agency. UNEP was subsequently created by the UN General Assembly and came into being in 1973, with headquarters in Nairobi, Kenya—the first UN agency to be based in a developing country. The organization has never grown large—employing about two hundred professionals with supporting staff—but it has been important in raising global consciousness and instigating programs for environmental protection.

UNEP is a form of rule-making agency. Its fifty-eight-member governing council makes recommendations, proposes standards, and initiates discussions leading to international treaties. In this respect it is comparable to rule-making organizations previously discussed in the areas of human rights, communication, transportation, and health. Rule-making in these and other functional areas can also be viewed through the lenses of a related concept frequently used by international relations theorists, that of *regimes*. The regime concept can be illustrated by application to UNEP and its role in the international system.

*Regimes,* in Stephen D. Krasner's frequently cited definition, are sets of "implicit or explicit principles, norms, rules, and decision-making procedures around which actors' expectations converge in a given area of international relations."[8] An international organization is not itself a regime but rather a structure within a regime that provides procedures for rule-making, dispute resolution, and other forms of interaction from which principles, norms, and rules may emerge. Within a given regime there may be many such structures. The regime actors are likely to include national government officials, staffs of international organizations, and representatives of affected private groups and entities.

Krasner's definition of "regime" leaves considerable room for different views of whether a particular regime has come into existence. "Norms" and "principles" are sometimes hard to define, and including implicit and explicit rules within the concept of regime may also make the regime itself difficult to define. In view of this problem, other writers have described regimes with particular multilateral agreements regulating state conduct (and private conduct as well, through government action) in a given issue area. Thus Oran Young speaks of specific (and separate) regimes for stratospheric ozone, greenhouse gases, biological diversity, and so on. In matters pertaining to the environment, the International Convention for the Regulation of Whaling and the Agreement on the Conservation of Polar Bears constitute regimes.[9] Thus, Peter Haas treats the Barcelona Convention for the Protection of the Mediterranean Sea Against Pollution as a particular regime within the environmental area.[10]

In this discussion we accept both concepts of a regime. UNEP, using the broader definition, functions within a regime consisting of the "principles, norms, rules, and decision-making procedures" relating to international environmental activities. Participants in this regime include the UNEP secretariat. Also included are staffs of other international organizations concerned with environmental effect (such as the Food and Agriculture Organization, WHO, and the International Oceanographic Commission). Members of environment-oriented NGOs and of the relevant scientific communities, officers of multinational corporations, and officials of national governments—more often technical specialists, but also on occasion, participants drawn from high political levels of government—also can be added.

Though small in size, UNEP has done much to shape the regime in which it operates. Its principal functions are gathering and disseminating information, encouraging governments to adopt environmentally sound policies, and promoting the development of international environmental law. Its information programs are extensive. Among them is the International Register of Potentially Toxic Chemicals, which makes available extensive information on chemical safety; INFOTERRA, a computer network, which provides names, addresses, and telex/telephone numbers of thousands of institutions and experts capable of giving answers to environmental questions; and the Global Environmental Monitoring System (GEMS). GEMS coordinates a network of monitoring stations in some 150 countries, providing information on climate and atmospheric conditions, renewable terrestrial resources, ocean and transboundary pollution, and the health consequences of pollution.

UNEP also devotes a substantial portion of its resources to seminars and other training sessions for government officials, as well as to technical cooperation. An important substantive emphasis of UNEP has been the relationship of environmental factors to economic development, health, and human settlements. Much of the technical assistance to developing countries focuses on environmentally sound ways to sustain forest productivity, animal and plant species, soils, and water supplies.

UNEP activities have also promoted the formation of more specific regimes through the development of international law. This includes the "hard" law of international treaties as well as the "soft" law of guidelines, principles, and standards for environmental management. Both are important. Hard law creates legal obligations; soft law helps build government consensus on appropriate goals and methods. Soft law could be regarded as creating regimes involving a lower level of commitment. Soft law standards have been formulated to provide guidance in such areas as weather modification, offshore mining and drilling, marine pollution from land-based sources, management of hazardous wastes, environmental impact assessment, and exchange of information on chemicals in international trade.

Multilateral treaties create particular regimes involving a relatively high degree of commitment. Some of those adopted with UNEP encouragement include the 1985 Vienna Convention and the 1987 Montreal Protocol (both dealing with protection of the stratospheric ozone layer) and the 1989 Basel Convention (trade in hazardous wastes). By 1990 UNEP's regional seas program had resulted in eleven regional conventions for marine environment protection. Two further treaties drafted with UNEP input were opened for ratification at the 1992 UNCED. A biodiversity treaty sought to preserve key plant and animal species by controlling the effect of deforestation, pollution, and misuse of resources. Another, much watered down at U.S. insistence, contained a non-specific commitment to limit the emission of the greenhouse gases believed to cause global warming. The global warming issue was revisited in Kyoto, Japan, and later in Bonn, Germany, in 1997. The United States again demonstrated reluctance to agree to climate treaties that would limit its carbon dioxide and methane emissions, which were described as one-quarter of the world's total. Fearing threats to the U.S. economy, American business groups continued to pressure government not to accede to international demands, thus weakening UNEP's role. With the inauguration of George W. Bush in January 2001, the Kyoto global warming treaty was formally repudiated. Under the Protocol agreed to in Kyoto in 1997, thirty-nine industrialized nations were required to cut emissions of six greenhouse gases to an average of 5.2 percent below 1990 levels by 2008–12. The United States was called upon to cut its greenhouse gas emissions by 7 percent. Bush questioned the science behind climate change, however, and canceled the actions of the Clinton administration. In March 2001 Bush reversed a pledge made during his election campaign to limit carbon dioxide emissions from U.S. power plants, arguing that the rule would be too costly. Bush's action was the clearest indication that U.S. involvement in UN-organized climate change talks was over. Moreover, the decision to abandon discussions on global warming came at a time when the amount of sea ice in the Arctic was declining steadily at a rate of about 9 percent each decade — a change that could adversely affect climate around the world.

But despite UNEP's difficulty in gaining support from the United States, it has not been without success. Although its desertification campaign failed, its regional seas program and negotiations on atmospheric ozone depletion resulted in international agreements. And given sustained opposition from the larger powers, UNEP has formed alliances with sympathetic NGOs, such as the World

Commission on Environment and Development. UNEP's budget has increased from $20 million in 1973 to more than $100 million thirty years later, but that sum was not judged significant considering its expanded responsibilities.

The focus on UNEP functions in this discussion does not obscure the fact that UNEP is only one structure within the broad global environmental regime, and but one of a number of international organizations, including the UN General Assembly and ECOSOC, having environmental functions. Most regime participants have no direct connection with UNEP. The UN Conference on Environment and Development, a highly publicized environmental meeting, was called by the UN General Assembly and had a structure quite distinct from UNEP. Although it owed something to UNEP initiative and to the international currents that UNEP had helped set in motion, UNCED drew its support and character from many different sources, governmental and nongovernmental. Indeed, while UNCED was meeting in Rio, nearly four thousand NGOs from 153 countries held their own parallel global forum at a nearby seaside park. This was symbolic of the array of participants in the regime, ranging from the fringes to the very core of the environmental movement.

UNEP occupies a special place in the development of the expanded environmental regime. Its mission has been that of communicator, educator, propagator, coordinator, and broker. If important change is to occur, it will be made possible by those who have the resources. UNEP thus has aimed at creating a regime within which the resources of others can be mobilized in support of environmental preservation. To accomplish this goal it has worked with environmental personnel in other international organizations to develop shared goals and perspectives, and often, joint activities. Even more important, UNEP has cultivated national constituencies in member states drawn from the scientific community, interested NGOs, and public officials with environmental responsibilities. By creating links with national groups and promoting international contacts among those groups, UNEP has helped to develop shared norms and expectations consonant with its own. At the national level, this transnational constituency has become an effective force in advising and persuading national governments to support UNEP activities. Although environmental activities are generally the work of other actors, UNEP, through its broker-communicator role, has played a crucial part in shaping the regime.

### Environmental Emergencies and Natural Disasters

In the matter of responding to natural disasters and environmental emergencies, the United Nations has developed an elaborate set of interlocking institutions that work within the UN Office for the Coordination of Humanitarian Affairs (OCHA). OCHA has the unique mandate of coordinating and mobilizing assistance within the international community to respond to various types of emergencies. OCHA's Disaster Response Branch functions every day all year and is responsible for an emergency hotline and operates a series of regional centers that develop situation reports for immediate action. Cash grants can be made available to governments confronted by crisis conditions, and UN Disaster Management Teams can be deployed to lend their expertise. A Military and Civil Defense Unit can activate aircraft and ships and call for the use of decontamination facilities (especially in nuclear, chemical, and biological crises) when needed. Field hospitals are also at the disposal of OCHA's military and civil defense units. With its Operation Coordination Center located in Geneva, Switzerland, and direct contact maintained with UN headquarters in New York, OCHA commands sufficient resources to function anywhere in the world. Moreover, OCHA links with the UN Disaster Assessment and Coordination Team, the latter a group of highly qualified and specially trained emergency management experts, and OCHA's own Disaster Response Branch on permanent standby for rapid activation. The latter team can be sent to a troubled area within hours of an emergency call. UNEP staff was added to this response team in 2000. Disasters usually require multidisciplinary efforts, and it is OCHA's job to promote interagency missions. Joint partnering with UNEP has led to the creation of a Joint UNEP/OCHA Environment Unit, situated in OCHA's Disaster Response Branch with ties to UNEP headquarters in Nairobi, Kenya. This combination has allowed the Unit to take advantage of the array of environmental expertise available in UNEP. In 2001 and 2002 plans moved forward for the formal training of UNEP staff for greater and more integrated involvement with the UN Disaster Assessment and Coordination Team. This successful UNEP/OCHA alliance serves as an important example of positive cooperation and collaboration between UN agencies.

## The Environment and Sustainable Development

Many challenges face the world community in the twenty-first century, but none is more important than achieving sustainable equilibrium between developing national economies, reducing poverty, promoting distributive justice, and protecting the planet's resources, commons, and life-support systems. The Nineteenth Special Session of the General Assembly in 1997 underscored the obstacles in achieving cooperation on existing agreements, especially measures outlined during the Earth Summit. Nevertheless, since 1992 there has been a proliferation of new actors in the area of environment and sustainable development that has expanded the base of participation in the United Nations. The world is becoming increasingly more urban, and the future of cities and towns will be determined through a synthesis of environmental, social, and economic development issues. The UN Commission on Sustainable Development has become the central forum for a plethora of specialized agencies seeking answers to questions of balance and harmonization. Moreover, from their joint endeavor have come many international environmental conventions, autonomous governing bodies, and secretariats.

But despite this dynamism and achievement, the overall record is not entirely positive. Need of developing countries for financial resources have not been met, and Official Development Assistance from donor governments in the developed world has in fact declined since the Rio Summit. The Global Environmental Facility, which is concerned with sustainable development projects, has not been adequately funded. And while UNEP and the World Bank devote considerably more resources to projects and programs associated with sustainable development and private or voluntary investment in such activities is also increasing, little progress has been made in creating innovative sources of financing for the future. What is needed is a more integrated systemic approach throughout the whole range of UN activities. Such a development requires closer interaction between UNEP and the UN Commission on Human Settlements. Also involved is the Inter-Agency Committee on Sustainable Development, which includes UNEP and the UN Center for Human Settlements (Habitat), as well as the Governing Council of UNEP and the Commission on Human Settlements that reports to the UN General Assembly.

The World Summit on Sustainable Development was held in Johannesburg, South Africa, in 2002, ten years after the 1992 Earth Summit in Rio de Janeiro. Its purpose was to reinvigorate sustainable development activities in the wake of ever deepening poverty and environmental degradation. The conference set new targets and new timetables, and the conferees generally agreed to take up the challenge with renewed vigor; yet even the basic steps were not taken. Seeking to move the issue away from governmental organizations and toward NGOs, treaty making was deemphasized for new and workable partnerships of the committed. But it was all too obvious that other pressing matters distracted the major actors, and in an environment of economic decline there was little in the way of resources to match the enthusiasm for the challenges that lay ahead.

UNEP, however, remained the environmental voice of the United Nations and the principal source of information for the UN Commission on Sustainable Development. The Nairobi Declaration adopted by the UNEP Governing Council in 1997 called for strengthening UNEP as the world community's coordination center on environmental issues. Only UNEP has the worldwide capacity to monitor and assess environmental matters through its several programs. So too, UNEP is the central agency concerned with the development of policy and law on environmental questions. It is also the bridge between science and policymaking and maintains an active association with national environmental organizations and agencies. UNEP therefore has been at the center of negotiations that have resulted in the drafting of important treaties that are related to the environment and sustainable development. Providing the world community with improved access to genuine environmental data and information, UNEP helps governments use environmental information for making decisions and planning actions for sustainable development.

## THE LAW OF THE SEA

The oceans constitute 70 percent of the earth's surface. In the past most of this area has been open to all states, but recent developments in the law of the sea have increased national control over large parts of world's waters. Most important are the rules expanding the breadth of the state's territorial sea, the creation of "exclusive economic zones" out to two hundred miles from a country's coastline, and the extension of national control over seabed resources. To stem these developments, efforts have been made to establish a form of world control over the open ocean seabed that is currently beyond national jurisdiction, a regime that states are most unwilling to accept anywhere else on earth. This latter issue is more than just a rule-making exercise to help regulate matters of technical, social, and economic interest. It is truly an experiment in peaceful political and territorial change that separates the global commons from notions of state sovereignty.

In centuries past the oceans were used for two main purposes—navigation and fishing. Although specific disputes over fisheries and navigation rights sometimes arose, the oceans were treated for the most part as a global commons not subject to the control of any single state. With the increased use of the oceans, made possible by new technology, the twentieth century saw a rising demand from states to extend national control over larger and larger ocean areas, as well as the seabed. While oil and fisheries have provided the primary motivation, the extension of national jurisdiction to areas that were formerly part of the high seas has had a considerable effect on navigation rights. In addition, intensive use of new technologies by contemporary seafarers creates problems of depleted fish supplies and increased maritime pollution.

These and other ocean problems have been attacked in a number of international forums. The International Maritime Organization (formerly known as the Intergovernmental Maritime Consultative Organization), founded in 1948 as a UN specialized agency, has produced important treaties dealing with maritime safety and pollution. UNEP encourages global and regional agreements to preserve the ocean environment. The UNESCO-sponsored Intergovernmental Oceanographic Commission promotes and coordinates scientific research, monitoring of the oceans, and international exchange of oceanographic data. The Food and Agriculture Organization also conducts research and provides technical assistance on fish as a food resource. The International Labor Organization makes recommendations and sponsors conventions dealing with maritime labor conditions. The International Whaling Commission, through international agreement, negotiations, and economic pressures exerted by sympathetic states, tries to preserve existing stocks of whales from extinction.

### Early Treaty-Drafting Conferences

While the attack on maritime-related problems has been highly splintered, by far the most ambitious effort to establish rules for the use of the oceans has occurred in UN-sponsored treaty-drafting conferences. As early as 1930 an international conference at The Hague tried to codify the law of the sea in treaty form but failed to reach agreement. In 1958 a UN Conference on the Law of the Sea (UNCLOS I) was more successful, producing four multilateral treaties: the Convention on the Territorial Sea and the Contiguous Zone, the Convention on the High Seas, the Convention on the Continental Shelf, and the Convention on Fishing and Conservation of the Living Resources of the High Seas. Each treaty entered into force among the ratifying states during the 1960s. Although the treaties codified much of the existing law of the sea, important issues remained unresolved, including the breadth of the territorial sea and the extent of coastal state jurisdiction over fishing rights.

The conventions on the territorial sea and the contiguous zone, the high seas, and fisheries addressed problems that had been at the heart of ocean law for centuries and codified long-standing rules of customary international law, adapted to modern circumstances. Jurisdiction over the continental shelf, on the other hand, was a new issue because technology had only recently made possible the exploitation of oil resources in subterranean areas of the ocean floor. The United States started the rush toward national jurisdiction with President Harry Truman's September 1945 proclamation claiming control over the natural resources of the seabed and subsoil of the U.S. continental shelf. Many states followed suit, and the 1958 convention embodied these claims in treaty law. The convention was extremely generous to coastal states, recognizing jurisdiction as far out as developing technology might permit exploitation of seabed resources.

A second UN conference (UNCLOS II), held in 1960, was unable to agree on disputed issues, and in subsequent years national jurisdiction over the oceans continued to expand. Several states, most of them in Latin America, went so far as to claim a territorial sea of two hundred miles, which included control over navigation as well as ocean and seabed resources. Others claimed an economic zone of varying distances that would not impinge on navigation rights.

## UNCLOS III

Faced with such diverse and extensive claims to national jurisdiction, the United Nations called a third UN Conference on the Law of the Sea (UNCLOS III). The initial impetus for this renewed UN effort is traceable to a remarkable speech before the 1967 General Assembly by Ambassador Arvid Pardo of Malta. The need for greater uniformity was obvious. The need to reconcile coastal state jurisdictional claims with flag state claims to "freedom of the seas" and every state's interest in what was left of the "global commons" was also apparent. The genius of Pardo's appeal was to join these concerns with the special needs of developing countries for additional sources of financial aid. To achieve these purposes, he proposed to set fixed limits to national jurisdiction and to declare the resources of the seabed and ocean floor beyond those limits "the common heritage of mankind." This common heritage would be managed by a seabed authority empowered to exploit its resources on behalf of all people, with particular emphasis on the needs of developing countries.

Preparations for the conference lasted six years, and drafting the convention took another nine years, from the first brief session held in December 1973 to the closing session in 1982. The new treaty embraced, modified, and amplified the four treaties drafted in 1958 at UNCLOS I. It also added important new provisions on exclusive economic zones, the rights of landlocked states, a regime for the common area beyond national jurisdiction, preservation of the marine environment, marine scientific research, and machinery for the settlement of disputes arising under the treaty.

A number of notable changes from previous law are written into the treaty. The breadth of the territorial sea, previously claimed at 3, 4, 6, 12, and up to 200 miles by different states, and not specified in the 1958 convention, was fixed at 12 miles, with an additional 12 miles of contiguous zone for enforcing regulations against smuggling. The 1958 convention set the contiguous zone at 12 miles from the coastline. The convention also provided an exclusive economic zone extending 200 miles from the coastline, in which coastal states had control over the economic resources of the sea and the subsoil beneath, but not jurisdiction over navigation. A limit was also put on the breadth of the continental shelf. Although various methods of calculation were given, coastal states were guaranteed jurisdiction over the seabed to a distance of 200 nautical miles, with a maximum in some cases of 350 miles. Any minerals extracted from the continental shelf beyond 200 miles were subject to a royalty, paid to an international authority, primarily for the benefit of developing states. The dispute settlement provisions were also noteworthy. Disputes arising under the law of the sea that were not settled by agreement were to be submitted to binding arbitration or judicial procedures. An International Tribunal for the Law of the Sea was created for that purpose.

The most controversial provisions turned out to be those setting aside the ocean floor beyond national jurisdiction (called the "Area") as the common heritage of humanity and creating an International Seabed Authority to administer it. Under the terms of the treaty, governments and private firms may obtain licenses to conduct mining operations in the Area, subject to fees, royalties, and production regulations. The Authority was also empowered to engage in undersea mining through an operating agency known as the Enterprise, and, as a condition to receiving the permit, national licensees must share technology with the Enterprise and give it first choice of mining tracts to exploit. The Authority was to be an autonomous international organization with its own assembly, council, and secretariat, governed by majority vote. A degree of minority protection was provided through requirements for extraordinary majorities on some issues.

Although the United States had earlier indicated that it would accept the seabed provisions of the treaty as part of the overall law of the sea package, the Reagan administration expressed reservations about the Seabed Authority and subsequently refused to sign the convention. The United States objected to the burdensome regulation of private corporations engaged in seabed mining, particularly the costs involved and production limits designed to protect land-based producers of the same minerals. The United States also feared being outvoted on critical issues by the Third World majority. Finally, there was concern that treaty amendment provisions might be used to exclude private enterprise entirely.

Despite this controversy, however, the Law of the Sea Convention represented the most ambitious scheme of codification and progressive development of international law ever attempted. New limits on the breadth of the territorial sea were assured. So too were the rules pertaining to exclusive economic zones. The right of transit through international straits that fell within national jurisdictions also was upheld. In accordance with the provisions of Article 308, the Convention entered into force on November 16, 1994, having acquired the necessary sixty formal state ratifications, although the United States was not one of them. The entry into force of the UN Convention on the Law of the Sea and the Agreement relating to the implementation of Part XI of the Convention caused the United Nations to redesign its program of information, advice, and assistance in this area. The UN Office of Legal Affairs assisted the various institutions created by the Convention, including the Commission on the Limits of the Continental Shelf, which held its initial meeting in June 1997. Moreover, the International Seabed Authority completed its initial organizational work and began to function in 1997, as did the International Tribunal for the Law of the Sea, which opened for serious business in 1998.

The United Nations celebrated the twentieth anniversary of the Convention of the Law of the Sea in 2002, by which time it had achieved near universality with 157 signatories and 138 states as ratified parties. The United States continued to avoid ratification of the document but agreed to adhere to most of its provisions. For the United Nations the Convention is a model in international treaty making, especially in regard to efforts at safeguarding the world's common resources and regulating the use of the high seas for the collective good of all peoples.

# INFORMATION AND PROMOTION

Every international organization gathers and disseminates information. This is an inevitable by-product of meetings, but it is also done systematically. Many organizations sponsor research in their technical areas and hold conferences for the exchange of information among scholars and experts, including representatives of governments and private groups. Many collect and publish statistical data supplied by research or by their members. All publish various reports of their activities.

## DAYS, YEARS, DECADES, AND WORLD CONFERENCES

International agencies also engage in promotional activities. Secretariats carry on various public information programs designed not only to inform but also to persuade. Speeches made in deliberative bodies have the same objectives. Although efforts at international consciousness-raising and promotion of worthy causes have become commonplace in international organizations, certain techniques repeatedly used by the United Nations merit special emphasis. They are the "day," the "week," the "year," the "decade," and the "world conference." (See Table 9-2.)

UN-sponsored days have become legion. Without being exhaustive, a representative list includes the International Day for the Elimination of Racial Discrimination (March 21), the International Day of Innocent Children Victims of Aggression (June 4), World Environment Day (June 5), the International Day Against Drug Abuse and Illicit Trafficking (June 26), International Literacy Day (September 8), International Peace Day (third Tuesday of September), World AIDS Day (December 1), Human Rights Day (December 10), International Day for Biological Diversity (December 29), and, of course, United Nations Day (October 24). The list of weeks is shorter but includes the Week of Solidarity with the Peoples Struggling against Racism and Racial Discrimination (beginning March 21) and Disarmament Week (October 24–30).

Nearly every year is now set aside for the promotion of some worthy cause. Thus 1990 was designated by the General Assembly as International Literacy Year, 1992 as International Space Year, 1993 as the International Year for the World's Indigenous Peoples, and 1994 as the International Year of the Family. The "decade" usually involves a more ambitious undertaking, with proposals for programs to achieve the purposes of the decade and periodic reports on progress. The first such decade was the UN Development Decade, 1961–70. The 1970s were subsequently declared the Second Development Decade, the 1980s the Third, and the 1990s the Fourth. The 1970s and the 1980s were also designated disarmament decades. A Decade to Combat Racism and Racial Discrimination was launched in 1973, and a Second Decade to Combat Racism in 1983. A UN Decade for Women was inaugurated in 1976, and in 1981 an International Drinking Water Supply and Sanitation Decade. A UN Decade of Disabled Persons began in 1983 and a World Decade for Cultural Development in 1988. The 1990s, in addition to the Fourth Development Decade, were also set aside for a Third Disarmament Decade, a UN Decade for International Law, an International Decade for the Eradication of Colonialism, and an International Decade for Natural Disaster Reduction. In 2003 the United Nations launched the Literacy Decade, noting that the matter was a part of the unfinished business of the twentieth century.

The world conference approach has already been noted in Chapter 3 in connection with the involvement of private groups with international organizations. Here we emphasize that UN-sponsored world conferences since the early 1970s—on such subjects as the environment, population, human rights, women, housing, energy resources, refugees, and development—have been staged primarily to raise the level of knowledge and international concern. Such meetings have the advantage of focusing on a single subject, commonly for two weeks or longer, and the governmental delegations are more heavily weighted with technical experts than generalist diplomats.

Secretary-General Kofi Annan's call for a Peoples' Millennium Assembly

Table 9-2  UN World Conferences, Decades, Years, Weeks, and Annual Days

| Date | Event |
|------|-------|
| **World Conferences** | |
| 1998 | World Conference on International Cooperation of Cities and Citizens for Cultivating an Eco-Society |
| 1998 | United Nations Diplomatic Conference of Plenipotentiaries on the Establishment of an International Criminal Court |
| 1999 | Third United Nations Conference on the Exploration and Peaceful Uses of Outer Space (UNISPAC III) |
| 2000 | Review Conference of the States Parties to the Treaty on the Non-Proliferation of Nuclear Weapons (NPT) |
| 2000 | Second World Conference on Natural Disaster Reduction |
| 2000 | Tenth United Nations Congress on the Prevention of Crime and the Treatment of Offenders |
| 2001 | World Conference on Racism and Racial Discrimination, Xenophobia and Related Intolerance |
| 2001 | Third United Nations Conference on the Least Developed Countries |
| **International Decades and Years** | |
| 1990s | International Decade for Natural Disaster Reduction |
| 1990s | Third Disarmament Decade |
| 1990–1999 | United Nations Decade of International Law |
| 1990–2000 | International Decade for the Eradication of Colonialism |
| 1991–2000 | Fourth United Nations Development Decade |
| 1991–2000 | Second Transport and Communications Decade in Africa |
| 1991–2000 | United Nations Decade against Drug Abuse |
| 1993–2002 | Second Industrial Development Decade for Africa |
| 1993–2002 | Asian and Pacific Decade of Disabled Persons |
| 1993–2003 | Third Decade to Combat Racism and Racial Discrimination |
| 1994–2004 | International Decade of the World's Indigenous People |
| 1995–2004 | United Nations Decade for Human Rights Education |
| 1997–2006 | United Nations Decade for the Eradication of Poverty |
| 1998 | International Year of the Ocean |
| 1998 | Fiftieth Anniversary of the Universal Declaration of Human Rights |
| 1999 | International Year of Older Persons |
| 1999 | Centennial of the First International Peace Conference |
| 2000 | International Year for the Culture of Peace |
| 2000 | International Year of Thanksgiving |
| 2001 | International Year of Volunteers |
| 2003 | United Nations Decade of Literacy |
| **Annual Days and Weeks** | |
| 8 March | United Nations Day for Women's Rights and International Peace |
| 21 March | International Day for the Elimination of Racial Discrimination |
| 21 March | Beginning Week of Solidarity with the Peoples Struggling against Racism and Racial Discrimination |
| 22 March | World Day for Water |
| 23 March | World Meteorological Day |
| 7 April | World Health Day |
| 23 April | World Book and Copyright Day |

TABLE 9-2    *(continued)*

| DATE | EVENT |
|---|---|
| ANNUAL DAYS AND WEEKS | |
| 3 May | World Press Freedom Day |
| 15 May | International Day of Families |
| 17 May | World Telecommunication Day |
| 25 May | Beginning Week of Solidarity with the Peoples of All Colonial Territories Fighting for Freedom, Independence and Human Rights |
| 31 May | World No-Tobacco Day |
| 4 June | International Day of Innocent Children Victims of Aggression |
| 5 June | World Environment Day |
| 17 June | World Day to Combat Desertification and Drought |
| 26 June | International Day against Drug Abuse and Illicit Trafficking |
| 26 June | International Day in Support of Victims of Torture |
| 1st Saturday of July | International Day of Cooperatives |
| 11 July | World Population Day |
| 9 August | International Day of the World's Indigenous People |
| 8 September | International Literacy Day |
| 16 September | International Day for the Preservation of the Ozone Layer |
| 3rd Tuesday of September | International Day of Peace |
| Last week in September | World Maritime Day |
| 1 October | International Day of Older Persons |
| 1st Monday of October | World Habitat Day |
| 9 October | World Post Day |
| 2nd Wednesday of October | International Day for Natural Disaster Reduction |
| 16 October | World Food Day |
| 17 October | International Day for the Eradication of Poverty |
| 24 October | United Nations Day |
| 24 October | World Development Information Day |
| 24–30 October | Disarmament Week |
| 16 November | International Day for Tolerance |
| 20 November | Africa Industrialization Day |
| 20 November | Universal Children's Day |
| 21 November | World Television Day |
| 29 November | International Day of Solidarity with the Palestinian People |
| 1 December | World AIDS Day |
| 2 December | International Day for the Abolition of Slavery |
| 3 December | International Day of Disabled Persons |
| 5 December | International Volunteer Day for Economic and Social Development |
| 7 December | International Civil Aviation Day |
| 10 December | Human Rights Day |
| 29 December | International Day for Biological Diversity |

SOURCE: UN Publications Service (http://www.un.org/events/refpap37.htm).

organized around the General Assembly session of the year 2000 captured the attention and provoked the imaginations of creative thinkers all over the world. His desire to enlist the services of NGOs representing the "peoples' interests" was honored. The building of global civil society, intimately linked with the organs of the United Nations, was a major pursuit that received the sanction of the member states but unfortunately suffered a significant setback after the events of September 11, 2001. Nonetheless, all world conferences, let alone the Peoples' Millennium Assembly, speak to the higher ideals of the United Nations and are often preceded by extensive preparation that normally includes negotiations on agreements or declarations to be approved at the different conferences. The Millennium Assembly, however, stands out because it attempted to lower the threshold for a broad range of popular representation by combining government bureaucracies with private organizations across a variety of social and economic sectors.

## EDUCATION, SCIENCE, AND CULTURE

Among international organizations the UN Educational, Scientific and Cultural Organization (UNESCO) has a special responsibility for the dissemination of information. Its activities are wide-ranging, which has been a source of both weakness and strength. The strength comes from the capacity to appeal to and gain support from many governmental and private constituencies with an interest in one or more of UNESCO's activities. The weakness lies in the dispersion of effort and the limited effects that result from spreading limited resources over a wide area.

A large share of UNESCO's resources has been devoted to technical assistance in education, particularly in programs for the elimination of illiteracy and for training in basic vocational skills essential to economic development. UNESCO had primary responsibility for organizing activities associated with the 1990 International Literacy Year and the 2003 Literacy Decade. In addition, UNESCO provides technical assistance for the promotion of the natural sciences and, to a lesser extent, the social sciences, the humanities, mass communication, and the development and preservation of national cultural heritages. It also promotes intergovernmental cooperation in research relating to the environmental sciences and natural resources. All of these programs are slanted heavily toward the needs of developing countries, and most are undertaken with financial assistance from the UN Development Program.

UNESCO has also produced a number of treaties in areas of concern to it, including an International Convention for the Protection of the World Cultural and National Heritage. It also is responsible for the Universal Copyright Convention; the Convention on the Free Flow of Educational, Scientific and Cultural Materials; and the Convention Against Discrimination in Education.

The strictly informational activities of UNESCO cover a staggering variety of topics. Titles in the catalog of UNESCO and UNESCO-sponsored publications number in the thousands. Periodical publications range in scope from the

UNESCO *Courier* (topical themes and events of popular interest) to the *International Social Science Journal, Diogenes* (humanities), *Nature and Resources, Prospects* (education), and *Museum.* These titles are illustrative, not exhaustive. Other publications include bibliographies, reports, histories (for instance, the multivolume *History of Africa* and *History of the Scientific and Cultural Development of Mankind*). It also has produced translations of literary masterpieces and special studies on all manner of subjects within UNESCO's areas of interest, as well as valuable statistical documentation in education, the social sciences, library services, mass communication, and other disciplines.

Another important informational activity, often fostered by means of conferences, is the promotion of interchange among scientists, scholars, and artists. To further this interchange, UNESCO has encouraged the formation of international professional societies and has often supported them through financial subventions. Scholarships and fellowships, educational exchange, elimination of barriers to the free flow of information, and improvement of mass communication systems are other elements of the UNESCO approach to dissemination of information. If UNESCO falls short in its efforts to spread education, science, and culture, it is not from lack of variety in its methods.

With such broad objectives, UNESCO's reach has necessarily exceeded its grasp. Falling short of goals need not bring a negative assessment; the task may simply be larger than the available resources. UNESCO has undoubtedly promoted the production and exchange of information in its various areas of activity, and its technical assistance programs have added something to national resources for education and development. Critics, nevertheless, have faulted the diffusion of its efforts and have suggested that it might have greater influence if its focus were sharper.

In response to these criticisms, UNESCO has tried to set priorities, but the pressures for diffusion of its efforts have been irresistible. First of all, its mandate is very broad—education, science, and culture can be construed to embrace almost anything—and the UNESCO Constitution posits the additional goal of contributing to a more peaceful world. Second, UNESCO constituencies—governmental and private—provide constant pressure for the continuation or addition of programs that have some benefit for them. For two decades or more, the Director-General of UNESCO has predominated in setting the direction for UNESCO's programs, and he is responsive to the groups that support him. These include scientists, scholars, and other private beneficiaries of UNESCO programs and, more important, the prevailing Third World majority in the UNESCO general conference and executive board, whose interests lie in expanding programs. A third reason for diffusion is UNESCO's bureaucracy, with its vested interest in proliferation and expansion. A reversal of the trend would cost some officials their jobs, while others might lose perquisites and prestige in the constituent communities they serve.

For the developed countries that pay most of the bills, the growth of UNESCO budgets has been a greater source of dissatisfaction than the abstract question of how many programs are too many. The United States, in particular, objected to budgetary increases during the 1970s and early 1980s, claiming that the UNESCO Director-General and his staff were not exercising proper restraint and that the UNESCO council and general conference were not holding him sufficiently accountable. Other problems also seriously eroded U.S. support for UNESCO. From the mid-1970s onward, the United States persistently objected to the "politicization" of UNESCO—particularly as expressed in Arab-sponsored resolutions criticizing Israel for its archaeological activity in Jerusalem or its educational policies in the West Bank. Washington vehemently objected to the attempt to isolate and exclude Israel from participation in UNESCO.

The United States also complained that UNESCO laid emphasis on group rights or "peoples rights," such as self-determination, at the expense of individual rights. A related U.S. concern was the Third World demand for a New International Information Order. The New Order was supposed to redress the imbalance and distortion in the movement of world information alleged to result from control of world news and information channels by the developed states and their powerful media organizations. The United States, in part, was concerned that the New International Information Order gave too much power to state-run media outlets and would legitimize greater government control over the global news media. In general, U.S. actions and opposition were not appreciated by a majority of UNESCO members, and during the Reagan presidency this ongoing quarrel caused Washington to reconsider its options.

On December 28, 1983, the United States informed the 161-member UNESCO body that it would withdraw at the end of the twelve-month period required by Charter law. Washington accused UNESCO of anti-American and anti-Western policies, but it was equally severe in its condemnation of the organ's financial and budgetary operations. The United States formally announced its withdrawal from UNESCO on December 19, 1984. (This was not the first and only instance of state dissatisfaction with the UN organ; there have been ten withdrawals and seven reentries since the creation of UNESCO.) The absence of the United States did not affect UNESCO's other members, however. Membership swelled to 188 member states and 4 associate members by 2002.

The aloofness of the United States meant a loss of almost 25 percent of UNESCO's budget, but the council made up much of the deficit by introducing a new schedule of payments that called for an increase in contributions by the member states. By 1998, Japan and Germany met the challenge and became the largest contributors to UNESCO. UNESCO's annual budget did not increase in the next six years, and staff and projects were reduced to meet the shortfall in revenue. Additional funding, however, was made available from several other UN programs and funds. Along with additional contributions from international regional banks and voluntary contributions, UNESCO sustained its activities. By the end of the century, UNESCO had authorized expenditures to education, the natural sciences, culture, communication and information, and social and human sciences. Despite budgetary challenges, UNESCO has remained a vital organization, sponsoring nearly five thousand grassroots clubs, associations, and centers that promote its ideals and perform unofficial tasks.

Although many in the U.S. Congress remained philosophically at odds with UNESCO, in September 2002 President Bush declared that the United States would resume its role in UNESCO. In 2001, Congress had urged the president to rejoin UNESCO and authorized $60 million in back dues payments. President Bush's announcement therefore was somewhat expected. With the United States once more onboard, in April 2003 the 166th session of UNESCO's Executive Board called for the first breakthrough budget in many years. Citing the war in Iraq and UNESCO's need to participate in the reconstruction of the Arab country, the 2004–05 budget was placed at $610 million, the largest in the organization's history.

## OTHER INFORMATION ACTIVITIES

Other international organizations also render informational services on which governments, businesses, the professions, and others throughout the world have come to rely. The Statistical Office of the United Nations, for example, publishes a number of annual basic reference works, including the *Statistical Yearbook,* the *Demographic Yearbook,* the *Yearbook of International Trade Statistics,* *World Energy Supplies,* and the *Yearbook of National Accounts Statistics.* The *UN Chronicle,* published quarterly (monthly before 1986) by the UN Department of Public Information, contains a review of major UN activities during the preceding quarter. The United Nations also issues periodicals on special subjects such as the *International Review of Criminal Policy* and the *International Social Service Review.* These and other regular UN publications are supplemented by numerous special reports. The specialized agencies likewise produce a multitude of facts in their own areas of competence and interest. When publications are considered together with the many conferences, seminars, and other meetings whose primary function is the spreading of knowledge, the informational services of the United Nations assume a wide scope indeed.

Units within the United Nations having special informational responsibilities include the UN Department of Public Information (DPI), the UN Institute for Training and Research (UNITAR), and the United Nations University. The DPI, with its information centers in many countries, supplies UN publications to the world and carries on a variety of public relations activities designed to present the organization in its most favorable light. In addition to the printed word, the DPI produces programs and public service advertisements for radio and television. UNITAR, established by the General Assembly in 1963, trains individuals for work in economic and social development and conducts training seminars for national government personnel concerned with the work of the United Nations. Its most visible activity is the publication of special studies undertaken by UNITAR staff, often in collaboration with visiting scholars. Since 1975 the United Nations University, with headquarters in Tokyo, has attempted to stimulate research on world problems and has provided fellowships for postgraduate training in collaboration with national research institutes and universities. It has established its own research and training centers, working through networks of cooperating institutions. Both UNITAR and the United Nations

University serve as links between the United Nations and the international academic community.

# INTERNATIONALLY ADMINISTERED PROGRAMS

International organizations widely use technical assistance to promote economic, social, and technical goals. (See Table 9-3 for a list of contemporary international organizations.) Reference has already been made to the technical assistance programs of the WHO and UNESCO in areas of their special interest, as well as to UN and ILO assistance in promoting human rights. While some organizations, such as the WHO, UNESCO, the ILO, and the Food and Agriculture Organization, have large programs of technical assistance, nearly every UN specialized agency offers technical assistance of some sort, financed variously from its regular budget, the UN Development Program, voluntary contributions, and other sources. Chapter 10 will discuss aid to developing countries in detail. Here we confine our examination to programs of international organizations for the aid of refugees and other people in need of emergency relief.

## EMERGENCY RELIEF

Since World War II international organizations have been continuously involved in programs for the relief of people in distress. If League of Nations efforts to protect refugees during the interwar years are included, the period of continuous involvement begins even earlier. Although the long-term problems of economic development absorb the greater part of UN resources, the organization and its related agencies have compiled a substantial record of accomplishment in meeting the short-term needs of selected groups of people in distress.

### UN Relief and Rehabilitation Administration

A direct forerunner of UN programs was the UN Relief and Rehabilitation Administration (UNRRA), an agency of the wartime United Nations that operated from November 1943 until it was disbanded in June 1947. During this period UNRRA expended nearly $4 billion, and at the peak of its activity it employed 27,800 people. The initiative and planning and 70 percent of the funds came from the United States, but the implementation involved the concerted action of many governments. Food, clothing, and medicine supplied by UNRRA filled a critical need for millions in Europe and Asia. In China alone, direct food relief was provided to an estimated ten million people. The process of rehabilitation also extended to the revival of agricultural and industrial production and to the support of public health programs, public education, and other social services. In addition, UNRRA assumed the responsibility for the care of millions of refugees and displaced persons.

UNRRA was terminated somewhat precipitately because the U.S. Congress

TABLE 9-3    International Organizations

WORLD ORGANIZATIONS

United Nations
UN Organizations and Affiliated organizations
   UNCTAD—UN Conference on Trade and Development
   UNESCO—UN Educational, Scientific and Cultural Organization
   UNICEF—UN Children's Fund
   FAO—Food and Agricultural Organization
   IAEA—International Atomic Energy Agency
   IBRD—International Bank for Reconstruction and Development
   ICAO—International Civil Aviation Organization
   International Criminal Court
   IDA—International Development Association
   IFC—International Finance Corporation
   ILO—International Labor Organization
   IHO—International Hydrological Organization
   IMO—International Maritime Organization
   IMF—International Monetary Fund
   Interparliamentary Union
   ITU—International Telecommunications Union
   Multinational Force and Observers (Sinai)
   Permanent Court of Arbitration, The Hague
   UNIDO—UN Industrial  Development Organization
   UPU—Universal Postal Union
   World Bank
   WHO—World Health Organization
   WIPO—World Intellectual Property Organization
   WMO—World Meteorological Organization
   WTO—World Trade Organization

OTHER INTERNATIONAL ORGANIZATIONS

ACP—African, Caribbean and Pacific (Lomé) Convention
APEC—Asia-Pacific Economic Cooperation
ATTAC—Association pour une Taxation des Transactions financières pour l'Aide aux
   Citoyens
Bureau International des Expositions (World's Fairs)
Commonwealth of Nations
Community of Portuguese-Speaking Countries
Companion Flag Organization
Euro-Atlantic Partnership Council
Explorers Club
Fisheries Inspections Ensigns
Francophonie—the organization of French-speaking countries
G77 Trade Information Network
IBI—Intergovernmental Bureau for Informatics
International Children's Day
International Committee of the Red Cross
International Co-operative Alliance
International Democrat Union
International Federation of Red Cross and Red Crescent Societies

(continued)

Table 9-3    *(continued)*

## Other International Organizations

International Gastronomy Flag
International Human Rights Campaign
International Union of Students
Interpol
Joshua Slocum Society
Max-Planck Gesellschaft (MPG)
Missions to Seafarers
NATO—North Atlantic Treaty Organization
Organization of Islamic Conference
OPEC—Organization of Petroleum Exporting Countries
Organization of World Heritage Cities
PRODOS Institute for Global Freedom Invention & Prosperity
Red Cross/Red Crescent
Rotary International
SOS Children's Villages
St. John's Ambulance
Unrepresented Nations and Peoples Organization
UPAEP—Postal Union of the Americas, Spain and Portugal
World Federation of Democratic Youth
World Service Authority
World Slavic Congress (WSC)
World Tourism Organization
World's Fairs (Bureau International des Expositions, BIE)

## International Sports Organizations

Fédération Internationale de Sport Universitaire (FISU) (International University
    Sports Federation)
IAFC—International Australian Football Confederation
International Blind Sports Federation
IOC—International Olympic Committee
IPC—International Paralympic Committee
PASO—Pan American Sports Association

## Regional Organizations

Europe
    Alps-Adriatic Working Community
    Black Sea Economic Cooperation
    Blue Flag (Beach Quality)
    CEFTA—Central European Free Trade Association
    CIS—Commonwealth of Independent States
    EU—European Union
    Eurocorps
    European Coal and Steel Community
    European Free Trade Association
    European Movement
    European River Commissions

TABLE 9-3   *(continued)*

REGIONAL ORGANIZATIONS

European Southern Observatory
Meuse-Rhine Euregio
NATO—North Atlantic Treaty Organization
Nordic Council
Paneuropa Union
Panceltic flag
WEU—Western European Union

Americas

OAS—Organization of American States
I-ADB—Inter-American Development Bank
CARICOM—Caribbean Community and Common Market
ANDEAN Community
Central American Parliament
Inter American Development Bank (IADB)
MERCOSUR, MERCOSUL (Southern Common Market)
North American Free Trade Area (NAFTA)
Organization of Central American States (ODECA)
Secretariat for Central American Economic Integration (SIECA)
South American Union (Unión Sudamericana)
Southern Common Market (MERCOSUR, MERCOSUL)
West Indies Federation
Yacht Racing Union of the Great Lakes

Africa

AU—African Union
ECOWAS—Economic Community of West African States
Inter Governmental Authority for Development
PATU—Panafrican Telephone Union
SADC—South African Development Community
Union Africaine et Malgache
Union of African States (1958–1962)
Union of Arab Maghreb

Asia

ADB—Asian Development Bank
APEC—Asia-Pacific Economic Cooperation Council
ASEAN—Association of South-East Asian Nations
Colombo Plan

North Africa & Middle East

LAS—League of Arab States
IDB—Islamic Development Bank
GCC—Gulf Cooperation Council
APPA—African Petroleum Producers Association

Oceania

Pacific Community, formerly SPC—South Pacific Commission

SOURCE: http://atlasgeo.span.ch/fotw/flags/flagorgs.html (last modified 14 June 2003).

decided to stop funding the organization. Congressional support had been undermined by persistent charges, not altogether without justification, of UNRRA inefficiencies and "political intrigue," as well as by well-founded suspicions that the Soviet Union was using UNRRA aid to consolidate its hold on Eastern Europe. UNRRA's demise created an alarming gap in the world's machinery for economic and social assistance to the most needy. Therefore, provisions had to be made for the assumption of UNRRA functions by other organizations. At the initiative of the UN General Assembly several important emergency organizations were created. One was the International Refugee Organization, which was established to deal with the refugee problem caused by World War II. Another was the UN International Children's Emergency Fund (UNICEF), which was supported by private donations and voluntary government contributions. It was formed specifically to administer relief programs for children in the war-devastated areas. Matters related to health issues were shifted to the responsibility of the WHO.

## Korean Relief and Reconstruction

War in Korea in the 1950s provided the setting for another UN relief operation of substantial proportions. Under a Security Council authorization the UN unified command administered a $450 million program of civilian and refugee relief. The U.S. government contributed more than $400 million of the total sum, and private U.S. agencies provided about half of the remainder. A longer-range program of reconstruction was authorized in December 1950 by a General Assembly resolution that established the UN Korean Reconstruction Agency (UNKRA). By the time UNKRA operations were phased out in 1960, to be replaced by massive amounts of direct U.S. aid, approximately $150 million had been expended for the rehabilitation of the South Korean economy and public services. The United States limited itself to 65 percent of the total UNKRA budget. Unlike some countries that absorbed large amounts of UN and U.S. aid, South Korea experienced remarkable postwar economic growth and industrialization.

## UN International Children's Emergency Fund

UNICEF was established in 1946 as a temporary organization to administer residual funds left over from UNRRA. Over the years, the approach that was so satisfactory in assisting the children of war-devastated areas also proved useful in tackling the problems of emerging and developing countries. The General Assembly gave UNICEF permanent status in 1953. (The words *International* and *Emergency* were deleted from the title when UNICEF was made permanent, but the acronym UNICEF was retained in preference to the less pronounceable UNCF.) The budget of UNICEF is raised mainly through voluntary government contributions, although a substantial portion comes through private donations and the sale of greeting cards. The fund has its own thirty-nation executive board, elected by ECOSOC, and its Executive Director and staff are a unit of the UN Secretariat.

The program's initial emphasis on emergency supplies of food, clothing, and medicines has shifted toward emphasis on longer-range programs for the benefit of children. UNICEF is still a source of drugs, insecticides, vaccines, and field equipment for disease-control campaigns, as well as food and medical supplies in emergency situations. But it is more than a supply program. UNICEF's grants-in-aid, usually matched by two or three times as much in local funds, are now available to governments for help in planning projects and training national personnel. As a condition of a grant, a government must agree to conduct the program as part of its permanent services wherever the need persists. UNICEF does not operate projects of its own, although it supervises the national programs it sponsors. UNICEF-aided projects are often conducted with the advice and cooperation of such other UN agencies as the WHO, FAO, UNESCO, and the ILO. Joint endeavors have included mass disease control, family education in better nutrition practices, teacher training and the local production of teaching materials, and the establishment of child welfare services. In recent decades UNICEF concentrated attention on programs to reduce infant mortality.

UNICEF still takes on emergency relief assignments. Aided by the International Red Cross, UNICEF coordinated most of the Western humanitarian assistance sent to Cambodia in the wake of its domestic upheavals and the 1978 Vietnamese invasion. In 1989 the UNICEF Executive Director was appointed as the representative of the UN Secretary-General to mobilize emergency aid to people displaced by civil war in the Sudan. But in July 1998, the head of UNICEF was compelled to acknowledge the agency's inadequacy in managing the massive relief operation. Members of the Sudan People's Liberation Army, long at war with the Sudanese government, cited rampant corruption within the aid mission and urged donor nations to investigate claims that Operation Lifeline Sudan, an umbrella organization of the United Nations, had squandered the resources of the mission. UNICEF was accused of failing to administer to the most desperate of Sudan's displaced population, estimated to be as high as 2.6 million. The admission by UNICEF that it had failed to adequately police the distribution of aid and that corrupt officials and dishonest aid handlers had used the assistance for their own purposes raised serious questions about the future of the program. Nonetheless, many selfless and courageous aid givers continued to function in the Sudan as the twenty-year-old conflict continued to take its human toll. For example, in February 2002 Sudanese government helicopters fired on a UN aid-dispensing station and killed seventeen people. UNICEF may have been poorly equipped to deal with the complicated situation in Sudan, but few organizations were prepared to place themselves in so conflicted a region. It was with good reason that UNICEF had received the Nobel Peace Prize in 1965.

Of keen interest to UNICEF was the coming into force in February 2002 of a convention banning the use of children in combat roles. Then in May 2002 the UN General Assembly held a Special Session devoted to children's issues and adopted by consensus an action plan for the promotion of children's health and education, as well as the effort aimed at preventing child abuse and exploitation. A General Assembly Committee on Social and Humanitarian Affairs also passed a resolution calling for the elimination of child labor and the protection of children against torture, sexual abuse, and slavery.

## Disaster Relief

Earthquakes, floods, famines, and other natural disasters have commonly evoked emergency aid from international sources, both public and private. Such aid has necessarily been provided on an ad hoc basis because the precipitating event is always unplanned. As early as 1965 the United Nations provided a small fund for use by the Secretary-General in meeting emergency needs arising from natural disasters. An Office of the Disaster Relief Coordinator (UNDRO) was established in 1971 following a particularly devastating earthquake in Peru and a tidal wave in Bangladesh the preceding year. UNDRO administers a fund for emergency relief, maintained on a continuing basis through voluntary contributions and applied to disasters resulting from both natural and human causes. It also provides planning assistance to prevent and minimize damage in countries subject to recurring normal disasters. UNDRO is not used to administer larger-scale relief operations, however. When famine reached crisis proportions in Ethiopia and other parts of Africa during the 1980s, the Secretary-General created a special Office of Emergency Operations in Africa to mobilize international aid, while UNDRO served a primarily reporting function. In 1991 the General Assembly established the position of UN Emergency Relief Coordinator at the undersecretary level to coordinate the activities of all UN agencies, including UNDRO, concerned with humanitarian emergency assistance.

## Reorganization

In 1997–98, Secretary-General Kofi Annan reorganized UN agencies and programs concerned with a broad range of human needs. His changes focused on making the United Nations leaner and more effective by consolidating several Secretariat bodies and eliminating waste, fraud, and mismanagement. They also involved shifting resources from administration to development and humanitarian needs. At the turn of the century, it was estimated that all the UN funds and programs, including UNICEF, had approximately $5 billion a year to spend on economic and social development, with major concern given to population policies, children, agriculture, food distribution, and refugees. In June 2001, further streamlining was attempted with the creation of the new UN Commission on Human Security. This was an effort to combine under a single unit matters concerned with peace and security, economic and social well-being, sustainable development, human rights, and other goals. A greater sense of coherence was the objective of the reorganization that was to go into effect just as the events of September 11 affected the world body.

## REFUGEES

The fiftieth anniversary of the 1951 UN Refugee Convention was celebrated in 2001. Considered a landmark in international refugee law, its drafters could never have contemplated the sustained and expanding nature of the refugee dilemma fifty years later. Believing they were addressing issues created by two twentieth-century world wars, little could they have known that the world of the twenty-first century would be witness to the largest refugee situation in all of history. Moreover, as funding to international agencies declined, the world was not necessarily able to respond effectively to the plight of millions forced to flee their homes and countries. A reduction to the problem, let alone a solution, did not seem in sight.

### Refugees and the League

In 1921 the League of Nations established the Office of High Commissioner for Refugees as a temporary agency to deal with the influx of nearly two million refugees from the Russian civil war into countries of Eastern and Central Europe. The hard shell of the problem had scarcely been dented when new streams of Greek, Armenian, and Assyrian refugees began to pour out of the tottering Ottoman Empire in 1922. Many years later, the League High Commissioner was still trying to cope with these problems when the Nazi persecutions of the 1930s produced a new flight of refugees from the Saar Valley in Germany as well as Austria and Czechoslovakia. A League agency that was intended to be temporary to meet what were thought to be the immediate needs of people displaced by the Great War quickly assumed the character of a permanent organization.

The homeless multitudes before World War II needed legal and political protection as well as relief and assistance with resettlement. The League High Commissioner and his small staff, however, never had the resources to render direct assistance on a significant scale. With a meager budget they could do little more than serve as an advocate with governments, work for uniform standards of legal protection, give advice to national governments, and attempt to coordinate the efforts of public and private agencies engaged in refugee relief. In the legal field one notable contribution was the Nansen Passport, named after Fridtjof Nansen, the first League High Commissioner. The Nansen Passport was a certificate issued to refugees by a national government on the recommendation of the High Commissioner and served as the equivalent of a regular passport, greatly facilitating refugee travel and resettlement throughout Europe. Though reluctant, many of the European states, especially those still holding colonies after the conflict, permitted the settlement of refugees in their midst, but none of them was prepared for the expression of radical nationalism in countries such as Germany and Austria where racial and ethnic exclusivity had taken hold. The harsh policies of the fascist states added to the dilemma of those seeking treatment for the refugee situation. By the mid-1930s Europe was awash in more refugees than immediately following the close of World War I.

## Refugees and World War II

World War II produced new millions of homeless people in Europe. The responsibility for massive refugee relief and repatriation was initially the responsibility of the military authorities and UNRRA. Of some eight million refugees and displaced persons in Allied-occupied zones at the time of the German surrender in 1945, five to six million were repatriated within a year through the prodigious efforts of military authorities, and numerous others were assimilated or resettled. Before it was phased out, UNRRA repatriated 750,000 additional refugees in the final years of operations.

## The International Refugee Organization

The International Refugee Organization (IRO) began operations in July 1947 as a specialized agency within the United Nations. During its term of existence, which expired in February 1952, the IRO spent nearly $400 million in assisting more than 1.6 million refugees who came under its mandate in Africa, the Americas, Asia, and Europe. Approximately 73,000 were repatriated, and more than 1 million were resettled abroad through the active advocacy and assistance of the IRO. At the termination of the IRO, most of the refugees remaining from its original mandate were the sick, the aged, and the disabled, for whom resettlement was especially difficult. A number of states argued for sustaining the life of IRO. The United States, however, which underwrote more than half of the IRO budget, insisted on the early termination date, claiming that the problem was now small enough to be handled by the countries of asylum and by voluntary organizations.

## The UN High Commissioner

It was in anticipation of the IRO's demise that the General Assembly created the Office of the UN High Commissioner for Refugees (UNHCR). UNHCR was meant to serve as a continuing focus for UN refugee activities.[11] Beginning operations in 1951, the High Commissioner was given the assignment of providing international protection for refugees and helping governments and voluntary organizations find permanent solutions through resettlement and assimilation. The High Commissioner's mandate excluded refugees receiving aid from other UN programs (such as the Palestine refugees) and refugees who have the rights of nationals in the country of asylum (for example, refugees from India to Pakistan, and vice versa). Otherwise the mandate extended to nearly all people outside their country of origin whose "well-founded fear of persecution for reasons of race, religion, nationality, or political opinion" prevents them from seeking the protection of the home country.

The High Commissioner's primary responsibility of providing international protection is carried out by promoting the adoption and supervising the application of international conventions and by encouraging governments to take other measures for the benefit of refugees. Of special importance is the 1951 Convention Relating to the Status of Refugees and its 1967 Protocol, which codified minimum rights in such matters as freedom of religion, access to courts, and the right to work, education, social security, and travel documents. The High Commissioner also provided material assistance to refugees from funds made available by voluntary contributions. States party to the 1951 Convention and/or to the 1967 Protocol numbered 137 in 2002. The number of implementing partners representing NGOs was 453 in 1997. Fifteen major donor countries traditionally have accounted for about 95 percent of UNHCR's total operating budget. UNHCR's expenditures have risen accordingly, from $3.5 million in 1965, to $544 million in 1990, to $900 million the following year, and to more than $1 billion annually since 1992. Nevertheless, the scaling back of donor contributions in 2000 left the UNHCR with a $100 million shortfall in 2001, and the situation has not improved despite the ever-growing numbers of refugees and displaced persons. Indeed, in 2001, the worldwide refugee population increased by approximately 1 million more refugees than in 1999. The refugee population was pegged at 14.5 million worldwide, and in addition to this number reported fleeing across borders, the UNHCR revealed that between 20 and 24 million people were internally displaced within their own countries and suffered the same deprivations as refugees. Adding to this condition were the 1.7 million who accepted voluntary repatriation between 2000 and 2002 but who remained in need of material assistance and security. Thus, by 2002 the total number of refugees in all categories was close to 40 million.

In the 1980s Africa was the locale of major UN refugee relief efforts, with an estimated 3 million refugees in various African countries. Their needs were highlighted by two International Conferences for Assistance to Refugees in Africa, held in 1981 (ICARA I) and 1984 (ICARA II). In a broader perspective, the refugees were simply one highly visible aspect of the emergency brought on by years of extended drought and other natural disasters, political turmoil, and economic mismanagement that had made Africa the object of world concern and concerted relief efforts. ICARA II recognized that the solution to refugee relief was closely tied to the development and revitalization of African economies.

The ensuing years brought no relief from refugee problems, either in Africa or the rest of the world, with the number of refugees growing steadily throughout the 1980s and 1990s and into the new millennium. In 2001 UNHCR estimated that there were 15,000 new refugees every day. Nearly half of the 5.5 million additions were from African countries, although the Philippines and Sri Lanka represented almost 1 million of the total. Some 140 countries were involved in or associated with this expanding and deepening human tragedy.

Thus, what had been envisioned fifty years earlier as a temporary office with a projected life span of three years had become one of the world's principal and permanent humanitarian agencies.

The UNHCR remains based in Geneva, Switzerland, but its offices are located in 115 countries. Moreover, its total force of approximately six thousand are essentially field workers functioning on a day-to-day basis in some of the most isolated, dangerous places in the world and under conditions of enormous stress. It is not surprising that the selfless nature and devotion to duty of the UNHCR workers has twice brought the Nobel Peace Prize to the agency, first in 1954 and again in 1981.

UNHCR's programs are approved and supervised by an Executive Committee composed of fifty member countries. Since the end of the Cold War, the UNHCR has moved beyond its mandate and also provides help to those forced to live in refugee-like situations. This category includes people who have been granted protection on a group basis, for example, the Kurds of northern Iraq; or on purely humanitarian grounds, for example, the Hutu from Rwanda who sought refuge in the former Zaire but who were not formally recognized as refugees. Still another category is displaced people who fled their homes but did not cross an international border. Such victims of civil war, as in Sarajevo and other besieged Bosnian communities, also received assistance from the UNHCR. Nevertheless, the agency is most concerned with people who no longer have the protection of their state and who are often detached from their families and communities of origin, such as the Kosovar Albanians who were subjected to ethnic cleansing in 1999.

UNHCR work is strictly humanitarian and nonpolitical. The agency not only cares for the world's most destitute population, it also guarantees "international protection," which means that no refugee can be involuntarily returned to a country where he or she has reason to fear persecution. UNHCR therefore is more inclined to assist large groups of refugees rather than individual cases. Thus, even the Dayton Peace Accords of 1995 authorized UNHCR to develop the modalities for the return of 2 million refugees and displaced persons that left Bosnia-Herzegovina. But the end of the Cold War not only provoked the breakup of Yugoslavia and the subsequent civil war, it also created the instabilities that forced some 5 million people in Eastern and Central Europe to seek asylum in Western European countries. In the four years of war and ethnic cleansing that consumed regions of the former Yugoslavia, some 3.5 million people received assistance from the UNHCR, 2.7 million in Bosnia-Herzegovina alone. Moreover, after diplomacy failed to resolve the Kosovo dilemma, NATO air attacks against Serbian military installations in March 1999 resulted in the Serbs intensifying their ethnic cleansing campaign against the Albanians living in the region. The flight of hundreds of thousands of Kosovar Albanians to neighboring countries presented still greater problems for the UN relief agencies as well as the international community.

The 1995–96 genocide in Rwanda and Burundi created one of the largest concentrations of refugees, with the UNHCR assisting almost 2 million people who moved to Tanzania and Zaire (now the Republic of the Congo). Between 2000 and 2003, still another million refugees were created by the civil strife in Liberia, Sierra Leone, and the Central African Republic, while hundreds of thousands more were displaced internally. And so the statistics read on and on, including 1.8 million Kurds, tens of thousands of Guatemalans, 800,000 Chechens, 100,000 East Timorese, 100,000 Sri Lankans, 540,000 Colombians, 2.5 million Congolese, the 2 million Afghans still living in Pakistan, and thousands of Tibetans. Nor are peace and tranquillity always the experience of refugees in asylum countries. Sexual violence, exploitation, and other forms of assault shadow the uprooted. UNHCR staff endeavor to shelter refugees from physical harm, but it can only hope to minimize, not eliminate, the horrors.

Nearly two-thirds of all refugees are found in two regions of the world: the Middle East and Africa. The remaining areas are South and Central Asia, Europe, East Asia and the Pacific, and the Americas. Ten countries have produced almost three-quarters of the world's refugees, with forty-two countries producing significant numbers (10,000 or more). The largest refugee population cited by the UNHCR in 2001 was the Palestinians; the next largest was Afghans, with more than 2 million still living in Pakistan from the once higher count of 4 million. These two groups are said to represent more than half of all the refugees but are left out of those listed as displaced persons. (Indeed, the distinction between "refugee" and "displaced person" has never been adequately addressed.) Among countries hosting refugees, high on the list is Yugoslavia. The United States is reported in sixth position, and remaining host countries of note are Guinea, Sudan (paradoxically also a creator of tens of thousands of refugees), Syria, and Lebanon (with another 800,000 Palestinians).

The UNHCR responds to the most desperate of the world's humanity, providing the basics of human survival—shelter, food, water, sanitation, and medical attention. It remains the only beacon of hope for people caught up in circumstances seldom of their own doing. Indeed, the tents made from blue plastic sheeting supplied by UNHCR have become an all-too-familiar symbol of an all-too-large portion of the world's people live under great stress.

Given the ubiquitous and persistent character of the world refugee dilemma, there appears little doubt it will be a major UN concern well into the future. It has therefore been contemplated to establish an early-warning system in which an international presence will be created in areas at risk and before communities are uprooted and opposed positions can no longer be reconciled. In 1998, the UNHCR experimented with a "preventive deployment" posture and dispatched specialist teams to the Central Asian republics of the former Soviet Union, where tensions resulting from independence had caused or threatened to cause fratricidal strife. Acknowledging that the search for long-term solutions was a political matter, to be managed by individual governments, UNHCR sought to purchase the necessary time to allow meaningful negotiations to develop. Where regional organizations are available, UNHCR is pleased to encourage their initiatives; it has been especially supportive in its relations with the Commonwealth of Independent States and the International

TABLE 9-4   Persons of Concern Who Fall under the Mandate of the UNHCR, Estimated Percentages within Total Population* by Region, January 2001

| REGION | PERCENTAGE |
| --- | --- |
| Africa | 38 |
| Middle East | 8 |
| South and Central Asia | 16 |
| Europe | 12 |
| Latin and North America | 8 |
| East Asia | 8 |
| Total* | 34,500,000 |

SOURCE: Compiled from Web site http://www.refugees.org/world/articles/50years_rr01_5.htm.

Note: According to the World Refugee Survey 2001, in 1995 there were approximately 35.6 million refugees worldwide. That number declined to 32.1 million in 1996 and to 29.9 million in 1997. In 1998 the number of refugees increased to 30.4 million, and in 1999 the number jumped to 35.1 million. Given UN projections of increases, notably by the UNHCR, the number of refugees and internally displaced people in 2002–2003 was probably closer to 40 million.

*Total population of all regions, January 2001: 34,500,000

Congress of Central American Refugees. UNHCR also believes it important to monitor the living and working conditions of returnees after repatriation, and community-based projects have been established to repair roads and bridges, increase the availability of clean water, and improve education and health care. Tools and seed packets also are distributed to resettled farmers to help reactivate the largely agricultural economies as well as help replenish the local food supply. (See Table 9-4 and Table 9-5.)

*Palestinian Refugees*

Since 1949 a UN Relief and Works Agency for Palestine Refugees in the Near East (UNRWA) has cared for Arab refugees of the several Arab-Israeli wars. Over the years it has absorbed more money than any other refugee program administered by the United Nations. Earlier organizations like UNRRA and the IRO had a modicum of satisfaction when refugee groups were reduced as a consequence of repatriation, resettlement, and assimilation. But UNRWA, which started with the approximately 900,000 Arabs that fled their homes during the first Arab-Israeli War in 1948–49, in 2003 claimed responsibility for more than 4 million people. Of these, approximately 1.7 million were in Jordan, 1.5 million in Gaza and the West Bank, and some 800,000 roughly divided between Lebanon and Syria (see Table 9-5). UNRWA education, health, relief, and social

TABLE 9-5    UNRWA Statistics for Distribution of Palestinian Registered Refugees by
Country and Area as of June 30, 2003

| LOCATION | | PERSONS | BABIES | FAMILIES |
|---|---|---|---|---|
| West Bank | Jericho | 16,656 | 296 | 3,659 |
| | Jerusalem | 194,182 | 1,385 | 44,918 |
| | Hebron | 151,395 | 2,533 | 31,548 |
| | Nablus | 278,521 | 3,155 | 60,474 |
| | Field Total | 654,971 | 7,582 | 143,562 |
| Gaza | Jabalia | 161,965 | 4,602 | 31,829 |
| | Rimal | 145,437 | 3,451 | 31,405 |
| | Zeitun | 116,681 | 2,843 | 30,124 |
| | Nuseirat | 106,700 | 2,659 | 21,953 |
| | Deir El-Balah | 76,406 | 1,868 | 16,291 |
| | Khan Yunis | 152,812 | 3,824 | 33,270 |
| | Rafah | 147,220 | 3,647 | 29,930 |
| | Field Total | 907,221 | 22,894 | 194,802 |
| Lebanon | Beirut | 48,417 | 293 | 13,457 |
| | Mountain | 78,400 | 486 | 20,724 |
| | Saida | 94,840 | 937 | 23,152 |
| | Tyre | 99,404 | 1,017 | 23,292 |
| | Tripoli | 54,835 | 610 | 12,110 |
| | Beqaa | 15,783 | 153 | 3,786 |
| | Field Total | 391,679 | 3,496 | 96,521 |
| Syria | Damascus | 321,037 | 5,634 | 74,170 |
| | South | 22,801 | 511 | 5,148 |
| | Homs-Hama | 35,883 | 574 | 8,773 |
| | North | 29,941 | 560 | 6,882 |
| | Field Total | 409,662 | 7,279 | 94,973 |
| Jordan | Amman South | 482,736 | 5,900 | 87,143 |
| | Irbed | 300,981 | 5,085 | 57,525 |
| | Amman North | 464,782 | 5,483 | 87,152 |
| | Zarka | 470,268 | 8,320 | 85,357 |
| | Field Total | 1,718,767 | 24,788 | 317,177 |
| | Agency Total | 4,082,300 | 66,039 | 847,035 |

SOURCE: UNRWA Publications and Statistics (http://www.un.org/unrwa/publications/statis 01
.html).

programs for the camp refugees covered 40 percent of the total refugee population. The largest service was in the realm of education, providing nine to ten
years of schooling for approximately 500,000 pupils in almost seven hundred
schools spread throughout the region. UNRWA employed a teaching staff of
approximately 13,000, virtually all of them Palestinians. UNRWA's health program involved a network of 125 clinics, treating about 6 million patients each
year, including specialized services in child health.

UNRWA's renewable mandate from the General Assembly, the last one in
effect through 2004, was funded almost entirely from voluntary contributions
from the international community. Most contributions are received in cash, although 7 percent of income also is received in kind, principally as donations of

food. Four percent of UNRWA income comes directly from UN bodies to cover staffing costs, including the ninety-eight international staff members connected with the UN Secretariat. Unlike the United Nations as a body, UNRWA has no system of assessed contributions. The list of major donors include members of the European Union, both collectively and individually (especially the Netherlands and Denmark), the United States (the largest single cash-donor country), the Nordic countries, and Japan. Although Saudi Arabia and Kuwait have made occasional contributions, the Arab states, while supporting UNRWA verbally, have not been particularly forthcoming with their donations. Saudi Arabia, however, may have reversed this trend with a generous contribution to UNRWA in 2003.

Despite all the attention and resources devoted to UNRWA, its regular budget is still considered underfunded. UNRWA's Assembly-approved budget for 2002 was $326.2 million, but available operative revenues were only $305.9 million, necessitating cuts in expenditures, notably in education. UNRWA has experienced nine consecutive years of budget deficits since 1993; its financial problems have been judged both chronic and structural, but the organization nonetheless has been slated to function at least until the formal establishment of a sovereign Palestinian state, possibly in 2005. UNRWA's operations have been negatively affected by this lack of funds, but they also suffer from the prevailing conflict with Israel and other political exigencies. Indeed, the United States contributed $95 million to UNRWA in 2003, calling UNRWA a force for stability in the Middle East and an irreplaceable partner in addressing emergency humanitarian needs in the West Bank and Gaza. But clearly, the U.S. action was tied to the Bush administration's Road Map to Peace between Israelis and Palestinians, and in part, its contribution was seen as a boost to the government of Abu Mazen in its contest with the forces represented by Yasir Arafat.

This was not the first time UNRWA was caught up in an Israeli-Palestinian peace process. UNRWA had become involved in the peace process brokered by the United States in the years after the 1993 accord between Israel and the PLO, an accord that transformed the PLO into the Palestinian Authority in Gaza and the West Bank. As Israel withdrew from numerous towns and villages in favor of the Palestinian Authority, UNRWA's work was made more, not less, demanding. The Agency developed a working relationship with the Authority, and on June 24, 1994, an exchange of letters between the Commissioner-General of UNRWA and Yasir Arafat allowed for a continuation of UNRWA's presence. UNRWA thereupon agreed to provide land, buildings, temporary shelter, and emergency humanitarian aid to assist the Palestinian Authority in establishing its operations in Jericho, the initial metropolitan area placed under PLO authority by the Israelis. It subsequently did the same in the additional towns and villages evacuated by the Israelis in 1995 and 1997. From that time forward, UNRWA developed effective relations with Arafat's Authority in the areas of education, health, relief, and social programs.

UNRWA also helped UN delegations further the peace process, and its headquarters was moved from Vienna to Gaza in 1995. A new headquarters building was designed in Gaza, and that shift alone involved an estimated $13.5 million. UNRWA continued to expand its mandate, and its Commissioner-General undertook the task of paying the salaries of nine thousand members of the Palestinian Police Force. The General Assembly approved that assistance but only through July 1995. UNRWA also accelerated the construction of schools, health clinics, and women's program centers. To make the territories more livable, UNRWA played a role in improving sanitation and roads and employed fifty-five hundred Palestinian laborers in Gaza alone. All this attention to the West Bank and Gaza did not deflect UNRWA from its other responsibilities, however. The refugee populations in Jordan, Lebanon, and Syria all had reason to expect UNRWA assistance, but the Agency's added responsibilities meant making heavier demands on the donor states. In effect, the promise of a Palestinian homeland had attracted more refugees to the territories, and UNRWA's task was made more, not less, burdensome by the prospects of an enhanced equilibrium in the region. By the turn of the century, 35 percent of the Palestinian refugees continued to live in camps in areas either administered by Israel, or by the Palestine Authority on the West Bank and Gaza, as well as in Arab host countries.

UNRWA was only one of three primary sources of financial support in the West Bank and Gaza. The Israeli Civil Administration in the territories and Palestinian NGOs (among which the most notable was Hamas [Harakat Al-Muqawama Al-Islamiya, or Islamic Resistance Movement]) were the other contributing bodies. The latter's funding came, in major part, from the oil-rich Arab states, which sponsored the development of schools, Koranic classes, health facilities, and other social services. Hamas also established the Islamic University in Gaza, and its financial base was larger than that of UNRWA after the 1991 Gulf War. It was not surprising, therefore, that both the Israeli authorities and UNRWA found it useful to work in harmony with the Palestinian NGOs, many of which had been organized by Hamas. The combined efforts of UNRWA, the Israeli government, and the NGOs provided for an annual financial distribution of almost $400 million for education, health, and other social services. Although it continued to employ several thousand teachers and provided schooling for almost half of the region's students, UNRWA activities were more directed toward health care, providing free basic medical services to more than 1 million registered refugees, or approximately half the population of the West Bank and Gaza. Since the appearance of the Palestinian Authority (after 1993) in the territories, however, the services rendered to the refugee community were disrupted by the competition, antagonism, and rivalry exhibited by major Palestinian actors. Hamas never accepted subordination to the Palestinian Authority/PLO leadership, and it, often violently, opposed Arafat's periodic and episodic negotiations with the Israeli government. The Palestinian Authority in turn tried to enforce its writ in the territories through harsh measures of governance. Although Hamas continued to emphasize its role as a deliverer of social services to the refugee population, its acknowledged militancy and refusal to accept the sovereign existence of Israel placed the Jewish state at risk and the Authority on the horns of a dilemma. Hamas was clearly the choice of the Palestinian majority, and Arafat's halting moves toward a settlement with Israel was hardly a boost to his popularity. UNRWA's work in such unsettled conditions was made considerably more complicated, and it has continued to function under severe limitations created by controversy and violence in the area into the twenty-first century.

## CONCLUSION

The contribution of expanding functional cooperation to international peace and security is highly speculative, but its contribution to economic and social well-being is subject to more concrete evaluation. Where interstate transactions have been of a technical and uncontroversial character, as in communication and transportation, the UN system has provided widely accepted standards for national conduct. In the areas of human rights, where the issue is less one of international cooperation than one of the conduct of the state within its own borders, standards have been set but not well observed. But even here, a little progress in securing compliance has been made, and the record of the ILO in upgrading labor standards, for instance, has been quite respectable. Substantial progress has also been made in creating international legal instruments for environmental protection. In the special area of the law of the sea, UN forums have contributed to a remarkable alteration of rules governing the use of the oceans and seabeds. International agencies have also promoted the exchange of useful information, and the services they render can stand on their own merits. Whereas most human needs are being met by individual and group action organized within a national setting, UN operations have in many local situations provided an important margin of difference for war victims, refugees, the socially underprivileged, and the economically deprived.

The tradition of decentralization bequeathed to the UN system has continued unabated, along with a steady proliferation of new agencies. This situation has given rise to criticisms of overlapping, duplication of effort, and irrational overall allocation of resources. There is no world budget for economic and social affairs. The United Nations and each specialized agency prepare their own budgets and programs within the limits that their memberships will collectively permit. Entrenched bureaucracies look out for their own bureaucratic interests. The Economic and Social Council was supposed to have a central coordinating function, but in practice it has been limited to discussion and liaison. Theoretically, governments could bring coordination to the system since the same governments for the most part hold membership in all the agencies of the UN system. But national governments are pluralistic institutions as well, and governmental policy toward a particular international function tends to be set by the government department with an interest in that function, whether health, education, the environment, oceans, or international trade. Government representatives to different international agencies often speak with different voices. If governments do not always coordinate their own policies effectively, there is little hope that they will provide effective coordination of the programs of many international agencies.

Some mitigating circumstances exist. Although no organization has the capacity to impose coordination, a degree of coordination has been introduced by cooperation across agency lines. An Administrative Committee on Coordination provides a forum in which representatives of the United Nations and specialized agency secretariats at the highest level can try to achieve a substantive meshing of their programs as well as greater uniformity in administrative matters. An International Civil Service Advisory Board, which serves the entire UN system, has helped establish uniformity in position classification, salaries and allowances, and pensions. Organizations engaged in related activities regularly interact at one another's meetings. Inter-secretariat liaison, by means of committees and other devices, is a standard operating procedure.

In defense of the system, one might even argue that the present pluralistic state of international society prevents consensus on any rational criteria for overall allocation between regional and universal levels and among individual programs on the same level. Greater centralization of resource allocation could result in different but not necessarily more rational matching of resources to needs.

The most formidable barriers to improved functional cooperation are in fact political and budgetary, not organizational. North-South divisions, as well as other political contests, have impinged on most of the functional activities, often turning their forums into ideological battlegrounds and shaping their programs to meet often political criteria that are unrelated. Cold War struggles have now subsided, but this has brought no corresponding upsurge in resources devoted to economic and humanitarian cooperation. In the long run, functional cooperation may provide cement for the foundations of world peace, but in the short run, functional growth depends on an expansion of the area of political agreement.

# NOTES

1. Useful commentaries on functionalist theory include James Patrick Sewell, *Functionalism and World Politics* (Princeton, NJ: Princeton University Press, 1960); Ernst B. Haas, *Beyond the Nation-State* (Stanford, CA: Stanford University Press, 1964); A. J. R. Groom and Paul Taylor, eds., *Functionalism: Theory and Practice in International Relations* (London: University of London Press, 1975); and Robert E. Riggs and I. Jostein Mykletun, *Beyond Functionalism: Attitudes Toward International Organization in Norway and the United States* (Minneapolis: University of Minnesota Press, 1979). An excellent brief analysis is "The Functional Approach to Peace," in Inis L. Claude Jr., *Swords into Plowshares,* 4th ed. (New York: Random House, 1971), pp. 378–407. For a recent study of international agencies set in a functionalist context, see Mark F. Imber, *The U.S.A., ILO, UNESCO, and IAEA: Politicization and Withdrawal in the Specialized Agencies* (London: Macmillan, in association with the Centre for International Policy Studies, University of Southampton, 1989).

2. See, for example, Simeon E. Baldwin, "The International Congresses and Conferences of the Last Century as Forces Working toward the Solidarity of the World," *American Journal of International Law* 1 (July 1907), pp. 565–78; Paul S. Reinsch, *Public International Unions, Their Work and Organization: A Study in International Administrative Law* (Boston: Ginn, 1911); J. A. Salter, *Allied Shipping Control: An Experiment in International Administration* (Oxford, UK: Clarendon Press, 1921); and Leonard S. Woolf, *International Government: Two Reports* (New York: Brentano, 1916). International functionalism is now most often identified with the Englishman David Mitrany, especially his small book *A Working Peace System: An Argument for the Functional Development of International Organization,* 1st ed. (London: Royal Institute of International Affairs, 1943). Mitrany published on this theme both before and after 1943.

3. For a more detailed classification of organization functions and decisions, see Robert W. Cox and Harold K. Jacobson, "The Framework for Inquiry," in Cox and Jacobson, *The Anatomy of Influence: Decision Making in International Organization* (New Haven, CT: Yale University Press, 1973), pp. 8–11; and Harold K. Jacobson, *Networks of Interdependence,* 2nd ed. (New York: Knopf, 1984), pp. 81–83.

4. *Report of the Secretary-General,* UN Document A/46/1 (1991), p. 9.

5. United Nations Focus Series, "Secretary-General Sets Course for Long-Awaited UN Revitalization," March 1, 1998, p. 4.

6. *Filartiga* v. *Pena-Irala,* 630 F.2d 876 (2d Cir. 1980); and see also *Rodriguez-Fernandez* v. *Wilkinson,* 505 F. Supp. 787 (D. Ian. 1980), as well as *Siderman* v. *The Republic of Argentina,* 965 F.2d 699 (9th Cir. 1992).

7. John W. McDonald, *Global Environmental Negotiations: The 1972 Stockholm Conference and Lessons for the Future,* The Project on Multilateral Negotiations of The American Academy of Diplomacy and The Paul H. Nitze School of Advanced International Studies, Johns Hopkins University, Working Paper Series WP-2, January 25, 1990, p. 5. See also John G. Ruggie, "On the Problem of 'The Global Problematique': What Roles for International Organizations?" reprinted in Richard A. Falk, Samuel S. Kim, and Saul H. Mendlowitz, *The United Nations and a Just World Order* (Boulder, CO: Westview Press, 1991), p. 459.

8. Stephen D. Krasner, "Structural Causes and Regime Consequences: Regimes as Intervening Variables," in Krasner, ed., *International Regimes* (Ithaca, NY: Cornell University Press, 1983), p. 2.

9. Oran R. Young, "The Politics of International Regime Formation: Managing Natural Resources and the Environment," *International Organization* 43, no. 3 (summer 1989), pp. 349–76. See also Oran R. Young, *International Cooperation: Building Regimes for Natural Resources and the Environment* (Ithaca, NY: Cornell University Press, 1989).

10. Peter M. Haas, "Do Regimes Matter? Epistemic Communities and Mediterranean Pollution Control," *International Organization* 43, no. 3 (summer 1989), pp. 377–403.

11. The first two decades of the UNHCR are recounted in Louise W. Holborn, *Refugees—A Problem of Our Time: The Work of the United Nations High Commissioner for Refugees, 1951–1972,* 2 vols. (Metuchen, NJ: Scarecrow Press, 1975). Another discussion is found in D. Gallagher, "The Evolution of the International Refugee System," *International Migration Review* 23 (fall 1989), pp. 579–98. The international legal status of refugees is treated in Guy S. Goodwin-Gill, *The Refugee in International Law* (Oxford, UK: Clarendon Press, 1983).

## SELECTED READINGS

Alston, Philip, ed. *The United Nations and Human Rights: A Critical Appraisal.* Oxford, UK: Clarendon Press, 1995.

Bacevich, Andrew J. *American Empire: The Reality and Consequences of U.S. Diplomacy.* Cambridge, MA: Harvard University Press, 2003.

Berkov, Robert. *The World Health Organization: A Study in Decentralized International Administration.* Geneva: Librairie E. Droz, 1957.

Buergenthal, Thomas. *Law-Making in the International Civil Aviation Organization.* Syracuse, NY: Syracuse University Press, 1969.

Choucri, Nazli, ed. *Global Changes: Environmental Challenges and Institutional Responses.* Cambridge, MA: MIT Press, 1993.

Codding, George A., Jr. *The Universal Postal Union.* New York: New York University Press, 1964.

Codding, George A., Jr., and Anthony M. Rutkowski. *The International Telecommunications Union in a Changing World.* Dedham, MA: Artech House, 1982.

Conway, Gordon. *The Doubly Green Revolution: Food for All in the 21st Century.* New York: Penguin, 1997.

Cox, Kevin R., ed. *Spaces of Globalization: Reasserting the Power of the Local.* New York: Guilford, 1997.

Cox, Robert W., and Harold K. Jacobson. *The Anatomy of Influence: Decision Making in International Organization.* New Haven, CT: Yale University Press, 1973.

Donnelly, Jack. *Human Rights and World Politics.* Boulder, CO: Westview Press, 1992.

Elhance, Aran. *Hydropolitics in the Third World: Conflict and Cooperation in International River Basins.* Washington, DC: U.S. Institute of Peace Press, 1999.

Feld, Werner J., and Robert S. Jordan. *International Organizations: A Comparative Approach.* 2nd ed. Westport, CT: Greenwood, 1988.

Ferris, Elizabeth G., ed. *Refugees and World Politics.* New York: Praeger, 1985.

Finkelstein, Lawrence S. *Politics in the United Nations System.* Durham, SC: Duke University Press, 1988.

Flood, Patrick J. *The Effectiveness of Human Rights Institutions.* Westport, CT: Praeger, 1998.

Forsythe, David P. *Human Rights and World Politics.* Rev. 2nd ed. Lincoln: University of Nebraska Press, 1989.

————. *The Internationalization of Human Rights.* Lexington, MA: Heath, 1991.

Gibson, John S. *International Organization, Constitutional Law, and Human Rights.* New York: Praeger, 1991.

Groom, A. J. R., and Paul Taylor. *Frameworks for International Cooperation.* London: Pinter, 1990.

Gustov, Mel. *Global Politics in the Human Interest.* Boulder, CO: Lynne Rienner, 1999.

Haas, Ernst B. *Beyond the Nation-State: Functionalism and International Organization.* Stanford, CA: Stanford University Press, 1964.

Haas, Peter M., Robert O. Keohane, and Marc A. Levy, eds. *Institutions for the Earth: Sources of Effective International Environmental Protection.* Cambridge, MA: MIT Press, 1993.

Hill, Martin. *The United Nations System: Coordinating Its Economic and Social Work.* Cambridge, UK: Cambridge University Press, 1978.

Holborn, Louise W. *The International Refugee Organization.* London: Oxford University Press, 1956.

————. *Refugees—A Problem of Our Time: The Work of the United Nations High Commissioner for Refugees, 1951–1972.* 2 vols. Metuchen, NJ: Scarecrow Press, 1975.

Hoogvelt, Ankie. *Globalization and the Postcolonial World: The New Political Economy of Development.* Baltimore, MD: Johns Hopkins University Press, 1997.

Hoy, Paula. *Players and Issues in International Aid.* West Hartford, CT: Kumarian Press, 1998.

Imber, Mark F. *The U.S.A., ILO, UNESCO, and IAEA: Politicization and Withdrawal in the Specialized Agencies.* London: Macmillan, in association with the Centre for International Policy Studies, University of Southampton, 1989.

International Bank for Reconstruction and Development. *World Development Indicators 1998.* Washington, DC: World Bank Publications, 1998.

Karns, Margaret P., and Karen A. Mingst, eds. *The United States and Multilateral Institutions: Patterns of Changing Instrumentality and Influence.* Boston: Unwin Hyman, 1990.

Kaufman, Natalie Hevener. *Human Rights Treaties and the Senate: A History of Opposition.* Chapel Hill: The University of North Carolina Press, 1990.

Keane, John. *Global Civil Society?* Cambridge, UK: Cambridge University Press, 2003.

Kimmerling, Baruch, and Joel S. Migdal. *The Palestinian People: A History.* Cambridge, MA: Harvard University Press, 2003.

Lipschutz, Ronnie D. *Global Civil Society and Global Environmental Governance.* Albany: State University of New York Press, 1996.

Meron, Theodore, ed. *Human Rights in International Law: Legal and Policy Issues.* 2 vols. Oxford, UK: Clarendon Press, 1984.

Morrell, James B. *The Law of the Sea: An Historical Analysis of the 1982 Treaty and Its Rejection by the United States.* Jefferson, NC: McFarland, 1991.

Mower, A. Glenn. *Regional Human Rights: A Comparative Study of the West European and Inter-American Systems.* Westport, CT: Greenwood Press, 1991.

Robertson, A. H., and J. G. Merrills. *Human Rights in the World: An Introduction to the Study of the International Protection of Human Rights.* 3rd ed. Manchester, UK: Manchester University Press, 1989.

Sanger, Clyde. *Ordering the Oceans: The Making of the Law of the Sea.* Toronto: University of Toronto Press, 1987.

Savage, James. *The Politics of International Telecommunication Regulation.* Boulder, CO: Westview Press, 1989.

Schaeffer, Robert K. *Understanding Globalization: The Social Consequences of Political, Economic, and Environmental Change.* Lanham, MD: Rowman and Littlefield, 1997.

Schiff, Benjamin N. *Refugees Unto the Third Generation: UN Aid to Palestinians.* Syracuse, NY: Syracuse University Press, 1995.

Sewell, James P. *UNESCO and World Politics.* Princeton, NJ: Princeton University Press, 1975.

Sokalski, Henryk J. *An Ounce of Prevention: Macedonia and the UN Experience in Preventive Diplomacy.* Washington, DC: U. S. Institute of Peace Press, 2003.

Soroos, Marvin S. *The Endangered Atmosphere: Preserving a Global Commons.* Columbia: University of South Carolina Press, 1997.

Storper, Michael. *The Regional World: Territorial Development in a Regional Economy.* New York: Guilford, 1997.

Taylor, Paul, and A. J. R. Groom, eds. *Global Issues in the United Nations' Framework.* London: Macmillan, 1989.

———. *International Institutions at Work.* London: Pinter, 1988.

Vosti, Stephen A., and Thomas Reardon. *Sustainability, Growth, and Poverty Alleviation.* Baltimore, MD: Johns Hopkins University Press, 1997.

Wang, James C. F. *Handbook on Ocean Politics and Law.* Westport, CT: Greenwood Press, 1992.

Weiss, Thomas G., and Leon Gordenker. *NGOs, the UN, and Global Governance.* Boulder, CO: Lynne Rienner, 1996.

Wells, Robert N., Jr., ed. *Peace by Pieces—United Nations Agencies and Their Roles: A Reader and Selective Bibliography.* Metuchen, NJ: Scarecrow Press, 1991.

Whitman, J., and D. Pocock, eds. *After Rwanda: The Coordination of United Nations Humanitarian Assistance.* New York: St. Martin's Press, 1996.

Williams, Douglas. *The Specialized Agencies and the United Nations: A System in Crisis.* New York: St. Martin's Press, 1987.

Zarjevski, Yefime. *A Future Preserved: International Assistance to Refugees.* New York: Pergamon Press, 1988.

# 10

PROMOTING ECONOMIC DEVELOPMENT

Promoting economic development may prove to be the decisive test of functional cooperation. To meet this global challenge, the United Nations, regional international organizations, and individual governments have launched programs aimed at helping developing countries prepare for the future. In no other area has the United Nations provided programs of such variety and scope. Approaches combine technical assistance and capital loans and grants within a broad range of educational, health, welfare, and internal improvement programs. The overall purpose is to build a base from which each society may hope to achieve sustainable economic development and improve the human condition. Despite the sincerity of these efforts, however, economic growth in most developing countries is slow and seldom measures up to expectations. Moreover, this disparity between expectations and realities has in turn produced a dangerous "frustration gap" that many observers of the contemporary scene feel contributes to social unrest, rebellion, and terrorism. Connected to the problem of stabilizing a volatile human population, therefore, is closing the gap between the vision of a better world and the reality of human despair and impoverishment. This also is the major challenge facing the United Nations.

## PROBLEMS OF DEVELOPMENT

The less developed world covers vast areas of the planet stretching eastward from Latin America through Africa and the Middle East to South and Southeast Asia and the islands of the Pacific littoral. Moreover, many of the new independent republics emerging from the breakup of the Soviet Union, as well as some East European and Balkan states, also fit this description. In meeting the problems of development, states are in some respects like individuals. No two individuals are exactly alike, but individuals living in poverty have many common characteristics and environmental problems that help explain their plight. Ending poverty for individuals depends not only on improving their economic lot but also on changing their thinking, their attitudes, their environment—in effect, their entire way of life.

In the years after World War II, improving living standards in the long-independent industrialized societies came to be accepted as a given. This fostered a belief that there was no limit to the ability of energetic and enlightened human beings to improve their lives still further, and in doing so assist others, recently independent, with their development. Synonyms for development have included "progress," "modernization," "industrialization," "economic growth," and "societal evolution." Whatever it is called, this question invariably arises: Why cannot the new but poor nations follow the same route to prosperity of the so-called developed nations? The answer, found throughout this chapter, is: They can, but. . . . It is to the "can" and "but" that we must turn our attention.

Leaders of developing countries are generally committed to emulating Western material values. What they really want, however, is the kind of production of wealth that the West enjoys. It is doubtful they also want the Western values that underpin that goal. Western work ethics, competitiveness, social mobility, and the freedom that goes along with democracy and capitalism are either not fully comprehended, or desirable. Societies are slowly giving way to modern demands, but commensurate changes in attitude and behavior are not always apparent. Moreover, whether changes in values will solve their problems and enrich the lives of tens of millions of people is a moot question. What is important is that they have caught a vision of plenty and affluence through the windows of the Western world, and they want to have a share in it.

After a century of hot and cold wars, new problems have complicated the process of helping Third World countries with their economic development. The "Second World," once thoroughly communist, has now embraced the principles of representative democracy and market capitalism and is attempting to put them into practice. In the process these states are seeking huge amounts of foreign aid from the West. These new aid recipients include not only the countries of Eastern Europe but also the former Soviet republics, all of which now are independent states. The former communist states have caught "development fever." More significant, they have become direct competitors with the Third World for the economic aid provided by the First World countries through the UN system.

## PROFILE OF A LESS DEVELOPED COUNTRY

An understanding of the problem of economic development may be grasped by examining the features that characterize most developing states. A picture of a typical developing state's base or starting point will highlight what needs to be done to achieve economic development. It also will point up the difficulties inherent in trying to assist a newly independent country to attain its lofty goals. A note of caution is in order, however, as great differences in size, population, resources, power supplies, native skills, and other natural and human variables exist in developing states as diverse as Brazil and Sierra Leone, Nigeria and Afghanistan. Moreover, the profile offered here of a developing country cannot be applied to oil-rich states in the Third World or to the developing states with extraordinary records of development, for instance, South Korea, Taiwan, and Singapore.

*First,* and most basic, to our profile is understanding that the state we speak of is poor, even if some people living there are extremely prosperous. Indeed even the poorest country has its rich element, but we must not allow this to distract us from our task. Millions of people in the Third World today live in conditions that can be described as absolute poverty. Although all Third World states are "less developed" than states in the First World, the poorest states are often referred to as the "least developed" or the Fourth World. Both the "less" and the "least" developed countries are referred to as LDCs.[1] The World Bank estimates that considerably more than one billion people in the developing world live in poverty, with incomes of less than $370 a year.

Poverty is a human tragedy for the hundreds of millions struggling to survive it; it is also an economic barrier to the process of development. Economic development is largely a function of turning savings into growth, and people living in grinding poverty have little capacity to save and invest. In addition, developed states are unlikely to invest in societies where mass consumer demand is nonexistent. The problem is circular: poverty leads to little or no savings, with a resulting low level of investment, which ensures the continuance of poverty. The central challenge of economic development in the poorer countries is to find a way to break this vicious circle.[2]

*Second,* the profile state is located to the south of most of the developed countries and has a tropical climate. More precisely, the poorest of the developing countries are with few exceptions located south of thirty degrees north latitude, which runs along the southern boundary of the United States and along the northern reaches of the African continent. Tropical jungles, vast mountain ranges, arid deserts, and wild bush country make up great portions of the landmass of these countries, forcing the people to carry on a daily struggle with nature to eke out a bare existence. High temperatures and humidity and soils leached by tropical rains make the job of wresting a living a precarious one. The profile state lacks the energy sources of coal and oil, although potential hydroelectric power sources exist in the form of great tropical rivers that wind through the mountains and jungles. In some Third World countries, tropical forests are being destroyed because wood is the only available energy supply for cooking and heating. Third World countries also suffer economically because of the high shipping costs that result from the great distances separating most of them from the world's industrial centers, which increase the prices of both their exports and their imports.

*Third,* the profile state is faced with population growth that often outpaces gains in productivity. The first benefits of modernization to reach many of the developing nations were drugs and medicines to save lives, chemicals to control mosquitoes and other disease carriers, and water-purifying agents. With better public health and sanitation, death rates plunged while traditionally high birthrates were hardly affected. The result is a population explosion that nullifies the economic benefits of modernization in those countries for all but the very rich.

TABLE 10-1    World Vital Events Per Time Unit, 2003

| TIME UNIT | BIRTHS | DEATHS | NATURAL INCREASE |
| --- | --- | --- | --- |
| Year | 128,758,963 | 55,508,568 | 73,250,395 |
| Month | 10,729,914 | 4,625,714 | 6,104,200 |
| Day | 352,764 | 152,078 | 200,686 |
| Hour | 14,699 | 6,337 | 8,362 |
| Minute | 245 | 106 | 139 |
| Second | 4.1 | 1.8 | 2.3 |

SOURCE: U.S. Bureau of the Census, International Data Base (http://www.census.gov/cgi-bin/ipc/pcwe).

Note: Figures may not sum to totals due to rounding.

Developing countries have now adopted programs to slow population growth and, with assistance from the UN Fund for Population Activities, have achieved modest success. Although birthrates are still extremely high in many countries, for the first time in human history birthrates are declining in every region of the world. Population control programs undoubtedly contributed to the decline. In some countries the decline also reflected the decline in fertility that normally accompanies the stage of development when incomes begin to rise and children are less an economic asset. For many families children are no longer necessary to ensure that some survive to care for parents in their old age. On a more somber note, population growth has also been slowed by the increased incidence of diseases such as AIDS and tuberculosis that in some Third World countries are at epidemic and pandemic levels.

Nevertheless, despite all the efforts and the conditions that have contributed to the decrease in the rate of overall population growth, by 2003 the world population was more than 6.3 billion. By contrast, world population had stood at less than 2.5 billion when the United Nations was organized in 1945. (See Table 10-1 for a glimpse into world population growth despite the evidence that the rate of growth is declining.) The less developed countries represented more than 5 billion of the world's total population of 6.3 billion in 2003, and demographic forecasts for total world population to attain 7 billion by 2010 are no longer mere projections.

Concerned with a variety of population issues, UN conferences on population were held in Rome in 1954, Belgrade in 1964, Bucharest in 1974, Mexico City in 1984, Cairo in 1994, and New York in 1999. Population issues also were raised at the Millennium Summit in 2000, the Third United Nations Conference on the Least Developed Countries in 2001, and the Second World Assembly on Aging in 2002. At the January 2003 Fifth Asian and Pacific Population Conference, a conference held once every ten years, it was noted that in 1963 only five countries had population policies. The region was in the midst of a population explosion, with an average total birthrate of 5.6 children per woman. In 2003 it was pointed out that virtually all member countries had population policies and all but seven had reduced birthrates, with many attaining a rate of 2.1 children per woman, the figure at which population stabilizes. Nevertheless, the Asia/Pacific region represented at the conference was home to 3.7 billion people, or 59 percent of the global population. Moreover, it remained home to the largest number of poor people worldwide, despite the remarkable advances made in controlling runaway population growth.

*Fourth,* the profile state often lacks the ability to support itself because of the low productivity of primitive agriculture. Peasant families tilling small plots with ancient farming technology or working on large estates for absentee landlords are living symbols of the plight of agriculture in such countries. Much of the profile state's farming is geared to a subsistence level, with little or no capability for developing a cash crop that could earn foreign exchange. Farming is intensive, with peasants crowded onto arable land in such numbers that the soil's fertility is low. Crop diseases, insects, wild animals and rodents, and unpredictable natural disasters in the form of droughts, floods, cyclones, and hurricanes can ruin the efforts of months of toil. Remedies have been attempted through land reform and technical assistance, but reform is problematic. Old ways die hard, and resources for changing them are scarce. The continuing flight of people from rural areas to teeming city slums testifies to the fact that low agricultural productivity persists.

*Fifth,* the profile state has a colonial background that has helped determine the direction of modernization and continues to affect the thought and action of its people. In many cases the rudimentary physical framework for development was laid out by the colonial power in the nineteenth century and the first half of the twentieth century. Surpassing the influence of that framework, however, is the lasting imprint that colonialism left on the attitudes and emotions of the people. The humiliation and sense of frustration fostered by foreign rule left the seeds of anti-Western feelings that remain today. In such states internal disunity often still exists as a holdover of a carefully cultivated colonial policy of "divide and rule" or as a result of boundary lines drawn by imperial design that sundered established communities or tribes and mixed traditional enemies within the same political unit. In societies lacking most of the internal impulses and capabilities necessary for modernization, the unity produced by the effort to end foreign rule produced a desire for change that independence and UN programs also have encouraged. Self-determination demands combined with retreating colonialism shaped the twentieth-century character of the United Nations. But the newly independent states that proudly assumed their roles in the world organization demonstrated particular opposition to domestic movements that used the same logic and demands in seeking their independence from the core entity. Civil wars continue to plague the new states in the twenty-first century. It needs reminding that in 1971 Bangladesh was only the first among the post–World War II countries to achieve independence as a consequence of a successful civil war. That war not only caused the dismemberment of the original Pakistan, it also reaffirmed Pakistani fears that India, which made the dismemberment possible, was determined to eliminate the consequences of the 1947 partition of the British Indian empire and absorb Pakistan within a united India.

*Sixth,* the profile state is built on the social fabric of a traditional society. Custom and tradition provide the social cement, and religion and conservative values provide the guidelines for human action. Small elite groups dominate the society and often oppose virtually all change because change would mean a loss of their status. Rigid class structures immobilize even the able and ambitious individual. Objective conditions of social stagnation are reinforced by group attitudes, requiring a revolution of perspectives as a prelude to modernity. No society completely abandons its traditional culture. Transitional societies in a state of vigorous change are called upon to reshape old values, resulting in cultural, social, political, and economic restlessness. Anomie and feelings of rootlessness are at the heart of the fundamentalist resurgence and the desire to rid society of all alien borrowings and impositions. Indeed, some of the roots of contemporary terrorism are watered by the frustrated aspirations of people wishing to return to a social condition that existed before the colonial experience. Interaction between the old and the new has fomented turmoil, revolution, and civil war as rival groups claim to offer people indigenous substitutes for the "new" ideologies imported from or imposed by foreign sources. The modernization process cannot successfully compete with emotional demands to purify society.

*Seventh,* the world profile state is characterized by high illiteracy. UNESCO's *Compendium of Statistics on Illiteracy: 1995 Edition,* released in 1997, identified the nine nations with the highest number of illiterate people as Bangladesh, Brazil, China, Egypt, India, Indonesia, Mexico, Nigeria, and Pakistan. Together, these nine countries in 2003 contained more than 700 million of the more than 1 billion people worldwide who were unable to read. Furthermore, educational needs to achieve modernization go beyond basic literacy to include technical, secondary, and university training. A university-trained elite exists in most of the underdeveloped countries, but it is extremely small in number and it consists for the most part of specialists in law, the humanities, and the social sciences. This elite provided the leadership in the march to independence, but a new elite of entrepreneurs, managers, scientists, engineers, and technicians is needed to exploit resources and organize the productive machinery.

*Eighth,* in its trade relations with the rest of the world, the profile state rests on a weak economic base. The export trade of most developing countries is based on the production or extraction of one or a few primary commodities. Living standards beyond the subsistence level provided by local agriculture depend on the export market for these commodities. Foreign exchange earnings needed for buying capital goods from advanced countries are limited by adverse world market conditions, including

- An oversupply of most primary commodities
- Competition from advanced states with greater productive efficiency
- Fluctuating prices resulting from speculation among buyers, changes in supply, and other conditions beyond the control of the developing states

- The introduction of synthetics and substitutes to replace natural commodities
- High shipping costs in getting commodities to distant markets
- Deteriorating terms of trade resulting in lower prices for primary commodity exports
- Higher prices for imports of manufactured consumer and capital goods

Recognition that the world economy is stacked against their interests has led the less developed countries to demand fundamental changes. The creation of a New International Economic Order (NIEO) at a summit meeting of the Non-Aligned Movement in the 1970s was aimed at leveling the playing field in some economic areas, but even this effort fell short as the more prosperous countries continued to distance themselves from the multitude of developing states.

*Ninth,* the profile state suffers from political instability. Most developing states are, or in the recent past have been, characterized by one-party, authoritarian regimes. In some of the new nations, early attempts to establish democratic systems failed when the promised bounty of independence could not be delivered, and an authoritarian regime was reinstituted. Opposition groups and parties have commonly been nonexistent, suppressed, or present in a highly innocuous form to provide the shadow but not the substance of a democratic system. In some states political activity has been largely confined to the capital city as an arena for heated rivalries among the political elite jockeying for positions of strength or attempting a coup. Throughout much of the Third World, changes of government through free elections have been rare occurrences. But some progress has been made through UN-supervised free elections in countries such as Nicaragua and Namibia. Nevertheless, building political stability remains one of the most difficult and frustrating problems facing the developing states.

*Tenth,* the people of the profile state are disproportionately subjected to epidemic and endemic diseases and other health problems. At least in part through the efforts of the World Health Organization, Third World peoples experienced improving health conditions during the 1950s, 1960s, and 1970s. With the increased use of vaccination and antibiotic drugs, developing countries were better able to combat communicable diseases during those decades. But in the mid-1980s and 1990s, HIV/AIDS quickly escalated into a pandemic in the developing countries where early diagnosis and treatment were lacking. HIV/AIDs virtually obliterated the gains achieved earlier in improving the health of the people of the developing areas. Recognized now as a disaster of global proportions, the disease has affected millions in Africa and threatens the lives of an unknown number in the most populous countries of India and China. Along with the emergence of AIDs in the 1980s and 1990s, drought, especially in Africa south of the Sahara, spawned widespread famine and left in its wake a reduced resistance to a variety of other diseases that the poorer countries could not cope with.

In summary, a typical developing state suffers from chronic mass poverty. Developing countries are swamped by a high percentage of young people in overpopulated societies with little access to jobs. Inefficient economies rest on outmoded agricultural foundations, and their international debts prevent financial stability. Undiagnosed and untreated diseases are ravaging the larger population, and customs and traditions also thwart change, especially when change involves making something positive of a colonial background. Illiteracy rates remain high, and the states' competitive position in world trade is poor or nonexistent. With a largely apathetic population, the governments of developing countries are too often corrupt and authoritarian, making balanced decision making virtually impossible. But as grim as the circumstances are in the developing states, an overriding urge to develop remains, and with help offered by other states, regional groups, and international organizations, strenuous efforts are ever being made to improve the lot of countless millions.

# A BLUEPRINT FOR ECONOMIC DEVELOPMENT

Governmental action to promote economic growth and modernization requires judicious planning so that strategies will match national needs and capabilities. Careful planning is also needed to ensure that resources provided through international agencies are put to productive use. Government programs cannot, however, provide a shortcut or easy route to modernization. Economic development has always been a slow and painful process. Despite unprecedented amounts of outside help from the United Nations and other sources, the job remains largely one of local initiative and self-help. The long Cold War–generated race between rival ideologies and their respective approaches to development has been brought to a close, with capitalism the clear winner in most of the world's former communist states. But within each developing society there is a still greater race to push development ahead of its two most dangerous competitors—hunger and mass frustration.

## PREPARING THE BASE

Except for certain natural factors not subject to human alteration, most of the characteristics of our profile state are susceptible to change and improvement. The proximate objective of every developing society is to reach the point from which the society will launch itself into an upward trend of steady, sustainable growth.

### Sociological and Political Changes

An adequate "takeoff" base requires a modernization of social and political institutions and practices. The following changes are fundamental to that objective.

   **1. *Attitudinal Changes*** In many countries a privileged elite will be challenged to adopt new attitudes favoring a modernization that may threaten its traditional status. The choice, however, is not always between self-instituted change and the status quo. The alternative may be a violent revolt that would sweep away all elements of entrenched privilege carried out by those in the society whose attitudes have changed more rapidly than those of the elite holders of wealth and power. Other critical value changes may involve new orientations toward "worldliness" and "getting ahead," the psychic satisfactions of work, the profit incentive, and other sometimes crass but essential motivations to economic advances.

**2. *Political Evolution*** Tangible societal changes must proceed apace of changing attitudes. First, political socialization must occur, taking the form of support for a minimally effective national political system. Government, a distant power that extracts taxes and drafts village youth for military service, must take on a new image through functions aimed at directing and servicing. Political leadership must be selected on the basis of abilities and policies rather than inherited status or wealth. A corps of administrators recruited and trained in modern governmental techniques must provide a degree of unity for the entire country, reaching even remote villages.

**3. *Educational Development*** Education may be the keystone in building a modern society. Not only do technicians of varying degrees of skills need to be trained, fundamental education in the "three Rs" must be imparted to a large portion of the population. Schools can serve an integrating function in selecting the best and most compatible traits of older traditions to mesh with those of the modern world. As in the advanced states, education must also provide a nationalizing force in developing a single language and in cultivating national myths, traditions, and popular heroes. Beyond the production of a literate, informed citizenry and a trained labor force, those people with access to secondary and college education must be trained and guided in managing the nation's changeover to a world of business, commerce, industry, and modern administration.

Unfortunately, many developing countries are unable or reluctant to devote the necessary resources to education, and pressures often exist to divert budgetary funds from education to projects that will show more "immediate" results. These countries also suffer from a "brain drain" that occurs when some of their best educated young people study at universities in the West and subsequently decide not to return.

**4. *Population Control*** Population control is widely perceived as crucial to developmental success but may in fact be primarily a problem of education and economic opportunities. Demographers speak of the self-limiting nature of the population explosion, noting that rising living standards in the advanced nations had the effect of reducing birthrates drastically. If preindustrialization birthrates had continued in Europe during the nineteenth and twentieth centuries, for example, some European countries would now have populations almost ten times larger. But in the developing world of today, population size is of such a magnitude that economic living standards in many countries cannot readily be raised to the point where self-limiting controls function in reducing the size of families.

One of the major issues confronting the United Nations in its efforts to control population is that of abortion. The Bali Declaration on Population and Sustainable Development adopted at a 1992 UN meeting served as the foundation upon which global population policies were formulated at the Cairo Conference on Population and Development in 1994. The Program of Action adopted at Cairo is still regarded as the blueprint for social and economic development around the world. Approved by the 179 nations participating at the Cairo conference, it was reaffirmed at the Bangkok Asia/Pacific Conference in 2003, and the latter reiterated that "in no case should abortion be promoted as a method of family planning." All governments recommitted themselves to strengthening women's health but to reduce the recourse to abortion through expanded and improved family planning services.

In the 1980s, the United States had declared that it would no longer support UN population control programs in countries such as China where the government administers a proabortion policy. But while U.S. assistance for international population control programs was reduced, it was not eliminated. That is, not until 1994 when conservatives gained control of the U.S. Congress and strenuous efforts were made to prevent U.S. funding from reaching UN population programs. Congressional attacks on the United Nations became more numerous, and the United States delayed meeting its financial obligations in major part to assure that no U.S. funds would be used for family planning projects. In April 1998, the Congress moved legislation that would allow the government to pay a portion of the country's arrears, but only if the United Nations demonstrated that the U.S. contribution would not be used for family planning activities. The Clinton administration also maneuvered round the congressional opposition to restore some funding for family planning on the assurance that the program would not include abortion on demand. George W. Bush assumed the U.S. presidency in January 2001, however, and almost immediately issued an order closing off the use of U.S. money for UN-sponsored or any other family planning organization operating in the international arena. What has been lost in this passionate debate is the awareness that birth control is a logical answer to the problem of abortion.

In a major program for population control supported by the United Nations, governmental and private organizations in India (the country with the highest birthrate) have distributed birth control information and also provided the means of contraception. Government programs have encouraged smaller families and even promised tangible rewards. In the West the approach is somewhat different. Programs in the developed countries center on the social and economic conditions, rather than on contraception or payoffs for holding the size of families to a certain number. Here attention is on prohibitions against child labor, policies and programs that emancipate women from male domination, social mobility leading to the economic independence of children from their parents, the mechanization of agriculture, and social insurance that can free parents from dependence on children in their old age. When large families are acknowledged to be an economic burden rather than an asset, when children can no longer be exploited for economic and dowry purposes, when large

TABLE 10-2   **European Population, 2000–2025**

| YEAR | POPULATION |
|------|------------|
| 2000 | 727,304,000 |
| 2005 | 720,898,000 |
| 2010 | 713,211,000 |
| 2015 | 704,506,000 |
| 2020 | 694,877,000 |
| 2025 | 683,533,000 |

SOURCE: UN World Population Prospects: Population Database (http://esa.un.org/unpp/p2k0data .asp), accessed Sept. 2003.

Note: Population based on medium fertility variant.

families are no longer accepted as a status symbol, it has been shown that population growth can be brought under control. The family planning initiatives in India have yet to bear fruit, but in Europe in 2003, the program to control population growth has produced not just stability but a decline in actual population numbers (see Table 10-2).

**5. Community Development** Finally, social change in local communities must be stressed. It is not enough that changes occur in capital cities. People who live in rural villages must discover that working together can enrich their lives, improve their living conditions, and reduce social barriers. Technical assistance in such areas as agriculture, health, education, the environment, and public works can enable people in local communities, often with local resources, to obtain some of the benefits of modernization. This requires that people improve individual skills, increase self-reliance, and learn the advantages and techniques of cooperative activity in local communities.

### Economic Changes

The central objective of modernization in all developing societies is economic betterment. Social and political changes are aimed mainly at making these societies more receptive to and more effective at promoting economic development. But the economic problem of achieving a modern economy remains, that is, how to move a poor country to the takeoff point for sustainable growth.

What are the economic variables in the development equation? How can an underdeveloped state marshal its forces in a collective economic offensive? A UN delegate once said of economic development, "It was easy enough to recognize what had to be done but difficult to decide how to go about it." Though no two states would proceed in exactly the same way, some common approaches can be suggested as "prescriptions for development." Remember, however, that much controversy exists over the best way to achieve development.

*Increase Agricultural Output* The objectives of greater farm productivity are (1) a healthier, better-fed, harder-working population, (2) increased foreign exchange earnings through exports, and (3) a savings—extracted from increased output—destined for investment. In the early stages of development, the peasant's food consumption may not increase, but food production must rise to support a growing urban workforce. The most useful means of expanding productivity fall into the category of improved farming technology—modern implements, fertilizers, insect and disease control, good seed stocks, weed control, and scientific farming techniques. In all of these areas, the United Nations has provided leadership, loans, grants, and special programs. Agrarian reform is another approach that has proved successful in a few societies. Basic to agrarian reform is land redistribution among the peasants, achieved by splitting up large estates. Although such a redistribution would increase incentives, the smaller holdings are often uneconomic because they cannot take advantage of economies of scale and because mechanization of such holdings is nearly impossible. Peasant cooperatives to encourage joint production, aided by a reform of inheritance laws that would end fragmentation of plots, may provide an answer to this dilemma. Credit to finance purchases of seeds and fertilizer is a critical element in efforts to boost production.

In 1979 the United Nations sought to expand credit for the rural poor through the creation of the International Fund for Agricultural Development (IFAD), which has since dispensed billions of dollars in project loans. IFAD mobilizes resources for agricultural development and makes them available to developing countries, especially those in the least developed category, or Fourth World. The latter receives assistance on terms that control transfers and expenditures. In major part, IFAD's finances initially came from the oil-producing Arab states and from several Western nations, but Middle East conflicts and a severe drop in oil prices during the 1980s and 1990s coupled with recessions in the West produced severe budget cuts in IFAD's operations.

*Develop Simple Industries* Agricultural production must be supplemented by the development of fisheries, mining, and raw material potentials. Most of the new nations have access to the world's oceans, and some have sizable inland lakes—both of which are sources for food rich in protein. Expansion in the production of primary commodities may help underdeveloped states to earn critically needed foreign exchange, although lower prices resulting from highly competitive conditions in the world commodity market may negate the advantages of increased production. Increased productivity, however, will enable such states to take advantage of periods of peak demand and high prices when the advanced countries are engaged in high levels of military spending or enjoy economic boom conditions. Finding a receptive market for their products generally has been more troublesome for Third World countries than increasing production of primary commodities.

*Invest in Social Overhead* A modern economy can be built only on a broad economic base or infrastructure. This means that each LDC professing modernization as a goal must be prepared to devote human and capital resources to the building of facilities for basic transport, communication, irrigation, and power supplies. The human resources needed to carry out such projects might be available if the labor surplus engaged in inefficient agricultural pursuits could be taken off the land, mobilized into construction units, and utilized in simple "social capital" projects. Added incentives underlying this approach may include reduced unemployment and increased agricultural production as labor-saving techniques are introduced. Also there is the need for an efficient use of foreign exchange to buy machinery from the industrial nations. Psychologically, the personal involvement of thousands of young people in social projects of this kind may help stimulate national pride and a surge of development spirit, thus giving purpose to lives in a condition of stasis. Recognizing that the world's youth population would increase from 738 million in 1975 to considerably more than 1 billion by 2005, the United Nations has been mindful of providing young people with positive tasks. International Youth Year was proclaimed in 1985 and a call went out to governments to produce meaningful jobs for young people. In 1998 the United Nations sponsored the World Conference of Ministers for Youth, and in 2002 the General Assembly Special Session on Children echoed this theme. Also emphasized was the need to guide young children so that they could develop in ways that later enabled them to contribute to overall development.

*Acquire Technical Skills*  Modern factories and transportation, communication, and power facilities can be operated only with skilled personnel. An industrializing society faces an enormous task in forging a new labor force of energetic and capable workers from a peasant society. Trainees must be supported out of the savings yielded from a surplus of production over consumption. Exceptions to this rule may be found in apprentice-type training programs and in the technical assistance rendered by advanced states or international institutions. New workers must adjust to the strict discipline of industrial life—regular hours, machine-dictated work speeds, and the rhythmic monotony of life on a production line. Managerial and administrative personnel will constitute a new elite, culled out of the indigenous population through ruthless competition for unprecedented rewards.

A vast new reservoir of skilled personnel became available with the end of the East-West Cold War in the early 1990s. In the newly independent countries of the former Soviet Union, as well as the countries of Eastern Europe now free from Soviet control, peoples' attention turned from war to peace and hence to development. So too in the countries of the West, great reductions in the production of armaments required individuals with engineering, managerial, and other skills to seek job opportunities in the mundane areas of human activity. Putting their skills to work for development required the retooling and the reapportioning of investment capital. In the developing countries it particularly meant remunerating skilled workers in convertible ("hard") currency, which was always in short supply in most developing countries.

The hiatus offered by the end of the Cold War, however, was interrupted by sustained hostilities in various Third World regions. The "peace" also was significantly jolted by the increased use of terror as a weapon in political contests between the more endowed nations and those people determined to weaken the hold of those nations on the world's destiny. In particular, the events of September 11, 2001, reinvigorated the armaments industries, especially in the United States, where many skilled defense and armaments workers went back into the war-making industries. Furthermore, the surplus of weapons experts in the republics of the former Soviet Union and the need to provide work to such individuals before terrorists or states with nuclear weapons ambitions might seek them out became more pressing after 2001. Under these circumstances it was difficult to entertain truly skilled and talented people in the developing world turning their attention to fundamental developmental needs. World conditions after 2001 also made it more difficult for aid workers and development specialists to utilize their skills for constructive purposes when many of the areas in which they were called to labor were overwhelmed by conflict.

*Foster Industrialization*  The capstone of the needed social, political, and economic changes can be summed up in the word *industrialization*. Industrialization tends to generate greater efficiency and productivity, which in turn results in increased trade and capital accumulation. Industrialization increases the capacity of a society to process primary commodities for marketing and consumption. In the West, nations embarked on policies of colonial expansion to secure dependable sources of raw materials and new markets for surplus manufactured products. Many leaders in developing states equate development and industrialization, and they stress the latter as the key to growth and prosperity. However, if industries are created before a proper base has been prepared, they will exist precariously in a modernizing enclave while the rest of the country and most of its people sink deeper into poverty. Sometimes overlooked by developing societies are nonindustrialized states, such as New Zealand and the Netherlands, that have managed high productivity and established exceptional living standards.

For a developing state to industrialize, it must import most of the necessary machinery, tools, and skills. Unlike social capital improvements, which often need sheer muscle power, industrial capital can be built locally only *after* some measure of industrialization has occurred. If modernizing states had the time and patience, they could follow the lead of the West in moving from primitive handicraft to more increasingly complex machines. It needs reminding, however, that such transformation occurred over a century or more, while in the developing societies of the twenty-first century the demand is for rapid action. The latter states are too far behind the more developed countries to accept the notion that modernization is an evolutionary not a revolutionary process, and indeed will require considerable time. The tide of rising expectations so apparent during the 1960s in the developing world continues to wash over the lands of the Third World, and there is little patience for those counseling a more deliberate process. Leaders of the developing nations, therefore, prefer to skip the successive steps of development and start with modern, sophisticated—even automated—factories. But there are drawbacks and a price to be paid for attempting to rush the development process. Since the more efficient factory uses less labor, the rise of a large, disgruntled, unemployed urban proletariat seems unavoidable. The dangerous by-product of that kind of industrialization is witnessed in worker unrest and repressive countermeasures by government. Experts from advanced nations who urge leaders to build simple, labor-intensive industries are nevertheless little appreciated and more than likely are suspected of having ulterior motives, or worse, neocolonialist attitudes. Adopting such proffered advice is deemed to be no better than their self-arrived-at conclusions, irrespective of the consequences.

Industrialization can produce many salutary results for an underdeveloped society. For one thing, manufactured goods become more readily available and cheaper for the masses. Foreign exchange formerly expended on imports of consumer items can be saved. Savings for investment should increase substantially once industrialization has begun because national income will be higher. Industrialized plants may also contribute to a local fabrication of capital goods. Despite its pitfalls and the problems it may create, industrialization may be a logical route for many developing countries to take in their attempted "great leap forward" to modernization. The extent, however, to which their people may view it as a singularly facile solution to problems of mass poverty is likely to be more an emotional than a rational reaction.

*Safeguard the Environment* Programs to industrialize may be short-term economic successes and yet in the long run prove to be environmental disasters. This issue was emphasized at the UN Conference on Environment and Development held in Rio de Janeiro in June 1992, as well as the Conference on Global Warming convened in Kyoto in 1997. The central message at Rio and Kyoto, as well as at the earlier 1972 Stockholm Conference on the Environment, was the need to act globally in dealing with such problems as the destruction of the ozone layer, the greenhouse effect, and the pollution of the oceans.

Many of the most direct and immediate problems, however, continue to be local and regional. In a number of Third World countries, forests are being destroyed as expanding populations desperately seek land for cultivation and fuel for cooking and warmth. The result is a creeping desertification as forests recede and ultimately disappear. This of course can be a global problem too because everyone breathes oxygen generated by the earth's great forests. Pollution or exhaustion of local water resources is also a problem in most parts of the world. Some water supplies have been victims of attempted development. The state of Uzbekistan, a former Soviet republic, is a case in point. Soviet planners, in their efforts to increase crop production, reversed the flow of waters feeding the Aral Sea with freshwater. Once the world's fourth largest lake, it has been turned into a smelly sewer, with less than half its former area and only one quarter of its volume. As a result, the huge harvest of fish and seafood that supported the Uzbek people for centuries has disappeared in virtually a single generation.

While Third World countries embark on ambitious development programs, the thirty most industrialized countries of the West continue to add huge quantities of pollution to the oceans, the land, and the atmosphere. The United States, with about 5 percent of the world's population, produces an estimated 25 percent of global pollution. Some developing states, especially in Africa, have permitted their territories to become dumping grounds for hazardous wastes from Western industrialized states. The 1992 Rio conference emphasized the need for a new game plan to eliminate poverty without environmental degradation. The catchphrase was "sustainable development," meaning progress that meets the needs of the present while not compromising the needs of future generations. Agreements signed at the conference on the ozone layer, global warming, and biodiversity indicated modest progress. Another international development of importance was the establishment in 1990 of a Global Environment Facility (GEF) to provide financing for environmental projects associated with the functioning of the World Bank, the IMF, the UN Development Program, and the UN Environment Programme. Sponsored by the World Bank with an initial fund of almost $1 billion, the GEF was particularly concerned with global warming, conservation of biodiversity, damage to the ozone layer, and protection of international waters.

Despite these apparent achievements, however, agreements like those at Kyoto in 1997 have still to go into force. Advanced industrialized countries agreed to cut the exhaust emissions from cars, industrial plants, households, and agricultural facilities by 5 percent (from 1990 levels) to stem the greenhouse effect of global warming. Kyoto, however, could not be put into force until it was signed and ratified by 55 states, including those that accounted for at least 55 percent of 1990 carbon dioxide emissions in industrialized countries. At the end of 1998, 60 countries had signed the Protocol, but only two—Fiji and Antigua and Barbuda—had actually ratified it. By 2002, however, 111 nations had ratified the agreement, including the 15 countries of the European Union and Japan. These acceptances brought the carbon dioxide emissions target within reach at 44.2 percent. The United States, responsible for 36.1 percent of greenhouse gas emissions, originally agreed to sign the document, but it also insisted it would not seek ratification until the developing countries pledged "meaningful participation," which meant nothing less than a reduction in the latter's development schedules. In response, the developing countries, led by China, India, and the Group of 77, argued they could not place limits on their growth at such a key moment in their own industrialization. With key industrialized states continuing to hold out, much hinged on Russia's ratification, which President Putin indicated could occur at any time. With Russia representing 17.4 percent of greenhouse gas emissions, its ratification would bring the Kyoto treaty into force no matter what the United States did. Unfortunately, the George W. Bush administration seemed to have no intention of ratifying the Kyoto Protocol. Bush declared that the treaty would cost Americans millions of jobs and billions of dollars, and the administration offered its own program for controlling emissions pollution. Most critics of the plan, however, argued that it would in fact add to the problem of global warming. President Bush in 2003 reiterated his belief that global warming was more a theory than a fact, and no matter the extent of international pressure, the United States intended to walk a separate path.

## PROMOTING INTERNATIONAL ACTION

The major responsibility for economic development quite naturally falls to the lot of individual developing states. Indeed, it would be difficult to discover a single "poor" state whose people did not regard economic betterment as the major objective and whose government did not regard it as the most pressing problem. Yet the need for outside help has become an accepted tenet of international economic orthodoxy, and "foreign aid" is widely regarded as a moral and political obligation of developed states. In response to numerous appeals, diverse programs of assistance have been established over more than five decades, starting with the Point Four Program of the United States in 1949. These international efforts, although based on converging interests of donors and recipients, have for the most part been shaped and directed by donor countries and have reflected their political, economic, military, moral, or community interests. This relationship between donors and recipients has produced problems of coordinating aid programs so that they will fit constructively with the developmental plans of the recipients. Major issues have arisen, and these issues have occasionally embroiled relations between giver and receiver. See Table 10-3 regarding vital rates and events seizing the developing countries in more recent years.

### SHOULD DONORS USE BILATERAL OR MULTILATERAL CHANNELS?

One such issue involves the means by which aid is funneled into developing economies. Although most financial aid comes from about a dozen capital-surplus countries, each contributor may use a variety of approaches in dispensing assistance.

Most donor states favor bilateral aid because they can exercise control over programs by imposing conditions on recipient states. In this way, industries competitive with those of the donor state can be discouraged, economic and social reforms can be encouraged, and counterpart funds can be required. Cold War ideological and political objectives were for many years critical determinants of the direction, kinds, and amount of bilateral aid. Donor governments also do not overlook propaganda advantages, as local populations can easily be made aware of the identity of their benefactor. Large amounts of foreign aid may permit the donor state to influence the recipient state's foreign policy. Moreover, directed trade patterns together with a need for spare parts may foster economic dependence.

Most developing countries prefer to receive aid through multilateral channels because this is likely to minimize interference in their domestic and foreign affairs. Exceptions to this preference are found in states that have a close and

TABLE 10-3    Less Developed Countries, Vital Rates and Events, 1991–2003

| YEAR | BIRTHS PER 1,000 POPULATION | DEATHS PER 1,000 POPULATION | RATE OF NATURAL INCREASE (%) | GROWTH RATE (%) |
|------|------|------|------|------|
| 1991 | 28.0 | 9.2 | 1.87 | 1.86 |
| 1992 | 27.2 | 9.1 | 1.81 | 1.76 |
| 1993 | 26.8 | 8.9 | 1.79 | 1.74 |
| 1994 | 26.5 | 8.9 | 1.75 | 1.71 |
| 1995 | 26.0 | 8.7 | 1.72 | 1.68 |
| 1996 | 25.6 | 8.7 | 1.69 | 1.65 |
| 1997 | 25.2 | 8.7 | 1.65 | 1.60 |
| 1998 | 24.7 | 8.6 | 1.61 | 1.58 |
| 1999 | 24.2 | 8.6 | 1.57 | 1.53 |
| 2000 | 23.6 | 8.5 | 1.51 | 1.48 |
| 2001 | 23.2 | 8.5 | 1.47 | 1.43 |
| 2002 | 22.9 | 8.5 | 1.44 | 1.40 |
| 2003 | 22.6 | 8.5 | 1.41 | 1.38 |

SOURCE: U.S. Bureau of the Census, International Data Base, 2003.

favorable relationship with major aid-givers. The United Nations probably offers the best hope for a fair and impartial aid program worked out through a partnership of donor and recipient countries, and most less developed countries have accorded this approach their full support. Donor countries, however, while participating in various UN assistance programs, have chosen to administer most of their aid through bilateral channels so as to retain full control over its distribution.

## SHOULD CAPITAL TRANSFERS HAVE PRIORITY?

An optimal aid program should match inputs of capital and technical assistance so that balanced growth can occur. This rarely happens even under the very best aid programs. Donor countries, while often generous to a fault in providing technical assistance, are reluctant to provide capital through government channels. But the leaders of the developing countries, under great pressure from their peoples to produce tangible results, clamor for capital.

Some less developed countries, such as the oil-producing states of the Organization of Petroleum Exporting Countries (OPEC), have large amounts of capital in the form of foreign exchange, whereas most developing states, especially in Africa, have very little capital and desperately seek to obtain more through UN programs. The addition of the former republics comprising the Soviet Union to the list of aid seekers has increased competition for scarce capital aid. Major capital aid programs outside of the UN system are almost wholly motivated by political and military considerations, such as U.S. aid to Israel and Egypt or to post-Taliban Afghanistan and U.S.-administered Iraq. Annual contributions to these countries amounting to many billions of dollars have been or are likely to be sustained well into the twenty-first century.

## SHOULD AID FUNDS BE GRANTED OR LOANED?

To give or to lend is a perennial problem facing aid-giving states and international institutions. In bilateral programs the United States has moved from a predominantly grant basis to a basis of mainly making low-interest loans, some at least partly repayable in local currencies. For many years the Soviet Union gave its aid in the form of long-term, low-interest loans, often repayable in local commodities. International institutions such as the World Bank generally extend short-term loans at moderate to high interest rates and expect repayment in hard currency.

Those favoring grants over loans argue that grants are more flexible than loans because they can be used to develop educational and other social overhead facilities. Loans, on the other hand, must ordinarily be used to expand self-liquidating productive facilities so that interest payments can be made and the principal of the loan amortized. Since grants do not have to be repaid, they have a minimally disturbing effect on the recipient country's balance of payments, unlike hard currency loans, which force the aid-receiving country to increase its exports or decrease its imports to obtain foreign exchange for installment payments. Grants, therefore, permit a better allocation of resources within a state and speed up economic growth by permitting a more rational application of aid funds.

The most compelling argument favoring loans over grants is that the need to repay loans with interest may encourage the recipient countries to devote the borrowed funds to productive projects rather than to monuments or imported luxury goods. Furthermore, within donor countries loans are generally more politically acceptable than grants.

Like most aid issues, that of loans versus grants poses a somewhat false dichotomy. Both grants and loans are needed in underdeveloped societies. Grants help develop substantial and suitable infrastructure, while loans provide the capital required for industrial growth and diversification. To increase the capacity of developing states to pay off loans, however, expanding world trade, open markets in the advanced countries, and higher prices for primary commodities are necessary.

## UN PROGRAMS

Economic development has become the major focus of debate in the General Assembly, the Economic and Social Council, and many subsidiary organs of the United Nations. Most UN programs have economic development as their basic objective, and most UN personnel administer development programs. Even such crucial questions as disarmament, collective security, and pacific settlement evoke an avalanche of words paying homage to economic development. Under constant pressures from less developed states, the developed states have agreed to participate in a variety of global programs.

The UN Charter says very little about economic development. Although economic cooperation is mentioned in a number of contexts, the only reference to economic *development* appears in Article 55, which provides, among other objectives, that "the United Nations shall promote: (a) higher standards of living, full employment, and conditions of economic and social progress and development." The Charter contains no authority to require any governmental or organizational action in the economic field, and aid programs must rest on a foundation of cooperation and voluntary contributions. The organization has in no way been deterred by the Charter's reticence on the subject of economic development, however, and a great variety of UN programs, resembling an "alphabet soup" of acronyms, have been established in three broad categories: planning and research, technical assistance, and capital financing.

## Building Support for Development

The leaders of most developing countries recognize that the principal responsibility for promoting economic advancement is theirs, that foreign aid and international cooperation are not substitutes for national action. But nations newly launched on programs of modernization lack the experience and sophistication needed to avoid costly mistakes and dead-end objectives. One of the most important approaches of the United Nations, consequently, has been to create opportunities for a meaningful dialogue between industrialized countries and countries seeking that status, and among the developing countries themselves. The dialogue has been carried on almost endlessly for many years, constituting a novel "school" for imparting desire, knowledge, judgment, and common sense to national purveyors of development schemes. The principal forums for carrying on the dialogue have been the Economic and Social Council (ECOSOC), the General Assembly in regular and special sessions, the Second (Economic and Financial) Committee of the Assembly, the informal forum of UN Headquarters, and countless conferences, committees, commissions, and agencies of the UN system.

The UN dialogue has also been a learning experience for the developed countries. From 1946 onward the chambers of the United Nations have echoed with the clamor of many voices. All seek to set forth views on the world's less fortunate and the urgency of economic development, the causes and cures for poverty, and the responsibilities of the more fortunate to alleviate poverty through substantial aid. The main cleavage between the developing states and the developed states has been over the approach to development, with the Western states advocating gradualist policies tested in their centuries-long development struggles and the developing states demanding rapid progress through shortcuts and massive technical and capital assistance programs. In the days of the Cold War the communist-bloc states increasingly joined the fray, offering until the late 1980s a socialist pattern as the best means for achieving progress.

Out of the debates have emerged not only a communication of existing ideas but also new approaches, increased knowledge, and a better understanding of the problems of development. This interchange has been complemented by special studies, by information gathering and analysis conducted by various secretariats, and by widespread publication of the findings. In fact, so extensive has been the research on problems of development that ECOSOC delegates have complained that they are being drowned in resolutions, reports, and discussions "beyond the analytical capacity and memory of the human brain." Computers have come into common use to help bring some semblance of order out of this chaos, but the search for shortcuts, new formulas, and sound plans continues.

## The Regional Commissions

On urging from the General Assembly, ECOSOC in 1947 established the Economic Commission for Europe (ECE) and the Economic Commission for Asia and the Far East (ECAFE) to give aid to countries devastated by the war. ECAFE became the Economic and Social Commission for Asia and the Pacific (ESCAP) in 1974. Latin American demands that economic development be recognized as a problem of equal importance resulted in the creation of the Economic Commission for Latin America (ECLA) in 1948, later changed to ECLAC with the addition of Caribbean nations in 1984. In 1958 the Economic Commission for Africa (ECA) was established to help plan and organize economic development drives for the new nations of that continent. Lack of regional harmony caused plans for a Middle East regional commission to be temporarily abandoned in the 1960s, but a new Economic and Social Commission for Western Asia (ESCWA) was established in 1974.

While all regional UN commissions foster economic cooperation among their members, each has an emphasis dictated by the special needs of the region. Headquartered in Geneva, the main concern of the ECE at the time of its establishment was the rebuilding of Western Europe from the devastation of World War II. With that task completed, the ECE directed its attention to the economic development of the economically weaker members of the European community and gave priority to economic cooperation between Western European nations and those of the former Soviet bloc in Eastern Europe.

From its Bangkok headquarters ESCAP has encouraged the creation of such developmental aids as the Asian Free Trade Area, the Mineral Resources Development Center, the International Pepper Community, the Asian Clearing Union, and the Asian Development Bank. It has also sponsored joint development projects, notably development of the Mekong River and Asian Highway.

ECLAC, with its central office in Santiago, Chile, has generated wide support in Latin America and is recognized for its contribution to the establishment of the Inter-American Development Bank, the Latin American Free Trade Association, the Central American Common Market, and other cooperative projects. It is also credited with spearheading the creation of the UN Conference on Trade and Development within the global UN system. ECLAC has fostered joint action in dealing with the many social problems affecting the modernization drive, such as birth control, child welfare, and housing.

The ECA, with headquarters at Addis Ababa, has in many respects the most difficult task of any regional commission. Its operations have been hampered by the abject poverty of many of its peoples and political rivalries among its members, many of which have ineffective and authoritarian governments. Nevertheless, it has helped to establish useful regional organizations in the areas of trade, banking, environmental protection, resource utilization, and political integration. Among these the African Development Bank has the better reputation for good management.

ESCWA is primarily a pan-Arab organization, with other countries in the Middle East—Iran, Israel, and Turkey—excluded from membership. When established in 1974, its headquarters were in Lebanon, but because of persistent war with Israel and much internal strife, the seat of operations was moved to Baghdad, Iraq. The lack of regional harmony had long worked against the establishment of a Middle East commission. How significant these problems were came to the fore when the United Nations undertook military action against the Iraqi regime of Saddam Hussein in 1991 and then the U.S.-led coalition uprooted that regime in 2003. Although ESCWA headquarters remained in Baghdad, virtually no development activities have been pursued.

Membership in the several regional commissions is not limited to states in the geographic region but includes others having special interests in the region. The nonregional members are for the most part industrialized states capable of contributing to the development of the region. The role of the commissions generally has been one of forging a regional outlook among diverse nations with different economic and social systems and, in some cases, with long histories of mutual hostilities. Cooperation within each of the regions has been fostered by numerous conferences, regular exchanges of information, the development of personal and government contacts, and an atmosphere of unity assiduously fostered by each commission's secretariat. Each of the commissions makes annual and special reports to ECOSOC, as well as recommendations to member governments and the specialized agencies on matters falling within their competence. Annual economic surveys of the commissions have served as bases for the development of "country plans" for the distribution of aid by donor countries' international organizations, and for the creation of new regional programs, such as the regional banks, common markets, and free trade associations. Annual sessions of the commissions have become major economic planning conferences with broad participation.

## The Development Decades of the Twentieth Century and Beyond

Four major UN campaigns to speed Third World development have taken the form of Development Decades for the 1960s, the 1970s, the 1980s, and the 1990s. The first was undertaken in 1961, when the Sixteenth General Assembly proclaimed a UN Development Decade to dramatize the organization's efforts, to call attention to the need for long-range planning, and to mobilize support for development. The Assembly set a target of raising the annual economic growth rate of developing countries from a 1960 average of about 3.5 percent to a 1970 minimum of 5 percent. The goal was not reached, but subsequent programs continued to dramatize UN development activities and the need for still greater efforts.

One major problem was the failure of many developing countries to carry out economic, political, and social reforms. Furthermore, development capital did not measure up to expectations. During the first two decades, the United Nations established the primary objective of transferring 1 percent of total GNP from each of the developed states to the developing states. In fact, such assistance fell from 0.51 percent of GNP in 1960 to less than 0.40 percent in the 1970s and 1980s. Burgeoning population growth further atrophied program goals by diverting attention within the developing countries to the need for increasing food production to avert famine and by emasculating aggregate national gains when measured in terms of per capita standards of living.

During the Third Development Decade the United Nations adopted a New International Development Strategy and also established a Substantial New Program of Action (SNPA) for the least developed countries. The strategy was aimed at getting each developed country to transfer 0.7 percent of its GNP each year to Third World development assistance. This was lower than the 1 percent of GNP demanded in the previous decades, but it was much higher than the actual development aid. SNPA also requested that donor countries contribute an additional 0.15 percent of GNP each year during the 1980s for the benefit of the poorest countries. It also strongly recommended that the industrialized countries convert their public loans to the poorest countries into outright grants. Supporters of SNPA argued that this would be a realistic approach because the alternative would probably be a general default by these countries.

The Fourth Development Decade was approved by the General Assembly in December 1990, along with an International Development Strategy to accelerate growth to the year 2000. The strategy emphasized human resources development, entrepreneurial innovation, and the energetic application of science and technology. The basic plan also called for political systems based on consent and respect for human rights, as well as social and economic rights. Third and Fourth World participants agreed to avoid despoiling the environment in their efforts to reduce the economic gap between them and the developed countries.

The Fourth Development Decade came at a propitious moment in the history of the United Nations and its development planning. The Cold War ended, and the developing states foresaw a great decline in world military expenditures that, according to the plan, would allow for the application of more significant resources to fight world poverty. The optimism was quickly shattered, however, by new regional and global political problems and enduring economic dilemmas that carried on into the twenty-first century.

*Promoting Industrial Development*

Some years into the First Development Decade (1966), the General Assembly established the UN Industrial Development Organization (UNIDO) "to promote the industrial development . . . and accelerate the industrialization of the developing countries, with particular emphasis on the manufacturing sector." The establishment of UNIDO revealed the emphasis that the developing states placed on industrialization, an emphasis that has not always been shared by the developed states. Opposed by many of the industrialized states, the creation of UNIDO nevertheless demonstrated the voting power of the Third World in the General Assembly. UNIDO therefore was not the beneficiary of substantial financial support from the developed countries.

UNIDO functioned as an "autonomous" organization within the United Nations until January 1, 1986, when it became a UN Specialized Agency. Its responsibilities were to strengthen, coordinate, and expedite international efforts to promote industrial development, through such activities as research, surveys, training programs, seminars, technical aid, and information exchange. Its main activity, however, was to apply continual pressure on the industrialized states to assist the developing states in their modernization drive. This role follows naturally because UNIDO's governing Industrial Development Board is elected by the General Assembly, and African, Asian, and Latin American states hold a majority of the Assembly seats. Examples of projects aided by UNIDO include the production of raw materials from sugarcane waste in Trinidad, the construction of a steel-rolling plant in Jordan, and the development of textile manufacturing in the Sudan. Dr. Abd-El Rahman Khane, a former Director-General of UNIDO, often proclaimed that the organization's goal was to have the Third World account for 25 percent of the world's industrial output by the year 2000. In 1975 it accounted for only 10 percent, and by 1990 it had not yet reached 11 percent. In support of the Industrial Development Decade for Africa, proclaimed in 1980, particular attention was focused on Africa, but wars, famine, disease, uncontrolled population growth, lack of skilled labor, and political corruption continued to inhibit real industrial growth.

UNIDO has been sustained despite opposition and the difficulties encountered in meeting declared goals. In 2003 the organization had 170 member states and headquarters in Vienna with a staff of 630. UNIDO also employed 123 staff members in the field and worked with more than 2,000 experts on short- and long-term assignments. With representation in 35 developing countries, the organization is active in promoting industrialization within transitional countries, and is a principal agent in the struggle against the marginalization of developing countries in an economically globalized world. During 2002 UNIDO's technical cooperation programs and projects totaled $81.8 million. Functioning under a new approach that called for integrated programs emphasizing the delivery of technical cooperation, UNIDO operated fifty-two programs at a cost of $103.8 million in 2002. Of these funds, 49.5 percent were allocated to Africa, 21.8 percent to the Arab region, and 28.7 percent to Central and Eastern Europe, Asia, and Latin America. Funding for UNIDO activities are in major part drawn from member states' assessed contributions.

## The Failed Role of Government: Changing Perspectives

At the end of the twentieth century it was apparent that development expectations had fallen far short of realities. While benefits are not to be discounted, developing countries' failures and limitations are substantial. Neither international nor regional organizations have achieved for states what they have been unable to do for themselves. State shortcomings are all too obvious, especially in their lack of capacity to fashion rules and institutions that deliver necessary goods and services to their citizens. Moreover, sustainable development, whether in economic or social matters, is impossible in the absence of successful governmental structures and processes. The shift away from the too-heavy dependence on the public sector to more assertive nongovernmental enterprises does not come naturally. But with government unable to meet the objectives of ever more complex societies, the emphasis has shifted to privatization. Government has been cast in a new set of roles, that of partner, catalyst, and facilitator. Structural adjustment policies demanded by the IMF in the developing nations have aimed at institutionalizing this reorientation. Structural adjustment, however, is no panacea, and its worse effects are usually visited upon already overburdened populations.

Development is no longer naively viewed as the inevitable consequence of good programs executed by good people. In hindsight, the central role of the state, which appeared to be the answer to the cyclic discontinuities of the marketplace and the supreme vehicle for the mobilization of human talents, was all too simple. Few countries had the developmental cadres or the circumstances to achieve desired outcomes. Moreover, inadequate experience in self-government exaggerated the roles of otherwise arbitrary rulers, and corruption in politics translated into corruption in modernization schemes. As a consequence, legions of development programs faltered or were suspended, and poverty endured.

Expanded government was a product of two world wars and a great depression in the older, more established and relatively advanced industrial nations. The retreat from empire following World War II and the proliferation of independent states without the basic experience of self-government meant that new nations would have to fend for themselves in an uncertain world. It also meant that governments, otherwise claiming to be democratically motivated, would monopolize power. In the absence of full-blown civil societies, with the masses little exposed to educational opportunities, with economic needs unanswered, and especially without a thriving middle class of commercial entrepreneurs, it was not surprising that governments dominated the popular will. Nor was it surprising that so-called development strategies were fashioned around state-dominant scenarios. In looking back on the development of the new states it is clear now that it was government that "developed." It was government and the public sector that became the primary consumer of national resources. It was government that decided where scarce resources would be placed, and what areas of development were to be given priority. This preeminence of officialdom did little to improve efficiency or the effectiveness of public delivery systems, but it went a long way to the modernization and expansion of the role of the armed forces in the new countries. Government existed to serve its own, not the people's, interest, and nowhere were the shortcomings and consequences of this arrogation of power in a centralized government better illustrated than in the Second World. There, communist systems, state-centric and absolutist, save for a few on the periphery of world affairs, came tumbling down in a heap between 1989 and 1991.

The epoch-making changes of the 1990s can only be compared with events immediately following the century's two catastrophic wars. But the end of the Cold War did not mean a better life for the world's impoverished people. State-dominated development strategies were brought into question as never before, but even with a new focus on privatization, government continued to play a central role, even if it was a central role that was modified by greater popular exposure and scrutiny in matters ranging from taxation to economic policies. Technological changes too opened opportunities to a global marketplace that at the turn of the century required public/private sector cooperation and greater transparency in the conduct of public affairs. Less tolerant of government failures, grassroots expression achieved a more audible voice, especially with the expansion of NGOs. The demand for greater government probity and accountability was matched by insistence that government be more effective in managing public goods such as property rights, infrastructure, basic health, and education. Decline in government authority, however, did not equate with a shift of priorities from state to people. Despite the emergence of more aggressive business groups as well as rank-and-file citizen organizations, there was no commensurate increase in public responsibility or civic consciousness. For the most part, only international relief agencies were left to tend to the needs of destitute peoples in developing countries that now in the twenty-first century were referred to as "failed states."

If the United Nations is to point out and help correct fault in its member states, it must first demonstrate its own capacity for self-improvement. In 1994 the UN Office of Internal Oversight Services (OIOS) was formed to help strengthen internal oversight of all UN activities. OIOS provides worldwide internal auditing, investigation, inspection, program monitoring, and evaluation and consulting services to all UN activities under the Secretary-General's authority. Since beginning operations in 1995 OIOS has exposed waste and fraud in the United Nations amounting to $198 million and recovered $87 million. OIOS has issued more than five thousand recommendations to improve internal controls and correct underlying obstacles to organizational efficiency and effectiveness. The overall implementation rate of OIOS recommendations is almost 80 percent; its use of quantitative and qualitative measures of program performance is a model for developing nations. It also may instill a greater sense of accountability, something desperately needed in emerging nations.

## TECHNICAL ASSISTANCE PROGRAMS

Technical assistance, which involves the teaching of skills and new technologies, is an indispensable instrument of any development program. Of the three main legs of the development stool—the infrastructure base, technical competence, and development capital—technical cooperation is the least controversial. It has consumed a sizable portion of the energies and funds of the advanced countries and of UN development programs. The transfer of any skill—from the most rudimentary to the most complex, from teaching a farmer how to wield a steel hoe most effectively to training technicians to run a nuclear power plant—falls within the scope of technical assistance. The most important categories are technological, managerial, administrative, educational, and medical, in all of which there has been a sharing of skills but a growing scarcity of technicians.

Some modern skills were transmitted to societies in the developing states during the nineteenth century and the first half of the twentieth century by colonizers and missionaries. League of Nations administrators also made a contribution, as did private business and philanthropic organizations. The initial government program of technical assistance on a substantial scale, however, began during World War II, when the United States sought to increase the production of primary commodities essential to the war effort through a major program of technical and cultural exchange with Latin American countries. U.S. experts in agriculture, mining, and education accepted in-service posts in Latin America, while large numbers of Latin Americans received training in the United States as medical doctors and technicians, engineers, agronomists, and public administrators. This program was phased out after the war, but in 1949 President Truman urged Americans to adopt "a bold new program for making the benefits of science and industrial progress available for the improvement and growth of under-developed areas." Set forth in his inaugural address as the last of four policies aimed at achieving peace and security in the world, Point Four was implemented by Congress in the Act for International Development. The Act provided for two programs: (1) an expanded program of technical assistance carried out through the United Nations and (2) a bilateral program of technical cooperation. With some changes in titles and administrative procedures, both programs continue today. Technical assistance can be broken down into two categories: one involves transferring knowledge and skills by sending individuals from developing countries abroad for training, and the other involves the importation and use of foreign experts.

## UN Development Program

The U.S. decision in 1949 to offer the underdeveloped world a large-scale technical assistance program led the General Assembly in November of that year to adopt an Expanded Program of Technical Assistance (EPTA). It went beyond the existing meager program and was financed through voluntary contributions rather than through the regular budget. Nine years later, in October 1958, the Assembly complemented the EPTA by establishing a Special Fund to lay the groundwork for encouraging capital flows into developing states. In November 1965 the Assembly combined the EPTA and Special Fund into a new UN Development Program (UNDP) to secure a unified approach. Although administratively joined, each maintains a distinctive approach to development within the UNDP.

*Expanded Program of Technical Assistance*

EPTA incorporates three main forms of assistance: (1) providing experts, including some from the underdeveloped countries themselves, to train cadres of technicians; (2) awarding fellowships for technical training in advanced countries; and (3) supplying limited amounts of equipment for training and demonstration purposes. Funds for EPTA, as for the Special Fund, come from voluntary contributions offered at annual pledging conferences. Contributions may be made in both local and hard currencies, but donors may not attach any conditions to the use of their contributions.

Funds are dispensed to approved projects sponsored by the United Nations or by specialized agencies that have been accepted as participating organizations of EPTA. These include the International Labor Organization, the Food and Agriculture Organization, UNESCO, the International Civil Aviation Organization, the World Health Organization, the International Telecommunication Union, the World Meteorological Organization, the International Atomic Energy Agency, the Universal Postal Union, the International Maritime Organization, and the World Bank. All are represented on the Inter-Agency Consultative Board for the Development Program, which coordinates all UN technical assistance and related programs. The IMF, although not participating directly in the program, works closely with the Consultative Board to deal with balance of payments problems affecting development programs.

Resident representatives in the field help governments develop sound programs and advise the Consultative Board on their feasibility in relation to local conditions. Offices around the globe coordinate technical assistance programs, function as "country representatives" for some of the specialized agencies, lend assistance on preinvestment surveys, and serve as a link between the United Nations and the recipient government.

UN technical assistance programs have been widely recognized as desirable and generally effective, and developing states have for the most part not been critical of the pace of UN technical assistance programs. Rather, their complaints have been directed primarily at the shortage of development capital.

*The Special Fund*

The Special Fund was a partial response to demands for capital transfers to supplement technical assistance and reflected a growing recognition by advanced states that the fruits of technical assistance would be increased if such assistance was supported by inputs of capital. The Special Fund, however, was only a compromise falling far short of the perennial demands of developing states for a massive development fund to provide capital grants and to be replenished annually at a contributory rate of 1 percent of the GNP of each industrialized state.

The Special Fund nonetheless embodied the concept of paving the way for increased private, national, and international investment. It was charged with conducting "preinvestment" surveys, discovering the wealth-producing potentials of not yet surveyed natural resources, establishing training and research institutes, and preparing "feasibility reports on the practicability, requirements, and usefulness" of development projects. Although EPTA and the Special Fund were to be coordinated, the Special Fund initially functioned independently in allocating money and determining priorities. The amalgamation of the two in the UNDP gave some assurance that both programs would operate thereafter under a single source of direction. The UNDP has become the world's largest agency for technical cooperation.

## UNDP

UNDP is a trusted development partner because it operates according to principles and values of the United Nations. Each country's control over its own future is respected while bringing countries together to work on shared tasks. The UNDP Executive Board, including representatives from thirty-six countries, is responsible for providing intergovernmental support to and supervision of the activities of UNDP and for ensuring that it is responsive to the needs of program countries. Today, UNDP is engaged in a range of projects from politics to security, public health, crime, and the environment.

In 2003, UNDP functioned in 166 countries, using a global network to help the UN system and its partners raise awareness and track progress while it connects countries to the knowledge and resources needed to achieve developmental objectives. Matters of democratic governance focus on building inclusive institutions to promote participation from among all classes of citizenry. Electoral and legislative systems, as well as the development of justice infrastructure and public administration, are high on the UNDP agenda. So too is poverty reduction through the development of pilot projects and by direct assistance to governments, civil society, and especially women seeking equality. Crisis prevention and recovery is another concern, as UNDP shares innovative approaches and deals with matters of early warning and conflict resolution. It also focuses on problems related to energy and the environment, with special interest in sustainable development. The revolution in communications is still another interest of UNDP as it tries to incorporate information and communications technology in its numerous programs. Without such policies people in the developing world would be left farther behind. In the area of health care, UNDP advocates placing HIV/AIDS at the center of national planning and budgets and is especially concerned with the creation of community-level support groups to combat the deadly disease. Finally, UNDP is a major actor in promoting gender equality and seeks to expose women to the political process, which is the only guarantee of their empowerment. Guided by the belief that development is a process of enlarging national choices, not just raising national incomes, UNDP seeks to ensure the most effective use of UN and international aid resources.

*Other Technical Assistance Programs*

The diversity of needs in the developing world has helped spawn a variety of special UN projects, each devoted to an attack on some particular problem of economic development not covered or covered inadequately by the general technical assistance program. To fill a need for top-level administrators in developing societies, an Operational, Executive, and Administrative Personnel Service (OPEX) was established in 1958 by the General Assembly. Internationally recruited experts were assigned under OPEX to governments with the proviso that their duties include training nationals to replace them. Another complementary personnel program emerged in 1963 when the General Assembly established the UN Institute for Training and Research (UNITAR). Fully operational by 1966, UNITAR specializes in conducting training seminars for new members of government delegations and their staffs and for individuals in UN-related civil service positions. UNITAR faculty is recruited through fellowship programs and through the voluntary participation of eminent scholars and politicians.

A number of programs, peripheral yet important to economic development, complete the UN effort to provide technical assistance. UN conferences on a host of topics such as population control, desertification, science and technology, environmental protection, world fisheries, and the role of women have been convened over the years to foster development attuned to the needs of particular regions and countries. An Industrial Development Center functions as a clearinghouse in the areas of economics and industrial technology, and an Economic Projections and Programming Center was established to develop long-term projections of world economic and industrial trends that could facilitate national planning. Both centers are located at UN Headquarters, although the latter center also operates through regional centers.

The World Food Program, set up in 1963 by the United Nations and the FAO, was called to provide food for economic and social development projects as well as to supply food in emergencies. Under this program food aid constitutes a partial substitute for cash wages for workers in such fields as mining, industry, community development, and irrigation. In the area of demography, the UN Population Commission conducts extensive research on population problems affecting the ability of states to develop and has sponsored several World Population Conferences. Other programs that contribute indirectly to technical cooperation include the UNICEF program for fostering the development of future leaders and technicians through food and educational programs for children. The United Nations itself trains political leaders in statecraft, and Secretariat technicians learn modern administrative techniques. Many other types of aid programs include provisions for technical assistance as well. For example, the World Bank has become active in technical assistance through project preparation, development programming, and the training of senior development officers.

A United Nations University that is headquartered in Tokyo carries on a fellowship program that is linked with national and regional development organizations in more than sixty countries. The University has supplied hundreds of scholars, scientists, and government officials to help fill knowledge gaps in the areas of poverty, famine, and resource management. Some of these fellows are experienced specialists, whereas others are graduate students, mainly from Third World countries.

### The Future of Technical Assistance

Technical assistance programs enable some nations to help other nations, making all of them better off. Donor countries benefit because poorer countries make better trading partners as their living conditions improve; furthermore, societies moving toward a brighter economic future are less prone to revolutionary violence. There has been little criticism of the principle of technical cooperation, from either developed or developing countries. Duplication and overlapping of jurisdictions have abounded in UN programs, however, as well as between these programs and bilateral and regional programs, and this has sometimes aroused petty jealousies and rivalries. Efforts within the United Nations to coordinate programs have been only partially effective, and future consolidations and partnership arrangements, such as those carried out by EPTA and the Special Fund through the UNDP, are needed in order to employ limited resources and personnel more advantageously. Finally, as already noted, no technical assistance program, no matter how well financed and administered, can achieve major development goals unless capital accumulation, investment, and transfers of technology move forward in tandem with it. We now turn our attention to the UN role of fostering the inflow of capital into developing economies to obtain the balance that is so essential for economic development.

## THE ROLE OF THE INTERNATIONAL MONETARY FUND

The world's monetary system, weakened during the period of economic nationalism of the 1930s, emerged from World War II in almost complete disarray. To promote a more orderly international payments system, the planners at the Bretton Woods Conference in 1944 drew up Articles of Agreement for an International Monetary Fund (IMF). The IMF, the World Bank (also a product of Bretton Woods), and the ill-fated International Trade Organization were to be the three legs on which international economic well-being would rest.

The IMF is one of the sixteen specialized agencies within the UN system. In 2003, 184 countries were members of the organization. Each member is represented on the organization's governing board, which meets annually to fix general policy. A Board of Governors (composed of ministers of finance or heads of central banks or other officials of comparable rank from all the member states) watches over the organization. Daily business is the responsibility of a 24-member Executive Board chaired by a Managing Director who is also administrative head of a staff of some 2,650 people from 140 countries. Voting is rarely made on the basis of formal balloting, and the Executive Board relies on the formation of consensus among its members. The IMF also has a Monetary and Financial Committee made up of twenty-four governors who represent constituencies or groups of countries. This Committee meets two times each year to advise the IMF on the functioning of the international monetary system. The Accounting Unit of the IMF operates with assets from Special Drawing Rights, worth approximately $293 billion in January 2003.

The main stated areas of IMF activity since 2001 are surveillance, financial assistance, and technical assistance, but its purposes are set forth in its original Articles of Agreement and include the following:

1. To promote international monetary cooperation.
2. To facilitate the expansion of international trade.
3. To promote exchange stability.
4. To assist in the establishment of a multilateral system of payments.
5. To give confidence to members by making its resources available to them.
6. To shorten the duration and lessen the degree of disequilibrium in members' balances of payments.

The architects of the Bretton Woods system intended that national currencies should be freely convertible with one another, avoiding the exchange control systems that emerged during the Great Depression and World War II. They also planned to avoid the wildly fluctuating exchange rates of the 1920s and 1930s by requiring each member country to establish and maintain a fixed value for its currency, tied directly or indirectly to the value of gold. The IMF would then help countries maintain their currency values by lending funds to cover temporary balance-of-payments deficits resulting from periods of weak demand for a state's currency. If long periods of either strong or weak demand created a "fundamental disequilibrium" in a state's payments position, that country could, with the IMF's permission, alter its exchange rate to reflect the real value of its currency on international markets. The IMF was not intended to be the principal source of lending to finance international trade but rather to supplement normal commercial sources.

This system mirrored the founders' concern that the world should not be allowed to slip back into the financial anarchy of the 1930s or retain strangling wartime controls. As in the proposals for a world trade system, the IMF's originators foresaw a new, orderly world of international finance based on a common code to guide the actions of member states and governed by an international institution that could determine exchange and payments policies. Since

1945 the IMF has contributed to greater financial order, but not without major crises to the system and severe pain to individual countries. Moreover, in the 1970s the IMF was forced to abandon the principle of fixed exchange rates tied to gold, as originally provided in the IMF articles. Instead, it shifted to floating rates set by market forces.

As the IMF operates today, it administers a code of conduct governing exchange rate policies and restrictions on payments, primarily in the interest of promoting freer exchange of currencies. It is also a forum for government consultation on major monetary questions. Beyond this it seeks to provide exchange stability by two means: by influencing currency values, and by permitting members to draw foreign exchange from the IMF to tide them over periods of serious financial hardship.

The concept underlying the use of the IMF as a pooling arrangement is fairly simple. All members contribute to a common bank of monetary reserves on which they can draw to overcome short-term disequilibriums in their balances of payments. The contributions are based on a quota system set according to a state's national income, gold reserves, and other factors related to ability to contribute. Initially, each member is required to contribute 25 percent of its quota in hard currency (presently, the U.S. dollar, British pound, euros for France and Germany, or Japanese yen)—the so-called *credit tranche*—but the remainder can be in its own currency. Each member has a right to purchase foreign exchange from the IMF in amounts equal to the value of its credit tranche, but the maximum may run much higher by agreement with the IMF. Other lending arrangements supplement the quota system, most designed to meet needs of developing countries. When a state withdraws an amount from the IMF for an emergency, it actually purchases the foreign exchange with its own domestic currency; when it repays the amount, it returns foreign exchange to the IMF for its own currency. In this way, the reserve pool as a revolving fund remains fairly constant in the total value of its holdings, but it is important to note that the amounts of different currencies will fluctuate depending on the demand for them.

The objective underlying the currency pool is to maintain fairly stable exchange values for members' currencies. When a member suffers a short-term deficit in its balance of payments that cannot be financed through commercial banks, purchases of foreign exchange from the IMF are ordinarily expected to carry it through the crisis. The IMF usually attaches conditions to large borrowings, designed to help remedy the problems that produced the large deficit. Such conditions may include commitments by the borrowing state to restrict domestic credit, allow more realistic exchange rates and price levels, balance its budget, and cut subsidies to state enterprises and less efficient sectors of its economy. Borrowers have frequently criticized IMF "conditionality," as it is called, because the financial discipline often has temporarily harsh effects on the domestic economy.

# UN DEVELOPMENT FINANCING PROGRAMS: THE WORLD BANK GROUP

Financial assistance for economic development within the UN system is in major part dispensed through loan programs associated with the World Bank Group, which consists of the International Bank for Reconstruction and Development (IBRD), the International Finance Corporation (IFC), the International Development Association (IDA), the Multilateral Investment Guarantee Agency (MIGA) and, the International Center for Settlement of Investment Disputes (ICSID). Although these five institutions function within the broad framework of the UN system, each is involved in its own fund-raising and decision-making operations. Developing states have repeatedly turned to the World Bank Group and the IMF for capital aid in the form of loans to supplement loans from national, regional, and private sources. IMF membership is a prerequisite for joining the World Bank Group, but a nation can join the IMF without joining the World Bank or its affiliated institutions.

## THE ROLE OF THE WORLD BANK GROUP

The agencies of the World Bank Group, along with the IMF, are responsible for almost all capital aid transfers to developing countries. Coordination between World Bank agencies and the IMF is managed through the World Bank/IMF Development Committee, which functions both as an advisory body to the two boards of governors and as an action body to encourage "foreign capital flows of all kinds" to developing states. Its membership includes finance and development ministers from the two boards of governors.

### The International Bank for Reconstruction and Development (IBRD)

Born from the 1944 Bretton Woods Conference, IBRD, or the World Bank as it is more commonly called, was created in 1945 and intended to be the central unit in UN lending operations. Since private international capital had virtually disappeared during the 1930s, the World Bank represented the prevailing attitude that some form of public international financing was essential as a supplement to private loans. Initially the World Bank devoted its resources to the urgent task of restoring Europe's war-torn economies, with only seven loans committed to developing countries by the end of 1949. The pace of development loans quickened, however, when the colonial empires crumbled and literally scores of new independent and sovereign states achieved freedom and self-government. With the emergence of the developing nations, World Bank loans rose by billions of dollars in each subsequent decade. By 2002 the World Bank's cumulative lending had reached $360 billion, almost all of it to developing countries.

The major focus of the World Bank in the twenty-first century is reducing poverty and improving living standards. The World Bank is run like a cooperative with its 185 member countries as shareholders. The number of shares a country has is based roughly on the size of its economy, with the United States the largest shareholder, followed by Japan, Germany, the United Kingdom, and France. The remaining shares are divided among the other member countries. Government shareholders in the bank are represented by a Board of Governors, composed of ministers of finance or ministers of development, who are the ultimate policymakers in the World Bank. Day-to-day decision making, however, is the responsibility of Executive Directors who work at Bank headquarters in Washington, D.C. Each government having membership in the World Bank Group is represented by an Executive Director, but only the five largest shareholders have direct representation. The other members in effect share nineteen Executive Directors. The World Bank President is traditionally a citizen of the largest shareholder, that is, the United States. Elected for five-year renewable terms, the President chairs meetings of the Board of Directors and is responsible for the overall management of the bank. The World Bank employs approximately ten thousand people, including economists, educators, environmental scientists, financial analysts, anthropologists, engineers, and numerous others with different specialized capacities. Employees come from approximately 160 countries, with more than three thousand staff members working in country offices.

Lending policies remain the responsibility of the Bank's Board of Governors, who are bound to the weighted-voting system based on subscribed capital. The World Bank makes "hard loans," repayable in convertible currency, and most of its loans have run for five to fifteen or twenty years at less than commercial rates of interest. Loans are made either to member governments or to private firms with a government guarantee. Loans to private firms have been minimal because companies have found it difficult to obtain their government's guarantee or have preferred not to get involved with governmental bureaucratic procedures. Moreover, the World Bank has no facilities for investigating and administering loan applications from small businesses. To meet this problem, the World Bank has granted loans to private banks and loan and investment agencies so that local banks can distribute those funds to private companies and local entrepreneurs.

The World Bank is operated by financial experts with banking experience and conveys a conservative image. It operates on sound principles of international finance, and its loan criteria are aimed at protecting its interests and those of its creditors. This image of soundness is necessary because most of the World Bank's loan funds are obtained not from governments but from borrowing in private capital markets. Loan applicants must use a "project" approach in which the applicant demonstrates that the loan will finance a carefully planned undertaking that will contribute to the productive and earning capacity of the country. For many years the World Bank frowned on social project loans (for building hospitals and schools or for slum clearance, for instance), general-purpose loans, and loans to meet rising debt or to resolve balance-of-payments problems, but it has given such loans increasing support in recent years. In fact, the World Bank's lending policies have changed substantially since the latter half of the 1980s and the 1990s, and it now encourages economic growth in major debtor countries of the Third World. For some years the World Bank limited its use of funds to "self-liquidating projects"—projects that would provide revenues large enough to service debt payments—but it now measures the repayment capacity of the nation's entire economy in making its loans. On average, World Bank loans have financed only 25 percent of the cost of projects, with other investors often joining the World Bank to provide the balance.

Over the years the World Bank has undergone a change, both in its self-image and in its operations, from a strictly financial institution to that of a development agency intimately concerned with solving problems of economic development. Instead of remaining aloof and merely passing judgment on loan applications, it now assists states in their development planning, helps prepare project proposals, and provides training for senior development officials. Its economic survey missions check resource and investment potentials in member countries and determine priorities for country and regional projects. The World Bank has also participated increasingly in consortium arrangements for financing major projects, with funds provided jointly by global, regional, and local public and private lending institutions. The World Bank has demonstrated that it can use its funds to secure the cooperation of political enemies on a mutually beneficial development plan, as in the joint development of a common river control system by India and Pakistan.

Despite the Bank's increased pace of activity, it has never been able to meet all the capital needs of developing states. For one thing, repayment of loans in hard currencies imposes heavy responsibilities on borrowing states that do not rank high as foreign exchange earners. Nevertheless, the World Bank of the twenty-first century is one of the world's largest sources of development assistance. Its primary focus today is helping the poorest people and the poorest countries. For example, it has become the largest funding agency of education programs to poverty-stricken nations. Bank-supported projects also have increased educational benefits for children in India, reduced tuberculosis infections in China, fought HIV/AIDS in Brazil, and helped relieve conditions that led to the financial disaster in East and Southeast Asia in the late 1990s.

### The International Finance Corporation (IFC)

From the start of the World Bank's operations, many observers recognized that some kind of affiliate was needed to help finance private investment. Such an affiliate would permit the stimulation of private companies by injections of international capital secured mainly from private sources. This kind of financing was provided by the establishment of the IFC in 1956, with a startup subscribed capital fund of $78 million. The IFC in 2003 had 175 members and a committed portfolio of $21.6 billion. In fiscal year 2002 it committed $3 billion to 204 companies in 75 countries. The IFC promotes the flow of capital from world money markets, stimulates the formation of investment capital within member countries, and encourages private enterprise and private investment opportunities. It makes loans and direct equity investments in private companies, including companies owned jointly by local and foreign interests. The IFC, for example, has entered into mixed equity loan commitments in such industries as steel, textiles, cement, jute, pulp, food processing, and pharmaceuticals. The IFC currently invests across a wide spectrum of sectors from capital markets, infrastructure, agribusiness, petrochemicals, and extractive industries to general manufacturing. Projects have been established in every geographic region, and opportunities are sought to invest in social service projects such as health care and education.

In an effort to get more private capital flowing into developing states, the IFC in 1989 established the International Securities Group (ISG) to provide investment banking services to clients in Third World countries. ISG functions (1) as an adviser in the issuance of securities; (2) as a partner, bringing companies from the developing world to international capital markets; and (3) as a provider of information to the world investment community on investment opportunities in emerging markets. As a result of IFC/ISG activities, by 1998 more than one thousand companies were listed on the stock exchanges in twenty developing countries. In this sense, IFC rejects anything resembling a "welfare" approach and seeks through pure capitalism to encourage economic growth and modernization.

IFC's mandate is to further economic development through the private sector. Working with business partners, it invests in sustainable private enterprises in developing countries and provides long-term loans, guarantees, and risk management and advisory services to its clients. IFC invests in projects in regions and sectors that are underserved by private investment. It also finds new ways to develop promising opportunities in markets deemed too risky by commercial investors in the absence of IFC participation. Obviously, IFC merely scratches the surface of world needs for public capital to stimulate private investment. Loans to small- and medium-sized companies are not necessarily included in its scope of operations, although it has encouraged members to establish local development banks to do this job and has offered to help finance them. The IFC itself has been authorized to borrow large sums from the World Bank. The result is effective but circular. The World Bank secures funds from private capital markets, lends some of these funds to the IFC, which in turn lends to country development banks, from which the funds return through direct loans to private businesses. Are these international and national institutional intermediaries really necessary? They obviously are, as they were created in response to urgent needs. Most investors refuse to risk their capital in developing states without governmental guarantee programs. The stage of sustainable growth may yet be reached by a developing country when substantial inflows of private funds occur without global, regional, or local institutional stimulation or direct protection. Both the IFC and ISG are in pursuit of that objective.

## The International Development Association (IDA)

In response to growing demands for a capital grants program and continuing criticism of the conservative nature of the World Bank's operations, in 1960 the IDA was established as a "soft loan" affiliate. The IDA was also a response by the United States (the idea was developed in the U.S. Congress) to a stepped-up Soviet aid/trade offensive. Although the IDA is a separate legal entity and its funds and reserves are separate from those of the World Bank, the management and staff of the two institutions are the same. The "soft loan" features of the IDA pertain to the long period for repayment, often fifty years. The slow amortization rate begins after a ten-year grace period, with 1 percent of the loan's principal repayable annually during the second ten years. In the remaining thirty years the rate is 3 percent payable annually. The low cost of the loan at no interest, but with a three-fourths of 1 percent annual service charge, makes it very attractive to borrowers. IDA loans really are not "soft," however. In one highly important respect, loans must be repaid in "hard" (convertible) foreign exchange. This usually means U.S. dollars or a currency freely convertible into dollars.

Developing states, recognizing the advantages of IDA's terms—especially the provision that no payments on a loan are due for ten years—quickly depleted the initial and subsequent subscriptions. As with World Bank loans, recipients of IDA funds must finance a portion of all loan projects, usually with local currency. The IDA's loans go mainly to government agencies in the poorest countries for projects similar to those funded in other developing countries by the World Bank. Whether IDA loans will continue to be paid off when the ten-year grace period ends depends in each case on a country's progress in economic development and its export trade. It will also depend on general world conditions—war or peace, boom or bust, population control or population explosion, the terms of trade, the development of synthetics, changes in consumer tastes, and numerous other unpredictable factors that may either ease repayments or, for all practical purposes, turn loans into grants. The IDA lends only to those countries that had a per capita income in 1995 of less than $905 and a lack of financial ability to borrow from the World Bank on market terms. In 1998, eighty countries were eligible to borrow from the IDA. Together these countries were home to 3.2 billion people, comprising 65 percent of the total population of the developing countries. Some 1.2 billion of these people survived on incomes of $1 or less a day. When a country passes the IDA eligibility threshold, it can no longer apply for the IDA's interest-free credits and must borrow from the World Bank at market-related rates. Some countries, however, like China and India, are eligible for a combination of World Bank loans and IDA credits. These countries are known as "blend borrowers." In 1998 there were seventeen blend borrowers. Countries that "graduated" from IDA eligibility included Costa Rica, Chile, Indonesia, and Morocco.

IDA cumulative lending since its founding in 1960 was $135 billion in 2003. In fiscal year 2002 the IDA loaned $8.18 billion for 133 operations in sixty-two countries. In the twenty-first century it stands next in importance to the World Bank in tending to the needs of the poorest countries. The IDA had 164 members in 2003, and contributions to IDA enable the World Bank to provide $6 billion to $7 billion per year in interest-free credits to the world's seventy-eight poorest countries. This support is vital because these countries have little or no capacity to borrow on market terms.

### The Multilateral Investment Guarantee Agency (MIGA)

A third affiliate of the World Bank Group, MIGA, came into being in 1988. MIGA's role is to encourage the flow of private equity capital to developing countries by insuring investments against losses resulting from political risks—war and civil strife, expropriation, government repudiation of contracts, and host government currency restrictions. MIGA also provides technical assistance to help countries disseminate information on investment opportunities and offers investment dispute mediation on request. With equity investments, or risk capital, recipient states have the benefit of capital infusion without incurring debt obligations. MIGA in 2003 had 163 members and cumulative guarantees of $10.34 billion. Fiscal year 2002 guarantees issued stood at $1.36 billion.

### The International Center for Settlement of Investment Disputes (ICSID)

Established in 1966, ICSID helps encourage foreign investment by providing international facilities for conciliation and arbitration of investment disputes. It therefore helps to encourage an environment of mutual confidence between states and foreign investors. A number of international agreements focused on investment refer to ICSID's arbitration facilities, and its expertise carries over to research and the publication of materials on arbitration law and foreign investment law. In 2003 ICSID had 139 members and 103 registered cases.

## THE WORLD BANK GROUP: AN EVALUATION

The World Bank Group operates on a professional, nonpolitical level. The activities of the World Bank and its four affiliates have offered advantages to almost every developing state, and indications are that the pace of their lending operations will accelerate in the decades ahead. Yet the Group's operations have been subject to extensive criticism. Control of World Bank Group operations by Western (former colonial) powers, through a voting system that is weighted on the basis of contributions, has aroused widespread suspicion of its motives and policies. Critics point out that the World Bank's loan terms are no bargain—that they are usually only slightly easier, and sometimes even harsher, than those of private banks. In many cases states borrow from the World Bank despite its high rates because their low credit rating prevents them from securing private loans. The IFC, it has been said, has never gained general acceptance in the advanced donor states, or for that matter in the developing world, as evidenced by relatively low-level funding to poorer countries. Its objective of furthering private investment by meshing capital from both the public and private sectors is a novel approach, but the total resources have been considered too modest to effectively stimulate growth capitalism within recipient states. The IDA has enjoyed a singular success in dispensing funds, probably because it comes closest to the capital grants system unsuccessfully sought by developing states. The IDA, however, is frequently "loaned out," with no funds available until a new pledging conference provides for a replenishment of reserve capital.

Despite criticism, the World Bank Group has retained the support of its members, whether developed or developing countries. The Group's loans have helped more than one hundred countries to finance useful development projects, and it has often successfully encouraged internal financial reforms within borrowing countries. This last role, sometimes referred to as "the art of development diplomacy," may go beyond domestic matters, as cited above in the World Bank's negotiation of the Indus River Agreement between India and Pakistan. Given the continuing capital needs for economic development in the world today and the failure of the UN Capital Development Fund, one can only conclude that the role of the World Bank Group will continue to expand.

## CONCLUSION ON ECONOMIC DEVELOPMENT

Where, on balance, do developing states stand today? What are the prospects for development in the decades ahead? Although more has been done to promote world economic development during the past four decades than in all the past cons of history, much more has been needed and expected. Progress, if defined as an improvement in mass standards of living, has failed to measure up to optimistic hopes. Agricultural output, while increasing substantially in some developing states, has barely kept pace with population growth, and millions of people remain undernourished. Famines in Africa during the 1980s and 1990s have extended into the new millennium. Unchecked, this situation may well prove a harbinger for much of the Third World, with the danger that undernourishment in many countries may turn first to more serious malnutrition and then to large-scale famine and disease of catastrophic proportions. In the area of housing, millions of new dwellings must be built each year merely to stay abreast of population growth. Education, despite extensive UN and national programs fostered by UNESCO, remains a major problem at all points on the educational scale—too many illiterate people, too few trained technicians, and a great paucity of university-trained professionals. Unemployment and underemployment also pose serious problems in many countries.

Although countries and subregions fail in their attempt to dent the problem of economic stagnation, a few have been making determined efforts to join the world of developed states. Some societies, however, have received huge infusions of aid but have failed to use that aid effectively, that is, to broaden the base of their economies or to integrate new productive enterprises with the demands of the world market. Indeed, too many well-intentioned efforts of the international community through bilateral, regional, and global programs have been scattered and largely uncoordinated and too often characterized by wasteful duplication and overlapping.

Clearly, most developing states prefer to receive aid through UN programs that leave them unencumbered politically and militarily, and most important, that avoid damaging national egos. The United Nations offers a partnership arrangement with assisted countries, cooperating in planning, developing, and administering aid programs that are somewhat freer of power rivalries than other aid programs. No other international organization can provide such a reservoir of development information and experience or possesses so many useful contacts that are beneficial to developing states. The United Nations also provides a natural focus for coordinating development programs, an "agitation chamber" for debating and stimulating action by member states, a forum for the exchange of information and ideas, and a repository of skills that are available to developing states. But the key objective of the great majority of members—obtaining the full support of the developed states for a large-scale capital grants program—has not been realized.

Nevertheless, a still higher profile is forecast for the UN system in the twenty-first century. Kofi Annan heads a spirited Secretariat team that is committed to new initiatives, and especially to making linkages between the United Nations and the global business community. Citing the need to address the forces of globalization, UN officials are concerned with both the positive and negative dimensions of the contemporary world economy. Cognizant that globalization in its current form can adversely affect developing nations, the Secretary-General has focused attention on the continuing North-South debate that highlights differences and gaps between wealthy and poor nations. In the middle of this exchange is the Third World's continuing dependence on the United Nations and the more affluent states' preference for the more intrusive World Bank and IMF. Sensitive to the issues behind this controversy, Kofi Annan has noted, "Unless we tackle the underlying distortions and imbalances in the global economy, unless we start the kind of global governance that is needed, we must expect more [political and military] conflicts and even more intractable ones."[3] Annan's words, spoken before September 11, 2001, reverberate today through the halls of the United Nations and throughout the world.

The United Nations therefore is engaged in forging even closer ties to the World Bank and IMF and encourages increased dialogue among global stakeholders. New forums have been fashioned to elevate high-level economic consultations between the Bretton Woods institutions and ECOSOC. A UN-sponsored meeting on finance and development elevated expectations among spokespeople from developing countries that the architecture of the world's financial institutions will be further adapted to focus more effort and resources on sustainable development projects and social issues. The creation of the UN Millennium Development Goals (see Chapter 9) is aimed at such future actions.

As the Millennium Summit convened in 2000, international programs aimed at helping poor nations develop and industrialize were failing in many countries, and radical changes were called for if the world was to come anywhere close to its targets. The Summit's *Human Development Report* of 2003 noted that instead of calling upon developing countries to cut back on public spending in favor of privatization, the IMF and World Bank must begin to press the richer countries for greater assistance. Despite a widespread assumption that all countries are making progress toward greater prosperity, the *Report* noted that fifty-four countries were poorer in 2003 than they were in 1990. Life expectancy also had fallen dramatically in thirty-four countries, primarily as a consequence of the HIV/AIDS epidemic, and twenty-one countries had less food available on a daily basis than at the beginning of the 1990s. Describing the decade of the 1990s as a "decade of despair," the *Report* questioned whether any of the Millennium Development Goals could be achieved despite all the oratory at the Millennium Summit. Reducing poverty by half by the year 2015, although a noble goal, was deemed to be a highly exaggerated statement of intention. UNDP Administrator Mark Malloch-Brown has said that only a "guerrilla assault" on the "Washington consensus" that makes the general policies in guiding the IMF and World Bank can reverse the present course and promise a more successful implementation of objectives. It is not enough that the IMF and World Bank tell countries to lower their sights; developing countries need the required assistance to achieve the Millennium Development Goals. Total reliance on market forces and increased trade, the *Report* cautions, will mean that many countries will never achieve their potential levels of development. Insisting that the public sector still has a major role in development, the *Report* again asked developed countries to revisit their roles in helping the world's poor countries realize higher standards of living for their people.

Although still determined to avoid the pressure employed by agencies of the United Nations on behalf of developing countries, the developed states nevertheless are forced by the events of September 11 to acknowledge that their policies are in need of change. Chastened by events that have produced the protracted war on terrorism, the most prosperous nations finally seem more inclined to listen to the concerns of developing nations. Moreover, no better forum than the United Nations exists for building bridges between North and South and between different societies and cultures. Thus, despite their reluctance to mix macroeconomic policy-making with particular financial and fiscal responsibilities, in the twenty-first century the more developed nations are compelled to demonstrate greater flexibility in their relations with developing countries. But even more so, the affluent states must find the formula that balances the financial and technical assistance needs of the many developing countries with those created by the post-2003 attempt to transform countries such as Iraq and Afghanistan into model nation-states. Finance ministers and central bank governors of the G-7 countries must give more attention to reducing uncertainty about the financial conditions prevailing in developing countries. They also must find the means to redistribute the risk of foreign lending to emerging market economies. The centerpiece for the new policy remains the abandonment of secrecy and a new emphasis on total transparency in fiscal and monetary dealings. Public and private corporations must be held to high standards of probity, and a newly reconstructed IMF must take responsibility for monitoring compliance with strict, international guidelines as well as demonstrating greater accountability. G-7 nations must accept responsibility for development projects that seldom have taken into account the most vulnerable groups—the abject poor, the illiterate, and marginalized minorities. Moreover, closing the distance between the developed and developing nations will require bringing the IMF and World Bank into more intimate association with the Group of 77.

Within the broad framework of the UN system, states have joined together to build institutional structures for economic and political cooperation. Some structures are rooted in the UN decision-making machinery of the Security Council and General Assembly, while others are located elsewhere in the system. Despite an emphasis on the decentralization of functions, all UN operational units have the primary goal of avoiding a return to narrow and bitter political and economic nationalism. But achievements in institution-building aside, the challenge to promote political stability and economic well-being through international action persists. With two-thirds of the world's people living in poverty, international cooperation as it has been practiced has its limits. Indeed, the earth's impoverished will begin to share the benefits of global economic cooperation only as more countries progress toward the goals of overall development and modernization. Toward this end, other more functional but nonetheless also central structures of the UN system, such as the IMF and World Bank Group, will be of central importance.

# NOTES

1. See "Redefining 'Least Developed Country,'" *Development Forum* 19, no. 3 (July–August 1991), p. 9. The UN Committee for Development Planning has defined LDCs as "those low-income countries that are suffering from long-term handicaps to growth, in particular low levels of human resource development and/or severe structural weaknesses." The World Bank in 1992 defined LDCs as those countries with a per capita income per year of $610 or less. General definitional characteristics for being accepted by the United Nations as a member of the "least developed" or poorest nations include (1) a per capita gross domestic product of approximately $200 a year, (2) a low life expectancy among the population, (3) literacy rates under 20 percent, and (4) a low contribution of manufacturing industries to GDP. It should be remembered that LDCs means "less developed countries" and also "least developed countries," with the former usage referring to the entire group of developing states, whereas the latter refers to the poorest of this group, sometimes referred to as the Fourth World. The least developed countries, according to UN classification, include Afghanistan, Angola, Bangladesh, Benin, Bhutan, Burkina Faso, Burundi, Cambodia, Cape Verde, Central African Republic, Chad, Comoros, Congo, Djibouti, Equatorial Guinea, Ethiopia, The Gambia, Ghana, Guinea, Guinea-Bissau, Haiti, Kiribati, Laos, Lesotho, Liberia, Madagascar, Malawi, Maldives, Mali, Mauritania, Mozambique, Myanmar (Burma), Nepal, Niger, Rwanda, Samoa, São Tomé and Príncipe, Sierra Leone, Solomon Islands, Somalia, Sudan, Tanzania, Togo, Tuvalu, Uganda, Vanuatu, Yemen, and Zambia.
2. See International Bank for Reconstruction and Development, *World Development Report, 1997* (Washington, DC: IBRD, 1997).
3. United Nations, *Development Update,* no. 26, January–February 1999, p. 1.

# SELECTED READINGS

Ali, Sheikh R. *The International Organizations and World Order Dictionary.* Santa Barbara, CA, and Oxford, UK: ABC-CLIO Press, 1992.

Berg, Robert J., and David F. Gordon, eds. *Cooperation for International Development: The United States and the Third World in the 1990s.* Boulder, CO: Lynne Rienner, 1989.

Culpeper, Roy. *The Multilateral Development Banks: Titans or Behemoths?* Boulder, CO: Lynne Rienner, 1997.

Delvin, Robert. *Debt and Crisis in Latin America.* Princeton, NJ: Princeton University Press, 1989.

Fry, Gerald W., and Galen R. Martin. *The International Development Dictionary.* Santa Barbara, CA, and Oxford, UK: ABC-CLIO Press, 1991.

———. *The International Education of the Development Consultant: Communicating with Peasants and Princes.* Oxford, UK: Pergamon Press, 1989.

Griffiths, Robert J., ed. *Annual Editions: Developing World 2003/2004.* 13th ed. Guilford, CT: McGraw-Hill/Dushkin, 2003.

Kapur, Devesh, John P. Lewis, and Richard Webb. *The World Bank: Its First Half Century. Volume I: History.* Washington, DC: Brookings Institution, 1997.

Kelly, Thomas J. *The Effects of Economic Adjustment on Poverty in Mexico.* Aldershot, UK: Ashgate, 1999.

Keohane, Robert O., and Mary A. Levy, eds. *Institutions for Environmental Aid: Pitfalls and Promise.* Cambridge, MA: MIT Press, 1996.

Kim, Samuel S. *The Quest for a Just World Order.* Boulder, CO: Westview Press, 1984.

Krueger, Anne O. *Perspectives on Trade and Development.* Chicago: University of Chicago Press, 1990.

Krueger, Anne O., Constantine Michalopoulos, and Vernon W. Ruttan. *Aid and Development.* Baltimore, MD: Johns Hopkins University Press, 1989.

MacDonald, Scott B., Margie Lindsay, and David L. Crum, eds. *The Global Debt Crisis: Forecasting for the Future.* London: Pinter, 1990.

Meller, Patricio, ed. *The Latin American Development Debate: Neostructuralism, Neomonetarism, and Adjustment Processes.* Boulder, CO: Westview Press, 1991.

Rapley, John. *Understanding Development: Theory and Practice in the Third World.* 2nd ed. Boulder, CO: Lynne Rienner, 2002.

Robinson, Thomas W., ed. *Democracy and Development in East Asia: Taiwan, South Korea, and the Philippines.* Washington, DC: AEI Press, 1991.

Seligson, Mitchell A., and John T. Passe-Smith. *Development and Underdevelopment: The Political Economy of Global Inequality.* Boulder, CO: Lynne Rienner, 1998.

Shihata, Ibrahim F. I., Franziska Tschofen, and Antonio R. Parra, eds. *The World Bank in a Changing World: Selected Essays.* Dordrecht: Martinus Nijhoff, 1991.

Ward, Barbara. *The Rich Nations and the Poor Nations.* New York: Norton, 1962.

Weaver, James H., Michael T. Rock, and Kenneth Kusterer. *Achieving Broad-Based Sustainable Development.* West Hartford, CT: Kumarian Press, 1996.

*World Development Report 1997.* Oxford, UK: Oxford University Press, 1997.

Young, Oran R. *Global Governance: Drawing Insights from the Environmental Experience.* Cambridge, MA: MIT Press, 1998.

# 11

## THE UNITED NATIONS
## IN THE TWENTY-FIRST CENTURY

If the United Nations did not exist it would have to be invented. It is the world's premier international organization and its numerous organs, agencies, programs, and projects embrace virtually every activity associated with life on this planet. In a world divided into nation-states and representing a vast array of interests, it is the United Nations that represents the common humanity of people everywhere. But above all, it is the United Nations that nurtures and encourages positive and constructive interaction between the many governments that speak for individual states.

Not everyone, however, believes the organization is a "noble experiment" in human cooperation. Indeed, for those who question the ubiquitous character of the United Nations, it continues to be judged a threat rather than a promise. Some states fear that the success of the United Nations translates into loss of national power and independence and that any delegation of what otherwise is considered exclusive state authority diminishes sovereignty and confuses and undermines constitutional order. Nowhere is criticism of the United Nations more vituperative than in the land that conceived it, and on whose soil its Headquarters is located.

Without the United States, the United Nations is a weak and lesser vehicle. Americans, however, have been among both the organization's strongest advocates and its most staunch critics. The United States throughout its history, but more so in the twentieth century, has been Janus-faced in its attitude toward international organization. Americans acknowledged the need for a world of accommodative spirit, a global civil society in which diversity was harmonized and celebrated; but at the same time, they also espoused a national uniqueness that set them apart from the many others around the world. When the United Nations was in its infancy, this dichotomy was less evident. Then, the United States, the only intact major survivor of World War II, set out to remodel the world; except for the obstacles strewn in its path by the Soviet Union, the United Nations was at the virtual beck and call of the United States, its clear and overwhelming majority not yet disturbed by the subsequent admission of scores of new nations.

The retreat from colonialism by the remaining imperial states transformed the world and the United Nations, and the U.S. monopoly in the international organization quickly faded. While posturing friendship and even alliance with the new countries, the United States found itself in a contest with the Soviet Union, which also sought the favor of the new states. Moreover, each new addition to the membership roll of the United Nations brought an agenda that represented exclusive interests, and oftentimes those interests clashed with others projected by the United States. This latter "rivalry" was best illustrated in the deliberations of the UN General Assembly, the one forum where the lesser powers were positioned to challenge the "mighty" and seek their own advantages.

Such challenges often came in the form of criticism and verbal abuse directed against the United States; and although it learned to parry each barb directed against it, the United States ceased to make the United Nations the preferred place from which to pursue U.S. foreign policy. In the 1970s the United States exchanged roles with the Soviet Union, and Washington far more than Moscow availed itself of the veto power in the Security Council. Outright rejection by the United States of majority decisions and resolutions in the General Assembly illustrated the profound changes occurring in the organization's performance. With the United Nations no longer an instrument of the big powers, the United States was more inclined to pursue its particular interests outside the purview of the world body. And the United States was not alone in this matter; the disputes that came before the United Nations seldom centered on any of the more prominent powers. But by contrast with the guarded demeanor of the world's major actors, the other nations, burdened by internal disorder or violated by the aggressive behavior of near and distant neighbors, welcomed and even invited UN intervention.

The passing of the Cold War accentuated the inchoate nature of many of the states born after World War II, and one or more of the Security Council's permanent powers felt compelled to prevent domestic disturbances from intensifying or spreading across international frontiers. Representative of the status quo power structure, the major members of the Security Council, but especially the United States, were eager to sustain an equilibrium that also was the basis for their own longevity. But the end of the Cold War also pointed to the instabilities in a world divided between "haves" and "have-nots." Although Russia replaced the Soviet Union on the Security Council and enjoyed the privileges that went with permanent power status, in other than strategic terms it too had become something akin to a Third World nation. Economically backward, its meager financial contribution to the United Nations dramatized its lesser place among the greater contemporary powers. On the other hand, Japan, which had assumed a UN financial responsibility only second to that of the United States, remained outside the select circle of major UN powers. So too reunified Germany, a key actor in Western Europe and the European Union, occupied a diminutive UN role.

Parallel and often more important decisions therefore were managed outside the framework of the United Nations. The G-7 countries that dominated the global economy functioned at a distance from the world organization. Here, Japan and Germany could share position with the United States, and Russia's admission to the club, sometimes described as "G-7 plus one," was more a gesture of realpolitik than recognition of Moscow's economic contribution. The existence of the G-7 forum and summit added little to the stature of the United Nations. Moreover, the International Monetary Fund and the World Bank were more likely to respond to the decisions of the G-7 than to those of the United Nations. The power of decision remained with the major actors in a wide range of economic and strategic matters, and the United Nations had to content itself with a status that, while not inconsequential, was nonetheless secondary to the actions and maneuvers of the most powerful among the national states.

The events of September 11, 2001, further exaggerated the inherent weakness of the United Nations, especially in reacting to the challenges to international peace. The terrorists, claiming to represent not a sovereign state but a vast community of believers, struck the United States with the stated purpose of destroying U.S. influence along a broad plane of global interests. Their targeting of the World Trade Center in New York City and the Pentagon in Washington signaled their intention to make protracted war on the one country still possessing ambitions of global hegemony. The U.S. reaction was predictable: It did not seek UN guidance or authority in responding to an act of open aggression. Declaring war on transnational terrorism, the Bush administration ordered U.S. forces to engage the enemy. The United Nations, its New York Headquarters just blocks from the site of the destroyed trade towers, declared its sympathy for its host country but was unprepared for this contemporary manifestation of war. The United Nations had been organized to maintain decorum between member states, and the violent actions of non-states did not fall within its range of operations.

Under normal circumstances the U.S.-led attack on Afghanistan would have been judged a violation of national sovereignty and an egregious affront to international law. But this was not a normal circumstance. Attention was riveted on eliminating a major source of terrorism. The United States therefore felt it was free to confront the threat to its security outside the rules and procedures of the United Nations. For the first time since its inception, the United Nations was not the institution primarily responsible for world peace. Although it had been organized with that objective in mind in 1945—indeed, with the belief that individual states were not by themselves capable of sustaining peace—the events of September 11 changed that essential purpose. With the threat to the peace emerging from non-stakeholder movements rather than from individual states, the United Nations was forced to come to grips with a new reality.

The United Nations was never meant to be a substitute for nation-states, rather seeing itself as the overall protector of the prevailing state system. But now it was forced to weigh its future amidst a contest between states seeking to preserve their integrity and the shadowy but disciplined terrorist elements whose stated purpose was the destruction of the prevailing order. The key to this confrontation became the United States, not the United Nations. This was a new form of warfare against a new kind of enemy. Global anarchists, convinced of their invincibility and unconcerned with protecting their base, were in position to acquire weapons of mass destruction and wanted the world to know they were intent on using them.

As the United Nations searched for a role in these new circumstances, the United States tried to rally the nations in a war on terrorism. For the first time since its formation in 1949, NATO invoked Article 5 of the Washington Treaty, which made an attack on one alliance member an attack on all. NATO provided troops for operations in Afghanistan, as did non-NATO members. The United Nations offered to assist with humanitarian relief and to help rebuild the Muslim nation while operations against remnants of Al-Qaeda and the Taliban were sustained. The United States, however, insisted that Afghanistan was only one campaign in a protracted war. In 2002–3, when Washington linked Iraq with the struggle against global terrorism, the United Nations refused to give its consent to broadening the conflict. The Bush administration publicized a direct connection between Saddam Hussein's Iraq and the war on terrorism and urged the Security Council to sanction still another theater of operations; but with few exceptions, UN member states refused to follow the U.S. lead. Despite this opposition, Washington proceeded, and in March 2003, without UN authorization, U.S. forces, assisted by a limited international coalition, invaded Iraq.

The U.S. action was meant to galvanize nations in a war on terrorism, but it had the opposite effect: the United Nations suffered division as never before. The United States was accused of making preemptive war, and the United Nations condemned the U.S. action, calling it unjustified, without provocation, and a violation of international law. Secretary-General Kofi Annan was most outspoken in his condemnation of the U.S. doctrine of preemption, asserting that supporting such actions would do more to elevate the threat of global anarchy than to combat worldwide terrorism.

UN rejection of the war in Iraq not only raised questions about the future of U.S. membership in the organization, it also brought into question the world body's future as a major actor in the struggle against global terrorism. The controversy that centered on the UN role in policing and restoring the economy of Iraq after the U.S. invasion found the Secretary-General in 2003 standing with those refusing to provide a blank check for Washington's actions. And because of the history of the matter, even the suggested restructuring of the UN's principal organs proved of questionable value. The crisis in Iraq and the threat posed by international terrorism revealed basic problems that challenged the very philosophy underpinning the world body.

## RETHINKING THE UNITED NATIONS IN THE AGE OF TERRORISM

Clearly, the United Nations needed structural as well as procedural reform. But the member states, both major and minor, were reluctant to alter Charter doctrine or reshape the organization to meet challenges not envisaged by the founders. The role of the permanent members on the Security Council continued to be debated, but there was little movement, for instance, in bringing Japan and Germany into the select circle. Even less attention was focused on eliminating the veto from the Security Council. The maintenance of the status quo in the organization's most critical organ signaled a form of stasis in which the organization followed the lead of important member states but could not be led into a new era of expanded cooperation. Indeed, the Secretary-General's call for greater cooperation and accommodation among the states was largely ignored in the fierce struggle to preserve sovereignty and freedom of action. Co-deployment was already an accepted principle when the events of September 11 aroused the world body to reexamine its limitations. Before the terrorist assault on the United States, the United Nations had accepted NATO's role in the Balkans and the ECOWAS police actions in West Africa. Regional responses to civil and cross-border conflict were judged useful, less costly, and more legitimate than conventional UN peacekeeping ventures. Even after September 11 the deployment of NATO forces in Afghanistan had a salutary effect on an already burdened United Nations. Of essential concern for the United Nations was the effectiveness of collective security, no matter how it was constituted. The central idea of the world body was the encouragement of joint efforts by states not seeking their own aggrandizement but dedicated to the maintenance and strengthening of international order. Secretary-General Kofi Annan's comments in October 2003 were directed at this need. Citing the rift between the United States and the United Nations caused by Washington's doctrine of pre-emption, Annan pleaded for recognition of the principle of "productive inter-dependence." Explaining that key assumptions on which international order had been based in 1945 were losing their relevance, the Secretary-General cited the deep divisions caused by the war in Iraq. Concerned that individual permanent powers were determined to ignore Security Council procedures, the central question appeared to be less an act of unilateralism and more the new sense of vulnerability that drives nations to take actions in defiance of international custom.

Never was the need for collective security greater than in an age where global anarchists threatened virtually all the international institutions invented to limit the uses of arbitrary power. Moreover, the UN Secretary-General replaced the major powers as the spokesman for global equilibrium in an era unfamiliar with the balance of power. Annan argued against individual actions that disrupted a fragile international decorum. Declaring that the United States needed the United Nations, the Secretary-General cited the pursuit of peace in scattered places such as Cambodia, Mozambique, El Salvador, Sierra Leone, Kosovo, and East Timor. He emphasized that no single nation, not even the United States, would be willing, let alone inclined, to shoulder such burdens alone. Acknowledging the validity of the reverse argument, he also stressed the inability of the United Nations to do its work without the United States. Annan expressed satisfaction that Washington had returned to the world organization in pursuit of sanction and cooperation for the ongoing operations in Iraq. The stress placed on Security Council resolutions offered by the United States—first to gain legitimacy for its action, and second to ask for material and financial support in pacifying and reconstructing Iraq—encouraged the Secretary-General to conclude that his pleadings were not in vain. The unanimous agreement to the U.S. resolution in October 2003 calling for lifting UN-imposed sanctions on Iraq was in many respects brokered by the Secretary-General to avoid deeper divisions among Security Council members, as well as among the member states in general. Such unanimous agreement, however, could not mask the damage done to international cooperation. Member states voting for the resolution did so more to shore up a weakened United Nations than to bring the nations into conformity with U.S. actions in Iraq. The forum represented by the United Nations retained its legitimacy as the only genuine institution promoting shared responsibility. Clearly, the many states large and small comprising the world organization had too much at stake to permit the further unraveling of its central core.

Again, the Secretary-General articulated the concerns of the nations, as he asked: "Can any one nation by itself tackle the problem of global warming or protecting the environment? Can any one nation advance the cause of human rights and bring to justice those guilty of war crimes and crimes against humanity? Can any one nation by itself win the war on terrorism, or prevent the spread of weapons of mass destruction, or stop the trafficking in illegal drugs?" [1] As a follow-up to his views on the state of international order, Annan went immediately to Madrid for the conference on funding Iraq's rehabilitation. Keynoting the plenary session of the seventy-eight nations assembled for the occasion, Annan called for laying aside past differences over the U.S. action. He advised the delegates to look toward the future and the need to combine their efforts. The Madrid conference was not destined to close the gap between the United States and the other nations, but the symbolism of the gathering could not be underestimated. Without the Secretary-General placing the imprimatur of the United Nations on the session, it is doubtful that states opposed to the U.S. doctrine of preemption would discern any responsibility in helping to bring order out of chaos.

Whereas it had become apparent that the war on terrorism would require resources not available to the United Nations, it was equally obvious that the United Nations was central to the maintenance of international order and correspondingly to the legitimacy of international systems and institutions. After September 11 the United States became more guarded in its relations with other nations. Fearful of the spread of weapons of mass destruction to adversarial states, President Bush described an "Axis of Evil" in the months after the terrorist attack. Including Iraq, Iran, and North Korea in this Axis, the administration let it be known that it had reason to question the actions of still other countries known to be in pursuit of weapons of mass destruction while supporting and even sponsoring terrorist organizations. Subsequently, concern that the Bush doctrine of preemption might be invoked beyond Iraq aroused deeper fears among UN members and officials within the UN Secretariat that the war on terrorism could not be contained.

It was in these dire circumstances that a genuine role for the United Nations began to emerge. In 2003, and again in March 2004, Annan pressured Iran to open its nuclear facilities to inspectors from the International Atomic Energy Agency and urged Teheran to respect international institutions that alone guaranteed its safety in a volatile world. Iran's publicly positive response to the Secretary-General's entreaties, its cooperation with officials of the European Union, and its acceptance of IAEA inspection went far in reducing the tension, but it did not defuse U.S. concerns. Annan's display of international diplomacy, however, went even further. It became evident that the purpose of the United Nations in the war on terrorism was not to muster forces to counter the phenomenon but rather to sustain the sincerity of the organization while the war was being pursued. To that end, the UN Counter-Terrorism Committee (CTC) was less an operative body than a sounding block for nations caught up in the struggle. Established by a Security Council resolution on September 28, 2001, under Chapter VII of the UN Charter, the CTC comprised the fifteen members of the Security Council and was mandated to increase the capability of states to fight terrorism. Not a sanctions committee or a watchdog on terrorist organizations, the CTC was charged to monitor state willingness to deny identified and potential terrorists finances and safe havens. The CTC also called upon states to share information, to cooperate with investigations, to arrest and prosecute terrorists, and to observe the relevant conventions and protocols related to combating terrorism. The CTC was committed to creating a global network of organizations working to thwart terrorist activities in every part of the world.

Of more immediate importance, however, was Annan's responsibility in developing a timetable and program for a UN Assistance Mission in Iraq. Not only was the Secretary-General's office responsible for assembling a future multinational peacekeeping force for Iraq, the Secretary-General also was mandated to hold a constitutional conference that would return Iraq to full sovereignty and help Iraqis create electoral processes. After initial hesitation, the United States had repeated its intention to transfer sovereignty to Iraq, and the urgency behind a more significant UN role was shown in the election of a new Spanish government in 2004. The first major statement from Madrid after the election was a declaration to withdraw Spain's forces from the coalition if the United Nations did not assume the peacekeeping function. In sum: Although the war on terrorism was a worldwide phenomenon, Iraq was made a key test of UN capacity not only to ensure the integrity of states but to give the United Nations a role in the ongoing war against terrorism. The UN's purpose, it was emphasized, lay in the promotion and encouragement of constructive and collective efforts against the perpetrators of disorder. Opinion remained strong that the United Nations was best equipped to tend to people in distress, and in so doing to emphasize the positive values reflected in the operation of international institutions.

# THE UNITED NATIONS
# AND THE DEFINITION OF TERRORISM

From the beginning of the phenomenon of terrorism that arose after World War II, the United Nations had been reluctant to seek measures promoting international cooperation for combating it. Some argued that terrorism was a scourge on the state system, while others asserted that it was a form of resistance in the pursuit of national liberation. Failure to define the scope and effect of international terrorism, around which condemnation of it could organize, provided terrorists with increased latitude and sometimes appeared to justify their actions. This inability to define terrorism has been traced to UN encouragement for wars of national liberation and the right of self-determination.

Colonialism was in retreat during the early decades of the United Nations, but it remained the central symbol, if not the enemy, of people still striving to achieve independence. Moreover, the United Nations more and more came to reflect the aspirations and objectives of those struggling against alien rulers. As these rulers released their grasp and newly sovereign states came into being, UN membership multiplied. The United Nations therefore came to reflect two contrary forms of world order: one was the expression of the major powers, notably the United States, given the tendency of the Soviet Union to associate with the former colonial people; the other was that of people in what had been casually described as the Third World. Differences along this divide had earlier separated the United States from the more numerous members of the United Nations, and nowhere were these differences more obvious than in the early attempt to define and counteract the emergence of a virulent form of international terrorism. Not only would there be no agreement on the term "terrorism," no consensus could be found for dealing with violence committed in the pursuit of political ends. Nor was agreement possible on the issue of violence that could not be confined to areas of actual tension. The United Nations, therefore, at an early period in the development of terrorist operations, and despite numerous protocols and conventions, could not find common ground on the task of distinguishing terrorists from liberators. Even more significant, it could not protect the innocent victims of terrorism.

Actions such as the hijacking of commercial aircraft and the threat posed to passengers who engaged in international travel received little attention from the United Nations. In 1972, Secretary-General Kurt Waldheim proposed including terrorism in all its permutations on the General Assembly agenda. Those states, almost without exception representing the Third World, that believed terrorism to be a form of legitimate violence in the pursuit of political objectives forcefully argued against it. Some members of the General Assembly opposed discussing the subject altogether. Waldheim nevertheless persisted, noting that "the scope of terrorist activity as well as its underlying causes had become increasingly international, and . . . modern technology had added a formidable dimension." Fereydoun Hoveyda, Iran's permanent representative to the United Nations and a key actor in bringing the issue of terrorism before the General Assembly, mirrored the Secretary-General's concerns. Hoveyda pointed to "the roots of terrorism" that lay in misery, frustration, grievance, and despair so deep that people became willing to sacrifice lives, including their own, to seek change.[2] Waldheim did not question the right of colonial and dependent peoples to seek their independence, but where liberation movements knew no bounds and victimized the innocent, he believed the situation became too serious to be ignored. The UN debate in search of a definition for terrorism proved fruitless, however, and the question was relegated to the Sixth (Legal) Committee of the General Assembly where it was hoped it could be treated with "dispassionate calm and objectivity."

The Sixth Committee held twenty-eight meetings during 1972–73 but failed to reach a consensus. The Committee enlisted the services of the Secretariat, which prepared a report in search of a definition for terrorism. A critical section of this document asserted that even when the use of force is legally and morally justified, the right of self-determination had its limits. This was especially true in the use of force against civilians, a long-recognized feature of the customary laws of war. But even here the opposition to such an interpretation had its supporters. Terrorist acts, it was argued, were no more than necessary "acts of communication" intended to show the determination and devotion of desperate people trying to counter the superior power arrayed against them. This argument asserted that terrorists were engaged in a "holy cause" more important than life itself.

Given such diverse opinion, the United Nations did little to address the dilemma of terrorism, which was therefore relatively freed from international scrutiny. Known perpetrators of such violence, such as the Palestine Liberation Organization and the African National Congress, were occasionally given substantial recognition by the General Assembly, and their leaders were permitted to address the plenary body. In this climate of confusion, terrorists became emboldened and spread and honed their tactics.

In 2004, the Sixth Committee was still searching for a definition of terrorism that would satisfy all its members and gain the approval of the General Assembly. Committee debate and the difficulties encountered in reaching a conclusion centered on those members wanting to outlaw all violence that affected people outside areas of immediate tension. This contrasted with those equating the use of violence, irrespective of its effect, as the outcome of legitimate frustrations. Hoveyda's comment in 1977 was prescient:

> As I review what was said in public debate and in the corridors [of the United Nations] it seems to me that it would have been possible to get agreement on a list of acts of terrorism disapproved generally, even by revolutionary leaders. I believe this holds especially for the taking of hostages and for the dispatch of letter bombs. A condemnation of such practices, I think, would have gone down even with states most concerned to defend those engaged in a struggle for national liberation and for the free exercise of their right of self-determination.

However, a proceeding that required that states first agree on what was meant by international terrorism proved incompatible with such an outcome.[3]

The terrorism of the 1970s—the "taking of hostages" and "dispatch of letter bombs"—can appear tame when compared with the suicide bombers of the twenty-first century. Yet, as a reading of Hoveyda suggests, had there been UN consensus on dealing with the subject in its more malleable form, perhaps the United Nations would be in a more secure position to deal with terrorism's dimensions after September 11.

# TERRORISM IN THE TWENTY-FIRST CENTURY

## A RELIGIOUS DIMENSION

As in war, terrorism often has a religious dimension, and religion and politics become entwined. This was seen repeatedly in conflicts in Northern Ireland, in the Nigerian civil war, in the partition of British India, and in Cyprus, as well as in the continuing conflicts in Chechnya, the Balkans, and the Middle East. The 1979 religion-dominated revolt against secular authority in Iran and the Mujaheddin (holy warrior) resistance to the Soviet invasion of Afghanistan that same year highlighted fears in the Muslim world that Islam was in danger. Muslim Pakistan's earlier dismemberment by Hindu-dominant India also contributed to these turbulent conditions, as did the war between a secularized Iraq and a religiously inspired Iran in 1980. The United Nations gave these religious dimensions only marginal attention, and the international organization was not sufficiently aware of their effect, especially on the Muslim worldview.

Religion is one of the array of components that make up terrorism. The United Nations was not created to deal with such matters, however. Nor was it structured to measure how member nations manage their domestic lives. Invariably, the United Nations operated outside the jurisdiction of the independent states, and it was not equipped to lecture to its members on matters of religion, local governance, or citizen behavior. Yet it was these very conditions that gave rise to contemporary terrorism and caused it to spill over frontiers, as terrorists of similar beliefs networked together. In many of the states that were the seedbeds for terrorism, UN member governments were inclined to encourage the flight of malcontents to distant places. Thus, without directly sponsoring terrorism, many states acted as incubators for terrorists.

Some member states also succumbed to that version of terrorism that emphasized the terrorist as a freedom fighter and martyr. The attack on the United States on September 11 did not elicit a uniform response among nations and their peoples. To some, the blow was directed at the power of the United States, and witnessing the last remaining superpower in distress was a welcome event. Such expression was muted in the halls of the United Nations, but there could be no mistaking the reality that some delegates felt a sense of justice.

## THE GLOBALIZATION OF TERROR

The United Nations also failed to address the linkages between the Cold War and conflicts on the periphery of superpower rivalry. Moreover, the United States and the Soviet Union were so caught up in their own test of wills that they too were incapable of reading events beyond their immediate range of interests. Treating conflicts in the Third World as reflections of their ideological rivalry, or as mere expressions of subnational objectives, the superpowers failed to comprehend the forces influencing a return to religion-based movements. Nor could the United Nations be faulted for not recognizing the motivation behind much of the sustained disorder. Born during the time of Cold War, the majority of UN member states were so preoccupied with their relations with the superpowers that they also failed to discern the popular shift away from dependence and toward a reassertion of self-identification. At the heart of the matter was the Westphalian concept of the secular state and its survival in the twenty-first century. This explains why the United Nations was not prepared for what followed the Cold War and why the debates about terrorism in the early 1970s were parroted during the 1980s and 1990s.

The post–Cold War world was again dominated by more or less the same powers that had been central to it. Above all, the United States set the tone for a reconfigured world. Globalization, the restructuring of the world economy, appeared to represent the changed world order. After the Gulf War of 1990–91, and following the almost immediate demise of the Soviet Union, President George Bush heralded the formation of a new "world order" and opined a new international environment overseen by the United States. The major threat to world peace supposedly had been removed, and the notion of a "peace dividend" appeared to usher in a new era of global development. Globalization became the new watchword, and the UN system was called upon to give it substance through its many institutions, not the least of which were the World Bank, the International Monetary Fund, and the World Trade Organization.

But another form of globalization—the globalization of terror—had also been nourished by the events that brought an end to East-West hostility, and this form of globalization gave a new dimension to the meaning of terror. What had been marginal in the context of the Cold War had become mainstream events when it ended. Few Third World issues had been resolved. The cultural clashes that had caused so much conflict did not diminish. National actors found themselves more challenged by long-ignored social conditions, and they were not prepared to address the networking of cultural experience by those who sensed a long-awaited opportunity to shape a destiny different from that driven by the United States and adopted by the United Nations.

For the terrorists who saw the United States as the principal threat to their ambitions, the United Nations was simply its handmaiden. The international organization's identity and role were so intertwined with the actions and policies of the United States that it too could not escape being judged as an extension of U.S. influence. Moreover, the events of September 11 revealed that when the global economy collides with the ambitions of global terrorists, the latter possess forces far greater than those projected by the UN member states. How the United Nations, its roots deep in the system of national states, responds to a world more changed by September 11 than by the end of the Cold War will reveal whether the international organization in fact has a future.

## THE UNITED NATIONS CHALLENGED

Established within a framework of national states, the United Nations was a manifestation of the international law that aimed at limiting the exclusive actions of sovereign states. But limitations were not something imposed from on high; states consented to the laws that bound them to one another, and reciprocity was the principle that elevated international above municipal law. States accepted international law because it compensated for their weakness or provided advantages that they otherwise could not realize.

The actions of the United States in Granada, Panama, and more recently Iraq raise questions about the progressive development of international law. They also undermine the purpose of world organization. The United Nations was meant to be the sum of its parts, but when one of its members becomes more than the sum of the other nations, the work of the United Nations is stunted and its function questioned. Washington made itself the enforcer of UN Security Council measures that were discussed but not acted upon by the collective body. Certainly in Iraq, the United States, whatever the rationale, violated the sovereign independence of another state and placed itself in judgment over the validity of the laws of another government. In a period of uncertainty, the many members of the United Nations demonstrated that although they may have been unclear on how to define terrorism, they knew how to condemn aggressive state unilateralism.

To the majority of UN members, no effort by the United States to link Baghdad with terrorism could justify the U.S.-led assault on a sovereign member of the international organization. As with Iraq's earlier invasion of Kuwait, the U.S. campaign also centered on regime change. And although the events of September 11 were used to justify the termination of a sovereign government, the United Nations refused to provide legitimacy for every action deemed to be a response to terrorism. Given the controversy, the United Nations avoided participating in the removal of Saddam Hussein's administration, and it was only at the close of hostilities that the United Nations pressured Washington to open the country to UN scrutiny. When Sergio Vieira de Mello, sent by Kofi Annan to oversee a UN role in Iraq, and many of his staff members were killed by a car bomb placed outside de Mello's Baghdad headquarters, it became clear that the United Nations, the most prominent extension of the international system, had by association become the enemy of those refusing to accept U.S. fiat.

The Baghdad attack was a blow to morale among UN workers, but it was more a symbolic terrorist act than a direct assault on the United Nations. Defined in terms of classic terrorism, the victims were not the real targets. Instead, this assault on the United Nations was initiated to point out the failure of U.S. peacekeeping in Iraq, to invite U.S. retaliation, and to demean the United Nations in the eyes of people who might look to it for solace and comfort. Moreover, bombings continued in and around Iraq's capital, including the headquarters of the International Red Cross. Kofi Annan's declaration that international organizations would continue their work was not unexpected, but the numbers of aid workers ending their operations and leaving Iraq was not insignificant. Not only aid-giving organizations were hesitant to put their personnel in harm's way; nations that might otherwise be counted upon to provide contingents for a multilateral force were most reluctant to do so. The U.S. invasion of Iraq had toppled Saddam's regime, but it also led to heavier resistance from those determined to deny the United States its objective of a terrorist-free, constitutional, self-governing Iraqi state. Washington's obvious difficulties in consolidating its gains in Iraq seemed to make a UN commitment to assist in the country's resurrection even more imperative.

## THE REALITIES OF THE GLOBAL CONDITION

While UN achievements have yet to be tallied in Iraq or Afghanistan, and the organization is constrained in coping with terrorism, it nevertheless remains the single body concerned with the physical health of the planet and the social and psychological health of all people. It needs restating that the United Nations stands at the apex of global actions in promoting the Universal Declaration of Human Rights. It possesses a unique role in economic development, the eradication of disease, and the improvement of nutritional and literacy standards as well as in advocating the rights of women and children. The United Nations is also in the vanguard of operations seeking to address the plight of ever-increasing numbers of refugees throughout the world. It must be given due credit for the creation of the International Criminal Court and for acting as the conscience of a world in protecting the natural environment. Committed to improved human conditions worldwide, the United Nations seeks answers to such widely disparate issues as sustainability, global drug trafficking, and overpopulation. It has long been considered key to the formation of global civil society. The United Nations remains seized of ambitious programs aimed at transforming the lives of people everywhere, especially the world's underclass. Humanity-centered concerns, such as greater understanding of cultural diversity, the quest for human solidarity, and improving the quality of life, merge with issues of development and especially sustainable economic welfare. Indeed, it is international civil society that helps limit an individual state's insatiable appetite for weapons and their inevitable deployment and use. In a world afflicted by a range of terror, it is civil society that continues to petition for disarmament and demands that governments eschew war as an instrument of national policy. At the heart of the United Nations is the belief that international civil society is the bedrock for the maintenance of humanitarian values in a troubled and confused world.

But the United Nations is still caught between its purpose and the fulfillment of its potential, that is, between aspiration and accomplishment. Irrespective of the revolutionary changes that have altered approaches to economic development, the character of poverty has not changed. Moreover, all indications point to a widening gulf between the prosperous few and the many abject poor. None of the strategies developed to close this gap have succeeded, whether launched by public or private sectors or combinations of them. In the initial decade of the twenty-first century, the distribution of wealth is so uneven that the imbalance has raised concerns of a more intense and widespread civil strife, resulting in increased episodes of international terrorism. Financial crises sweep across the globe, and economic dislocation raises questions about the success of globalization schemes, which present even more complicated challenges to political order in affluent and poor countries. The United Nations is hardly equipped to manage the magnitude of such problems, and even sovereign states have been limited in their ability to address the scale and complexity of social and economic disequilibrium.

Disintegrative forces, accelerated by perceived inequities and state-centric behaviors, continue to undermine world order. Internecine as well as cross-border conflicts energized by psychological and physical deprivation have produced the anarchic conditions that lead to alienation, collective despair, and ultimately acts of violence. Too often innocent people are wantonly abused and murdered, as occurred in Rwanda in the mid-1990s. Generally speaking, economic disequilibrium and social and psychological insecurities, in addition to failures of governance, provide ammunition for militant extremists that the United Nations cannot itself confront without the cooperation of member states.

The intertwining of religion with politics is not a recent phenomenon, but its contemporary characterization as a "clash of civilizations" may be overdrawn and will require particular scrutiny. The United Nations is not divided by religions or by the diversity of religious practices; it has always demonstrated tolerance in approaching the many peoples and cultures comprising the human family. The organization's stress on human rights begins with the understanding that in a world of many faiths, all are to be treated with equal respect. The one international organization that represents universal values and goals and that has demonstrated its impartiality in coping with state and civil disorder, the United Nations is also the best hope that civilizations can be reconciled and disparate cultures ensured security. This is how the war on terrorism must be approached. The olive branch has never been more important, and it is the United Nations that remains its custodian. States or groups or individuals that directly or indirectly provide financial contributions to disruptive elements in the name of faith must be called to answer to the United Nations, the only credible arbiter in contemporary times.

Terrorists are not born they are made. They also are sponsored by states that are determined to challenge the world power structure, and some of these states are members of the United Nations. It may be time for the United Nations to place a higher standard not only for membership in the organization but for retaining membership. If the day ever arrives when serious efforts will be directed at amending the UN Charter, the real test for the future of the United Nations will be found not in the *apportioning* of power but in the *neutralizing* of power. Universal membership had its special appeal in the waning days of World War II. With the failure of the League of Nations before them, the framers of the UN Charter examined the League's inability to maintain the cooperation of its members, or the ease with which vengeful states exploited the organization's lack of universality. The United Nations sought to avoid the mistakes of the older organization, but it made membership a right of passage rather than a test of a state's civil and civic responsibilities. With almost two hundred member states filling the halls of the United Nations, it is appropriate to ask the question—For what purpose does a nation claim a place in the world body?

## TOWARD WORLD ORDER

Pressured from within as well as without, the United Nations under the leadership of Secretary-General Kofi Annan introduced reforms aimed at closing the gap between the desirable and the possible, between aspiration and accomplishment, between stated purpose and realizable goals. Since 1997, the reorganization of the UN Secretariat has moved apace, but all internal changes were made dependent on the ability of member states to use the UN more effectively, and through the organization, to overcome differences that divided them from one another. Not prepared to wait for the latter, however, the UN Secretariat was engaged in assessing its strengths and weaknesses, and it charted new institutional structures that were intended to carry the UN's moral import through the first one hundred years of the twenty-first century.

For the Secretary-General and his staff of international civil servants, the United Nations remained the only international body representing the collective interest of the world's sovereign states. That reality translated into a universality of rights and obligations not found in any other arena, and where successful, offered the states a predictability of behavior reinforced by the rule of law. Guided by reciprocity and standardized rules that were unanimously accepted, it was the only forum where diversity of membership and disparate natural endowments met on an even playing field.

The UN's universal character offered governments unparalleled opportunities for interaction and negotiation, and no other international organization enjoyed so broad a mandate. No other international organization assumed responsibility for such a variety of issues burdening the world community. Only the United Nations was conceived to address so wide a spectrum of activities in so many critical areas simultaneously. Nevertheless, the United Nations seldom lived up to its kaleidoscopic billing. And as has been demonstrated, its operational mandate was too easily negated by the sheer lack of resources. Dependent on member states that often refused to honor individual commitments, the organization confronted seemingly unbridgeable gaps between needs, delivery, and expectations. Moreover, subject to manipulation by states with narrow agendas, the United Nations too often was trapped between its universal mandate and the exclusive interests of its members.

Constructed on the ashes of World War II, the foundation on which the United Nations rested was neither solid nor nourishing. Exposed to Cold War rivalries at the outset, the organization split into blocs and alliances that multiplied with the inclusion of the newly independent states. Regionalism and virulent nationalism prevented the organization from achieving its visionary objectives. Less a futuristic organization, the United Nations came to represent the peculiar interests of the different states that joined its ranks. All sought to maximize opportunities while paying lip service to the organization's universal purpose. Although far from its stated ideal, the United Nations nevertheless prevailed, developed innovative programs, notably in social and economic areas, and managed to survive the Cold War because none of its major members were inclined to abandon it. The end of the Cold War, however, focused new attention on the organization, and it came under increasing pressure to assume far greater and more complex responsibilities.

Amid conditions of political instability, a technological revolution in transportation, communication, and industry vastly increased the points of social contact across national boundaries and thus the opportunities for both cooperation and hostile collision. At the same time military technology substantially increased the penalties for those resorting to organized violence and provided added incentive to national states to avoid at least the most destructive forms of warfare. Faced with the social consequences of technological progress, particularly as they affected international relations, governments increasingly turned to international organization as a means of eliminating frictions and resolving differences through nonviolent means. Nonetheless, the states and international organizations were unprepared for the violence of terrorism and the means of the terrorists. Terrorists had demonstrated a capacity and a willingness to cause damage to the community of nations that the states in all their aggressive posturing refrained from doing.

The experience of more than one hundred years of functional international organizations, now greatly augmented by the growth and expansion of the UN system, did not yet show how to deal with the dilemma of nonstate terrorism. Member states must be ready to dig the foundation for the deeper integration of states before the contemporary concern given to global terrorism can be successfully addressed. States that choose to empathize with terrorists must decide what is in their best interest. Isolating terrorists and eliminating terrorism will require a degree of cross-cultural cooperation not yet on the horizon.

In the final analysis, the processes of international organization are geared to a world in which common problems must be attacked by multilateral means while making full allowance for the particular needs of national states. As vessels for common action, the processes made possible by the work of the United Nations can be adapted to generate the kind of cooperation that enhances the prerogatives and interests of member states. A more genuine community of nations is the goal of the United Nations, as well as the distant but attainable goal of freedom from fear, terror, and want. As it was determined by the diplomats who brought the United Nations into being in 1945, the collective effort of the world's nations can, if those nations wish it, steer a course to a brighter future, not for just the few but for people everywhere.

# NOTES

1. UN News Service, October 22, 2003.
2. Fereydoun Hoveyda, "The Problem of International Terrorism at the United Nations," *Terrorism: An International Journal* 1, no. 1 (1977), pp. 72–73.
3. Ibid., p. 82.

# SELECTED READINGS

Annan, Kofi. *The Quotable Kofi Annan: Selections from Speeches and Statements by the Secretary-General.* New York: United Nations Publications, 1998.

Bertrand, Maurice. *The Third Generation World Organization.* Dordrecht: Martinus Nijhoff, 1989.

Carnegie Commission on Preventing Deadly Conflict. *Preventing Deadly Conflict.* New York: Carnegie Corporation of New York, 1997.

Claude, Inis L., Jr. *States and the Global System.* New York: St. Martin's Press, 1988.

Coate, Roger A. *Unilateralism, Ideology, and U.S. Foreign Policy In and Out of UNESCO.* Boulder, CO: Lynne Rienner, 1989.

Cordesman, Anthony H. *The Iraq War: Strategy, Tactics, and Military Lessons.* Westport, CT: Praeger, 2003.

Finger, Seymour Maxwell. *American Ambassadors at the UN: People, Politics, and Bureaucracy in Making Foreign Policy.* New York: Holmes & Meier, 1988.

Finger, Seymour Maxwell, and Joseph R. Harbert, eds. *U.S. Policy in International Institutions.* Rev. ed. Boulder, CO: Westview Press, 1982.

Foreign Affairs Agenda. *The New Shape of World Politics: Contending Paradigms in International Relations.* New York: Council on Foreign Relations and Norton, 1997.

Franck, Thomas M. *Nation against Nation: What Happened to the U.N. Dream and What the U.S. Can Do about It.* New York: Oxford University Press, 1985.

Fromuth, Peter J., ed. *A Successor Vision: The United Nations of Tomorrow.* New York: UN Association of the United States of America, 1988.

Gati, Toby Trister, ed. *The US, the UN, and the Management of Global Change.* New York: New York University Press, 1983.

Gerson, Allan. *The Kirkpatrick Mission: Diplomacy Without Apology: America at the United Nations, 1981–1985.* New York: Free Press, 1991.

Karns, Margaret P., and Karen A. Mingst, eds. *The United States and Multilateral Institutions: Patterns of Changing Instrumentality and Influence.* Boston: Unwin Hyman, 1990.

Kegley, Charles W., ed. *The Long Postwar Peace.* New York: HarperCollins, 1991.

Maynes, Charles W., and Richard S. Williamson. *U.S. Foreign Policy and the United Nations System.* New York: Norton, 1996.

Muldoon, James P. *The Architecture of Global Governance.* Boulder, CO: Perseus, 2003.

Muller, Joachim, ed. *Reforming the United Nations: New Initiatives and Past Efforts.* Boston: Kluwer Law International, 1997.

Pinkney, Robert. *Democracy in the Third World.* Boulder, CO: Lynn Rienner, 2003.

Piszkiewicz, Dennis. *Terrorism's War with America: A History.* Westport, CT: Praeger, 2003.

Riggs, Robert E. *US/UN: Foreign Policy and International Organization.* New York: Appleton-Century-Crofts, 1971.

Rosenau, James N. *The United Nations in a Turbulent World.* International Peace Academy, Occasional Paper Series. Boulder, CO: Lynne Rienner, 1992.

Rosenau, James N., and Ernst-Otto Czempiel, eds. *Governance without Government: Order and Change in World Politics.* Cambridge, UK: Cambridge University Press, 1992.

Yoder, Amos. *The Evolution of the United Nations System.* New York: Crane Russak, 1989.

Zakaria, Fareed. *From Wealth to Power: The Unusual Origins of America's World Role.* Princeton, NJ: Princeton University Press, 1998.

Ziring, Lawrence. *Pakistan: At the Crosscurrent of History.* Oxford, UK: Oneworld Publications, 2003.

# Appendix

## THE CHARTER OF THE UNITED NATIONS

### WE THE PEOPLES OF THE UNITED NATIONS DETERMINED

to save succeeding generations from the scourge of war, which twice in our lifetime has brought untold sorrow to mankind, and

to reaffirm faith in fundamental human rights, in the dignity and worth of the human person, in the equal rights of men and women and of nations large and small, and

to establish conditions under which justice and respect for the obligations arising from treaties and other sources of international law can be maintained, and

to promote social progress and better standards of life in larger freedom,

### AND FOR THESE ENDS

to practice tolerance and live together in peace with one another as good neighbors, and

to unite our strength to maintain international peace and security, and

to ensure, by the acceptance of principles and the institution of methods, that armed force shall not be used, save in the common interest, and

to employ international machinery for the promotion of the economic and social advancement of all peoples,

### HAVE RESOLVED TO COMBINE OUR EFFORTS TO ACCOMPLISH THESE AIMS.

Accordingly, our respective Governments, through representatives assembled in the city of San Francisco, who have exhibited their full powers found to be in good and due form, have agreed to the present Charter of the United Nations and do hereby establish an international organization to be known as the United Nations.

### CHAPTER I
### PURPOSES AND PRINCIPLES

ARTICLE 1.

The Purposes of the United Nations are:

1. To maintain international peace and security, and to that end: to take effective collective measures for the prevention and removal of threats to the peace, and for the suppression of acts

of aggression and other breaches of the peace, and to bring about by peaceful means, and in conformity with the principles of justice and international law, adjustment or settlement of international disputes or situations which might lead to a breach of the peace;

2. To develop friendly relations among nations based on respect for the principle of equal rights and self-determination of peoples, and to take other appropriate measures to strengthen universal peace;

3. To achieve international cooperation in solving international problems of an economic, social, cultural, or humanitarian character, and in promoting and encouraging respect for human rights and for fundamental freedoms for all without distinction as to race, sex, language, or religion; and

4. To be a center for harmonizing the actions of nations in the attainment of these common ends.

ARTICLE 2.

The Organization and its Members, in pursuit of the Purposes stated in Article 1, shall act in accordance with the following Principles.

1. The Organization is based on the principle of the sovereign equality of all its Members.

2. All Members, in order to ensure to all of them the rights and benefits resulting from membership, shall fulfill in good faith the obligations assumed by them in accordance with the present Charter.

3. All Members shall settle their international disputes by peaceful means in such a manner that international peace and security, and justice, are not endangered.

4. All Members shall refrain in their international relations from the threat or use of force against the territorial integrity or political independence of any state, or in any other manner inconsistent with the Purposes of the United Nations.

5. All Members shall give the United Nations every assistance in any action it takes in accordance with the present Charter, and shall refrain from giving assistance to any state against which the United Nations is taking preventive or enforcement action.

6. The Organization shall ensure that states which are not Members of the United Nations act in accordance with these Principles so far as may be necessary for the maintenance of international peace and security.

7. Nothing contained in the present Charter shall authorize the United Nations to intervene in matters which are essentially within the domestic jurisdiction of any state or shall require the Members to submit such matters to settlement under the present Charter; but this principle shall not prejudice the application of enforcement measures under Chapter VII.

# CHAPTER II
# MEMBERSHIP

ARTICLE 3.

The original Members of the United Nations shall be the states which, having participated in the United Nations Conference on International Organization at San Francisco, or having previously signed the Declaration by United Nations of January 1, 1942, sign the present Charter and ratify it in accordance with Article 110.

ARTICLE 4.

1. Membership in the United Nations is open to all other peace-loving states which accept the obligations contained in the present Charter and, in the judgment of the Organization, are able and willing to carry out these obligations.

2.  The admission of any such state to membership in the United Nations will be effected by a decision of the General Assembly upon the recommendation of the Security Council.

### ARTICLE 5.

A Member of the United Nations against which preventive or enforcement action has been taken by the Security Council may be suspended from the exercise of the rights and privileges of membership by the General Assembly upon the recommendation of the Security Council. The exercise of these rights and privileges may be restored by the Security Council.

### ARTICLE 6.

A Member of the United Nations which has persistently violated the Principles contained in the present Charter may be expelled from the Organization by the General Assembly upon the recommendation of the Security Council.

## CHAPTER III
## ORGANS
### ARTICLE 7.

1.  There are established as the principal organs of the United Nations: a General Assembly, a Security Council, an Economic and Social Council, a Trusteeship Council, an International Court of Justice, and a Secretariat.
2.  Such subsidiary organs as may be found necessary may be established in accordance with the present Charter.

### ARTICLE 8.

The United Nations shall place no restrictions on the eligibility of men and women to participate in any capacity and under conditions of equality in its principal and subsidiary organs.

## CHAPTER IV
## THE GENERAL ASSEMBLY

### Composition
### ARTICLE 9.

1.  The General Assembly shall consist of all the Members of the United Nations.
2.  Each Member shall not have more than five representatives in the General Assembly.

### Functions and Powers
### ARTICLE 10.

The General Assembly may discuss any questions or any matters within the scope of the present Charter or relating to the powers and functions of any organs provided for in the present Charter, and, except as provided in Article 12, may make recommendations to the Members of the United Nations or to the Security Council or to both on any such questions or matters.

ARTICLE 11.

1. The General Assembly may consider the general principles of cooperation in the maintenance of international peace and security, including the principles governing disarmament and the regulation of armaments, and may make recommendations with regard to such principles to the Members or to the Security Council or to both.
2. The General Assembly may discuss any questions relating to the maintenance of international peace and security brought before it by any Member of the United Nations, or by the Security Council, or by a state which is not a Member of the United Nations in accordance with Article 35, paragraph 2, and, except as provided in Article 12, may make recommendations with regard to any such questions to the state or states concerned or to the Security Council or to both. Any such question on which action is necessary shall be referred to the Security Council by the General Assembly either before or after discussion.
3. The General Assembly may call the attention of the Security Council to situations which are likely to endanger international peace and security.
4. The powers of the General Assembly set forth in this Article shall not limit the general scope of Article 10.

ARTICLE 12.

1. While the Security Council is exercising in respect of any dispute or situation the functions assigned to it in the present Charter, the General Assembly shall not make any recommendation with regard to that dispute or situation unless the Security Council so requests.
2. The Secretary-General, with the consent of the Security Council, shall notify the General Assembly at each session of any matters relative to the maintenance of international peace and security which are being dealt with by the Security Council and shall similarly notify the General Assembly, or the Members of the United Nations if the General Assembly is not in session, immediately the Security Council ceases to deal with such matters.

ARTICLE 13.

1. The General Assembly shall initiate studies and make recommendations for the purpose of:
    a. promoting international cooperation in the political field and encouraging the progressive development of international law and its codification;
    b. promoting international cooperation in the economic, social, cultural, educational, and health fields, and assisting in the realization of human rights and fundamental freedoms for all without distinction as to race, sex, language, or religion.
2. The further responsibilities, functions and powers of the General Assembly with respect to matters mentioned in paragraph 1(b) above are set forth in Chapters IX and X.

ARTICLE 14.

Subject to the provisions of Article 12, the General Assembly may recommend measures for the peaceful adjustment of any situation, regardless of origin, which it deems likely to impair the general welfare or friendly relations among nations, including situations resulting from a violation of the provisions of the present Charter setting forth the Purposes and Principles of the United Nations.

ARTICLE 15.

1. The General Assembly shall receive and consider annual and special reports from the Security Council; these reports shall include an account of the measures that the Security Council has decided upon or taken to maintain international peace and security.

2. The General Assembly shall receive and consider reports from the other organs of the United Nations.

## ARTICLE 16.

The General Assembly shall perform such functions with respect to the international trusteeship system as are assigned to it under Chapters XII and XIII, including the approval of the trusteeship agreements for areas not designated as strategic.

## ARTICLE 17.

1. The General Assembly shall consider and approve the budget of the Organization.
2. The expenses of the Organization shall be borne by the Members as apportioned by the General Assembly.
3. The General Assembly shall consider and approve any financial and budgetary arrangements with specialized agencies referred to in Article 57 and shall examine the administrative budgets of such specialized agencies with a view to making recommendations to the agencies concerned.

## Voting
### ARTICLE 18.

1. Each member of the General Assembly shall have one vote.
2. Decisions of the General Assembly on important questions shall be made by a two-thirds majority of the members present and voting. These questions shall include: recommendations with respect to the maintenance of international peace and security, the election of the non-permanent members of the Security Council, the election of the members of the Economic and Social Council, the election of members of the Trusteeship Council in accordance with paragraph 1(c) of Article 86, the admission of new Members to the United Nations, the suspension of the rights and privileges of membership, the expulsion of Members, questions relating to the operation of the trusteeship system, and budgetary questions.
3. Decisions on other questions, including the determination of additional categories of questions to be decided by a two-thirds majority, shall be made by a majority of the members present and voting.

## ARTICLE 19.

A Member of the United Nations which is in arrears in the payment of its financial contributions to the Organization shall have no vote in the General Assembly if the amount equals or exceeds the amount of the contributions due from it for the preceding two full years. The General Assembly may, nevertheless, permit such a Member to vote if it is satisfied that the failure to pay is due to conditions beyond the control of the Member.

## Procedure
### ARTICLE 20.

The General Assembly shall meet in regular annual sessions and in such special sessions as occasion may require. Special sessions shall be convoked by the Secretary-General at the request of the Security Council or of a majority of the Members of the United Nations.

## ARTICLE 21.

The General Assembly shall adopt its own rules of procedure. It shall elect its President for each session.

## ARTICLE 22.

The General Assembly may establish such subsidiary organs as it deems necessary for the performance of its functions.

# CHAPTER V
# THE SECURITY COUNCIL

## Composition
### ARTICLE 23.

1.  The Security Council shall consist of eleven[1] Members of the United Nations. The Republic of China, France, the Union of Soviet Socialist Republics, the United Kingdom of Great Britain and Northern Ireland, and the United States of America shall be permanent members of the Security Council. The General Assembly shall elect six[2] other Members of the United Nations to be non-permanent members of the Security Council, due regard being specially paid, in the first instance to the contribution of Members of the United Nations to the maintenance of international peace and security and to the other purposes of the Organization, and also to equitable geographical distribution.
2.  The non-permanent members of the Security Council shall be elected for a term of two years. In the first election of non-permanent members, however, three shall be chosen for a term of one year. A retiring member shall not be eligible for immediate re-election.
3.  Each member of the Security Council shall have one representative.

## Functions and Powers
### ARTICLE 24.

1.  In order to ensure prompt and effective action by the United Nations, its Members confer on the Security Council primary responsibility for the maintenance of international peace and security, and agree that in carrying out its duties under this responsibility the Security Council acts on their behalf.
2.  In discharging these duties the Security Council shall act in accordance with the Purposes and Principles of the United Nations. The specific powers granted to the Security Council for the discharge of these duties are laid down in Chapters VI, VII, VIII, and XII.
3.  The Security Council shall submit annual and, when necessary, special reports to the General Assembly for its consideration.

## ARTICLE 25.

The Members of the United Nations agree to accept and carry out the decisions of the Security Council in accordance with the present Charter.

---

[1] Expanded to fifteen members by Charter amendment in 1965.
[2] Ten elective members, five chosen each year, provided for by Charter amendment in 1965.

## ARTICLE 26.

In order to promote the establishment and maintenance of international peace and security with the least diversion for armaments of the world's human and economic resources, the Security Council shall be responsible for formulating, with the assistance of the Military Staff Committee referred to in Article 47, plans to be submitted to the Members of the United Nations for the establishment of a system for the regulation of armaments.

## Voting
### ARTICLE 27.

1. Each member of the Security Council shall have one vote.
2. Decisions of the Security Council on procedural matters shall be made by an affirmative vote of seven[3] members.
3. Decisions of the Security Council on all other matters shall be made by an affirmative vote of seven[4] members including the concurring votes of the permanent members; provided that, in decisions under Chapter VI, and under paragraph 3 of Article 52, a party to a dispute shall abstain from voting.

## Procedure
### ARTICLE 28.

1. The Security Council shall be so organized as to be able to function continuously. Each member of the Security Council shall for this purpose be represented at all times at the seat of the Organization.
2. The Security Council shall hold periodic meetings at which each of its members may, if it so desires, be represented by a member of the government or by some other specially designated representative.
3. The Security Council may hold meetings at such places other than the seat of the Organization as in its judgment will best facilitate its work.

## ARTICLE 29.

The Security Council may establish such subsidiary organs as it deems necessary for the performance of its functions.

## ARTICLE 30.

The Security Council shall adopt its own rules of procedure, including the method of selecting its President.

## ARTICLE 31.

Any Member of the United Nations which is not a member of the Security Council may participate, without vote, in the discussion of any question brought before the Security Council whenever the latter considers that the interests of that Member are specially affected.

---

[3] Changed to nine members by Charter amendment in 1965.
[4] Changed to nine members by Charter amendment in 1965.

ARTICLE 32.

Any Member of the United Nations which is not a member of the Security Council or any state which is not a Member of the United Nations, if it is a party to a dispute under consideration by the Security Council, shall be invited to participate, without vote, in the discussion relating to the dispute. The Security Council shall lay down such conditions as it deems just for the participation of a state which is not a Member of the United Nations.

## CHAPTER VI
## PACIFIC SETTLEMENT OF DISPUTES

ARTICLE 33.

1. The parties to any dispute, the continuance of which is likely to endanger the maintenance of international peace and security, shall, first of all, seek a solution by negotiation, enquiry, mediation, conciliation, arbitration, judicial settlement, resort to regional agencies or arrangements, or other peaceful means of their own choice.
2. The Security Council shall, when it deems necessary, call upon the parties to settle their disputes by such means.

ARTICLE 34.

The Security Council may investigate any dispute, or any situation which might lead to international friction or give rise to a dispute, in order to determine whether the continuance of the dispute or situation is likely to endanger the maintenance of international peace and security.

ARTICLE 35.

1. Any Member of the United Nations may bring any dispute, or any situation of the nature referred to in Article 34, to the attention of the Security Council or of the General Assembly.
2. A state which is not a Member of the United Nations may bring to the attention of the Security Council or of the General Assembly any dispute to which it is a party if it accepts in advance, for the purposes of the dispute, the obligations of pacific settlement provided in the present Charter.
3. The proceedings of the General Assembly in respect of matters brought to its attention under this Article will be subject to the provisions of Articles 11 and 12.

ARTICLE 36.

1. The Security Council may, at any stage of a dispute of the nature referred to in Article 33 or of a situation of like nature, recommend appropriate procedures or methods of adjustment.
2. The Security Council should take into consideration any procedures for the settlement of the dispute which have already been adopted by the parties.
3. In making recommendations under this Article the Security Council should also take into consideration that legal disputes should as a general rule be referred by the parties to the International Court of Justice in accordance with the provisions of the Statute of the Court.

ARTICLE 37.

1. Should the parties to a dispute of the nature referred to in Article 33 fail to settle it by the means indicated in that Article, they shall refer it to the Security Council.

2. If the Security Council deems that the continuance of the dispute is in fact likely to endanger the maintenance of international peace and security, it shall decide whether to take action under Article 36 or to recommend such terms of settlement as it may consider appropriate.

## ARTICLE 38.

Without prejudice to the provisions of Articles 33 to 37, the Security Council may, if all the parties to any dispute so request, make recommendations to the parties with a view to a pacific settlement of the dispute.

# CHAPTER VII
# ACTION WITH RESPECT TO THREATS TO THE PEACE, BREACHES OF THE PEACE, AND ACTS OF AGGRESSION

## ARTICLE 39.

The Security Council shall determine the existence of any threat to the peace, breach of the peace, or act of aggression and shall make recommendations, or decide what measures shall be taken in accordance with Articles 41 and 42, to maintain or restore international peace and security.

## ARTICLE 40.

In order to prevent an aggravation of the situation, the Security Council may, before making the recommendations or deciding upon the measures provided for in Article 39, call upon the parties concerned to comply with such provisional measures as it deems necessary or desirable. Such provisional measures shall be without prejudice to the rights, claims, or position of the parties concerned. The Security Council shall duly take account of failure to comply with such provisional measures.

## ARTICLE 41.

The Security Council may decide what measures not involving the use of armed force are to be employed to give effect to its decisions, and it may call upon the Members of the United Nations to apply such measures. These may include complete or partial interruption of economic relations and of rail, sea, air, postal, telegraphic, radio, and other means of communication, and the severance of diplomatic relations.

## ARTICLE 42.

Should the Security Council consider that measures provided for in Article 41 would be inadequate or have proved to be inadequate, it may take such action by air, sea, or land forces as may be necessary to maintain or restore international peace and security. Such action may include demonstrations, blockade, and other operations by air, sea, or land forces of Members of the United Nations.

## ARTICLE 43.

1. All Members of the United Nations, in order to contribute to the maintenance of international peace and security, undertake to make available to the Security Council, on its call and in accordance with a special agreement or agreements, armed forces, assistance, and facilities,

including rights of passage, necessary for the purpose of maintaining international peace and security.

2. Such agreement or agreements shall govern the numbers and types of forces, their degree of readiness and general location, and the nature of the facilities and assistance to be provided.

3. The agreement or agreements shall be negotiated as soon as possible on the initiative of the Security Council. They shall be concluded between the Security Council and Members or between the Security Council and groups of Members and shall be subject to ratification by the signatory states in accordance with their respective constitutional processes.

## ARTICLE 44.

When the Security Council has decided to use force it shall, before calling upon a Member not represented on it to provide armed forces in fulfilment of the obligations assumed under Article 43, invite that Member, if the Member so desires, to participate in the decisions of the Security Council concerning the employment of contingents of that Member's armed forces.

## ARTICLE 45.

In order to enable the United Nations to take urgent military measures, Members shall hold immediately available national air-force contingents for combined international enforcement action. The strength and degree of readiness of these contingents and plans for their combined action shall be determined, within the limits laid down in the special agreement or agreements referred to in Article 43, by the Security Council with the assistance of the Military Staff Committee.

## ARTICLE 46.

Plans for the application of armed force shall be made by the Security Council with the assistance of the Military Staff Committee.

## ARTICLE 47.

1. There shall be established a Military Staff Committee to advise and assist the Security Council on all questions relating to the Security Council's military requirements for the maintenance of international peace and security, the employment and command of forces placed at its disposal, the regulation of armaments, and possible disarmament.

2. The Military Staff Committee shall consist of the Chiefs of Staff of the permanent Members of the Security Council or their representatives. Any Member of the United Nations not permanently represented on the Committee shall be invited by the Committee to be associated with it when the efficient discharge of the Committee's responsibilities requires the participation of that Member in its work.

3. The Military Staff Committee shall be responsible under the Security Council for the strategic direction of any armed forces placed at the disposal of the Security Council. Questions relating to the command of such forces shall be worked out subsequently.

4. The Military Staff Committee, with the authorization of the Security Council and after consultation with appropriate regional agencies, may establish regional sub-committees.

## ARTICLE 48.

1. The action required to carry out the decisions of the Security Council for the maintenance of international peace and security shall be taken by all the Members of the United Nations or by some of them, as the Security Council may determine.

2. Such decisions shall be carried out by the Members of the United Nations directly and through their action in the appropriate international agencies of which they are members.

## ARTICLE 49.

The Members of the United Nations shall join in affording mutual assistance in carrying out the measures decided upon by the Security Council.

## ARTICLE 50.

If preventive or enforcement measures against any state are taken by the Security Council, any other state, whether a Member of the United Nations or not, which finds itself confronted with special economic problems arising from the carrying out of those measures shall have the right to consult the Security Council with regard to a solution of those problems.

## ARTICLE 51.

Nothing in the present Charter shall impair the inherent right of individual or collective self-defense if an armed attack occurs against a Member of the United Nations, until the Security Council has taken measures necessary to maintain international peace and security. Measures taken by Members in the exercise of this right of self-defense shall be immediately reported to the Security Council and shall not in any way affect the authority and responsibility of the Security Council under the present Charter to take at any time such action as it deems necessary in order to maintain or restore international peace and security.

# CHAPTER VIII
# REGIONAL ARRANGEMENTS

## ARTICLE 52.

1. Nothing in the present Charter precludes the existence of regional arrangements or agencies for dealing with such matters relating to the maintenance of international peace and security as are appropriate for regional action, provided that such arrangements or agencies and their activities are consistent with the Purposes and Principles of the United Nations.
2. The Members of the United Nations entering into such arrangements or constituting such agencies shall make every effort to achieve pacific settlement of local disputes through such regional arrangements or by such regional agencies before referring them to the Security Council.
3. The Security Council shall encourage the development of pacific settlement of local disputes through such regional arrangements or by such regional agencies either on the initiative of the states concerned or by reference from the Security Council.
4. This Article in no way impairs the application of Articles 34 and 35.

## ARTICLE 53.

1. The Security Council shall, where appropriate, utilize such regional arrangements or agencies for enforcement action under its authority. But no enforcement action shall be taken under regional arrangements or by regional agencies without the authorization of the Security Council, with the exception of measures against any enemy state, as defined in paragraph 2 of this Article, provided for pursuant to Article 107 or in regional arrangements directed against renewal of aggressive policy on the part of any such state, until such time as the Or-

ganization may, on request of the Governments concerned, be charged with the responsibility for preventing further aggression by such a state.

2. The term enemy state as used in paragraph 1 of this Article applies to any state which during the Second World War has been an enemy of any signatory of the present Charter.

## ARTICLE 54.

The Security Council shall at all times be kept fully informed of activities undertaken or in contemplation under regional arrangements or by regional agencies for the maintenance of international peace and security.

# CHAPTER IX
# INTERNATIONAL ECONOMIC AND SOCIAL COOPERATION

## ARTICLE 55.

With a view to the creation of conditions of stability and well-being which are necessary for peaceful and friendly relations among nations based on respect for the principle of equal rights and self-determination of peoples, the United Nations shall promote:

a. higher standards of living, full employment, and conditions of economic and social progress and development;
b. solutions of international economic, social, health, and related problems; and international cultural and educational cooperation; and
c. universal respect for, and observance of, human rights and fundamental freedoms for all without distinction as to race, sex, language, or religion.

## ARTICLE 56.

All Members pledge themselves to take joint and separate action in cooperation with the Organization for the achievement of the purposes set forth in Article 55.

## ARTICLE 57.

1. The various specialized agencies, established by intergovernmental agreement and having wide international responsibilities, as defined in their basic instruments, in economic, social, cultural, educational, health and related fields, shall be brought into relationship with the United Nations in accordance with the provisions of Article 63.
2. Such agencies thus brought into relationship with the United Nations are hereinafter referred to as specialized agencies.

## ARTICLE 58.

The Organization shall make recommendations for the coordination of the policies and activities of the specialized agencies.

## ARTICLE 59.

The Organization shall, where appropriate, initiate negotiations among the states concerned for the creation of any new specialized agencies required for the accomplishment of the purposes set forth in Article 55.

ARTICLE 60.

Responsibility for the discharge of the functions of the Organization set forth in this Chapter shall be vested in the General Assembly and, under the authority of the General Assembly, in the Economic and Social Council, which shall have for this purpose the powers set forth in Chapter X.

## CHAPTER X
## THE ECONOMIC AND SOCIAL COUNCIL

### Composition
ARTICLE 61.

1. The Economic and Social Council shall consist of eighteen[5] Members of the United Nations elected by the General Assembly.
2. Subject to the provisions of paragraph 3, six[6] members of the Economic and Social Council shall be elected each year for a term of three years. A retiring member shall be eligible for immediate re-election.
3. At the first election, eighteen members of the Economic and Social Council shall be chosen. The term of office of six members so chosen shall expire at the end of one year, and of six other members at the end of two years, in accordance with arrangements made by the General Assembly.
4. Each member of the Economic and Social Council shall have one representative.

### Functions and Powers
ARTICLE 62.

1. The Economic and Social Council may make or initiate studies and reports with respect to international economic, social, cultural, educational, health, and related matters and may make recommendations with respect to any such matters to the General Assembly, to the Members of the United Nations, and to the specialized agencies concerned.
2. It may make recommendations for the purpose of promoting respect for, and observance of, human rights and fundamental freedoms for all.
3. It may prepare draft conventions for submission to the General Assembly, with respect to matters falling within its competence.
4. It may call, in accordance with the rules prescribed by the United Nations, international conferences on matters falling within its competence.

ARTICLE 63.

1. The Economic and Social Council may enter into agreements with any of the agencies referred to in Article 57, defining the terms on which the agency concerned shall be brought into relationship with the United Nations. Such agreements shall be subject to approval by the General Assembly.
2. It may coordinate the activities of the specialized agencies through consultation with and recommendations to such agencies and through recommendations to the General Assembly and to the Members of the United Nations.

---

[5] Expanded to twenty-seven members by Charter amendment in 1965 and to fifty-four members by Charter amendment in 1973.

[6] Changed to provide for the election of nine members each year by Charter amendment in 1965 and eighteen members each year by Charter amendment in 1973.

## ARTICLE 64.

1. The Economic and Social Council may take appropriate steps to obtain regular reports from the specialized agencies. It may make arrangements with the Members of the United Nations and with the specialized agencies to obtain reports on the steps taken to give effect to its own recommendations and to recommendations on matters falling within its competence made by the General Assembly.
2. It may communicate its observations on these reports to the General Assembly.

## ARTICLE 65.

The Economic and Social Council may furnish information to the Security Council and shall assist the Security Council upon its request.

## ARTICLE 66.

1. The Economic and Social Council shall perform such functions as fall within its competence in connection with the carrying out of the recommendations of the General Assembly.
2. It may, with the approval of the General Assembly, perform services at the request of Members of the United Nations and at the request of specialized agencies.
3. It shall perform such other functions as are specified elsewhere in the present Charter or as may be assigned to it by the General Assembly.

# Voting
## ARTICLE 67.

1. Each member of the Economic and Social Council shall have one vote.
2. Decisions of the Economic and Social Council shall be made by a majority of the members present and voting.

# Procedure
## ARTICLE 68.

The Economic and Social Council shall set up commissions in economic and social fields and for the promotion of human rights, and such other commissions as may be required for the performance of its functions.

## ARTICLE 69.

The Economic and Social Council shall invite any Member of the United Nations to participate, without vote, in its deliberations on any matter of particular concern to that Member.

## ARTICLE 70.

The Economic and Social Council may make arrangements for representatives of the specialized agencies to participate, without vote, in its deliberations and in those of the commissions established by it, and for its representatives to participate in the deliberations of the specialized agencies.

## ARTICLE 71.

The Economic and Social Council may make suitable arrangements for consultation with non-governmental organizations which are concerned with matters within its competence. Such arrangements may be made with international organizations and, where appropriate, with national organizations after consultation with the Member of the United Nations concerned.

## ARTICLE 72.

1. The Economic and Social Council shall adopt its own rules of procedure, including the method of selecting its President.
2. The Economic and Social Council shall meet as required in accordance with its rules, which shall include provision for the convening of meetings on the request of a majority of its members.

# CHAPTER XI
# DECLARATION REGARDING NON-SELF-GOVERNING TERRITORIES

## ARTICLE 73.

Members of the United Nations which have or assume responsibilities for the administration of territories whose peoples have not yet attained a full measure of self-government recognize the principle that the interests of the inhabitants of these territories are paramount, and accept as a sacred trust the obligation to promote to the utmost, within the system of international peace and security established by the present Charter, the well-being of the inhabitants of these territories, and, to this end:

a. to ensure, with due respect for the culture of the peoples concerned, their political, economic, social, and educational advancement, their just treatment, and their protection against abuses;
b. to develop self-government, to take due account of the political aspirations of the peoples, and to assist them in the progressive development of their free political institutions, according to the particular circumstances of each territory and its peoples and their varying stages of advancement;
c. to further international peace and security;
d. to promote constructive measures of development, to encourage research, and to cooperate with one another and, when and where appropriate, with specialized international bodies with a view to the practical achievement of the social, economic, and scientific purposes set forth in this Article; and
c. to transmit regularly to the Secretary-General for information purposes, subject to such limitation as security and constitutional considerations may require, statistical and other information of a technical nature relating to economic, social, and educational conditions in the territories for which they are respectively responsible other than those territories to which Chapters XII and XIII apply.

## ARTICLE 74.

Members of the United Nations also agree that their policy in respect of the territories to which this Chapter applies, no less than in respect of their metropolitan areas, must be based on the general principle of good-neighborliness, due account being taken of the interests and well-being of the rest of the world, in social, economic, and commercial matters.

# CHAPTER XII
# INTERNATIONAL TRUSTEESHIP SYSTEM

## ARTICLE 75.

The United Nations shall establish under its authority an international trusteeship system for the administration and supervision of such territories as may be placed thereunder by subsequent individual agreements. These territories are hereinafter referred to as trust territories.

## ARTICLE 76.

The basic objectives of the trusteeship system, in accordance with the Purposes of the United Nations laid down in Article I of the present Charter, shall be:

a. to further international peace and security;
b. to promote the political, economic, social, and educational advancement of the inhabitants of the trust territories, and their progressive development towards self-government or independence as may be appropriate to the particular circumstances of each territory and its peoples and the freely expressed wishes of the peoples concerned, and as may be provided by the terms of each trusteeship agreement;
c. to encourage respect for human rights and for fundamental freedoms for all without distinction as to race, sex, language, or religion, and to encourage recognition of the interdependence of the peoples of the world; and
d. to ensure equal treatment in social, economic, and commercial matters for all Members of the United Nations and their nationals, and also equal treatment for the latter in the administration of justice, without prejudice to the attainment of the foregoing objectives and subject to the provisions of Article 80.

## ARTICLE 77.

1. The trusteeship system shall apply to such territories in the following categories as may be placed thereunder by means of trusteeship agreements:
   a. territories now held under mandate;
   b. territories which may be detached from enemy states as a result of the Second World War; and
   c. territories voluntarily placed under the system by states responsible for their administration.
2. It will be a matter for subsequent agreement as to which territories in the foregoing categories will be brought under the trusteeship system and upon what terms.

## ARTICLE 78.

The trusteeship system shall not apply to territories which have become Members of the United Nations, the relationship among which shall be based on respect for the principle of sovereign equality.

## ARTICLE 79.

The terms of trusteeship for each territory to be placed under the trusteeship system, including any alteration or amendment, shall be agreed upon by the states directly concerned, including the mandatory power in the case of territories held under mandate by a Member of the United Nations, and shall be approved as provided for in Articles 83 and 85.

## ARTICLE 80.

1. Except as may be agreed upon in individual trusteeship agreements, made under Articles 77, 79, and 81, placing each territory under the trusteeship system, and until such agreements have been concluded, nothing in this Chapter shall be construed in or of itself to alter in any manner the rights whatsoever of any states or any peoples or the terms of existing international instruments to which Members of the United Nations may respectively be parties.
2. Paragraph 1 of this Article shall not be interpreted as giving grounds for delay or postponement of the negotiation and conclusion of agreements for placing mandated and other territories under the trusteeship system as provided for in Article 77.

## ARTICLE 81.

The trusteeship agreement shall in each use include the terms under which the trust territory will be administered and designate the authority which will exercise the administration of the trust territory. Such authority, hereinafter called the administering authority, may be one or more states or the Organization itself.

## ARTICLE 82.

There may be designated, in any trusteeship agreement, a strategic area or areas which may include part or all of the trust territory to which the agreement applies, without prejudice to any special agreement or agreements made under Article 43.

## ARTICLE 83.

1. All functions of the United Nations relating to strategic areas, including the approval of the terms of the trusteeship agreements and of their alteration or amendment, shall be exercised by the Security Council.
2. The basic objectives set forth in Article 76 shall be applicable to the people of each strategic area.
3. The Security Council shall, subject to the provisions of the trusteeship agreements and without prejudice to security considerations, avail itself of the assistance of the Trusteeship Council to perform those functions of the United Nations under the trusteeship system relating to political, economic, social, and educational matters in the strategic areas.

## ARTICLE 84.

It shall be the duty of the administering authority to ensure that the trust territory shall play its part in the maintenance of international peace and security. To this end the administering authority may make use of volunteer forces, facilities, and assistance from the trust territory in carrying out the obligations towards the Security Council undertaken in this regard by the administering authority, as well as for local defense and the maintenance of law and order within the trust territory.

## ARTICLE 85.

1. The functions of the United Nations with regard to trusteeship agreements for all areas not designated as strategic, including the approval of the terms of the trusteeship agreements and of their alteration or amendment, shall be exercised by the General Assembly.
2. The Trusteeship Council, operating under the authority of the General Assembly, shall assist the General Assembly in carrying out these functions.

# CHAPTER XIII
# THE TRUSTEESHIP COUNCIL

## Composition
## ARTICLE 86.

1. The Trusteeship Council shall consist of the following Members of the United Nations:
   a. those Members administering trust territories;
   b. such of those Members mentioned by name in Article 23 as are not administering trust territories; and

    c.  as many other Members elected for three-year terms by the General Assembly as may be necessary to ensure that the total number of members of the Trusteeship Council is equally divided between those Members of the United Nations which administer trust territories and those which do not.
2.  Each member of the Trusteeship Council shall designate one specially qualified person to represent it therein.

## Functions and Powers

### ARTICLE 87.

The General Assembly and, under its authority, the Trusteeship Council, in carrying out their functions, may:

a.  consider reports submitted by the administering authority;
b.  accept petitions and examine them in consultation with the administering authority;
c.  provide for periodic visits to the respective trust territories at times agreed upon with the administering authority; and
d.  take these and other actions in conformity with the terms of the trusteeship agreements.

### ARTICLE 88.

The Trusteeship Council shall formulate a questionnaire on the political, economic, social, and educational advancement of the inhabitants of each trust territory, and the administering authority for each trust territory within the competence of the General Assembly shall make an annual report to the General Assembly upon the basis of such questionnaire.

## Voting

### ARTICLE 89.

1.  Each member of the Trusteeship Council shall have one vote.
2.  Decisions of the Trusteeship Council shall be made by a majority of the members present and voting.

## Procedure

### ARTICLE 90.

1.  The Trusteeship Council shall adopt its own rules of procedure, including the method of selecting its President.
2.  The Trusteeship Council shall meet as required in accordance with its rules, which shall include provision for the convening of meetings on the request of a majority of its members.

### ARTICLE 91.

The Trusteeship Council shall, when appropriate, avail itself of the assistance of the Economic and Social Council and of the specialized agencies in regard to matters with which they are respectively concerned.

## CHAPTER XIV
## THE INTERNATIONAL COURT OF JUSTICE

### ARTICLE 92.

The International Court of Justice shall be the principal judicial organ of the United Nations. It shall function in accordance with the annexed Statute, which is based upon the Statute of the Permanent Court of International Justice and forms an integral part of the present Charter.

## ARTICLE 93.

1. All Members of the United Nations are *ipso facto* parties to the Statute of the International Court of Justice.
2. A state which is not a Member of the United Nations may become a party to the Statute of the International Court of Justice on conditions to be determined in each case by the General Assembly upon the recommendation of the Security Council.

## ARTICLE 94.

1. Each Member of the United Nations undertakes to comply with the decision of the International Court of Justice in any case to which it is a party.
2. If any party to a case fails to perform the obligations incumbent upon it under a judgment rendered by the Court, the other party may have recourse to the Security Council, which may, if it deems necessary, make recommendations or decide upon measures to be taken to give effect to the judgment.

## ARTICLE 95.

Nothing in the present Charter shall prevent Members of the United Nations from entrusting the solution of their differences to other tribunals by virtue of agreements already in existence or which may be concluded in the future.

## ARTICLE 96.

1. The General Assembly or the Security Council may request the International Court of Justice to give an advisory opinion on any legal question.
2. Other organs of the United Nations and specialized agencies, which may at any time be so authorized by the General Assembly, may also request advisory opinions of the Court on legal questions arising within the scope of their activities.

# CHAPTER XV
# THE SECRETARIAT

## ARTICLE 97.

The Secretariat shall comprise a Secretary-General and such staff as the Organization may require. The Secretary-General shall be appointed by the General Assembly upon the recommendation of the Security Council. He shall be the chief administrative officer of the Organization.

## ARTICLE 98.

The Secretary-General shall act in that capacity in all meetings of the General Assembly, of the Security Council, of the Economic and Social Council, and of the Trusteeship Council, and shall perform such other functions as are entrusted to him by these organs. The Secretary-General shall make an annual report to the General Assembly on the work of the Organization.

## ARTICLE 99.

The Secretary-General may bring to the attention of the Security Council any matter which in his opinion may threaten the maintenance of international peace and security.

## ARTICLE 100.

1. In the performance of their duties the Secretary-General and the staff shall not seek or receive instructions from any government or from any other authority external to the Organization. They shall refrain from any action which might reflect on their position as international officials responsible only to the Organization.
2. Each Member of the United Nations undertakes to respect the exclusively international character of the responsibilities of the Secretary-General and the staff and not to seek to influence them in the discharge of their responsibilities.

## ARTICLE 101.

1. The staff shall be appointed by the Secretary-General under regulations established by the General Assembly.
2. Appropriate staffs shall be permanently assigned to the Economic and Social Council, the Trusteeship Council, and, as required, to other organs of the United Nations. These staffs shall form a part of the Secretariat.
3. The paramount consideration in the employment of the staff and in the determination of the conditions of service shall be the necessity of securing the highest standards of efficiency, competence, and integrity. Due regard shall be paid to the importance of recruiting the staff on as wide a geographical basis as possible.

# CHAPTER XVI
# MISCELLANEOUS PROVISIONS

## ARTICLE 102.

1. Every treaty and every international agreement entered into by any Member of the United Nations after the present Charter comes into force shall as soon as possible be registered with the Secretariat and published by it.
2. No party to any such treaty or international agreement which has not been registered in accordance with the provisions of paragraph 1 of this Article may invoke that treaty or agreement before any organ of the United Nations.

## ARTICLE 103.

In the event of a conflict between the obligations of the Members of the United Nations under the present Charter and their obligations under any other international agreement, their obligations under the present Charter shall prevail.

## ARTICLE 104.

The Organization shall enjoy in the territory of each of its Members such legal capacity as may be necessary for the exercise of its functions and the fulfilment of its purposes.

## ARTICLE 105.

1. The Organization shall enjoy in the territory of each of its Members such privileges and immunities as are necessary for the fulfilment of its purposes.
2. Representatives of the Members of the United Nations and officials of the Organization shall similarly enjoy such privileges and immunities as are necessary for the independent exercise of their functions in connection with the Organization.

3. The General Assembly may make recommendations with a view to determining the details of the application of paragraphs 1 and 2 of this Article or may propose conventions to the Members of the United Nations for this purpose.

## CHAPTER XVII
## TRANSITIONAL SECURITY ARRANGEMENTS

### ARTICLE 106.

Pending the coming into force of such special agreements referred to in Article 43 as in the opinion of the Security Council enable it to begin the exercise of its responsibilities under Article 42, the parties to the Four-Nation Declaration, signed at Moscow, October 30, 1943, and France, shall, in accordance with the provisions of paragraph 5 of that Declaration, consult with one another and as occasion requires with other Members of the United Nations with a view to such joint action on behalf of the Organization as may be necessary for the purpose of maintaining international peace and security.

### ARTICLE 107.

Nothing in the present Charter shall invalidate or preclude action, in relation to any state which during the Second World War has been an enemy of any signatory to the present Charter, taken or authorized as a result of that war by the Governments having responsibility for such action.

## CHAPTER XVIII
## AMENDMENTS

### ARTICLE 108.

Amendments to the present Charter shall come into force for all Members of the United Nations when they have been adopted by a vote of two thirds of the members of the General Assembly and ratified in accordance with their respective constitutional processes by two thirds of the Members of the United Nations, including all the permanent members of the Security Council.

### ARTICLE 109.

1. A General Conference of the Members of the United Nations for the purpose of reviewing the present Charter may be held at a date and place to be fixed by a two-thirds vote of the members of the General Assembly and by a vote of any seven members of the Security Council. Each Member of the United Nations shall have one vote in the conference.
2. Any alteration of the present Charter recommended by a two-thirds vote of the conference shall take effect when ratified in accordance with their respective constitutional processes by two thirds of the Members of the United Nations including all the permanent members of the Security Council.
3. If such a conference has not been held before the tenth annual session of the General Assembly following the coming into force of the present Charter, the proposal to call such a conference shall be placed on the agenda of that session of the General Assembly, and the conference shall be held if so decided by a majority vote of the members of the General Assembly and by a vote of any seven members of the Security Council.

## CHAPTER XIX
## RATIFICATION AND SIGNATURE

ARTICLE 110.

1.  The present Charter shall be ratified by the signatory states in accordance with their respective constitutional processes.
2.  The ratifications shall be deposited with the Government of the United States of America, which shall notify all the signatory states of each deposit as well as the Secretary-General of the Organization when he has been appointed.
3.  The present Charter shall come into force upon the deposit of ratifications by the Republic of China, France, the Union of Soviet Socialist Republics, the United Kingdom of Great Britain and Northern Ireland, and the United States of America, and by a majority of the other signatory states. A protocol of the ratifications deposited shall thereupon be drawn up by the Government of the United States of America which shall communicate copies thereof to all the signatory states.
4.  The states signatory to the present Charter which ratify it after it has come into force will become original members of the United Nations on the date of the deposit of their respective ratifications.

ARTICLE 111.

The present Charter, of which the Chinese, French, Russian, English, and Spanish texts are equally authentic, shall remain deposited in the archives of the Government of the United States of America. Duly certified copies thereof shall be transmitted by that Government to the Governments of the other signatory states.

**In faith whereof** the representatives of the Governments of the United Nations have signed the present Charter.

**Done** at the city of San Francisco the twenty-sixth day of June, one thousand nine hundred and forty-five.

# NAME INDEX

Page numbers indicated in **bold type** indicate tables or figures.

Abbas, Mahmood, 295, 296
Abe, Nobuyasu, 331
Abu Mazen (Mahmood Abbas), 295, 296
Acheson, Dean, 359
Aidid, Mohammed Farah, 244
Akasi, Yasushi, 239
Amerasinghe, H. S., **49**
Annan, Kofi, 52, 83, 135, 149, 150, **151**, 153,
    155, 156, 159, 160–62, 184, 185, 186,
    187, 189, 190, 194, 197, 199, 208, 223,
    224, 226, 229, 236, 238, 250, 251, 255,
    312, 313, 329, 340, 349, 402, 405, 418,
    441, 442, 454, 510, 518, 519–20, 521,
    526, 527, 529
Arafat, Yasir, 98, 291, 292, 293, 294, 295,
    296, 463, 464
Aranha, Oswaldo, **48**
Arce, José, **48**
Arenales Catalán, Emilio, **48**
Aristide, Jean-Bertrand, 248, 249, 250

Baker, James, 109, 236
Baradei, Mohamed El, 343
Barak, Ehud, 292, 293, 294
Baruch, Bernard, 332
Belaúnde, Victor Andrés, **48**
Benítes, Leopoldo, **49**
bin Laden, Osama, 6, 191–92, 193, 209, 210,
    252
Bismarck, Otto von , 169
Blair, Tony, 195, 206
Blix, Hans, 194, 195, 197
Boland, Frederick H., **48**
Botha, P. W., 285
Bouteflika, Abdelaziz, **49**
Boutros-Ghali, Boutros, 52, 135, 149, 150,
    **151**, 153, 154–55, 156, 158–59, 214, 243,
    244, 245
Brooks, Angie E., **49**
Buergenthal, Thomas, **44**
Bush, George H. W., 109, 122, 188, 230, 243,
    306, 354, 525
Bush, George W., 5, 7, 119, 122–23, 154,
    179, 183, 184, 187, 193, 194, 195, 196,
    197, 198, 199, 200, 206, 230, 294, 337,
    343, 351, 367, 406, 433, 447, 462, 479,
    485, 518, 520

Butler, Richard, 186, 187
Byrnes, James F., 28

Caputo, Dante M., **50**
Carter, Jimmy, 290, 412
Castro, Fidel, 302
Choudhury, Humayan Rasheed, **49**
Churchill, Winston, 23, 25, 175
Clark, Wesley, 207–8
Claude, Inis L., 129
Clinton, Bill, 4, 122, 159, 179, 184, 186, 192,
    230, 244, 251, 292, 293, 309, 343, 351,
    352, 433, 479
Cordovez, Diego de, 149, 154, 304

de Klerk, F. W., 203, 285
de Marco, Guido, **50**, 53
Dhanapala, Jayantha, 331, 336
Drummond, Eric, 136, 158

Eden, Anthony, 24
Eisenhower, Dwight, 412
Elaraby, Nabi, **44**
Entezam, Nasrollah, **48**
Essy, Amara, **50**
Evatt, H. V., **48**

Fanfani, Amintore, **48**
Finger, Seymour Maxwell, 86
Florin, Peter, **49**, **50**
Foo Ping-sheung, 24
Franks, Tommy, 315
Frechette, Louise, 161
Freitas do Amaral, Diogo, **50**

Gandhi, Mahatma, 380
Ganev, Stoyan, **50**
Garba, Joseph Nanven, **50**
Gorbachev, Mikhail, 79, 182, 230, 368
Graham, Frank, 297
Guillaume, Gilbert, **44**
Gurirab, Theo-Ben, **50**
Gusmao, Xanana, 255

Haas, Ernst, 318
Haas, Peter, 432
Hambro, Edvard, **49**

Hammarskjöld, Dag, 10, 146, 149, **151**, 152, 153–54, 158, 214, 220, 222, 300
Han Seung-Soo, 50
Herzl, Theodor, 288
Higgins, Rosalyn, **44**
Hitler, Adolf, 326, 327
Holkeri, Harri, 50
Hollai, Imre, **49**
Hoveyda, Fereydoun, 522–24
Hull, Cordell, 24
Hun Sen, 239, 307–8
Hunte, Julian Robert, 50
Hussein (king of Jordan), 292
Hussein, Saddam, 6–7, 35, 179, 181–87, 189, 190, 193, 194, 195, 196, 198, 199, 200, 204, 205, 342, 355, 406, 491, 518, 526

Illueca, Jorge E., **49**
Insanally, Samuel R., 50
Ismail, Razali, **50**

Johnson, Lyndon, 297

Kabbah, Ahmed Tejan, 247, 248
Kabila, Joseph, 223
Kabila, Laurent, 223
Karadžić, Radovan, 243
Karzai, Hamid, 193, 210, 252, 253
Khasawneh, Awn Shawkat al-, **44**
Kavan, Jan, **50**
Kennedy, John F., 302, 354, 383
Khane, Abd-El Rahman, 491
Khan, Muhammad Ayub, 297
Khan, Muhammad Zafrulla, **48**
Khomeini, Ayatollah Ruholia Mussaui, 304, 305
Khruschev, Nikita, 302
Kim Il Sung, 353
Kirkpatrick, Jeane J., 129
Kittani, Ismat T., **49**
Kooijmans, Pieter H., **44**
Kormoma, Abudl G., **44**
Krasner, Stephen D., 431

Lake, Anthony, 251
Lie, Trygve, 149, **151**, 152, 153, 158
Liévano, Indalecio, **49**
Lytton (Lord), 16

Malik, Adam, **49**
Malik, Charles, **48**
Malloch-Brown, Mark, 511
Mandela, Nelson, 34, 204, 285–86
Manescu, Corneliu, **48**

Marker, Jamsheed, 312
Maza, José, **48**
Mbeki, Thabo, 223, 286
Milošević, Slobodan, 98, 207–8, 209, 275, 309, 405, 421
Mladic, Ratko, 243
Mobutu Sese Seko, 223, 392
Mojsov, Lazar, **49**
Molotov, Vyacheslav, 24
Mubarak, Hosni, 290
Mugabe, Robert, 288, 392
Munro, Leslie, **48**
Musharraf, Pervez, 299
Mussolini, Benito, 17

Nansen, Fridtjof, 455
Nasser, Gamal Abdel, 221, 290
Netanyahu, Benjamin, 291, 292
Nicholas II, Tsar, 325
Nimitz, Chester, 297
Nol, Lon, 307
Nujoma, Sam, 287–88

Omar, Mullah Mohammed, 192, 193, 209, 210, 252
Opertti, Didier, **50**
Ortega, Rudecindo, **48**
Owada, Hisashi, **44**

Padilla Nervo, Luis, **48**
Pandit, Vijaya Lakshmi, **48**
Pardo, Arvid, 438
Parra-Aranguren, Gonzalo, **44**
Pazhwak, Abdul Rahman, **48**
Pearson, Lester, **48**, 149, 220
Peres, Shimon, 291
Pérez de Cuéllar, Javier, 133, 135, 150, 152, 153, 154, 158, 271, 301, 304, 305, 306, 405
Perry, William, 347
Piniés, Jaime de, **49**
Pinochet, Augusto, 408
Plavsic, Biljana, 405
Pol Pot, 307, 308
Powell, Colin, 195, 196
Putin, Vladimir, 246, 338, 485

Quaison-Sackey, Alex, **48**
Quayle, Dan, 109
Qureira, Ahmad, 296

Rabin, Yitzhak, 291, 292
Rakhomonov, Imomali, 235
Ranariddh, Norodom, 307–8

Ranjeva, Raymond, **44**
Reagan, Ronald, 122, 230, 336, 351, 439
Rezek, José Francisco, **44**
Ritter, Scott, 185, 195
Romulo, Carlos P., **48**
Roosevelt, Eleanor, 412
Roosevelt, Franklin D., 17, 23, 25, 26, 171, 175, 332–33
Rumsfeld, Donald, 196

Sadat, Anwar Al-, 290
Salim, Salim A., **49**, 100, 150
Savimbi, Jonas, 233, 310
Selassie, Haile, 17
Shah, Zahir (king), 193
Sharon, Ariel, 294
Shastri, Lal Bahadur, 297
Shevardnadze, Eduard, 245
Shihabi, Samir S., **50**
Shi Jiuyong, **44**
Sihanouk, Norodom, 307, 308
Simma, Bruno, **44**
Slim, Mongi, **48**
Smith, Ian, 202
Smuts, Jan, 375
Sosa Rodríguez, Carlos, **48**
Spaak, Paul-Henri, **48**, 149
Stalin, Joseph, 25, 75, 175
Suharto, 390

Taylor, Charles, 233, 234, 310–11, 392
Thant, U, **151**, 152, 153, 154, 158, 221, 289, 301, 302
Thomas, Albert, 136, 158
Thorn, Gaston, **49**
Tito, Marshal (Josip Broz), 106, 420
Tomka, Peter, **44**
Trepczynski, Stanislaw, **49**
Truman, Harry, 28, 438, 496
Tubman, William V. S., 310
Turner, Ted, 153

Udovenko, Hennadiy, **50**

van Kleffens, Eelco N., **48**
Vereshchetin, Vladlen S., **44**
Vieira de Mello, Sergio, 199, 526

Waithayakon, Wan, **48**
Waldheim, Kurt, 100, 150, **151**, 152, 153, 158, 304, 522, 523
Wechmar, Rüdiger von, **49**
Wilhelm II, Kaiser, 169
Wilson, Woodrow, 13–14, 168, 169, 170, 325, 326, 374

Yeltsin, Boris, 351, 368
Yessin, Ahmad, 296
Young, Oran, 432

# SUBJECT INDEX

Page numbers indicated in **bold type** indicate tables or figures.

ABM. *See* antiballistic missile (ABM) treaty
abortion, 479
accidental nuclear war, 353–55
Acheson-Lilienthal Report, 332, 359
Act for International Development (U.S. Congress), 496
adjudication, dispute settlement, 267
administration, Secretariat, UN, 145–46
Administrative Committee on Coordination, ECOSOC, 61, 465
administrators, as political participants, 83–84
advisory opinions, ICJ, 276–77
AEC. *See* UN Atomic Energy Commission
Afghanistan
    after September 11, 252–54
    conflicts, 245
    sanctions against, 209–10
    Soviet intervention, 191–92, 303–4
    Soviet withdrawal, 231
    U.S. preemptive assault, 193
    U.S. role analyzed, 517, 518
Afghanistan Sanctions Committee, 210
AFL-CIO, 424
African Economic Council, 274
African National Congress (ANC), 80, 81, 285
African states
    Annan appointment, 150
    Boutros-Ghali appointment, 150
    decolonization, 379
    disaster relief, 454
    overlapping with other UN groups, **105**
    refugees, 457, 458–59
    regional groups, 102, **103**, 104
    UN professional personnel, **142**
    voting coinciding with United States, **111–12**
    *See also* Economic Commission for Africa
African Union, 274. *See also* Organization of African Unity (OAU)
agricultural productivity, 474, 481, 509
AIDS
    development planning, 498, 511
    LDCs, 476
    *See also* Joint UN Program on HIV/AIDS (UNAIDS)
air transportation, 427
Algerian question, 383, 386

Al-Quaeda organization
    Afghan campaign, 252–53
    Bush response to, 6
    Hussein link seen, 194
    origins of, 192
    Pakistan and, 299
    significance of, 370
    U.S. attack on, 123
American Convention on Human Rights (1978), 416
American Declaration of the Rights and Duties of Man (Bogotá, 1948), 416
American Neutrality Acts, 19
ANC. *See* African National Congress
Angola conflict, 232–33
    Cuban troops, 285, 287
    dispute settlement, 309–10
Angolan National Police, 232
annexation, 374
Antarctic Treaty (1959), **330**, 338–39
Antarctic Treaty System (ATS), **330**, 338–39
anthrax scares, 193–94
antiballistic missile (ABM) treaty, 337
anticolonial manifesto, 386–87
ANZUS (security pact, 1951), 212
apartheid
    conflict resolution, 282, 284–86
    domestic jurisdiction, 34
    sanctions against South Africa, 203–4
    *See also* South Africa
appeasement, 19
Arab group, overlapping with other UN groups, **105**
Arab-Israeli dispute
    Assembly majorities, 124
    categorizing, 202
    Emergency Session, 95
    history, 288–89, 379
    ICJ hearings, 268
    Iraqi proposal, 124
    Lebanon (UNIFIL), 215, **216**, 228–30
    Lebanon (UNOGIL), 154, **216**, 226, 227
    nuclear weapons, 341–42
    peacekeeping, 227–28
    peace process, 291–92
    refugees, 460–64
    Security Council, 271–72

Arab-Israeli dispute (*continued*)
  Six-Day War, 290
  UN Disengagement Observer Force, 215,
    **216,** 219, 227, 228
  UNEF I, **216,** 220–21
  UN Trace Supervision Organization
    (UNTSO), 215, **216,** 219
  U.S. veto, 98–99
  Zionism, 108–9, 288
Arab League
  collective security, 172
  dispute settlement, 274–75
  undermined, 213
arbitration, dispute settlement, 266–67
Argentina, boundary dispute, 267
arms control
  enforcement and sanctions, 365–66
  forums, 334–8
  inspection and enforcement, 365–66
  negotiations, 324
  ratio problems, 363–65
  threats of deception, 359–60
arms race
  end of the Cold War, 363
  nuclear proliferation, 344–45
  security issues, 358
  U.S.-Soviet, 333–34, 363
arms reduction. *See* arms control
arms regulation, 328
ASEAN. *See* Association of Southeast Asian
  Nations
Asian states
  Economic and Social Commission for West-
    ern Asia, 490, 491
  overlapping with other UN groups, **105**
  regional groups, 102, **103,** 104
  Southeast Asia Treaty Organization
    (SEATO, 1954), 212
  voting coinciding with U.S. votes, **113–15**
Asia and the Pacific
  UN professional personnel, **142**
  *See also* Economic and Social Commission
    for Asia and the Pacific, 490
Association of Southeast Asian Nations
  (ASEAN)
  caucusing group, 102
  terrorism, 163–64
Atlantic Charter, 23–24
atomic weapons, 327, 332–3
attitudinal changes, 477–78
Australia
  independence of East Timor, 213
  Solomon Islands conflict, 260–61
authoritarian regimes, 476

"Axis of Evil," 179, 343, 520
Axis Powers, 19, 20

Baghdad Pact, disintegration, 212
Bahrain, 301
balance of power
  collective security, 168–74
  concept of, 168
  League of Nations, 21
  World War I, 168–69
Balfour Declaration (1917), 288
Bali Declaration on Population and Sustainable Development (1992), 479
Bangkok Treaty, **331,** 340
Barre, Muhammad Siad, 243
Baruch Plan, 332–33, 359, 365
bilateral disputes, 319
bilateral or multilateral foreign aid, 486–87
BINGOs. *See* business international nongovernmental organizations
biodiversity treaties, 433
biological weapons. *See* chemical and biological weapons
Blair resolution, 195, 197
blend borrowers, 507
bloc politics, early UN, 27
Bonn Agreement, 253
Bosnia-Herzegovina
  conflicts, 239
  sanctions against Serbia, 206–9
Bretton Woods system, 500, 501
Bruce Committee (1939), 400–401
Brussels Conference (1890), 404
budgetary assessments. *See* finances
Bush administration
  coalition against Iraq, 99
  financial role, 5
  START II safeguards, 365
  unilateralism, 367
  U.S. role, 5
business international nongovernmental organizations (BINGOs), 79

Cairo Conference on Population and Development (1994), 479
Cambodia conflicts, **217,** 235–36, 303,
  307–8
  border disputes, 300
  conflict resolution, 307–8
  transitional governance, **217,** 238–39
Cambodian People's Party, 308
Capetown Agreements (1927, 1932), 284
capital transfers, 487
career service, 142–44

Caribbean Community and Common Market (CARICOM), 250
CARICOM. *See* Caribbean Community and Common Market
Caucasus, 309
caucusing groups, 102
CCD. *See* Conference of the Committee on Disarmament
CD. *See* Conference on Disarmament
CENTO (Central Treaty Organization, 1959), 212
Central African Republic conflict, **218**, 234
Central America, missions to, 236–37, 305–6
Central Asia, 309
Central Treaty Organization (CENTO, 1959), 212
Chechnya conflict, 246, 360–61, 393, 394
chemical and biological weapons, 355–56
chemical weapons
    Iraq, 189
    Organization for the Prohibition of Chemical Weapons, 61
children
    human rights, 409, **410**, 415
    Office of the Special Representative for Children in Armed Conflict, 161
    UNICEF, 452–54
    youth employment, 482
Chile
    boundary dispute, 267
    Pinochet dictatorship, 408
China, U.S. airmen, 300
China (Nationalist). *See* Taiwan
China (People's Republic of)
    attitude to UN, 4
    Korean War, 178, 181
    nuclear tests, 348
    Taiwan entry, 75, 78
    UNPREDEP veto, 97, 98, 99–100
    veto of Waldheim, 150, 152
CIS. *See* Commonwealth of Independent States
civil aviation, 427
civil servants, international, 83–84
    U.S. share, 127–28
civil service, international, 136–38
    career ideal, 142–44
    diversity and political support, 137–38
    impartiality, 144
    independence, 144–45
    International Civil Service Advisory Board, 465
    loyalty, 144
    origin, 136–37

civil society
    Annan emphasis, 153, 349
    international, 527
    as new superpower, 349
civil wars
    enforcement actions, 201, 202
    self-determination, 474
co-deployment principle, 21, 313, 519
coerced disarmament, 342–44
Cold War
    arms race, 327–29
    budgetary questions, 66
    decolonization, 380
    dispute settlement, 300–307, 318–19, **319**
    economic development, 492
    hot wars, 173
    ideological hostility, 360
    ILO, 423–24
    impact on UN, 530
    Korean War, 180–81
    NATO, 213
    origins, 2–3
    rivalry, 516
    security issues, 175
    Soviet Union, former, 2
    tension reduction, 356
    UN Charter, 181
    UN membership, 75
collective defense, 171
collective legitimization, 129
Collective Measures Committee, 180
collective sanctions, 211
collective security
    arms regulation, 328
    balance of power, 168–74
    commitment to, 172
    General Assembly, 51
    Gulf War (1990–91), 181–87
    Korean War, 176–81
    nature of, 171–73
    peacekeeping, 213–15
    terrorism, 519–21
    use of term, 171
    War on Iraq, 198
    war-prevention role, 167
    World War II, 23
collective security system, 171–72
    elements of, 172
    League of Nations, 22
    problems, 187–90
    prospects, 313
    war on Iraq, 196, 197
collective self-defense, 36, 171

colonialism
  demise of, 388–90
  divisions in UN, 522
  impact on LDCs, 474
  problems, 391
Commission for Conventional Armaments,
  334
Commission on Human Rights, 202, 413–14
Commission on Information from Non–Self-
  Governing Territories, 384–85, 387–88
Commission on the Limits of the Continental
  Shelf, 440
Committee of Twenty-Four, 388
commodity councils, 91
Commonwealth, British, bloc politics, 27
Commonwealth of Independent States (CIS)
  caucusing group, 102
  Chechnya conflict, 246
  dispute settlement, 275
  Georgia-Abkhazia, 217, 245–46, 309
  Tajikistan conflict, 235, 309
Communicable Disease Surveillance and Re-
  sponse (CSR), 430–31
communication, history, 10
communications network, 101–2
community development, 480
complementarity, principle of, 316
compliance, 127, 128–29
Comprehensive Nuclear Test Ban Treaty
  (1970), 331, 348, 349
  France, 281
  India-Pakistani conflict, 270, 298, 341
  participation, 361
Comprehensive Nuclear Test-Ban Treaty Orga-
  nization (CTBTO), 349
Concert of Europe, 170, 175
conciliation, dispute settlement, 266
Conference of the Committee on Disarmament
  (CCD), 335
Conference on Disarmament (CD), 335, 347
Conference on Environment and Development
  (Rio Summit, 1992), 81, 431, 434
Conference on Human Environment (1972),
  conference patterns, 81
Conference on International Organization,
  UN, (UNCIO), 26–27
Conference on Security and Cooperation in
  Europe (CSCE), 356, 357
conferences under UN auspices, 81–82, 441
  listed, 88–89, 442
conference support services, 162
conflict management, 318–19
Congo crises, 221–24
Congolese Rally for Democracy, 223

Connally Amendment, 279
consensual process, 9–10
  collective security, 172
  decision making, 44–45, 95–96, 100–101
  Korean War, 178
constitutional structure, 31–33
  Charter principles, 33–38
  See also UN Charter
Contact Group
  caucusing group, 102
  Kosovo conflict, 208
  nonalignment idea, 107
  Southern Africa conflict, 287
continental shelf, 281, 282, 438, 439, 440
Contra forces (Nicaragua), 237
controversy, resolution of, 148
Convention on Elimination of All Forms of
  Discrimination against Women, 409, 410,
  415
Convention for the Pacific Settlement of Dis-
  putes, 325
Convention on the Political Rights of Women,
  60–61
Convention on the Prohibition of the Develop-
  ment, Production, and Stockpiling of Bacteriological (Biological) and Toxin Weapons and on Their Destruction (1972),
  330, 355
Convention on the Prohibition of the Develop-
  ment, Production, Stockpiling, and Use of
  Chemical Weapons and Their Destruction
  (1997), 331, 356
Convention on the Prohibition of the Use,
  Stockpiling, Production, and Transfer of
  Anti-Personnel Mines and on Their Destruction (1997), 160, 331, 335, 357
Convention Relating to the Status of Refugees
  (1951), 457
cooperative tradition, 8
coordination, of social issues, 401
Côte d'Ivoire conflict, 219, 234–35
Cotonou Peace Agreement, 233
Council of Europe, 275, 417
Council of the International Maritime Organi-
  zation, 93
Council for South West Africa, 286
counterterrorism, 54, 162–64, 212
Court of Arbitration, Ethiopia-Eritrea, 251
credit tranche, 502
Crime Prevention, 161
crimes against humanity, 316
Croatia conflict, 242
CSCE. See Conference on Security and Coop-
  eration in Europe

CSR. *See* Communicable Disease Surveillance and Response
CTBTO. *See* Comprehensive Nuclear Test-Ban Treaty Organization
CTC. *See* UN Counter-Terrorism Committee
Cuba
  coercive measures proposal, 124
  U.S. embargo, 210, 211
Cuban missile crisis, 301–2, 353–54
cultural property return, 124
customary obedience, 126–27
Cyprus dispute, **216**, 224, 225–26

Dayton Accords, 207, 241, 309, 458
Decade of Human Rights Education (1995–2004), 418
decentralization, principle of, 401
  coordination issue, 464–65
decision making, 85
  consensual process, 9–10, 44–45, 95–96
  General Assembly, 53–55
  institutional setting, 90–108
  international organizations, 91–92
  member states, 74–75, 78–79
  national-level organizations, 85–90
  political instruments, 38–64
  private interest groups, 79–83
  procedural and substantive, 58
  Secretariat participation, 146–47
  Security Council, 58–59
  summarized, 38–39
Declaration by the United Nations (1942), 24
Declaration on the Denuclearization of Africa (1961), **331**, 339–40
Declaration on Fundamental Principles and Rights at Work (ILO), 422
Declaration on the Granting of Independence to Colonial Countries and Peoples (1960), 386–87, 388, 391
Declaration on the Human Environment (1972), 431
Declaration of Legal Principles Governing the Activities of States in the Exploration and Use of Outer Space, 350
Declaration of Philadelphia (1944), 422
Declaration regarding Non–Self Governing Territories, 383–84, 386
decolonization
  dispute settlement, 302, 320
  self-determination, 373
  significance, 390
  total, 383–90
  trusteeship stage, 379–83
  UN role, 374, 390–92

World War II effects, 378–79
defense budgets, national, 258
delegations, UN, 87, 89–90
demilitarization, 338–40
democracy, as political doctrine, 9–10
denuclearization, 339–40
Department of Disarmament Affairs, 160, 161, 329, 331–32
Department of Economic and Social Affairs, 162, **163**
Department of Peacekeeping Operations (DPKO), 214–15
developing countries. *See* less developed countries (LDCs)
development decades, 491–92
Development Dividend, 147
dictatorships, 392, 476
diplomacy, UN, 86–87, 89–90
  practice of, 148–49
  preventive, 214
  quiet, 148, 156
  Secretariat role, 148
disarmament
  approaches, 366–70
  confidence building, 351–53
  Department of Disarmament Affairs, 160, 161
  direct approach, 366–67
  end of the Cold War, 324, 367
  enforcement and sanctions, 365–66
  historical perspective, 325–32
  indirect approach, 367
  inspection systems, 365
  League of Nations, 21, 317, 325–27
  major international instruments (listed), **330–31**
  obstacles, 316–18, 357–66
  progress summarized, 338
  ratio problems, 363–65
  Russia, 351–52
  special conferences, 335–36
  terrorism, 369–70
  total, 368–69
  UN committees, 328–29
  UN department (DDA), 160, 161, 329, 331–32
  unilateral, 367–68
Disarmament Commission, 329, 334, 335, 336
disaster relief, 454
  Office of Emergency Relief Coordination, 161
displaced people, 458, 459
dispute settlement, 264–321
  bilateral disputes, 319
  case studies, 282, 284–300

dispute settlement (*continued*)
  Cold War, 300–307
  Cold War era, 318–19, **319**
  conclusions, 318–21
  disarmament, 316–18
  evaluated, 318–21
  humanitarian law, 314–16
  investment disputes center, 508
  among nonaligned, 320
  post–Cold War, 307–14
  procedures, 264–67
  regional settlement, 274–75
  Secretary-General, 148–49
  Third World, 320
  UN practice, 267–82
  unresolved disputes, 312–13
domestic jurisdiction, 33–35, 90–91
Dominican crisis, 227
DOMREP. *See* Mission of the Representative
  of the Secretary-General in the Dominican
  Republic
DPI. *See* UN Department of Public Information
DPKO. *See* Department of Peacekeeping
  Operations
drugs
  narcotic drugs treaties, 429
  Office of Drug Control, 161
Dumbarton Oaks Conference, 24–25
Dumbarton Oaks Proposals, 24–25, 26

Earth Summit, Agenda 21 blueprint, 54
Eastern Europe
  bloc solidarity, 110
  career service, 143
  end of the Cold War, 53
  human rights, 417–18
  overlapping with other UN groups, **105**
  regional groups, 102, **103**
  UN professional personnel, **142**
  voting coinciding with United States, **118**
East Timor conflict, 254–56, 312
  decolonization, 389–90
  *See also* Timor-Leste
ECAFE. *See* Economic Commission for Asia
  and the Far East
ECA. *See* Economic Commission for Africa
ECE. *See* Economic Commission for Europe
ECLAC. *See* Economic Commission for Latin
  America and the Caribbean
ECOMOG. *See* Economic Community of West
  African States Monitoring Group
Economic Commission for Africa (ECA),
  490–91

Economic Commission for Asia and the Far
  East (ECAFE), 490
Economic Commission for Europe (ECE), 490
Economic Commission for Latin America and
  the Caribbean (ECLAC), 490
Economic Community of West African States
  (ECOWAS), 233, 234
  dispute settlement, 275
  Sierra Leone, 247, 311
Economic Community of West African States
  Monitoring Group (ECOMOG), 233, 311
economic development, 470–509
  blueprint, 477–86
  conclusion, 509–12
  economic changes, 480–86
  ECOSOC, 59
  failed government role, 493–95
  financing programs, 503–9
  G-7 (with Russia, G-8), 512
  G-77, 106
  IMF role, 500–503
  NAM, 107
  problems of development, 470–77
  promoting, 486–88
  promoting international action, 486–88
  UN programs, 488–500
  World Bank Group, 503–9
economic liberalism, 9–10
Economic Projections and Programming Center, 499
economic regionalism, 37
economic rights, 406, 407
economic sanctions
  Gulf War (1990–91), 182, 184, 185
  Iraq, 160, 183, 184, 190–91
  League of Nations, 18, 174
  South Africa, 284
  weak-sanctions syndrome, 19
Economic and Social Commission for Asia
  and the Pacific (ESCAP), 490
Economic and Social Commission for Western
  Asia (ESCWA), 490, 491
Economic and Social Council (ECOSOC), 59
  commissions and agencies listed, **41**
  coordination responsibilities, 61, 464
  decision-making role, 60–61, 94
  economic development, 489
  enlargement, 32
  functions, 59–60
  human rights, 409
  membership, **43**, 93
  narcotics commission, 429–30
  NGOs, 80

origins, 400–401
ECOSOC. *See* Economic and Social Council
ECOWAS. *See* Economic Community of West African States
ECSWA. *See* Economic and Social Commission for Western Asia
education, technical skills, 482
educational development, 478
Egypt, Arab-Israeli conflict, 290
Egypt-Israel Peace Treaty (1979), 290
Eighteen-Nation Disarmament Committee (ENDC), 335, 345
elections
    Latin America, 236
    Third World, 476
El Salvador, 237, 306
emergency relief
    programs, 448, 452–55
    technical assistance, 448, 452–64
Emergency Special Sessions, 45, **47**
    on Palestine, 95
    political crises, 180–81
end of the Cold War
    arms race, 363
    budget issues, 68, 69, 127
    co-deployment principle, 21
    collective security, 181
    disarmament, 324, 367
    Eastern Europe, 53
    economic development, 495
    G-77, 106
    nuclear proliferation, 346–47
    peacekeeping, 230
    Security Council, 320, 516
ENDC. *See* Eighteen-Nation Disarmament Committee
enforcement actions
    arms control, 365–66
    U.S.-led war on Iraq, 200–202
environmental emergencies, 434–35
environmental issues
    economic development, 484
    environmental disasters, 484
    First World pollution, 484–85
    G-77, 106
    NGOs, 82
    regimes, 431–33
    Rio Summit, 485
    rules, 431
    sustainable development, 435–36
    UNEP links, 81
epidemic-prone and emerging infections, 430–31, 476

EPI. *See* Expanded Program on Immunization
EPTA. *See* Expanded Program of Technical Assistance
Equatorial Guinea, 301
Eritrea conflict, 250–51, 303
ESCAP. *See* Economic and Social Commission for Asia and the Pacific
Esquipulas II Agreement, 236–37
Ethiopia
    Eritrea conflict, 250–51
    League of Nations, 17–19
ethnic cleansing, Serbia, 206, 207, 208, 308–9
ethnic rivalry, 360–61
Europe, state system, 9–10
European Convention on Human Rights (1953), 417
European Union (EU)
    caucusing group, 102
    counterterrorism, 164
    euro adoption, 54
    international organizations, 84
    national loyalties, 399
    overlapping with other UN groups, **105**
    policy making, 146–47
    private lobbies, 81
Expanded Program on Immunization (EPI), 428
Expanded Program of Technical Assistance (EPTA), 496–97
export trade, 475–76

failed states, 495
FAO. *See* Food and Agriculture Organization
Federal Republic of Yugoslavia (FRY) conflict, 206–9
Final Act. *See* Helsinki Accord
finances, 65
    assessment problems, 65–67
    assessments related to voting strength, **68**
    budget procedures and politics, 69–71
    budget sizes, 127
    future problems, 71–72
    negative-growth, 162
    outstanding amounts, 128
    peacekeeping, 257–58, **259**
    potential income sources, 71
    Secretary-General role, 147
first-strike capability, 353
fishing, 437
FMLN. *See* Frente Farabundo Martí para la Liberación Nacional
Food and Agriculture Organization (FAO), 81, 437

foreign aid, 486–88
    capital transfers, 487
    grants or loans, 488
Four Policemen concept, 175
Fourteen Points, 14
France
    Algerian question, 383, 386
    Congo dispute, 224
    Greenpeace ship bombing, 301
    nuclear tests, 281, 301, 340, 348
    U.S. unilateralism, 191
    War on Iraq, 191, 199
French North Africa, 379
Frente Farabundo Martí para la Liberación
        Nacional (FMLN), 237
frustration gap, 470
FRY. See Federal Republic of Yugoslavia
functional commissions (listed), **41**
functional cooperation, organization of, 400–
        403
functionalists, 397
functionalist thought, 397–400
functional organizations, 397, 403–4

G-7 (with Russia, G-8)
    allies in War on Iraq, 198
    caucusing group, 102
    economic development, 512
    nonalignment idea, 107
    non-UN role, 516–17
GATT. See General Agreement on Tariffs and
        Trade
GEF. See Global Environmental Facility
GEMS. See Global Environmental Monitoring
        System
gender
    geographical distribution, **142**
    Office of the Focal Point for Women, 161
    Regional Commissions, 161–62
    Secretariat, 138, 139, **140**
    Special Adviser on Gender Issues, 161
    women in professional posts, **141**, 161–62
General Agreement on Tariffs and Trade
        (GATT), 61
General Assembly
    coalition structure, 123–25
    decision making, 53–55
    described, 39, **40**
    dispute settlement, 267–68, 272–73
    emergency sessions, **47**
    equality of members, 39, 42
    formal organization, 45, 47
    functions, 47, 51–53
    majority rule, 44–45

majority voting patterns, 123–24
membership, **43**, 52–53, 75
nonbinding recommendations, 94
parliamentary role, 42, 44
presidents (listed), **48–50**
procedures streamline proposal, 55
Reform Assembly, 160, 529
special sessions, **46**
voting, 94–96
general public, 152
Geneva Accords of 1988, 231, 304
Geneva Protocol of 1925, 355
genocide
    defined, 316
    humanitarian law, 313
    human rights conventions, 409, **411**
Genocide Convention, 51
Georgia conflict, **217**, 245–46, 309
Germany
    arms race, 325–27
    partition, 75
    UN role, 516
    See also Nazi Germany
Gibraltar, 388–89
Global Environmental Facility (GEF), 436,
        485
Global Environmental Monitoring System
        (GEMS), 432
Global Outbreak Alert and Response Net-
        work, 430
global warming, 83, 433
Goa conflict, 387
good offices, dispute settlement, 265–66
Great Britain
    parliamentary system comapred, 42
    war on Iraq, 195
great powers
    early security issues, 15
    Yalta Conference, 25–26
Greece, peacekeeping operations, 215, **216**
Greek city-states, 8
Greenpeace ship bombing, 301
Group of 77 (G-77)
    caucusing group, 102
    majority rule, 4
    origins, 104
    overlapping with other UN groups, **105**
    UN groups, 103–4, 106
groups, UN, 102–8
Guatemala conflict, **218**, 250
Gulf Cooperation Council, 305
Gulf War (first), 181–87
    Arab-Israeli conflict, 290–91
    domestic jurisdiction, 35

observer missions, 237–38
second Gulf War compared, 196, 197
Security Council, 5, 56
significance, 187–88
UN sanctions, 83

Hague Peace Conferences (1899 and 1907), 13, 170, 325
Haiti, elections observed, **217**, 236
Haiti conflict, 248–50, 306–7
Hamas, 295, 296
social services, 463–64
Hanseatic League, 8
health, international regulation, 427–31
Helms-Burton Act (U.S., 1996), 211
Helsinki Accord (1975), 356–57
Hesbollah, 229
HIV/AIDS. See AIDS
Hizb-ut Tahrir order, 235
Holy See, 75
horizontal federalism, 36
HRFOR. See UN Human Rights Force for Rwanda
humanitarian law, 313–16
human rights
covenants, 409, **410–11**
ECOSOC, 59, 60
enforcement actions, 201
goals and standards summarized, 415–16
Guatemala, 250
implementing, 412–15
labor standards, 422–24
law-making treaties, 409–12
major treaties, 415–16
NATO and Kosovo, 419–22
nature of, 406
new mandate, 160–61
NGOs, 83
regional institutions, 416–17
Resolution 1503 procedure, 414
rule-making, 404–7
U.S. policy trends, 412
Versailles Treaty, 404
voluntary norms, 407–9
See also Commission on Human Rights; Universal Declaration of Human Rights
Human Rights Commission. See Commission on Human Rights
Human Rights Committee, 414–15
hydrogen bombs, 333

IACHR. See Inter-American Commission on Human Rights

IAEA. See International Atomic Energy Agency
IBRD. See International Bank for Reconstruction and Development (IBRD); World Bank
ICAO. See International Civil Aviation Organization
Icelandic fishing limits, 281
ICJ. See International Court of Justice
ICSID. See International Center for Settlement of Investment Disputes
ICTR. See International Criminal Tribunal for Rwanda
ICTY. See International Criminal Tribunal for the Former Yugoslavia
IDA. See International Development Association
ideological hostility, Cold War, 360
IFAD. See International Fund for Agricultural Development
IFC. See International Finance Corporation
IFC. See International Finance Corporation (IFC)
IGOs. See international governmental organizations
illiteracy rates, 475
ILO. See International Labor Organization
IMF. See International Monetary Fund
independence. See decolonization
India
dispute settlement, 296–300
Goa conflict, 387
independence, 378
Kashmir conflict, 297–300
nuclear language, 354
nuclear tests, 270, 298, 341, 344, 349
Rann of Kutch arbitration, 267
UN India-Pakistan Observation Mission (UNIPOM), **216**, 226–27
UN Military Observer Group in India and Pakistan (UNMOGIP), **216**, 219–20
indigenous peoples, human rights, 419
individualism, 9–10
Indonesia
East Timor, 254–56
independence, 302
peacekeeping operations, 215, **216**
West Irian dispute, **216**, 224–25
Indo-Pakistan wars, 219–20
industrial development, 492–93
Industrial Development Center, 499
industrialization, 483–84
information
flows, 101–2

information (*continued*)
  power of secretariats, 157–58
  promotional activities, 440–41, **442–43**
  secretariats, international, 157–58
informational activities, 403
INFOTERRA, 432
inquiry (enquiry), dispute settlement, 266
integrity, 144
Inter-African Mission to Monitor the Bangui
  Agreements (MISAB), 234
Inter-American Commission on Human Rights
  (IACHR), 416–17
Inter-American Conference on Problems of
  Peace and War (Mexico City, 1945), 26
Inter-American Court of Human Rights, 416
Inter-American Judicial Committee, 416–17
Inter-American Treaty of Reciprocal Assis-
  tance (Rio Pact), 172, 212
INTERFET. *See* International Force in East
  Timor
Intergovernmental Oceanographic Commis-
  sion, 437
International Atomic Energy Agency (IAEA)
  Iran, 521
  Iraq monitoring, 124, 190, 194, 197, 342
  Libya inspections, 206
  North Korea, 179, 352
  safeguards, 346
  UN structure, 61
International Bank, 92
International Bank for Reconstruction and De-
  velopment (IBRD). *See* World Bank
International Center for Settlement of Invest-
  ment Disputes (ICSID), 508
International Civil Aviation Organization
  Council, 93
International Civil Aviation Organization
  (ICAO), 427
International Civil Service Advisory Board, 465
International Committee of the Red Cross, 84
International Conferences for Assistance to
  Refugees in Africa (ICARA I and II), 457
International Convention on the Suppression
  and Punishment of the Crime of Apart-
  heid (1973), 284
International Court of Justice (ICJ), 63–64
  advisory opinions, 276–77
  current (2003) docket, **283**
  decisions, 63–64, 94
  dispute settlement, 275–82
  election of judges, 57, 63
  judicial settlement, 267, 275–82
  jurisdiction, 277–79
  Lockerbie bombing, 205–6

  membership, **44**
  optional clause, 278–79
International Covenant on Civil and Political
  Rights, 409, **410**, 411, 414, 415
International Covenant on Economic, Social,
  and Cultural Rights, 409, **410**, 411–12,
  415
International Criminal Court
  Bush rejection, 123
  conference on establishment, 82
  human rights, 405–6
  mandate, 316
  Milošević trial, 98, 209
  origins, 314–16
  Preparatory Committee, 315–16
  Rome Statute, 315
  UN initiative, 527
  U.S. challenge, 98
  U.S. immunity agreements, 406
International Criminal Tribunal for the For-
  mer Yugoslavia (ICTY), 313–14
International Criminal Tribunal for Rwanda
  (ICTR), 313, 314
International Decade of the World's Indige-
  nous People (1995–2004), 419
International Development Association, 91
International Development Association (IDA),
  507–8
International Finance Corporation (IFC), 92,
  505–7
International Force in East Timor (INTERFET),
  255
International Frequency Registration Board,
  426
International Fund for Agricultural Development (IFAD), 481
international governmental organizations
  (IGOs), 79
  private group contacts, 81
international institutions
  emergence, 11–13
  patterns for early, 12
International Labor Code, 423
International Labor Organization (ILO)
  civil service, 136
  labor standards, 422
  maritime labor, 437
  membership, 93
  origins, 14
  private representation in, 79–80
  structure, 422–23
international law
  hard law, 432–33
  soft law, 433

UN challenged, 526
International Law Commission, 315
    codification, 51
International Maritime Organization (1948),
    437
International Monetary Fund (IMF), 500–
    502
    conditionality, 502
    currency pool, 502
    linkages, 138
    purposes, 501
    voting, 92
    World Bank Group, 503
International Office of Public Health (1907),
    428
international organizations
    functionalist thought, 398
    history, 8–9
    as participants, 84–85
    process, 10–11
    state system, 9–10
International Police Task Force, 241
international quasi-nongovernmental organi-
    zations (IQUANGOs), 79
International Refugee Organization (IRO),
    452, 456
International Register of Potentially Toxic
    Chemicals, 432
International Seabed Authority, 439
International Securities Group (ISG), 506
International Security Assistance Force (ISAF),
    Afghanistan, 193, 252–54
International Telecommunication Union (ITU),
    71, 425–27
International Telegraphic Union (1865), 11
International Tribunal for the Law of the Sea,
    439
International Tribunals, budget issues, 70
International Whaling Commission, 437
International Year of Indigenous People
    (1993), 419
International Youth Year (1985), 482
Interpol, 164
interstate relations, 36
intifada, 293, 296
INVO. See Iraq Nuclear Verification Office
IQUANGOs. See international quasi-
    nongovernmental organizations
Iran
    Bahrain conflict, 301
    claims tribunal, 267
    coerced disarmament, 343–44
    hostage crisis, 278
Iran-Iraq war, 231–32, 303, 304–5

Iraq
    coerced disarmament, 342
    Gulf War (1990–91), 181–87
    interim governing powers to U.S., 199
    invasion of Kuwait, 204
    Kuwait conflict, 237–38
    nonmilitary sanctions, 204–5, 210, 211, 520
    nuclear weapons, 341–42
    occupation, 197
    See also War on Iraq
Iraq Nuclear Verification Office (INVO), 190
IRO. See International Refugee Organization
ISAF. See International Security Assistance
    Force
ISG. See International Securities Group
Islamic Conference
    caucusing group, 102
    counterterrorism, 164
    Iran-Iraq, 305
    overlapping with other UN groups, 105
Islamic Jihad, 295
Israeli Civil Administration, 463
Israeli-Palestinian conflict
    decision making, 95
    Operation Defensive Shield, 294
    Operation Determined Path, 294
    Palestine, 288–96
    postwar, 379
    refugees, 462–63
    Road Map to Peace, 295
    self-determination, 385
    transformation, 292
ITU. See International Telecommunication
    Union
Ivory Coast conflict, 219, 234–35

Japan
    decolonization, 378
    UN role, 516
Joint Declaration on the Denuclearization of
    the Korean Peninsula, 179
Joint Declaration on the New Strategic Rela-
    tionship (2002), 338
Joint UN Program on HIV/AIDS (UNAIDS),
    429
Jordan, 379
judicial dispute settlement, 267, 275–82

Kashmir conflict, 219–20, 297–300
Kassebaum Amendment (U.S. Congress), 69
Kellogg-Briand Pact (1928), 16, 17, 20, 21
KFOR. See NATO Kosovo Force
Khmer Rouge, 303, 307
KLA. See Kosovo Liberation Army

Korea
    partition, 75
    relief and reconstruction, 452
Korean War
    Cold War, 180–81
    collective action, 176–78
    Security Council, 3
    Uniting for Peace Resolution (1950), 51,
        180–81
    UN membership, 75
Kosovo conflict
    bypassing the veto, 97–98
    China veto, 97
    domestic jurisdiction, 34
    human rights, 417, 419–22
    joint NATO deployment, 251–52
    NATO occupation, 309
    NATO supervision, 207–9, 213
    refugees, 458
    self-determination, 392–93, 394
    UNPREDEP mission, 241
Kosovo Liberation Army (KLA), 97–98, 207–
        8, 392–93, 420–21
Kuwait
    Gulf War (1990–91), 181–87
    Iraq invasion, 204, 237–38
Kyoto treaty on global warming, 82
    Bush rejection, 123, 433
    described, 485–86

labor, youth employment, 482
labor standards, 422–24
LAC. See Latin American and Caribbean group
laissez-faire, 9–10
landmine bans, 123, 127, 160
    conventions, 331, 357
languages
    Secretariat, 134
    working and official, 134
Latin America
    elections, 236
    nuclear-weapons-free zone, 339
    UN professional personnel, 142
Latin American and Caribbean group (LAC)
    economic commission, 490
    as group (listed), 104, 104
    overlapping with other UN groups, 105
    voting coinciding with U.S. votes, 115–16
law, authority of, 126
Law of the Sea, 436–37
    adoption, 51
    court, 439
    early treaty drafting, 437–38

G-77, 106
    potential income, 71
    regimes, 432, 433
Law of the Sea Convention (1994), 439–40
LDCs. See less developed countries
League of Arab States
    caucusing group, 102
    counterterrorism, 164
League of Nations
    actions, 16
    appraisal, 19
    autopsy, 21–23
    capsule history, 20–21
    civil service, 136
    colonialism, 391
    Covenant, 14, 15, 17–18, 20, 21, 26, 404
    demise, 20–21
    disarmament, 317, 325–27
    Ethopian case, 17–19
    failure, 172
    funding compared, 65
    innovations, 15–16
    Manchurian case, 16–17
    mandates system, 374–77
    organizational patterns, 400
    origins, 13–14
    refugees, 455–56
    Secretary-General, 158
    security functions, 16–19
    security system, 173–74
    significance, 317
    structure and functions, 14–15
    United States, 2, 16
League of Nations Covenant
    collective security, 171
    security system, 173–74
    staffing questions, 136
learning theories, 398
least developed countries, 472, 513n
Lebanon conflict, 228–30
less developed countries (LDCs), 470–71
    profile, 471–77
    Third World, 471
    See also Third World
Liberian conflict, 219, 234, 310
Liberians United for Reconciliation and De-
        mocracy, 233, 310
Libya
    independence, 303
    sanctions against, 205–6, 280
Likud Party, 294
Limited Test-Ban Treaty (1963), 347–49,
        362

Linas-Marcoussis Agreement, 234–35
literacy rates, 475
lobbying, 108
    pressure tactics, 109–10
Lukasa Protocol (1994), 232
Lytton Commission, 17

Macedonia conflict, 241
malaria control, 428
Manchuria, League of Nations, 16–17
mandate system, 374–77
mandatory sanctions, 203
mediation, dispute settlement, 266
membership
    geographic regions, 78, **79**
    growth, 1945-2003, 76–77
    higher standards, 529
    mini-state problem, 78
    partitioned states, 75
    vetoes, 99
member states
    decision making, 74–75, 78–79
    permanent representaives, 86–87, 89
merit principle, 139
MFO. See Multinational Force and Observers
Middle East
    economic development, 491
    independence, 378–79
    UN professional personnel, **142**
MIGA. See Multilateral Investment Guarantee
    Agency
migrant workers, human rights, **411**, 415
military alliances, 158, 170
    collective security, 171
    War on Iraq, 213
military-industrial complex, 359
military sanctions, 174–75
    demise of mandatory, 175–76
    Korean War, 177
military technology, 530
    research, 362–63
Millenium Report (2000), 135, 511
Millenium Summit (2000), 401–3, 511
MINUGUA. See UN Verification Mission in
    Guatemala
MINURSO peacekeeping force to Western Sa-
    hara, **217**, 236, 389
MIOPNUH. See UN Civilian Police Mission in
    Haiti
MISAB. See Inter-African Mission to Monitor
    the Bangui Agreements
Mission Planning Service, 215
Mission of the Representative of the Secretary-

General in the Dominican Repubic
    (DOMREP), **216**, 227, 250
missions, UN, 86–87, 89–90
MNCs. See multinational corporations
Montreal Convention for the Suppression of
    Unlawful Acts against the Safety of Civil
    Aviation (1971), 205, 280
MONUA. See UN Observer Mission in
    Angola
MONUC. See UN Organization Mission in
    the Democratic Republic of the Congo
moral condemnation, 202
Moscow Declaration on General Security
    (1943), 24
Moscow Treaty, 337–38
Mozambique conflict, **217**, 245
Multilateral Investment Guarantee Agency
    (MIGA), 508
multinational corporations (MNCs), 79
Multinational Force and Observers (MFO),
    227–28
Multinational Forces (MNFs), in Lebanon,
    228–29

Nairobi Declaration (1997), 436
Namibia
    conflict resolution, 286–88
    independence, 238, 285
    sanctions against South Africa, 203–4
NAM. See Non-Aligned Movement
Nansen Passport, 455
narcotic drugs treaties, 429
nationalism
    disarmament, 358–59
    early European, 9
    World War II, 23
nation-states
    behavior, 1
    early, 8
    European emergence, 9–10
NATO Kosovo Force (KFOR), 208, 252,
    421–22
NATO (North Atlantic Treaty Organization)
    Afghanistan, 254
    Bosnia, 207, 240
    cases against, 282
    collective security, 172
    counterterrorism, 164
    dispute settlement, 275
    end of Cold War, 213
    enlargement, 4, 172, 213, 337, 417
    extraction force, 97
    Kosovo conflict, 213

NATO (North Atlantic Treaty Organization) (*continued*)
Kosovo human rights, 420–22
Kosovo self-determination, 393
Operation Joint Guardian, 251–52
U.S. promotion, 110, 119
natural disasters, 434–35
navigation rights, 437
Nazi Germany
Holocaust, 288–89
League of Nations, 17, 19
*See also* Germany
negotiation, dispute settlement, 265
neocolonialism, 391
neoconservatives, 122
Netherlands, 302
New International Development Strategy, 492
new international economic order (NIEO), 399, 476
new world order, 525
NGOs. *See* nongovernmental organizations
Nicaragua
conflict, 236–37
Contras, 305–6
elections observed, **217**, 236
NIEO. *See* new international economic order
Non-Aligned Movement (NAM)
Boutros-Ghali appointment, 150
caucusing group, 104
goals, 106–7
Iran-Iraq War, 305
new international economic order, 476
overlapping with other UN groups, **105**
noncooperation with programs, as threat, 109
nongovernmental organizations (NGOs)
as actors, 79
government failures, 495
humanitarian affairs, 160
human rights, 414
role and functions, 82
UN collaboration, 152
nonmilitary sanctions, 174–75, 202
case studies, 202–10
policy improvements, 211–12
summary, 210–12
Non–Self-Governing Territories, 254, 383–84, 386
Nordic group
caucusing group, 102
overlapping with other UN groups, **105**
ᵀorth America and Caribbean, UN professional personnel, **142**
ᵗhern Alliance, 210

North Korea
coerced disarmament, 342–43
nuclear threat, 178–80, 352–53
North Sea continental shelf cases (1967–69), 281–82
North-South dialogue/divide, 104, 472
nuclear arms race, beginning, 332–34
nuclear blackmail, 346
nuclear-free zones, 339, 340
Nuclear Nonproliferation Treaty (1970)
conference (1995), 329
former Soviet states, 336–37
India-Pakistani conflict, 270, 297, 341
North Korea, 178–79
participation, 361
test ban, 329
*See also* Treaty on the Nonproliferation of Nuclear Weapons (1968)
nuclear proliferation, 340–44
arms race, 344–45
availability of weapons, 344
coerced disarmament, 342–44
efforts to halt, 345–47
end of the Cold War, 346–47
threat, 344–45
Nuclear Test Ban Treaty Organization, Preparation Committee, 61
nuclear tests
China, 348
eliminating, 347–49
France, 281, 301, 340, 348
India, 270, 298, 341, 344, 349
Pakistan, 270, 298, 341, 344
nuclear warheads, 351–53
nuclear weapons
avoiding accidental war, 353–55
Iraq, 189, 341–42
North Korea, 178–80, 341
nuclear club, 340–41
Nuclear Weapons–Free Zone Treaty, 274
Nuclear Weapons Nonproliferation Treaty (1995), **331**, 349
Nuremberg principle, 314
*Nutrition Report* (1937), 146

OAS. *See* Organization of American States
OAU. *See* Organization of African Unity
observer missions
after UNEF, 226–27
UNEF, **216**, 220–21
OCHA. *See* UN Office for the Coordination of Humanitarian Affairs (OCHA)
OECD. *See* Organization for Economic Cooperation and Development

Office of Development Financing, 147
Office of Drug Control, 161
Office of Emergency Operations in Africa, 454
Office of Emergency Relief Coordination, 161
Office of the Special Representative for Children in Armed Conflict, 161
oil-for-food program
  INVO funds, 190, 191
  occupation, 199
  sanctions approach, 205
  UNMOVIC funds, 194
OIOS. See UN Office of Internal Oversight Services
OMV (Ongoing Monitoring and Verification) inspections, 190
ONUCA. See UN Observer Group in Central America
ONUC. See UN Operation in the Congo
ONUMOZ. See UN Operation in Mozambique
ONUSAL. See UN Observer Mission in El Salvador
ONUVEN. See UN Observer Group for Verification of Elections in Nicaragua
OPANAL (Agency for the Prohibition of Nuclear Weapons in Latin America), 339
OPEC. See Organization of Petroleum Exporting Countries
operating programs, 403
Operational, Executive, and Administrative Personnel Service (OPEX), 499
Operation Desert Fox, 186
OPEX. See Operational, Executive, and Administrative Personnel Service
Optional Clause of the Statute, 63
Organization of African Unity (OAU)
  African Union, 274
  caucusing group, 102
  collective security, 172
  denuclearization, 339
  dispute settlement, 274, 275
  human rights, 160
  Liberia, 233, 310–11
  Sierra Leone, 247
Organization of American States (OAS)
  caucusing group, 102
  counterterrorism, 164
  dispute settlement, 274, 275
  Haiti, 250
  human rights, 416–17
  sanctions against Cuba, 211
Organization for Economic Cooperation and Development (OECD)
  caucusing group, 102
  regionalism concept, 37

Organization of the Islamic Conference, 305
Organization of Petroleum Exporting Countries (OPEC), 487
Organization for the Prohibition of Chemical Weapons, 61
Organization for Security and Cooperation in Europe (OSCE)
  caucusing group, 102
  CIS cooperation, 172
  elections in Bosnia, 207
  Kosovo, 97
  origins, 357
  Tajikistan, 235
OSCE. See Organization for Security and Cooperation in Europe
Oslo Accords, 291
Our Common Future (1987), 146
Outer Space Treaty, 330, 350–51
outer space, weapons in, 350–51

Pacific Islands trusteeship, 380, 381, 382
Pact of Paris (1928), 174
Pakistan
  dispute settlement, 296–300
  independence, 378
  Kashmir conflict, 297–300
  nuclear language, 354
  nuclear tests, 270, 298, 341, 344
  prisoners of war, 281
  Rann of Kutch arbitration, 267
  UN India-Pakistan Observation Mission (UNIPOM), 216, 226–27
  UN Military Observer Group in India and Pakistan (UNMOGIP), 216, 219–20
Palau, 382
Palestine
  Barak proposal, 293
  creation, 288
  partition, 289
  refugee issue, 293, 460–64, 461
  self-determination, 385
Palestine Authority
  membership, 75
  Palestine independence, 292
  UN aid, 462, 463
  UN status, 80–81
  U.S. veto, 98
Palestine Liberation Organization (PLO)
  first Gulf War, 291
  observer status, 80
  UN forces in Lebanon, 228–30
Palestinian National Covenant, 292
Pan American–Lockerbie bombing, 205–6, 280

parliamentary diplomacy, 89
parliamentary system, 42, 44
Partnership for Peace (PFP), 107, 213
*Pax Americana,* 2
PCIJ. *See* Permanent Court of International
    Justice
Peaceful Uses of Outer Space, 350
peacekeeping
    budget issues, 67, 69, 70, 128
    collective security, 213–15
    defined, 262n
    Department of Peacekeeping Operations
        (DPKO), 214–15
    early UN experiments, 215, 219–20
    enforcement, 260
    first preventive, 97
    future, 260
    Mission Planning Service, 215
    new mandate, 160
    peaceful dispute resolution, 37
    principal missions, 1947–2003, **216–19**
    retrospect and prospect, 256–61
    role, 214
    Secretary-General role, 148
    Security Council, 39
    Standby High Readiness Brigade, 214–15
    successes and failures, 230–56
    summarized, 257–58, **259**
    trends of 1990s, 4
    U.S. antipathy, 121–22
    U.S. budget share, 67, 70, 128
    women on staff, 162
    *See also* UN Special Commission (UNSCOM)
peace-loving
    identity, 74–75
    Yalta definition, 25
Peace Observation Commission, 180
Pearl Harbor, 22
People's Millenium Assembly, 153
People's Republic of Kampuchea (PRK), 307
Permanent Court of International Justice
    (PCIJ)
    case load, 276
    origins, 14
    replacing, 25
    successor, 63–64
Permanent Mandates Commission, 377, 381
personnel recruitment
    geographic distribution, 139, 141–42, **142**
    Secretariat, UN, 138–44
    status of women, **141**
hilippines, 378
 ʌsical coercion, 126
    ʌ. *See* Palestine Liberation Organization

Point Four Program (1949), 486, 496
Poland, 26
Policy Working Group on the United Nations
    and Terrorism, 164, 370
Polisario Front, 236
political evolution, 478
political instability, 476
population
    Europe trends, **480**
    UN Fund for Population Activities, 127,
        473
    UN Population Commission, 499
population control, 478–80
population growth, 472–74
    conferences, 473
    forecasts, **473**, 473
Portugal, 385
    colonies, 388
    East Timor, 254–56
postal service, 425
poverty, 401
    goals, 402
    least developed countries, 472
    widening gap, 528
power
    apportioning vs. neutralizing, 529
    collective security, 172
preemption doctrine, 191–200
    criticisms, 518
    nuclear weapons, 354–55
    rift over, 519, 520–21
    war on Iraq, 7, 101, 191–200
preemptive nuclear strikes, 344
Preparatory Commission, 27
Preparatory Committee, International Crimi-
    nal Court, 315–16
President of UN, 45, 47
    listed, **48–50**
preventive deployment, 459
preventive diplomacy, 214
primary commodities, 481
private interest groups, 79–83
    Secretariat links, 152
privatization, 495
PRK. *See* People's Republic of Kampuchea
procurement services, 162
professional societies, UN-sponsored, 445
professional staff, 139
    gender distribution, 139, **140, 141**
programs and funds (listed), **40**
promotional activities, 403, 440–41, **442–43**
propaganda barrier, 361–62
psychological warfare, 361–62
public debate, dispute settlement, 268

public relations, 152
Puerto Rico, 390

quiet diplomacy, 148, 156

racial discrimination, 409, **410**, 415
radio jamming, 426–27
Rapidly Deployable Mission Headquarters, 393
Rapid Reaction Force, 240
ratification of UN Charter, 27–28
Red Cross, 84
reforms
    program outlined, **163**
    Reform Assembly, 160, 529
    Secretariat, UN, 138
refugees, 455–64
    Africa, 457, 458–59
    by country, 459
    conferences, 457
    convention, 457
    human rights, 409, **411**
    International Refugee Organization, 452
    numbers, 457
    Palestine, 293
    technical assistance, 448, 452–64
    *See also* UN High Commissioner for
        Refugees (UNHCR)
regimes, defined, 431–32
Regional Commissions, gender balance,
    161–62
regional groups, 102, **103–4**
    overlapping with other UN groups, **105**
regional organizations
    arguments for, 37
    collective security, 212–13
    consultative status, 84
    dispute settlement, 274–75
    economic development, 490–91
    enforcing order, 36–37
    human rights, 416–18
    interstate cooperation, 36–38
    listed, **41**
    peacekeeping, 260
    technical agencies listed, **450–51**
    voting alignments, 102–8
regions, UN membership, 78, **79**
religious dimension to terrorism, 524, 528
research
    ECOSOC, 59–60
    military technology, 362–63
    Secretariat, 134, 146
    UN institute on disarmament, 329
research and training institutes (listed), **40**

resolutions, adoption of, 108–23
    consequences, 125–29
    as legitimizing force, 129
    Security Council, 121
    Soviet (now Russian) record, 110
    U.S. positions, 124–25
    U.S. views, 110, 124–25
revenue production, 71
Revolutionary United Front (RUF), 247, 248
revolution of rising expectations, 483
    frustration gap, 470
Revolving Credit Fund, 147
Rhodesia, sanctions against, 202–3, 211, 388
Rio Pact. *See* Inter-American Treaty of Recip-
    rocal Assistance
Rio Summit. *See* Conference on Environment
    and Development (Rio Summit, 1992)
river commissions, 11, 92
Rome Statute of the International Criminial
    Court, 315
roster organizations, 80
RUF. *See* Revolutionary United Front
rule-making, 403
    human rights, 404–7
Rush-Bagot Agreement (1817), 325
Russian Federation
    attitude to UN, 4
    current status, 516
    human rights, 417
    Kosovo conflict, 98
    UN interest, 230–31
    *See also* Chechnya conflict; Soviet Union,
        former
Rwanda
    assistance, **218**, 246
    conflict, **217**, 245, 246
    humanitarian law, 313, 314

SALT I. *See* Strategic Arms Limitation Talks
Salvadoran conflict, 237, 306
sanctions
    arms control, 365–66
    collective, 211
    mandatory, 203
    nonmilitary, 211–12
    physical force, 126
    *See also* Iraq, nonmilitary sanctions
SARS (severe acute respiratory syndrome),
    430
Saudi Arabia, wars on Iraq, 191
SDI. *See* Strategic Defense Initiative
SEATO (Southeast Asia Treaty Organization,
    1954), 212
Second World, 471

secretariats, international, 156
  administrative organization, 157
  importance, 133–34
  information, 157–58
  legal powers, 156–57
  neutrality, 158
  operating programs, 403
  organizational task, 159
  personal qualities, 158–59
  political environment, 159
  political leverage, 83–84
Secretariat, UN, 64
  budgeting, 134–35
  budget process, 67–68
  decision making, 146–47
  diversity issues, 137–38
  languages, 134
  linkages, 137–38
  offices listed, **41**
  personnel recruitment, 138–44
  political role, 145–59
  private group links, 152
  reforms, 138, 529
  research, 134
  staff recruitment, 134
  structure, 64
  tasks, 134
  workforce, 136–37, 138
Secretary-General, of agencies, administrative
    control, 157
Secretary-General for Management, 70
Secretary-General, UN
  backgrounds, **151**
  broad mandates, 146
  decision making, 147
  Deputy, 161
  dispute settlement, 148–49, 273
  expert opinion, 153
  future role, 510
  Pérez de Cuéllar's role, 133
  as political actor, 135
  political initiatives, 153–56
  political leadership, 149–56
  responsibilities, 64
  Security Council, 57
Security Council, 55–56
  composition, 56–57
  dispute settlement, 267–68, 269–72
  divisions within, 57
  enlargement, 32
  functions, 57
  Korean War, 3
  membership, **43**, 56–57

operations authorized, 120–21
peacekeeping, 258, 260
permanent representatives, 86–87
procedures, 58–59
reforms, 518–19
sanctions policy, 174–75
Secretary-General appointment, 149–50
top administrators, 142
U.S. voting dynamics, 120
veto power, 32, 96–101, **97**, 100
voting, 93, 96–97
voting dynamics, 108–23
security issues
  catch-22, 366
  disarmament, 358
  great powers, 15
  League of Nations, 15
  post–Cold War, 4
self-determination, 373–94
  civil wars, 474
  concept, 373
  future trends, 392–94
  manifesto, 386–87
  political crisis, 385–86
  terrorism, 394
September, 11, 2001 events
  Al-Qaeda, 192–93
  Bush response, 5, 6
  Counter-Terrorism Committee, 54
  described, 5, 123
  impact, 193
  Pakistani terrorists, 299
  UN approval, 123
  UN weakness, 517
  U.S. concerns, 156
Serbia
  dispute settlement, 308–9
  sanctions against, 206–9
  UN troops, 240
SHIRBRIG. *See* Standby High Readiness
    Brigade
Sierra Leone conflict, 246–48, 311–12
Six-Day War, 290
Six Nations Talks (2004), 180
slavery, human rights, 409, **410–11**
SNPA. *See* Substantial New Program of
    Action
social overhead, 481–82
Solomon Islands conflict, 260–61
Somalia conflict, **217**, 243–45, 311
  enforcement actions, 201
  U.S. critics, 230
Somaliland, 303

South Africa
  Angola and Cuba, 232
  colonialism, 375
  conflicts over apartheid, 282, 284–86
  human rights, 408
  Namibian independence, 238
  Namibia rule, 286
  nonmilitary sanctions against, 203–4, 211
  *See also* apartheid
Southeast Asia Treaty Organization (SEATO, 1954), 212
South Korea. *See* Korea; Korean War
South West African People's Organization (SWAPO)
  Angola, 232
  Namibia independence, 238
  observer status, 80, 81
  origins, 287
sovereign states
  defense budgets, 258
  disarmament, 358–59
  Dumbarton Oaks Proposals, 26
  early UN commitment, 24
  economic development, 493–95
  equality, 33, 92, 94
  Hague system, 13
  League of Nations, 15
  limits, 1
  terrorism, 517–18
  voting, 91–92
  World Court, 63
Soviet Nuclear Threat Reduction Act (1991), 346–47
Soviet Union, former
  Afghanistan, 191–92
  atomic weapons, 333
  budgetary questions, 66
  Cold War, 3
  collective security, 173
  Cuban missile crisis, 301–2
  decolonization, 380
  foreign aid, 488
  League of Nations, 20
  NAM, 107
  post-Soviet proliferation, 346–47
  Second World, 471
  shift in UN policy, 79
  U.S. grain sanctions, 210
  vetoes, 99, 100
  voting agreement with majority, **119, 120**
  *See also* Russian Federation
space cooperation, 350
Spain, 385

Special Commission on the Situation with Regard to the Implementation of the Declaration on the Granting of Independence to Colonial Countries and Peoples (1961), 388
Special Committee against Apartheid, 284
Special Fund, UN Development Program, 497–98
specialized agencies, 38
  budgets, 67
  ECOSOC coordination, 61
  listed, **41**
  NGO collaboration, 152
special programs, administration organization, 159
Special Sessions, 45, **46**
  budget issues, 69–70
  General Assembly listed, **88–89**
Standby High Readiness Brigade (SHIRBRIG), 214–15
START I, II. *See* Strategic Arms Reduction Talks
Star Wars. *See* Strategic Defense Initiative
state behavior, 1
State Department (U.S.), Bureau of International Affairs (IO), 85–86
stateless persons, human rights, 409, **411**
state system, Europe, 9–10
Statistical Office of the United Nations, 447
Stimson Doctrine, 17
Strategic Arms Limitation Talks (SALT II), 336
Strategic Arms Limitation Talks (SALT), 336
Strategic Arms Reduction Talks (START I), 336
Strategic Arms Reduction Talks (START II), 337–38
  inspection provisions, 364
Strategic Arms Reduction Talks (START III), 365
Strategic Defense Initiative (SDI, or "Star Wars"), 351
Strategic Offensive Reductions Treaty (SORT), 337–38, 347
structural adjustment policies, 494
Substantial New Program of Action (SNPA), 492
Sudan, 453
Suez crisis, **216**, 220–21
suicide bombings, 99
sustainable development, 402–3
  environmental issues, 435–36
  government role, 494
  Rio Summit, 485

SWAPO. *See* South West African People's
    Organization
Switzerland, membership, 63, 75

Taiwan, one China issue, 75, 78
Tajikistan conflict, 235, 309
Taliban
    Al-Qaeda link, 192
    origins, 231
    sanctions regime, 209–10
    Tajikistan, 235
Tashkent Agreement (1966), 226–27, 297
technical assistance, 495–96
    Expanded Program of Technical Assistance,
        496–97
    functional analysis, 399
    future, 500
    organizations listed, **449–50**
    other programs, 499–500
    refugees and relief, 448, 452–64
    UN Development Program, 496
technical skills, 482
telecommunications, 425–27
Ten-Nation Commission on Disarmament,
        334
terrorism
    after September 11, 5–6
    attack on UN, 526–27
    collective action, 177
    collective security, 201–2, 519–21
    Counter-Terrorism Committee, 54,
        162–64
    dilemma of defining, 522–24
    disarming, 369–70
    dispute settlement, 320
    globalization of, 525
    Israel, 294
    nonstate, 530
    nuclear threat, 345
    Pakistan, 299
    peacekeeping, 257
    religious dimension, 524
    rethinking UN role, 518–21
    Rome Treaty, 316
    self-determination, 394
    sovereign states, 517–18
    state sponsors, 370, 528–29
    UN working group, 370
    U.S. armaments industries, 483
    U.S. war on, 517–18
     st-ban talks/treaties, 334, 347
    ailand, border disputes, 300
    d World
        mical weapons, 355

coalitions, 124
defining terrorism, 522
disarmament, 328, 334–35
disputes among nonaligned, 320
dispute settlement, 320
elections, 476
environmental disasters, 484
less developed countries (LDCs), 471
majority voting, 95
new international economic order, 399
numerical dominance, 78
opposition to U.S., 272–73
Security Council role, 269
use of term, 104
voting power, 125
World Court, 279–80
*See also* less developed countries
Timor-Leste
    Australia, 213
    East Timor conflict, **219**, 254–56
    membership, 75
TNCs. *See* transnational corporations
tobacco use, 430
torture, 408
trade, 475–76
    Ethiopian case, 19
traditional societies, 475
transitional societies, 475
Transjordan, 379
translations, 445
transnational corporations (TNCs), 79
transportation, history, 10
Treaty on the Nonproliferation of Nuclear
        Weapons (1968), **330**, 345–46
    *See also* Nuclear Nonproliferation Treaty
        (1970)
Treaty of Pelindaba, 331
Treaty of Rarotonga (1987), **331**, 340
Treaty of Tlatelolco (1967), **330**, 339
Treaty of Westphalia (1648), 8, 9
Trusteeship Council, 381
    functions, 62
    membership, **43**, 62, 93
    nonbinding recommendations, 94
    petitions and visiting missions, 382, 383
trusteeship system
    functioning, 381–83
    nature, 381
    origins, 25, 379–81
    Security Council, 57
    territories listed, **376**
    UN role, 390–92
Truth and Reconciliation Commission, South
        Africa, 408

Truth and Reconciliation Committee, Sierra Leone, 248

Uganda conflict, **217**, 245, 246
UN Advance Mission in Cambodia (UNAMIC), **217**, 235–36, 307
UNAIDS. *See* Joint UN Program on HIV/AIDS
UNAMA. *See* UN Assistance Mission in Afghanistan
UNAMIC. *See* UN Advance Mission in Cambodia
UNAMIR. *See* UN Assistance Mission in Rwanda
UNAMSIL. *See* UN Assistance Mission to Sierra Leone
UN Angola Verification Mission (UNAVEM I), **216**, 232
UN Angola Verification Mission (UNAVEM II), **217**, 232
UN Angola Verification Mission (UNAVEM III), **218**, 232, 310
UNASOG (Libya-Chad), **218**, 245
UN Assistance Mission in Afghanistan (UNAMA), **219**, 253–54
origins, 193
UN Assistance Mission in Iraq, 521
UN Assistance Mission in Rwanda (UNAMIR), **218**, 246, 311
UN Assistance Mission to Sierra Leone (UNAMSIL), **218**, 247–48
UN Atomic Energy Commission (AEC), 332, 334
UNAVEM. *See* UN Angola Verification Mission (UNAVEM)
UN Charter
amendments, 32
Article 43 security force, 176, 189–90
Atlantic Charter origins, 23–24
Cold War, 181
collective security, 174–75
complete text, **535–56**
decolonization, 384
disarmament, 328
domestic jurisdiction, 33–35
drafting, 26–27
economic development, 488–89
human rights, 404
international civil service, 136
interpretation and development, 32–33
peace and security, 167
physical coercion, 126
principles, 33–38
regionalism, 36–37

Security Council, 57
universalism, 37–38
World Court, 63
*See also* constitutional structure
UNCIO. *See* Conference on International Organization, UN
UNCIP. *See* UN Commission on India and Pakistan
UNCI. *See* UN Commission for Indonesia
UN Civilian Police Mission in Haiti (MIPONUH), **218**, 249
UNCLOS. *See* UN Conference on the Law of the Sea
UN Commission on Human Security, 454
UN Commission on Human Settlements, 436
UN Commission on India and Pakistan (UNCIP), 297
UN Commission for Indonesia (UNCI), 215, **216**
UN Commission on Sustainable Development, 435
UN Conference on the Law of the Sea (UNCLOS I), 437–38
UN Conference on the Law of the Sea (UNCLOS II), 438
UN Conference on the Law of the Sea (UNCLOS III), 438–40
UN Conference on Trade and Development (UNCTAD), G-77 origins, 104
UN Council for Namibia, 286
UN Counter-Terrorism Committee (CTC), 54, 162–64, 521
UNCRO in Prevlaka, **218**, 241, 242
UNCTAD. *See* UN Conference on Trade and Development
UN Department of Disarmament Affairs (DDA), 329, 331–32
UN Department of Public Information (DPI), 152, 447
UN Development Group, 152
UN Development Program (UNDP), 498
budget procedures, 67
decentralized control, 401
EPTA, 496–97
intergovernmental organizations, 84
role, 498
Special Fund, 497–98
spending, 127
summarized, 54
technical assistance, 496
UN Disarmament Commission, 347
UN Disarmament Information Program, 329
UN Disengagement Observer Force (UNDOF), 215, **216**, 219, 227, 228

UNDOF. *See* UN Disengagement Observer Force
UNDP. *See* UN Development Program
UNDRO. *See* UN Office of the Disaster Relief Coordinator
UN Educational, Scientific, and Cultural Organization (UNESCO), 444–47
   budget assessments, 445–47
   decision making, 146
   private lobbies, 81
UNEF II. *See* UN Emergency Force (UNEF II)
UNEF I. *See* UN Emergency Force (UNEF I)
UNEF. *See* UN Emergency Force
UN Emergency Force (UNEF I), **216**, 220–21
UN Emergency Force (UNEF II), **216**, 227
UN Emergency Force (UNEF)
   Egypt (1967), 152
   Middle East (1956), 51–52, 146, 213, 214
UN Emergency Relief Coordinator, 454
UN Environment Programme (UNEP)
   decentralized control, 401
   origins, 431
   private links, 81
   regime, 431–33
   role, 434, 436
UNEP. *See* UN Environment Programme
UNESCO. *See* UN Educational, Scientific, and Cultural Organization
UNFICYP. *See* UN Peacekeeping Force in Cyprus
UNFPA. *See* UN Fund for Population Activities
UN Framework Convention on Climate Change (Kyoto, 1997), 82
UN Fund for Population Activities (UNFPA), 127, 473
UNGOMAP. *See* UN Good Offices Mission in Afghanistan
UN Good Offices Mission in Afghanistan (UNGOMAP), **216**, 231, 245
UNHCR. *See* UN High Commissioner for Refugees
UN High Commissioner for Refugees (UNHCR), 456–60, **460**
   budget issues, 67
   coordination, 83
   coordination with NGOs, 160
   Rwanda, 314
UN Human Rights Force for Rwanda (HRFOR), 314
UNICEF. *See* UN International Children's Emergency Fund
   nidad Revolucionaria Nacional Guatemalteca, 250

UNIDIR. *See* UN Institute for Disarmament Research
UNIDO. *See* UN Industrial Development Organization
UNIFIL. *See* UN Interim Force in Lebanon
UNIIMOG. *See* UN Iran-Iraq Military Observer Group
UNIKOM. *See* UN Iraq-Kuwait Observation Mission
unilateral disarmament, 367–68
unilateralism, U.S.
   Bush (2000) election, 122, 367
   Clinton policies, 4
   war on Iraq, 7, 99, 119
UN India-Pakistan Observation Mission (UNIPOM), **216**, 226–27
UN Industrial Development Organization (UNIDO), 492–93
UN inspection teams (UNSCOM) in Iraq
   biological and chemical arms, 189
   collective security, 183–87
   as evidence, 194
   failure, 190
   sanctions related, 205
UN Institute for Disarmament Research (UNIDIR), 329
UN Institute for Training and Research (UNITAR), 447, 499
UN Interim Force in Lebanon (UNIFIL), 215, **216**, 228
UN International Children's Emergency Fund (UNICEF), 452–54
   decentralization, 401
   origins, 452
   programs, 453
UN Iran-Iraq Military Observer Group (UNIIMOG), **216**, 231–32, 245, 305
UN Iraq-Kuwait Observation Mission (UNIKOM), **217**, 237–38, 245
   Baghdad cancels, 186
   collective security, 183
UNITAF. *See* UN Task Force in Somalia
UNITA (National Union for the Total Independence of Angola), 232–33, 310
UNITAR. *See* UN Institute for Training and Research
United Nations
   evaluated, 515
   first meeting, 26–27
   internal oversight office, 495
   origins, 1–2, 23–28
   purpose, 23
   U.S. ratification, 27–28

United Nations International Children's Education Fund (UNICEF)
  NGO coordination, 160
  spending, 127
United Nations University, 447–48, 500
United States
  airmen in China, 300
  budgetary assessments, 65–66, 66–67, 69
  constitution compared to UN Charter, 31–32
  family planning policy, 479
  human rights policy, 412
  international law, 526
  Janus-faced approach, 515
  Korean War, 177–78
  League of Nations, 2, 16, 19, 21–22
  peacekeeping, 256
  postwar policy, 2
  September 11 impact, 193
  trusteeship system, 380
  UNESCO, 445–47
  as UN godfather, 27
  unpaid dues, 52
  UN participation, 85–86
  veto power, 98–99
  voting agreement with majority, **119, 120**
United States–Iran Claims Tribunal, 267
United States Sinai Field Mission, 227
Uniting for Peace Resolution (1950), 51, 180–81
Universal Declaration of Human Rights (1948)
  50th anniversary, 161
  ECOSOC principles, 60
  revisited, 418–19
  UN at apex, 527
  voluntary norms, 407, 408
universalism, arguments for, 37–38
Universal Postal Union (UPU, 1874), 11, 93, 127, 425
UN Korean Reconstruction Agency (UNKRA), 452
UNKRA. See UN Korean Reconstruction Agency
UNMEE. See UN Mission in Ethiopia and Eritrea
UNMIBH in Bosnia-Herzegovina, **218**, 241–43
UNMIH. See UN Mission to Haiti
UNMIK. See UN Mission in Kosovo
UN Military Observer Group in India and Pakistan (UNMOGIP), **216**, 219–20, 227, 297, 298
UNMIL. See UN Mission in Liberia
UNMISET. See UN Mission of Support in East Timor

UN Mission in the Central African Republic (MINURCA), **218**, 234
UN Mission in Côte d'Ivoire (MINUCI), **219**, 234–35
UN Mission for East Timor (UNAMET), 254–55
UN Mission in Ethiopia and Eritrea (UNMEE), **219**, 251
UN Mission in Kosovo (UNMIK), **218**, 251
  tasks, 208–9
UN Mission in Liberia (UNMIL), **219**, 234, 310
UN Mission for the Referendum in Western Sahara (MINURSO), 236
UN Mission of Support in East Timor (UNMISET), **219**, 255, 312, 390
UN Mission to Haiti (UNMIH), **218**, 248–49
UN Mission for the Verification of Human Rights, 162
UNMOGIP. See UN Military Observer Group in India and Pakistan
UN Monitoring, Verification, and Inspection Commission (UNMOVIC)
  Iraq inspections, 35
  return to Iraq, 194, 197
  Secretary-General initiative, 155, 197
UNMOT. See UN Observer Mission to Tajikistan
UNMOVIC. See UN Monitoring, Verification, and Inspection Commission
UN Observer Group in Central America (ONUCA), **217**, 236–37, 245, 250, 306
UN Observer Group in Lebanon (UNOGIL), **216**, 226, 227
  Secretary-General initiative, 154
UN Observer Group for Verification of Elections in Haiti (ONUVEH), **217**, 236
UN Observer Group for Verification of Elections in Nicaragua (ONUVEN), **217**, 236, 306
UN Observer Mission in Angola (MONUA), **218**, 232–33, 310
UN Observer Mission in Georgia (UNOMIG), **217**, 245–46
UN Observer Mission in El Salvador (ONUSAL), **217**, 237, 250, 306
UN Observer Mission in Sierra Leone (UNOMSIL), 246–48, 311–12
UN Observer Mission to Tajikistan (UNMOT), **218**, 235, 309
UN Observer Mission to Uganda-Rwanda (UNOMUR), **217**, 245, 246, 311

UN Office for the Coordination of Humanitarian Affairs (OCHA), 434–35

UN Office of the Disaster Relief Coordinator (UNDRO), 454

UN Office of Internal Oversight Services (OIOS), 495

UNOGIL. See UN Observer Group in Lebanon

UNOMIL mission to Liberia, 310

UNOMSIL. See UN Observer Mission in Sierra Leone

UNOMUR. See UN Observer Mission to Uganda-Rwanda

UN Operation in the Congo (ONUC), 216, 222

UN Operation in Mozambique (ONUMOZ), 217, 245

UN Operation in Somalia (UNOSOM I), 217, 243, 311

UN Operation in Somalia (UNOSOM II), 217, 243–44, 311

UN Organization Mission in the Democratic Republic of the Congo (MONUC), 218, 223–24

UNOSOM. See UN Operation in Somalia

UN Peacekeeping Force in Cyprus (UNFICYP), 216, 224, 225–26, 227

UN Police Support Group (UNPSG), 242

UN Population Commission, 499

UNPREDEP. See UN Preventive Deployment Force

UN Preventive Deployment Force (UNPREDEP)
  China vote, 97
  in former Yugoslav Republic of Macedonia, 218, 241–43, 309

UNPROFOR. See UN Protection Force (UNPROFOR) in Croatia

UN Protection Force (UNPROFOR) in Croatia, 217, 239–41, 242, 308–9

UNPSG. See UN Police Support Group

UN Register of Conventional Arms, 331–32

UN Relief and Rehabilitation Administration (UNRRA), 448, 452, 456

UN Relief and Works Agency for Palestine Refugees in the Near East (UNRWA), 460–64

UN Relief and Works Agency (UNRWA)
  decentralized control, 401
  General Assembly, 38, 40
  support, 124

NRRA. See UN Relief and Rehabilitation Administration

RWA. See UN Relief and Works Agency

UNSCOB. See UN Special Committee on the Balkans

UNSCOM. See UN inspection teams (UNSCOM) in Iraq; UN Special Commission (UNSCOM)

UN Security Force (UNSF) in West New Guinea (West Irian), 216, 224–25

UNSF. See UN Security Force (UNSF) in West New Guinea (West Irian)

UNSMIH. See UN Support Mission in Haiti

UN Special Commission (UNSCOM)
  inspections in Iraq, 35, 342
  nuclear inspections, 342

UN Special Committee on the Balkans (UNSCOB), 215, 216

UN Strategy for the Millenium Development Goals, 402

UN Support Mission in Haiti (UNSMIH), 218, 249

UNTAC. See UN Transitional Authority in Cambodia

UNTAES. See UN Transitional Administration for Eastern Slavonia, Baranja, and Western Sirmium

UNTAET. See UN Transitional Administration in East Timor

UNTAG. See UN Transition Assistance Group

UN Task Force in Somalia (UNITAF), 243–44, 311

UNTEA. See UN Temporary Executive Authority

UN Temporary Executive Authority (UNTEA), 225

UNTMIH. See UN Transition Mission in Haiti

UN Trace Supervision Organization (UNTSO), 215, 216, 219, 227

UN Transitional Administration for Eastern Slavonia, Baranja, and Western Sirmium (UNTAES), 218, 241–42, 309

UN Transitional Administration in East Timor (UNTAET), 255

UN Transitional Authority in Cambodia (UNTAC), 217, 238–39, 307

UN Transition Assistance Group (UNTAG), 216, 238, 287

UN Transition Mission in Haiti (UNTMIH), 218, 249

UNTSO. See UN Trace Supervision Organization

UN Verification Mission in Guatemala (MINUGUA), 218, 250, 306

UN Yemen Observation Mission (UNYOM), 216, 226

UNYOM. *See* UN Yemen Observation Mission
UPU. *See* Universal Postal Union

value allocation, 399
Versailles Treaty, 14, 169–70
    disarmament, 325
    human rights, 404
veto power
    bypassing in Kosovo case, 97–98
    collective security, 175
    contemporary use, 98–101
    Security Council, 32, 96–97, **97**
    U.S. use, 98–99, 110, 516
Vienna Convention on Consular Relations
    (1963), 277
Vienna Convention on Diplomatic Relations
    (1961), 278
Vietnam, partition, 75
Vietnam War, 303
vital rates and events, 486, **487**
voluntary norms, 407–9
voting
    abstentions, 94
    Assembly majority patterns, 123–24
    background, 91
    exchange of information, 101–2
    General Assembly, 94–96
    groups coinciding with U.S., 110, **111–18**,
        **119**
    international arena, 91–94
    majority voting, 93, 94
    rule of unanimity, 92, 93
    Security Council, 96–97
    U.S. report on Assembly practices, 124
    weighted, 92–93

war, functional analysis, 399
war crimes, 313–16
War on Iraq
    collective security, 173
    collective security system, 196, 197
    doctrine of preemption, 191–200
    first Gulf War compared, 196, 197
    Great Britain, 195
    issues raised, 349
    military alliances, 213
    NAM, 107
    rationale, 6–7
    Secretary-General, 147, 155
    Security Council divisions, 57, 101
    UN enforcement issues, 200–202
    UN-U.S. split, 526
    U.S. unilateralism, 7, 99, 119, 191, 526

war crimes, 315
war-prevention role, 167
Warsaw Pact, dissolved, 213
Washington Naval Arms Limitation Treaty,
    326
Washington Naval Conference (1921), 326
Washington Treaty, 518
weapons of mass destruction
    human extinction, 368–69
    Iraq, in U.S. view, 194, 196, 197
    Libya, 206
    not found in Iraq, 200
    ratio problems, 364–65
    sanctions regime, 205
weeks, UN, 441, **442–43**
Western Europe, UN professional personnel,
    **142**
Western Europe and other states
    as group (listed), **104**
    overlapping with other UN groups, **105**
    on U.S. unilateralism, 119, 191, 199
    voting coinciding with U.S. votes, **116–17**
Western Sahara referendum, **217**, 236, 388
West Irian (now Irian Jaya) dispute, **216**, 224–
    25, 302
West New Guinea. *See* West Irian (now Irian
    Jaya) dispute
WFP. *See* World Food Program
WHO. *See* World Health Organization
women
    Convention on the Political Rights of
        Women, 60–61
    human rights and discrimination, 409, **410**,
        415
World Bank, 503–5
    decision making, 146
    dependence on member states, 159
World Bank Group
    evaluation, 508–9
    institutions, 503–8
    role, 503
    structure, 503
World Bank/IMF Development Committee,
    503
World Conference on Human Rights (1993),
    418
World Court. *See* International Court of Jus-
    tice (ICJ)
World Disarmament Campaign, 335
World Disarmament Conference (1932), 327
World Food Congresses, 81
World Food Program (WFP), 499
    Angola, 233

World Food Program (WFP) (*continued*)
  coordination, 83
  Ethiopia, 251
  Israel attack, 98
  NGO coordination, 160
  spending, 127
World Health Organization (WHO), 138, 428
World Meteorological Organization, 71, 350
world opinion, 129
World Summit for Social Development
    (Copenhagen, 1995), 401
World Summit on Sustainable Development
    (2002), 402–3, 436
World Trade Organization (WTO), 61
World War I
  balance of power, 168–69
  lessons, 13
World War II
  appeasement, 19
  effects on colonialism, 378–79
  refugees, 456
  U.S. mobilization, 22

World Zionist Organization, 288
WTO. *See* World Trade Organization
Wye River Accord (1998), 292

Yalta Conference, 25–26
Yemen civil strife, **216**, 226
youth employment, 482
Yugoslavia, former
  cases against NATO, 282
  dispute settlement, 308–9, 313–14
  human rights, 419–22
  peacekeeping, **217**, 239–41, 242
  refugees, 458
  sanctions against Serbia, 206–9
  UNPREDEP vetoed, 97

Zimbabwe
  colonialism, 388
  one-party rule, 392
  sanctions against Rhodesia, 202–3
Zionism, 108–9, 288